The Story of Christianity

VOLUME I

The Early Church to the Dawn of the Reformation

REVISED AND UPDATED

Also by Justo L. González

A History of Christian Thought, Volume 1: From the Beginnings to the Council of Chalcedon in A.D. 451

A History of Christian Thought, Volume 2: From Augustine to the Eve of the Reformation

A History of Christian Thought, Volume 3: From the Protestant Reformation to the Twentieth Century

The Story of Christianity, Volume 2

The Story of Christianity

VOLUME I

The Early Church to the Reformation

REVISED AND UPDATED

Justo L. González

HarperOne
An Imprint of HarperCollinsPublishers

HarperOne

HarperCollins Web site: http://www.harpercollins.com
HarperCollins®, ██® and HarperCollins™
are trademarks of HarperCollins

SECOND EDITION
Designed by Level C

Library of Congress Cataloging-in-Publication Data
is available upon request.

ISBN 978–0–06–185588–7

10 11 12 13 14   RRD(H)   10 9 8 7 6 5 4 3 2 1

To Catherine

Contents

Preface   xiii

Preface to the Revised and Updated Edition   xv

1   *Introduction*   1

PART 1: THE EARLY CHURCH
    Chronology   8

2   **The Fullness of Time**   13
    Judaism in Palestine   13
    Diaspora Judaism   17
    The Greco-Roman World   19

3   **The Church in Jerusalem**   25
    Unity and Diversity   25
    Religious Life   27
    The Waning of the Jewish Church   28

4   **Mission to the Gentiles**   31
    The Scope of the Mission   31
    Paul's Work   33
    The Apostles: Facts and Legends   36

5   **First Conflicts with the State**   41
    A New Jewish Sect   41
    Persecution Under Nero   43
    Persecution Under Domitian   46

6   **Persecution in the Second Century**   49
    The Correspondence Between Pliny and Trajan   49
    Ignatius of Antioch, the Bearer of God   51
    The Martyrdom of Polycarp   53

Persecution Under Marcus Aurelius   55
Toward the End of the Second Century   57

7   **The Defense of the Faith**   59
Base Rumors and Lofty Criticism   59
The Main Apologists   62
Christian Faith and Pagan Culture   63
The Arguments of the Apologists   66

8   **The Deposit of the Faith**   69
Gnosticism   70
Marcion   73
The Response: Canon, Creed, and Apostolic Succession   75
The Ancient Catholic Church   81

9   **The Teachers of the Church**   83
Irenaeus of Lyons   84
Clement of Alexandria   86
Tertullian of Carthage   88
Origen of Alexandria   93

10   **Persecution in the Third Century**   97
Persecution under Septimius Severus   97
Under Decius   100
The Question of the Lapsed: Cyprian and Novatian   102

11   **Christian Life**   105
The Social Origins of Early Christians   105
Christian Worship   107
The Organization of the Church   113
Missionary Methods   115
The Beginnings of Christian Art   117

12   **The Great Persecution and the Final Victory**   119

Suggested Readings   126

PART II: THE IMPERIAL CHURCH   129
Chronology   130

13   **Constantine**   131
From Rome to Constantinople   131
From the Unconquered Sun to Jesus Christ   137
From Persecution to Dominance   141

The Impact of the New Order 142
Reactions to the New Order 147

14 **Official Theology: Eusebius of Caesarea** 149

15 **The Monastic Reaction** 157
The Origins of Monasticism 158
The First Monks of the Desert 161
Pachomius and Communal Monasticism 165
The Spread of the Monastic Ideal 168

16 **The Schismatic Reaction: Donatism** 173

17 **The Arian Controversy and the Council of Nicea** 181
The Outbreak of the Controversy 182
The Council of Nicea 186

18 **The Pagan Reaction: Julian the Apostate** 193
Julian's Religious Policy 196

19 **Athanasius of Alexandria** 199
The Early Years 199
Through Many Trials 201
A Theological Agreement 205
Further Trials 207

20 **The Great Cappadocians** 209
Macrina 209
Basil the Great 211
Gregory of Nyssa 213
Gregory of Nazianzus 214

21 **Ambrose of Milan** 219
An Unexpected Election 219
The Bishop and the Throne 222

22 **John Chrysostom** 225
A Voice from the Wilderness 225
Return to the Wilderness 228

23 **Jerome** 233

24 **Augustine of Hippo** 241
A Tortuous Path to Faith 241
Minister and Theologian of the Western Church 246

25   **Beyond the Borders of the Empire**   253

26   **The End of an Era**   259
     Suggested Readings   261

PART III: MEDIEVAL CHRISTIANITY   263
     Chronology   264

27   **The New Order**   269
     The Germanic Kingdoms   269
     Benedictine Monasticism   277
     The Papacy   281
     The Arab Conquests   289

28   **Eastern Christianity**   295
     The Christological Debates to the Council of Chalcedon   296
     Further Theological Debates   302
     The Dissident Churches of the East   306
     Eastern Orthodoxy After the Arab Conquests   309

29   **Imperial Restoration and Continuing Decay**   315
     Charlemagne's Reign   315
     Theological Activity   318
     New Invasions   321
     Decay in the Papacy   323

30   **Movements of Renewal**   327
     Monastic Reform   327
     Canonical and Papal Reform   334
     The Papacy and the Empire in Direct Confrontation   338

31   **The Offensive Against Islam**   345
     The First Crusade   346
     Later History of the Crusades   349
     The Spanish Reconquista   351
     Consequences of the Offensive against Islam   352

32   **The Golden Age of Medieval Christianity**   357
     The Mendicant Orders   357
     One Flock Under One Shepherd   363
     Theological Activity: Scholasticism   369

Missionary Endeavors 380
Stones That Bear Witness: Architecture 381

33 **The Collapse** 387
New Conditions 387
The Papacy Under the Shadow of France 393
The Great Western Schism 402

34 **In Quest of Reformation** 407
The Conciliar Movement 407
John Wycliffe 411
John Huss 415
Girolamo Savonarola 421
The Mystical Alternative 425
Popular Movements 429

35 **Renaissance and Humanism** 433
The Later Course of Scholasticism 433
The Revival of Classical Learning 436
A New Vision of Reality 440
The Popes of the Renaissance 441

Suggested Readings 446

PART IV: THE BEGINNINGS OF COLONIAL CHRISTIANITY 447
Chronology 448

36 **Spain and the New World** 449
The Nature of the Spanish Enterprise 449
The Protest 452
The Caribbean 454
Mexico 455
Golden Castile 459
Florida 460
Colombia and Venezuela 462
The Four Corners of the Earth: The Incan Empire 465
La Plata 469

37 **The Portuguese Enterprise** 473
Africa 473
Toward the Rising Sun 476
Brazil 484

38   The New World and the Old   487

      Suggested Readings   491

      Appendix: The Ecumenical Councils   493

      Notes   495

      Index   497

      Credits   511

Maps
Palestine: Birthplace of Christianity   14
The Roman Empire   20
The Roman Empire under Diocletian   120
Constantine's path to absolute power   132
The birthplace of Donatism   177
Europe after the Invasions   270
The First Crusade   374
The Portuguese in Africa and the Orient   474

Preface

The reader will probably be surprised to learn that I regard this book in large measure as autobiographical. It is so first of all because, as José Ortega y Gasset said, each generation stands on the shoulders of its predecessors like acrobats in a vast human pyramid. Thus, to tell the story of those to whom we are heirs is to write a long preface to our own life stories.

But this book is also autobiographical in a second sense, for it deals with friends and companions with whom I have spent the last three decades. Since I first met Irenaeus, Athanasius, and the rest, and as I have read their writings and pondered their thoughts and deeds, they have accompanied me through the many turns and twists of life. Like contemporary friends, they have often been a joy, at other times a puzzlement, and even sometimes an aggravation. But still, they have become part of me, and as I write of them I am also aware that I am writing of my life with them.

It is customary in a preface to acknowledge those who have contributed to the writing of the book. This I find impossible, for I would have to name a long list of scholars, both living and dead—Origen, Eusebius, the Inca Garcilaso de la Vega, Harnack, and the host of unknown monks who copied and recopied manuscripts.

Among my contemporaries, however, there are two who I must mention. The first is my wife, Catherine Gunsalus González, Professor of Church History at Columbia Theological Seminary, in Decatur, Georgia, who has shared with me the last decade of my journey with the ancients, and whose reading and criticism of my manuscript have proven invaluable. The naming of the second is a sign of our times, for this is my live-in, full-time secretary of six years: the word processor on which I have prepared this manuscript. Many of the adjectives usually applied to typists in prefaces also apply to my word processor: patient, careful, uncomplaining, always ready to serve. Indeed, this secretary has typed and retyped my manuscript with no more protest than an occasional beep. However, as I write these very last words of my manuscript, an electric storm has forced me to take pen in hand once again, thus reminding me that we are not as far removed as we sometimes think from the time of Origen and Eusebius!

As I send this book out into the world, it is my hope that others will enjoy the reading of it as much as I have enjoyed the writing of it.

Preface to the Revised
and Updated Edition

It may seem odd that history needs to be revisited, revised, and rewritten; and yet it does. This is so, because history is never simply the bare past as it actually happened; it is the past as read through the sources that have survived, as selected by countless generations of historians, and as interpreted from our own present and from the future for which we hope. Thus, when I now read *The Story of Christianity* almost a quarter of a century after it was first written, I find much to reaffirm, but also much to revise. A few years after the first publication of this book, the Soviet Union collapsed. Then there was a resurgence of Islam, of which the rest of the world became aware as extreme and fanatical Muslims plotted and perpetrated acts of terrorism in every continent. Within Christianity itself, Pentecostalism and several similar movements took center stage through their growth both in traditionally Christian lands and in other regions. In many of those areas, new religions arose, many of them inspired by Christianity and taking some elements from it. The prospect of unprecedented ecological disaster finally gained the attention of governments and their leaders. The sustainability of the world economic order was severely questioned, no longer just by radical ideologues, but also by respected economists. The technology of communications has exploded. These developments—and many more—have shaped the way we look both at the future and at the past. Hence the need for a revised edition of this book.

The other compelling reason for such a revised edition is my desire to incorporate in *The Story of Christianity* a number of comments and suggestions that I have received during the intervening years. Some have come from colleagues who read and used this book in English. Others have come as a result of a number of translations making the book itself available to widely different cultures—for the very process of translation brings to light ambiguities that are not immediately noticeable in the original language. Students and colleagues reading *The Story* from widely divergent cultures—for instance, in Japan, in

Brazil, in Russia, in Korea—have widened my scope of what this book should include. I have not incorporated all their suggestions into the present edition (it is impossible to satisfy both those who want more on a given subject and those who want less!). But to all of them I am deeply grateful, particularly to students who have told me that a particular subject was not clear, or that they found another illuminating. Among those colleagues whose suggestions have proven valuable, I must again single out my wife, Catherine, who has read and reread my manuscript with unparalleled patience and wise advice. I must also express a particular word of gratitude to Professor James D. Smith III, of Bethel Seminary San Diego, whose many detailed suggestions have greatly improved the book.

As I send this new edition out into the world, I am acutely aware that it too will need to be revised; that history will have to be written anew again and again as generations succeed one another. It is thus my hope that this revised edition will inspire others to further revision as they enter into the fascinating dialogue between the present and the past that is the very essence of history: a dialogue in which the past addresses us, but does so in terms of our present questions.

I

Introduction

In those days a decree went out from Caesar Augustus that all the world should be enrolled.

LUKE 2:1

From its very beginning, the Christian message was grafted onto human history. The Good News Christians have proclaimed through the ages is that in Jesus Christ, and for our salvation, God has entered human history in a unique way. History is crucial for understanding not only the life of Jesus, but also the entire biblical message. A good deal of the Old Testament is historical narrative. The Bible tells the story of God's revelation in the life and history of the people of God. Without that story, it is impossible to know that revelation.

The New Testament writers are quite clear about this. The Gospel of Luke tells us that the birth of Jesus took place during the reign of Augustus Caesar, "when Quirinius was governor of Syria" (2:2). Shortly before, the same Gospel places the narrative within the context of Palestinian history, recording that it took place "in the days of Herod, king of Judaea" (1:5). The Gospel of Matthew opens with a genealogy that places Jesus within the framework of the history and hopes of Israel, and then goes on to date the birth of Jesus "in the days of Herod the king" (2:1). Mark gives less chronological detail, but still does affirm that Jesus began his ministry "in those days"—that is, the days of John the Baptist (1:9). The fourth gospel wishes to make clear that the significance of these events is not transitory, and therefore begins by stating that the Word who was made flesh in human history (1:14) is the same Word who "was in the beginning with God" (1:2). Finally, a similar note is sounded in the First Epistle of John, the opening lines of which declare that "that which was from the beginning" is also that "which we have heard, which we have seen with our eyes, which we have looked upon and touched with our hands" (1:1).

After completing his gospel, Luke continued the story of the Christian church in the book of Acts. He did not do this out of mere antiquarian curiosity, but rather out of some important theological considerations. According to

Luke and to the entire New Testament, the presence of God among us did not end with the ascension of Jesus. On the contrary, Jesus himself promised his followers that he would not leave them alone, but would send another counselor (John 14:16-26). At the beginning of Acts, immediately before the ascension, Jesus tells his disciples that they will receive the power of the Holy Spirit, by which they will be his witnesses "to the ends of the earth" (1:8). Then follow the events of Pentecost, which mark the beginning of the witnessing life of the church. Thus, the theme of the book commonly called *Acts of the Apostles* is not so much the deeds of the apostles, as the deeds of the Holy Spirit through the apostles (and others). Luke has left us two books, the first on the deeds of Jesus, and the second on the deeds of the Spirit.

But Luke's second book does not seem to have a conclusion. At the end, Paul is still preaching in Rome, and the book does not tell us what becomes of him or of the other leaders of the church. Luke had a theological reason for this, for in his view the story he was telling shall not come to an end before the end of all history.

What this means for those who share in Luke's faith is that the history of the church, while showing all the characteristics of human history, is much more than the history of an institution or of a movement. It is a history of the deeds of the Spirit in and through the men and women who have gone before them in the faith.

There are episodes in the course of that history in which it is difficult to see the action of the Holy Spirit. As our narrative unfolds, we shall find those who have used the faith of the church for their financial gain, or to increase their personal power. There will be others who will forget or twist the command-ment of love, or will persecute their enemies with a vindictiveness unworthy of the name of Jesus. At other times, it will appear to many of us that the church has forsaken the biblical faith, and some will even doubt that such a church can truly be called *Christian*. At such points in our narrative, it may do well to remember two things.

The first of these is that, while this narrative is the history of the deeds of the Spirit, it is the history of those deeds through sinners such as we are. This is clear as early as New Testament times, when Peter, Paul, and the rest are depicted both as people of faith and as sinners. And, if that example is not suffi-ciently stark, it should suffice to take another look at the "saints" to whom Paul addresses his First Epistle to the Corinthians!

The second is that it has been through those sinners and that church—and only through them—that the biblical message has come to us. Even in the darkest times in the life of the church, there were those Christians who loved, studied, kept, and copied the scriptures, and thus bequeathed them to us.

What those earlier Christians have bequeathed to us, however, is more than the text of scriptures. They have also left the illuminating record of their striving to be faithful witnesses under the most diverse of circumstances. In times of persecution, some witnessed with their blood, others with their writings, and still others with their loving acceptance of those who had weakened and later repented. In times when the church was powerful, some sought to witness by employing that power, while others questioned the use of it. In times of invasions, chaos, and famine, there were those who witnessed to their Lord by seeking to restore order, so that the homeless might find shelter, and the hungry might have food. When vast lands until then unknown were opened to European Christians, there were those who rushed to those lands to preach the message of their faith. Throughout the centuries, some sought to witness by the Word spoken and written, others by prayer and renunciation, and still others by the force of arms and the threat of inquisitorial fires.

Like it or not, we are heirs to this host of diverse and even contradictory witnesses. Some of their actions we may find revolting, and others inspiring. But all of them form part of our history. All of them, those whose actions we admire as well as those whose actions we despise, brought us to where we are now.

Without understanding that past, we are unable to understand ourselves, for in a sense the past still lives in us and influences who we are and how we understand the Christian message. When we read, for instance, that "the just shall live by faith," Martin Luther is whispering at our ear how we are to interpret those words—and this is true even for those of us who have never even heard of Martin Luther. When we hear that "Christ died for our sins," Anselm of Canterbury sits in the pew with us, even though we may not have the slightest idea who Anselm was. When we stand, sit, or kneel in church; when we sing a hymn, recite a creed (or refuse to recite one); when we build a church or preach a sermon, a past of which we may not be aware is one of the factors influencing our actions. The notion that we read the New Testament exactly as the early Christians did, without any weight of tradition coloring our interpretation, is an illusion. It is also a dangerous illusion, for it tends to absolutize our interpretation, confusing it with the Word of God.

One way we can avoid this danger is to know the past that colors our vision. A person wearing tinted glasses can avoid the conclusion that the entire world is tinted only by being conscious of the glasses themselves. Likewise, if we are to break free from an undue bondage to tradition, we must begin by understanding what that tradition is, how we came to be where we are, and how particular elements in our past color our view of the present. It is then that we are free to choose which elements in the past—and in the present—we wish to reject, and which we will affirm.

The opposite is also true. Not only is our view of the present colored by our history, but our view of history is also colored by the present and by the future we envision. Were the reader to compare this *Story* with earlier histories of the church, some differences would immediately become apparent. For one thing, this *Story* seeks to acknowledge the role of women throughout the life of the church in a way that most earlier histories did not. This is not because the author has any particular insight that others do not. It is simply because our age has become much more aware of the significant contribution of women to every era, and particularly to the life of the church. Likewise, it will become apparent that the way I tell the story here, it does not make the church of the North Atlantic its culmination. Again, this is not due to some particular insight of the author, but simply to the astonishing events of the last two centuries, when Christianity first became a truly universal religion, and then became more and more a religion no longer dominated by the North Atlantic. It is rather the obvious conclusion of anyone looking at the statistics of the last few decades, as will be seen in Volume 2. At a time when there are more Christians in the former "mission fields" than in the "mother churches," we must tell the story in a global way that was not necessary—and perhaps not even possible—in earlier generations. Thus, there are elements in the story that today seem most important to us, but were quite secondary to historians fifty years ago.

It is at this point that the *doing* of history converges with the *making* of it. When we study the life and work of past generations, and when we interpret it, we are *doing* history. But we must remember that we are reading the past in the light of our present, and also that future generations will read about our times as past history. In that sense, like it or not, both by our action and by our inaction, we are *making* history. This is both an exhilarating opportunity and an awesome responsibility, and it demands that we *do* history in order to be able to *make* it more faithfully. Every renewal of the church, every great age in its history, has been grounded on a renewed reading of history. The same will be true as we move ahead into the twenty-first century.

In this new century, as in every age, Christians face new and unexpected challenges. In seeking to be obedient in our response to such challenges, we have the resources of past times when other believers found themselves in similar situations. The response of the early church to a culture that often saw it with indifference or even contempt may provide guidance at a time when similar attitudes prevail in much of Western society. The manner in which the church in the fourth and fifth centuries responded to the migration of entire nations may provide insight into possible ways to interpret and to respond to the demographic upheavals of our time. The devotion of medieval scholastics and of Protestant Reformers may be an inspiration to budding scholars and theologians. The history of missions in the nineteenth century may well warn us of the pitfalls the church faces when it crosses cultural and social boundaries. In all of this, the past will illumine the present.

But the opposite is always true: As we look at those and other past times and events, we do so through the lens of our own time, our own concerns, our own hopes. History is not the pure past; history is a past interpreted from the present of the historian. Thus, our understanding of the early martyrs and heretics, of monastics, pastors, crusaders and scholars, as well as our understanding of everyday Christian life in the past, will be both marked and enriched by our present-day lenses.

It is into this dialogue that we now enter.

PART I

THE EARLY
CHURCH

Chronology

Emperors	Bishops of Rome*	Authors and Documents**	Events
Augustus (27 BCE–14 CE)		(Philo)	Jesus
Tiberius (14–37)			
Caligula (37–41)			
Claudius (41–54)		Paul's Epistles (Flavius Josephus)	Jews expelled from Rome
Nero (54–68)	Linus (?)	Mark	Persecution Jerusalem Christians flee to Pella (66)
Galba (68–69)			
Otho (69)			
Vitellius (69)			
Vespasian (69–79)		Matthew (?)	Fall of Jerusalem (70)
	Anacletus (?)	Luke—Acts (?)	
Titus (79–81)			
Domitian (81–96)		John (?)	
	Clement	Revelation	Persecution
Nerva (96–98)			
Trajan (98–117)			
	Evaristus Alexander Sixtus	Ignatius	Persecution

* Bishops whom the Roman Church does not recognize are in italics.
** Non-Christian authors are in parentheses.

Emperors	Bishops of Rome*	Authors and Documents**	Events
Hadrian (117–138)		Quadratus	Persecution
		Aristides	
	Telesphorus	Papias	
		(Epictetus)	Surge of Gnosticism
		Didache (?)	
		Gospel of the Hebrews	Marcion in Rome
	Hyginius	Psuedo-Barnabas (?)	
Antoninus Pius (138–161)	Pius	Basilides	
		Aristo of Pella (130)	
		Hermas (c. 150)	
		Martyrdom of Polycarp	
		Roman Symbol	
		Valentinus	
	Anicetus	Gospel of Peter	
		Muratorian Fragment (160)	Montanism
		Fronto of Cirta	
		Epitaph of Pectorius (?)	
		Ascension of Isaiah (?)	
		Odes of Solomon (?)	
Marcus Aurelius (161–180)	Justin (165)		Persecution
Lucius Verus co-emperor (161–169)	Soter	Hegesippus (154–166)	
		Lucian of Samosata	
		Tatian	
		II Enoch (?)	
	Eleuterus (?–189)	Athenagoras	Martyrs of Gaul (177)
Commodus	Theophilus of Antioch (Celus)		
		Irenaeus (c. 180)	
		Pantenus	Scillitan martyrs
	Victor (189–199)	Melito of Sardis (189)	Debate over date of Easter
Pertinax (193)		Tertullian (195–220)	
Didius Julian (193)			
Septimus Severus		Minucius Felix (?)	
	Zephyrinus (199–217)	Epitaph of Abercius	Persecution
		Perpetua and Felicitas	Syncretistic policy
		Clement of Alexandria (200–215)	Tertullian Montanist (207)

Emperors	Bishops of Rome*	Authors and Documents**	Events
Caracalla (211–217)			
Macrinus (217–218)	Calixtus (217–222)	Origen (215–253) (Plotinus)	
Elagabalus (218–222)			
Alexander Severus (222–235)	Urban (222–230) *Hippolytus* (222–235) Pontian (230–235)	Pseudo-Clementime (?)	Two bishops in Rome Origen in Palestine
Maximi (235–238)	Anterus (235–236) Fabian (236–250)		
Gordian I (238)			
Gordian II (238)			
Pupienus (238)	Sextus Julius Africanus		
Balbinus (238)			
Gordian III (238–244) Philip the Arabian (244–249)	Gospel of Thomas (?) Methodius Heraclas	Manicheism founded	
Decius (249–251)		Cyprian	Persecution
Hostilian (251)			
Gallus (251–253)	Cornelius (251–253) *Novatian* (251–258?)		Two bishops in Rome
Aemilian (253)	Lucius (253–254)	Didascalia (?)	
Valerian (253–259)	Stephen (254–257) Sixtus II (257–258)		
Gallienus (259–268)			
	Dionysius (260–268)	Dionysius of Alexandria Lucian of Antioch	Paul of Samosata bishop of Antioch
	Felix (269–274)	Gregory the Wonderworker Firmilian of Caesarea	
Claudius II (268–270)		Theognost	
Quintillus (270) Aurelian (270–275)		Gnostic papyri (?) Gospel of Bartholomew	
Tacitus (275–276) Florian (276)	Eutychian (275–283)		

Emperors	Bishops of Rome*	Authors and Documents**	Events
Probus (276–282)			
Carus (282–283)	Caius (283–296)		
Numerian (283–284)		Arnobius	
Carinus (283–285)			
Diocletian (284–305)			
Maximian (285–305)	Marcellinus (296–304)		
Constant Chlorus (292–306)		Pierius	Great Persecution
Galerius (292–311)			Edict of Toleration (311)
Maximinus Daia (305–313)	Marcellus (308–309)		
Constantine (306–337)	Eusebius (309–310)		
Severus (306–307)			
Maxentius (306–312)	Miltiades (311–314)		Battle of Milvian Bridge
Licinius (307–323)			Edict of Milan (313)
	Sylvester (314–335)		

2

The Fullness of Time

But when the time had fully come, God sent forth his Son, born of woman, born under the Law.

GALATIANS 4:4

The early Christians did not believe that the time and place of the birth of Jesus had been left to chance. On the contrary, they saw the hand of God preparing the advent of Jesus in all events prior to the birth, and in all the historical circumstances around it. The same could be said about the birth of the church, which resulted from the work of Jesus. God had prepared the way so that the disciples, after receiving the power of the Holy Spirit, could be witnesses "in Jerusalem and in all Judea and Samaria and to the ends of the earth" (Acts 1:8).

Therefore, the church was never disconnected from the world around it. The first Christians were first-century Jews, and it was as such that they heard and received the message. Then the faith spread, first among other Jews, and eventually among Gentiles both within and beyond the borders of the Roman Empire. In order to understand the history of Christianity in its early centuries, we must begin by looking at the world in which it evolved.

JUDAISM IN PALESTINE

Palestine, the land in which Christianity first appeared, has long been a land of strife and suffering. In ancient times, this was due mostly to its geographical position, at the crossroads of the great trade routes that joined Egypt with Mesopotamia, and Asia Minor with Arabia. As we read the Old Testament, we see that, as empires came and went, they cast a covetous eye on that narrow strip of land. For this reason, its inhabitants repeatedly suffered invasion, bondage, and exile. In the fourth century BCE, with Alexander and his Macedonian armies, a new contender entered the arena. Upon defeating the Persians, Alexander became master of Palestine. But his death followed shortly thereafter, and his vast empire was dismembered. For a long time, two of the resulting dynasties,

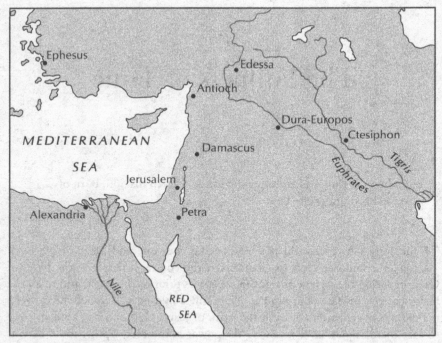

Palestine: Birthplace of Christianity.

one in Egypt and one in Syria, fought for possession of Palestine. The result was another period of unrest and political instability.

The conquests of Alexander—like most imperialist enterprises—sought to justify themselves on an ideological basis. He did not wish simply to conquer the world, but to unite and enrich it by spreading the insights of Greek civilization. The result, in which some elements of Greek origin combined with other elements taken from conquered civilizations in various forms and degrees, is known as *Hellenism*. Although the precise nature of Hellenism varied from place to place, it did provide the eastern Mediterranean basin with a unity that opened the way first to Roman conquest, and later to the preaching of the gospel.

But there were many Jews who did not regard Hellenism as a blessing. Since part of the Hellenistic ideology consisted of equating and mixing the gods of different nations, they saw in it a threat to Israel's faith in the One God. In a way, the history of Palestine from the time of Alexander's conquest to the destruction of Jerusalem in 70 CE may be seen as the constant struggle between Hellenizing pressures on the one hand and Jewish faithfulness to their God and their traditions on the other.

Under the leadership of Judas Maccabaeus, the Jews enjoyed a period of political freedom. Here he is seen as depicted by the fifteenth-century Italian painter Taddeo di Bartolo.

The high point of that struggle was the Jewish rebellion led by the family known as the Maccabees, in the second century BCE. For a while the Maccabees were able to gain a measure of religious and political independence. But eventually their successors gave way to the Hellenizing pressures of the Seleucids, who had succeeded Alexander in the rule of Syria. When some of the stricter Jews protested, they were persecuted. Partially as a result of all this, Rome eventually intervened. In 63 BCE, Pompey conquered the land and deposed the last of the Maccabees, Aristobulus II.

As Alexander had earlier, the Romans justified their imperial conquests by means of an ideology. Their calling was to civilize the world around them—which to them meant building and beautifying cities similar to Rome, and placing all of them under Roman rule and guidance. (Note that etymologically the word "civilization" may be understood as "cityfication".) Where there were no cities, they built new ones. And where there were ancient cities, they embellished them and erected public buildings in the style of Rome itself.

In general, Roman policies toward the religion and customs of conquered people were rather tolerant. Shortly after the conquest, the Roman government gave the descendants of the Maccabees a measure of authority, and used them in governing the land, giving them the titles of *high priest* and *ethnarch*. Herod the Great, appointed king of Judea by the Romans in 40 BCE, had a distant Maccabean claim, for he had married a woman of that lineage.

But the Roman brand of tolerance could not reconcile what appeared to be the obstinacy of the Jews, who insisted on worshiping only their God, and who threatened rebellion at the smallest challenge to their faith. Following general Roman policy, Herod built the city of Caesarea in honor of the emperor, and he had temples built in Samaria devoted to the worship of Roma and Augustus. But when he dared place a Roman eagle at the entrance of the Temple in Jerusalem there was an uprising, which he suppressed by force. His successors followed a similar policy, building new cities and encouraging the immigration of Gentiles.

This led to almost continuous rebellion. When Jesus was a child there was an uprising against Archelaus, Herod's son, who had to call in the Roman army. The Romans then destroyed a city in Galilee near Nazareth, and crucified two thousand Jews. It is to this rebellion that Gamaliel refers in Acts 5:37, as an example of useless revolt. The radical or Zealot party, tenaciously opposed to Roman rule, continued unabated in spite of such atrocities—and perhaps because of them—and played an important role in the great rebellion that broke out in 66 CE. Once again the Roman legions were called in, and in the year 70 they took Jerusalem and destroyed the Temple. Several years later the last stronghold of Jewish resistance, the rock fortress of Massada, was conquered after a heroic defense.

In the midst of such suffering and so many vicissitudes, Jewish religion took different shapes, and several parties appeared. The best known, both because the gospels refer to it repeatedly and because later Judaism evolved from it, is the party of the Pharisees. They were the party of the populace, who did not enjoy the material benefits of Roman rule and Hellenistic civilization. To them, it was important to be faithful to the Law, and for that reason they studied and debated how the Law was to be applied in every conceivable situation. This has led to the charge that they were legalistic. That may be true to a degree. But one must remember that by their emphasis on the Law they sought to make the faith of Israel relevant to everyday situations, and to new circumstances under Roman rule and Hellenizing threats. Besides this, they held some doctrines, such as the final Resurrection and the existence of angels, which the more conservative Jews declared to be mere innovations.

Those more conservative Jews were the Sadducees. By and large, they belonged to the Jewish aristocracy, and they were conservative in both politics and religion. In matters of religion, their interest centered on the Temple, which they held with the support of the Romans, who in turn found the political conservatism of the Sadducees much to their liking. The Sadducees rejected many of the doctrines of the Pharisees as unwarranted innovations.

This means that one must take care not to exaggerate the opposition of Jesus and the early Christians to the Pharisees. A great deal of the friction between Christians and Pharisees was due to the similarity of their views, rather than to their difference. Moving among the common people, Jesus and his followers had more opportunities to rub shoulders with the Pharisees than with the Sadducees.

There were many other sects and groups within first-century Judaism. The Zealots have already been mentioned. Another important group was the Essenes, an ascetic sect to which many attribute the production of the Dead Sea Scrolls. This group, and probably others like it, sought to obey the Law by withdrawing from the rest of society, and often had a very intense expectation that the end was near.

On the other hand, this diversity of tendencies, sects, and parties should not obscure two fundamental tenets of all Jews: ethical monotheism and eschatological hope. Ethical monotheism means that there is only one God, and that this God requires, just as much as proper worship, proper relationships among human beings. The various parties might disagree as to the exact shape of such relationships, but they all agreed on the need to honor the only God with the whole of life.

Eschatological hope was another common tenet in the faith of Israel. Most kept the messianic hope, and firmly believed that the day would come when God would intervene in order to restore Israel and fulfill the promise of a Kingdom of peace and justice. Some thought that they were to speed its coming by the force of arms. Others were convinced that such matters should be left entirely in the hands of God. But all looked to a future when God's promises would be fulfilled.

Of all these, the best equipped to survive after the destruction of the Temple were the Pharisees. Their roots went back to the time of the Exile, when it was not possible to worship in Jerusalem, and religious life perforce centered on the Law. The same was true of the millions of Jews who lived in distant lands in the first century. Not being able to attend worship regularly in the Temple, they developed the synagogue, where the Law and the traditions of Israel were studied, and where the dispersed Jews experienced community and strengthened their resolve to live as the faithful people of God even in dispersion. When the Temple was destroyed in 70 CE the Sadducees received a mortal blow, while the theological tradition of the Pharisees continued to bloom into modern Judaism.

DIASPORA JUDAISM

For centuries before the birth of Jesus, the number of Jews living outside of Palestine had been increasing. Dating back to the Old Testament times there were numerous Jews in Persia and Mesopotamia. In Egypt, they had even built a temple in the seventh century BCE, and another five centuries later. By the time of Jesus, there were sizable Jewish communities in every major city in the Roman Empire. These Jews, scattered far and wide, but with strong emotional and religious connections with the land of their ancestors, are called the *Diaspora* or *Dispersion*.

This mosaic from Tunisia, depicting the Menorah, is one of many archaeological remains of the Diaspora.

Diaspora Judaism is of crucial importance for the history of Christianity, for it was one of the main avenues through which the new faith expanded throughout the Roman Empire. Furthermore, Diaspora Judaism unwittingly provided the church with one of the most useful tools of its missionary expansion, the Greek translation of the Old Testament.

One of the common traits of Diaspora Judaism was that many of its members had forgotten the language of their ancestors. For this reason, it was necessary to translate the Hebrew scriptures into languages that the members understood—Aramaic in the Eastern wing of the Diaspora and Greek in its Western wing, within the borders of the Roman Empire. Following Alexander's conquests, Greek had become the common language of the majority of people living in the Mediterranean. Egyptians, Jews, Cypriots, and even Romans used Greek to communicate with one another. Therefore, it was natural that when the Jews of the Diaspora began losing their Hebrew they would translate the scriptures into Greek.

This translation originated in Alexandria—the main city in Egypt—and is called the *Septuagint*, or the *Version of the Seventy* (or *LXX*), named as such because of an ancient legend that told of seventy Jewish scholars commissioned to translate the scriptures. After working independently, they found that their translations agreed exactly. The obvious purpose of the legend was to legitimize the translation as divinely inspired.

In any case, the Septuagint was of enormous importance to the early church. It is the version of scripture quoted by most New Testament authors, and it profoundly influenced the formation of early Christian vocabulary—including the very name of "Christ," which was the Septuagint word for "Anointed One" or

"Messiah." When the early Christians began their missionary spread, they used the Septuagint as a ready-made means of arguing with the more traditional Jews who did not accept their teachings, and also as a means of communicating their message to the Gentiles. For this and other reasons, the Jewish community produced other versions that were not as readily suitable for Christian use, and, in effect, left the church in sole possession of the Septuagint.

Due to the Diaspora, Judaism was forced to come to terms with Hellenism in a manner that could be avoided in Palestine itself. Particularly in Alexandria, there was a movement within Judaism that sought to show the compatibility between the ancient faith and the best of Hellenistic culture. As early as the third century BCE, attempts were made to retell the history of Israel following the accepted patterns of Hellenistic historical writing. But the high point of this entire tradition was the work of Philo of Alexandria, a contemporary of Jesus who sought to show that the best of pagan philosophy agreed with the Hebrew scriptures. He claimed that, since the Hebrew prophets antedated the Greek philosophers, the latter must have drawn from the wisdom of the former. According to Philo, such points of agreement are many, for ultimately the teachings of the philosophers coincide with those of scripture. The difference is that scripture speaks figuratively. This in turn means that it is to be understood by means of allegorical interpretation. Through such interpretation, Philo tried to prove that the God of scripture is the same as the One of the philosophers, and that the moral teachings of the Hebrews are basically the same as those of the best among the Greek philosophers. This sort of argument provided ample ammunition for the early Christians in their efforts to show to the pagan world that their faith was credible.

THE GRECO-ROMAN WORLD

The Roman Empire had brought to the Mediterranean basin an unprecedented political unity. Although each region kept some of its ancient laws and customs, the general policy of the empire was to encourage as much uniformity as possible without doing unnecessary violence to the uses of each area. In this they followed the example of Alexander. Both Alexander and the Roman Empire succeeded to a remarkable degree, and therefore Roman law and Hellenistic culture comprised the context in which the early church took shape.

The political unity wrought by the Roman Empire allowed the early Christians to travel without having to fear bandits or local wars. When reading about Paul's journeys, we see that the great threat to shipping at that time was bad weather. A few decades earlier, an encounter with pirates was much more to be feared than any storm. In the first century, well-paved and well-guarded roads ran to the most distant provinces—even though most trade and travel took

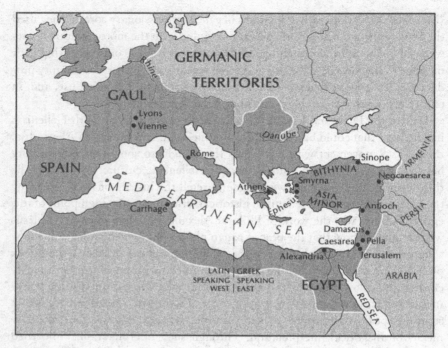

The Roman Empire

place by water. Since trade flourished, travel was constant; thus Christianity
often reached a new region, not through the work of missionaries or preachers,
but rather through traveling traders, slaves, and others. In that sense, the political circumstances favored the spread of Christianity.

But other aspects of those circumstances were a threat and a challenge to the
early Christians. In order to achieve greater unity, imperial policy sought religious uniformity by following two routes: *syncretism* (the indiscriminate mixing
of elements from various religions) and emperor worship.

Rome had a vested interest in having its subjects from different lands believe that, although their gods had different names, they were ultimately the
same gods. To the Roman Pantheon (temple of all gods) were added numerous
gods from different lands. The same roads and sea lanes that served Christian
missionary expansion were also traveled by people of all sorts of traditions and
beliefs. These traditions and beliefs mingled in the plazas and markets of the
cities, to the point that their original form was barely recognizable. Syncretism became the fashion of the time. In that atmosphere, Jews and Christians
were seen as unbending fanatics who insisted on the sole worship of their One
God—an alien cyst that must be removed for the good of society.

Although the Roman Empire was famous for its roads, most long-distance trade and travel took place via water, employing ships such as this one, depicted in a mosaic in the ruins of Ostia, the harbor city of ancient Rome.

The syncretism of the times could also been seen in what historians now call "mystery religions." These were not based on the ancient Olympian deities, but on others which seemed to be much more personal. In earlier times, people generally had followed the religion of their birthplace. But now, after the conquests of Alexander and of Rome, which gods one was to serve became a matter of personal choice. Therefore, one did not belong to a mystery religion by birth, but rather by initiation. Most of these religions were based on myths regarding the origin of the world, the sustenance of life, and the life of the deity. From Egypt came the myth of Isis and Osiris, which explained the fertility of the Nile and all other fertility. Greece contributed rites that from time immemorial had been celebrated near Athens. The cult of Mithra, a god of Indo-Iranian origin, was very popular in the army. Others worshiped the Great Mother of Semitic origin. Given the syncretism of all these religions, soon they were so intermingled that today it is exceedingly difficult for historians to determine which doctrine or practice arose in which context. Since the deities of the mysteries were not exclusivistic, like the God of Jews and Christians, many people who were initiated into various of these cults borrowed elements from one to the other.

But it was another element in Roman religion that eventually became the

The Great Mother of the Gods, commonly known as Cybele, came to Greece and Rome from Asia Minor.

reason for persecution. This was the worship of the ruling emperor. Roman authorities saw this as a means of unity and a test of loyalty. To refuse to burn incense before the emperor's image was a sign of treason or at the very least of disloyalty. When Christians refused to burn incense before the emperor's image, they did so as a witness to their faith; but the authorities condemned them as disloyal and seditious people.

To communicate their faith in the midst of Hellenistic culture, Christians found two philosophical traditions particularly attractive and helpful: Platonism and Stoicism.

Socrates, Plato's teacher, had been condemned to death, as an incredulous corrupter of youth. Plato wrote several dialogues in his defense, and by the first century Socrates was considered one of the greatest sages of antiquity. Socrates, Plato, and many other philosophers had criticized the ancient gods, and had taught about a supreme being, perfect and immutable. Furthermore, both Socrates and Plato believed in the immortality of the soul. And Plato affirmed that, far above this world of fleeting things, there was a higher world of abiding truth. All of this many early Christians found attractive and useful in their attempts to respond to charges that they were ignorant and unbelieving. Although at first these philosophical traditions were used for interpreting the faith to outsiders, soon they began influencing the manner in which Christians understood their own faith—which would eventually result in bitter theological debates.

Something similar happened with Stoicism. This philosophical school, slightly younger than Platonism, held to very high moral standards. The early Stoics—in the third century BCE—were materialists who believed that all things were made out of fire, and determinists who were convinced that all they could do was to train themselves to assent to the inexorable laws that rule events. By the time Christianity appeared on the scene, however, Stoicism had evolved to the point where it had religious overtones, and some of its philosophers spoke of using their wisdom to guide the course of events. In any case, all Stoics believed that the purpose of philosophy was to understand the law of nature, and to obey and adjust to it. The wise person is not one who knows a great deal, but rather one whose mind is so attuned to the universal law that reason prevails. When this happens, passions subside, and the philosopher approaches the ideal of *apatheia*—life without passions. The virtues one must cultivate are four: moral insight, courage, self-control, and justice. These, however, are different facets of the life of wisdom, and therefore a failure in one of them is a failure in all. Stoics were also critical of the religion of their time, which many saw as a way to have the gods justify the desires of their worshipers rather than as a call to virtue. They rejected the traditional parochialism of earlier Greek culture, insisting on the universality of the law of reason and calling themselves citizens of the world.

Again, all this was very attractive to Christians, whose criticism of the religion and morals of the time was rarely well received. The church, which many Christians called a "new race" because it drew its members from all races, was living proof of the universal unity of humankind. The Stoic notion of natural law as the guide to wisdom was soon taken up by Christian apologists and moralists who argued that the Christian life was life according to that law. In response to prejudice, ridicule, and even martyrdom, the Stoic ideal of *apatheia* called believers to steadfastness. And many of the arguments that Stoic philosophers had used against the gods were now taken up by Christians.

This was the world into which Christianity was born. The presence of Judaism in various parts of the world, the order of the Roman Empire, and Hellenistic civilization provided avenues for the proclamation of the new faith; but they also provided obstacles and even dangers. In the next chapters, we shall see how the early Christians followed those avenues, attempted to overcome those obstacles, and responded to those dangers.

3

The Church in Jerusalem

And with great power the apostles gave their testimony to the
resurrection of the Lord Jesus, and great grace was upon them all.

ACTS 4:33

The Book of Acts affirms that from the very beginning there was a strong
church in Jerusalem. But then that very book moves on to other matters,
and tells us very little about the later history of that Christian community. The
rest of the New Testament offers a few other bits of information. But it, too,
deals mostly with the life of the church in other parts of the empire. Yet, by
piecing together what the New Testament tells us with information gathered
from other authors, one can come to a general idea of the life of that earliest
Christian community and its later history.

UNITY AND DIVERSITY

The earliest Christian community is often idealized. Peter's firmness and
eloquence at Pentecost tend to eclipse his wavering on what ought to be done
with the Gentiles who wished to join the church. The possession of all things
in common, commendable as it may be, did not abolish all tensions between
various groups, for "the Hellenists murmured against the Hebrews because their
widows were neglected in the daily distribution" (Acts 6:1).

These last words do not refer to a conflict between Jews and Gentiles, for
Acts makes clear that at that time there were still no Gentiles in the church. It
was rather a conflict between two groups of Jews: those who kept the customs
and language of their ancestors, and those who were more open to Hellenistic
influences. In Acts, the people in the first group are called "Hebrews," and the
others are the "Hellenists." In response to this crisis, the twelve called an assembly that appointed seven men "to serve tables." Exactly what this meant is
not altogether clear, although there is no doubt that the idea was that the seven
would have administrative tasks, and that the twelve would continue preaching and teaching. In any case, it would seem that all seven were Hellenists, for

In Jerusalem, shortly after Pentecost, Christians had to deal with the diversity in their midst.

they had Greek names. Thus, the naming of the seven appears as an attempt to give greater voice in the affairs of the church to the Hellenistic party, while the twelve, all "Hebrews," would continue being the main teachers and preachers.

The seventh chapter of Acts tells the story of Stephen, one of the seven. There is a hint (Acts 7:47-48) that his attitude toward the Temple was not entirely positive. In any case, the Jewish Council—the Sanhedrin—composed mostly of anti-Hellenistic Jews, refuses to listen to him and condemns him to death. This contrasts with the treatment given by the same council to Peter and John, who were released after being beaten and told to stop preaching (Acts 5:40). Furthermore, when persecution finally broke out and Christians had to flee Jerusalem, the apostles were able to remain. When Saul left for Damascus to seek out Christians who had taken refuge there, the apostles were still in Jerusalem, and Saul seemed to ignore them. All of this would seem to indicate that the earliest persecution was aimed mostly at what were called *Hellenistic* Christians, and that the Hebrews had much less difficulty. It is later, in chapter 12, that we are told of Herod (not the council) ordering the death of James, and the arrest of Peter.

Immediately after the death of Stephen, Acts turns to Philip, another of the seven, who founded a church in Samaria. Peter and John are then sent to supervise the life of that new community. Thus, a church is being born beyond the confines of Judea, and that church, although not founded by the apostles, still acknowledges their authority. This is a pattern that would often be repeated as the church extended to new areas.

By its ninth chapter, Acts becomes increasingly interested in Paul, and we hear less and less of the church in Jerusalem. What was happening was that the Hellenistic Jewish Christians were serving as a bridge to the gentile world, and that Gentiles were joining the church in such numbers that they soon overshadowed the earlier Jewish Christian community. For this reason most of our story will deal with Gentile Christianity. And yet, we should not forget that earliest of churches, of which we have only fragmentary glimpses.

RELIGIOUS LIFE

The earliest Christians did not consider themselves followers of a new religion. All of their lives they had been Jews and they still were. This was true of Peter and the twelve, of the seven, and of Paul. Their faith was not a denial of Judaism but was rather the conviction that the messianic age had finally arrived. According to Acts, Paul would say that he was persecuted "because of the hope of Israel" (Acts 28:20)—meaning the coming of the Messiah. The earliest Christians did not reject Judaism, but were convinced that their faith was the fulfillment of the Messiah whom Jews over the ages had been anticipating.

For this reason, Christians in Jerusalem continued to keep the Sabbath and attend worship at the Temple. To this they added the observance of the first day of the week, in which they gathered to break bread in celebration of the resurrection of Jesus. Those early communion services did not center on the Lord's passion, but rather on his victory through which a new age had dawned. It was much later—centuries later—that the focus of Christian worship shifted toward the death of Jesus. As a celebration of the resurrection of Jesus, in the earliest Christian community the breaking of the bread took place "with glad and generous hearts" (Acts 2:46)—the word "generous" probably referring to the sharing of food.

There were indeed times set aside for sorrow for one's sins, in particular during the two weekly days of fasting, which the church adopted from Jewish practice. At an early date, however, at least some Christians began fasting, not on Mondays and Thursdays, like the Jews, but rather on Wednesdays and Fridays. It may be that this shift took place in commemoration of the betrayal and the crucifixion.

In that early church, authority was vested primarily in the twelve (although some scholars suggest that this emphasis on the authority of the apostles appeared slightly later, as part of an effort to tighten up the system of authority

In an illustration found in an Egyptian manuscript of Acts, circa 400 CE, the loop on the cross is shaped in the manner of an ancient hieroglyph meaning life.

within the church). Of the apostles, Peter and John seem to have been foremost, for Acts gives several indications of this, and they are two of the "pillars" to whom Paul refers in Galatians 2:9.

The third such pillar, however, was not one of the twelve. He was James, the brother of the Lord. According to Paul (1 Cor. 15:7), the risen Jesus had appeared to James. Whether because of his blood ties with Jesus, or for some other reason, James soon became the leader of the church in Jerusalem. Later, when church leaders were uniformly given the title *bishop*, it was said that James was the first bishop of Jerusalem. Although the title is clearly erroneous, it is probably true that he was the leader of the church in Jerusalem.

THE WANING OF THE JEWISH CHURCH

Soon persecution grew fiercer and more general. Herod Agrippa, the grandson of Herod the Great, ordered the death of James the brother of John—not to be confused with James the brother of Jesus and head of the community. When this move was well received by his subjects, Herod had Peter arrested, but he escaped. In 62 CE the other James, the brother of Jesus, was killed by order of the high priest, even against the desire and advice of some of the Pharisees.

Soon thereafter, the leaders of the Christian community in Jerusalem decided to move to Pella, a city beyond the Jordan River, the population of which was mostly Gentile. This move seems to have been prompted, not only by persecution at the hands of the Jews, but also by Roman suspicion regarding the exact nature of the new religious sect. At that time, Jewish nationalism had reached the boiling point, and in 66 CE, a rebellion broke out four years later that would lead to the destruction of Jerusalem by the Roman armies. Christians were followers of one who they said was of the line of David, and who had been crucified by Roman authorities for supposedly claiming that he was King of the Jews. They were led first by James, the brother of the crucified, and then, after the death of James, by Simeon, another relative of Jesus. To allay the suspicions that all of this created, the church decided to remove to Pella. But in spite of this such suspicions continued, and Simeon was eventually killed by the Romans, although it is not clear whether this was due to his Christian faith or to his claim to Davidic lineage. In any case, the result of all this was that the ancient Jewish church, rejected by both Jews and Gentiles, found itself in increasing isolation. Although by 135 CE a number of Jewish Christians had returned to Jerusalem, their relationship with the rest of Christianity had been almost entirely severed, and leadership had passed to Gentile Christians.

In the desolate regions beyond the Jordan, Jewish Christianity made contact with various groups that had also abandoned orthodox Judaism. Lacking contact with the rest of the church, that Jewish Christian community followed its own course, and was often influenced by the many sects among which it lived. When, in later centuries, Gentile Christians deigned to write a few words about that forgotten community, they would speak of its heretics and its strange customs, but they would have little of positive value to say about that church, which faded out of history in the fifth century. It may be to some of them that Irenaeus referred when writing in the second century about some whom he calls "Ebionites" and who "circumcise, continue obeying the prescriptions of the

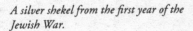
A silver shekel from the first year of the Jewish War.

Law, and are so much influenced by Judaism that they worship Jerusalem as God's dwelling."[1]

Meanwhile, the church—now dominated by Gentiles—continued appealing to Jews throughout the Roman Empire. It continued claiming that its faith was the fulfillment of Judaism, and that Jews should therefore accept Christianity. At the same time, there was always the inclination among some Christians—even Gentile Christians—to go back to their Jewish roots in ways that the leadership of the church considered inappropriate. Furthermore, at that time some Jewish groups were also seeking converts among the Gentiles, and were thus in direct competition with the church. As a result, the Jewish-Christian polemic continued long after the church had become mostly Gentile. Many Christians wrote treatises and preached sermons against Judaism. Many of these were not really directed against Jews themselves, but rather at Christians who might be attracted to Judaism. Yet those treatises and sermons did promote among Christians an anti-Jewish attitude that would have nefarious consequences in subsequent times.

4

Mission to the Gentiles

I am not ashamed of the Gospel: it is the power of God for salvation to everyone who has faith, to the Jew first and also to the Greek.

ROMANS 1:16

Those Christians whom Acts calls "Hellenists," while Jewish, showed a degree of openness to Hellenistic culture. Since they were the first to be persecuted in Jerusalem, they were the first to be scattered throughout the neighboring towns, and thus they were also the first to take the Christian message to those areas.

THE SCOPE OF THE MISSION

According to Acts 8:1, these Christians "were all scattered throughout Judea and Samaria." Acts 9:32-42 speaks of visits by Peter to the Christian communities in Lydda, Sharon, and Joppa, all in Judea. Acts 8 tells of the work of Philip in Samaria, the conversion of Simon Magus; and the visit of Peter and John. As early as Acts 9, we are also told that some of the fleeing Christians were scattered as far as Damascus, well beyond the borders of Judea. And Acts 11:19 adds further that "those who were scattered because of the persecution that arose over Stephen traveled as far as Phoenicia and Cyprus and Antioch." This does not mean that the mission was extended to the Gentiles, for Acts explains that they went to all these areas "speaking the Word to none except Jews."

The mission of Philip in Samaria, and the conversion of the Ethiopian eunuch, are possibly the first indications of the church's willingness to receive non-Jews. But the issue is finally faced in Acts 10, in the episode of Peter and Cornelius, which eventually leads the church of Jerusalem to the surprised conclusion: "Then to the Gentiles also God has granted repentance unto life" (Acts 11:18). Immediately thereafter we are told that something similar happened in Antioch, with the result that Barnabas was sent by the church in Jerusalem to investigate the matter, and "when he came and saw the grace of God, he was glad" (Acts 11:23). These various events show that, according to Acts, while

A medieval illuminated manuscript depicting Pentecost shows the Spirit coming to the apostles in tongues of fire.

the earliest Christian expansion was mostly the result of the witness of those Jewish Christians of Hellenistic tendencies who had to flee Jerusalem, the mother church approved of their work, both among Hellenistic Jews and among Gentiles.

Naturally, this did not solve all problems, for there was always the question of whether Gentile converts to Christianity had to obey the Law of Israel. After some hesitation, the church in Jerusalem accepted them, declaring that "it has seemed good to the Holy Spirit and to us to lay upon you no other burden than these necessary things: that you abstain from what has been sacrificed to idols and from blood and from what is strangled and from unchastity" (Acts 15:28-29). This, however, did not end the matter, for Paul's Epistles are full of evidence that there were for a time those who insisted on greater strictures.

Furthermore, one should note that most of these first Gentile converts were not completely alien to Judaism. They were what Jews often called "God-fearers"—people who had come to believe in the God and the ethical teachings of Israel, but for one reason or another had not joined the ranks of Israel by becoming "proselytes." In Acts, both the Ethiopian eunuch and Cornelius were such God-fearers. And, in Antioch of Pisidia, Paul and Barnabas were enthusiastically received by the Jewish community until they proved to be too ready to accept "others who fear God" into the ranks of the people of God (Acts 13).

PAUL'S WORK

It is not necessary to retell here all of Paul's travels, to which the book of Acts devotes several chapters. It should suffice to say that, for some unknown reason, Barnabas went to Tarsus to look for Paul, and together they spent a year in Antioch, where the followers of Jesus were first called "Christians." Then during a number of voyages, first with Barnabas and then with others, Paul took the gospel to the island of Cyprus, to several cities of Asia Minor, to Greece, to Rome, and perhaps—according to a tradition that cannot be confirmed—to Spain.

But to say that Paul took the gospel to those areas is not to imply that he was the first to do so. The Epistle to the Romans shows that there was a church in the imperial capital before Paul's arrival. Furthermore, the spread of Christianity in Italy was such that when Paul arrived at the small seaport of Puteoli there were already Christians there.

Therefore, Paul's significance to the early spread of Christianity ought not to be exaggerated. Although the New Testament speaks a great deal of Paul and his journeys, there were many others preaching in various regions. Barnabas and Mark went to Cyprus. The Alexandrine Jew Apollos preached in Ephesus and Corinth. And Paul himself, after complaining that "some preach Christ from envy and rivalry," rejoices that by all these Christ is proclaimed (Phil. 1:18).

Paul's greatest and most unique contribution to the shaping of early Christianity was not so much in the actual founding of churches. Rather, it was in the Epistles that he wrote in connection with that activity, since those Epistles eventually became part of Christian scripture, and thus have had a decisive and continuing impact on the life and thought of the Christian church.

Paul is often shown with a book of his Epistles.

The missionary task itself was undertaken, not only by Paul and others whose names are known—Barnabas, Mark, et al.—but also by countless and nameless Christians who went from place to place taking with them their faith and their witness. Some of these, like Paul, traveled as missionaries, impelled by their faith. But mostly these nameless Christians were merchants, slaves, and others who traveled for various reasons, but whose travel provided the opportunity for the expansion of the Christian message.

Finally, while speaking of Paul's work, it is important to point out that, while he felt called to preach to the Gentiles, according to Acts his usual procedure upon arriving at a new town was to go to the synagogue and the Jewish community. Again, he did not believe that he was preaching a new religion, but rather of the fulfillment of the promises made to Israel. His message was not that Israel had been abandoned by God, but rather that now, through the resurrection of Jesus, the age of the Messiah had dawned, and that therefore the way was open for Gentiles to join the people of God. This message would have been quite appealing to God-fearers who now found that they could join the people of God without undergoing circumcision or following the dietary Laws of Israel.

The growth of the Gentile church brought about a number of changes, particularly in the life of worship. When Christians were expelled from the synagogues as false Jews, they began gathering in private houses, at least on Sunday for the breaking of the bread, but often more frequently for instruction and for joint support in the increasingly difficult task of living as Christians in a hostile world. When most converts were either Jews or God-fearers, the church could take for granted that they already knew most of the fundamentals of Christian faith and ethics—the worship of only one God, creation of all things by this God, chastity, honesty, etc. But as increasing numbers of Gentiles sought to join the church it was found necessary to provide for them more extensive periods of teaching and training before they were admitted into the church by baptism. Thus, the catechumenate arose. As part of this process, the service came to be divided in two main parts: the "service of the Word," and the "service of the table." In the former, extensive portions of scripture were read and interpreted both to guide those who were already baptized and for the instruction of catechumens. Then those who were not yet baptized were dismissed, and the congregation proceeded to the service of the table—communion. While we have some indications that this process was already taking place quite early, the process continued throughout the first three centuries, and therefore it is in Chapter 11 that we shall look more carefully into early Christian worship.

THE APOSTLES: FACTS AND LEGENDS

The New Testament gives no indication as to the career of most of the apostles. Acts tells of the death of James, the brother of John. But that very book, after following Paul's career for a number of years, abruptly leaves him while preaching in Rome, awaiting trial. What became of Paul, Peter, and the other apostles? From an early date, traditions began to appear claiming that one or another of them had preached in a particular region, or had suffered martyrdom in one way or another. Most of these traditions are no more than the result of the desire of a church in a particular city to claim an apostolic origin. Others are more worthy of credit.

Of all these traditions, the most trustworthy is the one that affirms that Peter was in Rome, and that he suffered martyrdom in that city during Nero's persecution. On these points, several writers of the first and second centuries seem to agree. We are also told that he was crucified—according to one version, upside-down—and this seems to be implied by the otherwise obscure words in John 21:18-19.

The case of Paul is somewhat more complex. The book of Acts leaves him while preaching in Rome. Ancient writers agree that he died in Rome—probably beheaded, as befitted a Roman citizen—at the time of Nero. But others say that he undertook some journeys that are not mentioned in Acts, including one trip to Spain. Some have tried to join these two traditions by supposing that Paul went to Spain between the end of Acts and the Neronian persecution. But this explanation encounters chronological difficulties. At best, all that can be said is that nothing is known for certain between the end of the book of Acts and Paul's death during the reign of Nero.

The task of reconstructing John's later career is complicated by the frequency with which the name of John appears in early records. There is an ancient tradition that claims that John was killed in a pot of boiling oil. But the book of Revelation places John, at about the same time, in exile on the island of Patmos. Another very trustworthy tradition speaks of John as a teacher at Ephesus, where he died around the year 100. All this indicates that there were at least two people with the same name, and that later tradition confused them. A second-century Christian writer—Papias of Hierapolis—affirms that there were indeed two persons by the name of John in the early church: one the apostle, and another an elder at Ephesus, who received the visions on Patmos. It is clear, from the enormous difference in their use of the Greek language, that the John of Revelation did not write the Fourth Gospel—commonly known as the Gospel of John. In any case, there was indeed toward the end of the first century, in the city of Ephesus, a Christian teacher named John, whose authority was great in all of the churches of Asia Minor.

According to one of many traditions about the apostles, Peter sent seven deacons to evangelize Spain. Bas-relief in the Cathedral of Ávila.

Late in the second century, a development took place that greatly hinders the task of the historian who seeks to discern the later career of the apostles. The churches in every important city began claiming apostolic origins. In its rivalry with Rome and Antioch, the church in Alexandria felt the need to have a founder with apostolic connections, and thus the tradition appeared that Saint Mark had founded the church there. Likewise, when Constantinople became a capital city in the empire, its church too needed apostolic roots, and thus it was claimed that Philip had preached in Byzantium, the ancient site on which Constantinople was later built.

There are other traditions regarding apostolic activities that are worthy of note, if not for their truthfulness, at least for their popularity and their significance for later history. This is particularly true of the traditions regarding the origins of Christianity in Spain and in India. Christians in Spain have claimed that their land was evangelized, not only by Paul, but also by James and by seven envoys sent by Peter. The legend regarding Peter's missionaries to Spain appeared first in the fifth century, but it was not as influential as that of James's visit to the country, which originated three centuries later. According to this tradition, James proclaimed the gospel, without much success, in Galicia and Saragossa. On his way back, the Virgin appeared to him standing on a pillar, and gave him words of encouragement. This is the origin of the *Virgen del Pilar*, still venerated by many in the Spanish tradition. Upon his return to Jerusalem, James was beheaded by Herod, and then his disciples took his remains back to Compostela in Spain, where they are supposedly buried to this day.

This legend has been of great significance for the later history of Spain, for Saint James (in Spanish, *Santiago*) became the patron saint of the nation. During the wars against the Moors, *Santiago* was often the battle cry to which various small kingdoms would rally. At the same time, pilgrimages to the shrine of Saint James in Compostela played an important role both in European religiosity and in the unification of northern Spain. The Order of Saint James also played a significant role in Spanish history. Thus, although it is highly unlikely that James ever gave any thought to Spain, the legends regarding his visit were very influential in the later history of that country.

The tradition that claims Thomas visited India leaves historians somewhat baffled. It appears for the first time in the *Acts of Thomas*, which may have been written as early as the end of the second century. But already it is embellished with legendary tales that make the entire account suspicious. We are told that an Indian king, Gondophares, was seeking an architect to build a palace, and that Thomas, who was no architect, offered himself for the job. When the king found that Thomas was giving to the poor the money allotted for the construction of the palace, he had the apostle put in prison. But then Gondophares's brother, Gad, died and came back from the dead. Upon his return he told his brother of the magnificent heavenly palace that he had seen, which was being built through Thomas's gifts to the poor. The king was then converted and baptized, and Thomas moved on to other parts of India, until he died as a martyr.

Historians have found that much in this legend is of questionable authenticity, and have often discarded the whole of it as fictitious, for history had no record of Gondophares or of any of the other details of the story. More recently, however, coins have been found that prove that there was indeed a ruler by that name, and that he had a brother named Gad. This, coupled with the undeniable antiquity of Christianity in India, and with the fact that at the time there was significant trade between India and the Near East, makes it more difficult to reject categorically the possibility that Thomas may have visited that land, and that the story may have been embellished with all kinds of legendary details later. In any case, it is significant that from a relatively early date there was a church in India, and that this church has long claimed Thomas as its founder.

In conclusion, it is certain that some of the apostles—particularly Peter, John, and Paul—did travel proclaiming the gospel and supervising the churches that had been founded, either by them or by others. Perhaps other apostles, such as Thomas, did likewise. But most of the traditions regarding apostolic travels date from a later period, when it was believed that the apostles divided the world among themselves, and when the church in each country or city sought to claim apostolic origins. In truth, most missionary work was not carried out by the apostles, but rather by the countless and nameless Christians who for different reasons—persecution, business, or missionary calling—traveled from place to place taking the news of the gospel with them.

5

First Conflicts with the State

I know that you have but little power, and yet you have kept my word
and have not denied my name.

REVELATION 3:8B

From its very beginnings, Christianity was no easy matter. The Lord whom
Christians served had died on the cross, condemned as a criminal. Soon
thereafter Stephen was stoned to death following his witness before the Council
of the Jews. Then James was killed at Herod Agrippa's order. Ever since then,
and up to our own days, there have been those who have had to seal their witness with their blood.

Yet, the reasons for persecution, and the manner in which it has been carried
out, have varied. Already in the early decades of the life of the church there was
a certain development in these matters.

A NEW JEWISH SECT

The early Christians did not believe that they were following a new religion.
They were Jews, and their main difference with the rest of Judaism was that
they were convinced that the Messiah had come, whereas other Jews continued awaiting his advent. Therefore, the Christian message to Jews was not
that they should abandon their Jewishness. On the contrary, now that the
messianic age had begun, they were to be better Jews. Likewise, their early
proclamation to the Gentiles was not an invitation to accept a newly born
religion, but rather to become participants in the promises made to Abraham
and his descendents. Gentiles were invited to become children of Abraham by
faith, since they could not be so by flesh. This invitation was made possible
because, since the time of the prophets, Judaism had held that through the
advent of the Messiah all nations would be brought to Zion. For those early
Christians, Judaism was not a rival religion to Christianity, but the same faith,
even though those who followed it did not see or believe that the prophecies
had been fulfilled.

From the point of view of those Jews who rejected Christianity, the situation was understood in a similar manner. Christianity was not a new religion, but a heretical sect within Judaism. As we have seen, first-century Judaism was not a monolithic entity, but included various divergent sects and opinions. Therefore, when Christianity entered the scene, Jews saw it as simply another sect.

The attitude of those Jews toward Christianity is best understood by placing ourselves in their situation, and seeing Christianity from their perspective, as a new heresy going from town to town tempting good Jews to become heretics. Furthermore, many Jews believed, with some biblical foundation, that the reason why they had lost their independence and been made subjects of the Roman Empire was that the people had not been sufficiently faithful to the traditions of their ancestors. Nationalistic and patriotic sentiment was aroused by the fear that these new heretics could once more bring the wrath of God upon Israel.

For these reasons, in most of the New Testament it is the Jews who persecute Christians, who in turn seek refuge under the wing of Roman authorities. This happens, for instance, when some Jews in Corinth accuse Paul before Proconsul Gallio, saying that "this man is persuading men to worship God contrary to the Law," to which Gallio answers, "If it were a matter of wrongdoing or vicious crime, I should have reason to hear you, O Jews; but since it is a matter of questions about words and names and your own law, see to it yourselves; I refuse to be a judge of these things" (Acts 18:14-15). Later, when there is a riot because some claim that Paul has brought a Gentile to the Temple, and some Jews try to kill the apostle, it is the Romans who save his life.

Thus, Romans, Jews, and Christians agreed that what was taking place was a conflict among Jews. As long as things were relatively orderly, Romans preferred to stay out of such matters. But when there was a riot or any disorderly conduct, they intervened to restore order, and sometimes to punish the disorderly.

A good illustration of this policy was the expulsion of Jews from Rome by Emperor Claudius, around the year 51 CE Acts 18:2 mentions this expulsion, but does not explain the reason for it. Suetonius, a Roman historian, says that Jews were expelled from the capital city for their disorderly conduct "because of Chrestus." Most historians agree that "Chrestus" is none other than *Christus*, and that what actually took place in Rome was that Christian proclamation caused so many riots among Jews that the emperor decided to expel the lot. At that time, Romans still saw the conflict between Christians and Jews as an internal matter within Judaism.

But the distinction between Christians and Jews became clearer as the church gained more converts from the Gentile population, and the ratio of Jews in its ranks diminished. There are also indications that, as Jewish nationalism increased and eventually led to rebellion against Rome, Christians—particularly the Gentiles among them—sought to put as much distance as possible between themselves and that movement. The result was that Roman authorities began to become cognizant of Christianity as a religion quite different from Judaism.

This new consciousness of Christianity as a separate religion was at the root of two and a half centuries of persecution by the Roman Empire, from the time of Nero to the conversion of Constantine. Roman authorities had dealt with Judaism long enough to understand that for most Jews their refusal to worship the emperor or the gods was not an act of rebellion against established authorities, and that such rebellion would only take place when those authorities sought to impose their gods on the Jews. As a result, Jews were normally exempt from the expectation that they worship the emperor. Thus, as long as Christianity was considered a variant of Judaism, its adherents would not normally be required to worship the emperor, and their refusal to do so would not be considered an act of rebellion or disobedience, but a matter of religious conviction. But once it became clear that not all Christians were Jews, and that this new religion was spreading throughout the empire, authorities would demand that Christians, like any other subjects of the empire, show their loyalty by worshiping the emperor.

The history of Jewish-Christian relations in the first years of Christianity has had fateful consequences. While Christianity appeared as a heretical sect within Judaism, the latter tried to suppress it, as can be seen in various books of the New Testament—books, it should be added, written by Christian Jews. Since that time, however, Jews have not been in a position where it was possible for them to persecute Christians—in fact, the opposite has often been the case. When Christianity became the official religion of the majority, there were those who, on the basis of what the New Testament says about the opposition of Judaism to Christianity, and without any regard for the different historical circumstances, declared the Jews to be a rejected race, persecuted them, and even massacred them. Such an attitude would have been abhorrent to Paul, who claimed that he was being persecuted "for the hope of Israel."

PERSECUTION UNDER NERO

Thanks to his mother's intrigues, Nero reached the Roman throne in October of 54. At first he was a reasonable ruler, not entirely unpopular, whose laws in favor of the dispossessed were well received by the Roman populace. But he became increasingly infatuated by his dreams of grandeur and his lust for pleasure, and surrounded himself with a court where all vied to satisfy his every whim. Ten years after his accession to the throne, he was despised by the gen-

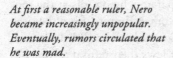

*At first a reasonable ruler, Nero
became increasingly unpopular.
Eventually, rumors circulated that
he was mad.*

eral population as well as by the poets and artists, who were offended by the
emperor's claim that he was one of them. Soon the rumor began circulating that
he was mad.

Such was the state of affairs when, on the night of June 18, 64 CE, a great
fire broke out in Rome. It appears that Nero was several miles away, in his
palace at Antium, and that as soon as he heard the news he hurried to Rome,
where he tried to organize the fight against the fire. He opened to the homeless the gardens of his palace, as well as other public buildings. In spite of
this, there were those who suspected the emperor, whom many believed was
mad, of having ordered that certain sections of the city be put to the torch.
The fire lasted six days and seven nights, and then flared up sporadically for
three more days. Ten of the fourteen sections of the city were destroyed. In
the midst of their sufferings, the people clamored for justice. Soon the rumor
arose—and persists to this day in many history books—that Nero had ordered
the city destroyed so he could rebuild it according to his fancy. The Roman
historian Tacitus, who may well have been present at the time, records several
of the rumors that circulated, but seems inclined to believe that the fire began
accidentally in an oil warehouse.

More and more, the people began to suspect the emperor. A rumor circulated that he had spent most of the time during the fire atop a tower on the
Palatine, dressed as an actor, playing his lyre and singing about the destruction
of Troy. Then the story was that, in his presumptuousness as a poet, he had ordered the city destroyed so that the fire would inspire in him a great epic poem.
Nero tried to allay such suspicions, but it soon became clear that he would not
succeed in this as long as there was no one else to blame. Two of the areas that

had not burned had many Jewish and Christian residents. Therefore, the emperor decided to blame the Christians.

Tacitus tells the story:

> In spite of every human effort, of the emperor's largesse, and of the sacrifices made to the gods, nothing sufficed to allay suspicion nor to destroy the opinion that the fire had been ordered. Therefore, in order to destroy this rumor, Nero blamed the Christians, who are hated for their abominations, and punished them with refined cruelty. Christ, from whom they take their name, was executed by Pontius Pilate during the reign of Tiberius. Stopped for a moment, this evil superstition reappeared, not only in Judea, where was the root of the evil, but also in Rome, where all things sordid and abominable from every corner of the world come together. Thus, first those who confessed [that they were Christians] were arrested, and on the basis of their testimony a great number were condemned, although not so much for the fire itself as for their hatred of humankind.[2]

These words from Tacitus are of great value, for they are one of the most ancient extant indications of how pagans viewed Christians. Reading these lines, it is clear that Tacitus did not believe that the fire in Rome was set by Christians. Furthermore, he did not approve of Nero's "refined cruelty." But, all the same, this good and cultured Roman believed a great deal of what was being said about the "abominations" of Christians and their "hatred of humankind." Tacitus, and other authors writing contemporaneously, do not detail these supposed "abominations." Second-century authors would be more explicit. But, in any case, Tacitus believed the rumors, and thought that Christians hated humankind. This last charge makes sense if one remembers that all social activities—the theater, the army, classic literature, sports—were so entwined with pagan worship that Christians often felt the need to abstain from them. Therefore, to the eyes of a Roman such as Tacitus, who loved his culture and society, Christians appeared as haters of humankind.

But Tacitus goes on:

> Before killing the Christians, Nero used them to amuse the people. Some were dressed in furs, to be killed by dogs. Others were crucified. Still others were set on fire early in the night, so that they might illumine it. Nero opened his own gardens for these shows, and in the circus he himself became a spectacle, for he mingled with the people dressed as a

charioteer, or he rode around in his chariot. All of this aroused the mercy of the people, even against these culprits who deserved an exemplary punishment, for it was clear that they were not being destroyed for the common good, but rather to satisfy the cruelty of one person.[3]

Once again the pagan historian, while showing no love for Christians, indicates that the reason for this persecution was not justice, but the whim of the emperor. These lines are also one of the few surviving pagan testimonies of the cruel tortures to which those early martyrs were subjected.

It is difficult to know the extent of the Neronian persecution. Christian writers from the latter part of the first century, and early in the second, recall the horrors of those days. It is also very likely that both Peter and Paul were among the Neronian martyrs. On the other hand, there is no mention of any persecution outside the city of Rome, and therefore it is quite likely that this persecution, although exceedingly cruel, was limited to the capital of the empire.

Although at first Christians were charged with arson, soon they were persecuted for merely being Christian—and for all the supposed abominations connected with that name. Ancient writers tell us that Nero issued an edict against Christians. But such an edict, if it ever existed, is no longer extant.

In 68 CE, Nero was deposed by a rebellion that gained the support of the Roman senate, and killed himself. The persecution ceased, although nothing was done to rescind whatever laws Nero had passed against Christians. A period of such political turmoil followed that the year 69 is known as the year of four emperors. Eventually, Vespasian gained control of the government, and during his reign and that of his son Titus Christians were generally ignored by the authorities.

PERSECUTION UNDER DOMITIAN

Domitian, who became emperor after Titus, at first paid no particular attention to Christians. Why he eventually turned against them is not clear. It is a fact that he loved and respected Roman traditions, and that he sought to restore them. Christians, in their rejection of Roman gods and of many Roman traditions, stood in the way of Domitian's dreams, and this may have been one of the causes of persecution.

Jews also found themselves in trouble with the emperor. Since the Temple had been destroyed in 70, Domitian decided that all Jews should remit to the imperial coffers the annual offering they would otherwise have sent to Jerusalem. Some Jews refused to obey, while others sent the money but made clear that Rome had not taken the place of Jerusalem. In response, Domitian enacted strict laws against Judaism, and insisted on the offering in even harsher terms.

Christians were seen as enemies of society, in part because they abstained from activities and spectacles such as those that took place in the Roman Colosseum.

Since at that time the distinction between Jews and Christians was not clear in the minds of Roman authorities, imperial functionaries began persecuting any who followed "Jewish practices." Thus began a new persecution, which seems to have been directed against both Jews and Christians.

As in the case of Nero, it does not appear that this persecution was uniformly severe throughout the empire. In fact, it is only from Rome and Asia Minor that there are trustworthy reports of persecution at this time.

In Rome, Flavius Clemens and his wife Flavia Domitilla, who may have been related to the emperor, were executed. They were accused of "atheism" and of "Jewish practices." Since Christians worshiped an invisible God, pagans often declared them to be atheists. Therefore, it is likely that Flavius Clemens and Domitilla died because they were Christians. If so, these are the only two Roman martyrs of this persecution whose names are known. But several ancient writers affirm that there were many martyrs, and a letter that the church in Rome addressed to the Corinthians—*First Clement*—speaks of "the continuous and unexpected evils which have come upon us."

In Asia Minor, this persecution resulted in the writing of the book of Revelation, whose author was exiled on the island of Patmos. There are indications that many were killed, and for generations the church in Asia Minor remembered the reign of Domitian as a time of trial.

In the midst of persecution, Revelation displays a much more negative attitude toward Rome than the rest of the New Testament. Paul had instructed Christians in Rome to obey the authorities, whom he declared to have been ordained by God. But now the seer of Patmos speaks of Rome as "the great harlot . . . drunk with the blood of the saints and the blood of the martyrs of Jesus" (Rev. 17:1, 6). Furthermore, the hope of a new, heavenly city found in Revelation is the counterpart of the present earthly city; over against the city of Rome, "Babylon the great," or "the great harlot," Christians should look to the new Jerusalem, coming from heaven, where God will wipe all tears from their eyes.

Fortunately, when persecution broke out Domitian's reign was coming to an end. Like Nero, Domitian was increasingly seen as a tyrant. His enemies conspired against him, and he was murdered in his own palace. The Roman senate then decreed that his name should be erased from every inscription, so that there would be no memory of him. In this his enemies succeeded, for history has long seen Domitian as a madman lusting for power and recognition as a divine being. Christian historians have also contributed to this, for they have been convinced that anyone who persecuted Christians must have been a tyrant and a madman. Today, historians are vindicating Domitian's memory as a relatively good ruler. As for Christians, after Domitian's fall no one seems to have taken notice of them, and therefore they were granted a few years of relative peace.

6

Persecution in the Second Century

Now I begin to be a disciple. . . . Let fire and cross, flocks of beasts, broken bones, dismemberment, come upon me, so long as I attain to Jesus Christ.

IGNATIUS OF ANTIOCH

Although the Roman Empire began persecuting Christians from the time of Nero, throughout the first century the details of such persecutions are scarce. By the second century, however, records begin to afford a clearer view of the issues involved in the persecutions, and of the attitudes of Christians toward martyrdom. Of these, the most dramatic are the *Acts of the Martyrs*, which retell the arrest, trial, and execution of various martyrs. Some of these include so many trustworthy details about the trials that they seem to have been taken, in part at least, from official court records. Sometimes we are told that the writer was present at the trial and death of the martyr, and historians are inclined to believe that it was indeed so. On the other hand, a number of these supposed *Acts of the Martyrs* clearly were penned at a much later date, and deserve little credit. But, in any case, the genuine "acts" are among the most precious and inspiring documents of early Christianity. Secondly, we learn of the attitude of Christians toward martyrdom through other Christian writings. Of these, the most valuable is probably the set of seven letters that the aged Bishop Ignatius of Antioch wrote on his way to martyrdom. Finally, the second century offers further glimpses into the attitude of Roman authorities vis-à-vis the new faith. In this context, the correspondence between Pliny and Trajan is most illuminating.

THE CORRESPONDENCE BETWEEN PLINY AND TRAJAN

In III CE, Pliny the Younger was appointed governor of Bithynia, on the northern shore of modern-day Turkey. From various sources, it would appear that Pliny was a just man with a profound respect for Roman law and traditions.

But in Bithynia he had to deal with an unexpected problem. There were many Christians in the region—so many, in fact, that Pliny discovered that the pagan temples were almost deserted, and that the sellers of animals for sacrifice found few buyers. When somebody sent the new governor a list of Christians, Pliny began inquiries, for he knew that this religion was illegal.

The governor had the accused brought before him, and thus began learning of the beliefs and practices of Christians. Many declared that they were not Christians, and others said that, although they had followed the new faith for a time, they had abandoned it. Of these Pliny required only that they pray to the gods, burn incense before the image of the emperor, and curse Christ—things he had heard true Christians would never do. Once they met these requirements, he simply let them go.

Those who persisted in their faith posed a different problem. Pliny's practice was to offer them three opportunities to recant, while threatening them with death. If they refused, he had them executed, not so much for being Christians as for their obstinacy. If they were Roman citizens, he had them sent to Rome, as the law required.

But Pliny considered himself a just man, and therefore felt obliged to find out what crimes, besides sheer obstinacy, Christians committed. All he could learn was that Christians gathered before dawn to sing to Christ "as to a god," and to join in an oath not to commit theft, adultery, or any such sins. They also used to gather for a common meal, but had discontinued this practice when the authorities had outlawed secret meetings. Not quite convinced that this was the whole truth, Pliny put two female Christian ministers to torture. But they simply confirmed what he already knew.

The question then was, should Christians be punished for concrete crimes, or should the very name "Christian" be considered a crime? Not knowing what course to follow, Pliny suspended the proceedings and wrote Emperor Trajan for further instructions.

The emperor's response was brief. When it comes to the punishment of Christians, there is no general rule that is equally valid in all circumstances. On the one hand, the nature of their crime is such that the state should not waste time seeking them out. On the other hand, if they are accused and refuse to recant, they should be punished. Those who are willing to worship the gods should be pardoned without further inquiries. Finally, anonymous accusations should be disregarded, for they are a bad legal precedent and are "unworthy of this age."

Almost a hundred years later, the legal mind of Tertullian, a Christian in North Africa, rebelled against the injustice of such an edict, which was still in force:

What a necessarily confused sentence! It refuses to seek them out, as if they were innocent, and orders that they be punished as if they were guilty. It pardons, and yet is cruel. It ignores, and yet punishes. Why do you circumvent your own censure? If you condemn, why do you not inquire? And, if you do not inquire, why do you not also absolve?[4]

Yet, although Trajan's decision seemed to lack logic, it did not lack political sense. He understood what Pliny was saying: that Christians, by the mere fact of being such, were not committing any crime against society or against the state. Therefore, the resources of the state should not be wasted in seeking them out. But, once accused and brought before the authorities, Christians had to be forced to worship the gods of the empire, or face punishment. Otherwise, imperial courts would lose their authority. In other words, Christians were not punished for crimes committed before being brought to trial, but for what seemed their contempt of Roman courts. Those who openly refused to worship the gods and the emperor had to be punished, first, because the dignity of the courts required it; and, second, because in refusing to worship the emperor they seemed to be denying his right to rule.

The policies Trajan outlined in his response to Pliny were followed far beyond the borders of Bithynia, and long after Trajan's death. Throughout the second century, and part of the third, it was imperial policy not to seek out Christians, but still to punish them when they were brought before the authorities. That this was true even before the correspondence between Pliny and Trajan may be seen in the circumstances surrounding Ignatius's seven letters.

IGNATIUS OF ANTIOCH, THE BEARER OF GOD

About the year 107, the elderly bishop of Antioch, Ignatius, was condemned to death by the imperial authorities. Since great festivities were being planned in Rome in celebration of a military victory, Ignatius was sent to the capital so that his death might provide entertainment for the people. On his way to martyrdom, he wrote seven letters that are among the most valuable documents informing our knowledge of early Christianity.

Ignatius was probably born around 30 or 35 CE, and was well over seventy when his life ended in martyrdom. In his letters, he repeatedly calls himself "the bearer of God," as if this were a title by which he was known—and this is an indication of the high respect in which he was held among Christians. Much later, by making a slight change in the Greek text of his letters, people began speaking of Ignatius as "he who was borne by God," and thus arose the legend that he was the little child whom Jesus picked up and placed in the midst of his disciples. In any case, by the beginning of the second century

A sixth-century mosaic depicting scenes in Antioch.

Ignatius had great prestige in the entire Christian community, because he was bishop (the second after the apostles) of one of the most ancient churches, that of Antioch.

Nothing is known about the arrest and trial of Ignatius, nor of who it was that brought an accusation against him. From his letters, it is clear that there were several factions in Antioch, and that the elderly bishop had tenaciously opposed those doctrines he found heretical. It is not clear whether he was accused before the authorities by a pagan, or by a dissident Christian who sought to undo him. In any case, for one reason or another, Ignatius was arrested, tried, and condemned to die in Rome.

On their way to Rome, Ignatius and the soldiers guarding him passed through Asia Minor. A number of Christians from that area came to see him. Ignatius was able to see them and converse with them. He even had a Christian amanuensis with him who wrote the letters he dictated. Since Ignatius could receive visitors who were obviously guilty of the same crime of which he stood convicted, it is clear that there was no general persecution of Christians throughout the empire at this time, but that only those brought before the courts were condemned.

Ignatius's seven letters are the outcome of these visits. He had received the bishop, two elders, and a deacon from the church in Magnesia. From Tralles, Bishop Polybius had come. Ephesus had sent a delegation headed by Bishop Onesimus—who may well have been the same person about whom Paul wrote to Philemon. To each of these churches, Ignatius addressed a letter from Smyrna. Later, from Troas, he wrote three other letters: one to the church of Smyrna, another to its Bishop Polycarp, and a third to the church in Philadelphia. But the most significant letter in helping us understand the nature of persecution and martyrdom in the second century is the one that Ignatius wrote from Smyrna to the church in Rome.

Somehow, Ignatius had heard that Christians in Rome were considering the possibility of freeing him from death. He did not look upon this with favor. He was ready to seal his witness with his blood, and any move on the part of Christians in Rome to save him would be an obstacle to his goal. He therefore wrote to them:

> I fear your kindness, which may harm me. You may be able to achieve what you plan. But if you pay no heed to my request it will be very difficult for me to attain unto God.

As Ignatius goes on to say, his purpose is to be an imitator of the passion of his God, Jesus Christ. As he faces the ultimate sacrifice, Ignatius believes that he begins to be a disciple; and therefore all that he wants from Christians in Rome is that they pray, not that he be freed, but that he may have the strength to face every trial,

> . . . so that I may not only be called a Christian, but also behave as such. . . . My love is crucified. . . . I no longer savor corruptible food . . . but wish to taste the bread of God, which is the flesh of Jesus Christ . . . and his blood I wish to drink, which is an immortal drink. . . . When I suffer, I shall be free in Jesus Christ, and with him shall rise again in freedom. . . . I am God's wheat, to be ground by the teeth of beasts, so that I may be offered as pure bread of Christ.

And the reason why Ignatius is willing to face death with such courage is that he will thereby become a witness:

> If you remain silent about me, I shall become a word of God. But if you allow yourselves to be swayed by the love in which you hold my flesh, I shall again be no more than a human voice.[5]

Shortly thereafter, Bishop Polycarp of Smyrna wrote to the Christians in Philippi asking for news regarding Ignatius. The answer from the Philippians has been lost, although it seems certain that Ignatius died as he expected shortly after his arrival in Rome.

THE MARTYRDOM OF POLYCARP

Although very little is known of Ignatius's martyrdom, there is much more information regarding that of his younger friend, Polycarp, when his time came almost half a century later. It was the year 155, and the policy that Trajan had outlined for Pliny was still in effect. Christians were not sought out; but if they were accused and they refused to worship the gods, they had to be punished.

We know of events in Smyrna through the work of a writer who claims to have witnessed them. It all began when a group of Christians was brought before the authorities, and they refused to worship the gods. Under the cruelest of tortures they remained firm, we are told, because "resting in Christ they scorned the pains of the world." When Germanicus, an elderly Christian, was brought to trial, he was told that he should take into account his old age and recant, rather than submit to torture and death. To this he responded that he had no desire to continue living in a world where the injustices that he had just seen took place. And, to show how deeply he meant his words, he called on the beasts to come to him and kill him. This act of courage further aroused the anger of the mob, which began to shout: "Death to the atheists!" (referring to those who had no visible gods) and "Bring Polycarp!"

When the old bishop learned that he was being sought, he followed the advice of his flock, and hid for several days. But after having moved to another hiding place, and still being discovered, he decided that his arrest was the will of God, refused to flee any further, and calmly awaited those who came after him.

The proconsul who presided at his trial tried to persuade him to worship the emperor, urging him to consider his advanced age. When Polycarp refused, the judge ordered him to cry: "Out with the atheists!" To this Polycarp responded by pointing at the crowd around him and saying: "Yes. Out with the atheists!" Again the judge insisted, promising that if he would swear by the emperor and curse Christ he would be free to go. But Polycarp replied: "For eighty-six years I have served him, and he has done me no evil. How could I curse my king, who saved me?"

Thus, the dialogue went on. When the judge threatened him with being burned alive, Polycarp simply answered that the fire that the judge could light would last only a moment, whereas the eternal fire would never go out. Finally, we are told that after he was tied to the post in the pyre, he looked up and prayed out loud: "Lord Sovereign God . . . I thank you that you have deemed me worthy of this moment, so that, jointly with your martyrs, I may have a share in the cup of Christ. . . . For this . . . I bless and glorify you. Amen."[6]

Many years earlier, Ignatius of Antioch had advised young Bishop Polycarp regarding his duties as bishop and the need to be firm in his faith. Now Polycarp showed himself a worthy recipient of Ignatius's advice, and a follower of his example.

One significant note in this entire account is that Polycarp fled and hid when he learned that he was being sought. We are also told in the same account that a certain Quintus, who offered himself as a martyr, weakened at the last moment and abandoned the faith. This was important for those early Christians, who believed that martyrdom was not something that one chose, but something for which one was chosen by God. Those who were so chosen were strengthened by Christ who suffered with them, and for that reason were able to stand firm. Their firmness was not of their own doing, but of God. On the other hand, those who ran forward and offered themselves for martyrdom—the "spontaneous"—were false martyrs, and Christ would desert them.

But not all Christians agreed with the author of the *Martyrdom of Polycarp*. Throughout the entire period of persecutions, there were occasional spontaneous martyrs. And, when they remained firm to the end, they found the approval of many. This may be seen in another document of the same time, the *Apology* by Justin Martyr, in which we are told that at a Christian's trial two others came forth in his defense, and all three died as martyrs. In telling this story, Justin does not give the slightest indication that the martyrdom of the two who were spontaneous was less valid than that of the one originally accused.

PERSECUTION UNDER MARCUS AURELIUS

Marcus Aurelius, who became emperor in 161, possessed one of the most enlightened minds of his age. He was not, like Nero and perhaps Domitian, enamored with power and vainglory. On the contrary, he was a refined man who left behind a collection of *Meditations,* written for his private use, which are literary masterpieces of the time. He expresses some of the ideals with which he tried to rule his vast empire:

> Think constantly, both as a Roman and as a man, to do the task before you with perfect and simple dignity, and with kindness, freedom, and justice. Try to forget everything else. And you will be able to do so if you undertake every action in your life as if it were the last, leaving aside all negligence and the opposition of passion to the dictates of reason, and leaving aside also all hypocrisy, egotism, and rebelliousness against your own lot.[7]

Under such an emperor, it could be expected that Christians would enjoy a period of relative peace. And yet, the same emperor who expressed such lofty ideals regarding government also ordered that Christians be persecuted. In the only reference to Christianity in his *Meditations,* the emperor praises those souls who are ready to abandon their bodies when the time comes, rather than cling to life. He then goes on to say that this attitude is praiseworthy only when it is the outcome of reason, "and not of obstinacy, as is the case with Christians."

Furthermore, as a child of his age, this enlightened emperor was also a superstitious man. He constantly sought the advice of seers, and before every significant undertaking sacrifices had to be offered. During the early years of his reign, there seemed to be an endless string of invasions, floods, epidemics and other disasters. Soon the explanation arose that Christians were to blame, for they had brought the wrath of the gods upon the empire. It is impossible to know for certain whether the emperor believed this explanation; but, in any case, he fully supported the persecution, and favored the revival of the old religion. Perhaps, like Pliny, what he found most objectionable in Christians was their stubbornness.

One of the most informative documents from this time tells of the martyrdom of the widow Felicitas and her seven sons. Felicitas was one of the consecrated widows (that is, women who devoted all their time to work for the church, which in turn supported them). Her work was such that some pagan priests decided to put an end to it by accusing her before the authorities. When the prefect tried to persuade her to abandon her faith, first with promises and then with threats, she answered that he was wasting his time, for "while I live, I shall defeat you; and if you kill me, in my death I shall defeat you all the more." He then tried to persuade her sons. But she encouraged them to stand firm, and none of them flinched before the worst threats. Finally, the record of the inquest was sent to Marcus Aurelius, who ordered that they should die in different sections of the city—probably to appease various gods.

Another martyr during this persecution was Justin, perhaps the best Christian scholar of the time, who had founded a school in Rome where he taught what he called "the true philosophy"—Christianity. He had recently bested a famous pagan philosopher in a public debate, and there are indications that it was this philosopher who accused him. In any case, Justin died as a martyr in Rome—although the accounts of his martyrdom did not appear until much later, and therefore the details are questionable.

Further insight into this persecution comes to us through a letter that the churches of Lyons and Vienne, in Gaul, sent to their fellow Christians in Phrygia and Asia Minor. It seems that at first all that was done in those cities was to forbid Christians to visit public places. But then one day a mob began following them on the street, shouting at them and pelting them. Finally, several Christians were arrested and taken before the governor to be tried. There a certain Epagathus emerged from among the mob members and offered to defend the Christians. Asked if he was one of them, he said that he was, and he was then added to the group of the accused.

The writers of the letter explain that persecution had appeared unexpectedly, "like a bolt of lightning," so that many were not prepared. Some of them weakened and "left the womb of the church like abortive ones."

The rest, however, stood firm, and this in turn increased the wrath of the governor and the mob. Torture was ordered. A certain Sanctus, when tortured, simply answered, "I am a Christian." The more he was tortured, the more he persisted in saying nothing but these words. Moved by this and many other signs of courage, some who had earlier denied their faith returned to confess it and die as martyrs. We are not told how many died, but the letter does say that the place where Christians were being held was so full that some died of suffocation before the executioners could get to them.

These are only a few examples of what took place under the reign of the enlightened Marcus Aurelius. There are several other accounts of martyrdoms still extant. One must suppose that the accounts that have survived tell only a part of the story of what actually happened throughout the empire.

TOWARD THE END OF THE SECOND CENTURY

Marcus Aurelius died in 180 and was succeeded by Commodus, who had begun to rule jointly with him eight years earlier. Although Commodus did not issue any edicts against persecution, the storm abated during his reign, and the number of martyrs was relatively low. After the death of Commodus, there was a period of civil war, and Christians were once again ignored in favor of more pressing matters. Finally, in 193, Septimius Severus became master of the empire. At first, Christians were able to live in peace under his reign. But eventually he too added his name to the growing list of those who had persecuted the church. However, since this was early in the third century, we shall return to it at another point in our narrative.

In summary, during the entire second century Christians were in a precarious position. They were not constantly persecuted. Sometimes they were persecuted in some areas of the empire, and not in others. Since the general policy of the empire was that outlined by Trajan—Christians were not to be sought, but, if brought before the authorities, they must be forced to recant or be punished—the good will of their neighbors was very important. If any believed the evil rumors about them, they would be accused, and persecution would break out. For this reason it was very important to show that those rumors were untrue, and to give pagans a better and more favorable understanding of Christianity. This was the task of the apologists, to whom we now turn.

However, before we move on to that chapter of our "story," it is important to note that, in contrast with much of what we have often been told, it was not usually the worst emperors, and sometimes some of the best, who persecuted Christians. This will become more apparent as the third century advances, and belies the notion that persecution was usually due either to corrupt authorities or to evil and inept rulers. For a number of reasons, some of them justified,

A mosaic depicts the legend of martyrs left to freeze to death in Sebaste.

the authorities saw in Christianity a movement with subversive overtones, and therefore sought to suppress it, not because they were corrupt or ill-informed, but rather as a matter of policy in defense of the integrity of the state.

7

The Defense of the Faith

We do not seek to flatter you . . . but request that you judge on the basis
of a proper and thorough investigation.

JUSTIN MARTYR

Throughout the second century, and well into the third, there was no systematic persecution of Christians. It was illegal to be a Christian; but those
who followed the new faith were not sought out by the authorities. Persecution
and martyrdom depended on local circumstances, and particularly on the good
will of neighbors. If for any reason someone wished to harm a Christian, all that
had to be done was to present an accusation. Such may well have been the case
with Justin, who seems to have been accused by his rival, Crescentius. At other
times, as in Lyons and Vienne, it was a mob, fired by all sorts of rumors about
Christians, that demanded that they be arrested and punished.

Given such circumstances, Christians felt the need to refute rumors and
misconceptions regarding their beliefs and practices. Even if their arguments
did not convince others of the truth of Christianity, it was believed that something very tangible would be gained if false reports were dispelled. Such was the
task of some of the ablest Christian thinkers and writers, known as the "apologists"—that is, defenders. Some of their arguments have been in continuous
usage through the centuries.

BASE RUMORS AND LOFTY CRITICISM

Many of the rumors that the apologists sought to dispel were based on misun-
derstandings of Christian practice or teaching. Thus, for instance, Christians
gathered every week to celebrate what they called a "love feast." This was
done in private, and only the initiates (those who had been baptized) were
admitted. Furthermore, Christians called each other "brother" and "sister,"
and there were many who spoke of their spouses as their "sister" or "brother."
Joining these known facts, non-Christians imagined Christian worship as an
orgiastic celebration filled with Christians eating and drinking to excess, then

extinguishing the candles, and venting their lusts in indiscriminate and even incestuous unions.

Communion also gave rise to another rumor. Since Christians spoke of being nourished by the body and blood of Christ, and since they also spoke of him as a little child, some came to the conclusion that, as an initiation rite, Christians concealed a newborn in a loaf of bread, and then ordered the neophyte to cut the loaf. When this was done, they all joined in eating the warm flesh of the infant. The new initiate, who had unwittingly become the main perpetrator of the crime, was thus forced to remain silent. Such rumors were made more credible because it was commonly known that when Christians found an abandoned infant they would pick it up and take it home with them.

Some even claimed that Christians worshiped an ass. This was an old rumor about Judaism that was now extended to include Christians, and make them an object of mockery. Illustrating this, a graffito has been found in which a man with the head of an ass is crucified, while another looks at him in adoration. The inscription reads, "Alexamenos worships God."

Such notions—and many other similar ones—were fairly easy to refute, for it sufficed to show that Christians followed principles of conduct that were not compatible with such wild imaginings. Much more difficult to refute was the criticism of a number of cultured pagans who had taken the trouble to learn about Christianity and claimed that it was intellectually wanting. Although it attacked Christianity on numerous levels, this criticism boiled down to one main point: Christians were an ignorant lot whose doctrines, although preached under a cloak of wisdom, were foolish and even self-contradictory. This seems to have been a common attitude among the cultured aristocracy, to whom Christians were a despicable rabble.

During the reign of Marcus Aurelius, one such intellectual, Celsus, wrote a refutation of Christianity called *The True Word*. There he expressed the feelings of those who, like him, were wise and sophisticated:

In some private homes we find people who work with wool and rags, and cobblers, that is, the least cultured and most ignorant kind. Before the head of the household, they dare not utter a word. But as soon as they can take the children aside or some women who are as ignorant as they are, they speak wonders. . . . If you really wish to know the truth, leave your teachers and your father, and go with the women and the children to the women's quarters, or to the cobbler's shop, or to the tannery, and there you will learn the perfect life. It is thus that these Christians find those who will believe them.[8]

At about the same time, the pagan Cornelius Fronto wrote a treatise against Christians that unfortunately has been lost. But the Christian writer Minucius Felix may be quoting him when he puts the following words in the mouth of a pagan:

> If you still have even a modicum of wisdom or shame, cease searching the heavenly regions, and the goals and secrets of the universe. It is enough that you watch where you walk. This is especially true of people such as you, who lack education and culture, and are crude and ignorant.[9]

Thus, the enmity against Christianity on the part of many cultured pagans was not a purely intellectual matter, but was deeply rooted in class prejudice. The cultured and sophisticated could not conceive of the possibility that the Christian rabble could know a truth that was hidden from them. Their main objection was that Christianity was a religion of barbarians who derived their teaching, not from Greeks or Romans, but from Jews, a primitive people whose best teachers never rose to the level of Greek philosophers. If anything good is to be found in Jewish scripture—they said—that is because the Jews copied it from the Greeks.

Furthermore—the argument went on—the Jewish and Christian God is ridiculous. Its followers claim on the one hand that God is omnipotent, high above every creature. But on the other hand they depict God as a busybody who is constantly delving into human affairs, who goes into every home listening to what is said and even checking what is being cooked. This is sheer contradiction and nonsense.

In any case, the worship of this God destroys the very fiber of society, because those who follow this religion abstain from most social activities, claiming that participation in them would be tantamount to worshiping false gods. If such gods are indeed false, why fear them? Why not join in their worship like sensible people, even if one does not believe in them? The truth of the matter is that Christians, while claiming that the gods are false, continue fearing them as true.

As to Jesus, it should suffice to remember that he was a criminal condemned by Roman authorities. Celsus even claims that Jesus was the illegitimate son of Mary with a Roman soldier. If he was truly Son of God, why did he allow himself to be crucified? Why did he not destroy all his enemies? And, even if Christians could answer such questions, Celsus asks further:

> What could be the purpose of such a visit to earth by God? To find out what is taking place among humans? Does he not know everything? Or

is it perhaps that he knows, but is incapable of doing anything about evil unless he does it in person?[10]

Also, these Christians preach—and truly believe—that they will rise again after death. It is on the basis of that belief that they face death with an almost incredible obstinacy. But it makes no sense to leave this life, which is certain, for the sake of another, which is at best uncertain. And the doctrine of a final resurrection itself is the high point of Christian nonsense. What will happen to those whose bodies were destroyed by fire, or eaten by beasts or by fish? Will God scour the world after bits and pieces of each body? What will God do with those parts of matter that have belonged to more than one body? Will they be given to their first owner? Will that leave a gap in the risen bodies of all later owners?

Such arguments, and many similar ones, could not be set aside by mere denial. It was necessary to offer solid refutation. This was the task of the apologists.

THE MAIN APOLOGISTS

The task of responding to such criticism resulted in some of the most remarkable theological works of the second century, a tradition that continued for many years thereafter. At this point, however, it will suffice to deal with the apologists of the second century and the beginning of the third.

Probably the earliest surviving apology is the *Letter to Diognetus,* whose unknown author—perhaps a certain Quadratus mentioned by ancient historians—seems to have lived early in the second century. Shortly thereafter, before 138, Aristides wrote an apology that has been rediscovered in modern times. But the most famous of the early apologists was Justin, to whose martyrdom reference was made in the preceding chapter, and who is also one of our earliest sources describing Christian worship—to which we shall return later. Justin had lived through a long spiritual pilgrimage, from school to school, until he found in Christianity what he called "the true philosophy." Three of his works are extant: two apologies—which are really two parts of a single work—and a *Dialogue with Trypho,* a Jewish rabbi. One of Justin's disciples, Tatian, wrote an *Address to the Greeks,* and at about the same time Athenagoras composed *A Plea for the Christians* and a treatise *On the Resurrection of the Dead.* Later in the century, Theophilus, bishop of Antioch, wrote three books *To Autolycus,* which dealt with the doctrine of God, the interpretation of scripture, and Christian life. All these apologies of the second century were written in Greek, as was also the refutation *Against Celsus,* which Origen wrote in the third century.

In Latin, the two earliest apologies are *Octavius,* by Minucius Felix, and Tertullian's *Apology.* To this day, scholars are not agreed as to which of these two apologies was written first, although it is clear that whoever wrote the later one was indebted to his predecessor.

By reading all of these apologies, historians can discern the main objections that pagans raised against Christianity, as well as the manner in which the most cultured members of the church responded to them, and how Christian theology developed in the very act of responding to pagan objections.

CHRISTIAN FAITH AND PAGAN CULTURE

Since they were accused of being uncultured barbarians, Christians were forced to take up the issue of the relationship between their faith and pagan culture. All Christians agreed that the worship of the gods, and everything related to that worship, must be rejected. This was the reason why they abstained from many civil ceremonies, in which sacrifices and vows were made to the gods. This, together with pacifist convictions, also led many Christians to the conclusion that they could not be soldiers, for members of the military were required to offer sacrifices to the emperor and the gods. Likewise, there were many Christians who objected to the study of classical literature, where the gods played an important part, and where all sorts of immorality was ascribed to them. To be a Christian required a commitment to the sole worship of God, and any deviation from that commitment was a denial of Jesus Christ, who in the final judgment would deny the apostate who had denied him.

While all agreed on the need to abstain from idolatry, not all agreed on what should be a Christian's attitude toward classical pagan culture. This included the work and thought of philosophers such as Socrates, Plato, Aristotle, and the Stoics, whose wisdom is admired by many to this day. To reject all of this would be to set aside some of the highest achievements of the human intellect; to accept it could be seen as a concession to paganism, an inroad of idolatry into the church.

Therefore, on the question of the value of classical culture, Christians took two opposite tacks. Some insisted on a radical opposition between Christian faith and pagan culture. Typical of this attitude was Tertullian, who summarized it in a famous phrase. "What does Athens have to do with Jerusalem? What does the Academy have to do with the Church?"[11] What prompted him to write these lines was his conviction that many of the heresies that circulated in his time were the result of attempts to combine pagan philosophy with Christian doctrine.

But even apart from the question of possible heresy, there were those who gloried in the "barbarian" origin of Christianity, over against the claims of classical culture and philosophy. Such was the case of Tatian, Justin Martyr's most famous disciple, whose *Address to the Greeks* is a frontal attack on all that the Greeks consider valuable, and a defense of the "barbaric" Christians. Because Greeks called all those who did not speak their language "barbarians," Tatian began by pointing out to them that they were not in agreement as to how Greek was to be spoken, for each region had its own dialect. Furthermore, argued Tatian, these people who claim that their tongue is the greatest of human creations have also invented rhetoric, which is the art of selling words for gold to the highest bidder, and which thus results in the defense of untruth and injustice.

All that the Greeks have that is of any value—so said Tatian—they have taken from barbarians: they learned astronomy from the Babylonians, geometry from the Egyptians, and writing from the Phoenicians. And the same is true of philosophy and religion, since the writings of Moses are much older than those of Plato, and even than those of Homer. Therefore, any agreement between the culture which is supposedly Greek and the religion of the Hebrew and Christian barbarians is the result of the Greeks having learned their wisdom from the barbarians. And what makes matters worse is that the Greeks, in reading the wisdom of the barbarians, misunderstood it, and thus twisted what the Hebrews knew as truth. As a consequence, the supposed wisdom of the Greeks is but a pale reflection and caricature of the truth that Moses knew and Christians preach.

If this is what Tatian says about the best of classical culture, one can imagine what he has to say about the pagan gods. Homer and the other Greek poets tell shameful things about them, such as adultery, incest, and infanticide. How are we to worship such gods, clearly inferior to us? Finally, Tatian adds, let it not be forgotten that many of the statues that the pagans worship are in fact representations of prostitutes whom the sculptors used as models. Thus, the very pagans who say that Christians belong to the lower social strata are in fact worshiping people of the lower classes!

But not all Christians took the same stance. On becoming a Christian, Justin did not cease being a philosopher, but rather took upon himself the task of doing "Christian philosophy," and a major part of that task as he saw it was to show and explain the connection between Christianity and classical wisdom. Thus, he did not share Tatian's negative attitude toward philosophy. But this does not mean that he was willing to compromise his faith or that he was lacking in conviction, for when the time came for him to stand up for his faith he did so with courage, and thus earned the title of *Justin Martyr*.

Justin claimed that there were several points of contact between Christianity and pagan philosophy. The best philosophers, for instance, spoke of a supreme

This vase by Greek artist Duris depicts a school scene.

being from which every other being derives its existence. Socrates and Plato affirmed life beyond physical death; and Socrates showed the strength of that affirmation in the manner in which he died. Plato knew that there are realities beyond those of the present world, and thus posited another world of eternal realities. Justin claimed that the philosophers were basically correct on all these points, although he did not always agree on the manner in which they understood them. For instance, in contrast to the philosophers, Christian hope is not based on the immortality of the soul, but rather on the resurrection of the body. But in spite of such differences, Justin insisted that there were in the philosophers glimpses of truth that could not be explained as mere coincidence.

How, then, can one explain this partial agreement between the philosophers and Christianity? For Justin, the answer is to be found in the doctrine of the Logos. This is a Greek word that means both "word" and "reason." According to a tradition of long standing in Greek philosophy, the human mind can understand reality because it shares in the Logos or universal reason that undergirds all reality. For instance, if we are able to understand that two and two make four, the reason for this is that both in our minds and in the universe there is a Logos, a reason or order according to which two and two always make four. The Fourth Gospel affirms that in Jesus, the Logos or Word was made flesh. Thus, according to Justin, what has happened in the incarnation is that the underlying reason behind the universe, the Logos or Word of God, has come in the flesh.

According to the Fourth Gospel, this Logos is "the true light that enlightens" everyone. This means that, even before the incarnation, he is the source of all true knowledge. Paul had already said (1 Cor. 10:1-4) that the ancient Hebrews' faith rested on none other than Christ, who had been revealed to them even before the incarnation. Now Justin added that there were also among the pagans those who knew the same Logos, however remotely. Whatever truth there is in the writings of Plato was granted to him by the Logos of God, the same Logos who was incarnate in Jesus. Therefore, in a way, Socrates, Plato, and the other sages of antiquity "were Christians," for their wisdom came from Christ. This is not to say, however, that the incarnation was not needed, for those philosophers of old knew the Logos "in part," while those who have seen him in his incarnation know him "fully."

What Justin thus did was to open the way for Christianity to claim whatever good it could find in classical culture, in spite of its having been pagan. Following his inspiration, there soon were other Christians who tried to build additional bridges between their faith and ancient culture. Their work, and the dangers inherent therein, will be discussed elsewhere in this narrative.

THE ARGUMENTS OF THE APOLOGISTS

Justin's use of the doctrine of the Logos provided a basic framework within which Christians could claim whatever they wished from the rich lode of classical culture. But there still remained the need to refute the various objections raised against Christianity. Although it is impossible to list here all such refutations, some examples will give a general idea of the nature of the arguments of the apologists.

When accused of being atheists because they had no visible gods, Christians responded that in that case many of the greatest philosophers and poets were also atheists. To support that statement it sufficed to quote the ancient writers who had affirmed that the gods were human inventions, and that their vices were worse than those of their worshipers. Aristides suggested that such gods had been invented precisely in order to give full rein to human vice. Also, a common argument was that the idols, often made of gold and precious stones, had to be guarded against thieves. How can a god that must be protected provide any protection? How can a god made by human hands be above humans? On these points orthodox Christianity held to the doctrine of monotheism and divine creation that it had learned from its Jewish background.

To the objections raised against the final resurrection, the apologists responded by having recourse to divine omnipotence. If God made all bodies out of nothing, why would it be impossible for the same God to create them anew, even after they have been dead and scattered?

To the accusations that Christians are immoral, the apologists respond that this is not true, and that it is rather the pagans who are immoral. It is in this context that Justin Martyr provides one of the earliest descriptions of Christian worship, which we shall have occasion to quote later on. How can anyone believe that our worship is orgiastic and incestuous, when the rules of our conduct are such that even evil thoughts must be cast aside? It is the pagans who tell such things of their gods, and even practice them under the guise of worship. How can anyone believe that we eat children, when we reject every form of bloodshed? It is the pagans who leave their unwanted children exposed to the elements, to die of cold and hunger.

Finally, Christians were accused of being subversive, for they refused to worship the emperor and thus destroyed the very fiber of society. The apologists answered that it was true that they refused to worship the emperor or any other creature, but that in spite of this they were loyal subjects of the empire. What the emperor needs—they said—is not to be worshiped, but to be served; and those who serve him best are those who pray for him and for the empire to the only true God.

It is at this latter point that one feels that perhaps the Christian apologists did not quite understand the depth of objections of people such as Celsus. From the point of view of Celsus, no matter how faithful to the emperor and the empire Christians thought they were, they were in fact subverting the very fiber of society by withdrawing from its main civic and religious functions, and thus acting as if they were not valid or even evil. Furthermore, the church, particularly through its bishops and their correspondence, was creating an empire-wide network at a time when the government was very suspicious of all societies or gatherings not organized by the state. These subversive undertones of Christian teaching and practice formed the basis of continued persecution by some of the most able emperors of the second and third centuries, and explain the fact that as Roman officials attained a fuller understanding of Christianity persecution, rather than declining, became ever fiercer.

In conclusion, the writings of the apologists witness to the tensions in which early Christians lived. While rejecting paganism, they had to deal with the valuable elements in the culture it had produced. While accepting the truth to be found in the philosophers, they insisted on the superiority of Christian revelation. While refusing to worship the emperor, and even while persecuted by the authorities, they continued praying for the emperor and admiring the greatness of the Roman Empire. These tensions were admirably expressed in the *Address to Diognetus*:

> Christians are no different from the rest in their nationality, language or customs. . . . They live in their own countries, but as sojourners. They fulfill all their duties as citizens, but they suffer as foreigners. They find their homeland wherever they are, but their homeland is not in any one place. . . . They are in the flesh, but do not live according to the flesh. They live on earth, but are citizens of heaven. They obey all laws, but they live at a level higher than that required by law. They love all, but all persecute them.[12]

8

The Deposit of the Faith

Error never shows itself in its naked reality, in order not to be discovered.
On the contrary, it dresses elegantly, so that the unwary may be led to
believe that it is more truthful than truth itself.

IRENAEUS OF LYONS

The many converts who joined the early church came from a wide variety
of backgrounds. This variety enriched the church and gave witness to the
universality of its message. But it also resulted in widely differing interpretations of that message. Such different interpretations should not surprise us, for
at the time Christianity was still ill-defined—to the point that it would probably be better to speak of "Christianities," in the plural. There certainly were
in it varying views and emphases, as any reader of the New Testament can still
see when comparing, for instance, the Gospel of Mark with John, Romans, and
Revelation. But, were all the existing views and interpretations equally valid or
acceptable? Was there not the danger that, within the still undefined limits of
Christianity, there would be interpretations that would threaten its integrity?
The danger was increased by the syncretism of the time, which sought truth,
not by adhering to a single system of doctrine, but by taking bits and pieces
from various systems. The result was that, while many claimed the name of
Christ, some interpreted that name in a manner that others felt obscured or
even denied the very core of his message. In response to such threats, what
would become known as orthodox Christianity began to define itself by reaffirming such elements of its Jewish heritage as the doctrines of creation, of the
positive value of the created world, of the rule of God over all of history, of
the resurrection of the body—a doctrine learned from the Pharisees—and a
coming final reign of God. In order to reaffirm such doctrines, it developed a
series of instruments—creeds, the canon of scripture, apostolic succession—
that would set limits on orthodoxy and would long remain central themes in
Christian life and teaching. Thus, even those whose views were eventually re-

jected by the church at large, and came to be known as *heretics*, left their mark on the church and the way it understood itself.

GNOSTICISM

Of all the differing interpretations of Christianity, none seemed as dangerous, nor as close to victory, as was Gnosticism. This was not a well-defined organization in competition with the church; rather, it was a vast and amorphous movement that existed both within and outside of Christianity. Within Judaism, partly as a response to the fall of Jerusalem and the destruction of the Temple in 70, some embraced Gnostic ideas, thus giving birth to a Gnostic Judaism that contradicted much of traditional Jewish teachings—particularly regarding divine creation and the goodness of the created world. Likewise, when Gnosticism incorporated the name of Christ and other items from the Judeo-Christian tradition into its diverse systems, it did so in such terms that other Christians felt that some crucial elements of their faith were being denied.

For centuries, practically the only sources that historians had for the study of Christian Gnosticism were the descriptions of the *heresiologists*—Christian writers arguing against Gnosticism and its tenets. The few existing fragments of Gnostic writings did not suffice to correct or evaluate what the heresiologists told us. Then, in 1945, a large collection of Gnostic writings was discovered in Nag Hammadi, in Egypt. This included, among other things, the fairly early *Gospel of Thomas*, and the later *Gospel of Truth* of Valentinus—a leading Gnostic whose teachings had been described, and also somewhat distorted, by the heresiologists. For a number of reasons, it was not until the 1970s that these writings became generally known and available to scholars as well as to the public at large. These and other discoveries—including the *Gospel of Judas*, published in 2006—have both corrected and reinforced much of what the heresiologists told us.

The name *Gnosticism* is derived from the Greek word *gnosis*, which means "knowledge." According to the Gnostics, they possessed a special, mystical knowledge, reserved for those with true understanding. That knowledge was the secret key to salvation.

Although the writings of the heresiologists give the impression that Gnosticism was mostly a collection of idle speculations about the origins of all things, both spiritual and material, salvation—and not speculation—was the main concern of the Gnostics. Drawing from several sources, the Gnostics came to the conclusion that all matter is evil, or at best unreal. A human being is in reality an eternal spirit (or part of the eternal spirit) that somehow has been imprisoned in a body. Since the body is a prison to the spirit, and since it misleads us as to our true nature, it is evil. Therefore, the Gnostic's final goal is to escape

*Many Gnostics saw a symbol of opposition
to the evil god of creation in the serpent
(shown here inscribed beside a secret word
on a Gnostic coin).*

from the body and this material world in which we are exiled. This image of exile is crucial for Gnosticism. The world is not our true home, but rather an obstacle to the salvation of the spirit—a view which, although officially rejected by orthodox Christianity, has frequently been part of it.

How, then, is the origin of the world and of the body to be explained? Gnosticism affirmed that originally all reality was spiritual. The Supreme Being had no intention of creating a material world, but only a spiritual one. Thus, a number of spiritual beings were generated. It is at this point that the "endless genealogies" that the heresiologists describe find their place in the various Gnostic systems. Gnostic teachers did not agree as to the exact number of spiritual beings standing before the original spiritual "abyss" and the present world, with some systems positing up to 365 such spiritual beings or "eons." In any case, one of these eons, far removed from the Supreme Being, fell into error, and thus created the material world. According to one system, for instance, Wisdom, one of the eons, wished to produce something by herself, and the resulting "abortion" was the world. That is what the world is in Gnosticism: an abortion of the spirit, and not a divine creation.

But, since this world was made by a spiritual being, there are still "sparks" or "bits" of spirit in it. It is these that have been imprisoned in human bodies and must be liberated through gnosis.

In order to achieve that liberation, a spiritual messenger must come to this world, to waken us from our dream or spiritual confusion. Our spirits are asleep within our bodies, being driven by the impulses and passions of the body, and someone must come from beyond to remind us who we really are and to call us to struggle against our incarceration. This messenger brings the gnosis, the secret knowledge and inspiration necessary for salvation. Above us are the heavenly spheres, each ruled by an evil power whose aim is to impede our progress to the spiritual realm. In order to reach the spiritual "fullness," or *pleroma*, we must break through each of those spheres. The only way to do this is to have the secret knowledge that opens the way—much like a spiritual password. The heavenly messenger has been sent precisely to give us that knowledge, without which there is no salvation.

In Christian Gnosticism—one should always remember that there were also non-Christian Gnostics—that messenger is Christ. What Christ has then done is to come to earth in order to remind us of our heavenly origin, and to give us the secret knowledge without which we cannot return to the spiritual mansions.

Since Christ is a heavenly messenger, and since body and matter are evil, most Christian Gnostics rejected the notion that Christ had a body like ours. Some said that his body was an appearance, a sort of ghost that miraculously seemed to be a real body. Many distinguished between the heavenly "Christ" and the earthly "Jesus," apparently believing that the latter was merely the shell in which Christ appeared. In some cases, this was coupled with the notion that Jesus did have a body, but that this was of a "spiritual matter," different from ours. Most denied the birth of Jesus, which would have put him under the power of the material world. All these notions are various degrees of what the church at large called *Docetism*—a name derived from a Greek word meaning "to seem"—for all of them implied, in one way or another, that the body of Jesus appeared to be fully human, but was not.

According to several Gnostic teachers, not all human beings have a spirit. Some are purely carnal, and thus are irreparably condemned to destruction when the physical world comes to an end. On the other hand, the imprisoned sparks of the spirit within those whom the Gnostics call "spiritual" will necessarily be saved and return to the spiritual realm. In order to do this, they must learn the secret knowledge of the truly illumined, that is, the Gnostic teachers.

Meanwhile, how is this life to be lived? At this point, the heresiologists say that the Gnostics gave two divergent answers. Most declared that, since the body is the prison of the spirit, one must control the body and its passions and thus weaken its power over the spirit. But, according to some heresiologists, there were also some who held that, since the spirit is by nature good and cannot be destroyed, what we are to do is to leave the body to its own devices and let it follow the guidance of its own passions. Thus, while some Gnostics were extreme ascetics, others may have been libertines.

It is difficult to reconstruct the social composition or the religious life of Gnostic communities or schools. For one thing, most of them held that their gnosis was secret, and therefore even their own writings leave historians wondering as to their worship and community life. Even their social composition is in question. Most historians agree with Giovanni Filoramo's assessment that Gnostic societies were "clubs, confined and restricted to intellectuals," and that they were "the expression of an economically expanding and socially mobile provincial society."[13] But the very fact that the Nag Hammadi documents are in Coptic would seem to indicate that it had also made significant inroads among the lower classes, for Egyptian society in Hellenistic times was highly stratified, with those who spoke Copt at the very bottom of society, and with very little social mobility.

One point is certain: In many Gnostic circles women had a prominence they did not have in society at large. Part of the reason for this was that, since it is the spirit and not the body that is important, the shape of one's body has little to do with eternal realities. Also, in many of the genealogies of eons with which Gnostics explained the origin of the world, there were female as well as male eons. It is quite possible that it was partly in response to this feature in Gnosticism that orthodox Christianity began restricting the role of women in the church, for it is clear that in first-century Christianity women had roles in the church that the second century began to deny them.

Gnosticism was a serious threat to Christianity throughout the second century. The main leaders of the church tenaciously opposed it, for they saw in it a denial of several crucial Christian doctrines, such as creation, incarnation, the death of Jesus through crucifixion, and resurrection. For that reason, the church at large devised methods to combat it. But before we turn to those methods, we must pause to look at another teacher whose doctrines, similar to Gnosticism yet different from it, were seen as a particular threat.

MARCION

Marcion, whose father was bishop of Sinope on the southern coast of the Black Sea, knew Christianity from an early age. But he profoundly disliked both Judaism and the material world. He thus developed an understanding of Christianity that was both anti-Jewish and anti-material. He went to Rome, around the year 144, and there he gathered a following. But eventually the church at large came to the conclusion that his doctrines contradicted several fundamental points in Christian doctrine. He then founded his own church, which lasted for several centuries as a rival to the orthodox church.

Since Marcion was convinced that the world is evil, he came to the conclusion that its creator must be either evil or ignorant—or both. But instead of positing a long series of spiritual beings, as the Gnostics did, Marcion proposed a much simpler solution. According to him, the God and Father of Jesus is not the same as Yahweh, the God of the Old Testament. It was Yahweh who made this world. The Father's purpose was to have only a spiritual world. But Yahweh, either through ignorance or out of evil intent, made this world and placed humankind in it—a theme that one finds in many Gnostic writings as well.

This means that the Hebrew scriptures are indeed inspired by a god, although this is Yahweh, and not the Supreme Father. Yahweh is an arbitrary god, who chooses a particular people above all the rest. And he is also vindictive, constantly keeping an account on those who disobey him, and punishing them. In short, Yahweh is a god of justice—and of an arbitrary justice at that.

Over against Yahweh, and far above him, is the Father of Christians. This God is not vindictive, but loving. This God requires nothing of us, but rather gives everything freely, including salvation. This God does not seek to be obeyed, but to be loved. It is out of compassion for us—Yahweh's creatures— that the Supreme God has sent his Son to save us. But Jesus was not really born of Mary, since such a thing would have made him subject to Yahweh. Rather, he simply appeared as a grown man during the reign of Tiberius, and his body was not made of material flesh. Naturally, at the end there will be no judgment, since the Supreme God is absolutely loving, and will simply forgive us.

All of this led Marcion to set the Hebrew scriptures aside. If the Old Testament was the Word of an inferior god, it should not be read in the churches, nor used as the basis of Christian instruction. In order to fill this gap, Marcion compiled a list of books that he considered true Christian scriptures. These were the Epistles of Paul—according to Marcion, one of the few who had really understood Jesus' message—and the Gospel of Luke, who had been Paul's companion. All other ancient Christian books were plagued by Jewish views. As to the many quotations from the Old Testament in Luke and Paul, Marcion explained them away as interpolations—the handiwork of Judaizers seeking to subvert the original message.

Marcion posed an even greater threat to the church than did the Gnostics. Like them, he rejected or radically reinterpreted the doctrines of creation, incarnation, and resurrection. But he went beyond them in that he organized a church with its own bishops and its own scripture. For a number of years, this rival church achieved a measure of success, and even after it was clearly defeated it lingered on for centuries.

THE RESPONSE:
CANON, CREED, AND APOSTOLIC SUCCESSION

Marcion's list was the first attempt to put together a "New Testament." When early Christians spoke of "Scripture," what they meant was the Hebrew scriptures, usually in the Greek version known as the Septuagint (Syriac-speaking Christians used a similar translation into their language). It was also customary to read in church passages from one or several of our present four Gospels, as well as from the Epistles—particularly Paul's. Since there was no approved list, different Gospels were read in different churches, and the same was true of other books. But Marcion's challenge required a response; and thus the church at large began to compile a list of sacred Christian writings. This was not done in a formal manner, through a council or special meeting. What actually happened was that a consensus developed gradually. While very soon there was general agreement as to the basic books to be included in the canon of the New Testament, it took a long time to come to an absolute consensus on every minor detail.

There was no question, except among Gnostics and Marcionites, that the Hebrew scriptures were part of the Christian canon. This was important as proof that God had been preparing the way for the advent of Christianity, and even as a way of understanding the nature of the God who had been revealed in Jesus Christ. Christian faith was the fulfillment of the hope of Israel, and not a sudden apparition from heaven.

As to what is now called the "New Testament," the Gospels were the first to attain general recognition. It is important to note that those early Christians decided to include more than one Gospel in their canon. Apparently, churches in some cities or regions had a particular Gospel which was most closely connected to their history and traditions. Such was the case, for instance, with the Gospel of Luke in Antioch and the surrounding area. As contact among these churches developed, they began sharing their manuscripts and traditions, and thus the acceptance and use of a variety of Gospels came to be seen as a sign of the unity of the church. At a later time, many have pointed out the inconsistencies among the four Gospels in matters of detail. The early Christians were well aware of these differences, and that was precisely one of the main reasons why they insisted in using more than one book. They did this as a direct response to the challenge of Marcion and Gnosticism. Many Gnostic teachers claimed that the heavenly messenger had trusted his secret knowledge to a particular disciple, who alone was the true interpreter of the message. Thus, various Gnostic groups had a book that claimed to present the true teachings of Jesus. Such were, for instance, the *Gospel of Thomas* and the *Gospel of Truth* of the Valentinian Gnostics. Marcion used the Gospel of Luke, from which he had deleted all references to Judaism or to the Hebrew scriptures. In response to this situation, the church at large sought to show that its doctrines were not based on the supposed witness of a single apostle or Gospel, but on the consensus of the entire apostolic tradition. The very fact that the various Gospels differed in matters of detail, but agreed on the basic issues at stake, made their agreement a more convincing argument. Against Marcion's expurgated Gospel of Luke, the church offered the consensus of a number of Gospels—sometimes three, and sometimes four, since the Fourth Gospel was somewhat slower in gaining universal acceptance. Against the secret traditions and private interpretations of the Gnostics, the church had recourse to an open tradition, known to all, and to the multiplicity of the witness of the Gospels.

It is important to realize that in the first four or five centuries of Christianity there were dozens—perhaps hundreds, most of them now lost—of Gospels and writings about the acts of Mary and the apostles. It is not true, however, that such writings were trying to find their way into the canon, and that the church suppressed some of them. The truth is that the non-canonical Gospels fall into two categories. Some of them, dating mostly from the second century—with the possible exception of the *Gospel of Thomas,* some of whose material may have been earlier—are Gnostic Gospels. Each of these was considered scripture by a particular group which rejected all others, and therefore had no interest in including their book in the nascent canon of the New Testament. They were never considered part of a canon either by the orthodox Christian community—which rejected them—or by their own proponents—who rejected the notion that there could be more than one inspired Gospel. The second category, mostly dating from the third century or later, includes pious stories about Jesus. The church never rejected these. It simply did not include them in the canon— the list of sacred books—of the New Testament. They continued to be read, with little opposition, for centuries, and it is not uncommon to find in medieval cathedrals depictions of episodes taken from such documents. One example of many is the *Protoevangelium of James,* which tells the story of Mary's parents, Anna and Joachim—a story that came to be an accepted part of Christian tradition, and which is often found in medieval art and literature.

Next to the Gospels, the book of Acts and the Pauline Epistles enjoyed early recognition. Thus, by the end of the second century the core of the canon was established: the four Gospels, Acts, and the Pauline Epistles. On the shorter books that appear toward the end of the present canon, there was no consensus until a much later date; but there also was little debate. The book of Revelation, widely accepted by the third century, was questioned after the conversion of Constantine, for its words about the prevailing culture and the empire seemed too harsh. It was in the second half of the fourth century that a complete consensus was achieved regarding exactly which books ought to be included in the New Testament, and which ought not to be included. Even then, this was not decided by an official council nor by any other decision-making body, but was rather a matter of consensus—which in itself shows that very few considered this a burning issue. Furthermore, in this entire process the guiding concern was not theology in the abstract sense, but the life of worship, for the main question was, is this book to be read when the church gathers for worship?

Another element in the church's response to heresies was the use of various creeds, particularly in baptism. Quite often the church in a particular city had its own creedal formula, although similar to others in neighboring cities. Apparently what happened was that a "daughter" church used the formula it had learned from the "mother church," although with some variations. On this basis, scholars have classified ancient creeds into "families," and such families can then be used to trace the relationship among various churches.

One of these creeds was an earlier and shorter formulation of what we now call the Apostles' Creed. The notion that the apostles gathered before beginning their mission and composed this creed, each suggesting a clause, is pure fiction. The truth is that its basic text was put together, probably in Rome, around the year 150. Due to its use in Rome, the ancient form of the Apostles' Creed is called "R" by scholars. At the time, however, it was called "the symbol of the faith." The word *symbol* in this context did not mean what it does to us today; rather, it meant "a means of recognition," such as a token that a general gave to a messenger, so that the recipient could recognize a true messenger. Likewise, the "symbol" put together in Rome was a means whereby Christians could distinguish true believers from those who followed the various heresies circulating at the time, particularly Gnosticism and Marcionism. Any who could affirm this creed were neither Gnostics nor Marcionites.

One of the main uses of this "symbol" was in baptism, where it was presented to the candidate in the form of a series of three questions:

Do you believe in God, the Father almighty?
Do you believe in Christ Jesus, the Son of God, who was born of the Holy Ghost and of Mary the Virgin, who was crucified under Pontius Pilate, and died, and rose again at the third day, living from among the dead, and ascended unto heaven and sat at the right of the Father, and will come to judge the quick and the dead?
Do you believe in the Holy Ghost, the Holy Church, and the resurrection of the flesh?

This is the core of what historians call "the old Roman symbol," or simply *R*. It is obvious that this creed—like most ancient creeds—has been built around the trinitarian formula that was used in baptism. Since one was baptized "in the name of the Father, of the Son, and of the Holy Ghost," these questions were posed as a test of true belief in the Father, the Son, and the Holy Ghost.

Closer scrutiny reveals that this early creed is directed against Marcion and the Gnostics. First of all, the Greek word *pantokrator,* usually translated as "almighty," literally means "all ruling." What is meant here is that there is nothing—and certainly not the material world—which falls outside of God's rule. (Other ancient creeds say "Creator of all things visible and invisible.") The distinction between a spiritual reality that serves God and a material reality that does not is rejected. This world, its matter and its physical bodies, are part of the "all" over which God reigns. This emphasis on divine creation and rule over it and over all of history was one of the many points derived from Jewish tradition that Christians continue to hold and consider central to their faith.

The creed's most extensive paragraph is the one dealing with the Son. This is because it was precisely in their christology that Marcion and the Gnostics differed most widely from the church. First of all, we are told that Jesus Christ is the "Son of God." Other ancient versions say "Son of the same" or "His Son," as does our present creed. The important point here is that Jesus is the Son of the God who rules over this world and over all reality, and who is the creator of all things. The birth "of Mary the Virgin" is not there primarily in order to stress the virgin birth—although, quite clearly, that is affirmed—but rather to affirm the very fact that Jesus was born, and did not simply appear on earth, as Marcion and others claimed. The reference to Pontius Pilate is not there to put the blame on the Roman governor, but rather to date the event, thus insisting that it was a historical, datable event. And docetism is further denied by declaring that Jesus "was crucified . . . died, and rose again." Finally, it is affirmed that this same Jesus will return "to judge"—a notion that Marcion would never accept.

The third clause, although less explicit because the needs of the time did not require it to be extensive, also shows the same concern. The *holy church* is affirmed because, over against the Gnostics with their many schools and Marcion with his own church, Christians were beginning to underscore the authority of the church. And the "resurrection of the flesh" is a final rejection of any notion that the flesh is evil or of no consequence.

While an analysis of *R* helps us understand the original purpose of the Apostles' Creed, it is important to realize that this incipient form of the Apostles' Creed was only one of several creedal statements employed at the time in con-

The final judgment, a traditional theme in Christian teaching, was denied by Marcion, who claimed that the God of true Christianity does not judge or condemn.

nection with baptism. Churches that had strong connections with Rome, such as those in North Africa and Gaul, used variant forms of *R*. But the churches in the Eastern portion of the empire—in areas such as Syria, Egypt, and Asia Minor—had their own creedal formulas. Thus, while *R* was the basis for the Apostles' Creed, the Baptismal Creed of Caesarea, or some other creed of the same family, and was the basis for the Nicene Creed—which, as we shall see, was formulated in the fourth century and is the most widely accepted of the ancient creeds.

Although the canon of the New Testament and the various creeds were valuable instruments in the struggle against heresy, the debate finally came to the issue of the authority of the church. This was important, not simply because someone had to decide who was right and who was wrong, but because of the very nature of the issues at stake. All agreed that the true message was the one taught by Jesus. The Gnostics claimed that they had some secret access to that original message, through a succession of secret teachers. Marcion claimed that he had access to that message through the writings of Paul and Luke—which, however, had to be purged of what did not agree with Marcion's views regarding the Old Testament. Over against Marcion and the Gnostics, the church at large claimed to be in possession of the original gospel and the true teachings of Jesus. Thus, what was debated was in a way the authority of the church against the claims of the heretics.

At this point, the notion of apostolic succession became very important. What was argued was simply that, if Jesus had some secret knowledge to communicate to his disciples—which in fact he did not—he would have entrusted that teaching to the same apostles to whom he entrusted the churches. If those apostles had received any such teaching, they in turn would have passed it on to those who were to follow them in the leadership of the various churches. Therefore, had there been any such secret teaching, it should be found among the direct disciples of the apostles, and the successors of those disciples, the bishops. But the truth was that those who could now—that is, in the second century—claim direct apostolic succession unanimously denied the existence of any such secret teaching. In conclusion, the Gnostic claim that there is a secret tradition with which that they have been entrusted , is false.

In order to strengthen this argument, it was necessary to show that the bishops of the time were indeed successors of the apostles. This was not difficult, since several of the most ancient churches had lists of bishops linking them with the apostolic past. Rome, Antioch, Ephesus, and others had such lists. Present-day historians do not find such lists absolutely trustworthy, for there are indications that in some churches—Rome among them—there were not at first "bishops" in the sense of a single head of the local church, but rather a collegiate group of officers who sometimes were called "bishops" and sometimes "elders"— presbyters. In any case, be it through actual bishops or through other leaders, the fact remains that the orthodox church of the second century could show its connection with the apostles in a way Marcion and the Gnostics could not.

Does this mean that only churches that could show such apostolic connections were truly apostolic? Not so, since the issue was not that every church could prove its apostolic origins, but rather that they all agreed on the one faith, and could jointly prove that this faith was indeed apostolic. At a later date, the idea of apostolic succession was carried further, with the notion that an ordination was valid only if performed by a bishop who could claim direct apostolic succession. When first developed, late in the second century, the principle of apostolic succession was inclusive rather than exclusive: over against the closed and secret tradition of the Gnostic teachers, it offered an open and shared tradition that based its claim, not on a single favorite disciple of Jesus, but on the witness of all the apostles and of the churches founded by them.

This common witness was further strengthened by the network connecting bishops and resulting in a high degree of collegiality. While bishops were elected by the faithful in each city, the custom soon developed that after such election the prospective bishop would send a statement of faith to neighboring bishops, who would then vouch for his orthodoxy. As a sign of this, several of those neighboring bishops would participate in the consecration of their new colleague.

THE ANCIENT CATHOLIC CHURCH

The original meaning of *Catholic church* referred to this episcopal collegiality, as well as with the multiform witness to the gospel in several canonical gospels. The word *catholic* means "universal," but it also means "according to the whole." To separate itself from the various heretical groups and sects, the ancient church began calling itself "Catholic." This title underscored both its universality and the inclusiveness of the witness on which it stood. It was the church "according to the whole," that is, according to the total witness of all the apostles and all the evangelists. The various Gnostic groups were not "Catholic" because they could not claim this broad foundation. Indeed, those among them who claimed apostolic origins did so on the basis of a hypothetical secret tradition handed down through a single apostle. Only the Church Catholic, the church "according to the whole," could lay claim to the entire apostolic witness. This was the warranty of the church's orthodoxy, and this was the reason why "Catholic" eventually became a synonym for *orthodox* or "correct teaching." Ironically, through an evolution that took centuries, debates regarding the true meaning of *catholic* came to be centered on the person and authority of a single apostle—Peter.

9

The Teachers of the Church

Ours is the great Teacher of all wisdom, and the whole world, including
Athens and Greece, belongs to Him.

CLEMENT OF ALEXANDRIA

During the early decades of the life of the church, most of what Christians
wrote addressed a concrete problem or specific issue. This is true, for
instance, of the Pauline Epistles, each of which was prompted by a particular
circumstance, and in none of which Paul attempts to discuss the entire body of
Christian doctrine. After the apostolic age, the same was true for a while. The
various writers of that period whose work has been preserved are given the joint
title of *apostolic fathers*, and each of their writings deals with very specific issues.
This is the case of the epistles of Ignatius of Antioch, to which we have already
referred. Likewise, late in the first century, Clement of Rome wrote an *Epistle
to the Corinthians,* prompted by problems similar to those which Paul had already addressed in his letters to the same church. The *Didache* or *Teaching of
the Twelve Apostles*—not really written by them, but by an unknown Christian
at an uncertain time and place—is a manual of discipline giving guidelines for
Christian life and worship. The *Shepherd of Hermas*, written by a brother of
the bishop of Rome in the middle of the second century, deals mostly with the
forgiveness of sins after baptism. In summary, all the writings of the so-called
apostolic fathers deal with a single issue, and none of them seeks to expound the
totality of Christian doctrine. The same is true of Justin and the other apologists who wrote in the second half of the second century. Most of their writings
deal with the issue of persecution. And none of them looks at the totality of
Christian doctrine.

But toward the end of the second century the challenge of Marcion and
the Gnostics required a different response. The heretics had created their own
systems of doctrine, and to this the church at large had to respond by having
some of its teachers offer equally cogent expositions of orthodox belief. Precisely
because the speculations of the heretics were vast in scope, the response of

Christian teachers was equally vast. This gave rise to the first writings in which one can find a fairly complete exposition of Christian truth. These are the works of Irenaeus, Clement of Alexandria, Tertullian, and Origen.

IRENAEUS OF LYONS

Irenaeus was a native of Asia Minor—probably Smyrna—where he was born around the year 130. There he was a disciple of Polycarp, of whose martyrdom we have already told in an earlier chapter. Throughout his life, Irenaeus was a fervent admirer of Polycarp, and in his writings he often speaks of an "old man"—or a presbyter—whose name is not given, but who is probably Polycarp. In any case, unknown reasons led Irenaeus to migrate to Lyons, in what is today southern France. There he became a presbyter, and as such was sent to Rome with a message for the bishop of that city. While he was in Rome, persecution broke out in Lyons and nearby Vienne—these are the events discussed in Chapter 5—and Bishop Photinus perished. Upon his return to Lyons, Irenaeus was elected bishop of the church in that city. He served as such until his death, probably as a martyr, in 202.

Irenaeus was above all a pastor. He was not particularly interested in philosophical speculation nor in delving into mysteries hitherto unsolved, but rather in leading his flock in Christian life and faith. Therefore, in his writings he did not seek to rise in great speculative flights, but simply to refute heresy and instruct believers. Only two of his works survive: *Demonstration of Apostolic Preaching,* and *Exposure and Refutation of Knowledge Falsely So-Called* (also known as *Against Heresies).* In the first of these, he instructs his flock on some points of Christian doctrine. In the latter, he seeks to refute Gnosticism. In both, his goal is to expound the faith that he has received from his teachers, without adorning it with his own speculations. Therefore, the writings of Irenaeus are an excellent witness to the faith of the church toward the end of the second century.

Irenaeus, who sees himself as a shepherd, also sees God as above all a shepherd. God is a loving being who creates the world and humankind, not out of necessity nor by mistake—as Gnostics claimed—but out of a desire to have a creation to love and to lead, like the shepherd loves and leads the flock. From this perspective, the entirety of history appears as the process whereby the divine shepherd leads creation to its final goal.

The crown of creation is the human creature, made from the beginning as a free and therefore responsible being. That freedom is such that it allows us to become increasingly conformed to the divine will and nature, and thus to enjoy an ever-growing communion with our creator. But, on the other hand, the human creature was not made from the beginning in its final perfection. Like a true shepherd, God placed the first couple in Eden. They were not mature beings, but were rather "like children," with their own perfection as such. This means that God's purpose was that human beings would grow in communion with the divine, eventually surpassing even the angels.

The angels are above us only provisionally. When the divine purpose is fulfilled in the human creature, we shall be above the angels; for our communion with God will be closer than theirs. The function of angels is similar to that of a tutor guiding the first steps of a prince. Although the tutor is temporarily in charge of the prince, eventually the prince will rule even the tutor.

Humankind is to be instructed, not only by the angels, but also by the "two hands" of God: the Word and the Holy Spirit. Led by those two hands, humans are to receive instruction and growth, always with a view to an increasingly close communion with God. The goal of this process is what Irenaeus calls "divinization"—God's purpose is to make us ever more like the divine. This does not mean, however, that we are somehow to be lost in the divine, nor that we shall ever be the same as God. On the contrary, God is so far above us that no matter how much we grow in our likeness to the divine we shall always have a long way to go.

But one of the angels was jealous of the high destiny reserved for humankind, and for that reason led Adam and Eve into sin. As a result of sin, the human creature was expelled from paradise, and its growth was thwarted. From that point on, history has unfolded under the mark of sin.

Although the actual course of history is the result of sin, the fact that there is history is not. God always had the purpose that there be history. The situation in paradise, as described in Genesis, was not the goal of creation, but its beginning.

From this perspective, the incarnation of God in Jesus Christ is not merely a response to sin. On the contrary, God's initial purpose included being united with humankind. In fact, the future incarnate Word was the model that God followed in making humans after the divine image. Adam and Eve were so created that, after a process of growth and instruction, they could become like the incarnate Word. What has happened because of sin is that the incarnation has taken on the added purpose of offering a remedy for sin, and a means for defeating Satan.

Even before the incarnation, and from the very moment of the first sin, God has been leading humanity toward closer communion with the divine. For this reason, God *curses* the serpent and the earth, but only *punishes* the man and the woman. At the very moment of the fall, God is working for human redemption.

Israel has an important role in the drama of redemption, for it is in the history of the chosen people that the two "hands of God" have continued their work, preparing humankind for communion with God. Therefore, the Old Testament is not the revelation of a God alien to the Christian faith, but is rather the history of the unfolding redemptive purposes of the same God whom Christians know in Jesus Christ.

At the proper time, when humankind had received the necessary preparation, the Word was incarnate in Jesus Christ. Jesus is the "second Adam" because in his life, death, and resurrection a new humanity has been created, and in all his actions Jesus has corrected what was twisted because of sin. Furthermore, Jesus has defeated Satan, and this in turn has enabled us to live in renewed freedom. Those who are joined to him in baptism, and nourished in his body through communion, are also participants in his victory. Jesus Christ is literally the head of the church, which is his body. This body is nourished through worship—particularly communion—and is so joined to its head that it is already receiving the first benefits of Christ's victory. In his resurrection, the final resurrection has dawned, and all who are part of his body will partake of it.

Even at the end, when the Kingdom of God is established, God's task as shepherd will not be finished. On the contrary, redeemed humanity will continue growing into greater communion with the divine, and the process of divinization will go on eternally, taking us ever closer to God.

In conclusion, what we find in Irenaeus is a grand vision of history, so that the divine purposes unfold through it. The focal point of that history is the incarnation, not only because through it God's word has straightened the twisted history of humankind, but also because from the very beginning the union of the human with the divine was the goal of history. God's purpose is to be joined to the human creature, and this has taken place in a unique way in Jesus Christ.

CLEMENT OF ALEXANDRIA

The life story and the interests of Clement of Alexandria were very different from those of Irenaeus. Clement was probably born in Athens, the city that had long been famous for its philosophers. His parents were pagans; but young Clement was converted in unknown circumstances, and then undertook a vast search for a teacher who could give him deeper instruction in the Christian faith. After extensive travels, he found in Alexandria a teacher who satisfied his thirst for knowledge. This was Pantaenus, of whom little is known. Clement remained in Alexandria, and when his teacher died Clement took his place as the main Christian instructor in Alexandria. In 202, when Septimius Severus was emperor, persecution broke out, and Clement had to leave the city. He then traveled along the Eastern Mediterranean—particularly Syria and Asia Minor—until his death in 215.

Alexandria, where Clement spent most of his career, was the most active intellectual center of the time. Its Museum, or temple of the muses, with its adjacent library, was similar to our modern universities, in that it was a meeting place for scholars in various fields. Furthermore, because it was also a trade center, Alexandria was a meeting place, not only for scholars and philosophers, but also for charlatans and adventurers. Therefore, the syncretistic spirit of the time reached its high point in that city at the mouth of the Nile.

It was in that context that Clement studied and taught, and therefore his thought bears the mark of Alexandria. He was not a pastor, like Irenaeus, but rather a thinker and a searcher; and his goal was not so much to expound the traditional faith of the church—although he did hold that faith—as to help those in quest of deeper truth, and to convince pagan intellectuals that Christianity was not the absurd superstition that some claimed it was.

In his *Exhortation to the Pagans,* Clement shows the gist of his theological method in making use of Plato and other philosophers. "I seek to know God, and not only the works of God. Who will aid me in my quest? . . . How then, oh, Plato, is one to seek after God?" Clement's purpose in the passage is to show his pagan readers that a good part of Christian doctrine can be supported by Plato's philosophy. Thus, pagans would be able to approach Christianity without taking for granted, as many supposed, that it was a religion for the ignorant and the superstitious.

But the reason why Clement calls upon Plato is not only that it is convenient for his argument. He is convinced that there is only one truth, and that therefore any truth to be found in Plato can be none other than the truth that has been revealed in Jesus Christ and in scripture. According to him, philosophy was given to the Greeks just as the Law was given to the Jews. Both have the purpose of leading to the ultimate truth, now revealed in Christ. The classical philosophers were to the Greeks what the prophets were to the Hebrews. With the Jews, God has established the covenant of the Law; with the Greeks, that of philosophy.

How can one see the agreement between scripture and the philosophers? At first sight, there seems to be a great distance between the two. But Clement was convinced that a careful study of scripture would lead to the same truth that the philosophers have known. The reason for this is that scripture is written allegorically or, as Clement says, "in parables." The sacred text has more than one meaning. The literal sense ought not to be set aside. But those who are content with it are like children who are content with milk and never grow to adulthood. Beyond the literal sense of the text there are other meanings that the truly wise must discover.

There is a close relationship between faith and reason, for one cannot function without the other. Reason builds its arguments on first principles which cannot be proven, but are accepted by faith. For the truly wise, faith is the first principle, the starting point, on which reason is to build. But Christians who are content with faith, and do not use reason to build upon it, are again like children who are forever content with milk.

Clement contrasts such people, who are satisfied with the rudiments of faith, with the wise person or, as he says, the "true Gnostic." Those who are wise go beyond the literal meaning of scripture. Clement himself saw his task, not as that of a shepherd leading a flock, but rather as that of the "true Gnostic" leading others of similar interests. Naturally, this tends to produce an elitist theology, and Clement has often been criticized on this account.

It is not necessary to say a great deal about the actual content of Clement's theology. Although he sees himself as an interpreter of scripture, his allegorical exegesis allows him to find in the sacred text ideas and doctrines that are really Platonic in inspiration. God is the Ineffable One about which one can only speak in metaphors and in negative terms. One can say what God is not. But as to what God is, human language can do no more than point to a reality that is beyond its grasp.

This Ineffable One is revealed to us in the Word or Logos, from whom the philosophers as well as the prophets received whatever truth they knew, and who has become incarnate in Jesus. On this point, Clement follows the direction set earlier by Justin. The main difference is that, while Justin used the doctrine of the Logos to show to pagans the truth of Christianity, Clement uses the same doctrine to call Christians to be open to the truth in philosophy.

In any case, Clement's importance does not lie in the manner in which he understands one doctrine or another, but rather in that his thought is characteristic of an entire atmosphere and tradition that developed in Alexandria and that would be of great significance for the subsequent course of theology. Later in this chapter, when discussing Origen, we shall see the next step in the development of that theological tradition. It is also interesting to note that Clement is the author of the oldest Christian hymn whose authorship is known—a hymn whose translation by Lowell Mason in 1831, now commonly sung, begins "Shepherd of tender youth, guiding in love and truth."

TERTULLIAN OF CARTHAGE

Tertullian was very different from Clement. He seems to have been a native of the North African city of Carthage. Although he spent most of his life there, it was in Rome that he was converted to Christianity when he was about forty years old. Having returned to Carthage, he wrote a number of treatises in defense of the faith against the pagans, and in defense of orthodoxy against various heresies. Many of his works are important for a number of different reasons. For instance, his treatise *On Baptism* is the oldest extant treatise on that subject, and is an important source for our knowledge of early baptismal practices.

And his work *To His Wife* gives us an interesting glimpse into marriage among second-century Christians.

Tertullian was a lawyer, or at least had been trained in rhetoric, and his entire literary output bears the stamp of a legal mind. In an earlier chapter, we have quoted his protest against the "unjust sentence" of Trajan, ordering that Christians should not be sought out, but should be punished if brought before the authorities. Those lines read like the argument of a lawyer appealing a case before a higher court. In another work, *On the Witness of the Soul,* Tertullian places the human soul on the witness stand and, after questioning it, comes to the conclusion that the soul is "by nature Christian," and that if it persists in rejecting Christianity this is due to obstinacy and blindness.

The treatise where Tertullian's legal mind shines is *Prescription against the Heretics.* In the legal language of the time, a *Prescription* could mean at least two things. It could be a legal argument presented before the case itself was begun, in order to show that the trial should not take place. If, even before the actual case was presented, one of the parties could show that the other had no right to sue, or that the suit was not properly drawn, or that the court had no jurisdiction, the trial could be canceled. But the same word had a different meaning when one spoke of a "long-term prescription." This meant that if a party had been in undisputed possession of a property for a certain time, that party became the legal owner, even if at a later time another party claimed it.

Tertullian uses the term in both senses, as if it were a case of a suit between orthodox Christianity and the heretics. His aim is to show, not simply that the heretics are wrong, but rather that they do not even have the right to dispute with the church. To this end, he claims that scriptures belong to the church. For several generations the church has used the Bible, and the heretics have not disputed its possession. Even though not all of scripture belonged originally to the church—for a large part of it was written by the Jews—by now it does. Therefore, the heretics have no right to use the Bible. They are latecomers who seek to change and to use what legally belongs to the church.

In order to show that scripture belongs to the church, it suffices to look at the various ancient churches where scripture has been read and interpreted in a consistent manner since the days of the apostles. Rome, for instance, can point to an uninterrupted line of bishops joining the present time—the late second century—to the apostles Peter and Paul. And the same is true of the church in Antioch as well as of several others. All of these apostolic churches agree in their use and interpretation of scripture. Furthermore, by virtue of their very origin the writings of the apostles belong to the apostolic churches.

Since scripture belongs to the churches which are the heirs to the apostles, the heretics have no right to base their arguments on it. Here Tertullian uses the term *prescription* in the other sense. Since heretics have no right to interpret scripture, any argument with them regarding such interpretation is out of place. The church, as the rightful owner of scripture, is the only one that has the right to interpret it.

This argument against the heretics has repeatedly been used against various dissidents throughout the history of Christianity. It was one of the main arguments of Catholics against Protestants in the sixteenth century. In Tertullian's case, however, one should note that his argument was based on showing continuity, not only of formal succession, but also of doctrine, through the generations. Since this continuity of doctrine was precisely what was debated at the time of the Reformation, the argument was not as powerful as in Tertullian's time.

But Tertullian's legalism goes beyond arguments such as this. His legal mind leads him to affirm that, once one has found the truth of Christianity, one should abandon any further search for truth. As Tertullian sees the matter, a Christian who is still searching for further truth lacks faith.

> You are to seek until you find, and once you have found, you are to believe. Thereafter, all you have to do is to hold to what you have believed. Besides this, you are to believe that there is nothing further to be believed, nor anything else to be sought.[14]

This means that the accepted body of Christian doctrine suffices, and that any quest for truth that goes beyond that body of doctrine is dangerous. Naturally, Tertullian would allow Christians to delve deeper into Christian doctrine. But anything that goes beyond it, as well as anything coming from other sources, must be rejected. This is particularly true of pagan philosophy, which is the source of all heresy, and is nothing but idle speculation.

> Miserable Aristotle, who gave them dialectics! He gave them the art of building in order to tear down, an art of slippery speech and crude arguments . . . which rejects everything and deals with nothing.[15]

In short, Tertullian condemns all speculation. To speak, for instance, of what God's omnipotence can do is a waste of time and a dangerous occupation. What we are to ask is not what God could do, but rather what has God in fact done. This is what the church teaches. This is what is to be found in scripture. The rest is idle and risky curiosity.

This, however, does not mean that Tertullian does not use logic against his adversaries. On the contrary, his logic is often inflexible and overwhelming, as in the case of the *Prescription*. But the strength of his arguments is not so much in his logic as in his rhetoric, which sometimes leads him to sarcasm. For instance, in writing against Marcion he tells his opponent that the God of the church has made this entire world and all its wonders, whereas Marcion's god has not created a single vegetable. And then he goes on to ask, what was Marcion's god doing before its recent revelation? Is the divine love that Marcion touts an affair of the last minute? Thus, through a unique combination of mordant irony and inflexible logic, Tertullian became the scourge of heretics and the champion of orthodoxy.

Yet, around the year 207, that staunch enemy of heresy, that untiring advocate of the authority of the church, joined the Montanist movement. Why Tertullian took this step is one of the many mysteries of church history, for there is little in his own writings or in other contemporaneous documents that tells us of his motives. It is impossible to give a categorical answer to the question of why Tertullian became a Montanist. But it is possible to note the affinities between Tertullian's character and theology, on the one hand, and Montanism on the other.

Montanism is named after its founder, Montanus, who had been a pagan priest until his conversion to Christianity in 155. At a later time he began prophesying, declaring that he had been possessed by the Holy Spirit. Soon two women, Priscilla and Maximilla, also began prophesying. This in itself was not new, for at that time, at least in some churches, women were allowed to preach or prophesy. What was new, and gave rise to serious misgivings, was that Montanus and his followers claimed that their movement was the beginning of a new age. Just as in Jesus Christ a new age had begun, so was a still newer age beginning in the outpouring of the Spirit. This new age was characterized by a more rigorous moral life, just as the Sermon on the Mount was itself more demanding than the Law of the Old Testament. At least some Montanists affirmed that this more rigorous law included celibacy.

The rest of the church opposed the preaching of the Montanists not because they prophesied, but because they claimed that with them the last age of history had dawned. According to the New Testament, the last days began with the advent and resurrection of Jesus, and with the giving of the Holy Spirit in Pentecost. As years went by, this emphasis on the last days being already here was progressively forgotten, to the point that in the twenty-first century many find it surprising. But in the second century the conviction of the church was very much alive, that the last days had already begun in Jesus Christ. Therefore to claim, as the Montanists did, that the end was beginning then, with the giving of the Spirit to Montanus and his followers, was to diminish the significance of the events of the New Testament, and to make of the gospel one more stage in the history of salvation. These were the consequences of Montanism that the church could not accept.

Tertullian seems to have been attracted by Montanist rigorism. His legal mind sought perfect order, where everything was properly done. In the church at large, in spite of all its efforts to do the will of God, there were too many imperfections that did not fit Tertullian's frame of mind. The only way to explain the continuing sin of Christians was to see the church as an intermediate stage, to be superseded by the new age of the Spirit. Naturally, such dreams were doomed to failure, and some ancient writers tell us that toward the end of his days Tertullian was sufficiently disappointed with Montanism to found his own sect—which those ancient writers call the *Tertullianists*.

Even after he became a Montanist, Tertullian continued his campaign against doctrinal error. Probably the most significant of the works that he wrote during this period is his brief treatise *Against Praxeas*, where he coined formulas that would be of great importance in later trinitarian and christological debates.

Little or nothing is known of Praxeas. Some scholars believe that there never was such a person, and that *Praxeas* was another name for Calixtus, the bishop of Rome, whom Tertullian prefers to attack under a fictitious name. Whoever Praxeas was, it is clear that he was influential in the church of Rome, and that there he had sought to explain the relationship between Father, Son, and Holy Spirit in a manner that Tertullian found inadmissible. According to Praxeas, the Father, the Son, and the Holy Spirit were simply three modes in which God appeared, so that God was sometimes Father, sometimes Son, and sometimes Holy Spirit—at least, this is what may be inferred from Tertullian's treatise. This is what has been called *Patripassianism* (the doctrine that the Father suffered the passion) or *Modalism* (the doctrine that the various persons of the Trinity are "modes" in which God appears).

Since Praxeas had also curtailed Montanist influence in Rome, Tertullian opens his treatise with typical mordancy: "Praxeas served the Devil in Rome in two ways: expelling prophecy and introducing heresy, evicting the Spirit and crucifying the Father."[16]

But Tertullian then moves on to explain how the Trinity is to be understood. It is in this context that he proposes the formula "one substance and three persons." Likewise, when discussing how Jesus Christ can be both human and divine, he speaks of "one person" and "two substances" or "natures," the divine and the human. The manner in which he explains the meaning of the terms "person" and "substance" is drawn mostly from their legal use. Later theologians would explicate the same words in metaphysical terms. In any case, it is significant that, in both the trinitarian and the christological questions, Tertullian coined the formulas that would eventually become the hallmark of orthodoxy.

For all these reasons, Tertullian is a unique personality in the story of Christianity. A fiery champion of orthodoxy against every sort of heresy, in the end he joined one of the movements that the church at large considered heretical. And, even then, he produced writings and theological formulas that would be very influential in the future course of orthodox theology. Furthermore, he was the first Christian theologian to write in Latin, which was the language of the Western half of the empire, and thus he may be considered the founder of Western theology.

ORIGEN OF ALEXANDRIA

Clement's greatest disciple, and the last of the four Christian teachers to be considered in this chapter, was Origen. In contrast with Clement, Origen was the son of Christian parents. His father suffered martyrdom during the persecution of Septimius Severus—the same persecution that forced Clement to leave the city. Origen, who was still a young lad, wished to offer himself for martyrdom. But his mother hid his clothes and he was forced to remain at home, where he wrote a treatise on martyrdom addressed to his imprisoned father.

Shortly thereafter, when Origen was still in his late teens, the bishop of Alexandria, Demetrius, entrusted him with the task of training catechumens—that is, candidates for baptism. This was a very serious responsibility, and young Origen, whose genius was exceptional, soon became famous. After teaching catechumens for a number of years, he left that task to some of his best disciples, and devoted himself entirely to running a school of Christian philosophy that was very similar to those founded by the great classical philosophers. There he lectured, not only to Christians who came from afar to listen to him, but also to enlightened pagans drawn by his fame, such as the mother of the emperor and the governor of Arabia.

For a number of reasons, including jealousy, conflict arose between Demetrius and Origen. The final result was that the latter had to leave his native city and settle at Caesarea, where he continued writing and teaching for another twenty years.

Finally, during the persecution of Decius (discussed in the next chapter), Origen had the opportunity to show the strength of his faith. Given the nature of that persecution, Origen was not put to death, but was tortured to such a point that he died shortly after having been released. He died in Tyre, when he was about seventy years old.

Origen's literary output was enormous. Since he was aware of the manner in which diverse versions of scripture differed, he compiled the *Hexapla*. This was an edition of the Old Testament in six columns: the Hebrew text, a Greek transliteration from the Hebrew—so that a reader who did not know that ancient language could at least have some idea of its pronunciation—and four different Greek translations. To this was added an entire system of symbols indicating variants, omissions, and additions. Besides this great scholarly work, Origen wrote commentaries on many books of the Bible, the already cited apology *Against Celsus,* and a great systematic theology called *De principiis*—("On First Principles"). Part of this great literary production was achieved through dictation, and it is even said that at times he would simultaneously dictate seven different works to as many secretaries.

The spirit of Origen's theology is very similar to that of his teacher, Clement. It is an attempt to relate Christian faith to the philosophical tradition that was then current in Alexandria, Platonism. He was aware of the danger of abandoning Christian doctrine in favor of the teachings of the philosophers, and thus declared that "nothing which is at variance with the tradition of the apostles and of the church is to be accepted as true." This tradition includes first of all the doctrine that there is only one God, creator and ruler of the universe, and therefore the Gnostic speculations regarding the origin of the world are to be rejected. Secondly, the apostles taught that Jesus Christ is the Son of God, begotten before all creation, and that his incarnation is such that, while becoming human, he remained divine. As to the Holy Spirit, Origen declares that apostolic tradition is not entirely clear, except in affirming that the Spirit's glory is no less than that of the Father and the Son. Finally, the apostles taught that at a future time the soul will be rewarded or punished according to its life in this world, and that there will be a final resurrection of the body, which will rise incorruptible.

However, once these points have been affirmed, Origen feels free to rise in great speculative flights. For instance, since the tradition of the apostles and of the church gives no details as to how the world was created, Origen believes that this is a fair field of inquiry. In the first chapters of Genesis there are two stories of creation, as Jewish scholars had noted even before the time of Origen. In one of these stories, we are told that humankind was created after the image and likeness of God, and that "male and female created He them." In the second, we are told that God made Adam first, then the animals, and then formed the woman out of Adam's rib. In the Greek version of the first narrative, the verb describing God's action is "to create," whereas in the second it is "to form" or "to shape." What is the meaning of these differences? Modern scholars would speak of the joining of separate traditions. But Origen simply declares that there are two narratives because there were in fact two creations.

According to Origen, the first creation was purely spiritual. What God first created were spirits without bodies. This is why the text says "male and female"—that is, with no sexual differences. This is also why we are told that God "created," and not that God "formed."

God's purpose was that the spirits thus created would be devoted to the contemplation of the divine. But some of them strayed from that contemplation and fell. It was then that God made the second creation. This second creation is material, and it serves as a shelter or temporary home for fallen spirits. Those spirits who fell farthest have become demons, while the rest are human souls. It was for these human souls—fallen preexistent spirits—that God made the bodies we now have, which God "shaped" out of the earth, making some male and some female.

This implies that all human souls existed as pure spirits—or "intellects," as Origen calls them—before being born into the world, and that the reason why we are here is that we have sinned in that prior, purely spiritual existence. Although Origen claims that all this is based on the Bible, it is clear that it is derived from the Platonic tradition, where similar ideas had been taught for a long time.

In the present world, the Devil and his demons have us captive, and therefore Jesus Christ has come to break the power of Satan and to show us the path we are to follow in our return to our spiritual home. Furthermore, since the Devil is no more than a spirit like ours, and since God is love, in the end even Satan will be saved, and the entire creation will return to its original state, where everything was pure spirit. However, since these spirits will still be free, there is nothing to guarantee that there will not be a new fall, a new material world, and a new history, and that the cycle of fall, restoration, and fall will not go on forever.

In evaluating all of this, one has to begin by marveling at the width of Origen's mental scope. For this reason, he has had fervent admirers at various times throughout the history of the church. One must also remember that Origen proposes all of this, not as truths to be generally accepted, nor as something that will supersede the doctrines of the church, but as his own tentative speculations, which ought not to be compared with the authoritative teaching of the church.

However, once this has been said, it is also important to note that on many points Origen is more Platonist than Christian. Thus, for instance, Origen rejects the doctrines of Marcion and of the Gnostics, that the world is the creation of an inferior being; but then he comes to the conclusion that the existence of the physical world—as well as of history—is the result of sin. At this point there is a marked difference with Irenaeus, for whom the existence of history was part of the eternal purpose of God. And when it comes to the preexistence of souls, and to the eternal cycle of fall and restoration, there is no doubt that Origen strays from what Christianity has usually taught.

As one studies the writings of these great teachers of the church, it is evident that different trends or theological tendencies are beginning to emerge. First,

Irenaeus reflects the sort of theology that will become dominant in his native area of Asia Minor as well as in Syria. This is a theology dominated by the story of what God has done, is doing, and will do. It sees salvation as union with the Christ who has conquered death—a union established by baptism and fed by communion. Secondly, particularly in Alexandria, a theological trend is emerging whose main concern is to show the connection between Christianity and the best of classical philosophy. This theology is dominated by the quest for philosophical, unchanging truth. For it, salvation consists in being so illumined by God as to be able to return to the spiritual world. Finally, in the Latin-speaking West Tertullian is the first exponent of a theology that will be profoundly concerned over moral issues—sometimes to the point of legalism—and for which salvation is attained by moral purity. In later centuries, these three theologies would continue evolving. The Latin-speaking West, dominated by a theological outlook patterned after Tertullian's, would be involved in repeated debates on how to preserve the purity of the church, and much later—particularly in the sixteenth century—over the role of works in salvation. The Greek-speaking East would soon be divided by differences reflecting the tradition expounded by Irenaeus on the one hand, and the philosophical outlook of Origen on the other.

IO

Persecution in the Third Century

> The present confession of the faith before the authorities has been all the
> more illustrious and honorable because the suffering was greater. The
> struggle intensified, and the glory of those who struggled grew with it.
>
> CYPRIAN OF CARTHAGE

In the last years of the second century, the church had enjoyed relative peace.
The empire was involved in civil wars and in defending its borders against
barbarian inroads, and therefore had paid scant attention to Christians. Trajan's
old principle, that Christians were to be punished if they refused to worship
the emperor and the gods, but that they ought not to be sought out, was still in
force. Therefore, whatever persecution existed was local and sporadic.

In the third century, things changed. Trajan's policy was still valid, and
therefore the threat of local persecution was constant. But over and beyond that
there were new policies that deeply affected the life of the church. The emperors
who created and applied these policies were Septimius Severus and Decius.

PERSECUTION UNDER SEPTIMIUS SEVERUS

Early in the third century, the reigning emperor, Septimius Severus, had managed to put an end to a series of civil wars that had weakened the empire. But
even so, it was not easy to govern such a vast and unruly domain. The "barbarians" who lived beyond the borders of the Rhine and the Danube were a
constant threat. Within the empire there were dissident groups, and there was
always the danger that a legion might rebel and name its own emperor, thus
precipitating a new civil war. Faced with such difficulties, the emperor felt the
need for religious harmony within his territories, and thus settled on a policy
of promoting syncretism. He proposed a plan to bring all his subjects together
under the worship of *Sol invictus* (the "Unconquered Sun")—and to subsume
under that worship all the various religions and philosophies then current. All
gods were to be accepted, as long as one acknowledged the Sun that reigned
above all.

This policy soon clashed with what seemed the obstinacy of two groups that refused to yield to syncretism: Jews and Christians. Septimius Severus then decided to stop the spread of those two religions, and thus outlawed, under penalty of death, all conversions to Christianity or to Judaism—for at that point both religions were gaining numerous converts. This was in addition to the still existing threat of Trajan's legislation.

The net result was an increase in local persecutions akin to those of the second century, to which was now added a more intensive persecution aimed directly at new converts and their teachers. Therefore, the year 202, when the edict of Septimius Severus was issued, is a landmark in the history of persecutions. There is a tradition affirming that Irenaeus suffered martyrdom in that year. It was also at that time that a group of Christians, including Origen's father, were killed in Alexandria. Since Clement was a famous Christian teacher in that city, and since the imperial edict was particularly directed against those who sought new converts, he had to seek refuge in areas where he was less known.

The most famous martyrdom of that time is that of Perpetua and Felicitas, which probably took place in 203. It is possible that Perpetua and her companions were Montanists, and that the account of their martyrdom comes from the pen of Tertullian. In any case, the martyrs were five catechumens—that is, five people who were preparing to receive baptism. This agrees with what is known of the policies of Septimius Severus. These five people—some of whom were in their teens—were charged, not with being Christians, but with recently converting, and thus disobeying the imperial edict.

Perpetua is the heroine of the *Martyrdom of Saints Perpetua and Felicitas.* She was a young, well-to-do woman nursing her infant child. Her companions were the slaves Felicitas and Revocatus, and two other young men, Saturninus and Secundulus. A great deal of the text of the *Martyrdom* is placed on the lips of Perpetua, and some scholars believe that she may actually have spoken most of these words. When Perpetua and her companions were arrested, her father tried to persuade her to save her life by abandoning her faith. She answered that, just as everything has a name and it is useless to try to give it a different name, she had the name of Christian, and this could not be changed.

The judicial process was a long and drawn-out affair, apparently because the authorities hoped to persuade the accused to abandon their faith. Felicitas, who was pregnant when arrested, was afraid that her life would be spared for that reason, or that her martyrdom would be postponed and she would not be able to join her four companions. But the *Martyrdom* tells us that her prayers were answered, and that in her eighth month she gave birth to a girl who was then adopted by another Christian woman. Seeing her moan in childbirth, her jailers asked how she expected to be able to face the beasts in the arena. Her answer is typical of the manner in which martyrdom was interpreted: "Now my sufferings are only mine. But when I face the beasts there will be another who will live in me, and will suffer for me since I shall be suffering for him."[17]

The account then reports that the three male martyrs were the first to be put in the arena. Saturninus and Revocatus died quickly and bravely. But no beast would attack Secundulus. Some of them refused to come out to him, while others attacked the soldiers instead. Finally, Secundulus himself declared that a leopard would kill him, and so it happened.

We are then told that Perpetua and Felicitas were placed in the arena to be attacked by a crazed cow. Having been hit and thrown by the animal, Perpetua asked to be able to retie her hair, for loose hair was a sign of mourning, and this was a joyful day for her. Finally, the two bleeding women stood in the middle of the arena, bid each other farewell with the kiss of peace, and died by the sword.

Shortly thereafter, for reasons that are not altogether clear, persecution abated. There were still isolated incidents in various parts of the empire, but the edict of Septimius Severus was not generally enforced. In 211, when Caracalla succeeded Septimius Severus, there was a brief persecution; but this again did not last long, and was mostly limited to North Africa.

The next two emperors, Elagabalus (218–222) and Alexander Severus (222–235), pursued a syncretistic policy similar to that of Septimius Severus. But they did not attempt to force Jews and Christians to accept syncretism, or to stop seeking converts. It is said that Alexander Severus had on his private altar, jointly with his various gods, images of Christ and of Abraham. His mother, Julia Mammea, went to hear Origen lecture in Alexandria.

Under Emperor Maximin there was a very brief persecution in Rome. At that time the church in that city was divided, and the two rival bishops, Pontianus and Hippolytus, were sent to work in the mines. But again the storm passed, and it was even rumored—with little basis in fact—that Philip the Arabian, who ruled the empire from 244 to 249, was a Christian.

In short, during almost half a century, persecution was rare, while the number of converts to Christianity was great. For this entire generation of Christians, the martyrs were worthy of great admiration, but they had lived in times past, and those evil times were not likely to be repeated. Every day there were more Christians among the aristocracy, and the ancient rumors about Christian immorality had little credence among the masses. Persecution was a distant memory, both painful and glorious.

Then the storm broke.

UNDER DECIUS

In 249, Decius took the imperial purple. Although Christian historians have depicted him as a cruel person, the truth is that Decius was simply a Roman of the old style, whose main goal was to restore Rome to her ancient glory. There were several factors contributing to the eclipse of that glory. The barbarians beyond the borders were increasingly restless, and their incursions into the empire were growing more and more daring. There was a serious economic crisis. And the ancient traditions associated with the classical times of Roman civilization were generally forgotten.

To a traditional Roman such as Decius, it seemed obvious that one of the reasons for all this was that the people had abandoned the ancient gods. When all adored the gods, things went better, and the glory and power of Rome were on the increase. By neglecting the gods, Rome had provoked their displeasure, and had been itself neglected by them. Therefore, if Rome's ancient glory was to

Decius believed that Rome must return to its gods.

All were required to have a certificate attesting that they had offered sacrifice to the gods. This is one such certificate.

be restored, it was necessary to restore also its ancient religion. If all the subjects of the empire would worship the gods, perhaps the gods would once again favor the empire.

This was the basis of Decius's religious policy. It was no longer a matter of rumors about Christian immorality, nor of punishing the obstinacy of those who refused to worship the emperor. It was rather an entire religious campaign for the restoration of ancestral religion—a religion that was being particularly undermined by Christianity. What was at stake, as Decius saw it, was the survival of Rome itself. Those who refused to worship the gods were practically guilty of high treason.

Given these circumstances, Decius's persecution was very different from earlier ones. The emperor's purpose was not to create martyrs, but apostates. Almost fifty years earlier, Tertullian had declared that the blood of the martyrs was a seed, for the more it was spilled the greater the number of Christians. The exemplary deaths of Christians in those early years had moved many who had witnessed them, and therefore persecution seemed to encourage the spread of Christianity. If, instead of suffering martyrdom, Christians were forced to recant, this would deprive Christianity of the heroic witness of the martyrs, and would be a victory for Decius's goal of restoring paganism.

Although Decius's edict has been lost, it is clear that what he ordered was not that Christians as such ought to be persecuted, but rather that the worship of the gods was now mandatory throughout the empire. Following the imperial decree, everyone had to offer sacrifice to the gods and to burn incense before a statue of Decius. Those who complied would be given a certificate or *libellum* attesting to that fact. Those who did not have such a certificate would then be considered outlaws who had disobeyed the imperial command.

The imperial decree found Christians unprepared for the new challenge. The generations that had lived under constant threat of persecution were now past, and the new generations were not ready for martyrdom. Some ran to obey the

imperial command. Some bought false certificates declaring that they had sacrificed before the gods, when in fact they had not. Others stood firm for a while,
but when brought before the imperial authorities offered the required sacrifice
to the gods. And there was a significant number who resolved to stand firm and
refuse to obey the edict.

Since Decius's goal was to promote the worship of the gods, rather than to
kill Christians, those who actually died as martyrs were relatively few. What
the authorities did was to arrest Christians and then, through a combination
of promises, threats, and torture, to try to force them to abandon their faith.
It was under this policy that Origen was imprisoned and tortured. And Origen's case found hundreds of counterparts throughout the empire. This was no
longer a sporadic or local persecution, but one that was systematic and universal. As proof of the widespread application of the imperial decree, certificates
of having sacrificed have survived from some rather remote parts of the empire.

One of the results of this persecution was that a new title of honor appeared
within the church, that of the "confessor." Until that time, practically all who
were taken before the authorities and remained firm had become martyrs.
Those who offered sacrifice to the gods and to the emperor were apostates. Due
to the policies established by Decius, there were now those who remained firm
in their faith, even in the midst of cruel torture, but who never received the
crown of martyrdom. Those who had confessed the faith in such circumstances
were then called "confessors," and were highly respected by other Christians.

Decius's persecution was brief. In 251 Gallus succeeded him, and his policies
were set aside. Six years later Valerian, a former companion of Decius, began a
new persecution. But he was captured by the Persians, who took him prisoner,
and the church enjoyed another forty years of relative peace.

THE QUESTION OF THE LAPSED:
CYPRIAN AND NOVATIAN

In spite of its brief duration, the persecution under Decius was a harsh trial
for the church. This was due, not only to the persecution itself, but also to the
problems that had to be faced after it. In short, the great question before the
church was what to do about the "lapsed"—those who, in one way or another,
had weakened during the persecution. There were several complicating factors.
One was that not all had fallen in the same manner nor to the same degree.
The case of those who ran to offer sacrifice as soon as they were told of the
imperial decree was hardly the same as that of those who purchased fraudulent
certificates, or those others who had weakened for a moment, but had then reaffirmed their faith and asked to rejoin the church while the persecution was still
in progress.

Given the great prestige of the confessors, some thought that they were the ones with authority to determine who among the lapsed ought to be restored to the communion of the church, and how. Some confessors, particularly in North Africa, claimed that authority, and began restoring some of the lapsed. This met with the opposition of many bishops who claimed that only the hierarchy had the authority to restore the lapsed, and that only it could do so in a uniform and just manner. Still others were convinced that both the confessors and the bishops were showing too much leniency, and that the lapsed ought to be treated with greater rigor. In the debate surrounding this question, two people played crucial roles: Cyprian and Novatian.

Cyprian had become a Christian when he was about forty years old, and shortly thereafter had been elected bishop of Carthage. His favorite theologian was Tertullian, whom he called "the master." Like Tertullian, he was trained in rhetoric, and he could easily overwhelm his opponents with his arguments. His writings are among the best Christian literature of the time.

Cyprian, who had become a bishop shortly before the persecution, thought that his duty was to flee to a secure place with other leaders of the church, and continue guiding the flock through an extensive correspondence. As was to be expected, many interpreted this decision as an act of cowardice. The church of Rome, for instance, had lost its bishop in the persecution, and the clergy of that city wrote to Cyprian questioning his decision. He insisted that he had fled for the good of his flock, and not out of cowardice. As a matter of fact, his valor and conviction were amply proven a few years later, when he gave his life as a martyr. But meanwhile his own authority was questioned, and there were many who claimed that the confessors of Carthage, who had suffered for their faith, had more authority than he did, particularly when it came to the question of the restoration of the lapsed.

Some of these confessors thought that the lapsed should be readmitted directly, with no other requirement than their own declaration of repentance. Soon some of the presbyters, who had other reasons for disliking their bishop, joined the confessors, and the outcome was a schism that divided the church in Carthage and throughout the neighboring areas. Cyprian then called a *synod*—that is, a gathering of the bishops of the region—which decided that those who had purchased or otherwise obtained certificates without actually having sacrificed would be immediately readmitted to the communion of the church. Those who had sacrificed would only be readmitted on their deathbeds, or when a new persecution gave them the opportunity to prove the sincerity of their repentance. Those who had sacrificed and showed no repentance would never be readmitted. All these actions were to be taken by the bishops, and not by confessors. These decisions ended the controversy, although the schism continued for some time.

The main reason why Cyprian insisted on the need to regulate the readmission of the lapsed into the communion of the church was his own understanding of the church. The church is the body of Christ, and will share in the victory of its Head. Therefore, "outside the church there is no salvation," and "no one can have God as Father who does not have the church as mother." By this he did not mean that one had to be in total agreement with the hierarchy of the church—he himself had his own clashes with the hierarchy of Rome. But he did believe that the unity of the church was of supreme importance. Since the actions of the confessors threatened that unity, Cyprian felt that he had to reject those actions and to insist on the need for a synod to decide what was to be done with the lapsed.

Besides this, Cyprian was an admirer of Tertullian, whose writings he studied assiduously. Tertullian's rigorism had an influence on Cyprian, and he revolted against the idea of restoring the lapsed too easily. The church was to be a community of saints, and the idolaters and apostates had no place in it.

Novatian was more rigorous than Cyprian. He clashed with the bishop of Rome, Cornelius, because in his opinion the lapsed were being readmitted too easily. Years earlier, there had been in the same city a similar conflict between Hippolytus, a noted theologian, and bishop Calixtus, because the latter was willing to forgive those guilty of fornication who repented, and Hippolytus insisted that this should not be done. At that time the result was a schism, so that there were two bishops in Rome. In the case of Novatian's protest the result was the same. As in so many other cases, the issue was whether purity or forgiving love should be the characteristic note of the church. The schism of Hippolytus did not last long, but the Novatianist schism did continue for several generations.

The significance of these episodes is that they show how, due to its concern for its own purity, and to its understanding of sin as a debt owed to God, the Western church was repeatedly embroiled in debates regarding how that purity should be sustained while still having the church be a community of love. As a result, the restoration of the lapsed was one of the main concerns of the Western church from a very early date. The question of what should be done about those baptized Christians who sinned divided the Western church repeatedly. It was out of that concern that the entire penitential system developed. Much later, the Protestant Reformation was in large measure a protest against that system.

II

Christian Life

... not many of you were wise according to worldly standards, not many
were powerful, not many of noble birth; but ... God chose what is weak
in the world to shame the strong.

I COR. 1:26-27

When telling the story of Christianity, one must always remember that the
sources themselves are not a fair representation of all that was taking
place. Since most of the surviving documents deal with the work and thought
of the leaders of the church, or with persecution and conflicts with the state,
there is always the tendency to forget that these writings present only a partial
picture, saying little of the life and faith of the rank and file, or of their religious
practices. Furthermore, when one attempts to reconstruct the rest of the picture, one is faced with an almost total lack of sources, and must be content with
piecing together bits of information.

THE SOCIAL ORIGINS OF EARLY CHRISTIANS

The complaint of the pagan writer Celsus was quoted earlier: Christians were
ignorant folk whose teaching took place, not in schools nor in open forums,
but in kitchens, shops, and tanneries. Although the work of Christians such
as Justin, Clement, and Origen would seem to belie Celsus's words, the fact
remains that, in general, Celsus was telling the truth. Wise scholars among
Christians were the exception rather than the rule. It is significant that in his
apology *Against Celsus* Origen does not contradict Celsus on this score. From
the perspective of cultured pagans such as Tacitus, Cornelius Fronto, and
Marcus Aurelius, Christians were a despicable rabble.

They were not entirely wrong, for recent sociological studies indicate that
the vast majority of Christians during the first three centuries belonged to the
lower echelons of society, or at least did not fit well in the higher ranks. According to the witness of the Gospels, Jesus spent most of his time with poor, ill,
and despised people. Paul, who belonged to a higher social class than most of

This shrine, found in a relatively humble dwelling in Herculaneum, attests to the presence of Christians there in the first century, when the city was destroyed by the Vesuvius.

the earliest disciples, does say that the majority of Christians in Corinth were ignorant, powerless, and of obscure birth. The same is generally true during the first three centuries of the life of the church. Although there were Christians of relatively high rank, such as Domitilla—if she indeed was a Christian—and Perpetua, it is likely that for each of these there were hundreds or perhaps thousands of Christians of humbler status and less instruction.

It was mostly out of this rank and file that legends and writings arose with a very different tone from that of Justin and the other Christian scholars. Foremost among these writings are some of the Apocryphal Gospels and some of the Acts of various apostles and of the Virgin. This includes the Acts of Peter, the Epistle of Jesus to King Abgar, the correspondence between Mary and Ignatius of Antioch, the Gospel of Bartholomew, and many others. The miraculous plays a central role in these writings, even to the point of the ridiculous. Thus, for instance, in one of the Apocryphal Gospels, young Jesus amuses himself by breaking the water jars of his playmates and throwing the pieces into a well. When the other boys burst into tears, saying that their parents will punish them for having broken the jars, Jesus orders the water to return the broken jars and these come up unscathed. Or, when Jesus wishes to be atop a tree, he does not climb like other boys. He simply orders the tree to bend down to him, sits on it, and tells the tree to return to its original position.[18]

However, this naive credulity should not lead one to underestimate those common Christians. A comparison of their theology with that of more cultured Christians does not always favor the latter. Thus, for instance, the active, sovereign, and just God who is depicted in many of these apocryphal writings is closer to the God of scripture than is the ineffable and distant One of Clement of Alexandria. Furthermore, while the great apologists made every effort to prove to the authorities that their faith was not opposed to imperial policies, there are indications that some common Christians were well aware that there was an unavoidable clash between the goals of the empire and the divine purpose. When one of these Christians was taken before imperial authorities, we are told that he refused to acknowledge the authority of the emperor, and declared that Christ was "my Lord, the emperor over all kings and all nations." Finally, while some of the more cultured Christians tended to spiritualize Christian hope, in the faith of the common people there was still the vision of a Kingdom that would supplant the present order, of a new Jerusalem where God would wipe away the tears of those who were suffering under the social order of the empire.

CHRISTIAN WORSHIP

Worship was one point at which Christians of all social classes had a common experience. As we reconstruct that experience, we must rely mostly on documents left behind by Christian leaders. But, since common Christians partook of the same services, here we have a rare glimpse at the life of all Christians.

We are told in the book of Acts that from the very beginning the early church had the custom of gathering on the first day of the week for the breaking of bread—the Eucharist or Lord's Supper. The reason for gathering on the first day of the week was that this was the day of the resurrection of the Lord. Therefore, the main purpose of this service of worship was not to call the faithful to repentance, or to make them aware of the magnitude of their sins, but rather to celebrate the resurrection of Jesus and the promises of which that resurrection was the seal. For this reason, Acts describes those gatherings as happy occasions:

This painting, found in a catacomb, depicts an early communion service. Communion was the central act of Christian worship.

they "ate their food with glad and generous hearts, praising God and having the goodwill of all the people" (Acts 2:46-47). Those early communion services did not focus their attention on the events of Good Friday, but rather on those of Easter. A new reality had dawned, and Christians gathered to celebrate that dawning and to become participants in it.

From that time, and throughout most of its history, the Christian church has seen in communion its normal and highest act of worship. Only after the Protestant Reformation in the sixteenth century—and in many cases much later—did it become common practice in many Protestant churches to focus their worship on preaching rather than on communion.

Besides the well-known but scant data offered by the New Testament, it is possible to reconstruct early Christian worship by piecing together information from a number of extant documents. Although these writings come from different times and places, and therefore there are differences and inconsistencies in what they tell us, it is possible to draw from them a general picture of the typical service of communion.

The most remarkable characteristic of those early communion services was that they were celebrations. The tone was one of joy and gratitude, rather than sorrow and repentance. In the beginning, communion was part of an entire meal. Believers brought what they could, and after the common meal there were special prayers over the bread and the wine. However, by the beginning of the second century the common meal was being set aside, perhaps for fear of persecution, or in order to quell the rumors about orgiastic "love feasts," or perhaps simply because the growing number of believers made it necessary. But even then, the original tone of joy remained.

Two of the earliest witnesses we have regarding Christian worship come from Governor Pliny the Younger of Bythinia and from Justin Martyr—both already mentioned in the context of the persecutions of the second century. What Justin says about worship is rather brief:

The day that is commonly called Sunday all those [believers] who live in the cities or the fields gather, and in their meetings as much as time allows is read from the *memoirs of the apostles* or from the writings of the prophets. Then, once the reader is through, the one presiding offers a verbal exhortation, urging us to follow these beautiful examples. Immediately after this, we all stand as one and raise our prayers, after which—as I have already said—bread, wine, and water are offered, and the president, as he is able, also sends to God his prayers and thanksgiving, and all the people respond, "Amen." Now follows the distribution and partaking of the nourishment that has been consecrated by thanksgiving, and they are sent by means of the deacons to those who are not present. Those who can and will, freely give what seems best to them, and the offering is given to the president. With this he helps orphans and widows, those who are in need because of illness or any other reason, those who are in prison, sojourners, and, in short, the president provides for any who are in need. We hold this general gathering on Sunday, because it is the first day, in which God, transforming darkness and matter, created the world, and also the day in which Jesus Christ, our Savior, rose from the dead.[19]

From these and other sources we know that at least since the second century there were two main parts in a communion service. First there were readings of scripture and commentaries on them, with prayers and hymn singing. Since at that time it was almost impossible for an individual Christian to possess a copy of scripture, this first part of the service was often the only way in which believers came to know the Bible, and therefore this part of the service was rather extensive—sometimes lasting for hours. Then, after dismissing those who were not baptized with a prayer and blessing, came the second part of the service, communion proper, which opened with the kiss of peace. After the kiss, the bread and wine were brought forth and presented to the one presiding, who then offered a prayer over the elements. In this prayer, often lengthy, the saving acts of God were usually recounted, and the power of the Holy Spirit was invoked over the bread and the wine. Then the bread was broken and shared, the common cup was passed, and the meeting ended with a benediction. This service was also the occasion for the sharing with those in need, for whom an offering was collected. Elsewhere, Justin also says that

The baptistery of the church at Dura-Europos.

"whatever we have we make common, and this we share with those who are in need."[20]

Another early custom was to gather for communion at the tombs of the faithful. This was the function of the catacombs. Some authors have dramatized the "church of the catacombs," depicting these as secret places where Christians gathered in defiance of the authorities. This is at best an exaggeration. The catacombs were cemeteries whose existence was well known to the authorities, for Christians were not the only ones with such subterranean burial arrangements. Although on occasion Christians did use the catacombs as hiding places, the main reason why they gathered there was not that they feared the authorities, but rather two others. First, although the church was not recognized by the government, and therefore could not own property, funeral societies were allowed, and these could own cemetery property. In some cities Christians organized themselves into such funeral societies, and therefore it made sense for them to gather at their cemeteries. But even more importantly, many heroes of the faith were buried there, and Christians believed that communion joined them not only among themselves and with Jesus Christ, but also with their ancestors in the faith.

This was particularly true in the case of martyrs. As early as the middle of the second century, it was customary to gather at their tombs on the anniversary of their deaths, and there to celebrate communion. Once again, the idea was that they too were part of the church, and that communion joined the living and the dead in a single body. It was this practice that gave rise to saints' days—which usually celebrated, not their birthday, but the day of their martyrdom. (The custom of gathering relics of martyrs seems to have begun fairly early. In the mid-second century, the *Martyrdom of Polycarp* tells us that Polycarp's bones "would have been more precious to us than pearls.")

More frequently than in catacombs or cemeteries, Christians gathered in private homes. There are indications of this in the New Testament. Later, as congregations grew, some houses were exclusively devoted to divine worship. Thus, the oldest Christian church, found in the excavations of Dura-Europos and built before 256, seems to have been a private dwelling that was converted into a church.

Another consequence of the growth of congregations was that it soon became impossible for all Christians in a particular city to gather together for worship. Yet the unity of the body of Christ was so important that it seemed that something was lost when in a single city there were several congregations. In order to preserve and symbolize the bond of unity, the custom arose in some places to send a piece of bread from the communion service in the bishop's church—the *fragmentum*—to be added to the bread to be used in other churches in the same city. Also, in order to preserve and symbolize the unity of Christians all over the world, each church had a list of bishops of other churches, both near and far, for whom prayer was to be made during communion. These lists were usually written on two writing tablets hinged or strung together, as was then customary for such notes and for some official communications. These sets of tablets were called "diptychs," and at a later date the deletion of someone's name from a church's diptychs became a matter of grave importance. Just as the bond of unity was sealed by the inclusion of a name, that bond was broken by deleting a name.

At the beginning, the Christian calendar was rather simple and was basically a weekly calendar. Every Sunday was a sort of Easter, and a day of joy; and every Friday was a day of penance, fasting, and sorrow. Rather early, for reasons that are not altogether clear, Wednesday also became a day of fasting. There was a very special Sunday, once a year, the day of resurrection, the greatest of Christian celebrations. Unfortunately, Christians were not in agreement as to when the great day was to be celebrated, for some thought it should be set in accordance with the Jewish Passover, while others believed that it should always be celebrated on a Sunday. By the second century there were bitter debates about the matter. To this day, although for other reasons, not all churches agree on the manner in which the date of Easter Sunday is to be determined.

Part of what took place at Easter was the baptism of new converts and their being added to the congregation. Justin tells us that "once those who have believed have been washed and joined us, we take them to where those who

A fifth-century baptistery in the ruins of Ephesus.

are called brothers and sisters are gathered, in order to offer fervent prayers for ourselves, for the recently illumined, and for all others all over the world. [. . .] Then there is the kiss of peace, the president is given bread and a cup of wine and water . . . ," and the Eucharist is celebrated.[21]

In preparation for these events, that usually took place at Easter, there was a time of fasting and penance. This is the origin of our present-day Lent. Pentecost, a feast of Jewish origin, was also celebrated by Christians from a very early date.

The earliest feast day in connection with the birth of Jesus was January 6, Epiphany, the day of his manifestation. This was originally the celebration of the birth itself. Later, particularly in some areas of the Latin-speaking West, December 25 began to take its place. This latter date was actually a pagan festival which, after the time of Constantine (the fourth century), was preempted by the celebration of Christmas.

Baptism was, besides communion, the other great event of Christian worship. As has already been said, in order to partake of communion one had to be baptized. In Acts we are told that people were baptized as soon as they were converted. This was feasible in the early Christian community, where most converts came from Judaism or had been influenced by it, and thus had a basic understanding of the meaning of Christian life and proclamation. But, as the church became increasingly Gentile, it was necessary to require a period of preparation, trial, and instruction prior to baptism. This was the "catechumenate," which by the beginning of the third century lasted up to three years. During that time, catechumens received instruction on Christian doctrine, and were to give signs in their daily lives of the depth of their conviction. As the date approached for their baptism, they were taught the meaning of the creed or baptismal formula that they would be asked to affirm at their baptism. Finally, shortly before being baptized, they were examined and added to the list of those to be baptized.

Baptism was usually administered once a year, on Easter Sunday. Early in the third century it was customary for those about to be baptized to fast on Friday and Saturday, and to be baptized very early Sunday morning, which was the time of the resurrection of Jesus. The candidates were completely naked, the men separate from the women. On emerging from the waters, the neophytes were given white robes, as a sign of their new life in Christ (see Col. 3:9-12 and Rev. 3:4). Then they were anointed, thus making them part of the royal priesthood.

After all the candidates were baptized, they went in procession to the meeting place, where the neophytes joined the rest of the congregation and partook of communion for the first time. The newly baptized were then given water to drink, as a sign that they were thoroughly cleansed, both outside and inside. And they were also given milk and honey, as a sign of the Promised Land into which they were now entering.

Baptism was normally performed by immersion or with the neophyte kneeling in the water, and then having water poured over the head. The *Didache* or *Teaching of the Twelve Apostles*, a document of uncertain date, prefers that it be done in "living"—that is, running—water. But where water was scarce it could be administered by pouring water three times over the head, in the name of the Father, the Son, and the Holy Spirit.

To this day, scholars are not in agreement as to whether the early church baptized infants. By the late second or early third century, there are texts indicating that at least sometimes the children of Christian parents were baptized as infants. But all earlier documents, and many later ones, provide such scant information that it is impossible to decide one way or the other.

THE ORGANIZATION OF THE CHURCH

It is clear that early in the second century there were three distinct positions of leadership in the church: bishop, presbyter—or elder—and deacon. Some historians have claimed that this hierarchy is apostolic in origin; but the extant documents would seem to point in an opposite direction. Although the New Testament does refer to bishops, presbyters, and deacons, these three titles do not appear together, as if they were three clearly defined functions or offices that always existed together. In fact, the New Testament would seem to indicate that the organization of local churches varied from place to place, and that for a certain time the titles of "bishop" and "elder"—or presbyter—were interchangeable. There are also some historians who are inclined to believe that some churches—Rome among them—were not led by a single bishop, but rather by a group of leaders who were sometimes called "bishops" and sometimes "presbyters."

As has already been explained, the emphasis on the authority of bishops and on apostolic succession was in response to the challenge of heresies in the late second and early third centuries. As the church became increasingly Gentile, the danger of heresies rose, and this in turn led to a greater stress on episcopal authority.

The roles of women in positions of leadership in the early church deserves special attention. It is clear that by the end of the second century the official leadership of the church was entirely masculine. But the matter is not quite as clear in earlier times. Particularly in the New Testament, there are indications that women also had positions of leadership. Philip had four daughters who "prophesied"—that is, who preached. Phoebe was a female deacon in Cenchreae, and Junia was counted among the apostles. What actually seems to have taken place is that during the second century, in its efforts to combat heresy, the church centralized its authority, and a by-product of that process was that women were excluded from positions of leadership. But still in the early years of the second century, Governor Pliny informed Trajan that he had ordered that two Christian female ministers—*ministrae*—be tortured.

When speaking of women in the early church, mention should be made of the particular role of widows. The book of Acts says that the primitive church helped support the widows in its midst. This was in part an act of obedience to the repeated Old Testament injunction to care for the widow, the orphan, the poor, and the sojourner. But it was also a matter of practical necessity, for a widow deprived of means of support either had to remarry or to seek refuge with her children. In either case, if the new husband or the child was not a Christian, the widow would be severely limited in her Christian life. Therefore, it soon became customary for the church to support its widows, and to give them particular responsibilities. In an earlier chapter, the story was told of a widow whose ministry was such that she enraged the pagans, and therefore became a martyr. Other widows devoted themselves to the instruction of catechumens. Eventually, the meaning of the word "widow" within the church changed and came to refer not just to a woman whose husband had died but also to any unmarried woman who was supported by the community and who in turn performed some particular functions within it. Some were women who chose to remain unmarried in order to perform their ministry. It is then that one begins to find such strange phrases as "the virgins who are called widows." Eventually, this would give rise to feminine monasticism, which developed earlier than its masculine counterpart.

The church also began celebrating marriages at least by the beginning of the

*An early Christian depiction of a
marriage ceremony. The caption reads,
"May you live in God."*

second century—when Ignatius of Antioch wrote to Polycarp that all marriages should take place with the knowledge of the bishop. It is understandable that devout couples would wish to consecrate their union. But apparently marriages in the church also had another function: to acknowledge unions that were not strictly legal. According to the law of the time, the social status—and the accompanying rights—of a couple was determined by the status of a husband. In the early church women tended to be of higher social standing than men, and therefore official, legal marriages among believers could have serious civil consequences, depriving the wife of some of her rights and standing. The solution was to perform church marriages that had no official or civil sanction.

MISSIONARY METHODS

Although it is impossible to give exact statistics, the enormous numerical growth of the church in its first centuries is undeniable. This leads us to the question of what methods it used to achieve such growth. The answer may surprise some modern Christians, for the ancient church knew nothing of "evangelistic services" or "revivals." On the contrary, in the early church worship centered on communion, and only baptized Christians were admitted to its celebration. Therefore, evangelism did not take place in church services, but rather, as Celsus said, in kitchens, shops, and markets. A few famous teachers, such as Justin and Origen, held debates in their schools, and thus won some converts among the intelligentsia. But the fact remains that most converts were made by anonymous Christians whose witness led others to their faith. The most dramatic form taken by such witness was obviously that of suffering unto death, and it is for this reason that the word "martyr," which originally meant

A fourth-century Roman mosaic of Christ found in a villa in St. Mary Dorset, England. Note the Chi Rho monogram behind his head. This became a common Christian symbol after the time of Constantine.

"witness," took on the meaning that it has for us today. Finally, some Christians were reputed for their miracles, which also won converts.

The most famous of these miracle workers was Gregory Thaumaturgus—a name that means "wonderworker." He was from the region of Pontus on the southern coast of the Black Sea, and had been converted through the learned witness of Origen. But upon returning to Pontus and becoming bishop of Neocaesarea, his great evangelistic success was due, not to his theological arguments, but to the miracles that he was said to perform. These were mostly miracles of healing, but we are also told that he could control the course of a river in flood, and that the apostles and the Virgin appeared to him and guided his work. Gregory was also one of the first to use a missionary method that has appeared again and again in later times: he substituted Christian festivals for the old pagan ones, and made sure that the Christian celebrations outdid the others.

Another surprising fact about the early expansion of Christianity is that, after the New Testament, very little is said of any missionaries going from place to place, as Paul and Barnabas had done. It is clear that the enormous spread of the gospel in those first centuries was not due to full-time missionaries, but rather to the many Christians who traveled for other reasons—slaves, merchants, exiles condemned to work in the mines, and the like.

Finally, one should note that Christianity spread mainly in the cities, and that it penetrated the rural areas slowly and with much difficulty. By the year 100, 64 percent of port cities in the Roman Empire had a church, as did 24 percent of inland cities. By the year 180, these figures had increased to 86 percent and 65 percent, respectively.[22] It was long after Constantine that Christianity could claim most of the rural population of the empire. (Actually, the word *paganus*—"pagan"—originally had nothing to do with religion, but was used to refer to an uncouth, rural person. It was after most city dwellers became Christian that the ancient religion, which now existed mostly in the countryside, was dubbed *paganism.*)

THE BEGINNINGS OF CHRISTIAN ART

Since at first Christians gathered in private homes, it is not likely that there were in their meeting places many decorations or symbols alluding to the Christian faith. If there were any, they certainly have not survived. But as soon as Christians began having their own cemeteries—the catacombs—and their own churches—such as the one in Dura-Europos—Christian art began to develop. This early art is found mostly in simple frescoes—paintings on walls—in catacombs and churches, and in the carved sarcophagi—stone coffins—in which some of the wealthier Christians were buried.

Since communion was the central act of worship, scenes and symbols referring to it are most common. Sometimes what is depicted is the Lord's Supper in the upper room. In other cases there is simply a basket containing fish and bread.

The fish was one of the earliest Christian symbols and for that reason appears frequently in communion scenes as well as in other contexts. The significance of the fish, apart from its connection with the miraculous feeding of the multitudes, was that the Greek word for fish—*ICHTHYS*—could be used as an acrostic containing the initial letters of the phrase: "Jesus Christ, Son of God, Savior." For this reason the fish appears, not only in representational art, but also in some of the most ancient Christian epitaphs. Thus, for instance, the epitaph of Abercius, bishop of Hierapolis toward the end of the second century, says that faith nourished Abercius with "a fresh water fish, very large and pure, fished by an immaculate virgin" (Mary, or the church?). And other similar epitaphs speak of "the divine race of the heavenly fish," and "the peace of the fish."

Other scenes in primitive Christian art refer to various biblical episodes: Adam and Eve, Noah in the ark, water coming out of the rock in the desert, Daniel in the lions' den, the three young men in the fiery furnace, Jesus and the Samaritan woman, the raising of Lazarus, and so forth. Generally, what one finds is very simple art, more allusive than realistic. For example, Noah is often depicted as standing in a box that is hardly large enough to keep him afloat.

In conclusion, the ancient Christian church was composed mostly of humble folk for whom the fact of having been adopted as heirs of the King of Kings was a source of great joy. This was expressed in their worship, in their art, in their life together, and in their valiant deaths. The daily life of most of these Christians took place in the drab routine in which the poor in all societies must live. But they rejoiced in the hope of a new light that would destroy the dark injustice and idolatry of their society.

12

The Great Persecution
and the Final Victory

I am concerned only about the law of God, which I have learned. That
is the law which I obey, and in which I shall overcome. Besides that law,
there is no other.

THELICA, MARTYR

After the persecutions of Decius and Valerian, the church enjoyed a long
period of relative peace. Early in the fourth century, however, the last and
worst persecution broke out. The reigning emperor was Diocletian, who had reorganized the empire and brought renewed prosperity. Part of Diocletian's reor-
ganization had consisted of placing the government on the shoulders of a team
of four emperors. Two of these had the title of *augustus*: Diocletian himself in
the East, and Maximian in the West. Under each of them there was a junior
emperor with the title of *caesar*: Galerius under Diocletian, and Constantius
Chlorus under Maximian. Thanks to Diocletian's political and administrative
gifts, this division of power worked quite well as long as he held ultimate authority. Its main purpose, however, was to ensure an orderly process of succession; for Diocletian planned that a "caesar" would succeed his "augustus," and
that then the remaining emperors would appoint someone to fill the vacancy
left by the promoted caesar. Diocletian hoped that this would avert the frequent
civil wars that racked the empire over the question of succession. As we shall
see, this hope proved futile.

In any case, under Diocletian's administration the empire was enjoying relative peace and prosperity. Apart from recurring skirmishes along the borders,
only Galerius had to undertake significant military campaigns, one along the
Danube River and another against the Persians. Among the team of emperors,
it seems that only Galerius had given any indication of enmity toward Christianity. Both Diocletian's wife, Prisca, and their daughter, Valeria, were Christians. The peace of the church seemed assured.

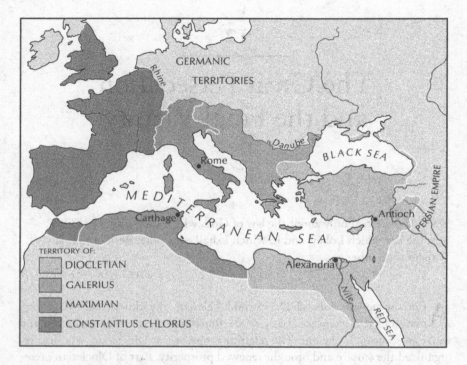

GERMANIC
TERRITORIES

Rhine

Danube

BLACK SEA

PERSIAN EMPIRE

Rome•

M E D I T E R R A N E A N   S E A

Carthage•

•Antioch

TERRITORY OF:

DIOCLETIAN

GALERIUS

MAXIMIAN

CONSTANTIUS CHLORUS

Alexandria•

Nile

RED SEA

The Roman Empire under Diocletian.

The first difficulties probably arose in the army. There was no general agreement among Christians regarding military service, for, while most church leaders of the time said that Christians should not be soldiers, there were many believers among the legions. In any case, around the year 295 a number of Christians were condemned to death, some for refusing to join the army, and others for trying to leave it. Galerius viewed this attitude of Christians toward military service as a serious danger, for it was conceivable that at a critical moment Christians in the army would refuse to obey orders. Therefore, as a measure required for military morale, Galerius convinced Diocletian that all Christians should be expelled from the legions. Diocletian's edict did not require any additional penalty for Christians besides expulsion from the ranks of the military. But in some areas, probably due to an excess of zeal on the part of some officers who did not wish to see their ranks thinned, there were attempts to force Christian soldiers to deny their faith. The result was a number of executions, all of them in the army of the Danube, under the command of Galerius.

After these events, Galerius seems to have become increasingly prejudiced against Christians, and in 303 he finally convinced Diocletian to issue a new edict against them. At least, this is what historian Eusebius of Caesarea tells us, for Eusebius himself made every effort not to blame the other emperors at the time—of which Diocletian was one—for the persecutions. Even then, the purpose was not to kill Christians, but to remove them from positions of responsibility within the empire. It was then ordered that Christians be dismissed from any government position, and that all Christian buildings and books be destroyed. At the beginning, there were no sterner measures. But soon the conflict grew worse, for many Christians refused to turn over their sacred writings, and in such cases they were tortured and condemned to death.

Then fire broke out twice in the imperial palace. Galerius accused the Christians of having set it, out of revenge for the destruction of their meeting places and the burning of their books. Some Christian writers of the period suggest that Galerius himself was responsible for the fires, which he had set in order to blame the Christians. Whatever the case may be, Diocletian's fury was not slow in coming, and it was decreed that all Christians in the imperial court must offer sacrifice before the gods. Prisca and Valeria complied, but the Grand Chamberlain Dorotheus and several others suffered martyrdom. Throughout the empire houses where Christian met and sacred writings were being set to the torch, and there were areas where overzealous officials followed the emperor's example and put Christians to death. The only area where there seems to have been a slight respite was the territory under the rule of Constantius Chlorus, where persecution was limited to tearing down some church buildings—at least, this is what we are told by Eusebius, who wished to present Constantius in the best possible light.

The situation grew worse. There were disturbances in some areas, and Diocletian became convinced that Christians were conspiring against him. He then decreed, first, that all the leaders of the churches be arrested and, somewhat later, that all Christians must offer sacrifice to the gods.

Thus was unleashed the most cruel of all the persecutions that the ancient church had to endure. Following the example of Decius, efforts were made to encourage Christians to abandon their faith. Accustomed as they were to the relative ease of several decades, many Christians succumbed. The rest were tortured with refined cruelty, and eventually killed in a variety of ways. A number were able to hide, and some of these took the sacred books with them. There were even a few who crossed the border into Persia—thus appearing to confirm the worst suspicions as to their lack of loyalty.

While all this was taking place, Galerius aspired to the supreme position

Diocletian's persecution was the most cruel that the ancient church had to endure. To the real stories of torture and martyrdom were added many others that were probably legendary. Here we see one of those doubtful events that were repeatedly retold by devout Christians and often depicted in art: the crucifixion of Acacius and his companions, by Francisco Gallego (1440–1507).

within the empire. In 304 Diocletian became ill and, although he survived, he felt weak and tired. Galerius went to him and apparently induced him to abdicate. He also secured Maximian's abdication by threatening to invade his neighbor's territories with his clearly superior army. In 305 both Diocletian and Maximian abdicated, while Galerius and Constantius Chlorus took the title of augustus. The two caesars under them, Severus and Maximinus Daia, were Galerius's inept creatures.

These arrangements, however, were not well received by many in the legions, where the sons of Constantius and Maximian, Constantine and Maxentius, were very popular. Young Constantine lived for years in Diocletian's court, and later in Galerius's, apparently as a hostage to insure the loyalty of his father Constantius Chlorus. But he escaped—or, according to some historians, was released—and joined his father, who had pleaded ill health in asking that his son be sent to him. When Constantius died, the troops refused to obey the designs of Galerius and proclaimed Constantine as their augustus. Meanwhile, Maxentius had taken Rome, and Severus, who ruled in the ancient capital, committed suicide. Galerius invaded the territories held by Maxentius; but his troops began to pass over to his rival's side, and he was forced to return to the Eastern portion of the empire, where his support was stronger. Finally, in desperation, Galerius appealed to Diocletian, asking him to come out of retirement and establish order. But Diocletian declared that he was quite happy growing cabbages in his retirement, and refused to resume the government of the empire—although he was willing to lead the necessary negotiations among the various rivals. The final result was a very unstable arrangement, which included the appointment of a new augustus, Licinius. By then the claimants to various parts of the empire were too numerous to list here, and further civil wars were clearly inevitable. Meanwhile Constantine, the son of Constantius Chlorus, was simply biding his time and strengthening his position in his territories in Gaul and Great Britain.

In the midst of such political chaos, persecution continued, although its impact depended upon the policies set by each emperor in each region. In the West, most of the territory was under the effective control of Constantine and Maxentius, and neither of these two emperors enforced the decrees against Christians, which they saw as the work of their rival Galerius. Galerius and his main protégé, Maximinus Daia, continued persecuting Christians. Maximinus sought to perfect the policies of Galerius by having Christians maimed and put to work in stone quarries. But then many of the condemned began organizing new churches in their places of punishment, and Maximinus had them killed or deported anew. The lists of martyrs grew longer and longer, and there seemed to be no end in sight.

Then help came from an unexpected quarter. Galerius became ill with a painful disease and, perhaps convinced by those Christians who said that this was a punishment from God, grudgingly decided to change his policy. According to Christian historian Eusebius of Caesarea, on April 30, 311, Galerius proclaimed:

> With all the laws which we have decreed for the good of the state, we have sought to restore the ancient rules and traditional discipline of the Romans. We have particularly sought to have Christians, who had abandoned the faith of their ancestors, return to the truth. . . . After the promulgation of our edict ordering all to return to the ancient customs, many obeyed for fear of danger, and we were forced to punish others. But there are still many who persist on their opinions, and we are aware that they neither worship nor serve the gods, nor even their own god. Therefore, moved by our mercy to be benevolent toward all, it has seemed just to us to extend to them our pardon, and allow them to be Christians once again, and once again gather in their assemblies, as long as they do not interfere with public order.
>
> In another edict we shall instruct our magistrates regarding this matter.
>
> In return for our tolerance, Christians will be required to pray to their god for us, for the public good, and for themselves, so that the state may enjoy prosperity and they may live in peace.[23]

Such was the edict that ended the most cruel persecution that the church had to suffer from the Roman Empire. Soon prisons were opened, and forth came a multitude of people bearing the marks of torture, but thankful for what they saw as an intervention from on high.

Galerius died five days later, and Christian historian Lactantius, who made it a point to show that those who persecuted Christians died horrible deaths, declared that his repentance came too late.

The empire was then divided among Licinius, Maximinus Daia, Constantine, and Maxentius. The first three recognized one another, and declared Maxentius to be a usurper. As to their policies toward Christians, Maximinus Daia was the only one who soon began anew the persecution that Galerius had ended.

But a great political change was about to take place which would put an end to persecution. Constantine, who during the previous intrigues and civil wars had limited his intervention to diplomatic maneuvering, began a campaign that would eventually make him master of the empire. Suddenly, when least

Constantine became sole emperor, and with his leadership a new age began for the church.

expected to do so, Constantine gathered his armies in Gaul, crossed the Alps and marched on Rome, Maxentius's capital. Taken by surprise, Maxentius was unable to defend his strongholds, which Constantine's troops rapidly occupied. All that he could do was to collect his army before Rome, and there fight the invader from Gaul. Rome itself was well-defended, and if Maxentius had chosen the wiser course, and remained behind the city walls, perhaps history would have taken a different turn. But instead, he consulted his augurs, who advised him to present battle.

According to two Christian chroniclers who knew Constantine, on the eve of the battle he had a revelation. One of our sources, Lactantius, says that it was in a dream that Constantine received the command to place a Christian symbol on the shields of his soldiers. The other chronicler, Eusebius, says that the vision appeared in the sky, with the words "in this you shall conquer." In any case, the fact remains that Constantine ordered that his soldiers should use on their shield and on their standard or *labarum* a symbol that looked like the superimposition of the Greek letters chi and rho. Since these are the first two letters of the name, "Christ," this *labarum* could well have been a Christian symbol. Although eventually Christians saw in this the great moment of Constantine's conversion, historians point out that even after this event Constantine continued worshiping the Unconquered Sun. In truth, Constantine's conversion was a long process, to which we shall return in the next chapter.

The important fact is that Maxentius was defeated, and that as he fought on the Milvian bridge he fell into the river and drowned. Constantine thus became master of the entire Western half of the empire.

Once his campaign had begun, Constantine moved rapidly. After the battle of the Milvian bridge, he met with Licinius at Milan, and there concluded an alliance with him. Part of what was agreed there was that the persecution of Christians would stop, and that their buildings, cemeteries, and other properties would be returned to them. This agreement, commonly known as the *Edict of Milan*, marks the date usually given for the end of persecutions (313 CE), although in truth Galerius's edict was much more important, and even after the *Edict of Milan* Maximinus Daia continued his policy of persecution. Eventually, through a series of steps that will be told in the next chapter, Constantine became sole emperor, and persecution came to an end.

Whether this was in truth a victory, or the beginning of new and perhaps greater difficulties, will be the theme of many of the chapters to follow. Whatever the case may be, there is no doubt that the conversion of Constantine had enormous consequences for Christianity, which was forced to face new questions. What would happen when those who called themselves servants of a carpenter, and whose great heroes were fisherfolk, slaves, and criminals condemned to death by the state, suddenly saw themselves surrounded by imperial pomp and power? Would they remain firm in their faith? Or would it be that those who had stood firm before tortures and before beasts would give way to the temptations of an easy life and of social prestige? These were the burning issues that the Christian church had to face in the next period of its history.

SUGGESTED READINGS

Lewis Ayres, Andrew Louth, and Frances M. Young, eds. *The Cambridge History of Early Christian Literature*. Cambridge, UK: Cambridge University Press, 2004.

Henry Bettenson, ed. *Documents of the Christian Church*. London: Oxford, several editions.

E. C. Blackman. *Marcion and His Influence*. London: S.P.C.K., 1948.

Gillian Clark. *Christianity and Roman Society*. Cambridge, UK: Cambridge University Press, 2004.

E. R. Dodds. *Pagan and Christian in an Age of Anxiety*. Cambridge: University Press, 1968.

W. H. C. Frend. *The Early Church*. Philadelphia: J. B. Lippincott, 1966.

Robin Lane Fox. *Pagans and Christians*. Now York: Knopf, 1987.

Justo L. González. *A History of Christian Thought,* Vol. I. Nashville: Abingdon, 1970.

Edgar J. Goodspeed. *A History of Early Christian Literature*. Chicago: University of Chicago Press, 1966. Revised and enlarged by Robert M. Grant.

Christopher Hall. *Learning Theology with the Church Fathers*. Downers Grove, IL: InterVarsity, 2002.

R. P. C. Hanson. *Tradition in the Early Church*. London: SCM, 1962.

Hans Jonas. *The Gnostic Religion*. Boston: Beacon Press, 1958.

Josef A. Jungman. *The Early Liturgy to the Time of Gregory the Great*. London: Darton, Longman & Todd, 1959.

Hans Lietzmann. *The Beginnings of the Christian Church*. London: Lutterworth, several editions.

Hans Lietzmann. *The Founding of the Church Universal*. London: Lutterworth, several editions.

Ramsay MacMullen. *Christianizing the Roman Empire (A.D. 100-400)*. New Haven: Yale University Press, 1984.

Margaret M. Mitchell and Frances M. Young, eds. *The Cambridge History of Christianity: Volume 1: Origins to Constantine*. Cambridge, UK: Cambridge University Press, 2006.

Jaroslav Pelikan. *The Christian Tradition,* Vol. I. Chicago: University of Chicago Press, 1971.

Rodney Stark. *The Rise of Christianity: A Sociologist Reconsiders History*. Princeton: Princeton University Press, 1996.

Gérard Vallée. *The Shaping of Christianity: The History and Literature of Its Formative Centuries (100-800)*. New York: Paulist, 2001.

Robert B. Workman. *Persecution in the Early Church*. London: Epworth Press, reprint, 1960.

PART II

THE IMPERIAL CHURCH

Chronology

Emperors	Bishops of Rome*	Events**
(306–337) Constantine	Sylvester (314–335)	Edict of Milan (313)
		Arian controversy begins
		Pachomius's first foundation (324)
		Council of Nicea (325)
		Constantinople founded (330)
	Marcus (335–336)	
Constantine II (337–340)	Julius (337–352)	
Constantius II (337–361)		
Constans (337–350)	Liberius (352–366)	Arianism at its apex
Julian (361–363)	*Felix II (353–365)*	Pagan reaction
Jovian (363–364)		
Valentinian I (364–392)		
Valens (364–378)	Damasus (366–383)	†Eusebius of Caesarea and Athanasius (373)
Gratian (375–383)	*Ursinus (366–367)*	Battle of Adrianople (378)
Valentinian II (375–392)	Siricius (384–399)	†Basil the Great (379)
		†Macrina (380)
Theodosius (379–395)		†Council of Constantinople (381)
Maximus (383–388)		
		†Gregory of Nazianzus (389)
Eugenius (392–394)		†Gregory of Nyssa (395?)
Arcadius (395–408)		†Martin of Tours and Ambrose (397)
Honorius (395–423)	Anastasius (399–401)	
Theodosius II (408–450)		
		Fall of Rome (410)
	Zosimus (417–418)	
		†Jerome (420)
		†Augustine (430)

*Bishops whom the Roman church does not recognize are in italics
**Dagger (†) indicates that year given is year of death.

13

Constantine

> The eternal, holy and unfathomable goodness of God does not allow us
> to wander in darkness, but shows us the way of salvation. . . . This I have
> seen in others as well as in myself.
>
> CONSTANTINE

We left Constantine at the moment when, after defeating Maxentius at the
Milvian bridge, he joined Licinius in ordering the end of persecution.
Although we have already indicated that eventually he became sole ruler of the
Roman Empire, it now remains to outline the process by which he achieved
that goal. The question of the nature and sincerity of his conversion must also
be discussed. But what is of paramount importance for the story of Christianity is not so much how sincere Constantine was, or how he understood the
Christian faith, as the impact of his conversion and his rule both during his
lifetime and thereafter. That impact was such that it has even been suggested
that throughout most of its history the church has lived in its *Constantinian era*,
and that even now, in the twenty-first century, we are going through crises connected with the end of that long era. Whether or not this is true is a question
to be discussed when our narrative comes to the present day. In any case, Constantine's religious policies had such enormous effect on the course of Christianity that all of Part II may be seen as a series of reactions and adjustments in
response to those policies.

FROM ROME TO CONSTANTINOPLE

Long before the battle at the Milvian bridge, Constantine had been preparing
to extend the territories under his rule. To that end, he took great care to develop a strong base of operations in Gaul and Great Britain. He spent over five
years strengthening the borders along the Rhine, where the barbarians were a
constant threat, and courting the favor of his subjects by his just and wise government. This did not make him an ideal ruler. His love of luxury and pomp
was such that he built a grandiose and ornate palace in his capital city—Trier—

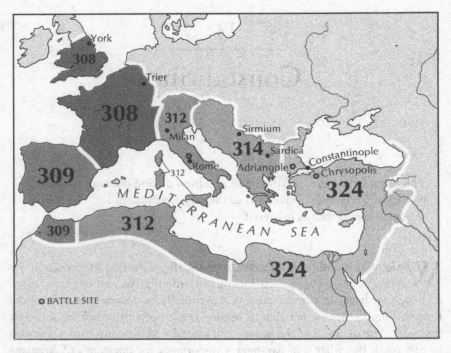

Constantine's path to absolute power.

while neglecting public works to such an extent that the drainage system of the nearby fields failed, and the vineyards that were the backbone of the local economy were flooded. Yet, he seems to have had that rare gift of rulers who know just how far they can tax their subjects without losing their loyalty. By securing the borders against barbarian incursions, Constantine won the gratitude of many in Gaul. Frequent and extravagant shows in the circus gained the support of those who preferred violence and blood—the barbarian captives thus sacrificed were so many that a chronicler of the times affirms that the shows lost some of their interest because the beasts grew tired of killing.

An astute statesman, Constantine challenged his rivals one at a time, always protecting his flanks before making his next move. Thus, although his campaign against Maxentius seemed sudden, he had been preparing for it, both militarily and politically, for many years. His military preparations were such that in his campaign against Maxentius he committed only one-fourth of his resources, thus making sure that during his absence there would not be a major barbarian invasion, or a revolt in his own territories. In the field of diplomacy, he had to make sure that Licinius, who was Maxentius's neighbor to the east,

Constantine would leave his mark on the Christian church for more than a thousand years.

would not take advantage of Constantine's campaign to invade and lay claim to some of Maxentius's territories. In order to preclude that possibility, Constantine offered his half-sister Constance in marriage to Licinius, and he may also have made a secret agreement with his future brother-in-law. This would seem to cover his flank. But even then, he waited until Licinius was involved in a conflict with Maximinus Daia before launching his own invasion of Italy.

The victory at the Milvian bridge gave Constantine control of the Western half of the empire, while the East was still partitioned, split between Licinius and Maximinus Daia. His meeting with Licinius in Milan seemed to strengthen their alliance, and forced Licinius to direct his efforts against their common rival, Maximinus Daia. Licinius moved rapidly. Maximinus was still near Byzantium—later Constantinople, and now Istanbul—when his enemy appeared before him with a smaller army and defeated him. Maximinus was forced to flee, and died shortly thereafter.

The empire was then divided between Licinius, who ruled over the entire area east of Italy, including Egypt, and Constantine, who controlled Italy as well as Western Europe and the western portion of North Africa. Since the two emperors were related by marriage, there was hope that the civil wars had

Licinius was Constantine's brother-in-law, and his main rival.

come to an end. But the truth was that both Licinius and Constantine sought to rule the whole empire, which, in spite of its vastness, was too small for the two of them. For a while, each of the two rivals devoted himself to consolidate his power and to prepare for the inevitable conflict.

Finally, hostilities broke out. A conspiracy to murder Constantine was discovered, and the ensuing investigation implicated a relative of Licinius who had fled to his kinsman's territories. Licinius refused to send his relative to Constantine to be executed, and eventually declared war on Constantine. Although Christian historians have usually laid all the blame for this conflict on Licinius, the truth is that Constantine wished to go to war with his brother-in-law, but was able to make his rival appear as the aggressor. Finding himself militarily outmaneuvered by Constantine, Licinius had to sue for peace. Once again, Constantine showed that he was an able statesman and a patient man, and was content with taking most of Licinius's European territories.

A period of peace followed. Once again, Constantine used the time to consolidate his power in the newly conquered territories. Instead of residing in the West, he established his headquarters first in Sirmium and later in Sardica (now Sofia). Both cities were located in recently conquered territories, and thus Constantine was able to keep an eye on Licinius and to strengthen his rule over the area.

The truce lasted until 322, although there was an ever-increasing tension between the two emperors. The main reason for conflict was still the ambition of both men, which found expression in the question of what titles and honors were to be given to their sons. But by the time war finally broke out, the question of religious policy had also become a bone of contention.

Licinius's religious policy needs to be clarified, for after Constantine's victory some Christian writers, in order to justify his actions against Licinius, made the latter appear in a bad light. For a number of years after the Edict of Milan, Licinius took no measures against Christians. Actually, a contemporary Christian writer, in telling the story of Licinius's victory over Maximinus Daia, makes it sound very similar to Constantine's victory over Maxentius—including a vision. But Christianity in Licinius's territories was divided over a number of issues, and such divisions led to public disorders. When Licinius used his imperial powers to assure peace, there were groups of Christians that considered themselves wronged, and who began thinking of Constantine as the defender of the true faith, and as "the emperor whom God loved." Licinius was not a Christian, but there are indications that he feared the power of the Christian God; and therefore, when he learned that his subjects were praying for his rival, he felt that this was high treason. It was then that he took measures against some Christians, and this in turn gave Constantine the opportunity to present himself as the defender of Christianity against Licinius the persecutor.

In 322, Constantine invaded Licinius's territories, using the pretext that he was in pursuit of a band of barbarians who had crossed the Danube. Licinius interpreted this, rightly or wrongly, as an intentional provocation, and prepared for war by gathering his troops at Adrianople, where he awaited Constantine's somewhat smaller armies.

Contemporary chroniclers affirm that Licinius feared the magical power of Constantine's *labarum,* and that he ordered his soldiers to avoid looking at the Christian emblem, and not to direct a frontal attack against it. If this is true, it must have demoralized his troops. In any case, after a long and bloody battle, Constantine's smaller army won the day and Licinius fled to Byzantium. His wife Constance—probably accompanied by Bishop Eusebius of Nicomedia, who will have an important role to play as our story unfolds—went in his name to her brother Constantine, who promised to spare Licinius's life in exchange for his abdication. Shortly thereafter, Licinius was murdered. Constantine was now sole master of the empire.

Constantine would reign for the next thirteen years, until his death in 337. Compared with the previous civil wars, this was a period of rebuilding and prosperity. But there was always political uneasiness, and quite a few people were condemned to death for real or supposed conspiracies against the emperor—among them his oldest son, Crispus, who had commanded his father's fleet in the war against Licinius, and whom Constantine ordered executed.

Constantine had not sought absolute power for the mere pleasure of it. He also dreamed, like Decius and Diocletian before him, of restoring the ancient glory of the empire. The main difference was that, whereas Decius and Diocletian had sought that end through a restoration of paganism, Constantine believed that it could best be achieved on the basis of Christianity. Some of the staunchest opponents of this policy were in Rome, particularly in its Senate, where the members of the old aristocracy bemoaned the eclipse of their ancient gods and privileges. Several years before his final struggle with Licinius, Constantine had clashed with the interests of the Roman Senate. Now, as absolute master of the empire, he set out on a bold course: he would build a "New Rome," an impregnable and monumental city, which would be called Constantinople—that is, "City of Constantine."

It may well have been during his campaign against Licinius that Constantine became aware of the strategic value of Byzantium. That city was at the very edge of Europe, where it almost touched Asia Minor. Thus, it could serve as a bridge between the European and the Asian portions of the empire. Furthermore, if properly fortified, Byzantium would control the Bosporus, through which all shipping had to pass in its way from the Mediterranean to the Black Sea. A peace treaty made with Persia several decades earlier was about to expire, and the emperor felt the need to establish his headquarters near the Eastern border. But at the same time the Germanic tribes on the Rhine were always a threat, and therefore it would not be wise for the emperor to settle too far from the West. For all these reasons, Byzantium seemed the ideal location for the new capital. Constantine's choice—for which he took no credit, claiming that he was following instructions from God—proved to be most wise, for the city that he founded would play a strategic role for centuries to come.

But ancient Byzantium was too small for the grandiose dreams of the great emperor. Its walls, built during the reign of Septimius Severus, were scarcely two miles long. Aping the ancient legend of Romulus and Remus and the founding of Rome, Constantine went to the fields far beyond the ancient walls, and with his lance marked the route that the new walls should follow. This was done amid great ceremonies in which both Christians and pagan priests took part. When those who followed the emperor, seeing him walk far into the countryside, asked him how far he intended to go, he is said to have answered: "As far as the One who walks ahead of me." Naturally, Christians in his entourage would have understood these words to refer to their God, whereas pagans would have taken them to mean one of their gods, or perhaps the Unconquered Sun. By the end of the ceremonies, Constantine had set aside a vast area, capable of holding a teeming multitude.

Construction began immediately. Since the materials and skilled artisans available were not sufficient to meet Constantine's timetable, things such as statues, columns, and so on were brought from various cities. Constantine's agents scoured the empire in search of anything that could embellish the new capital. Years later, Jerome would say that Constantinople was dressed in the nakedness of the rest of the empire. A number of statues of pagan gods were taken from their ancient temples and placed in such public places as the hippodrome, the public baths, or the squares. Thus, used as mere ornaments, the ancient gods seemed to have lost their old power.

Perhaps the most famous statue thus taken to Constantinople was the sculpture of Apollo said to be the work of Phidias, one of the greatest sculptors of all time. This was placed in the middle of the city, atop a huge stone column brought from Egypt, and which was reputed to be the largest such monolith in the world. To make it even taller, the column was placed on a marble pedestal that was over twenty feet high. The entire monument measured approximately 125 feet from top to bottom. But the statue itself no longer represented Apollo, for a new head, that of Constantine, had been placed upon it.

Other great public works were the basilica of Saint Irene—that is, holy peace—the hippodrome, and the public baths. Also, a great palace was built for the emperor, and the few noble families agreed to move from Old Rome were given replicas of their ancestral mansions.

All this, however, did not suffice to populate the new city. To that end, Constantine granted all sorts of privileges to those who came to live there, such as exemption from taxes and from military service. Soon it became customary to give free oil, wheat, and wine to the citizens of Constantinople. The result was that the city grew at such an incredible rate that a century later, under Theodosius II, it was necessary to build new walls, for the population had outgrown the ones that in Constantine's time had seemed excessively ambitious.

As will be seen in future chapters of this history, Constantine's decision to found a new capital had enormous consequences, for shortly thereafter the Western portion of the empire—old Rome included—was overrun by the barbarians, and Constantinople became the center that for a thousand years kept alive the political and cultural inheritance of the old empire. Since its capital was in ancient Byzantium, this Eastern Roman Empire is also called the Byzantine Empire.

FROM THE UNCONQUERED SUN TO JESUS CHRIST

The nature of Constantine's conversion has been the subject of many debates. Shortly after the events told in this chapter, there were Christian authors—one of whom we shall meet in the next chapter—who sought to show that the emperor's conversion was the goal toward which the history of the church and of the empire had always been moving. Others have claimed that Constantine was simply a shrewd politician who became aware of the advantages to be drawn from a "conversion."

Both interpretations are exaggerated. It suffices to read the documents of the time to become aware that Constantine's conversion was very different from that of other Christians. At that time, people who were converted were put through a long process of discipline and instruction, in order to make certain that they understood and lived their new faith, and then they were baptized. Their bishop became their guide and shepherd as they sought to discover the implications of their faith in various situations in life.

Constantine's case was very different. Even after the battle of the Milvian bridge, and throughout his entire life, he never placed himself under the direction of Christian teachers or bishops. Christians such as Lactantius—tutor to his son Crispus—formed part of his entourage. Hosius, bishop of Cordoba, became for a time his liaison with other ecclesiastical leaders. But Constantine reserved the right to determine his own religious practices, and even to intervene in the life of the church, for he considered himself "bishop of bishops." Repeatedly, even after his conversion, he took part in pagan rites in which no Christian would participate, and the bishops raised no voice of condemnation.

The reason for this was not only that the emperor was both powerful and irascible, but also that, in spite of his policies favoring Christianity, and of his repeated confession of the power of Christ, he was not technically a Christian, for he had not been baptized. In fact, it was only on his deathbed that he was baptized. Therefore, any policy or edict favoring Christianity was received by the church as the action of one who was friendly or even inclined to become a Christian, but who had not taken the decisive step. And any religious or moral deviations on Constantine's part were seen in the same light, as the unfortunate actions of one who, while inclined to become a Christian, was not one of the faithful. Such a person could receive the advice and even the support of the church, but not its direction. This ambiguous situation continued until Constantine's final hour.

On the other hand, there are several reasons why Constantine should not be seen as a mere opportunist who declared himself in favor of Christianity in order to court the support of Christians. First of all, such a view is rather anachronistic, for it tends to see Constantine as a forerunner of modern politicians. At that time, even the most incredulous did not approach religious matters with such a calculating attitude. Secondly, if Constantine had been such an opportunist, he chose a poor time to seek the support of Christians. When he put the Chi-Rho on his *labarum*, he was preparing to go to battle for the city of Rome, center of pagan traditions, where his main supporters were the members of the old aristocracy who considered themselves oppressed by Maxentius. Christians were stronger, not in the West, where the battle was to be fought, but in the East, to which Constantine would lay claim only years later. Finally, it should be pointed out that whatever support Christians could give Constantine was of doubtful value. Given the ambivalence of the church toward military service, the number of Christian soldiers in the army, particularly in the West, was relatively small. Among the civilian population, most Christians belonged to the lower classes, and thus had scarce economic resources to put at the disposal of Constantine. After almost three centuries of tension with the empire, it was impossible to predict what would be the attitude of Christians before such an unexpected thing as a Christian emperor.

The truth is probably that Constantine was a sincere believer in the power of Christ. But this does not mean that he understood that power in the same way in which it had been experienced by those Christians who had died for it. For him, the Christian God was a very powerful being who would support him as long as he favored the faithful. Therefore, when Constantine enacted laws in favor of Christianity, and when he had churches built, what he sought was not the goodwill of Christians, but rather the goodwill of their God. It was this God who gave him the victory at the Milvian bridge, as well as the many that followed. In a way, Constantine's understanding of Christianity was similar to Licinius's, when the latter feared the supernatural power of his rival's *labarum*. The difference was simply that Constantine had laid claim to that power by serving the cause of Christians. This interpretation of Constantine's faith is supported by his own statements, which reveal a sincere man with a meager understanding of the Christian faith.

This did not prevent the emperor from serving other gods. His own father had been a devotee of the Unconquered Sun. While not denying the existence of other gods, the worship of the Unconquered Sun was addressed to the Supreme Being, whose symbol was the sun. During most of his political career, Constantine seems to have thought that the Unconquered Sun and the Christian God were compatible—perhaps two views of the same Supreme Deity— and that the other gods, although subordinate, were nevertheless real and relatively powerful. On occasion, he would consult the oracle of Apollo, accept the title of High Priest that had traditionally been the prerogative of emperors, and partake of all sorts of pagan ceremonies without thinking that he was thus betraying or abandoning the God who had given him victory and power.

Constantine was a shrewd politician. His power was such that he could favor Christians, build churches, and even have some images of gods moved to Constantinople to serve as ornaments in his dream city. But if he had attempted to suppress pagan worship, he would soon have had to face an irresistible opposition. The ancient gods were far from forgotten. Christianity had made very little progress among the old aristocracy and the rural masses. There were in the army many followers of Mithras and other gods. The Academy of Athens and the Museum of Alexandria, the two great centers of learning of the time, were devoted to the study of ancient pagan wisdom. An imperial decree could not undo all this—not yet, anyway. And in any case the emperor himself, who saw no contradiction between the Unconquered Sun and the Incarnate Son, was not inclined to issue such a decree.

Given these circumstances, Constantine's religious policy followed a slow but constant process. It is likely that this process responded both to the demands of political realities and to Constantine's own inner development, as he progressively left behind the ancient religion and gained a better understanding of the new. At first, he simply put an end to persecution and ordered that confiscated Christian property be returned. Shortly thereafter he gave new signs of favoring Christianity, such as donating to the church the Lateran palace in Rome, which had belonged to his wife, or putting the imperial posts at the service of bishops traveling to attend the Synod of Arles in 314. At the same time, he sought to keep good relations with those who followed the ancient religions, and most especially with the Roman Senate. The official religion of the empire was paganism. As head of that empire Constantine took the title of Supreme Pontiff or High Priest, and performed the functions pertaining to that title. On coins minted as late as 320 one finds the names and symbols of the ancient gods, as well as the monogram for the name of Christ—the Chi-Rho that Constantine had used for the first time at the Milvian bridge.

The campaign against Licinius gave Constantine occasion to appear as the champion of Christianity. He was now moving into the territories where for quite a time the church had counted the greatest number of adherents. After defeating Licinius, Constantine appointed a number of Christians to high positions in government. Since his tensions with the Roman Senate were growing, and that body was promoting a resurgence of paganism, Constantine felt increasingly inclined to favor Christianity.

In the year 324 an imperial edict ordered all soldiers to worship the Supreme God on the first day of the week. This was the day on which Christians gathered to celebrate the Resurrection of their Lord. But it was also the day of the Unconquered Sun, and therefore pagans saw no reason to oppose such an edict. A year later, in 325, the great assembly of bishops that would later be known as the First Ecumenical Council gathered at Nicea.[24] That assembly was called by the emperor, who once again put the imperial posts at the disposal of the traveling bishops.

The founding of Constantinople was a further step in that process. The very act of creating a "New Rome" was an attempt to diminish the power of the ancient aristocratic families of Rome, who were mostly pagan. The raiding of pagan temples for statues and other objects with which to embellish the new capital was a blow to paganism, many of whose ancient shrines lost the gods that were objects of local devotion. Even Christian writers acknowledged that this was accomplished through an unwarranted use of force, and that people often complied for fear of retribution. At the same time, the building of new and sumptuous churches contrasted with the sacking of the old temples.

In spite of all this, almost to his dying day Constantine continued functioning as the High Priest of paganism. After his death, the three sons who succeeded him did not oppose the Senate's move to have him declared a god. Thus, the ironic anomaly occurred, that Constantine, who had done so much to the detriment of paganism, became one of the pagan gods—and to compound the irony, the Eastern church considers him a saint, thus resulting in a saint who is also a pagan god!

FROM PERSECUTION TO DOMINANCE

Although Constantine was certainly an important turning point in the life of the church—to the extent that one may properly speak of a "Constantinian era" stretching from his time until the early twentieth century—he did not make Christianity the official religion of the empire. Constantine himself remained a pagan priest, as befitted his role as emperor, and was not baptized until he was about to die. His sons Constantine II, Constantius, and Constans were baptized, and certainly several of their edicts favored Christianity. But their rule was marked by dissension as the church was bitterly divided over the issue of Arianism (a view of Christ and the Godhead that will be discussed in Chapter 17) and imperial religious policies focused on that dispute. In 356, Constantius, by then sole emperor, declared the worship of images to be a capital crime; but the law was generally ignored. Then Constantine's nephew Julian—who had been baptized—led a pagan reaction, and is therefore commonly known as "the Apostate." After Julian's reign, Jovian and Valentinian II continued the earlier policy of supporting Christianity—most often in its Arian version—while not taking stern measures against paganism. Christianity and paganism were generally on an equal footing before the state, both allowed and both supported by it. It was in the last years of the reign of Emperor Gratian (375–383), who had called on Theodosius (379–395) to share his rule, that decisive measures were taken to place paganism at a disadvantage. In 382, Gratian decreed an end to governmental financial support for paganism and its priests, and he also ordered that the altar to the goddess Victory be removed from the Senate-House. In 391, Theodosius outlawed pagan sacrifices and ordered the temples closed or devoted to public use. In 392, all pagan worship—private as well as public—was forbidden.

Yet the greatest threat to the ancient religion was the manner in which overzealous bishops and mobs took these decrees as license to use force against paganism. Even before the time of Constantine, some fanatical Christians used violence against pagan worship, as attested by the Council of Elvira in Spain in 305, whose sixtieth canon orders that "if any are killed as a result of having destroyed idols, they should not be counted among the martyrs." Now, as Christianity was favored by the empire, and paganism lost its protection, the use of force against pagans—and Jews—was seldom punished. Distinguished and even saintly bishops such as Martin of Tours destroyed pagan temples and other places of worship. There is ample evidence of violence committed by Christians against pagans, and of pagans' resistance to the new order. In Alexandria, Bishop Theophilus—whom we shall encounter again as one of the most unscrupulous of John Chrysostom's enemies—claimed possession of all pagan temples, sacked them, and then paraded part of his loot. His pagan opponents gathered in the ancient temple to Serapis, where they held and crucified a number of Christians. Theophilus appealed to the authorities, who besieged and eventually took the temple. Theophilus then brought in the monks from the desert to demolish it. Similar incidents were repeated in Carthage, in Palestine, and elsewhere.

Perhaps the most telling sign of the change that was taking place is the very word "paganism." The ancient religion had no name, except those of the various gods. After the events of the fourth century, it was relegated to the most remote areas of the empire and, as we have seen, the word for *rustic*, (*"paganus"*), which some Christians had used pejoratively with regard to their opponents, came to refer to those who followed the ancient, now rural, religion.

THE IMPACT OF THE NEW ORDER

The most immediate consequence of Constantine's conversion was the cessation of persecution. Until then, even at times of relative peace, Christians had lived under the threat of persecution, and what was for many the hope of martyrdom. After Constantine's conversion, that threat and that hope dissipated. The few pagan emperors who reigned after him did not generally persecute Christians, but rather tried to restore paganism by other means. But the immediate impact of that conversion on the life of the church went far beyond the obvious cessation of persecution. In this regard, a series of imperial edicts granted the church and its leaders' privileges whose echoes may still be seen in some areas in the twenty-first century. One of this was tax exemption for church properties, as well as making it legal to bequeath property to the church. Over the long run, this would mean that the church would come to own vast lands and other riches. The bishops—at the time there were about eighteen hundred of them—as well as other clergy were also granted exemption from taxes, from military conscription, and from the days of labor that others were forced to devote to public works. First on the occasion of the Synod of Arles in 314, then of the

Council of Nicea in 325, and eventually as a matter of normal policy, bishops were granted free access to the imperial posts. Constantine also sought to legislate on matters of personal conduct—particularly sexual morality—in ways that seem to have been influenced by Christian teaching. But in this regard his efforts had as scant results as many other similar efforts throughout the history of the church. At the same time, the new privileges, prestige and power now granted to church leaders soon led to acts of arrogance and even to corruption. Historian Theodoret refers to a certain Lucius, who bought his position as bishop of Alexandria "as if it were a mere worldly dignity"—a practice that would later be called simony—and other ancient authors attest to similar practices elsewhere. As bishops came to have judicial powers, bribes were offered, and often accepted. While this was far from general practice, it bespoke of the new dangers now threatening the church—dangers it has often faced when it has been powerful and prestigious.

As for the laity, there is no doubt that the experience of conversion became less dramatic or fateful than it had been in earlier times. There is ample evidence of increasing syncretism and superstition. Archeologists have found proof of this in tombs in various areas of the empire, where people were buried with a combination of Christian and pagan symbols and religious artifacts. When people became ill, they often had recourse to ancient magical practice, much to the chagrin of many a Christian preacher. Gladiatorial combats persisted, and some Christians now attended—as they also attended plays that had earlier been forbidden to them.

The decree ordering the first day of the week to be devoted to worship—apparently both of Christ and of the Unconquered Sun—made it possible for Christians to gather more easily, no longer having to meet in the early hours of the morning, before work. This, and the influence of civil ceremonies and pomp, had an influence on Christian worship, which in the actual practice of religion was the point at which most rank and file Christians probably felt the impact of the new order.

Until Constantine's time, Christian worship had been relatively simple. At first, Christians gathered to worship in private homes. Then they began to gather in cemeteries, such as the Roman catacombs. By the third century there were structures set aside for worship such as the house in Dura-Europos mentioned in Chapter 11.

After Constantine's conversion, Christian worship began to be influenced by imperial protocol. Incense, which was used as a sign of respect for the emperor, began appearing in Christian churches. Officiating ministers, who until then had worn everyday clothes, began dressing in more luxurious garments—and soon were called "priests," in imitation of their pagan counterparts, while the communion table became an "altar"—in opposition to the instructions found earlier in the *Didache*. Likewise, a number of gestures indicating respect, which were normally made before the emperor, now became part of Christian worship. An interesting example of this had to do with prayer on Sundays. At an earlier time, the practice was not to kneel for prayer on Sundays, for that is the day of our adoption, when we approach the throne of the Most High as children and heirs to the Great King. Now, after Constantine, one always knelt for prayer, as petitioners usually knelt before the emperor. The custom was also introduced of beginning services with a processional. Choirs were developed, partly in order to give body to that procession. Eventually, the congregation came to have a less active role in worship.

Already in the second century, it had become customary to commemorate the anniversary of a martyr's death by celebrating communion where the martyr had been buried. Now churches were built in many of those places. Eventually, some came to think that worship was particularly valid if it was celebrated in one of those holy places, where the relics of a martyr were present. As a consequence, some began to unearth the buried bodies of martyrs in order to place them—or part of them—under the altar of one of the many churches that were being built. Others began claiming revelations of martyrs who had not been known, or who had been almost forgotten. Some even said that they had received visions telling them where a particular martyr was buried—as in the case of Ambrose and the supposed remains of Saints Gervasius and Protasius. Eventually, the relics of saints and of New Testament times were said to have miraculous powers. Empress Helena, the mother of Constantine, gave special impetus to this entire development when, in a pilgrimage to the Holy Land, she claimed to have discovered the very cross of Christ. Soon this cross was said to have miraculous powers, and pieces of wood claiming to come from it were found all over the empire.

While these developments were taking place, many leaders of the church viewed them with disfavor, and tried to prevent superstitious extremes. Thus, a common theme of preaching was that it was not necessary to go to the Holy Land in order to be a good Christian, and that the respect due to the martyrs should not be exaggerated. But such preaching was unequal to the task, for people were flocking into the church in such numbers that there was little time to prepare them for baptism, and even less to guide them in the Christian life once they had been baptized. In contrast to earlier times, when there was a far-reaching program of teaching and training for new converts, the church now found itself overwhelmed by the numbers of those requesting baptism, and unable to give them proper training and supervision. The long term of training and teaching before receiving baptism was dramatically shortened, and soon

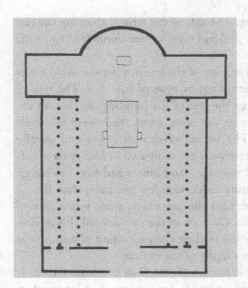

Floor plan of a typical basilica.

many went to the baptismal font with very little idea of its significance. Many of these new converts brought with them beliefs and customs that the earlier church would have considered unacceptable—to which numerous sermons attacking superstition among believers give ample witness.

The churches built in the time of Constantine and his successors contrasted with the simplicity of churches such as that of Dura-Europos. Constantine himself ordered that the Church of Saint Irene—Holy Peace—be built in Constantinople. Helena, his mother, built in the Holy Land The Church of the Nativity in Bethlehem and another one on the Mount of Olives. Similar churches were built in the major cities of the empire, sometimes by imperial command, and sometimes simply following the example of the new capital. On occasion, local residents were ordered to contribute to the building of churches with labor and materials. This policy continued under Constantine's successors, most of whom sought to perpetuate their memory by building great churches. Although most of the churches built by Constantine and his first successors have been destroyed, there is enough evidence to offer a general idea of their basic plan—which in any case was copied in a number of subsequent churches that still stand.

Some of these churches had an altar in the center, and their floor plan was polygonal or almost round. But most of them followed the basic rectangular plan of the "basilica." This was an ancient word which referred to the great public—or sometimes private—buildings whose main part was a great room divided lengthwise into naves by two or more rows of columns. Since these structures provided the model for church buildings during the first centuries after Constantine's conversion, such churches came to be known as "basilicas."

In general, Christian basilicas had three main parts: the atrium, the naves, and the sanctuary. The atrium was the entryway, usually consisting of a rectangular area surrounded by walls. In the middle of the atrium was a fountain where the faithful could perform their ablutions—ritual washing—before entering the main part of the building. The side of the atrium abutting the rest of the basilica was called the narthex, and had one or more doors leading to the naves.

The naves were the most spacious section of the basilica. In the middle was the main nave, set aside from the lateral ones by rows of columns. The roof of the main nave was usually higher than the rest of the building, so that on the two rows of columns separating it from the other naves there were tall walls with windows that provided light. The lateral naves were lower and usually narrower than the main one. Since there were normally two or four rows of columns, some basilicas had a total of three naves, and others had five—although there were some basilicas with up to nine naves, very few had more than five.

Toward the end of the main nave, near the sanctuary, there was a section reserved for the choir, usually fenced in. On each of the two sides of this section there was a pulpit, which was used for the reading and exposition of scripture as well as for the main cantor during the singing of the Psalms.

The sanctuary was at the end of the nave, with the floor at a higher level. It ran on a direction perpendicular to the nave, and was somewhat longer than the rest of the basilica was wide, thus giving the entire floor plan the shape of a cross or T. In a place near the middle of the sanctuary was the altar, where the elements were placed for the celebration of communion.

The back wall of the sanctuary, directly behind the main nave, was semicircular, thus forming the apse—a concave space behind the altar. Against the wall of the apse there were benches for the officiating ministers. If it was the main church of a bishop, amid these benches there was a chair for the bishop, the "cathedra"—which gave rise to the word "cathedral." On some occasions, the bishop would preach seated on the cathedra.

The inside of the basilica was richly adorned with polished marble, lamps and tapestries. But the characteristic medium of Christian art during that period—and long thereafter in the Eastern church—was the mosaic. Walls were covered with pictures made of very small colored pieces of stone, glass, or porcelain. Usually these mosaics represented scenes from the Bible or from Christian tradition. Sometimes there was also a mosaic of the person who had paid for the building, and this person is often depicted in the act of presenting a small replica of the basilica. Naturally, the main wall to be decorated was that of the apse. This usually was a great mosaic representing either the Virgin with the Child on her lap, or Christ seated in glory, as supreme ruler of the universe. This depiction of Christ, known as the *pantokrator* ("universal ruler")—shows the impact of the new political situation on Christian art, for Christ is depicted as sitting on a throne, very much like a Roman emperor.

Near the basilica stood other buildings. The most important of these was the baptistery, large enough to accommodate several dozen people. The main feature within the baptistery, usually at the center, was the baptismal pool, into which one descended by a series of steps. Its shape usually had symbolic value— round or womb-shaped to signify the new birth, shaped as a coffin to symbolize the death of the old person and the rising of a new one, octagonal to remind believers that in Christ a new age, "the eighth day of creation," had dawned, etc. Here baptism was celebrated, normally by immersion, by pouring, or by a combination of the two, where those to be baptized knelt in the water, and then had water poured over them in the name of the Father, the Son, and the Holy Spirit. (Actually, these were the normal ways of administering baptism at least until the ninth century. Baptism by dabbing water on the head had been practiced long before that, but usually only in extreme conditions of poor health, deathbed baptisms, or scarcity of water. It was in the colder areas of Western Europe, in the ninth century, that this alternate form of baptism became more common. In Italy baptism by immersion was continued until the thirteenth century, and the Eastern churches—Greek, Russian, and so forth—still baptize by immersion.)

In the middle of the baptistery a great curtain separated the room in two, one side for men and the other for women—for in the fourth century one still descended to the waters naked, and was given a white robe on rising from them.

All this serves to illustrate what was taking place as a result of Constantine's conversion. The ancient church continued its traditional customs. Communion was still the central act of worship, celebrated every Sunday. Baptism was still generally by entering into the water, and kept a great deal of its ancient symbolism. But changes brought about by the new situation could be seen everywhere. Thus, the great question that the church faced at this time was to what degree and how it should adapt to the changed circumstances.

REACTIONS TO THE NEW ORDER

One of the results of the new situation was the development of what may be called an "official theology." Overwhelmed by the favor that the emperor was pouring on them, many Christians sought to show that Constantine was chosen by God to bring the history of both church and empire to its culmination, where both were joined. Typical of this attitude was church historian Eusebius of Caesarea.

Others took the opposite tack. For them, the fact that the emperors now declared themselves Christian, and that for this reason people were flocking to the church, was not a blessing, but rather a significant loss. Some who tended to look at matters under this light, but did not wish to break communion with the rest of the church, withdrew to the desert, there to lead a life of meditation and asceticism. Since martyrdom was no longer possible, these people believed that the true athlete of Christ must continue training, if no longer for martyrdom, then for monastic life. The fourth century thus witnessed a massive exodus of the most devout Christians to the deserts of Egypt and Syria. This early monastic movement will be the subject of Chapter 15.

Others with a negative reaction to the new state of affairs felt that the best course was simply to break communion with the church at large, now become the imperial church, which was to be considered sinful and apostate. To these we shall turn in Chapter 16.

Among those who remained in the church, withdrawing neither into the desert nor into the schism, there was a great deal of intellectual activity. As in every such period, there were some who proposed theories and doctrines that the rest of the church felt it had to reject. Most important of these was Arianism, which gave rise to bitter controversies regarding the doctrine of the Trinity. In Chapter 17 we shall discuss these controversies up to the year 361, when Julian became emperor.

Julian's reign marked the high point of another attitude toward Constantine's conversion: pagan reaction. Chapter 18 will deal with that reign and the attempt to revitalize paganism.

Most Christians, however, reacted to the new situation with neither total acceptance nor total rejection. Most church leaders saw the new circumstances as offering unexpected opportunities, but also great dangers. Thus, while affirming their loyalty to the emperor, as most Christians had always done, they insisted that their ultimate loyalty belonged only to God. Such was the attitude of the great *fathers* of the church—a misnomer, for there were also mothers among them. Since both danger and opportunity were great, these leaders faced a difficult task. Perhaps not all of their decisions and attitudes were wise; but even so, this was an age of giants who would shape the church and its theology for centuries to come.

14

Official Theology:
Eusebius of Caesarea

Looking westward or eastward, looking over the whole earth, and even looking at heaven, always and everywhere I see blessed Constantine leading the same empire.

EUSEBIUS OF CAESAREA

Eusebius of Caesarea was in all probability the most learned Christian of his time. He was also one of the most ardent admirers of Constantine and his work, as may be seen in the words quoted above. For this reason he has sometimes been depicted as a spineless man who allowed himself to be swayed by the glitter of imperial power. But things are not so simple when one considers his entire career.

Eusebius was born around the year 260, most likely in Palestine, where he spent most of his early years. He is known as Eusebius "of Caesarea" because, although it is not certain that he was born there, it was in that city that he spent most of his life and that he served as bishop. Practically nothing is known of his parents, and it is impossible to determine whether he grew up in a Christian home or was converted as a youth.

In any case, the person who left a deep impression on Eusebius was Pamphilus of Caesarea. Pamphilus was a native of Berytus—now Beirut, in Lebanon—who had studied in Alexandria under Pierius, a famous teacher who was carrying on Origen's work in that city. After holding some important posts in Berytus, Pamphilus went to Caesarea, probably at the request of the bishop of that city. The church of Caesarea had kept Origen's library, and Pamphilus spent long hours working with it and adding to it. In this task he was aided by several others who were moved by Pamphilus's intellectual curiosity and profound faith. One of those captivated by the scholar from Berytus was young Eusebius, who acknowledged his debt by calling himself "Eusebius of Pamphilus."

Pamphilus, Eusebius, and several others spent several years working as a team, probably living in the same room and pooling their economic resources. Eventually, the disciple outdid the master, and Eusebius traveled far and wide in quest of documents regarding Christian origins. During that period of joint work, Pamphilus and Eusebius wrote several works, although most of them have now been lost.

But their peaceful and scholarly life would come to an end. It was still the time of persecutions, and the threat that had always loomed on the horizon now became the storm of the great persecution under Diocletian. By June of 303, the persecution made itself felt in Caesarea, in the first martyrdom in many years. From then on, the storm grew worse. In 305 Maximinus Daia, a bitter enemy of Christianity, achieved imperial rank. Two years later, Pamphilus was arrested. But then there was a lull in the storm, and the great Christian scholar simply remained in prison for more than two years before being condemned to death. During that time, he and Eusebius collaborated on a five-book *Defense of Origen,* to which Eusebius added a sixth book after his teacher's martyrdom.

Eusebius himself was not arrested. Why this was so is not clear. At least on two occasions he left the city, and one may suppose that part of his reason for doing so may have been to avoid arrest. At that time, most Christians held that there was no shame in hiding during a time of persecution, for martyrdom was something for which one had to be chosen by God. In any case, Eusebius did not suffer personally during the persecution, although his teacher and many of his companions died as martyrs.

In the midst of such evil times, Eusebius carried on with what would become his most important work, his *Church History.* This work, which he later revised, became of great importance to future church historians. Without it, a great deal of the story that we have been telling would have been lost. It was Eusebius who collected, organized, and published practically all that is now known about many of the people and events in the life of the early church. Without him, our knowledge of the early history of Christianity would be reduced by half.

Finally, in 311, things began to change. First came an edict by Galerius that granted tolerance to Christians. Then Constantine defeated Maxentius, and Constantine and Licinius, meeting at Milan, put an end to persecution. From the point of view of Eusebius and his surviving companions, what was taking place was a direct intervention by God, something similar to the events of Exodus. From then on Eusebius—and probably a vast number of other Christians whose opinions were not set down in writing—began looking upon Constantine and Licinius as the instruments of the divine design. When hostilities finally broke out between the two emperors, Eusebius was convinced that Licinius had become insane and begun to persecute Christianity. Only Constantine, and he alone, remained as God's chosen instrument.

The Arch of Constantine, next to the Roman Colosseum, is one of the few remaining monuments from Constantine's reign.

A few years before Constantine became sole emperor, Eusebius had been elected bishop of Caesarea. This was a great responsibility, for persecution had disbanded his flock, which he now had to gather and organize anew. Furthermore, the bishopric of Caesarea had jurisdiction not only over the church in the city itself, but also over the rest of Palestine. Now become a pastor and administrator, Eusebius had little time for his literary and scholarly pursuits.

He had been bishop of Caesarea for a number of years when a new storm came to break the peace of the church. This was not a matter of persecution by the government, but rather a bitter theological debate that threatened to rend the church asunder: the Arian controversy over the divine status of Jesus. Since this will be the subject of an upcoming chapter, it is not necessary to discuss it here. Let it suffice to say that Eusebius's role in the controversy was not beyond reproach. The reason for this, however, was not that he was a hypocrite or an opportunist. It was rather that Eusebius never fully understood what was at stake. For him, the peace and unity of the church were of prime importance. Therefore, although at first he seemed to be inclined toward Arianism, at the Council of Nicea he took an opposite stance, only to waver again once the council had disbanded. Since he was a famous bishop and scholar, many looked to him for direction, and his confusion—which was probably shared by many of lesser intellectual gifts—did little to bring the controversy to a happy conclusion.

Eusebius had met Constantine years before, when the future emperor visited Palestine with Diocletian's court. In Nicea, at the time of the council, Eusebius saw the emperor seeking the unity and well-being of the church. On a number of other occasions he had interviews and correspondence with the emperor. He probably came to know the ruler best when Constantine and his court went to Jerusalem for the dedication of the newly built Church of the Holy Sepulchre. The festivities on that occasion were part of the celebration of the thirtieth anniversary of Constantine's reign. The Arian controversy was still boiling, and the bishops who gathered for the great dedication—first at Tyre and then at Jerusalem—were deeply interested in it, as was the emperor. Eusebius, as bishop of the principal city in the area, played an important role in the proceedings, and delivered a speech in praise of Constantine. This speech, still extant, is one of the reasons why some accuse him of sheer flattery. But, when judged in terms of what was then customary in such situations, Eusebius's speech appears rather moderate in its praise of the emperor.

In any case, Eusebius was neither a close friend nor a courtier of Constantine. He spent most of his life in Caesarea and the surrounding area, busy with ecclesiastical affairs, while Constantine spent his time either in Constantinople or in other parts of the empire. The contacts between the two were brief and intermittent. Since Eusebius was admired by many of his colleagues, the emperor cultivated his support. And, since Eusebius was convinced that, after the great trials of his earlier years, Constantine had been raised up by God, he did not hesitate to support the emperor. Furthermore, it was after Constantine's death in 337 that Eusebius wrote his lines of highest praise for the ruler who had brought peace to the church. Therefore, his actions are not so much those of a flatterer as those of a rather uncritical, but grateful, man. And even in this regard, Eusebius was more measured than some of his contemporaries, for chroniclers of the time tell us that there were Christians who went so far as to offer sacrifices to the statue of Constantine!

Eusebius's gratitude, however, went far beyond its most obvious expressions in words of praise. His understanding of what had taken place in the person of Constantine left a mark on his entire work, and particularly in the way in which he understood the history of the church up to his time. The final draft of his *Church History* did not simply seek to retell the various events in the earlier life of the church. It was really an apology that sought to show that Christianity was the ultimate goal of human history, particularly as seen within the context of the Roman Empire. Similar notions had appeared earlier, when Christian writers in the second century declared that all truth comes from the same Logos who was incarnate in Jesus Christ. According to such authors as Justin and Clement of Alexandria, both philosophy and the Hebrew scriptures were given as a preparation for the gospel. Also circulating was the idea that the empire itself, and the relative peace that it brought to the Mediterranean basin, had been ordained by God as a means to facilitate the dissemination of the Christian faith. Others, such as Irenaeus, had held that the entirety of human history from the time of Adam and Eve had been a vast process by which God had been training humankind for communion with the divine. What Eusebius then did was to bring together these various ideas, showing them at work in the verifiable facts of the history of both the church and the empire. The history that thus resulted was no mere collection of data of antiquarian interest, but rather a further demonstration of the truth of Christianity, which is the culmination of human history.

In support of that thesis, Constantine's conversion was the keystone. According to Eusebius, the main reason for persecution was that Roman authorities did not see that Christianity was the crowning touch on the best Roman traditions. Faith and the empire, like faith and philosophy, were not really incompatible. On the contrary, the Christian faith was the culmination of both philosophy and the empire. Therefore, Constantine's religious policies were important to Eusebius's understanding of history, not simply because they were advantageous for the church, but for much deeper reasons. The new situation was living and convincing proof of the truth of the gospel, to which all human history pointed.

This theological perspective made it very difficult for Eusebius to take a critical stance on the events of his time. He seems to have been aware of some of Constantine's shortcomings, especially his irascible and sometimes even bloodthirsty temperament. But, apparently in order not to weaken his argument, Eusebius simply remains silent about such things.

The importance of all this is not merely in what Eusebius says or does not say about Constantine. Far beyond that, Eusebius's work is an indicator of the degree to which, even unwittingly, Christian theology was being shaped by the new circumstances, even to the point of abandoning some of its traditional themes.

Three examples should suffice to illustrate the manner in which theology was being accommodated to fit the new situation. First of all, it is clear that, in the New Testament as well as in the early church, it was affirmed that the gospel was first of all good news to the poor, and that the rich had particular difficulty in hearing it and receiving it. Actually, one of the theological issues that caused some concern for earlier Christians was how it was possible for a rich person to be saved. But now, beginning with Constantine, riches and pomp came to be seen as signs of divine favor. The next chapter will show that the monastic movement was in part a protest against this accommodating understanding of the Christian life. But Eusebius—and the thousands of others for whom he probably spoke—does not seem to have been aware of the radical change that was taking place as the persecuted church became the church of the powerful, nor of the dangers involved in that change.

Likewise, Eusebius described with great joy and pride the ornate churches that were being built. But the net result of those buildings, and of the liturgy that evolved to fit them, was the development of a clerical aristocracy, similar to the imperial aristocracy, and often as far from the common people as were the great officers of the empire. The church imitated the uses of the empire, not only in its liturgy, but also in its social structure.

Finally, the scheme of history that Eusebius developed led him to set aside or at least to postpone a fundamental theme of early Christian preaching: the expectation of the full Reign of God. Although Eusebius does not go as far as to say so explicitly, in reading his works one receives the impression that now, with Constantine and his successors, the plan of God has been fulfilled. No longer will Christians have to decide between serving the coming reign and serving the present one—which has become a representative and agent of the Reign of God. Beyond the present political order, all that Christians are to hope for is their own personal transference into the heavenly kingdom. Christian hope came to be relegated to the future life or to the distant future, and seemed to have little to do with the present world. Religion tended to become a way to gain access to heaven, rather than to serve God in this life and the next. The earlier notion, that in the resurrection of Christ the new age has dawned, and that by baptism and the Eucharist Christians become participants in it, was now abandoned, and Christian hope was now limited to the individual's life after death. Since the time of Constantine, and due in part to the work of Eusebius and of many others of similar theological orientation, there was a tendency to set aside or to postpone the hope of the early church, that its Lord would return in the clouds to establish a Kingdom of peace and justice. In subsequent times, and as long as the Constantinian era endured, most individuals and movements that rekindled eschatological hope were branded as heretics and subversives, and condemned as such. It would be only as the Constantinian era approached an end, particularly in the twentieth and twenty-first centuries, that eschatology would once again become a central theme in Christian theology.

Although the life of Eusebius illustrates the changes that were taking place, this is not to say that he was solely responsible for them. On the contrary, the entire history of the period would seem to indicate that Eusebius, although more articulate than most, was simply expressing the common feeling among Christians, for whom the advent of Constantine and of the peace he brought about was the final triumph of Christianity over its enemies. Those Christians were not able to express their opinions with Eusebius's elegance and erudition; but they were the ones who, step by step, shaped the church in the years to come. Eusebius is not the creator of what we have called "official theology," but rather the mouthpiece of the thousands of Christians who, like him, were overawed by God's mercy in finally delivering the church from persecution. But not all Christians regarded the new circumstances with like enthusiasm, as the next chapters will amply show.

15

The Monastic Reaction

> Monks who leave their cells, or seek the company of others, lose their
> peace, like the fish out of water loses its life.
>
> ANTHONY

The new position of the church after Constantine's peace was not equally received by all. Over against those who, like Eusebius of Caesarea, saw the more recent events as the fulfillment of God's purposes, there were those who bemoaned what they saw as the low level to which Christian life had descended. The narrow gate of which Jesus had spoken had become so wide that countless multitudes were hurrying through it—many seeming to do so only in pursuit of privilege and position, without caring to delve too deeply into the meaning of Christian baptism and life under the cross. Bishops competed with one another over prestigious positions. The rich and powerful seemed to dominate the life of the church. The tares were growing so rapidly that they threatened to choke out the wheat.

For almost three hundred years, the church had lived under the constant threat of persecution. All Christians were aware of the possibility that some day they might be taken before Roman authorities, and there placed before the awesome choice between death and apostasy. During the prolonged periods of quiet in the second and third centuries, there were those who forgot this; and when persecution did arrive, they proved too weak to withstand the trial. This in turn convinced others that security and comfortable living were the greatest enemies of faithfulness, and that these enemies proved stronger during periods of relative peace. Now, when the peace of the church seemed assured, many of these people saw that very assurance as a snare of Satan.

How was one to be a true Christian in such circumstances? When the church joins the powers of the world, when luxury and ostentation take hold of Christian altars, when the whole of society is intent on turning the narrow path into a wide avenue, how is one to resist the enormous temptations of the times? How is one to witness to the crucified Lord, to the one who had nowhere to lay

From the beginning, many of the monastics were women and some of them served as models for other women as well as for men.

his head, at a time when many leaders of the church live in costly homes, and when the ultimate witness of martyrdom is no longer possible? How to over-come Satan, who is constantly tempting the faithful with the new honors that society offers?

Many found an answer in the monastic life: to flee from human society, to leave everything behind, to dominate the body and its passions, which give way to temptation. Thus, at the very time when churches in large cities were flooded by thousands demanding baptism, there was a veritable exodus of other thou-sands who sought beatitude in solitude.

THE ORIGINS OF MONASTICISM

Even before Constantine's time, there had been Christians who, for various reasons, had felt called to an unusual style of life. Reference has already been made to the "widows and virgins"—that is, to those women who chose not to marry or to remarry, and to devote all their time and energies to the work of the church. Some time later, Origen, following the Platonic ideal of the wise life, made arrangements to live at a mere subsistence level, and led a life of extreme asceticism. It is said that he even took literally the Word of Christ about those who have made themselves "eunuchs for the Kingdom." Also, although Gnos-ticism had been rejected by the church, its influence could still be felt in the widely held notion that there was a fundamental opposition between the body

and the life of the spirit, and that therefore in order to live fully in the spirit it was necessary to subdue and to punish the body.

Thus, monasticism has roots both within the church and outside of it. From within the church, monasticism was inspired by Paul's words, that those who chose not to marry had greater freedom to serve the Lord. This impulse toward celibacy was often strengthened by the expectation of the return of the Lord. If the end was at hand, it made no sense to marry and to begin the sedentary life of those who are making plans for the future. At other times, there was an additional reason for celibacy: since Christians are to witness to the coming Kingdom, and since Jesus declared that in the Kingdom "they neither marry nor are given in marriage," those who choose to remain celibate in the present life are a living witness to the coming Kingdom.

A number of outside influences also played a part in the development of Christian monasticism. Several schools of classical philosophy held that the body was the prison or the sepulcher of the soul, and that the latter could not be truly free as long as it did not overcome the limitations of the body. Stoic doctrine, very widespread at the time, held that passions are the great enemy of true wisdom, and that the wise devote themselves to the perfecting of their souls and the subjugation of their passions. Several religious traditions in the Mediterranean basin included sacred virgins, celibate priests, eunuchs, and others whose lifestyle set them apart for the service of the gods. This sense that the body—and particularly sexual activity—was somehow evil or unworthy of those devoted to holiness became so widespread that in an attempt to curb this extreme practice, the Council of Nicea, in 325 CE, ordered that any among the

The temptations of Anthony became the subject of much religious art. Here we see them depicted by a German engraver of the fifteenth century.

clergy who had castrated themselves be deposed, and no one be admitted into the clergy who had done such a thing. But according to ancient chroniclers even at that council there were already some who wished to order clerical celibacy—a move that was defeated by the impassioned opposition of bishop Paphnutius, widely respected for his steadfastness during the persecution and his own celibate life. Thus, the ideals of early Christian Monasticism arose both from Scripture and from other sources quite alien to Christianity.

THE FIRST MONKS OF THE DESERT

Although there were early monastics throughout the Roman Empire, it was the desert—especially the Egyptian desert—that provided the most fertile soil for the growth of monasticism. The very word *monk* is derived from the Greek word *monachos,* which means "solitary." One of the driving motivations for the early monks was the search for solitude. Society, with its noise and its many activities, was seen as a temptation and a distraction from the monastic goal. The term "anchorite," which soon came to mean a solitary monk, originally meant withdrawn or even fugitive. For these people, the desert was attractive, not so much because of its hardship, but rather because of its inaccessibility. What they sought was not burning sands, but rather an oasis, a secluded valley, or an abandoned cemetery, where they would not be disturbed by others.

There are indications that the early Christian monastic movement was often associated with a parallel movement of individuals who abandoned their villages fleeing from the hardships imposed by the government, particularly taxation. At about the same time that early Christian monasticism flourished, the population of rural Egyptian villages dwindled, as people found it impossible to fulfill all the obligations that the government imposed on them and fled to more inaccessible areas. These too were fugitives or anchorites, and it was not always possible to distinguish between them and those who fled to the desert in search of greater holiness.

It is impossible to tell who was the first monk—or nun—of the desert. The two who are usually given that honor, Paul and Anthony, owe their fame to two great Christian writers, Jerome and Athanasius, who wrote about them, each claiming that his protagonist was the founder of Egyptian monasticism. But the truth is that it is impossible to know—and that no one ever knew—who was the founder of the movement. Monasticism was not the invention of an individual, but rather a mass exodus, a contagion, which seems to have suddenly affected thousands of people. In any case, the lives of Paul and Anthony are significant, if not as those of founders, certainly as typical of the earliest forms of monasticism.

Jerome's life of Paul is very brief, and almost entirely legendary. But still, the nucleus of the story is probably true. Toward the middle of the third century, fleeing persecution, a young man named Paul went to the desert, where he found an abandoned hiding place for counterfeiters. There he passed the rest of his life, spending his time in prayer and living on a diet that consisted almost exclusively of dates. According to Jerome, Paul lived in such conditions for almost a century, and his only visitors during that time were the beasts of the desert and the elderly monk, Anthony. Although this may be somewhat exaggerated, it does point to the ideal of solitude that was so important to the early monastics.

According to Athanasius, Anthony was born in a small village on the left shore of the Nile, the son of relatively wealthy parents. Most likely he was a Copt—a descendant of the ancient Egyptians, who now suffered oppression and discrimination from Greeks and Romans alike. When they died, Anthony was still young, and his inheritance was sufficient to permit a comfortable life both for him and for his younger sister, for whom he now took responsibility. His plans were simply to live off his inheritance, until a reading of the gospel in church had such an impact on him that he felt compelled to change his life. The text that day was the story of the rich young ruler, and the words of Jesus were very clear to Anthony, who was relatively rich: "If you would be perfect, go, sell what you possess and give to the poor, and you will have treasure in heaven" (Matt. 19:21). In response to those words, Anthony disposed of his property and gave the proceeds to the poor, reserving only a portion for the care of his sister. But later he was moved by the words of Jesus in Matthew 6:34: "do not be anxious about tomorrow." He then disposed even of the small reserve fund that he had kept for his sister, placed her under the care of the virgins of the church, and left for the desert.

Anthony spent his first years of retreat learning the monastic life from an old man who lived nearby—which shows that Anthony was not the first Christian anchorite. These were difficult times for the young monk, for often he missed the pleasures he had left behind, and began to feel sorry for having sold all his goods and withdrawn to the desert. When he was thus tempted, Anthony had recourse to stricter discipline. Sometimes he would fast for several days; at other times he would limit his food to a single meal a day, after sunset.

After several years, Anthony decided that it was time to leave his elderly teacher and the other neighboring monks from whom he had learned monastic discipline. He then went to live in a tomb in an abandoned cemetery, where he subsisted on the bread some kind souls brought him every few days. According to Athanasius, at this time Anthony began having visions of demons that accosted him almost continuously. At times, his encounter with these demons was such that it resulted in a physical struggle that left him sore for days.

Finally, when he was thirty-five years old, Anthony had a vision in which God told him not to fear, for he would always be able to count on divine aid. It was then that Anthony decided that the tomb in which he lived was not sufficiently distant from society, and moved farther into the desert. He found an abandoned fort where he now fixed his residence. Even there the demons followed him, and the visions and temptations continued. But Anthony was now convinced that he had God's help, and the struggle became more bearable.

However, it was not only demons that pursued the monastic athlete. He was pursued by other monks who were desirous to learn from him the discipline and wisdom of prayer and contemplation. And he was also pursued by the curious and the ailing, for by then he was becoming famous as a saint and a worker of miracles. Again and again the elderly anchorite withdrew to ever more desolate places, but he was repeatedly found by those who sought him. He finally gave up this struggle and agreed to live near a number of disciples, on condition that they would not visit him too frequently. In exchange, Anthony would visit them periodically and talk with them about monastic discipline, the love of God, and the wonders of contemplation.

On two occasions, however, Anthony did visit the great city of Alexandria. The first was when the great persecution broke out under Diocletian, and Anthony and several of his disciples decided to go to the city in order to offer up their lives as martyrs. But the prefect decided that such ragged and disheveled characters were not worthy of his attention, and the would-be martyrs had to be content with speaking words of encouragement to others.

Anthony's second visit to Alexandria took place many years later, during the Arian controversy regarding the divinity of the Son of God. The Arians claimed that the holy hermit had sided with them, and against Athanasius, and Anthony decided that the only way to undo such false rumors was to appear in person before the bishops gathered in Alexandria. According to Athanasius, the elderly monk, who had to speak in Coptic because he knew no Greek—and who probably was also illiterate—spoke with such wisdom and conviction that he confounded the Arians.

Finally, toward the end of his days, Anthony agreed to have two younger monks live with him and take care of him. He died in 356, after instructing his two companions to keep the place of his burial secret and to send his cloak—his only possession—to bishop Athanasius in Alexandria.

Both Paul and Anthony went to the desert before the time of Constantine— and even then, there were others already there. But when Constantine came to power, the life these hermits had led became increasingly popular. Some travelers who visited the region declared, with obvious exaggeration, that the desert was more populated than some cities. Others speak of twenty thousand women and ten thousand men leading the monastic life in a single area of Egypt. Similar figures are sometimes given for the arid regions of Cappadocia, in what is now Turkey, where monks dug caves in the soft stone of the region. No matter how exaggerated these figures may be, one fact is certain: those who fled society for the withdrawn life of the hermit were legion.

The harsh mountains of Cappadocia were riddled with caves where monks dwelled.

Their life was extremely simple. Some planted gardens, but most of them earned their living weaving baskets and mats that they then traded for bread and oil. Apart from the ready availability of reeds, this occupation had the advantage that while weaving one could pray, recite a psalm, or memorize a portion of scripture. The diet of the desert consisted mostly of bread, to which were occasionally added fruit, vegetables, and oil. Their belongings were limited to the strictly necessary clothing, and a mat to sleep on. Most of them frowned on the possession of books, which could lead to pride. They taught each other, by heart, entire books of the Bible, particularly the Psalms and books of the New Testament. And they also shared among themselves edifying anecdotes and pearls of wisdom coming from the most respected anchorites.

The spirit of the desert did not fit well with that of the hierarchical church whose bishops lived in great cities and enjoyed power and prestige. Many monks were convinced that the worst fate that could befall them was to be made a priest or a bishop—it was precisely at this time, and partly as a result of the changes brought about after Constantine's conversion, that Christian ministers began to be called "priests." Although some monks were ordained, this was done almost always against their will or in response to repeated entreaties from a bishop of known sanctity, such as Athanasius. This in turn meant that many anchorites would go for years without partaking of communion, which from the very beginning had been the central act of Christian worship. In some areas, churches were built in which the nearby hermits gathered on Saturday and Sunday. On Sunday, after communion, they would often have a common meal, and then part for another week.

On the other hand, this sort of life was not free of temptations. As years went by, many monks came to the conclusion that, since their life was holier than that of most bishops and other leaders of the church, it was they, and not those leaders, who should decide what was proper Christian teaching. Since many of these monks were fairly ignorant and prone to fanaticism, they became the pawns of others with more education, power, and cunning who used the zeal of the desert hosts to their own ends. In the fifth century, this came to the point where rioting monks would seek to impose by force and violence what they considered to be orthodox doctrine.

PACHOMIUS AND COMMUNAL MONASTICISM

The growing number of people withdrawing to the desert, and the desire of most of them to learn from an experienced teacher, gave rise to a new form of monastic life. Anthony was repeatedly compelled to flee from those who sought his help and guidance. Increasingly, solitary monasticism gave way to a communal form of the monastic life. Those who lived in such communities still called themselves "monks"—that is, solitary—but by this they meant, not that they lived completely alone, but that they lived in solitude from the world. This form of monasticism is called "cenobitic"—a name derived from two Greek words meaning "communal life."

As in the case of solitary monasticism, it is impossible to name the founder of cenobitic monasticism. Most probably it appeared simultaneously in various places, brought about, not so much by the creative genius of one person as by the pressure of circumstances. The completely solitary life of the early monastics was not well suited for many who went to the desert. Furthermore, if the center of Christian life is love, there is some question as to how one living absolutely alone, seldom having to deal with other people, practices love of neighbor. Thus, cenobitic monasticism was born both out of the natural tendency of monastics to gather around particularly saintly leaders, and out of the very nature of the gospel.

Although not its founder, Pachomius deserves credit as the organizer who most contributed to the development of cenobitic monasticism. Pachomius was born around the year 286, in a small village in southern Egypt. His parents were pagans, and he seems to have known little about Christianity before being taken from his home and forced to join the army. He was very saddened by his lot, when a group of Christians came to console him and his companions. The

young recruit was so moved by this act of love that he vowed that, if he somehow managed to leave the military, he too would devote himself to serve others.
When quite unexpectedly he was allowed to leave the army, he sought someone
to instruct him in the Christian faith and to baptize him. Some years later, he
decided to withdraw to the desert, where he asked an old anchorite to be his
teacher.

For seven years young Pachomius lived with the anchorite, until he heard a
voice commanding him to move. His old teacher helped him build a shelter, and
there Pachomius lived by himself until his younger brother, John, joined him.
Together, the two brothers devoted themselves to prayer and contemplation.

But Pachomius was not satisfied, and he constantly asked God to show him
the way to better service. Finally, he had a vision in which an angel told him
that he was to serve humankind. Pachomius rejected the vision, declaring that
he had come to the desert to serve God, not humans. But the message was
repeated and Pachomius, perhaps remembering his early vows when he was a
soldier, decided to change the direction of his monastic life.

With his brother's help, he built a large enclosure, sufficient for a number of
monks, and recruited what would be the first members of the new community.
Pachomius hoped to teach them what he had learned of prayer and contemplation, and also to organize a community in which all would help one another.
But his recruits had not been properly selected, discipline broke down, and
eventually Pachomius expelled the lot.

He then began a second attempt at communal monasticism. The earlier attempt had failed because his recruits said that he was too demanding. In this
new attempt, rather than relaxing his discipline, he was more rigorous. From
the very beginning, he demanded that any who wished to join the community
must give up all their goods and promise absolute obedience to their superiors.
Besides, all would work with their hands, and none would be allowed to consider any task unworthy. The basic rule was mutual service, so that even those
in authority, in spite of the vow of absolute obedience which all had made, had
to serve those under them.

The monastery that Pachomius founded on these bases grew rapidly, to the
point that during his lifetime nine such communities were established, each
with several hundred monks. Meanwhile, Mary, Pachomius's sister, founded
similar communities for women. At that time, there were some in city churches
who felt that the institution of the widows and virgins was no longer necessary,
and as a result many of these women left the cities and joined other women in
monastic communities, often in the desert. According to witnesses who visited
the region, in some areas in Egypt there were twice as many women monastics
as there were men.

Each of these monasteries was encircled by a wall with a single entrance. Within the enclosure there were several buildings. Some of them, such as the church, the storehouse, the refectory, and the meeting hall, were used in common by the entire monastery. The rest were living quarters in which monks were grouped according to their responsibilities. Thus, for instance, there was a building for the gatekeepers, who were responsible for the lodging of those who needed hospitality, and for the admission and training of those who requested to join the community. Other such buildings housed the weavers, bakers, cobblers, and so forth. In each of them there was a common room and a series of cells, one for every two monks.

The daily life of a Pachomian monk included both work and devotion, and Pachomius himself set an example for the rest by undertaking the most humble tasks. For the devotional life, Paul's injunction to "pray without ceasing" was the model. Thus, while the bakers kneaded the bread, or the cobblers made shoes, all sang psalms, recited passages of scripture, prayed either aloud or in silence, meditated on a biblical text, and so forth. Twice a day there were common prayers. In the morning the entire community gathered to pray, sing psalms, and hear the reading of scripture. In the evening they had similar services, although now gathered in smaller groups in the common rooms of the various living quarters.

The economic life of Pachomian communities was varied. Although all lived in poverty, Pachomius did not insist on the exaggerated poverty of some anchorites. At the tables there was bread, fruit, vegetables, and fish—but never meat. What the monks produced was sold in nearby markets, not only in order to buy food and other necessary items, but also in order to have something to give the poor and any sojourners who came by. In each monastery there was an administrator and an aide, and these had to render periodic accounts to the administrator of the main monastery, where Pachomius lived.

Since every monk had to obey his superiors, the hierarchical order was clearly defined. At the head of each housing unit there was a superior, who in turn had to obey the superior of the monastery and his deputy. And above the superiors of the various monasteries were Pachomius and his successors, who were called "abbots" or "archimandrites." When Pachomius was about to die, his monks vowed obedience to whomever he would choose as his successor, and thus was established the custom that each abbot would name the person to succeed him in absolute command of the entire organization. This new abbot's authority was final, and he could name, transfer, or depose the superiors of all the communities in the entire system.

Twice a year, all Pachomian monks gathered for prayer and worship, and to deal with any issues necessary to maintain proper order of the communities.

The organization was also kept together by frequent visits to all monasteries by the abbot or his representative. Pachomius and his followers never accepted ecclesiastical office, and therefore there were no ordained priests among them. On Sundays a priest would come to the monastery and celebrate communion.

In the women's communities, life was organized in a similar fashion. While each was headed by a woman, the male abbot of the original community—Pachomius and his successors—ruled over them just as they did over the male Pachomian communities.

Those who wished to join a Pachomian community simply appeared at the gate of the enclosure. This was not easily opened to them, for before being admitted to the gatekeepers' house candidates were forced to spend several days and nights at the gate, begging to be let in. Thus, they were required to show both the firmness of their resolve and their humility and willingness to obey. When the gate was finally opened, the gatekeepers took charge of the candidates, who lived with them for a long period, until they were considered ready to join the community in prayer. Then they were presented to the assembly of the monastery, where they sat at a special spot until a place was found for them in one of the houses, and a role assigned to them in the ongoing life of the monastery.

A surprising fact about the entire process of admission to the Pachomian communities is that many of the candidates who appeared at the gates and were eventually admitted had to be catechized and baptized, for they were not Christians. This gives an indication of the enormous attraction of the desert in the fourth century, for even pagans saw in monasticism a style of life worth pursuing. To what degree such attraction was religious, and to what degree it is an indication of the harsh living conditions of the rural poor in Egypt, it is impossible to tell. Significantly, however, the vast majority of those who fled to the Egyptian desert were Copts, that is to say, the descendants of the ancient Egyptians who were now at the lowest echelon of Egyptian society.

THE SPREAD OF THE MONASTIC IDEAL

Although the roots of monasticism are not to be found exclusively in Egypt, that was where the movement gained most momentum in the fourth century. Devout people from different regions went to Egypt, some to remain there and others to return to their countries with the ideals and practices they had learned in the desert. From Syria, Asia Minor, Italy, and even Mesopotamia, pilgrims went to the land of the Nile and on their return spread the story and the legends of Paul, Anthony, Pachomius, and countless others. Throughout the Eastern portion of the empire, wherever there was a suitable place, a monk fixed his abode. Some exaggerated the ascetic life by ostentatious acts, such as spending their lives atop a column of a ruined temple. But others brought to the church a sense of discipline and absolute dedication that was very necessary in what seemed the easy times after Constantine.

However, those who most contributed to the spread of the monastic ideal were not the anchorites who copied the ways of the Egyptian desert and sought secluded places where they could devote themselves to prayer and meditation, but rather a number of bishops and scholars who saw the value of the monastic witness for the daily life of the church. Thus, although in its earliest times Egyptian monasticism had existed apart and even in opposition to the hierarchy, eventually its greatest impact was made through some of the members of that hierarchy.

Several of those who thus contributed to the spread of monasticism were of such importance that we shall deal with them in upcoming chapters. But it may be well to point out here their significance for the history of monasticism. Athanasius, besides writing the *Life of Saint Anthony,* repeatedly visited the monks in the desert, and when he was persecuted by imperial authority he found refuge among them. Although he himself was not a monk, but a bishop, he sought to organize his life in such a way that it would reflect the monastic ideals of discipline and renunciation. When exiled in the West, he made known to the Latin-speaking church what was taking place in the Egyptian desert. Jerome, besides writing the *Life of Paul the Hermit,* translated Pachomius's *Rule* into Latin, and he himself became a monk—although an unusually scholarly one. Since Jerome was one of the most admired and influential Christians of his time, his works and his example had a significant impact on the Western church, which thus became more interested in the monastic spirit. Basil of Caesarea—known as Basil the Great—found time in the midst of all the theological debates in which he was involved to organize monasteries where time was given both to devotion and to the care of the needy. Answering questions addressed to him by monks, he wrote a number of treatises which, although not originally intended as monastic rules, eventually were quoted and used as such. Soon the harsh lands of his native Cappadocia—in what is today central Turkey—became populated by monastics. Augustine, the great bishop of Hippo, partly owed his conversion to reading Athanasius's *Life of Saint Anthony,* and lived as a monk until he was forced to take a more active role in the life of the church. Even then, he organized the priests who worked with him into a semi-monastic community, and thus provided inspiration for what would later be called the Canons of St. Augustine.

But the most remarkable example of the manner in which a saintly and monastic bishop contributed to the popularity of the monastic ideal was Martin of Tours. The *Life of Saint Martin,* written by Sulpitius Severus, was one of the most popular books in Western Europe for centuries and was one of the most influential elements in the shaping of Western monasticism.

Martin was born around the year 335 in Pannonia, in what is now Hungary. His father was a pagan soldier, and during his early years Martin lived in various parts of the empire—although the city of Pavia, in northern Italy, seems to have been his most frequent place of residence. He was very young when he decided to become a Christian, against his parents' will, and had his name included in the list of catechumens. His father, in order to force him away from his Christian contacts, had him enrolled in the army. It was the time when Emperor Julian—later known as the Apostate—led his first military campaigns. Martin served under him for several years. During this period, an episode took place that ever since has been associated with the name of Martin.

Martin and his friends were entering the city of Amiens in what is now France when an almost naked and shivering beggar asked them for alms. Martin had no money for him, but he took off his cape, cut it in two, and gave half to the beggar. According to the story, later in his dreams Martin saw Jesus

The story of Martin dividing his cape to share with the beggar soon became a common theme in Christian art.

coming to him, wrapped in half a soldier's cape, and saying: "Inasmuch as you did it to one of the least of these my brethren, you did it to me." This episode became so well known, that ever since Martin is usually represented in the act of sharing his cape with the beggar. This is also the origin of the word *chapel*—for centuries later, in a small church, there was a piece of cloth reputed to be a portion of Martin's cape. From that piece of cape—*capella*—the little church came to be called a "chapel," and those who served in it, "chaplains."

Shortly after the incident at Amiens, Sulpitius Severus tells us, Martin was baptized, and two years later he was finally able to leave the army. He then visited the learned and saintly bishop Hilary of Poitiers, who became a close friend. Several different tasks and vicissitudes took him to various parts of the empire, until finally he settled just outside the city of Tours, near Poitiers. There he devoted himself to the monastic life, while the fame of his sanctity spread through the region. It was said that God performed great works through him, but he always refused to count himself as anything more than an apprentice in the Christian life.

When the bishopric of Tours became vacant, the populace wanted to elect Martin to that position. The story goes that some of the bishops present at the election opposed such an idea, arguing that Martin was usually dirty, dressed in rags, and disheveled, and that his election would damage the prestige of the office of bishop. No agreement had been reached when it was time to read the Bible, and the person assigned for that task was nowhere to be found. Then one of those present took the book and began reading where it fell open: "By the mouth of babes and infants, thou hast founded a bulwark because of thy foes, to still the enemy and the avenger" (Ps. 8:2). The crowd took this to be a direct message from heaven. Martin, the filthy and unseemly man whom the bishops scorned, had been chosen by God to silence the bishops. Without further ado, Martin was elected bishop of Tours.

But the new bishop was not ready to abandon his monastic ways. Next to the cathedral, he built a small cell where he devoted all his free time to the monastic life. When his fame was such that he could find no peace in that cell, he moved back to the outskirts of the city, and from there he would carry on his pastoral tasks.

When Martin died, many believed that he was a saint. His fame and example led many to the conviction that a true bishop ought to be like him. Thus, the monastic movement, which at first was in great measure a protest against the worldliness and the pomp of bishops, eventually left its imprint on the idea itself of the episcopate. For centuries—and in some quarters to the present time—it was thought that a true bishop should endeavor to achieve the monastic ideal as much as possible. In that process, however, monasticism itself was changed, for whereas those who first joined the movement fled to the desert in quest for their own salvation, as years went by monasticism would become— particularly in the West—an instrument for the charitable and missionary work of the church.

Already in these early stages, the monastic movement had shown its ability to evolve in various directions. From the solitude of the early anchorites, it evolved into large communities, some with hundreds of members. A movement that at first eschewed books and learning soon enrolled scholars such as Jerome, Augustine, and Basil. Originally a lay movement that tended to reject much of the life of the organized church, it was soon embraced by bishops, and eventually set the ideal standard for all bishops. This adaptability would continue through the ages. In the ensuing centuries, monastics would become missionaries, scholars, teachers, preservers of ancient cultural traditions, settlers of new lands, and even soldiers.

In all of this, there was a common thread: the conviction that the ideal Christian life was one of personal poverty and sharing of goods. The earlier practice of Christian communities in general, of sharing goods among its members, now became the hallmark of monasticism, something expected of monks and nuns, but not of the rest of the church. Now that almost all the population had become Christian, most were excused from such sharing, while monastics continued that earlier tradition. Thus arose a distinction between two levels of Christians which would mark most of the history of the church—a distinction reinforced by the vows of celibacy and obedience that only monastics took.

The Schismatic Reaction:
Donatism

> What is debated between the Donatists and us is, where is to be found
> this body of Christ which is the church? Are we to seek the answer in our
> own words, or in those of the Head of the body, our Lord Jesus Christ?
>
> AUGUSTINE OF HIPPO

While those who followed the monastic way of life expressed their dissatisfaction with the new order by withdrawing to the desert, others simply declared that the church at large had been corrupted, and that they were the true church. Of several splinter groups with similar views, the most numerous were the Donatists.

The Donatist controversy was one more instance in which the church was divided over the question of the lapsed and how they ought to be restored. After each period of violent persecution, the church had to face the issue of what to do with those who had yielded their faith, but who now sought to be restored to the communion of Christians. Although there were similar issues and schisms in the East, it was mostly in the Latin-speaking West, with its emphasis on law and order, that such schisms were most common and lasting. In the third century, this had resulted in the schism of Novatian in Rome; and in North Africa, Cyprian, bishop of Carthage, had to defend his episcopal authority against those who held that the confessors were the ones who should determine how the lapsed were to be restored. Now, in the fourth century, the debate over the restoration of the lapsed became particularly virulent in North Africa.

The persecution had been very violent in that region, and the number of those who had yielded was great. As in other cases, those who had yielded had not done so to the same degree. Some bishops avoided further persecution by handing over to the authorities heretical books, and leading them to believe that these were Christian scriptures. Others turned in the genuine scriptures, claiming that in so doing they were avoiding bloodshed, and that this was their responsibility as pastors. Many, both clergy and lay, succumbed to imperial pressure and worshiped the pagan gods—indeed, the number of the latter was such that some chroniclers state that there were days when the pagan temples were full to overflowing.

On the other hand, there were many Christians who remained firm in their faith, and as a result suffered imprisonment, torture, and even death. As earlier, those who survived imprisonment and torture were called "confessors," and were particularly respected for the firmness of their faith. In Cyprian's time, some of the confessors had been too ready to readmit the lapsed, without any consultation with the authorities of the church. Now, after Constantine's conversion, a significant number of confessors took the opposite tack, insisting on greater rigor than the church was applying. These more demanding confessors claimed that the lapsed were not only those who had actually worshiped the gods, but also those who had handed the scriptures to the authorities. If changing a tittle or a jot in scriptures was such a great sin, argued the confessors, is it not an even greater sin to turn the sacred text over to be destroyed? Thus, some bishops and other leaders were given the offensive title of *traditores*—that is, those who had handed over or betrayed, a title often applied to Judas.

Such was the state of affairs when, shortly after the end of persecution, the very important bishopric of Carthage became vacant. The election fell on Caecilian. But he was not popular with the rigorist party, which elected Majorinus as his rival. In these elections there were intrigues and unworthy maneuvers on both sides, so that each was justified in claiming that his rival's election had been irregular. When Majorinus died shortly after being made rival bishop of Carthage, his party elected Donatus of Casae Nigrae, who became their leader for almost half a century, and from whom the Donatist movement eventually derived its name.

Naturally, the rest of the church was profoundly disturbed by this schism in North Africa, for it was possible to acknowledge only one bishop of Carthage. The bishops of Rome and of several other important cities declared that Caecilian was the true bishop of Carthage, and that Majorinus and Donatus were usurpers. Constantine, who was greatly interested in keeping the church together so that it could help unify his empire, followed the lead of these bishops, and sent instructions to his officers in North Africa, that they should acknowledge only Caecilian and those in communion with him. This had important practical consequences, for Constantine was issuing legislation in favor of Christianity, such as tax exemption for the clergy. On the basis of his instructions to North Africa, only those in communion with Caecilian could enjoy these benefits—or receive any of the gifts that Constantine was offering to the church.

Carthage, now in ruins, was the center of Roman rule and of church life in North Africa.

What were the causes of the Donatist schism? The foregoing is only the outward history of its beginnings. But in truth the schism had theological, political, and economic roots. The theological justification, and immediate cause of the schism, had to do with the issue of dealing with those who yielded during a time of persecution. According to the Donatists, one of the three bishops who had consecrated Caecilian was a *traditor*—that is, had delivered scriptures to the authorities—and therefore the consecration itself was not valid. Caecilian and his party responded by claiming, first, that the bishop was not a *traditor* and, second, that even had he been one, his action in consecrating Caecilian would still have been valid. Thus, besides the factual question of whether or not this particular bishop—and others in communion with Caecilian—had yielded, there was the additional issue of whether an ordination or consecration performed by an unworthy bishop was valid. The Donatists declared that the validity of such an act depended on the worthiness of the bishop performing it. Caecilian and his followers responded that the validity of the sacraments and of other such acts cannot be made to depend on the worthiness of the one administering them, for in that case all Christians would be in constant doubt regarding the validity of their own baptism or of the communion of which they had partaken. Since it is impossible to know the inner state of the soul of a minister offering such sacraments, there would be no way to dispel doubt regarding their validity.

The Donatists, on their part, insisted that Caecilian, whose consecration had been flawed by the participation of a *traditor*, was not really a bishop, and that for that reason all those whom he had ordained were false ministers, whose sacraments had no validity. Furthermore, the other bishops whose consecration was not in no doubt had sinned by joining in communion with people such as Caecilian and his party. In consequence, their sacraments and ordinations were no longer valid.

Given the two positions, if a member of Caecilian's party decided to join the Donatists, a new baptism was required, for the Donatists claimed that a baptism administered by their opponents was not valid. But, on the other hand, those who left the Donatist party were not rebaptized by Caecilian and his followers, who held that baptism was valid regardless of the worth of the person administering it.

Besides the matter of the validity of sacraments administered by an unworthy person, the debate had to do with two very different conceptions of the church. The Donatists held that the church, being the bride of Christ, had to be pure and holy, while their opponents pointed to the parable of the wheat and the tares, which suggests that it is best for the disciples not to try to adjudge who is worthy and who is not, but rather leave that judgment to the Lord. For one party, the holiness of the church consisted of the holiness of its members; for the other, it was grounded in the holiness of its Lord. For the Donatists, what gave authority to a priest or bishop was his personal holiness; for their opponents, such authority was derived from the office—which was a common principle of Roman law.

These were the main theological issues involved in the debate. But when one reads between the lines of the documents of the time, one becomes aware that there were other causes of conflict often obscured by the theological debates. Thus, it appears that among the Donatists there were some who had delivered the scriptures to the authorities, and even some who had made an entire inventory of all the objects that the church used in worship, in order to give that inventory to the authorities. Yet, these people were accepted among the Donatists. Furthermore, one of the first leaders of Donatism was a certain Purpurius, who had murdered two nephews. Thus, it is difficult to believe that the real source of enmity of the Donatists toward the rest of the church was their concern for purity.

It is a fact that the two parties soon separated along social and geographical lines. In Carthage and its immediate surroundings—Proconsular Africa— Caecilian and his followers were strong. But farther west, in Numidia and Mauritania, the Donatists were very popular. Numidia and Mauritania were agricultural areas. A great deal of their produce was exported to Italy through

The birthplace of Donatism.

Carthage. The net result was that as middle-men the Carthaginians, with less labor and risk, made more money from the crops than those who actually raised them. Furthermore, Numidia and Mauritania were much less Romanized than Carthage and the area around it. Many in the less Romanized areas retained their ancestral language and customs, and saw Rome and everything connected with it as a foreign and oppressive force. In Carthage, on the other hand, there was a strongly Latinized class of landowners, merchants, and military officers, and it was this class that reaped most of the benefits of trade and other contacts with Italy. For these people, good relations with Rome as well as with the rest of the empire were of paramount importance. But in Carthage itself, as well as in its outlying districts, there were numerous people among the lower classes whose feelings were similar to those of the Numidians and Mauritanians.

Long before the advent of Constantine, Christianity had made significant inroads in Numidia, among the lower classes of Proconsular Africa, and in Mauritania, though to a lesser degree. The new faith of these converts was a force even the empire could not overcome. At the same time, fewer members of the Romanized classes of Carthage had embraced Christianity. This brought into the Christian community some of the class tensions of the rest of society. But at that time those who were converted—particularly those of the higher classes—had to break many of their social contacts, and therefore the tensions within the church were not as great as they could have been.

This situation changed drastically with the advent of Constantine and the peace of the church. Now one could be both a good Roman and a good Christian. Following the lead of the emperor, the Romanized classes flocked to the church. Others from the same social strata who had been converted earlier saw this as a positive development, for their earlier decision was now corroborated by that of other important people. But Christians from the lower classes tended to see the new developments as a process of corruption of the church. What these Christians had always hated in the Roman Empire was now becoming part of the church. Soon the powerful—those who controlled politics and the economy—would also control the church. It seemed necessary to resist that process, and to remind the newly converted powerful that when they were still worshiping pagan gods, the supposedly "ignorant" Numidians, Mauritanians, and others knew the truth.

All this may be seen in the various stages of the conflict. Caecilian was elected with the support of the Romanized Christians of Carthage. His election was opposed by the lower classes in Proconsular Africa, and by almost all of the people and the clergy of Numidia. Before he had even had time to study the issues being debated, Constantine decided that Caecilian's party represented the legitimate church. The same was decided by the bishops of the great Latin cities—and eventually by those of Greek cities. On the other hand, the Donatists were quite willing to accept the support of those members of the Numidian clergy who had weakened during the persecution.

This does not mean that from its origins Donatism was consciously a political movement. The early Donatists were not opposed to the empire, but to "the world"—although for them many of the practices of the empire were worldly. They repeatedly sought to persuade Constantine that he had erred in deciding in favor of Caecilian. Even as late as the reign of Julian, during the second half of the century, some Donatists hoped that Roman authorities would see the error of their ways, and come to the support of the movement.

Around the year 340, there appeared among the Donatists a group called the *circumcellions*—a name of debatable origin, which probably means that they had their headquarters in martyrs' shrines. They were mostly Numidian and Mauritanian Donatist peasants who resorted to violence. Although sometimes they have been depicted as no more than bandits masquerading as people driven by religious motives, the truth is that they were religious to the point of fanaticism. They were convinced that there was no death more glorious than that of the martyrs, and that now that persecution in the old style had ended, those who died in battle against the perverters of the faith were also martyrs. In some cases, this quest for martyrdom rose to such a pitch that people committed mass suicide by jumping off cliffs. This may well be fanaticism; but it is not opportunistic hypocrisy.

The circumcellions became an important factor in the schism. Sometimes the Donatist leaders in the towns tried to disassociate themselves from this radical party. But at other times, when they needed activist troops, they appealed to the circumcellions. The time came when many villas and land holdings in secluded places had to be abandoned. The rich and those who represented the empire did not dare travel though the countryside without heavy escort. More than once, the circumcellions appeared at the very gates of fortified towns. Credit suffered, and trade almost came to a standstill.

In response, Roman authorities had no recourse but to use force. There were persecutions, attempts to persuade the dissidents, massacres, and military occupation. All to no avail. The circumcellions were the expression of a deep discontent among the masses, and the empire was unable to stamp out the movement. As we shall see later on, shortly thereafter the Vandals invaded the area, thus putting an end to Roman rule. But even under the Vandals the movement continued. In the sixth century, the Eastern Roman Empire—with its capital in Constantinople—conquered the region. But the circumcellions continued. It was only after the Muslim conquest late in the seventh century that Donatism and the circumcellions finally disappeared.

In conclusion, Donatism—particularly its radical branch, the circumcellions—was a response to the new conditions brought about by the conversion of Constantine. While some Christians received the new order with open arms, and others withdrew to the desert, the Donatists simply broke with the church that had now become an ally of the empire. Even so, the serious theological questions they had raised about the nature of the church and the validity of the sacraments would force other Christians, notably Saint Augustine, to deal with these issues. It was partly in response to the Donatists that Augustine and others developed their doctrine of the church, their view of the validity of sacraments, and the Just War Theory. Thus, as is often the case, those whom the rest of the church eventually rejected as heretics and schismatics left their mark in the theology that was developed in order to refute them.

17

The Arian Controversy and
the Council of Nicea

And [we believe] in one Lord Jesus Christ, the Son of God, begotten
from the Father as the only-begotten, that is, from the substance of
the Father, God from God, light from light, true God from true God,
begotten, not made, being of one substance with the Father.

CREED OF NICEA

From its very beginnings, Christianity had been involved in theological
controversies. In Paul's time, the burning issue was the relationship between Jewish and Gentile converts. Then came the crucial debates over Gnostic
speculation. In the third century, when Cyprian was bishop of Carthage, the
main point at issue was the restoration of the lapsed. All of these controversies
were significant, and often bitter. But in those early centuries the only way to
win such a debate was through solid argument and holiness of life. The civil
authorities paid scant attention to theological controversies within the church,
and therefore the parties in conflict were not usually tempted to appeal to those
authorities in order to cut short the debate, or to win a point that had been lost
in a theological argument.

After the conversion of Constantine, things changed. Now it was possible to
invoke the authority of the state to settle a theological question. The empire had
a vested interest in the unity of the church, which Constantine hoped would
become the "cement of the empire." Thus, the state soon began to use its power
to force theological agreement upon Christians. Many of the dissident views
that were thus crushed may indeed have threatened the very core of the Christian message. Had it not been for imperial intervention, the issues would probably have been settled, as in earlier times, through long debate, and a consensus
would eventually have been reached. But there were many rulers who did not
wish to see such prolonged and indecisive controversies in the church, and who
therefore simply decided, on imperial authority, who was right and who should

be silenced. As a result, many of those involved in controversy, rather than seeking to convince their opponents or the rest of the church, sought to convince the emperors. Eventually, theological debate was eclipsed by political intrigue.

The beginning of this process may be seen already in the Arian controversy, which began as a local conflict between a bishop and a priest, grew to the point that Constantine felt obliged to intervene, and resulted in political maneuvering by which each party sought to destroy the other. At first sight, it is not a very edifying story. But upon closer scrutiny what is surprising is not that theological debate became entangled in political intrigues, but rather that in the midst of such unfavorable circumstances the church still found the strength and the wisdom to reject those views that threatened the core of the Christian message.

THE OUTBREAK OF THE CONTROVERSY

The roots of the Arian controversy are to be found in theological developments that took place long before the time of Constantine. Indeed, the controversy was a direct result of the manner in which Christians came to think of the nature of God, thanks to the work of Justin, Clement of Alexandria, Origen, and others. When the first Christians set out to preach their message throughout the empire, they were taken for ignorant atheists, for they had no visible gods. In response, some learned Christians appealed to the authority of those whom antiquity considered eminently wise: the classical philosophers. The best pagan philosophers had taught that above the entire cosmos there was a supreme being, and some had even declared that the pagan gods were human creations. Appealing to such respected authorities, Christians argued that they believed in the supreme being of the philosophers, and that this was what they meant when they spoke of God. Such an argument was very convincing, and there is no doubt that it contributed to the acceptance of Christianity among the intelligentsia.

But this was also a dangerous argument. It was possible that Christians, in their eagerness to show the kinship between their faith and classical philosophy, would come to the conviction that the best way to speak of God was not in the manner of the prophets and other biblical writers, but rather in the manner of Plato, Plotinus, and the rest. Since those philosophers conceived of perfection as immutable, impassible, and fixed, many Christians came to the conclusion that such was the God of scripture.

Two means were found to bring together what the Bible says about God and the classical notion of the supreme being as impassible and fixed: allegorical interpretation of scriptural passages, and the doctrine of the Logos. Allegorical interpretation was fairly simple to apply. Wherever scripture says something

Medieval art sometimes depicted the Trinity as a single body with three faces.

"unworthy" of God—that is, something that is not worthy of the perfection of the supreme being of the philosophers—such words are not to be taken literally. Thus, for instance, if the Bible says that God walked in the garden, or that God spoke, one is to remember that an immutable being does not really walk or speak. Intellectually, this satisfied many minds. But emotionally it left much to be desired, for the life of the church was based on the faith that it was possible to have a direct relationship with a personal God, and the supreme being of the philosophers was in no way personal.

There was another way to resolve the conflict between the philosophical idea of a supreme being and the witness of scripture. This was the doctrine of the Logos, as developed by Justin, Clement, Origen, and others. According to this view, although it is true that the supreme being—the "Father"—is immutable, impassible, and so on, there is also a Logos, Word, or Reason of God, and this is personal, capable of direct relationships with the world and with humans.

Thus, according to Justin, when the Bible says that God spoke to Moses, what it means is that the Logos of God spoke to him.

Due to the influence of Origen and his disciples, these views had become widespread in the Eastern wing of the church—that is, that portion of the church that spoke Greek rather than Latin. The generally accepted view was that, between the immutable One and the mutable world, there was the Word, or Logos, of God. It was within this context that the Arian controversy took place.

The controversy itself began in Alexandria, when Licinius was still ruling in the East, and Constantine in the West. The bishop of Alexandria, Alexander, clashed over several issues with Arius, who was one of the most prestigious and popular presbyters of the city. Although the points debated were many, the main issue at stake was whether the Logos, the Word of God, was coeternal with God. The phrase that eventually became the Arian motto, "there was when He was not," aptly focuses on the point at issue. Alexander held that the Word existed eternally with the Father; Arius argued that the Word was not coeternal with the Father. Although this may seem a very fine point, what was ultimately at stake was the divinity of the Word. Arius claimed that, strictly speaking, the Word was not God, but the first of all creatures. It is important to understand at this point that Arius did not deny that the Word existed before the incarnation. On the preexistence of the Word, all were in agreement. What Arius said was that, before anything else was made, the Word had been created by God. Alexander argued that the Word was divine, and therefore could not be created, but rather was coeternal with the Father. In other words, if asked to draw a line between God and creation, Arius would draw that line to include the Word in creation, while Alexander would draw it in a manner that would place all of God's creation on one side and the eternal Word on the other.

Each of the two parties had, besides a list of favorite proof-texts from the Bible, logical reasons that seemed to make the opponents' position untenable. Arius, on the one hand, argued that what Alexander proposed was a denial of Christian monotheism—for, according to the bishop of Alexandria, there were two who were divine, and thus there were two gods. Alexander retorted that Arius's position denied the divinity of the Word, and therefore also the divinity of Jesus. From its very beginning, the church had worshiped Jesus Christ, and Arius's proposal would now force it either to cease such worship, or to declare that it was worshiping a creature. Alexander concluded that, since both alternatives were unacceptable, Arius was proven wrong.

Although these were the issues debated in the course of the controversy, quite possibly at the heart of the matter was also the question of how it is that Christ saves. For Alexander, and particularly for those who subsequently defended his

A city gate in Nicea, now in ruins.

views—especially Athanasius—Christ has achieved our salvation because in him God has entered human history and opened the way for our return to him. Apparently Arius and his followers felt that Christ's role as Savior was imperiled by such a view, for Jesus had opened the way for salvation by his obedience to God, and such obedience would be meaningless if he himself was divine, and not a creature.

The conflict became public when Alexander, claiming that such was his authority and his responsibility as a bishop, condemned Arius's teachings and removed him from all posts in the church in Alexandria. Arius did not accept this judgment, but rather appealed both to the people of Alexandria and to a number of prominent bishops throughout the Eastern portion of the empire who had been his fellow students in Antioch. Soon there were popular demonstrations in Alexandria, with people marching in the streets chanting Arius's theological refrains. The bishops to whom Arius had appealed—who called themselves *fellow Lucianists* in honor of their common teacher in Antioch— wrote letters declaring that the deposed presbyter was correct, and that it was Alexander who was teaching false doctrine. Thus, the local disagreement in Alexandria threatened to divide the entire Eastern church.

Such was the state of affairs when Constantine, who had just defeated Licinius, decided to intervene. His first step was to send Bishop Hosius of Cordoba, his advisor in ecclesiastical matters, to try to reconcile the two parties. When Hosius reported that the dissension could not be resolved by mere amicable entreaties, Constantine decided to take a step that he had been considering for some time: he would call a great assembly or council of Christian bishops from all parts of the empire. Besides dealing with a number of issues that required the establishment of standard policies, this great council—to meet in Nicea, a city within easy reach of Constantinople—would resolve the controversy that had broken out in Alexandria.

THE COUNCIL OF NICEA

It was the year 325 when the bishops gathered in Nicea for what would later be known as the First Ecumenical—that is, universal—Council. The exact number of bishops present is not known—the figure given in ancient chronicles (318) is doubted by some scholars, since it coincides with the number of those circumcised in Abraham's time—but there were approximately three hundred, mostly from the Greek-speaking East, but also some from the West. In order to see that event in the perspective of those who were there, it is necessary to remember that several of those attending the great assembly had recently been imprisoned, tortured, or exiled, and that some bore on their bodies the physical marks of their faithfulness. And now, a few years after such trials, these very bishops were invited to gather at Nicea, and the emperor covered their expenses to do so. Many of those present knew of each other via hearsay or through correspondence. But now, for the first time in the history of Christianity, they had before their eyes physical evidence of the universality of the church. In his *Life of Constantine,* Eusebius of Caesarea, who was present, describes the scene:

There were gathered the most distinguished ministers of God, from the many churches in Europe, Libya [i.e., Africa] and Asia. A single house of prayer, as if enlarged by God, sheltered Syrians and Cilicians, Phoenicians and Arabs, delegates from Palestine and from Egypt, Thebans and Libyans, together with those from Mesopotamia. There was also a Persian bishop, and a Scythian was not lacking. Pontus, Galatia, Pamphylia, Cappadocia, Asia, and Phrygia sent their most outstanding bishops, jointly with those from the remotest areas of Thrace, Macedonia, Achaia, and Epirus. Even from Spain, there was a man of great fame [Hosius of Cordoba] who sat as a member of the great assembly. The bishop of the Imperial City [Rome] could not attend due to his advanced age; but he was represented by his presbyters. Constantine is the first ruler of all time to have gathered such a garland in the bond of peace, and to have

Although Constantine was not yet baptized, he presided over the great council of bishops.

presented it to his Savior as an offering of gratitude for the victories he had won over all his enemies.[25]

In this euphoric atmosphere, the bishops discussed the many legislative matters that had to be resolved with the end of persecution. They approved standard procedures for the readmission of the lapsed and for the election and ordination of presbyters and bishops, and for establishing the order of precedence of the various episcopal sees. They also decreed that bishops, presbyters, and deacons could not move from one city to another—a rule soon to be ignored.

But the most difficult issue that the council had to face was the Arian controversy. On this score, there were several different groups whose positions and concerns had to be taken into account.

There was first of all a small number of convinced Arians, led by Eusebius of Nicomedia. (This bishop, who played a central role throughout the early years of the controversy, is not to be confused with the historian, Eusebius of Caesarea, who was also present at the council.) Since Arius was not a bishop, he was not allowed to sit in the council, and it was Eusebius of Nicomedia who spoke for him and for the position that he represented. This small group was convinced that what Arius taught was so patently correct that all that was needed was a clear exposition of the logic of the argument, and the assembly would vindicate Arius and rebuke Alexander for having condemned his teachings.

In direct opposition to the Arian party, there was another small group of bishops who were convinced that Arianism threatened the very core of the Christian faith, and that therefore it was necessary to condemn it in no uncertain terms. The leader of this group was, not surprisingly, Alexander of Alexandria. Among his followers was a young man who, being only a deacon, could not sit in the council, but who would eventually become famous as the champion of Nicene orthodoxy: Athanasius of Alexandria.

Most of the bishops from the Latin-speaking West had only a secondary interest in the debate, which appeared to them as a controversy among Eastern followers of Origen. For them, it was sufficient to declare that in God there were, as Tertullian had said long before, "three persons and one substance."

Another small group—probably numbering no more than three or four—held positions approaching *patripassianism*, that is, that the Father and the Son are the same, and that therefore the Father suffered the passion. These bishops agreed that Arianism was wrong, but their own doctrines were also rejected later in the course of the controversy, as the church began to clarify what it meant by trinitarian doctrine.

In truth, the vast majority of those present did not belong to any of these groups. They bemoaned the outbreak of a controversy that threatened to divide the church at a time when persecution had finally come to an end and new opportunities and challenges needed to be met. It seems that at the beginning of the sessions these bishops hoped to achieve a compromise that would make it possible to move on to other matters. A typical example of this attitude was that of Eusebius of Caesarea, the learned historian whose erudition gained him great respect among his fellow bishops.

According to the reports of those present, what changed matters was the exposition that Eusebius of Nicomedia made of his own views—which were also those of Arius. When the bishops heard his explanation, their reaction was the opposite of what Eusebius of Nicomedia had expected. The assertion that the Word or Son was no more than a creature, no matter how high a creature, provoked angry reactions from many of the bishops: "You lie!" "Blasphemy!" "Heresy!" Eusebius was shouted down, and we are told that the pages of his written speech were snatched from his hand, torn to shreds, and trampled underfoot.

The mood of the majority had now changed. Earlier they hoped to deal with the issues at stake through negotiation and compromise, without condemning any doctrine. Now they were convinced that they had to reject Arianism in the clearest way possible.

At first the assembly sought to do this through a series of passages of scripture. But it soon became evident that by limiting itself to biblical texts the council would find it very difficult to express its rejection of Arianism in unmistakable terms. It was then decided to agree on a creed that would express the faith of the church in such a way that Arianism was clearly excluded. The exact process they followed is not entirely clear. Eusebius of Caesarea, for reasons that scholars still debate, proposed the creed of his own church. Constantine suggested that the word *homoousios*—to which we shall return—be included in the creed. (Did Constantine know enough about the discussion to come up with this word, or was it suggested to him by his ecclesiastical advisor Hosius of Cordoba, as some suspect?) Eventually, the assembly agreed on a formula that was based on the creed of Caesarea, but with a number of additions that clearly rejected Arianism:

> We believe in one God, the Father Almighty, maker of all things visible and invisible.
>
> And in one Lord Jesus Christ, the Son of God, the only-begotten of the Father, that is, from the substance of the Father, God of God, light of light, true God of true God, begotten, not made, of one substance [homoousios] with the Father, through whom all things were made, both in heaven and on earth, who for us humans and for our salvation descended and became incarnate, becoming human, suffered and rose again on the third day, ascended to the heavens, and will come to judge the living and the dead.
>
> And in the Holy Spirit.
>
> But those who say that there was when He was not, and that before being begotten He was not, or that He came from that which is not, or that the Son of God is of a different substance [hypostasis] or essence [ousia], or that He is created, or mutable, these the Catholic church anathematizes.[26]

This formula, with a number of additions later, and without the anathemas of the last paragraph, provided the basis for what is now called the Nicene Creed, which is the most universally accepted Christian creed. (The Apostles' Creed, being Roman in origin, is known and used only in churches of Western origin—which include the Roman Catholic Church and those stemming from the Protestant Reformation. The Nicene Creed, on the other hand, is acknowledged both by these Western churches and by those of the East, including Greek Orthodox, Russian Orthodox, and the like.)

When one reads the formula as approved by the bishops at Nicea, it is clear that their main concern was to reject any notion that the Son or Word—Logos—was a creature, or a being less divine than the Father. This may be seen first of all in affirmations such as: "God of God, light of light, true God of true God." It is also the reason why the creed declares that the Son is "begotten, not made." Note that the Creed began by declaring that the Father is "maker of all things visible and invisible." Thus, in declaring that the Son is "begotten, not made," he is being excluded from those things "visible and invisible" made by

The Council of Nicea as depicted in the Nüremberg Chronicle.

the Father. Furthermore, in the last paragraph, those are condemned who declare that the Son "came from that which is not"—that is, out of nothing, like the rest of creation. Also, in the text of the creed itself, we are told that the Son was begotten "from the substance of the Father."

The key word, however, and the one that was the subject of much controversy, is *homoousios* ("of the same substance"). This was intended to convey that the Son is just as divine as the Father. But it also provided the main reason for subsequent resistance to the Nicene Creed, for it seemed to imply that there is no distinction between Father and Son, and thus left the door open for Patripassianism.

The bishops gathered at Nicea hoped that the creed on which they had agreed (together with the clear anathemas appended to it) would put an end to the Arian controversy, and proceeded to sign it. Very few—Eusebius of Nicomedia among them—refused to sign. The assembly declared those who did not heretical, and deposed them. But Constantine added his own sentence to that of the bishops: He banished the deposed bishops from their cities. He probably intended only to avoid further unrest. But this addition of a civil sentence to an ecclesiastical one had serious consequences, for it established a precedent for the intervention of secular authority on behalf of what was considered orthodox doctrine.

In spite of what the bishops had hoped, the Council of Nicea did not end the controversy. Eusebius of Nicomedia was an able politician, and we are even told that he was distantly related to the emperor. His strategy was to court the approval of Constantine, who soon allowed him to return to Nicomedia. Since the emperor's summer residence was in Nicomedia, soon Eusebius was able to present his case once again before Constantine. Eventually, the emperor decided that he had been too harsh on the Arians. Arius himself was recalled from

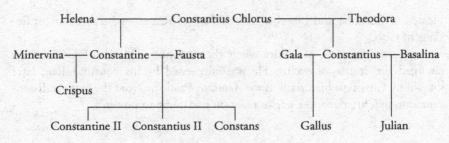

The Family of Constantine

exile, and Constantine ordered the bishop of Constantinople to restore him to communion. The bishop was debating whether to obey the emperor or his conscience, when Arius died.

Alexander of Alexandria died in 328, and was succeeded by Athanasius, who had been present at the Council of Nicea as a deacon, and who would now become the champion of the Nicene cause. He soon became so identified with that cause that the later history of the Arian controversy is best told by following Athanasius's life. This will be the subject of Chapter 19, and therefore it is not necessary to follow the subsequent course of the controversy in any detail here. Let it suffice to say that Eusebius of Nicomedia and his followers managed to have Athanasius exiled by order of Constantine. By then, most of the Nicene leaders were also banished. When Constantine finally asked for baptism, on his deathbed, he received that sacrament from Eusebius of Nicomedia.

After a brief interregnum, Constantine was succeeded by three of his sons: Constantine II, Constans, and Constantius II. Constantine II ruled over Gaul, Great Britain, Spain, and Morocco. Constantius's territory included most of the East. And Constans was allotted a strip of land between his two brothers, including Italy and North Africa. At first the new situation favored the Nicene party, for the eldest of Constantine's three sons took their side, and recalled Athanasius and the others from exile. But then war broke out between Constantine II and Constans, and this provided an opportunity for Constantius, who ruled the East, to follow his pro-Arian inclinations. Once again Athanasius was exiled, only to return when, after the death of Constantine II, the West was united under Constans, and Constantius was forced to follow a more moderate policy. Eventually, however, Constantius became sole emperor, and it was then that, as Jerome said, "The entire world woke from a deep slumber and discovered that it had become Arian." Once again the Nicene leaders had to leave their cities, and imperial pressure was such that eventually even the elderly

Hosius of Cordoba and Liberius—the bishop of Rome—signed Arian confessions of faith.

Such was the state of affairs when the unexpected death of Constantius changed the course of events. He was succeeded by his cousin Julian, later known by Christian historians as *the Apostate*. Profiting from the endless dissension among Christians, the pagan reaction had come to power.

18

The Pagan Reaction: Julian the Apostate

This is how that very humane prince [Constantius] dealt with us, although we were close relatives. Without benefit of trial, he killed six of our common cousins, my father, who was his uncle, another uncle on my father's side, and my older brother.

JULIAN THE APOSTATE

Julian had many reasons to dislike both Constantius and the Christian faith that he professed. At the time of Constantine's death, most of the dead emperor's close relatives had been massacred. The only notable exceptions were the three brothers who inherited the throne, and their cousins Julian and his older half-brother Gallus. The circumstances in which these crimes were committed are not altogether clear, and therefore it might be unfair to lay the blame on Constantius. It is clear that after Constantine's death there was some question as to who would succeed him, and that the army then killed most of his relatives—not in order to set up another dynasty, but rather in order to make sure that power would belong indisputably to Constantine's three surviving sons. Of these, only Constantius was then in Constantinople, where the massacre took place, and for that reason the common opinion was that he had ordered, or at least condoned, the death of his relatives.

Whatever the case may be, Julian was convinced that his cousin was guilty. Julian's father was a half-brother of Constantine, and therefore Julian was a first cousin to the three new emperors. Of Julian's vast family, only he and his half-brother Gallus survived. He later declared that Gallus was spared because he appeared to be mortally ill at the time, and that Julian himself was allowed to live because he was only six years old and thus was no threat to the throne. It is possible that Constantius himself ordered that these two cousins be spared, for they were too young to lead a rebellion and, if Constantine's three sons died

Julian, known in posterity as the Apostate, was in fact an able ruler who sought to restore the glories and traditions of ancient Rome.

without issue, these younger cousins could provide an orderly succession to the throne.

Meanwhile, both Gallus and Julian were kept away from the court. While Gallus devoted himself to physical exercise, his younger brother became increasingly interested in philosophical studies. Both were baptized and received Christian instruction, and during their exile from court both were made "readers" of the church.

Eventually, Constantius had to call on Gallus, for in 350 CE he had become sole ruler of the empire, and he had no children who could aid him in government or succeed him to the throne. In 351, Constantius gave Gallus the title *caesar*, that is, of junior emperor, and put vast territories under his rule. But Gallus did not turn out to be an able ruler, and there were rumors that he was conspiring against his cousin. A few years after having made him caesar, Constantius had him arrested and beheaded.

Meanwhile, Julian had continued his philosophical studies in Athens, a city famous as the seat of much of ancient wisdom. There he knew Basil of Caesarea, a devout Christian who would eventually become one of the greatest bishops of his time. It was also there that Julian became interested in the ancient-mystery religions. He had definitively abandoned Christianity, and sought after truth and beauty in the literature and religion of classical Greece.

Julian pursued his philosophical studies in Athens.

Constantius decided to set aside the bad experience he had had with Gallus and called his one surviving relative to share his power, giving him the title of caesar and appointing him to rule in Gaul. No one expected Julian, who had spent his life among books and philosophers, to be a great ruler, and in any case Constantius granted him very little support. But Julian surprised his contemporaries. His administration in Gaul was exemplary. And, when the occasion arose to lead a campaign against the barbarians, he proved that he was an able general and gained great popularity in the army.

All of this was not entirely to Constantius's liking, for he feared that Julian might seek possession of the throne. Tensions increased between the two cousins. When Constantius, who was preparing a campaign against Persia, called the troops in Gaul to the East, they rebelled and proclaimed Julian *augustus*, that is, supreme emperor. As soon as Constantius was free of the Persian threat, he marched against Julian and his rebellious troops. At the moment war seemed unavoidable, and both sides were braced for it, Constantius died. Julian had no difficulty marching to Constantinople and claiming the rule of the whole empire. It was the year 361.

Julian's first action was to seek revenge against those most responsible for his misfortunes, and against those who had sought to keep him away from the seat of power. To that end he named a court that was theoretically independent, but that in truth responded to the wishes of the emperor. This court condemned several of his worst enemies to death.

Apart from this, Julian was an able ruler, who managed to establish order in the chaotic administration of his vast domains. Yet it is not for such actions that he is most remembered, but rather for his religious policy, which earned him the title by which history knows him: the Apostate.

JULIAN'S RELIGIOUS POLICY

Julian sought both to restore the lost glory of paganism, and to impede the progress of Christianity. Since the time of Constantine, paganism had lost a great deal of its ancient splendor. Constantine himself had not persecuted paganism, nor sought to force the conversion of pagans. But he had sacked ancient temples in order to obtain works of art to use in decorating his new capital city. Under his sons, there were a number of laws passed favoring Christianity. By the time Julian became sole emperor, the ancient temples were practically empty, and there were pagan priests dressed only in rags, trying to supplement their meager incomes in dozens of ways and paying scant attention to the ancient rites.

Julian wished to bring about a total restoration and reformation of paganism. To that end he ordered that everything that had been taken from the temples be returned to them. Following the example of the Christian church, he organized the pagan priesthood into a hierarchy similar to that of the church at that time. Thus, he divided his entire empire into regions, each with an archpriest who was above all the pagan priests in that region. The various archpriests of each region were under the high priest of the province. And these high priests were under a supreme priest, who was Julian himself. All members of this priestly hierarchy were to lead an exemplary life, and to be concerned, not only with worship, but also with acts of charity directed at those in need. While rejecting Christianity, Julian had actually learned a great deal from it.

While this vast program of religious renewal was being organized, Julian took more direct steps to restore the ancient worship of the gods. He saw himself as chosen by them to do this work; and therefore, while he waited for the entire empire to return to its ancient faith, he was committed to render unto the gods the worship and the sacrifices that others did not render. By his order there were massive sacrifices in which the gods were offered hundreds of bulls and other animals at a time. But Julian, who was a wise ruler, was well aware that his restoration of paganism was not as popular as he would have liked. People mocked his new ceremonies, even while participating in them. For that reason it seemed necessary, not only to promote paganism, but also to hinder Christianity, its most powerful rival.

To this end Julian took a series of measures, in all justice, however, it is necessary to insist that he never decreed persecution against Christians. There were Christian martyrs in a number of places, but this was due, not to imperial command, but rather to mob actions or to overzealous local officials. Julian himself was convinced that persecution of Christians would not help his cause.

Rather than persecuting Christians, Julian followed a two-pronged policy of hindering their progress and ridiculing them. On the first score, he passed laws forbidding Christians to teach classical literature. Thus, while prohibiting what was to him a sacrilege, he prevented Christians from using the great works of classical antiquity to spread their faith, as they had been doing since the time of Justin in the second century. Secondly, Julian set out to ridicule Christians, whom he called "Galileans." With this in mind he wrote a work *Against the Galileans,* in which he demonstrated that he knew the Bible, and mocked both its contents and the teachings of Jesus. Although this work has been lost, its impact was such that eighty years later Bishop Cyril of Alexandria found it necessary to write a rebuttal in which he acknowledges that part of the power of Julian's arguments stemmed from his having been Christian, and thus knowing the Bible and Christian doctrine. Apparently one of Julian's main arguments was that the "Galileans" had twisted and misinterpreted Jewish scripture. Such arguments needed to be reinforced by policy and thus, Julian decided to rebuild the Temple in Jerusalem, not out of any particular affinity toward Judaism, but rather out of the necessity for a practical rebuttal to the common Christian argument that the destruction of the Temple had been the fulfillment of prophecies in the Old Testament.

All of these projects were moving along as rapidly as possible, when death overtook him quite unexpectedly. Julian was leading his troops in a campaign against the Persians when he was fatally wounded by an enemy spear. A famous legend, but one lacking all historical foundation, claims that his last words were: "Thou hast conquered, Galilean!"

19

Athanasius of Alexandria

> The results of the incarnation of the Savior are such and so many, that
> anyone attempting to enumerate them should be compared to a person
> looking upon the vastness of the sea and attempting to count its waves.
>
> ATHANASIUS OF ALEXANDRIA

Among those who were present at the Council of Nicea there was a young man, so dark and short that his enemies would later call him "the black dwarf." This was Athanasius, Alexander's secretary, who would soon become one of the central figures in the controversy, and the champion of Nicene orthodoxy. He was one of the great leaders—or "Fathers"—of the fourth century, whose biographies we now turn to as the best way to understand the events of that time.

THE EARLY YEARS

The time and place of Athanasius's birth are not known, although it is likely that he had rather obscure origins in a small town or village on the shore of the Nile River. Since he spoke Coptic, the language of the original inhabitants of the area who had been successively conquered by the Greeks and the Romans, and his complexion was dark, like that of the Copts, it is very likely that he belonged to that group, and that therefore he was a member of the lower classes in Egypt. He certainly never claimed to be of high birth, nor to be well versed in the subtleties of Greco-Roman culture.

During his early years he was in close contact with the monks of the desert. Jerome affirms that he gave a cloak to Paul the Hermit; and Athanasius himself, in his *Life of Saint Anthony,* says that he used to visit that famous monk and wash the old man's hands. This last detail has led some to venture the suggestion that when he was a child Athanasius served Anthony. Whatever the case may be, there is no doubt that throughout his life Athanasius kept in close contact with the monks of the desert, who repeatedly gave him support and asylum.

Though mocked as "the black dwarf," Athanasius was a theological giant.

From the monks, Athanasius learned a rigid discipline that he applied to himself, and an austerity that earned him the admiration of his friends and even the respect of many of his enemies. Of all the opponents of Arianism, Athanasius was to be feared most. The reasons for this were not to be found in subtlety of logical argument, nor in elegance of style, nor even in political perspicacity. In all these areas, Athanasius could be bested by his opponents. His strong suit was in his close ties to the people among whom he lived, and in living out his faith without the subtleties of the Arians or the pomp of so many bishops of other important sees. His monastic discipline, his roots among the people, his fiery spirit, and his profound and unshakable conviction made him invincible.

Even before the Arian controversy broke out, Athanasius had written two works, *Against the Gentiles* (meaning the pagans) and *On the Incarnation of the Word,* which offered clues as to the nature of his theology. The speculations of Clement or of Origen are not to be found here. These works show the deep conviction that the central fact of Christian faith, as well as of all human history, is the incarnation of God in Jesus Christ. The presence of God amidst humankind, made human: that is the heart of Christianity as Athanasius understood it.

In a memorable passage, he speaks of the incarnation in terms of an imperial visit to a city. The emperor resides in one of the houses in the city. As a result, the particular house, as well as the entire town, receives special honor and protection. Bandits stay away from such a place. Likewise, the Monarch of the Universe has come to visit our human city, living in one of our houses, and thanks to such a presence we are all protected from the attacks and wiles of the Evil One. Now, by virtue of that visit from God in Jesus Christ, we are free to be what God intends us to be—that is, beings capable of living in communion with the divine.

Clearly, the presence of God in history was the central element in the faith of Athanasius. Therefore, it is not surprising that he saw Arianism as a grave threat to the very heart of Christianity. What Arius taught was that the one who had come to us in Jesus Christ was not truly God, but a lesser being, a creature. Such a notion was unacceptable to Athanasius—as it also was to the monks who had withdrawn to the desert for the love of God Incarnate, and to the faithful who gathered to participate in worship under Athanasius's leadership. For Athanasius, for the monks, and for many of the faithful, the Arian controversy was not a matter of theological subtleties with little or no relevance. In it, the very core of the Christian message was at stake.

When Alexander, the bishop of Alexandria, was on his deathbed, all took for granted that he would be succeeded by Athanasius. But the young man, whose purpose was to live in peace offering the sacraments and worshiping with the people, fled to the desert. It is said that, shortly before he died, Alexander asked for his younger friend, probably in order to indicate that he wished him to be the next bishop of Alexandria. But Athanasius was still in hiding. Finally, several weeks after the death of Alexander, and against his own wishes, Athanasius was made bishop of Alexandria. The year was 328, the same year in which Constantine revoked the sentence banishing Arius. Arianism was regaining ground, and the battle lines were being drawn.

THROUGH MANY TRIALS

Eusebius of Nicomedia and the other Arian leaders knew that Athanasius was one of their most formidable enemies. They soon began to take steps to assure his downfall, circulating rumors that he dabbled in magic, and that he was a tyrant over the Christian flock in Egypt. As a result, Constantine ordered him to appear before a synod gathered at Tyre, where he was to answer to grave charges brought against him. In particular, he was accused of having killed a certain Arsenius, a bishop of a rival group, and having cut off his hand in order to use it in rites of magic. A chronicle with a flair for the dramatic reports that Athanasius went to Tyre as ordered, and after hearing the charges brought against him he brought into the room a man covered in a cloak. After making sure that several of those present knew Arsenius, he uncovered the face of the hooded man, and his accusers were confounded when they realized that it was Athanasius's supposed victim. Then someone who had been convinced by the rumors circulating against the bishop of Alexandria suggested that perhaps

Athanasius had not killed Arsenius, but had cut off his hand. Athanasius waited until the assembly insisted on proof that the man's hand had not been cut. He then uncovered one of Arsenius's hands. "It was the other hand!" shouted some of those who had been convinced by the rumors. Then Athanasius uncovered the man's other hand and demanded: "What kind of a monster did you think Arsenius was? One with three hands?" Laughter broke out through the assembly, while others were enraged that the Arians had misled them.

Free from the accusations made before the Synod of Tyre, Athanasius decided to go on to Constantinople in order to present his case before the emperor. Eusebius of Nicomedia had a great deal of influence at court, and Athanasius found it impossible to gain access to the emperor. He then took bolder steps. One day when Constantine was out for a ride, the tiny bishop of Alexandria simply jumped in front of the emperor's horse, grabbed its bridle, and did not let it go until he had been granted an audience. Perhaps such methods were necessary, given the political situation at court. But they served to convince Constantine that Athanasius was indeed a dangerous and impulsive fanatic. Therefore, he was willing to listen some time later, when Eusebius of Nicomedia told him that Athanasius had boasted that he could stop the shipments of wheat from Egypt to Rome. On the basis of Eusebius's accusation, Constantine sent Athanasius away from Alexandria, banishing him to the city of Trier, in the West.

But shortly thereafter Constantine died—after having been baptized by Eusebius of Nicomedia—and was succeeded by his three sons Constantine II, Constans, and Constantius. The three brothers decided that all exiled bishops—there were a number of them—could return to their sees.

Yet Athanasius's return to Alexandria was not the end, but rather the beginning, of a long period of struggle and repeated exiles for him. There was an Arian party in Alexandria, and these people now claimed that Athanasius, who had been away, was not the legitimate bishop. The rival claimant, a certain Gregory, had the support of the government. Since Athanasius was not willing to give him the church buildings, Gregory decided to take them by force, and the result was a series of disorders of such magnitude that Athanasius decided that, in order to avoid further violence, it was best for him to leave the city. There were also indications that the authorities blamed him for the disorders. This was confirmed when he reached the port and was refused passage because the governor had forbidden it. Eventually he convinced one of the captains, who smuggled him out of the port and took him to Rome.

Athanasius's exile in Rome was fruitful. Both the Arians and the Nicenes had requested support from Julius, the bishop of Rome. Athanasius was able to present the Nicene position in person, and he soon gained the support of the

Roman clergy, who took up the Nicene cause against the Arians. Eventually, a synod gathered in the ancient capital declared that Athanasius was the legitimate bishop of Alexandria, and that Gregory was a usurper. Although this did not mean that Athanasius could return to Alexandria immediately, it did signal the support of the Western church for the Nicene cause, and for Athanasius in particular.

After the death of Constantine II, Constans became sole emperor in the West, and he then asked Constantius, who ruled in the East, to permit the return of Athanasius to Alexandria. Since at that particular moment Constantius needed the support of his brother, he granted the request, and Athanasius was able to return to Alexandria.

Gregory's mismanagement in Alexandria had been such that the people received Athanasius as a hero or a liberator. It is possible that one of the factors involved in this situation was that Gregory and the Arian party represented the more Hellenized higher classes, whereas Athanasius was the man of the people. In any case, he was given a noisy and joyous welcome. Besides the inhabitants of the city, many monks came from the desert to join in the celebrations. With such show of support, Athanasius was free from the attacks of his enemies for approximately ten years. During that time he strengthened his ties with other defenders of orthodoxy, particularly through abundant correspondence. It was also at this time that he wrote a number of treatises against Arianism.

But Emperor Constantius was a committed Arian, and felt the need to rid himself of this champion of the Nicene faith. As long as Constans was alive, Constantius would endure the presence of Athanasius, who counted on the support of the Western emperor. In addition, a certain Magnentius tried to usurp imperial power, and Constantius had to gather all of his resources against this new rival.

Finally, in 353 CE, Constantius, who now ruled the whole empire, felt sufficiently secure to unleash his pro-Arian policy. Through threats and the use of force, an increasing number of bishops accepted Arianism. It is said that when Constantius ordered a synod to condemn Athanasius and was told that this was not possible, since the canons of the church did not permit them to condemn someone without a hearing, the emperor responded: "My will also is a canon of the church." On that ominous threat, many of the bishops signed the condemnation of Athanasius. Those who refused were banished.

If the chroniclers of the time are to be believed, Constantius feared the power Athanasius enjoyed in Alexandria, and for that reason sought to remove him from that city without actually banishing him. Athanasius received a letter in which the emperor granted him an audience that had never been requested. The bishop answered politely that there must have been an error, for he had

*Constantius II, named after his grandfather
Constantius Chlorus, eventually became sole heir to
Constantine. His support for Arianism was such that, as
Nicene theologian Jerome would say, "The world woke
up as from a slumber, and discovered itself to be Arian."*

not requested such an honor, and did not wish to waste the emperor's valuable time. Constantius then ordered a concentration of troops in Alexandria. When the legions were in place and any revolt could be crushed, the governor ordered Athanasius, in the name of the emperor, to leave the city. Athanasius responded by producing the old imperial order in which he was given permission to return. There must be a mistake, he told the governor, since the emperor would not contradict himself.

Shortly thereafter, when Athanasius was celebrating communion in one of the churches, the governor ordered the building to be surrounded and suddenly burst into the room leading a group of armed soldiers. Chaos ensued, and Athanasius ordered the congregation to sing Psalm 136, with its refrain: "For His mercy endureth forever." The soldiers pushed their way through the crowd, while some sang and others sought to escape. The clergy who were present formed a tight circle around Athanasius, who refused to flee until his flock was safe. But at that point he fainted, and somehow the clergy carried him to safety.

From that moment, Athanasius seemed to have become a ghost. He was sought everywhere, but the authorities could not find him. He had taken refuge among the monks of the desert, his faithful allies. These monks had means of communication among themselves, and whenever the officers of the empire approached the bishop's hideout, he was simply transferred to a safer place.

For five years, Athanasius lived among the monks in the desert. During those five years, the Nicene cause suffered severe setbacks. Imperial policy openly favored the Arians. Several synods were forced to declare themselves in favor of Arianism. Eventually, even Hosius of Cordoba and Liberius of Rome, both well advanced in years, were forced to sign Arian confessions of faith. Although many bishops and other church leaders were convinced that Arianism was unacceptable, it was difficult to oppose it when the state supported it so decisively. The high point for Arianism came when a council gathered in Sirmium openly rejected the decisions of Nicea. This was what orthodox leaders called the "Blasphemy of Sirmium."

Unexpectedly, Constantius died and was succeeded by his cousin Julian. Since the new emperor had no interest in supporting either side of the controversy, he simply canceled all orders of exile against all bishops. He was apparently hoping that the two parties would weaken each other while he moved forward toward his goal of restoring paganism. One of the consequences of this action was that Athanasius was able to return to Alexandria, where he undertook a much-needed campaign of theological diplomacy.

A THEOLOGICAL AGREEMENT

During the course of the controversy, Arianism had become increasingly technical and abstract. Among its defenders were many who had been trained in the best of Greek logic, and who therefore offered ever subtler arguments in defense of their position. On the basis of such arguments, Athanasius would clearly be bested. But the reason why he opposed Arianism—and the core of his arguments against it—had little to do with such speculations. His concern was rather with the core Christian tenet that Jesus is the Savior of humankind, the restorer of that which had fallen. While it is possible that in its early stages Arianism was also concerned primarily with the doctrine of salvation, it soon moved on to the field of speculative argument. This, which seemed to be its strength, would actually be its downfall, for it left Athanasius and his supporters in possession of the central issue of salvation. Along these lines, Athanasius argued that the corruption of humanity as the result of sin was such that a new creation was required, a radical reformation and restoration of what had been destroyed by sin. The work of salvation is no lesser than the work of creation. Therefore, the one responsible for our re-creation can be no lesser than the one responsible for our creation.

Athanasius was also willing to move beyond doctrinal or verbal formulae, and seek clarification and accord on the real issues at stake. He had come to the conclusion that many opposed the Nicene Creed because they feared that the assertion that the Son was of the same substance as the Father could be understood to mean that there is no distinction between the Father and the Son. Therefore, some preferred not to say "of the same substance," but rather "of a similar substance." The two Greek words were *homoousios* (of the same substance) and *homoiousios* (of a similar substance). The Council of Nicea had declared the Son to be *homoousios* with the Father. But now many were saying that they would rather affirm that the Son was *homoiousios* with the Father.

The Church of Saint Irene in Constantinople, where the Second Ecumenical Councill gathered in 381 and finally reaffirmed the doctrine of the Trinity.

At an earlier time, Athanasius had insisted on the Nicene formula, declaring that those who said "of a similar substance" were as heretical as the Arians. But now the elderly bishop of Alexandria was ready to see the legitimate concern of those Christians who, while refusing Arianism, were not ready to give up the distinction between the Father and the Son.

Through a series of negotiations, Athanasius convinced many of these Christians that the formula of Nicea could be interpreted in such a way as to respond to the concerns of those who would rather say, "of a similar substance." Finally, in a synod gathered in Alexandria in 362 CE, Athanasius and his followers declared that it was acceptable to refer to the Father, Son, and Holy Spirit as "of one substance" as long as this was not understood as obliterating the distinction among the three, and that it was also legitimate to speak of "three substances" as long as this was not understood as if there were three gods.

Also, just as the followers of Arius had once used chants to promote their views, now the Nicene party did likewise, composing hymns that affirmed the doctrine of the Trinity. Most famous among these are "O Splendor of God's Glory Bright," by Ambrose (c.339–397; see Chapter 21) and "Of the Father's Love Begotten," by Aurelius Prudentius (348–c.413).

On the basis of this understanding, most of the church rallied in its support of the Council of Nicea, whose doctrine was eventually ratified at the Second Ecumenical Council, gathered in Constantinople in 381 CE. But Athanasius would not live to see the final victory of the cause to which he devoted his life.

FURTHER TRIALS

Although Julian did not wish to persecute Christians, the news that arrived from Alexandria disturbed him. His efforts to restore paganism were met with the staunch resistance of Athanasius, who by now had become a popular hero. If imperial policy were to succeed in Alexandria, it was necessary to exile its bishop once again. It soon became clear to Athanasius that Julian wanted to remove him not only from Alexandria, but also from Egypt. Athanasius knew that he could not remain in the city, where there was no place to hide, and therefore resolved to seek refuge once again among the monks.

Aware that Athanasius was planning to hide in the desert, the imperial authorities sought to arrest him. According to some biographers, Athanasius was being carried up the Nile River on a ship. "Have you seen Athanasius?" shouted some soldiers from a a faster ship overtaking his. "Yes," Athanasius answered quite truthfully. "He is just ahead of you, and if you hurry you shall overtake him." Soon the other ship was lost ahead of Athanasius.

As we have seen, Julian's reign did not last long. He was succeeded by Jovian, who was an admirer of Athanasius. Once again the bishop of Alexandria returned from exile, although he was soon called to Antioch to counsel the emperor. When he finally returned to Alexandria, it seemed that his long chain of exiles had come to an end.

But Jovian died in a few months and was succeeded by Valens, a staunch defender of Arianism. Fearing that the emperor would take measures against the orthodox in Alexandria if he remained in the city, Athanasius resolved to leave once again. It soon became evident, however, that Valens was not eager to tangle with the bishop who had bested both Constantius and Julian. Athanasius was thus able to return to Alexandria, where he remained until death claimed him in 373 CE.

Although Athanasius never saw the final victory in the cause to which he devoted his life, his writings clearly show that he was convinced that in the end Arianism would be defeated. As he approached old age, he saw emerge around himself a new generation of theologians devoted to the same cause. Most remarkable among these were the Great Cappadocians, to whom we now turn our attention.

20

The Great Cappadocians

Not for all, my friends, not for all is it to philosophize about God, since
the subject is neither that simple nor that lowly. Not for all, nor before
all, nor at all times, nor on all themes, but rather before some, at some
times and with some bounds.

GREGORY OF NAZIANZUS

The region of Cappadocia was in Eastern Anatolia, lands that now belong
to Turkey. There lived three church leaders known as the Great Cappadocians: Basil of Caesarea, the theologian known as "The Great"; his brother
Gregory of Nyssa, famous for his works on mystical contemplation; and their
friend Gregory of Nazianzus, a poet and orator, whose many hymns have
become traditional in the Greek-speaking church. But before turning our attention to them, justice requires that we deal with another person just as worthy,
although often forgotten by historians who tend to ignore the work of women.
This remarkable woman was Macrina, the sister of Basil and Gregory of Nyssa,
and someone who should certainly be counted among the Great Cappadocians.

MACRINA

The family in which Macrina, Basil, and Gregory were raised had deep Christian roots reaching back at least two generations. Their paternal grandparents
had spent seven years hiding in the forest during the Decian persecution. In
that exile, they were accompanied by several members of their household, including their two sons, Gregory and Basil. Gregory (who subsequently became
the uncle of our Cappadocians) was a bishop. His brother Basil, the father of
Macrina and her brothers, became a famous lawyer and teacher of rhetoric. His
wife was the daughter of a Christian martyr. Thus, the grandparents of our
Cappadocians, both on the maternal and paternal sides, had been Christians,
and one of their uncles a bishop.

Macrina was twelve years old when her parents decided to make arrangements for her marriage, as was then customary. They settled on a young relative

who was planning to become a lawyer, and Macrina acquiesced. Everything was ready when the groom died, quite unexpectedly. Thereafter, Macrina refused to accept any other suitor, and eventually vowed herself to celibacy and to a life of contemplation.

Some two or three years before Macrina's engagement, Basil had been born. He was a sickly child whose survival was in doubt for a time. The elder Basil, who had always wanted a son, gave this one the best education available, in the hope that he would continue in his father's footsteps as a lawyer and orator. Young Basil studied first at Caesarea, the main city in Cappadocia; then in Antioch and Constantinople; and finally in Athens. It was in the ancient Greek city that he met Gregory, who would eventually become bishop of Nazianzus, as well as Prince Julian, later dubbed "the Apostate."

After such studies, Basil returned to Caesarea, puffed up with his own wisdom. His studies, as well as his family's prestige, guaranteed him a place of importance in Caesarean society. Soon he was offered a position teaching rhetoric.

It was then that Macrina intervened. She bluntly told her brother that he had become vain, acting as if he were the best inhabitant of the city, and that he would do well in quoting fewer pagan authors and following more of the advice of Christian ones. Basil shrugged off his sister's comments, telling himself that, after all, she was rather unlearned.

Then tragic news arrived. Their brother Naucratius, who was living in retirement in the country, had died unexpectedly. Basil was shaken. He and Naucratius had been very close. In recent times their paths had diverged, for Naucratius had forsaken worldly pomp, while Basil had devoted himself wholeheartedly to them. The blow was such that Basil changed his life entirely. He resigned his teaching position and all other honors, and he asked Macrina to teach him the secrets of religious life. A short time earlier their father had died, and it was now Macrina who offered her bereaved family strength and consolation.

Macrina sought to console her family by leading their thoughts to the joys of religious life. Why not withdraw to their holdings in nearby Annesi, and live there in renunciation and contemplation? True happiness is not found in the glories of the world, but in the service of God. That service is best rendered when one breaks all ties with the world. Dress and food must be as simple as possible, and one should devote oneself entirely to prayer. Thus, what Macrina proposed was a life similar to that of the ascetics of the desert.

Macrina, her mother, and several other women withdrew to Annesi while Basil, following the desires of his sister, left for Egypt in order to learn more about the monastic life. Since Basil eventually became the great teacher of monasticism in the Greek-speaking church, and since it was Macrina who awakened his interest in it, it could be said that she was the founder of Greek monasticism.

Macrina spent the rest of her life in monastic retreat in Annesi. Years later, shortly after Basil's death, their brother Gregory of Nyssa visited her. Her fame was such that she was known simply as "the Teacher." Gregory left a record of that visit in his dialogue with her, *On the Soul and the Resurrection*, the main arguments and assertions of which may well have been Macrina's. He opens that work by informing us that "Basil, great among the saints, had departed from this life and gone to God, and all the churches mourned his death. But his sister the Teacher still lived and therefore I visited her." Gregory, however, was not easily consoled on finding his sister suffering from a severe asthma attack on her deathbed. "The sight of the Teacher," he wrote, "reawakened my pain, for she too was about to die."

She let him shed his tears and express his pain, and then consoled him, reminding him of the hope of resurrection. Finally, she died in great peace. Gregory closed her eyes, led the funeral service, and went out to continue the work that his sister and brother had entrusted to him.

BASIL THE GREAT

Years earlier, Basil had returned from Egypt, Palestine, and other lands where he had gone to study the monastic life, and had settled near Annesi. He and his friend Gregory of Nazianzus founded a community for men similar to the one Macrina had created for women. He believed that community life was essential, for one who lives alone has no one to serve, and the core of monastic life is service to others. He himself made it a point to undertake the most disagreeable tasks in the community. He also wrote rules to be followed in the monastic life. Since all the legislation in the Greek church regarding monastic life is based on the teachings of Basil, he is usually regarded as the father of Eastern monasticism.

But Basil had lived as a monk for little more than six years when he was ordained a presbyter against his will. He soon had conflicts with the bishop of Caesarea, and rather than creating greater difficulties decided to return to his monastic community. He remained there until Valens became emperor. Since the new emperor was Arian, the bishop of Caesarea decided to set aside his differences with Basil and call on the holy monk to assist him in the struggle against Arianism.

When Basil arrived at Caesarea, conditions were very difficult. Bad weather had destroyed the crops, and the rich were hoarding food. Basil preached against such practices, and sold all his properties in order to feed the poor. If

Basil, seen here in an eleventh-century fresco, became the leader of the Nicene party.

all would take only what they needed, he said, and give the rest to others, there would be neither rich nor poor:

> If one who takes the clothing off another is called a thief, why give any other name to one who can clothe the naked and refuses to do so? The bread that you withhold belongs to the poor; the cape that you hide in your chest belongs to the naked; the shoes rotting in your house belong to those who must go unshod.[27]

Basil joined these claims with action. On the outskirts of Caesarea, he created what his friend Gregory of Nazianzus would call "a new city." There the hungry were fed, the ill cared for, and the unemployed given employment. For the support of this new city—which was called Basiliad—Basil collected resources from the well-to-do, telling them that this was their opportunity to invest their resources in a treasure in heaven, beyond the reach of thieves and moths.

When the bishop of Caesarea died, the election of his successor became a focal point for the struggle between the orthodox and the Arian. Basil's prestige was such that he seemed to be the most likely candidate. The Arian party found only one point at which Basil was vulnerable: his questionable health. The orthodox responded that they were electing a bishop, not a gladiator. Eventually, Basil was elected.

The new bishop of Caesarea knew that his election would lead to conflicts with the emperor, who was Arian. Soon Valens announced his intention to visit Caesarea. The Nicene party knew from bitter experience in other cities that Valens used such visits in order to strengthen Arianism.

Many imperial officers arrived at Caesarea in order to prepare Valens's visit. The emperor had ordered them to subdue the new bishop through a combination of promises and threats. But Basil was not easy to subdue. Finally, in a heated encounter, the praetorian prefect lost his patience and threatened Basil with confiscating his goods, and with exile, torture, and even death. Basil responded, "All that I have that you can confiscate are these rags and a few books. Nor can you exile me, for wherever you send me, I shall be God's guest. As to torture you should know that my body is already dead in Christ. And death would be a great boon to me, leading me sooner to God." Taken aback, the prefect said that no one had ever spoken to him thus. Basil answered, "Perhaps that is because you have never met a true bishop."

Finally, the emperor arrived. When he took a bountiful offering to the altar, thus showing his favor to the city, no one went forth to receive it. The emperor had to wait for the bishop, who finally accepted his offering, making it very clear that it was he who was favoring the emperor.

After these events, Basil was able to devote his time to his tasks as a bishop. He was particularly interested in organizing and spreading the monastic life, and in advancing the Nicene cause. Through a vast correspondence and several theological treaties, he made a significant contribution to the reaffirmation of trinitarian doctrine and the definitive rejection of Arianism. But, like Athanasius, he was unable to see that final victory, for he died a few months before the Council of Constantinople confirmed the Nicene doctrine in 381.

GREGORY OF NYSSA

Basil's younger brother, Gregory of Nyssa, was of a completely different temperament. While Basil was tempestuous, inflexible, and even arrogant, Gregory preferred silence, solitude, and anonymity. He had no desire to become the champion of any cause. Although he had a solid education, it was not of the quality of Basil's. For a time, he wanted to be a lawyer and a rhetorician, but he did not embrace these goals with great enthusiasm.

Whereas Basil and his friend Gregory of Nazianzus fervently took up monastic life, Gregory of Nyssa married a young woman with whom he seems to have been very happy. Years later, after his wife died and he too had taken the monastic life, he wrote a treatise titled *On Virginity,* which featured arguments characteristic of him. According to him, he who does not marry does not have to suffer the pain of seeing his wife going through childbirth nor the greater pain of losing her. For him, the monastic life was a way to avoid the pains and struggles of active life. He became known for his mystical life and for the writings in which he described that life and gave directives for those wishing to follow it.

But the struggles of the time were too urgent and too bitter to pass by a person such as Gregory. His brother Basil forced him to become bishop of Nyssa, which was little more than a village. Valens and the Arians continued using all their power against the orthodox party. Such strife was too much for Gregory, who went into hiding. But in spite of this, after the death of both Valens and Basil, Gregory became one of the main leaders of the Nicene party. As such he was received by the Council of Constantinople in 381.

Although he was a quiet and humble person, his writings show the inner fire of his spirit. And his careful explications of Nicene doctrine contributed to its triumph in Constantinople.

After that great council, Emperor Theodosius took him as one of his main advisors in theological matters, and Gregory was thus forced to travel throughout the empire, and even to Arabia and Mesopotamia. Although there was great value in this work, Gregory always saw it as a hindrance, keeping him away from the life of contemplation.

Finally, being assured that the Nicene cause was firmly established, Gregory returned to the monastic life, hoping that the world would leave him alone. In this he was so successful that the date and circumstances of his death are not known.

GREGORY OF NAZIANZUS

The other great Cappadocian theologian was Gregory of Nazianzus, whom Basil had met when they were fellow students. Gregory was the son of the bishop of Nazianzus, also called Gregory, and his wife Nona—for at that time bishops were often married. The elder Gregory had been an Arian, but Nona had brought him to orthodoxy. As in the case of Basil, Gregory's family was very devout, to such a point that many of them have subsequently received the title of "saint"—Gregory himself, his parents Gregory the elder and Nona, his brother Caesarius, his sister Gorgonia, and his cousin Amphilochius.

Gregory spent most of his youth in study. After some time in Caesarea, he went to Athens, where he remained some fourteen years, and where he met both

In a ninth-century manuscript of the sermons of Gregory of Nazianzus, he and others are depicted fleeing from the Arians.

Basil and Prince Julian. He was thirty years old when he returned to his home country and joined Basil in the monastic life. Meanwhile, his brother Caesarius had become a famous physician in Constantinople, where he served both Constantius and Julian without letting himself be moved by the Arianism of the former or the paganism of the latter.

Back in Nazianzus, Gregory was ordained a presbyter, although he did not wish it. He fled to Basil's monastic community, where he stayed for some time, but eventually returned to his pastoral duties in Nazianzus. At that point he delivered a famous sermon on the duties of a pastor. He began: "I have been overcome, and I confess my defeat," and declared that his reluctance to serve as a pastor was due in part to his interest in the contemplative life, and in part to his fear that he would be unequal to the task, for "it is difficult to practice obedience; but it is even more difficult to practice leadership."

From then on, Gregory became more involved in the controversies of the time. When Basil made him bishop of a small hamlet, Gregory felt that his friend had imposed on him, and their friendship was sorely strained. It was a sad time for Gregory, marked by the deaths of Caesarius, Gorgonia, Gregory the Elder, and Nona. Alone and bereaved, Gregory left the church that had been entrusted to him, in order to have time for quiet meditation. He was in his retreat when the news arrived of the death of Basil, with whom he had never been reconciled.

Gregory was in shock. But eventually he felt compelled to take a leading role in the struggle against Arianism, in which Basil had sought his help with

This bas-relief at the base of an obelisk in Constantinople—now Istanbul—shows Emperor Theodosius holding a wreath for the victor in the games. At his sides stand his heirs, Honorius and Arcadius.

relatively little success. In 379 CE, he appeared in Constantinople. At that time Arianism enjoyed the total support of the state, and in the entire city there was not a single orthodox church. Gregory began celebrating orthodox services in the home of a relative. When he ventured in the streets, the mob pelted him. Repeatedly, Arian monks broke into his service and profaned the altar. But he stood firm, strengthening his small congregation with hymns he composed, some of which have become classics of Greek hymnody.

Finally, the tide changed. Late in the year 380, Emperor Theodosius made his triumphal entry into Constantinople. He was an orthodox general who soon expelled all Arians from the high positions that they had used to further their cause. A few days later, the new emperor asked Gregory to visit the cathedral of Hagia Sophia with him. It was an overcast day, broken only by a ray of sunlight that hit on Gregory. Some of those present believed this to be a sign from heaven and began shouting, "Gregory, bishop, Gregory, bishop!" Since this fit his policy, Theodosius gave his approval. Gregory, who did not wish to become a bishop, was finally convinced. The obscure monk from Nazianzus was now patriarch of Constantinople.

A few months later, the emperor called a council that gathered in Constantinople and over which Gregory presided, as bishop of the city. This task was not to his liking, for he said that the bishops behaved like a swarm of hornets.

When some of his opponents pointed out that he was already bishop of another place, and that therefore he could not be bishop of Constantinople, Gregory promptly resigned the position he had never sought. Nectarius, the civil governor of Constantinople, was elected bishop in his stead, and occupied that position with relative distinction until he was succeeded by John Chrysostom, to whom we shall return.

As for Gregory, he returned to his homeland, where he spent his time composing hymns and devoting himself to his pastoral duties. When he heard that Theodosius planned to call another council and asked him to preside over it, he flatly refused. He lived away from all civil and ecclesiastical pomp until he died when he was some sixty years old.

The Council of Constantinople reaffirmed the doctrine of Nicea regarding the divinity of the Son, and added that the same ought to be said about the Holy Spirit. Thus, it was this council that definitively proclaimed the doctrine of the Trinity. Its decisions, and the theology reflected in them, were in large measure the result of the work of the Cappadocian Fathers. In this regard, their main contribution was in clarifying the difference between *ousia* ("essence") and *hypostasis*—a word that literally means "substance" but which the Cappadocians defined as the translation of the Latin *persona*. Thus, the Latin West and the Greek East came to agree on a common formula: one essence—or *ousia*—in three persons—or *hypostases*.

It is difficult for us today to understand the vehemence with which people in the fourth century debated such matters, and we tend therefore to discount them as the heated lucubrations of overzealous theologians. But we should not dismiss the matter so easily. That the debate profoundly touched people's lives is indicated in Gregory of Nazianzus's comment, that one could not even get one's shoes repaired without getting into a discussion regarding whether the Son was *homoousios* or *homoiousios* to the Father. At the other end of the social spectrum, for fifty years after the Council of Nicea most emperors embraced the Arian cause and staunchly opposed the Nicene. What was at stake was much more than idle speculation. Ultimately, the issue was, can God truly be present in a carpenter executed by the empire as a criminal, or is God more like the emperor on his throne? One should not wonder, then, that so many emperors preferred the Arian view. Eventually, a compromise was reached whereby the Carpenter was declared to be truly divine, but was now represented much more often as the exalted Pantokrator—the exalted emperor sitting on a throne and ruling the entire world—than as a carpenter.

21

Ambrose of Milan

God ordered all things to be produced so that there would be common
food for all, and so that the earth would be the common inheritance of
all. Thus, nature has produced a common right, but greed has made it
the right of a few.

AMBROSE OF MILAN

The fourth century, so rich in great Christian leaders, produced none whose
career was more dramatic than that of Ambrose of Milan.

AN UNEXPECTED ELECTION

It was in the year 373 that the death of the bishop of Milan threatened the peace
of that important city. Auxentius, the dead bishop, had been appointed by an
Arian emperor who had exiled the previous bishop. Now that the bishop's seat
was vacant, the election of a successor could easily turn into a riot, for both
Arians and orthodox were determined that one of their number would be the
next bishop of Milan.

In order to avoid a possible riot, Ambrose, the governor of the city, decided
to attend the election. His efficient and fair rule had made him popular, and
he had reason to hope for higher office in the service of the empire. But first he
must deal wisely with the potentially explosive situation in Milan. Therefore, he
appeared at the church, where tempers were beginning to flare, and addressed
the crowd. He was trained in the best of rhetoric, and as he spoke calm was
restored.

Suddenly, from the midst of the crowd, a child cried, "Ambrose, bishop."
This caught the fancy of the crowd, and the insistent cry was heard: "Ambrose,
bishop; Ambrose! Ambrose!"

Such an election was not part of Ambrose's plans for his career, and therefore
he had recourse to various devices in order to dissuade the people. When that
strategy failed, he repeatedly attempted to escape from the city, but was unsuccessful. Finally, when it became clear that the emperor was gratified with the

Ambrose fled in an attempt to avoid being made bishop of Milan.

election of his governor, and would be very displeased if Ambrose insisted on his refusal, he agreed to be made bishop of Milan. Since he was only a catechumen, and therefore was not even baptized, it was necessary to perform that rite, and then to raise him through the various levels of ministerial orders. All this was done in eight days, and he was consecrated bishop of Milan on December 1, 373.

Although Ambrose had not sought the office of bishop, he felt that it was a responsibility to which he must devote his best efforts. To help him in his administrative chores, he called on his brother, Uranius Satyrus, who was governor of another province. (Their sister Marcellina was also a devout Christian; she led a semi-monastic life in Rome.) Ambrose also undertook the study of theology with the help of Simplicianus, a priest who had taught him the basics of Christian doctrine, and whom Ambrose now called to be his tutor in theology. His keen mind aided him in this undertaking. People commented on his ability to read without muttering the words, which was rare at the time. Soon he was one of the best theologians in the Western church, although his work consisted mostly of sermons and other expositions of scripture, and in making available to the Latin-speaking West the theology of the Greek-speaking East. For this he was exceptionally well qualified, for he had been well versed in the Greek language and an admirer of its literature long before he began studying theology. Along these lines, he contributed to the development of trinitarian theology in the West by popularizing the work of the Cappadocians—particularly Basil's treatise *On the Holy Ghost*. He also emphasized the centrality of the incarnation, which he discussed in pastoral rather than in speculative terms: "He became a small babe so that you could be fully grown, perfect human beings; he was wrapped in swaddling clothes so that you might be freed from the bonds of death; he came to the manger to bring you to the altar; he was on earth so that you might be in heaven."[28] Ambrose was also very much involved in the formation of the clergy that would work with him, and to this end wrote *Duties of the Clergy*, a treatise that was influential in shaping the understanding of Christian ministry long after Ambrose's death.

Shortly after Ambrose's consecration, the nearby region was ravaged by a band of Goths who had crossed the border with imperial permission but had then rebelled. Refugees flocked to Milan, and there was news of many captives for whom the Goths were demanding ransom. Ambrose's response was to order that funds be raised for the refugees and for ransoming the captives by melting some of the golden vessels and other ornaments the church possessed. This created a storm of criticism, particularly among the Arians, who were eager to find him at fault and accused him of sacrilege. Ambrose answered:

> It is better to preserve for the Lord souls rather than gold. He who sent the apostles without gold also gathered the churches without gold. The church has gold, not to store it, but to give it up, to use it for those who

The ruins of the ancient baptistery, under the cathedral of Milan, where Ambrose probably baptized Augustine.

are in need. . . . It is better to keep the living vessels, than the golden ones.²⁹

Likewise, in writing about the duties of pastors Ambrose told them that true strength consists in supporting the weak against the strong, and that they should invite to their feasts not the rich who could reward them but rather the poor who could not.

Among the many who went to listen to him preach, there was a young teacher of rhetoric who had taken a long and tortuous spiritual pilgrimage, and who was so entranced by the bishop's words that he returned to his mother's faith, which he had abandoned many years before. Eventually, the young man, whose name was Augustine, was baptized by Ambrose, who does not seem to have been aware of the exceptional gifts of his convert, who one day would become the most influential theologian of the West since the apostle Paul.

THE BISHOP AND THE THRONE

The Western portion of the empire was ruled by Gratian and his half-brother Valentinian II. Since the latter was still a child, Gratian was also regent in his domain. Gratian was then killed in a rebellion, and the usurper, Maximus, threatened to take Valentinian's territories. The boy emperor was defenseless, and therefore, in a desperate move, he and his mother Justina sent Ambrose as an ambassador to Maximus. The bishop was successful, and the expected invasion was averted.

In spite of this, relations between Ambrose and Justina were not good. The empress was Arian and insisted on having a basilica where Arian worship could be celebrated. On that point, Ambrose was adamant. He would not have a holy place desecrated by heretical worship, nor would he allow the empress's power to be used to further the Arian cause in Milan. Thus followed a long series of memorable confrontations. At one point, Ambrose and his followers were besieged by imperial troops surrounding a disputed church. While those outside threatened the besieged with the clash of arms, Ambrose rallied his flock by singing hymns and psalms. Finally, Justina sought an honorable retreat by demanding that, if not the church, at least its sacred vases be delivered to the emperor. After all, had not Ambrose done as much for a mob of refugees and captives? Again the bishop refused, and answered:

I can take nothing from the temple of God, nor can I surrender what I received, not to surrender, but to keep. In so doing I am helping the emperor, for it is not right for me to surrender these things, nor for him to take them.³⁰

It was in the midst of such confrontations with imperial power that Ambrose ordered that an ancient burial ground under one of the churches be dug up. There two skeletons were found, probably dating back long before the Christian Era. But someone remembered hearing as a child about two martyrs, Protasius and Gervasius, and immediately the remains were given those names. Soon rumors were circulating about the miracles performed by the "sacred relics," and the people rallied even more closely around their bishop.

Eventually, with the apparent connivance of Justina, Maximus invaded Valentinian's territories. Part of the arrangement was probably that Maximus would rid the empress of the annoying bishop of Milan. But the Eastern emperor, Theodosius, intervened and defeated Maximus. When Valentinian was killed, probably by some who sought his power, Theodosius intervened once again, and thus became sole ruler of the empire.

Theodosius was a Nicene Christian—it was under his auspices that the Council of Constantinople gathered in 381 CE and reaffirmed the decisions of Nicea. But in spite of this, and now for other reasons, he clashed with Ambrose on two separate occasions. Both times he had to yield before the firmness of the bishop, although in all fairness one must say that the first time justice was on Theodosius's side.

The first clash took place when some overzealous Christians in the small town of Callinicum burned a synagogue. The emperor decided that they be punished, and that they also must rebuild the synagogue. Ambrose protested that a Christian emperor should not force Christians to build a Jewish synagogue. After several stormy interviews, the emperor yielded, the synagogue was not rebuilt, and the arsonists were not punished. This was a sad precedent, for it meant that in an empire calling itself Christian, those of a different faith would not be protected by the law.

The other conflict was different, and in it justice was on Ambrose's side. There had been a riot at Thessalonica, and the commandant of the city had been killed by the rioters. Ambrose, who knew the irascible temperament of the emperor, went to him and counseled moderation. Theodosius seemed convinced, but later his wrath was rekindled, and he decided to make an example of the disorderly city. He sent word that the riot had been forgiven, and then, by his order, the army trapped those who had gathered at the circus or arena to celebrate the imperial pardon, and slaughtered some seven thousand of them.

Upon learning of these events, Ambrose resolved to demand clear signs of repentance from the emperor. Although the details are not clear, one of Ambrose's biographers tells us that the next time Theodosius went to church in Milan, the bishop met him at the door, raised his hand before him, and said, "Stop! A man such as you, stained with sin, whose hands are bathed in the blood of injustice, is unworthy, until he repents, to enter this holy place, and to partake of communion."[31]

At that point, some courtiers threatened violence. But the emperor acknowledged the truth in Ambrose's words, and gave public signs of repentance. He also ordered that from that time on, if he ever decreed that someone be put to death, the execution be delayed for thirty days.

After that clash, relations between Theodosius and Ambrose were increasingly cordial. Finally, when the emperor knew that death was near, he called to his side the only man who had dared to censure him in public.

By then Ambrose's fame was such that Fritigil, the Germanic queen of the Marcomanni, had asked him to write for her a brief introduction to the Christian faith. After reading it, Fritigil resolved to visit the wise man in Milan. But on her way she learned that Ambrose had died—on April 4, 397, Easter Sunday.

22

John Chrysostom

How think you that you obey Christ's commandments, when you spend
your time collecting interest, piling up loans, buying slaves like livestock,
and merging business with business? . . . And that is not all. Upon all
this you heap injustice, taking possession of lands and houses, and
multiplying poverty and hunger.

JOHN CHRYSOSTOM

One hundred years after his death, John of Constantinople was given the
name by which subsequent generations would know him: Chrysostom—
"the golden-mouthed." That was a title he well deserved, for in a century that
gave the church such great preachers as Ambrose of Milan and Gregory of
Nazianzus, John of Constantinople stood above all the rest, a giant above the
giants of his time.

But for John Chrysostom the pulpit was not simply a podium from which
to deliver brilliant pieces of oratory. It was rather the verbal expression of his
entire life, his battlefield against the powers of evil, an unavoidable calling that
eventually led to exile and to death itself.

A VOICE FROM THE WILDERNESS

He was above all a monk. Before becoming a monk he was a lawyer, trained in
his native Antioch by the famous pagan orator Libanius. It is said that when
someone asked the old teacher who should succeed him, he responded: "John,
but the Christians have laid claim on him."

Anthusa, John's mother, was a fervent Christian who loved her child with a
deep and possessive love. She was quite happy when her lawyer son, then twenty
years of age, asked that his name be added to the list of those training for baptism. Three years later, when he completed the time of preparation that was
then required, he was baptized by Bishop Meletius of Antioch. Once again his
mother rejoiced. But when he told her that he intended to withdraw from the

His contemporaries described Chrysostom as short, with a wide and furrowed forehead, and deep-set eyes.

city and follow the monastic way she was adamant, and made him promise that he would never leave her as long as she lived. It may well be that some of these experiences are reflected in his later sermons on topics such as marriage and the family.

John's way of solving the tension between his monastic vocation and his mother's possessiveness was simply to turn their home into a monastery. There he lived with three like-minded friends until, after his mother's death, he joined the monks in the Syrian mountains. He then spent four years learning the discipline of monastic life, and two more rigorously practicing it in complete solitude. Later, he himself would admit that such a life was not the best kind of training for the shepherd's task. "Many who have gone from monastic retreat to the active life of the priest or the bishop are completely unable to face the difficulties of their new situation."[32]

In any case, when John returned to Antioch after his six years of monastic withdrawal, he was ordained deacon, and then a presbyter shortly thereafter. As such, he began preaching, and soon his fame was widespread throughout the Greek-speaking church.

In 397, the bishopric of Constantinople became vacant, and the emperor ordered that John be taken to the capital city to occupy that prestigious position. But his popularity in Antioch was such that the authorities feared a riot, and therefore kept the imperial decree secret. They simply invited the famous preacher to visit a small chapel on the outskirts of the city, and when he was there they ordered him into a carriage, in which he was forcefully taken to the capital. There he was consecrated bishop early in 398.

Constantinople was a rich town, and one given to luxury and intrigue. The great Emperor Theodosius was dead, and the two sons who had succeeded him, Honorius and Arcadius, were indolent and inept. Arcadius, who supposedly ruled the East from the capital city of Constantinople, was in fact ruled by a certain Eutropius, the palace chamberlain, who used his power to satisfy his own ambition and that of his cronies. Eudoxia, the empress, felt humiliated by the chamberlain's power, although in fact it was Eutropius who had arranged her marriage to Arcadius. The intrigues that enveloped everything in that city had also had a hand in John's elevation to the patriarchal throne, for Patriarch Theophilus of Alexandria had been actively campaigning in favor of a fellow Alexandrine, and John had been given the post through Eutropius's intervention.

The new bishop of Constantinople was not completely aware of all of this. From what we know of his character, it is probable that, had he been aware, he would have acted just as he did. The former monk was still a monk, and could not tolerate the manner in which the rich inhabitants of Constantinople sought to wed the gospel with their own luxuries and comforts.

His first task was to reform the life of the clergy. Some priests who claimed to be celibate had in their homes what they called "spiritual sisters," and this was an occasion of scandal for many. Other clergymen had become rich, and lived with as much luxury as the potentates of the great city. The finances of the church were in a shambles, and the care of the flock was largely unattended. John took all of those issues head on. He ordered that the "spiritual sisters" move out of the priests' homes, and that the latter lead an austere life. Church finances were placed under a system of detailed scrutiny. The luxury items that adorned the bishop's palace were sold in order to feed the hungry; and the clergy received orders to open the churches at such times as were convenient not only for the wealthy, but also for those who had to work. Obviously, all these measures gained him both the respect of many and the hatred of others.

But such a reformation could not be limited to the clergy. It was necessary that the laity also be called to lead lives more in accordance with gospel mandates. Therefore, the golden-mouthed preacher thundered from the pulpit:

The gold bit on your horse, the gold circlet on the wrist of your slave, the gilding on your shoes, mean that you are robbing the orphan and starving the widow. When you have passed away, each passer-by who looks upon your great mansion will say, "How many tears did it take to build that mansion; how many orphans were stripped; how many widows wronged; how many laborers deprived of their honest wages?" Even death itself will not deliver you from your accusers.[33]

RETURN TO THE WILDERNESS

The powerful could not abide that voice that challenged them from the pulpit of Hagia Sophia, the church of Saint Sophia—the largest in Christendom. Eutropius, who had made him bishop, expected special favors and concessions. But John was convinced that Eutropius was simply another Christian in need of having the gospel clearly and unambiguously preached. The result was that Eutropius repented, not of his sin, but rather of his error in having brought the meddlesome preacher from Antioch.

Finally a storm broke out over the right of asylum. Some fled from the tyranny of Eutropius and took refuge in Hagia Sophia. The chamberlain simply sent soldiers after them. But the bishop proved unbending, and did not allow the soldiers into the sanctuary. Eutropius protested before the emperor, but Chrysostom took his cause to the pulpit and for once Arcadius did not bow before the requests of his favorite. After that, the influence of the chamberlain waned, and many attributed this to his clash with the bishop.

Shortly thereafter, a series of political circumstances precipitated Eutropius's downfall. The people were jubilant, and soon there were mobs demanding vengeance against the one who had oppressed and exploited them. The chamberlain's only recourse was to run to Hagia Sophia and embrace the altar. When the mob came after him, Chrysostom stood in its way, and invoked the same right of asylum that he had invoked earlier against Eutropius. Thus, Chrysostom was led to defend the life of his erstwhile enemy, first against the people, then against the army, and finally against the emperor himself. The crisis came to an end when the former chamberlain, not trusting what seemed the weak defenses of the church, fled from his refuge, and was captured and killed by some of the many he had wronged.

But Chrysostom had made many more enemies among the powerful. Eudoxia, the emperor's wife, resented the bishop's growing power. Besides, what was being said from the pulpit of Hagia Sophia was not to her liking—it fitted her too well. When Chrysostom described the pomp and the folly of the powerful, she felt the people's eyes staring at her. It was necessary to silence that voice from the wilderness that had brought such wild ravings to the elegant Hagia Sophia. With that in mind, the empress made special grants to the church. The bishop thanked her. And continued preaching.

Then the empress had more direct methods of recourse. When Chrysostom had to leave the city in order to attend to some matters in Ephesus, Eudoxia joined Theophilus of Alexandria in plotting against the meddling preacher. Upon his return, Chrysostom found himself the object of a long list of ridiculous charges brought before a small gathering of bishops convened by Theophilus. He paid no attention to them, but simply went about his preaching and his management of the church. Theophilus and his partisans found him guilty, and asked Arcadius to banish him. Prodded by Eudoxia, the weak emperor agreed to that request, and ordered Chrysostom to leave the city.

The situation was tense. The people were indignant. The bishops and other clergy from neighboring towns gathered at the capital, and pledged their support to the bishop. All that he had to do was to give the order, and they would convene as a synod that would condemn Theophilus and his followers. This could be coupled with a popular uprising that would shake the very foundations of the empire. One word from the eloquent bishop, and the entire conspiracy against him would crumble. Arcadius and Eudoxia were aware of this and made ready for war. But Chrysostom was a lover of peace, and therefore made ready for exile. Three days after receiving the imperial edict, he bid farewell to his friends and followers and surrendered to the authorities.

The populace was not ready to give up without a struggle. The streets were boiling with rumors of mutiny. Arcadius, Eudoxia, and the army did not dare show themselves in public. That night, in what was taken as a sign of divine wrath, the earth quaked. A few days later, in response to the fearful and urgent pleas of Eudoxia, Chrysostom returned to the city and to his pulpit, where he was received with shouts of acclamation.

Although the bishop had returned, the causes of the conflict were not resolved. After a few months of additional intrigue, confrontation, and humiliation, Chrysostom received a new order of exile. Once again he refused to heed the advice of his friends, and quietly surrendered to the soldiers who came after him, rather than stirring up a riot that would cause the people further suffering.

But the riot was inevitable. Mobs flocked to Hagia Sophia and the surrounding area. The army was ordered to quell the disturbance, and in the ensuing struggle the cathedral and several public buildings nearby caught fire and were destroyed. The cause of the fire was never discovered. But during the inquest many of Chrysostom's supporters were tortured, and his best-known friends were banished—although to areas distant from him.

Meanwhile, the preacher with the golden mouth was lead to exile in the remote village of Cucusus. Since he lacked a pulpit there, he took up the pen, and the world was moved. Innocent, the bishop of Rome, took up Chrysostom's cause, and many followed his example. The emperor's actions were criticized from every quarter; Theophilus of Alexandria had no support but that of a few timid souls who dared not oppose imperial power. As the controversy became widespread, the little town of Cucusus seemed to become the center of the world. Empress Eudoxia had died, and some hoped that Emperor Arcadius would reverse his policy. But he did not, and a number of bishops supported the imperial policy by agreeing to the banishment of the famous preacher. But in the West, Pope Innocent and many others were convinced that a great injustice was being committed, and appealed to Arcadius's Western counterpart, Honorius. The latter sent a Latin delegation to the East armed with a letter to Arcadius indicating that they should be granted full respect, and that a synod should be convened in Salonika to discuss the charges brought against John. If the Latin delegation was then convinced that the cause against John was just, Honorius would break communion with him. But if, on the contrary, the deposition of John was found to be unjust, Arcadius should restore communion with him—and by implication return him to his see in Constantinople. This threatened not only Arcadius's policies, but also that of the important bishops who had come to power by supporting them—including the patriarchs of Alexandria and of Antioch. Therefore the Latin delegation received what in its report to Innocent it called a "Babylonian treatment"—it is not clear whether on orders from the court in Constantinople, or from John's ecclesiastical rivals, who needed the embassy to fail. The members of the delegation were imprisoned, tortured, offered a bribe of three-thousand gold pieces—which they refused—and sent home in a leaky boat that soon began to sink. In their report to Innocent, they said that the soldiers told them that the captain of the ship had been given orders to see that they did not make it home. But eventually, after changing ships, they did return to Italy. Meanwhile, a number of John's most influential supporters simply disappeared, being secretly exiled to various remote areas and fortresses.

Finally, even Cucusus seemed too near a place of exile, and Chrysostom was ordered removed even farther, to a cold and unknown hamlet on the shores of the Black Sea. The soldiers guarding him, being aware that their charge did not have the good will of the crown, paid no attention to his failing health, and during the journey drove him to exertions well beyond his strength. Soon the banished bishop became seriously ill. When he perceived that death was near, he asked to be taken to a small church by the roadside. There he took communion, bid farewell to those around him, and preached his briefest but most eloquent sermon: "In all things, glory to God. Amen."

In Constantinople and elsewhere, people felt that a great injustice and even a sacrilege had been committed. John's staunchest supporters refused the authority of the new bishop and of those in communion with him—particularly the patriarchs of Alexandria and of Antioch—and the schism ended only when, thirty-one years after his death, John's memory was restored, and his body brought back to Constantinople amid great pomp and celebration.

As we compare the lives of Chrysostom and Ambrose, we see an indication of what would be the future course of the churches in the East compared with the West. Ambrose faced the most powerful emperor of his time, and won. Chrysostom, on the other hand, was deposed and banished by the weak Arcadius. From then on, the Latin-speaking church of the West would become increasingly powerful, as it filled the vacuum left by the crumbling empire. In the Greek-speaking East, on the other hand, the empire would last another thousand years. Sometimes weak, and sometimes strong, this Eastern offshoot of the old Roman Empire—the Byzantine Empire—would zealously guard its prerogatives over the church. Theodosius was not the last Western emperor to be humbled by a Latin-speaking bishop. And John Chrysostom was not the last Greek-speaking bishop banished by an Eastern emperor.

23

Jerome

I frankly confess that I get carried away with indignation. I cannot listen
to such sacrilege with patience.

JEROME

N one of the great personalities of the fourth century is more intriguing than
Jerome. He is outstanding, not for his sanctity, like Anthony, nor for his
keen theological insight, like Athanasius, nor for his firmness before the authorities, like Ambrose, nor even for his preaching, like Chrysostom, but rather for
his titanic and endless struggle with the world and with himself. Although he is
known as "Saint Jerome," he was not one of those saints who are granted the joy
of God's peace in this life. His holiness was not humble, peaceful, and sweet,
but rather proud, stormy, and even bitter. He always strove to be more than
human, and therefore had little patience for those who appeared indolent, or
who dared criticize him. Those who suffered his sharp attacks were not only the
heretics of his time, as well as the ignorant and the hypocritical, but also John
Chrysostom, Ambrose of Milan, Basil of Caesarea, and Augustine of Hippo.
Those who disagreed with him were "two-legged asses." But in spite of this attitude—and perhaps to a large measure because of it—Jerome earned a place
among the great Christian figures of the fourth century. Even so, throughout
the history of Christian art he has been depicted as a sour ascetic, often contemplating a skull.

He was born around 348 CE, in an obscure corner of northern Italy. He was
younger than many of the great figures of the fourth century. But it has been
aptly said that Jerome was born an old man, and therefore he soon considered
himself older than his contemporaries. More surprisingly, they came to regard
him as an imposing and ancient institution.

He was an ardent admirer of classical learning, and felt that this love for an
essentially pagan tradition was sinful. His inner turmoil on this score peaked
when, during a serious illness, he dreamed that he was at the final judgment and
was asked: "Who are you?" "I am a Christian," Jerome answered. But the judge

retorted: "You lie. You are a Ciceronian." After that experience, Jerome resolved to devote himself fully to the study of scripture and of Christian literature. But he never ceased reading and imitating the style of the classical pagan authors.

He was also obsessed with sex. Upon retiring to the monastic life, he hoped to be rid of that burden. But even there he was followed by his dreams and by the memories of dancers in Rome. He sought to suppress such thoughts by punishing his body, and by an exaggeratedly austere life. He was unkempt, and even came to affirm that, having been washed by Christ, there was no need to ever wash again. And yet that did not suffice. In order to fill his mind with something that would take the place of the pleasures of Rome, he decided to study Hebrew. That language, with its strange alphabet and grammar, seemed barbaric to him. But he told himself that, since the Old Testament was written in it, it must be divine.

Eventually Jerome conceded that he was not made for the life of a hermit and returned to civilization probably before three years were up. In Antioch he was ordained a presbyter. He was at Constantinople before and during the Council of 381. He returned to Rome, where Bishop Damasus, a good judge of human nature, made him his private secretary and encouraged him to engage in further study and writing. It was also Damasus who first suggested to him the project that would eventually occupy most of his time, and would become his greatest monument: a new translation of scripture into Latin. Although Jerome did some work on this project while in Rome, he pursued it most actively later in his life.

Meanwhile, he found a great deal of help amidst a group of rich and devout women who lived in the palace of a widow, Albina. Besides Albina, the most prominent members of the group included her widowed daughter Marcella, Ambrose's sister Marcellina, and the scholarly Paula, who—with her daughter Eustochium—would play a leading role in the rest of Jerome's life. The bishop's secretary visited that house regularly, for in its women he found devoted disciples, some of whom became accomplished students of Greek and Hebrew. It was in that company that Jerome felt most free to discuss the scholarly questions that occupied his mind—particularly questions having to do with the text of the Bible.

It is significant that Jerome, who never had any close male friends, and who was obsessed with sex, found such solace in this group of women. Perhaps he felt at ease because they did not dare compete with him. In any case, it was they who came to know the sensitivity that he desperately sought to hide from the rest of the world.

However, Jerome was not a tactful man, and he soon made enemies among the leaders of the church in Rome. When Damasus died, late in 384, Jerome lost his staunchest defender. Siricius, the new bishop, had little use for Jerome's

Jerome, who had no male friends and who was obsessed with sex, did however find solace in the friendship of Paula and her daughter Eustochium.

Seventeenth-century Spanish painter Juan Martín Cabezalero presents Jerome as an inspired interpreter and translator of scripture.

scholarship. When one of Paula's daughters died, Jerome's enemies, whom he had criticized for their comfortable life, claimed that her death was due to the rigors recommended by Jerome. Finally, he decided to leave Rome and go to the Holy Land—or, as he said, "from Babylon to Jerusalem."

Paula and Eustochium followed him, taking a different route, on a joint pilgrimage to Jerusalem. From there, Jerome went on to Egypt, where he visited the Alexandrine scholars as well as the desert dwellings of the monks. By 386 he had returned to Palestine, where both he and Paula had decided to settle and devote themselves to the monastic way of life. Their goal, however, was not the extreme asceticism of the desert monks, but rather a life of moderate austerity, spent mostly in study. Since Paula was rich, and Jerome was not lacking in means, they founded two monastic houses in Bethlehem, one for women under Paula's leadership, and another for men under Jerome's supervision. He then furthered his education in Hebrew, in order to translate the Bible, while he taught Latin to the children of the neighborhood, and Greek and Hebrew to Paula's nuns.

Above all, however, he devoted himself to the work that would be his great literary monument: the translation of the Bible into Latin. By then there were other translations, but these had been done on the basis of the Septuagint—the ancient translation of the Hebrew text into Greek. What Jerome then undertook was a direct translation from Hebrew. After many years of work, interrupted by a voluminous correspondence and by the calamities that shook the Roman world, Jerome completed this enormous task.

Jerome's version, commonly known as the *Vulgate,* eventually became the standard Bible of the entire Latin-speaking church. Particularly successful was his translation of the Hebrew Psalms into excellent Latin poetry. These Psalms were given wider use and circulation when used in Gregorian chant, to the point that they were still in use in the liturgy long after the Vulgate had been supplanted by more modern translations.

But at first the Vulgate was not as well received as Jerome had wished. The new translation, naturally enough, altered the favorite texts of some people, and many demanded to know who had given Jerome authority to tamper with scripture. Furthermore, many believed the legend that the Septuagint had been the work of independent translators who, upon comparing their work, found themselves in total agreement. That legend had long been used to argue that the Septuagint was just as inspired as the Hebrew text. Therefore, when Jerome published a version that disagreed with the Septuagint, there were many who felt that he lacked respect for the inspired Word of God.

Such criticism did not come only from ignorant believers, but also from some very learned Christians. From North Africa, Augustine of Hippo (the great theologian to whom we shall devote the next chapter) wrote:

> I pray you not to devote your energies to translating the sacred books to Latin, unless you do as you did earlier in your translation of the book of Job, that is, adding notes that show clearly where your version differs from the Septuagint, whose authority has no equal. . . . Besides, I cannot

imagine how, after so long, someone can find in the Hebrew manuscripts anything which so many translators did not see before, especially since they knew Hebrew so well.[34]

At first Jerome did not answer Augustine's letter—nor a second one. Augustine insisted on the matter, writing again and blaming Jerome for scandalizing the faithful. As an example of the evils caused by Jerome's translation, he refers to the manner in which Jerome translated the name of the plant that provided shade for the prophet Jonah. The traditional version—based on Greek—called it a *gourd*. Jerome translated it as *ivy*. Augustine reports:

> A certain bishop, our brother, ordered that your translation be employed in the church he leads. People were surprised that you translated a passage in Jonah in a very different way than they were used to singing [in church] for generations. There was a riot, particularly since the Greeks claimed that the passage was wrong. . . . So you see the consequences of supporting your translation on manuscripts that cannot be verified by known languages [that is, Greek or Latin, rather than Hebrew].[35]

When Jerome finally responded to Augustine's letters, he implied that Augustine was simply a young man seeking to make a name for himself by criticizing his elders. While at first appearing to praise Augustine's learning, Jerome subtly indicated that he was doing Augustine a favor by not pursuing the controversy, for a debate between the two of them would be an unequal contest. In the course of the letter, he proceeded to crush Augustine's arguments, eventually telling him that "you don't even understand what you are asking about,"[36] and calling his opponents—apparently including Augustine among them—*cucurbitarians*, or "gourdists."

Although most of Jerome's controversies ended in wounds that never healed, the outcome was different in this particular case. Years later, Jerome felt the need to refute the doctrine of the Pelagians—which will be discussed in the next chapter—and to that end he had recourse to Augustine's works. His next letter to the wise bishop of North Africa expressed an admiration that he reserved for very few.

At first glance, Jerome appeared to be an extremely insensitive person whose only concern was his own prestige. But in truth he was very different than he appeared, and his rigid facade hid a sensitive spirit. No one knew this as well as did Paula and Eustochium. But Paula died in 404, and Jerome felt alone and desolate. His grief was all the greater, for he was convinced that it was not only his end that approached, but that of an era. A few years later, on August 24, 410,

A few months after the death of Eustochium, Jerome took his last Communion and died.

Rome was taken and sacked by the Goths under Alaric's command. The news shook the world. Jerome heard of it in Bethlehem, and wrote to Eustochium:

> Who could have believed that Rome, built by the conquest of the world, would fall? That the mother of many nations has turned to her grave? . . . My eyes are dim by my advanced age . . . and with the light that I have at night I can no longer read Hebrew books, which are difficult even during the day for the smallness of their letters.[37]

Jerome survived for almost ten more years. They were years of loneliness, pain, and controversy. Finally, a few months after the death of Eustochium, who had become as a daughter to him, the tired scholar went to his rest.

24

Augustine of Hippo

> When I thought of devoting myself entirely to you, my God . . . it was
> I that wished to do it, and I that wished not to do it. It was I. And since
> I neither completely wished, nor completely refused, I fought against
> myself and tore myself to pieces.
>
> AUGUSTINE OF HIPPO

"Take up and read. Take up and read. Take up and read." These words, probably shouted by a playing child, floated over the fence of the garden in Milan and struck the ears of a dejected professor of rhetoric who sat under a fig tree and cried, "How long, Lord, how long? Will it be tomorrow and always tomorrow? Why does my uncleanliness not end this very moment?" The child's words seemed to him words from heaven. Shortly before, elsewhere in the garden, he had put down a manuscript he was reading. Now he returned to the spot, took up the manuscript, and read the words of Paul: "Not in reveling and drunkenness, not in debauchery and licentiousness, not in quarreling and jealousy. But put on the Lord Jesus Christ, and make no provision for the flesh, to gratify its desires." Responding to these words, Augustine—for that was the name of the rhetorician—made a decision that he had been postponing for a long time: he devoted himself to the service of God. Soon he abandoned his career as a professor, and set out on a course that would eventually make him one of the most influential figures in the entire history of Christianity.

In order to understand the scope and meaning of the experience in the garden of Milan, one must follow Augustine's career to that point.

A TORTUOUS PATH TO FAITH

Augustine was born in 354 CE, in the little town of Tagaste, in North Africa. His father was a minor Roman official who followed the traditional pagan religion. But his mother, Monica, was a fervent Christian, whose constant prayer for her husband's conversion was eventually answered. Augustine does not seem to have been very close to his father, whom he hardly mentions in his writings.

But Monica did play an important role—sometimes even an overwhelming one—in the life of her only son.

Both parents were aware of their child's exceptional gifts, and therefore sought for him the best education possible. To that end they sent him to the nearby town of Madaura until their resources ran out, when Augustine had to abandon his studies and return to Tagaste. There, according to his own report, he "wandered with my companions through the public squares of Babylon and wallowed in their mud as if it were cinnamon and precious ointments."[38] With these friends, he boasted of his sexual adventures—real or imagined—and joined in capers that he would one day rue as the sign of his own sinfulness.

Eventually, thanks to the support of a certain Romanianus, he was able to travel to Carthage to pursue his studies. Augustine was some seventeen years old when he arrived at the great city that for centuries had been the political, economic, and cultural center of Latin-speaking Africa. Although he did not neglect his studies, he also set out to enjoy the many pleasures that the city offered. Soon he had a concubine who bore him a child. He named the boy Adeodatus, meaning "given by God"—or "by a god."

As all young men of his time preparing for careers as lawyers or public functionaries, Augustine was a student of rhetoric. The purpose of this discipline was to learn to speak and to write elegantly and convincingly. Truth was not at issue. That was left for professors of philosophy. But among the many ancient works that students of rhetoric had to read were those of Cicero, the famous orator of classical Rome. And Cicero, besides being a master of language, was a philosopher. Thus, it was reading Cicero that Augustine came to the conviction that proper speech and style were not sufficient. One must also seek truth.

That search led the young student to Manichaeism. This religion was Persian in origin, having been founded by a certain Mani in the third century. According to Mani, the human predicament is the presence in each of us of two principles. One, which he calls *light*, is spiritual. The other, *darkness*, is matter. Throughout the universe there are these two principles, both eternal: light and darkness. Somehow—Manichaeans explained it through a series of myths—the two have mingled, and the present human condition is the result of that admixture. Salvation then consists in separating the two elements, and in preparing our spirit for its return to the realm of pure light, in which it will be absorbed. Since any new mingling of the principles is evil, true believers must avoid procreation. According to Mani, this doctrine had been revealed in various fashions to a long series of prophets, including Buddha, Zoroaster, Jesus, and Mani himself.

In Augustine's time, Manichaeism had spread throughout the Mediterranean basin. Its main appeal was its claim to be eminently rational. Like Gnosticism

No other theologian in the Western church has been as influential as Augustine.

earlier, Manichaeism based many of its teachings on astronomical observation. Besides, part of its propaganda consisted of ridiculing the teachings of Christianity, particularly the Bible, whose naïveté and primitive language it mocked.

Manichaeism seemed to address Augustine's difficulties with Christianity, which centered on two issues. The first was that, from the point of view of rhetoric, the Bible was a series of inelegant writings—some even barbaric—in which the rules of good style were seldom followed, and where one found crude episodes of violence, rape, deceit, and the like. The second was the question of the origin of evil. Monica had taught him that there was only one God. But Augustine saw evil both around and in himself, and had to ask about the source of such evil. If God was supreme and pure goodness, evil could not be a divine creation. And if, on the other hand, all things were created by the divine, God could not be as good and wise as Monica and the church claimed. Manichaeism offered answers to these two points. The Bible—particularly the Old Testament—was not in fact the Word of the eternal principle of light. Nor was evil a creation of that principle, but of its opposite, the principle of darkness.

For these reasons, Augustine became a Manichee. But there were always doubts, and he spent nine years as a "hearer," without seeking to join the ranks of the "perfect." When, at Manichaean gatherings, he vented some of his doubts, he was told that his questions were very profound, and that there was a great Manichaean teacher, a certain Faustus, who could answer them. When the much-anticipated Faustus finally arrived, he turned out to be no better than the other Manichaean teachers. Disappointed, Augustine decided to carry on his quest in different directions. By then, after spending some time back in Tagaste, Augustine had returned to Carthage as a teacher; but his students in Carthage were an unruly lot, and a career in Rome seemed more promising. But that did not turn out as he had hoped, for his students in the capital city, although better behaved, were slow in paying for his services. He then moved on to Milan, where there was a need for a teacher of rhetoric.

In Milan, Simplicianus—the same person on whom Ambrose had called to be his tutor in theology—introduced him to the writings of the Neoplatonists. Apparently, he did this in the hope that Neoplatonism would open the way for Augustine to return to his mother's faith—a hope that eventually proved to be well-founded. As a result of his readings, Augustine became a Neoplatonist. Neoplatonism, very popular at the time, was a philosophy with religious overtones. Through a combination of study, discipline, and mystical contemplation, it sought to reach the ineffable One, the source of all being. The goal of the Neoplatonist was the ecstasy that one experienced when lost in such contemplation. Unlike Manichaean dualism, Neoplatonism affirmed that there was only one principle, and that all reality was derived from it through a series of emanations—much like the concentric circles that appear on the surface of the water when hit by a pebble. Those realities that are closer to the One are superior, and those that are more removed from it are inferior. Evil then does not originate from a different source, but consists simply in moving away from the One. Moral evil consists in looking away from the One, and turning one's gaze to the inferior realms of multiplicity. This seemed to answer Augustine's vexing questions as to the origin of evil. From this perspective, one could assert that a single being, of infinite goodness, was the source of all things, and at the same time acknowledge the presence of evil in creation. Evil, though real, is not a "thing," but rather a direction away from the goodness of the One. Also, Neoplatonism helped Augustine to view both God and the soul in incorporeal terms—which Manichaeism had not done for him.

There remained another doubt: How can one claim that the Bible, with its crude language and its stories of violence and falsehood, is the Word of God? Providing an answer to this question was the role of Ambrose in Augustine's life. Monica, who was with the latter in Milan, insisted that he should hear Ambrose's sermons. As a professor of rhetoric, Augustine agreed to attend the services led by the most famous speaker in Milan. His initial purpose was not to hear what Ambrose had to say, but to see how he said it. However, as time went by he found that he was listening to the bishop less as a professional, and more as a seeker. Ambrose interpreted many of the passages that had created difficulties for Augustine allegorically. Since allegorical interpretation was perfectly acceptable according to the canons of rhetoric, Augustine could find no fault in this. And it certainly made scripture appear less crude, and therefore more acceptable.

By then, Augustine's major intellectual difficulties with Christianity had been solved. But there were other difficulties of a different sort. He could not be a lukewarm Christian. Were he to accept his mother's faith, he would do it wholeheartedly, and he would devote his entire life to it. Furthermore, due to the prevalence of the monastic ideal, and to his own Neoplatonic perspective, Augustine was convinced that, were he to become a Christian, he must give up his career in rhetoric, as well as all his ambitions and every physical pleasure. It was precisely this last requirement that seemed most difficult. As he later wrote, at that time he used to pray, "Give me chastity and continence; but not too soon."

At this point a battle raged within himself. It was the struggle between willing and not willing. He had already decided to become a Christian. But not too soon. He could no longer hide behind intellectual difficulties. Furthermore, from all quarters came news that put him to shame. In Rome the famous philosopher Marius Victorinus, who had translated the works of the Neoplatonists into Latin, had presented himself at church and made a public profession of his faith. Then came news of two high civil servants who, upon reading Athanasius's *Life of Saint Anthony*, had abandoned career and honor in order to follow the hermit's example. It was then, unable to tolerate the company of his friends—or himself—that Augustine fled to the garden, where his conversion took place.

After his conversion, Augustine took the necessary steps to embark on a new life. He requested baptism, which he and his son Adeodatus received from Ambrose. He resigned from his teaching post. And then, with Monica—who had dogged him most of his life, hoping both that he would become a Christian and that he would marry well and advance in his career, Adeodatus and a group of friends, he set out for North Africa, where he planned to spend the rest of his days in monastic retreat. Monica had persuaded Augustine to dismiss his concubine of many years—whose name he does not even mention. The return to Africa was interrupted at the seaport of Ostia, where Monica became ill and died. Augustine was so overcome with grief that it was necessary for him and his companions to remain in Rome for several months.

When they finally reached Tagaste, Augustine sold most of the property that he had inherited, gave some of the money to the poor, and with the rest he settled at Cassiciacum with Adeodatus—who died shortly thereafter—and a few friends whose goal was mystical contemplation and philosophical inquiry. Their objective was not the extreme rigorism of the monks of the desert, but rather an orderly life, with no unnecessary comforts, and devoted entirely to prayer, study, and meditation.

It was at Cassiciacum that Augustine wrote his first Christian works. They still bore a Neoplatonic stamp, although he was slowly coming to appreciate the difference between Christian teaching and some elements in Neoplatonism. He hoped that the few dialogues he wrote at Cassiciacum would be only the beginning of many years devoted to the philosophical life.

MINISTER AND THEOLOGIAN OF
THE WESTERN CHURCH

But this was not to be, for his fame was spreading, and there were some who had other plans for his life. In 391, he visited the town of Hippo in order to talk to a friend whom he wished to invite to join the small community at Cassiciacum. While at Hippo he attended church, and Bishop Valerius, who saw him in the congregation, preached about how God always sends shepherds for the flock, and then asked the congregation to pray for God's guidance in case there was among them someone sent to be their minister. The congregation responded exactly as the bishop had expected, and Augustine, much against his will, was ordained to serve with Valerius in Hippo. Four years later, he was made bishop jointly with Valerius, who feared that another church would steal his catch. Since at that time it was forbidden for a bishop to leave his church for another, Augustine's consecration to serve as a bishop jointly with Valerius guaranteed that he would spend the rest of his days at Hippo. (Although apparently neither Augustine nor Valerius was aware of it, there was also a rule against having more than one bishop in a single church.) Valerius died a short time later, and left Augustine bishop of Hippo.

As a minister and as a bishop, Augustine sought to retain as much as possible of the lifestyle of Cassiciacum. But now his energies had to be directed less toward contemplation, and more toward his pastoral responsibilities. It was with those responsibilities in view that he wrote most of the works that made him the most influential theologian in the entire Latin-speaking church since New Testament times.

Many of Augustine's first writings were attempts to refute the Manichaeans. Since he had helped lead some of his friends to that religion, he now felt a particular responsibility to refute the teachings that he had supported earlier. use those were the main points at issue, most of these early works dealt with the authority of scripture, the origin of evil, and free will.

The question of the freedom of the will was of particular importance in the polemics against the Manichaeans. They held that everything was predetermined, and that human beings had no freedom. Against such views, Augustine became the champion of the freedom of the will. According to him, human freedom is such that it is its own cause. When we act freely, we are not moved by something either outside or inside of us, as by a necessity, but rather by our own will. A decision is free inasmuch as it is not the product of nature, but of the will itself. Naturally, this does not mean that circumstances do not influence our decisions. What it does mean is that only that which we decide out of our own will, and not out of circumstance or out of an inner necessity, is properly called "free."

This was important in order to be able to solve the difficulties having to do with the origin of evil. Augustine insisted that there is only one God, whose goodness is infinite. How, then, can one explain the existence of evil? By simply affirming that the will is created by God, and is therefore good, but that the will is capable of making its own decisions. It is good for the will to be free, even though this means that such a free will can produce evil. The origin of evil, then, is to be found in the bad decisions made by both human and angelic wills—those of the demons, who are fallen angels. Thus, Augustine was able to affirm both the reality of evil and the creation of all things by a good God.

This, however, does not mean that evil is ever a *thing*. Evil is not a substance, as the Manichaeans implied when speaking of it as the principle of darkness. It is a decision, a direction, a negation of good.

Another movement that Augustine had to refute was Donatism. The reader will remember that this movement centered in North Africa, where Augustine was now a pastor. Therefore, throughout his career Augustine had to deal with the various issues raised by the Donatists. One of these was the question of whether ordinations conferred by unworthy bishops were valid. To this, Augustine responded that the validity of any rite of the church does not depend on the moral virtue of the person administering it. If it were so, Christians would live in constant doubt as to the validity of their baptism. No matter how unworthy the celebrant, the rite is still valid, although obviously the celebrant is at fault. On this point, most of the Western church through the centuries has agreed with Augustine, whose views on the church and on the validity of sacraments became normative in the West.

It was also in trying to deal with the Donatist issue that Augustine developed his Just War Theory. As has already been said, some Donatists—the circumcellions—had turned to violence. The entire movement had social and economic roots of which Augustine was probably not aware. But he was certain that the depredations of the circumcellions must cease. He thus came to the conclusion that a war may be just, but that in order for it to be so certain conditions must be fulfilled. The first is that the purpose of the war must be just—a war is never just when its purpose is to satisfy territorial ambition, or the mere exercise of power. The second condition is that a just war must be waged by properly instituted authority. This seemed necessary in order to prevent personal vendettas. In later centuries, however, this principle would be applied by the powerful in order to claim that they had the right to make war on the powerless, but that the powerless could not make war on them. Actually, this could already be seen in the case of the circumcellions, who according to Augustine did not have the right to wage war on the state, whereas the state had the right to wage war on them. Finally, the third rule—and the most important one to Augustine—is that, even in the midst of the violence that is a necessary part of war, the motive of love must be central.

It was, however, against the Pelagians that Augustine wrote his most important theological works. Pelagius was a monk from Britain who had become famous for his piety and austerity. He saw the Christian life as a constant effort through which one's sins could be overcome and salvation attained. Pelagius agreed with Augustine that God has made us free, and that the source of evil is in the will. As he saw matters, this meant that human beings always have the ability to overcome their sin. Otherwise, sin would be excusable.

But Augustine remembered when he both willed and did not will to become a Christian. This meant that human will was not as simple as Pelagius characterized it. There are times when the will is powerless against the hold sin has on it. The will is not always its own master, for it is clear that the will to will does not always have its way, nor can the will do that which its fallen condition does not permit it even to imagine.

According to Augustine, the power of sin is such that it takes hold of our will, and as long as we are under its sway we cannot move our will to be rid of it. The most we can accomplish is to struggle between willing and not willing, which does little more than show the powerlessness of our will against itself. The sinner can will nothing but sin. Within that condition, there certainly are good and bad choices; but even the best choices still fall within the category of sin.

This does not mean, however, that freedom has disappeared. The sinner is still free to choose among various alternatives. But all of these are sin, and the one alternative that is not open is to cease sinning. In Augustine's words, before the fall we were free both to sin and not to sin. But between the fall and redemption the only freedom left to us is the freedom to sin. When we are redeemed, the grace of God works in us, leading our will from the miserable state in which it found itself to a new state in which freedom is restored, so that we are now free both to sin and not to sin. Finally, in the heavenly home we shall still be free, but only free not to sin. Again, this does not mean that all freedom is destroyed. On the contrary, in heaven we shall continue to have free choices. But none of them will be sin. At that point, our minds will be so overwhelmed by the goodness of God that sin will be as unimaginable as not sinning is now.

Back to the moment of conversion, how can we make the decision to accept grace? According to Augustine, only by the power of grace itself, for before that moment we are not free not to sin, and therefore we are not free to decide to accept grace. The initiative in conversion is not human, but divine. Furthermore, grace is irresistible, and God gives it to those who have been predestined to it.

In contrast, Pelagius claimed that each of us comes to the world with complete freedom to sin, or not to sin. There is no such thing as original sin, nor a corruption of human nature that forces us to sin. Children have no sin until they, out of their own free will, decide to sin.

The controversy lasted several years, and eventually Pelagianism was rejected. It simply did not take into account the terrible hold of sin on human will, nor the corporate nature of sin, which is manifest even in infants before they have opportunity to sin for themselves. Augustine's views, however, did not gain wide acceptance. He was accused of being an innovator. In southern

France, where opposition to Augustine was strongest, Vincent of Lerins argued that one should believe only what has been held "always, everywhere, and by all"—criteria that Augustine's critics claimed his doctrines did not meet. Many contested Augustine's view that the beginning of faith is in God's action rather than in a human decision. These opponents of Augustine's doctrine of predestination have been called, somewhat inexactly, "Semi-Pelagians."(They could also be called "Semi-Augustinians.") Through a process that took almost a century, Augustine was reinterpreted, so that theologians came to call themselves "Augustinian" while rejecting his views on irresistible grace and predestination. In 529, the Synod of Orange upheld Augustine's doctrine of the primacy of grace in the process of salvation, but left aside the more radical consequences of that doctrine. It was thus that subsequent generations—with notable exceptions— interpreted the teachings of the great bishop of Hippo.

Two of Augustine's writings are particularly significant. The first is his *Confessions*, a spiritual autobiography, addressed in prayer to God, which tells how God led him to faith through a long and painful pilgrimage. It is unique in its genre in all of ancient literature, and even to this day it witnesses to Augustine's profound psychological and intellectual insight.

The other work worthy of special mention is *The City of God*. The immediate motive impelling Augustine to write it was the Fall of Rome in 410 CE. Since there were many who still clung to ancient paganism at that time, some charged that Rome had fallen because it had abandoned its ancient gods and turned to Christianity. It was to respond to such allegations that Augustine wrote *The City of God*, a vast encyclopedic history in which he claims that there are two cities—that is, two social orders—each built on a foundation of love. The city of God is built on the love of God. The earthly city is built on the love of self. In human history, these two cities always appear mingled with each other. But in spite of this there is between the two of them an irreconcilable opposition, a fight to the death. In the end, only the city of God will remain. Meanwhile, human history is filled with kingdoms and nations, all built on love of self, which are no more than passing expressions of the earthly city. All of these kingdoms and nations, no matter how powerful, will wither and pass away, until the end of time, when only the city of God will remain standing. In the case of Rome in particular, God allowed it and its empire to flourish so that they served as a means for spreading the gospel. Now that this purpose has been fulfilled, God has let Rome follow the destiny of all human kingdoms, which is simply punishment for their sins. But even so, Christians do well to learn even the history of the human city, for—as Augustine says in another treatise—"all we may learn about the past helps us understand the Scriptures."[39]

A woodcut in a 1489 edition of Augustine's City of God *depicts him writing the book, and also shows the contrast between the two cities. Note the devils in the earthly city mocking the angels in the heavenly.*

Augustine was the last of the great leaders of the Imperial church in the West. When he died, the Vandals were at the gates of Hippo, announcing a new age. Therefore, Augustine's work was, in a way, the last glimmer of a dying age.

And yet, his work was not forgotten among the ruins of a crumbling civilization. On the contrary, through his writings he became the teacher of the new age. Throughout the Middle Ages, no theologian was quoted more often than he was, and he thus became one of the great doctors of the Roman Catholic Church. But he was also the favorite theologian of the great Protestant Reformers of the sixteenth century. Thus, Augustine, variously interpreted, has become the most influential theologian in the entire Western church, both Protestant and Catholic.

25

Beyond the Borders of the Empire

Abgarus, King of Edessa, greetings to Jesus, the good Savior who has appeared in Jerusalem: I have heard of you and the many cures that you effect with no help of medicines or herbs. . . . I have also heard that the Jews conspire against you and seek to do you harm. Please know that, although small, my city is noble, and suffices for the two of us.

ABGARUS, KING OF EDESSA
(PURPORTEDLY IN A LETTER TO JESUS)

Up until this point our attention has centered on the history of Christianity within the borders of the Roman Empire. There is ample reason for this, for Christianity was born within that empire, and most of today's Christians—Catholic, Protestant, and Eastern Orthodox—trace their heritage to the early development of the church within those borders. However, it is important to remember that this is not the whole story, for while Christianity was developing within the Roman Empire it was also taking root in lands beyond the reach of Roman rule. Among the Germanic "barbarians" of the north, Christianity gained a foothold long before the barbarians themselves broke into the Roman Empire. But the most impressive expansion was toward the east, and there are Christians in the twenty-first century who trace their origins to those early churches beyond the Eastern borders of the empire. In the eastern reaches of the Roman Empire, and beyond toward the east, Syriac was the language most commonly used for trade and international communication, and it provided the channel for the expansion of Christianity. This language was closely akin to the Aramaic spoken in Palestine and by Jews in the Eastern Diaspora. Long before the advent of Christianity, most Jews had ceased speaking Hebrew, and many could not even understand the reading of scripture in the synagogue. Thus, the practice arose of translating the sacred text into Aramaic, at first orally, and then in written form—in documents known as *Targums*. This practice, which paralleled the rise of Christianity, provided early Aramaic-speaking Christians with ready-made versions of at least part of the Hebrew scripture, much as the

Septuagint provided Greek-speaking Christians with a similar instrument. At some point around the second century, a Syriac translation of both the Old and New Testaments appeared, and came to be known as the Peshitta—(*peshitta* means "simple"), which thus reminds us of *Vulgate*, which has a similar meaning. At least part of the Old Testament was quite possibly the work of Jewish translators, but it is clear Christians—most likely Jewish Christians—played an important role in the process of translation. Tatian—the disciple of Justin Martyr who has already been mentioned as one of the early apologists—had attempted to harmonize the four Gospels into a single one, taking some elements from each, and leaving out others. This edited compilation of the four Gospels was known as the *Diatessaron*—meaning "according to the four"—and was the subject of much controversy among Syriac-speaking Christians, for some preferred it to the four canonical Gospels and others rejected it altogether—a controversy that was not quickly resolved, for the *Diatessaron* was still read in some Syriac churches as late as the seventh century.

From a very early date, Christianity spread eastward following the lines of Syriac trade and culture. Its most notable early success was in the city of Edessa—in the eastern reaches of what is now Turkey. This city became Christian, apparently during the rule of King Abgarus IX (179–216), long before the Roman Empire embraced Christianity, and thus seems to have been the earliest Christian state. Soon the legend arose that the conversion of Edessa had taken place much earlier, during Jesus's lifetime, and that King Abgarus V, who suffered from leprosy, had sent a letter to Jesus asking that he come and cure his leprosy. Instead of coming personally, Jesus sent Thaddeus, his disciple, with a letter to Abgarus. The latter was cured, embraced Christianity, and urged his subjects to do likewise. The legend probably dates from the time of Abgarus IX, for the words of Jesus quoted in the correspondence are taken from Tatian's *Diatessaron*. At any rate, by the fourth century the legend was well-established, for Eusebius of Caesarea mentions it and quotes from the letters in question. The letter supposedly written by Jesus soon became a popular talisman. Translated into Greek, Latin, Arabic, Copt, and Slavonic, people would carry it into battle, or during epidemics, as a talisman to save them from injury or disease. At any rate, long before the conversion of Constantine the kings of Edessa, and most of their subjects, were Christian.

In the nearby region of Adiabene there appears to have been a Christian community quite early in the second century. The royal family that ruled there had been converted to Judaism during the reign of Emperor Claudius (41–54), and most of the area had embraced that faith. Apparently a number of these Jews became Christians, for there is evidence of a Christian community there early in the second century.

After Edessa, the next state to embrace Christianity was Armenia. Armenia was a buffer state between Persia and the Roman Empire, and as such had a turbulent history often determined by the policies of those mighty powers constantly at war. Persia's policy was to engulf Armenia within its empire, while Rome preferred to have Armenia as an independent buffer state protecting its Eastern borders. As a result, Armenians tended to favor Rome in its rivalry with Persia. The founder of Christianity there was Gregory Lusavorich—the Illuminator, who had been converted in Caesarea of Cappadocia while he and his relative, King Tradt III, were in exile in the Roman Empire. When conditions changed and Tradt was restored to the throne, Gregory and other Christian converts also returned to Armenia. There, after many sufferings and difficulties, including imprisonment, he converted Tradt and baptized him on Epiphany, January 6, 303 CE. Thus, the rulers of this nation had become Christians before Constantine. Eventually, the rest of the population was converted, and the Bible was translated into Armenian. Furthermore, from Armenia Christianity expanded into the kingdom of Georgia, on the Caucasus River—according to historian Rufinus, as the result of a series of miracle healings brought about through the prayers of a female slave to the queen.

Ethiopian Christianity originated in Egypt, and has always had strong connections with the church in that land. In the fourth century the brothers Frumentius and Edessius, who would become the founders of Ethiopian Christianity, had been shipwrecked near the region, captured by the Ethiopians, and eventually set free. But Frumentius went to Alexandria, had Athanasius consecrate him as a bishop, and returned to the kingdom of Aksum, which would later become the core of Ethiopia. After nearly a century of missionary work, mostly by Christians from Egypt, the king was converted, and he was soon followed by the rest of the country. When the Council of Chalcedon condemned Dioscorus and other Alexandrines as heretics for holding that there is in Christ only a divine, and not a human, nature (see Chapter 28), Ethiopian Christians followed the example of most Egyptian Christians, and rejected the decisions of the council. Thus, they became Monophysite, maintaining that Christ had only one nature, and to this day remain the largest of the so-called Monophysite churches. Its most famous monuments are the churches cut into the rock in Lalibela.

Christianity had also crossed the border into Mesopotamia and Persia at a very early date, probably taken there by Syriac-speaking merchants and other travelers. At first, Christianity grew particularly in Mesopotamia, where Syriac was widely spoken, and where Christians could therefore make ample use of Syriac literature being produced in Antioch and Edessa. The Parthian dynasty that ruled the Persian Empire early in the Christian Era practiced a measure of religious tolerance, and Christianity seems to have grown rapidly, to the point that it was present in every province of the empire. Then, in 224, the Sassanid dynasty came to power in Persia, and most of its rulers began persecuting Christianity as a foreign religion. At the edges of the Roman Empire, there was an important theological school in the city of Nisibis, on the Euphrates River—a city that was under Roman rule until the Persians conquered it in 363. The earliest church building that archeologists have found was built in Dura-Europos, in modern-day Syria, and dates from the third century (see illustration in Chapter 12). In the fourth century, as the Roman Empire became Christian, official Persian opposition to Christianity increased, for now Christians were often seen as Roman sympathizers. At some point in the middle of the fourth century, in his *Demonstration on Persecution*, the great Persian Christian sage Aphrahat attested to the conditions in which the Persian church lived. There, after listing all those in the Old and New Testament who suffered for their faith, and arguing that Jesus is the paradigm which the ancients foreshadowed and Christians now follow, he speaks of the great persecution of "our Western brethren" under Diocletian, and the great change that had taken place there, as a sign of hope for the persecuted Persian church. Eventually, after the Councils of Ephesus (431) and Chalcedon (451), most Persian Christians rejected the decisions regarding the two natures of Christ of made by one or the other of these two councils, thus asserting their independence from Rome and gaining a measure of tolerance. They then joined the ranks of Eastern dissident churches. Some of these were dubbed "Monophysite," for they claimed that Christ had only one nature, his humanity having been absorbed into the divine nature. Others were called "Nestorian," for they followed the teachings of Nestorius, who emphasized the distinction between the divine and the human natures in Christ. These controversies will be explained more fully in Chapter 28.

Christianity was present in Arabia by the second century, for we know of contacts between Christians in Alexandria and their counterparts in Arabia, and of visits by Christian teachers, bishops, and other travelers from Alexandria to Arabia. As Christianity gained strength in neighboring regions, Arabia became a point of contact and conflict among three slightly different versions of Christianity, one coming from the Greek-speaking portion of the Roman Empire, and supported by that empire, another from Persia and a third from Ethiopia. To this mix was added the presence of at least one ancient Christian Gnostic sect—the Elkesaites. By the seventh century, this was the confused and confusing picture of Christianity that Muhammad came to know and to reject.

We have already seen that there is a tradition claiming that the apostle Thomas founded the church in India. It is difficult to ascertain exactly when Christianity arrived in India, because in some ancient texts Arabia is referred to as India. For example, we are told that around the year 180 Pantaenus, a famous Christian teacher in Alexandria, went to "India," and one of the participants at the Council of Nicea in 325 was "John the Persian, of all Persia and great India." At any rate, there are documents that clearly show that Christianity was firmly implanted in India by the beginning of the fifth century.

In the West, the most notable expansion beyond the borders of the empire took place in Ireland. There Christianity had gained a strong foothold before the downfall of the empire. Although the spread of Christianity to Ireland probably occurred via several channels, it is usually attributed to St. Patrick. As a young lad, Patrick had been captured in Great Britain by Irish raiders, and had served as a slave in Ireland. After an adventuresome escape and many other vicissitudes, he had a vision calling him to serve as a missionary to his former captors. Back in Ireland, he met with various perils, but eventually experienced great success, and the inhabitants were baptized in droves. Soon monasteries were founded, and the learning of antiquity became one of their major interests. Since Ireland was later bypassed by the wave of barbarian invasions that swept Europe, its monasteries were among the main sources from which the territories of the ancient Roman Empire regained much of the classical knowledge and literature that had been lost during the invasions.

Finally, mention must be made of Arian expansion among the Germanic tribes to the north of Constantinople. When Constantius was emperor and therefore Arianism enjoyed the support of the empire, a number of Arian missionaries crossed the Danube River and began a mission among the Goths. Foremost among these missionaries was Ulfila, whose name, often spelled *Wulfila,* means "little wolf." While there are many details in Ulfila's life on which the various sources do not agree, it appears that he was not a full-blooded Goth, for at least one of his parents seems to have been Cappadocian. He apparently grew up as a Christian, although the sources differ as to whether this was as an Arian or as a Nicene orthodox. He did not remain long as a missionary among the Goths, for after a few years he and some of his flock moved to Moesia (in what is now Bulgaria), apparently in order to escape persecution. His great contribution to Gothic Christianity was in developing an alphabet for the language of the Goths, and then translating the Bible into it.

At the same time, there were many Goths serving in the imperial guard in Constantinople, and many of these were converted to Christianity before returning to their country. Since most of this contact had taken place when Arianism was on the upswing, it was to Arianism that the Goths had been converted. Then more of their neighbors followed suit. The result was that, by the time of the great invasions, many of the invaders were Christians, although of the Arian persuasion. While the subtle differences between Arianism and

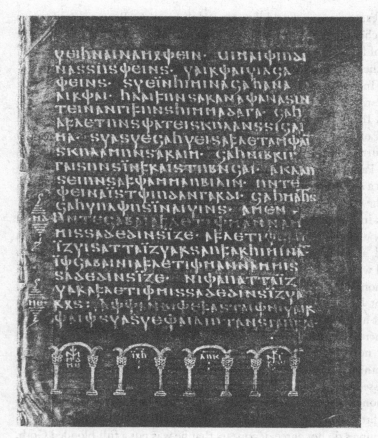

Fragments of the Gothic version of the Gospels by Ulfila still survive.

Nicene Christianity seem to have been of little interest to these Germanic peoples, Arianism did provide them with a church and a hierarchy that were independent of both Rome and Constantinople, and therefore fostered a sense of identity that they would take into the territories they conquered. Thus, it was as they became assimilated into Roman culture and traditions that most of them abandoned Arianism and converted to Nicene Christianity.

Thus, while it was within the confines of the Roman Empire that Christianity attained some of its most notable victories, by the time the Western Roman Empire came to an end there were already Christians as far east as India, as far south as Ethiopia, and as far north as Ireland. These churches, though often forgotten today, would continue to play an important role in the history of Christianity.

26

The End of an Era

The world goes to ruin. Yes! But in spite of it, and to our shame, our
sins still live and even prosper. The great city, the capital of the Roman
Empire, has been devoured by a great fire, and all over the earth Romans
wander in exile. Churches which once were revered are now but dust and
ashes.

JEROME

When Augustine died, the Vandals were laying siege to the city of Hippo.
Shortly thereafter, they were masters of the northern coast of Africa,
except Egypt. A few years earlier, in 410 CE, Rome had been taken and sacked
by Alaric and his Goths. Even earlier, at the battle of Adrianople in 378, an
emperor had been defeated and killed by the Goths, whose troops had reached
the very walls of Constantinople before turning to the West, where the empire
was more vulnerable. The ancient empire, or rather its Western half, was
crumbling. For centuries, Roman legions had been able to hold the Germanic
people behind their borders at the Rhine and the Danube. In Great Britain, a
wall separated the Romanized area from that which was still in control of the
barbarians. But now the floodgates were open. In a series of seemingly endless
waves, sometimes invited by Roman officials who sought their military support,
Germanic hordes crossed the frontiers of the empire, sacked towns and cities,
and finally settled in areas that had been part of the Roman Empire. There they
founded their own kingdoms, many of them supposedly subject to the Roman
Empire—which theoretically continued to exist until the deposition of the last
emperor in 476—but in truth independent. Their impact was such that their
memory is still present in the names of many of the regions in Europe where
each group settled: Germany, named after the Germanic invaders, France, England, Lombardy (named after the Franks, Angles, and Lombards) and many
others. The Western Roman Empire had come to an end, even though most of
its conquerors would eventually speak languages derived from the Latin of the

Alaric, king of the Goths, took and sacked Rome in 410—an event that produced consternation throughout the empire and a date that would long stand as a historical landmark.

empire, and even though various European leaders would claim to be the true successors of the ancient caesars for another fifteen centuries.

The imperial church, which Constantine had inaugurated, continued existing for another thousand years in the Byzantine Empire. Not so in the West, for it would be a long time before Western Europe could once again experience the political unity and relative peace that it had known under Roman rule. It would also take centuries to rebuild much that had been destroyed, not only in terms of roads, buildings, and aqueducts, but also in terms of literature, art, and knowledge of the physical world. In all of these fields, it was the church that provided continuity with the past. It became the guardian of civilization and of order. In many ways, the church filled the vacuum left by the demise of the empire. Centuries later, when the empire was resurrected in the West, this was accomplished through the action of the church, and it was the pope who crowned its emperor.

Meanwhile, there were new challenges to be met. Many of the invaders were pagan, and therefore the conquered felt the need to teach their faith to their victors. Slowly, through the unrecorded witness of thousands of Christians, the invaders accepted the Christian faith, and eventually from their stock came new generations of leaders of the church.

Furthermore, since many of the invaders had previously been converted to Arian Christianity, the issue of Arianism, which had been considered virtually dead for decades, once again came to the foreground in the West—where Arianism had never been a real issue. Eventually, yielding to the influence of those whom they had conquered, all of these Arian people would come to accept the Nicene faith. But this was not done without a great deal of struggle and suffering.

Out of all of this, a new civilization would arise, one which was heir to classical Greco-Roman antiquity as well as to Christianity and to Germanic traditions. This process took the thousand years known as the Middle Ages, to which we must now turn.

SUGGESTED READINGS

Douglas Burton-Christian. *The Word in the Desert: Scripture and the Quest for Holiness in Early Christian Monasticism*. New York: Oxford University Press, 1993.

Chrysostomus Baur. *John Chrysostom and His Time*. 2 vols. Westminster, Maryland: Newman, 1959, 1960.

Gerald Bonner. *St. Augustine of Hippo: Life and Controversies*. London: SCM, 1963.

Hans von Campenhausen. *The Fathers of the Greek Church*. New York: Pantheon, 1959.

Hans von Campenhausen. *Men Who Shaped the Western Church*. New York: Harper & Row, 1964.

Augustine Casiday and Frederick W. Norries, eds. *The Cambridge History of Christianity: Volume 2: Constantine to c. 600*. Cambridge, UK: Cambridge University Press, 2007.

Hermann Doerries. *Constantine the Great*. New York: Harper & Row, 1972.

F. Homes Dudden. *The Life and Times of St. Ambrose*. 2 vols. Oxford: Clarendon, 1935.

W. H. C. Frend. *The Donatist Church: A Movement of Protest in Roman North Africa*. Oxford: Clarendon, 1952.

Robert Payne. *The Fathers of the Western Church*. New York: Viking, 1951.

Robert Payne. *The Holy Fire: The Story of the Fathers of the Eastern Church*. London: Skeffington, 1958.

Marjorie Strachey. *Saints and Sinners of the Fourth Century*. London: William Kimber, 1958.

Laura Swan. *The Forgotten Desert Mothers: Sayings, Lives, and Stories of Early Christian Women*. New York: Paulist Press, 2001.

Helen Waddell. *The Desert Fathers*. Ann Arbor: University of Michigan Press, 1957.

PART III

MEDIEVAL CHRISTIANITY

Chronology

Western Emperors*	Eastern Emperors*	Popes**	Events
Honorius (395–423)	Theodosius II (408–450)	Innocent (401–417) Celestine (422–432)	Fall of Rome (410)
			†Augustine (430) Council of Ephesus (431)
	Marcian (450–457)	Leo (440–461)	Council of Chalcedon (451) Leo before Attila (453) Vandals sack Rome (455)
	Leo (457–474)		
Romulus Augustulus (475–476)	Zeno (474–491)	Felix II (483–492)	Odoacer ends western empire (476) Henoticon (482)
	Anastasius (491–518)		Clovis is baptized (496)
		Symmachus (498–514)	
	Justin (518–527)	Hormisdas (514–523) John (523–526)	†Boethius (524) †Theodoric (526)
	Justinian (527–565)		Belisarius takes Carthage (533)
		Vigilius (537–555)	II Council of Constantinople (553) Lombards invade Italy (568)
		Pelagius II (579–590)	Conversion of Recared (589)

*Only the names of the most important rulers and popes are included.
**The names of popes not now acknowledged as such by the Roman church are in italics.
†Dagger indicates date of death.

Western Emperors*	Eastern Emperors*	Popes**	Events
		Gregory (590–604)	Monte Cassino destroyed (589)
			Augustine in England (597)
	Heraclius (610–641)		Mohammed flees to Medina (622)
		Honorius (625–638)	Muhammad takes Mecca (630)
			†Muhammad (632)
			†Isidore of Seville (636)
			Synod of Whitby (663)
	Constantine IV (668–685)		III Council of Constantinople (680–681)
	Justinian II (685–695; 705–711)	Sergius (687–701)	Moors in Spain (711)
		Gregory II (715–731)	
	Leo III (717–741)	Gregory III (731–741)	Battle of Tours (732)
	Constantine V (741–775)	Zacharias (741–752)	
		Stephen II (752–757)	
		Adrian (772–795)	Charlemagne attacks Saxons (772)
	Leo IV (775–780)		
	Constantine VI (780–797)		II Council of Nicea (787)
		Leo III (795–816)	
	Irene (797–802)		
Charlemagne (800–814)	Nicephorus (802–811)		
Louis the Pious (814–840)			
			Norsemen take Paris (845)
		Nicholas I (858–867)	Photius partriarch (857)
			Cyril and Methodius in Moravia (863)
Charles the Bald (875–877)			
Charles the Fat (881–887)			
			King of Bulgaria becomes "czar" (917)
			Patriarchate of Bulgaria (927)

Western Emperors*	Eastern Emperors*	Popes**	Events
Henry (933–936)			
Otto (936–973)			
			Conversion of Olga of Russia (950)
Otto II (973–983)			
Otto III (983–1002)			
Henry II (1002–1024)			
Conrad II (1024–1039)			
Henry III (1039–1056)			
		Leo IX (1049–1054)	East-West schism (1054)
Henry IV (1056–1106)		Victor II (1055–1057)	
		Stephen IX (1057–1058)	
		Nicholas II (1058–1061)	Hugh abott of Cluny (1049–1109)
		Alexander II (1061–1073)	Battle of Hastings (1066)
			Casnossa (1077)
		Gregory VII (1073–1085)	Anselm archbishop of Canterbury (1093)
		Urban VI (1088–1099)	Council of Clermont (1095)
			†El Cid (1099)
			Crusaders take
		Paschal II (1099–1118)	Jerusalem (1099)
Henry V (1106–1125)			
		Calixtus II (1119–1124)	Concordat of Worms (1122)
			Abelard condemned (1141)
			Fall of Edessa (1144)
		Alexander III (1159–1181)	†Bernard of Clairvaux (1153)
			†Peter Lombard (1160)
			Fall of Jerusalem (1187)
		Innocent III (1198–1216)	
	LATIN EMPIRE (1204–1261)		
Otto IV (1208–1215)			Battle of Navas de Tolosa (1212)
			IV Lateran Council (1215)

Western Emperors*	Eastern Emperors*	Popes**	Events
Frederick II (1215–1250)			
			St. Dominic (1221) St. Francis (1226)
		Gregory IX (1227–1241)	
			Bonaventure and Thomas Aquinas (1274)
		Celestine V (1294) Boniface VIII (1294–1303)	End of crusader presence in Holy Land (1291)

Kings of France***	Kings of England***	Popes**	Events
Philip IV (1285–1314)	Edward I (1272–1307)		*Clerics laicos* (1296) *Unam sanctam* (1302) Pope's humiliation at Anagni (1303)
		Benedict XI (1303–1304) Clement V (1305–1314)	
	Edward II (1307–1327)		Beginning of "Babylonian Captivity" (1309) Suppression of Templars (1312)
Philip V (1316–1322)		John XXII (1316–1334)	
Charles IV (1322–1328)	Edward III (1327–1377)		Eckhart (1327)
Philip VI (1328–1350)		Benedict XII (1334–1342)	Hundred Years' War (1337–1453)
		Clement VI (1342–1352)	
John II (1350–1364)			Occam (1349)
		Innocent VI (1352–1362)	
Charles V (1364–1380)		Urban V (1362–1370)	
	Richard II (1377–1399)	Gregory XI (1370–1378)	End of "Babylonian Captivity" (1377)
		Urban VI (1378–1389)	Great Western Schism (1378)

***At this point, it is more important to follow the kings of France and England than the emperors.

Kings of France***	Kings of England***	Popes**	Events
Charles VI (1380–1422)		*Clement VII* (1378–1394)	Wycliffe condemned at Oxford (1380) †Ruysbroeck (1381) †Wycliffe (1384)
		Boniface IX (1389–1404) *Benedict XIII* (1394–1423)	
	Henry IV (1399–1413)		Huss rector at Prague (1402)
		Innocent VII (1404–1406) Gregory XII (1406–1415) *Alexander V* (1409–1410) *John XXIII* (1410–1415)	Council of Pisa (1409) Huss called to Rome (1410)
	Henry V (1413–1422)		Lollard rebellion (1413–1414) Council of Constance (1414–1418) †Huss (1415)
Charles VII (1422–1461)	Henry VI (1422–1461)	Martin V (1417–1431) Eugene IV (1431–1447)	First crusade ag. Hussites (1420) End of Great Schism (1423) †Joan of Arc (1431) Council of Basel (1431–1449) Council of Ferara-Florence (1438–1445)
		Nicholas V (1447–1455)	Fall of Constantinople (1453)
Louis XI (1461–1483)	Edward IV (1461–1483)		
		Sixtus IV (1471–1484)	†Hans Bohm (1476)
Charles VIII (1483–1498)			
		Alexander VI (1492–1503)	
	Henry VII (1485–1509)		Columbus in America (1492) †Savonarola (1498)
		Julius II (1503–1513)	
	Henry VIII (1509–1547)		
		Leo X (1513–1521)	

27

The New Order

If only to this end have the barbarians been sent within Roman
borders, . . . that the church of Christ might be filled with Huns and
Suevi, with Vandals and Burgundians, with diverse and innumerable
peoples of believers, then let God's mercy be praised . . . even if this has
taken place through our own destruction.

PAULUS OROSIUS

The Fall of the Western Roman Empire created a number of independent
kingdoms, each of which was of great significance for the subsequent history of the church in its territory. It also gave new functions and power to two
institutions that had begun to develop earlier: monasticism and the papacy.
Finally, new invasions, this time from the southeast, posed new challenges for
Christianity. Each of these developments merits separate consideration.

THE GERMANIC KINGDOMS

Although the "barbarians" appeared to the Romans as looters with their minds
set on destruction, most of them really aspired to settle within the borders of
the Roman Empire, and there to enjoy some of the benefits of a civilization that
until then they had only known from afar. Thus, after a period of wandering,
each of the major invading bodies settled in a portion of the empire—some
because that was the territory they fancied, and others simply because they had
been pushed into that land by other invaders.

It is not necessary for our purposes here to follow the wanderings and even-
tual settling down of each Germanic group. However, in order to give an idea
of such wanderings, and of the Germanic impact on various parts of the former
Roman Empire, it may be well to consider some of the larger and most influential groups.

The Vandals, who crossed the Rhine in 407, wandered across France and
Spain, crossed the Straits of Gibraltar in 429, and took Carthage in 439. By then

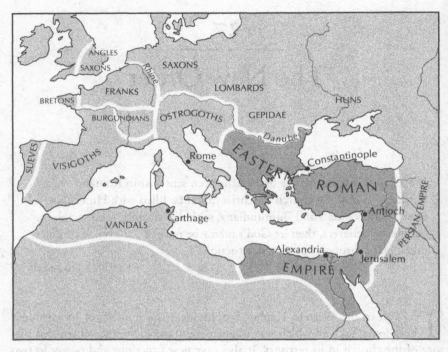

Europe after the Invasions.

they were virtual masters of all the northern coast of Africa from the Straits to the borders of Egypt. They then took to the sea and occupied Sicily, Corsica, and Sardinia. In 455, they sacked the city of Rome, and the destruction they wrought was even greater than that of the Goths forty-five years earlier. Their rule in North Africa was disastrous for the church. They were Arians—that is, they rejected the essential and eternal divinity of Jesus—and under their rule repeated persecutions broke out against both Catholics and Donatists—who were still debating the issues discussed in chapter 16.

Finally, after almost a century of Vandal rule, the area was conquered by General Belisarius, of the Byzantine Empire. That empire, with its capital in Constantinople, was enjoying a brief renaissance under the leadership of Emperor Justinian, whose dream was to restore the ancient glories of the Roman Empire. The Eastern invaders from Constantinople, whom North Africans called "Greeks," brought in still another form of Christianity which, although agreeing in doctrine with that of the Western Catholics, showed marked differences in terms of culture and daily practices. The net result was that, when North Africa was conquered by the Muslims late in the seventh century, they found Christianity badly divided, and it eventually disappeared.

The Visigoths—another Germanic group and one of two main branches of the Goths mentioned above—defeated the Romans at the battle of Adrianople in 378, then swept through the Balkans, and took Rome in 410. By 415 they were in Spain, and they ruled that country until they were overthrown by the Muslims early in the eighth century. The political history of their kingdom was chaotic. Only fifteen of their thirty-four kings died of natural causes or in the field of battle. The rest were either murdered or deposed. They too were Arian, but they did not persecute the orthodox in their territories to the extent that the Vandals did in theirs. It soon became evident that the orthodox descendants of the conquered inhabitants were the guardians of ancient culture, and that their participation was necessary in order to provide the kingdom with a measure of stability. This led to the conversion of the Visigothic King Recared (586–601) to Nicene Orthodoxy, which he solemnly embraced at a great assembly in Toledo, in 589 CE. After the king, the vast majority of the nobles became Catholic, and Arianism soon disappeared.

The outstanding Christian leader of the entire history of the Visigothic kingdom was Isidore of Seville. He was a scholar who sought to preserve as much as possible of ancient culture. His book *Etymologies* is a veritable encyclopedia that shows the state of knowledge at his time, not only in religious matters, but also in astronomy, medicine, agriculture, and practically every other field of knowledge. Although one of the best, it is typical of the writings of the time, for all Isidore could do was to collect and classify the wisdom of the past, with very little by way of original thought. Yet, it was through the works of scholars such as Isidore that the Middle Ages learned of the glories and the wisdom of antiquity.

After the conversion of Recared, the church played the role of legislator for the Visigothic kingdom. In this it provided a measure of order, although in reading the decrees of its councils one cannot but cringe at the injustice and the inequalities that reigned. For instance, a council gathered at Toledo in 633 decreed that priests could only marry with their bishops' permission, and that if any disobeyed, the priest was to be condemned to "do penance for some time," while his wife was to be taken away and sold by the bishop.

The legislation regarding Jews was similar. The same council—whose president was Isidore of Seville, the most enlightened man of his time—decreed that Jews should not be forced to convert to Christianity, but that those who had been forcibly converted earlier would not be allowed to return to the faith of their ancestors, for this would be blasphemy. Furthermore, such converts were forbidden any dealings with Jews who retained their ancient faith, even if they were their closest relatives. And if any of them were found to be observing some

Germanic and Christian traditions were combined. On this money box there are scenes of the magi and of the Germanic hero Wieland.

of their traditional practices, particularly "the abominable circumcisions," their children were to be taken away from them. Furthermore, any Jew who was found to be married to a Christian woman had to choose between conversion and leaving his wife and children. If the case was reversed, and the wife was Jewish and refused conversion, the marriage was void, and she had to leave the children with the father.

Even after the conversion of Recared, and in spite of the efforts of the church, the Visigothic kingdom continued to be politically unstable and plagued with violence and arbitrariness. King Recesvinth (649–672), for instance, killed seven hundred of his enemies, and distributed their wives and children among his friends. Finally, under King Roderick (710–711), the Muslims invaded Spain and put an end to Visigothic rule. By then, however, Christianity had become so rooted in the country, that it became the rallying point in the long struggle to re-conquer the peninsula from the Muslim Moors.

During most of the fifth century, Gaul was divided between two invading groups: the Burgundians, who were Arians, and the Franks, who were still pagans. The Burgundians, however, did not persecute the Catholics, as did the Vandals in North Africa. On the contrary, they imitated their customs, and soon many Burgundians had accepted the Nicene faith of their Catholic subjects. In 516, King Sigismund was converted to orthodox trinitarian doctrine, and soon the rest of the kingdom followed suit.

The Franks (whose country came to be known as "France") were at first an unruly alliance of independent tribes, until a measure of unity was brought by the Merovingian dynasty named after its founder, Meroveus. Clovis, Meroveus's grandson and the greatest of the Merovingian line, was married to a Christian Burgundian princess, and on the eve of a battle promised that he would be converted if his wife's God gave him victory. As a result, on Christmas Day, 496 CE, he was baptized, along with a number of his nobles. Shortly thereafter, most of the Franks were also baptized.

In 534, the Burgundians were conquered by the Franks, and thus the whole region was united. The later Merovingians, however, were weak kings, and by the seventh century the actual government was in the hands of "chamberlains" who in reality were prime ministers. One of these, Charles Martel (that is, "the Hammer") led the Frankish troops against the Muslims, who had taken Spain, crossed the Pyrenees, and threatened the very heart of Europe. He defeated them at the battle of Tours (or Poitiers) in 732. By then he was virtual king, but did not claim that title. It was his son, Pepin the Short, who decided that the time had come to rid himself of the useless King Childeric III—known as "the Stupid." With the consent of Pope Zacharias, he forced Childeric to abdicate and become a monk. He was then anointed king by Bishop Boniface, who was acting under papal instructions. This was of paramount importance for the subsequent history of Christianity, for Pepin's son, Charlemagne, would be the greatest ruler of the early Middle Ages, one who sought to reform the church, and who was crowned emperor by the pope.

Throughout this process, the role of the church was often compromised. Under powerful kings such as Clovis, ecclesiastical leaders seemed to be content to support and obey the ruler. Soon it became customary for kings to decide who should occupy a vacant bishopric. This was understandable, since extensive holdings of land went with the office of bishop, and therefore a bishop was also a great lord. Shortly before anointing Pepin, Boniface complained to the pope that the Frankish church was practically in the hands of lay lords, that many of the bishops acted as lords rather than as pastors, and that the notion of a council of bishops gathered to bring order and renewal to the life of the church was unheard of in the Frankish kingdom. Such conditions would continue until the time of Charlemagne.

Great Britain had never been entirely under Roman control. Emperor Hadrian had built a wall separating the southern portion of the island, which was part of the Roman Empire, from the north, where the Picts and Scots retained their independence. When disaster threatened the Roman possessions on the continent, the legions were withdrawn from Great Britain, and many of the inhabitants left with them. Those who remained were soon conquered by the

From the island of Iona missionaries went forth throughout Scotland and beyond.

Angles and the Saxons, who eventually founded the seven kingdoms of Kent, Essex, Sussex, East Anglia, Wessex, Northumbria, and Mercia. These invaders were pagans, although there always remained a part of the earlier population that retained the Christian faith of Roman times.

At the same time as some of the various Germanic invasions were taking place, the Irish church was flourishing. Since it retained much of its earlier faith and culture, Ireland soon began sending missionaries to other countries, most notably to Scotland. The most famous of these missionaries was Columba, who settled on the small island of Iona with twelve companions, probably in 563 CE. The monastery that they founded there became a center of missions to Scotland, where there soon were several other houses patterned after the Iona community. Eventually, these missions moved south, to territories held by Angles and Saxons.

An important and lasting consequence of the influence of Irish Christianity on the rest of Europe was the spread of the practice of private or auricular confession to a priest, which had originally developed in Ireland, and was often accompanied by manuals for confessors. It is also interesting to note that the popular hymn "Be Thou My Vision" is a translation of a Celtic prayer or *lorica* to thwart the evil influence of the Druids—*Rob tu mo bhoile.*

For reasons that are not altogether clear, there were a number of differences between this Scotch-Irish Christianity and that which had evolved in the former territories of the Roman Empire. Instead of being ruled by bishops, the Scotch-Irish church was under the leadership of the heads of monastic communities. They also differed on the manner in which a number of rites should be performed, and on the date of Easter. A sign of resistance on the part of the Scotch-Irish monks was to wear a different tonsure, shaving the front instead of the crown of their head—as did other monks. Eventually, this practice was outlawed.

The other form of Christianity—the one reflecting and following the customs of the rest of Europe—had always been present in Great Britain among those who kept the traditions of Roman times, but it gained momentum when Christians on the continent became interested in Great Britain. A biographer of Gregory the Great—to whom we shall return later on in this chapter—records an incident in which young Gregory, who was then living as a monk in Rome, saw some blond young men who were to be sold as slaves.

"What is the nationality of these lads?" Gregory asked.

"They are Angles," he was told.

"Angels they are in truth, for their faces look like such. Where is their country?"

"In Deiri."

"*De ira* ["from wrath"] they are indeed, for they have been called from wrath to God's mercy. Who is their king?"

"Aella."

"Alleluia! In that land must the name of God be praised."

This dialogue possibly never took place. But it is certain that Gregory was interested in the land of the Angles, and he may have considered going there as a missionary. He became pope in 590, and nine years later sent a mission to the Angles under the leadership of Augustine, a monk from the same monastery to which Gregory had belonged. When they realized the difficulties that lay ahead, Augustine and his companions considered giving up the enterprise. But Gregory would hear nothing of it, and they were forced to continue. Finally they arrived at the kingdom of Kent, whose king, Ethelbert, was married to a Christian. At first they did not have much success. But eventually Ethelbert himself was converted, and increasing numbers of his subjects followed suit. Augustine then became the first archbishop of Canterbury (the capital of Kent). One by one, the various kingdoms became Christian, and Canterbury became the ecclesiastical capital for all of England.

Soon, however, there were conflicts between those who followed this form of Christianity, and those who belonged to the Scotch-Irish tradition. In Northumbria, we are told that this conflict became serious, for the king followed Scotch-Irish tradition, and the queen held to the Roman one. Since the date for

there will always be somebody fighting on your behalf

Easter differed, one of them was fasting while the other was feasting. In order to solve the difficulties, a synod was held at Whitby in 663. The Scotch-Irish stood fast on the traditions they said they had received from Columba. The Roman missionaries and their partisans retorted that St. Peter's tradition was superior to Columba's, for the apostle had received the keys to the Kingdom. On hearing this, we are told, the king asked those who defended the Scotch-Irish position:

> "Is it true what your opponents say, that St. Peter has the keys to the
> Kingdom?"
> "Certainly," they answered.
> "Then there is no need for further debate. I shall obey Peter. Otherwise,
> when I arrive at heaven he might close the doors on me and keep
> me out."

As a result, the Synod of Whitby decided in favor of the European tradition, and against the Scotch-Irish. Similar decisions were made throughout the British Isles. But this was not due simply to the naïveté of rulers, as the incident at Whitby would seem to imply. It was really the almost inevitable result of the pressure and prestige of the rest of Western Christendom, seeking uniformity throughout the church.

In Italy, the Germanic invasions brought a chaotic situation. Although in theory there were emperors in Rome until 476, these in truth were no more than puppets of various Germanic generals. Finally, in 476, Odoacer, leader of the Germanic Heruli, deposed the last emperor, Romulus Augustulus, and wrote to Zeno, the emperor at Constantinople, telling him that now the empire was reunited. At first Zeno was flattered by this, and he even gave Odoacer the title of "patrician." But soon there were conflicts, and the emperor decided to rid himself of the Heruli by inviting the Eastern Germanic Ostrogoths to invade Italy. This was done, and for a short while Italy was under the rule of the Ostrogoths.

Since the Ostrogoth invaders were Arian, the older population of Italy, which followed the Nicene or Catholic faith, looked to Constantinople for support. This in turn made the Ostrogoth rulers suspect that their subjects plotted treason. For this reason, the orthodox were often persecuted, although usually not on religious grounds, but rather on charges of conspiracy. It was thus that Boethius, the most learned man of the time, was put in jail by King Theodoric. While in prison he wrote his most famous work, *On the Consolation of Philosophy*, which debates predestination and free will, as well as why evil men prosper while good men are ruined. In 524 he was executed, jointly with his father-in-law Symmachus. Two years later, Pope John died in prison. Since then, Boethius, Symmachus, and John were considered martyrs of the Roman Church, and the tension between the ancient population and the Ostrogoths grew. Finally, when the Byzantine Empire, under Justinian, had a short period of renewed grandeur, Justinian's general Belisarius invaded Italy and, after twenty years of military campaign, he and others put an end to the kingdom of the Ostrogoths.

But in 568 the Lombards invaded Italy from the north. As Constantinople began losing some of the power it had gained under Justinian, there was the danger that the Lombards would overrun the peninsula. Thus, by the middle of the eighth century, the popes, aware that they could expect little help from Constantinople, began to look to the north for help. Thus developed the alliance between the papacy and the Frankish kingdom that would eventually lead to the crowning of Charlemagne as emperor of the West.

In summary, from the fifth to the eighth century Western Europe was swept by a series of invasions that brought chaos to the land, and destroyed a great deal of the learning of antiquity. The invaders brought with them two religious challenges that until then seemed to be matters of the past: paganism and Arianism. Eventually, both pagans and Arians were converted to the faith of those whom they conquered. This was the Nicene faith, also called "orthodox" or "catholic." In the process of that conversion, and also in an effort to preserve the wisdom of ancient times, two institutions played a central role, and thus were strengthened. These two institutions, to which we now turn, were monasticism and the papacy.

BENEDICTINE MONASTICISM

We have already seen that when the church was joined to the empire, and thus became the church of the powerful, there were many who found in monasticism a way to live out the total commitment that had been required in earlier times. Although this movement was particularly strong in Egypt and other portions of the Eastern empire, it also found followers in the West. This Western monasticism, however, tended to differ from its Eastern counterpart on three points. First, Western monasticism tended to be more practical. It did not punish the body for the sole purpose of renunciation, but also to train it, as well as the soul, for a mission in the world. Columba and Augustine of Canterbury are examples of this practical bent of Western monasticism. Secondly, Western monasticism did not place the premium on solitude that was typical in the East. From the beginning, Western monasticism sought ways to organize life in community. Finally, Western monasticism did not live in the constant tension with the hierarchy of the church that was typical of Eastern monasticism. Except in times of extreme corruption of the hierarchy, monasticism in the West has been the right arm of popes, bishops, and other ecclesiastical leaders.

The main figure of Western monasticism in its formative years—in many ways, its founder—was Benedict, who was born in the small Italian town of. Nursia around 480 CE. Thus, he grew up under the rule of the Ostrogoths. Since his family belonged to the old Roman aristocracy, he was well aware of the tensions between orthodox and Arian, and the persecutions that the former suffered. When he was about twenty years old, he resolved to become a hermit, and went off to live in a cave. Then followed a period of extreme asceticism, as he sought to overcome the temptations of the flesh. Eventually his fame grew and, as had happened earlier in Egypt with other admired monks, a group of disciples gathered around him. When the place proved unsuitable for his purposes, Benedict moved the small community to Monte Cassino, a place so remote that there still was a sacred grove, and the local inhabitants continued celebrating ancient pagan worship. Benedict and his followers cut the grove, overturned the pagan altar, and built a monastic foundation in that very place. Shortly thereafter his sister Scholastica settled nearby and founded a similar community for women. Eventually, Benedict's fame was such that the Ostrogothic king went to visit him. But the monk had nothing but harsh words and dire prophecies for the man whom he considered a tyrant.

Benedict's greatest significance, however, was in the *Rule* that he gave to his community. Although fairly brief, this document would determine the shape of monasticism for centuries. Rather than extreme asceticism, what the *Rule* seeks is a wise ordering of the monastic life, with strict discipline, but without undue harshness. Thus, while many of the monks of the desert lived on bread, salt, and water, Benedict prescribed that his monks would have two meals a day, each with two cooked dishes, and at times with fresh fruits and vegetables. Also, each monk was to receive a moderate amount of wine every day. And, in addition to his bed, each monk should have a cover and a pillow. All this was to be done only in times of abundance, for in times of scarcity monks should be content with whatever was available.

There are, however, two elements of the monastic life that are crucial for Benedict. These are stability and obedience. The first means that monks are not free to go from one monastery to another as they please. Each monk must remain for the rest of his life in the monastery that he has initially joined, unless ordered to go to another place. The commitment to stability on the part of Benedictine monks proved one of the sources of the institution's great relevance in a time of chaos.

Secondly, the *Rule* insists on obedience. First of all, this means obedience to the *Rule* itself. But the abbot is also to be obeyed "without delay." This means not only instant obedience, but also that an effort is to be made to make that

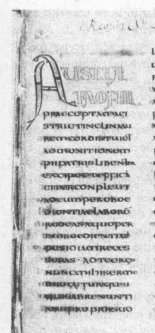

The oldest surviving manuscript of the Rule of St. Benedict.

obedience willing. If what is commanded is impossible, the monk is to explain to the abbot why it is so. If, after such explanation, the superior insists on the command, it is to be obeyed as well as possible. The abbot, however, must not be a tyrant, but is himself subject to God and to the *Rule*. The word "abbot" means "father," and as such should the abbot behave.

An errant monk is to be admonished secretly. If after two such admonitions he does not repent, he is to be reprimanded before the community. The next step is excommunication, which means being barred, not only from communion, but also from the meals in common and from every contact with the other monks. If he is still unrepentant, he is to be whipped. If even this is to no avail, he is to be sorrowfully expelled from the community. Even then, if he repents, he is to be received again. This, up to three times, for after the third expulsion the monastery will be forever closed to him. In short, the *Rule* is not written for venerable saints, such as the heroes of the desert, but for fallible human beings. This may have been the secret of its success.

The *Rule* also insists on physical labor, which is to be shared by all. Except in exceptional cases of illness or of unique gifts, all will take turns in every task.

For instance, there will be weekly cooks, and in order to show that this work is not to be despised, the change of cooks will take place in one of the services of worship. Also, the ill, the elderly, and the very young will receive special consideration in the assignment of tasks. On the other hand, those who come from wealthy families will receive no special treatment on that account. If it is necessary for some reason to establish an order of priority in the monastery, this will be done according to the length of time that each has been part of the community. Thus, whereas poverty for earlier monasticism was a form of private renunciation, Benedict sought to achieve through it the creation of a new order within the community. A monk's poverty welds him to the community, in which all are of equal poverty, and on which all must depend for all their needs.

The core of the monastic life as Benedict conceived it was prayer. Periods were assigned each day for private prayer, but most of the devotions took place in the chapel. There the monks were to gather eight times a day, seven during daytime, and once in the middle of the night, for the Psalmist says: "seven times a day I praise thee" (Ps. 119:164) and "At midnight I rise to praise thee" (Ps. 119:62).

The first gathering for prayer took place in the early hours of dawn, and was followed by seven others. These hours, kept by most monastic houses during the Middle Ages, were called *matins, lauds, prime, terce, sext, none, vespers,* and *compline.* Most of the time at each of these gatherings was devoted to reciting the Psalms and to readings of other portions of scripture. The Psalms were distributed so that all would be recited in the course of a week. The other readings depended on the time of day, the day of the week, and the liturgical season. As a result, most monks came to know the entire Psalter by heart, as well as other portions of scripture. Since many of the laity who had the necessary leisure followed similar devotional practices, they too acquired great familiarity with various parts of the Bible, as they appeared in their *breviaries*—books containing the material to be read at various hours. The eight hours of prayer came to be called canonical hours, and their celebration the Divine Office.

Although Benedict himself had little to say about study, soon this was one of the main occupations of Benedictine monks. In order to celebrate the Divine Office, books were needed. Monks became adept at copying both the Bible and other books, and thus preserved them for subsequent generations. Their houses also became teaching centers, particularly for the many children who were placed under their care in order to be trained as monks. And many also served as hospitals and pharmacies, or as hostels where a weary traveler could find shelter.

Eventually, monasteries also had a profound economic impact, for many were established on marginal lands that were brought into production by the

Besides centers of study, monasteries provided medical services, producing and administering medicines and taking care of the sick.

labor of the monks. Thus, countless acres were added to the agricultural land of Europe. Furthermore, in a society where the wealthy considered manual labor demeaning, the monasteries showed that the highest intellectual and spiritual achievements could be coupled with hard physical labor.

Although the monastic movement had many followers in Western Europe before Benedict's time, it was Benedict's *Rule* that eventually became widespread. In 589, the monastery that Benedict had founded at Monte Cassino was looted and burned by the Lombards. Most of the monks fled to Rome, taking their *Rule* with them. It was there that Gregory, who would later become pope, came to know them. Soon their *Rule* was followed by many in the city of Rome. Augustine, the missionary to England, took the *Rule* with him to the British Isles. With the support of the papacy, the Benedictine *Rule* spread throughout the Western church. The many monasteries that followed it, although not organized into a formal "order," were thus united by common practices and ideals.

THE PAPACY

The second institution which, jointly with monasticism, gave unity and continuity to the Middle Ages was the papacy. The word *pope* simply means "father," and in early times was used to refer to any important and respected bishop. Thus, there are documents referring to Pope Cyprian of Carthage, or to Pope

Athanasius of Alexandria. In the West the title was eventually reserved for the bishops of Rome, but in the East it continued to be used with more liberality. In any case, what is important is not the origin of the title of pope, but rather how the bishop of Rome came to enjoy the authority that he had in the Middle Ages, and still has in the Roman Catholic Church.

The origins of episcopacy in Rome are not altogether clear. Most scholars agree that Peter did visit Rome, and that there is at least a very high probability that he died there. But the various lists of the early bishops of Rome, mostly dating from late in the second century, do not agree among themselves. While some claim that Clement was Peter's successor, others name him as the third bishop after the apostle's death. This has led some scholars to suggest the possibility that in the beginning Rome did not have a single bishop, but rather a "collegiate episcopacy"—a group of bishops who jointly led the church. While such a theory is open to debate, it is clear that during the early centuries the numerical strength of Christianity was in the Greek-speaking East, and that churches such as Antioch and Alexandria were much more important than the one in Rome. Even in the West, the theological leadership of the church was in North Africa, which produced such figures as Tertullian, Cyprian, and Augustine.

It was the Germanic invasions that brought about the great upsurge in the pope's authority. In the East, the empire continued existing for another thousand years. But in the West the church became the guardian of what was left of ancient civilization, as well as of order and justice. Thus, the most prestigious bishop in the West, that of Rome, became the focal point for regaining a unity that had been shattered by the invasions.

A prime example of this is Leo "the Great," who has been called the first "pope" in the modern sense. Later, we shall see his participation in the theological controversies of the time—most notably the controversy on the relationship between divinity and humanity in Christ. In that participation it is clear that Leo's opinion was not generally accepted simply because he was the bishop of Rome, and that it took a politically propitious moment for his views to prevail. Since Leo intervened in controversies that took place mostly in the East, many Eastern bishops—as well the most Byzantine emperors—saw this as an unwarranted attempt on the part of the bishop of Rome to expand the range of his authority. It was only when more favorable emperors came to power that Leo's positions were more generally accepted. This in turn resulted in growing prestige for the papacy.

In the West, however, things were different. In 452 Italy was invaded by Attila and his Huns, pagans from Eastern Europe who had first sought to conquer Constantinople, but whom the Byzantine authorities had diverted toward the West—in part by offering them gold. They took and sacked the city of Aquileia. The road to Rome was open to them, for there was no army between them and the ancient capital. The Western emperor was weak both in character and in resources, and the East had given indications that it was unwilling to intervene. It was then that Leo left Rome and marched to meet "the Scourge of God." What was said in that interview is not known. Legend has it that Attila saw Saints Peter and Paul marching with the pope, and threatening the Hun. Whatever was said, Attila decided not to attack Rome, and turned toward the north, where he died shortly thereafter.

Leo was still Bishop of Rome in 455, when the Vandals sacked the city. At that time, he was unable to stop the invaders. But it was he who led the negotiations with the Vandal leader, Genseric, and thus avoided the burning of the city.

Needless to say, these episodes—and others like it—gave Leo great authority in the city of Rome. That he was able to do these things was due both to his personal gifts and to the political situation of the time, when the civil authorities proved incapable of performing their duties. But in Leo's mind there was a deeper reason. He was convinced that Jesus had made Peter and his successors the rock on which the church was to be built, and that therefore the bishop of Rome, Peter's direct successor, is the head of the church. Thus, in Leo's writings one finds all the traditional arguments that would repeatedly be mustered in favor of papal authority.

Leo died in 461 and was succeeded by Hilarius, who had been his close associate, and who continued his policies. But under the next pope, Simplicius, conditions changed. In 476, Odoacer deposed the last Western emperor, and thus began in Italy a long period of political chaos. In theory, Italy was now part of the Eastern Roman Empire. But there were constant tensions between the popes and the Eastern emperors, mostly having to do with the theological controversies to which we shall return shortly. Eventually, this resulted in a schism between East and West that would take several years to heal. This schism was further aggravated by the invasion of Italy by the Ostrogoths. Since they were Arian, tensions between them and the earlier population were unavoidable. By 498, these tensions resulted in the existence of two rival popes, one supported by the Ostrogoths and the other by Constantinople. There were violent riots in the streets of Rome, where the followers of one pope clashed with the followers of the other. At long last, after a series of synods, the conflict was resolved.

The new pope was Hormisdas (514–523), and under his leadership a series of negotiations finally ended the schism with Constantinople. Meanwhile, the Byzantine Empire was enjoying its brief resurgence under the leadership of Emperor Justinian. It was then that Belisarius invaded Italy and put an end to the kingdom of the Ostrogoths. But this did not bring a favorable change for the church in Italy, for the emperor and his functionaries tried to impose there a situation similar to that which existed in the Eastern empire, where the church was almost completely subject to the state. The next few popes, for as long as Byzantium held sway, were mere puppets of Justinian and of his empress, Theodora. Those who dared follow an independent policy soon felt the consequences of imperial wrath.

As part of this revival of the Byzantine Empire, Justinian rebuilt in Constantinople the cathedral of Saint Sophia, Hagia Sophia—dedicated to Christ as Holy Wisdom. It is said that when he beheld the finished product he boasted: "Solomon, I have outdone thee!" This structure still stands, although now surrounded by minarets built after the Turkish contest.

Byzantine power over Italy did not last long. Only six years after the last stronghold of the Ostrogoths had been conquered, the Lombards invaded the area. Had they been united, they would soon have conquered all of it. But after their first victories they broke up into several rival groups, and this slowed their advance. After Justinian's death in 565, Byzantine power began to wane, and Constantinople could no longer maintain a strong army in Italy. Thus, those who had not been conquered by the Lombards, although still technically part of the Eastern empire, were forced to take measures for their defense. In Rome,

This mosaic in the cathedral Hagia Sophia shows Constantine (on the right) presenting his city to Jesus and the Virgin, and Justinian (on the left) doing likewise with the cathedral of Saint Sophia.

the popes became responsible for the preservation of the city against the Lombard threat. When Benedict I died in 579, the Lombards were besieging the city. His successor, Pelagius II, saved it by buying the Lombards off. Then, since no help was forthcoming from Constantinople, he turned to the Franks, hoping that they would attack the Lombards from the north. Although these initial negotiations did not come to fruition, they pointed to the future, when the Franks would become the main support of the papacy.

The next pope, Gregory, was one of the ablest men ever to occupy that position. We have already met him as the person who sent Augustine and his companions in a mission to England. He was born in Rome around 540, apparently to a family of the old aristocracy. At that time Justinian reigned in Constantinople, and his generals were fighting the Ostrogoths in Italy. Belisarius, Justinian's ablest general, had been recalled to Constantinople, and the war dragged on. The Ostrogoth king, Totila, took the offensive for a short time. In 545, he besieged Rome, which surrendered the next year. At that time, archdeacon Pelagius (later Pope Pelagius II) went out to meet the victorious king and obtained from him a measure of mercy. It is likely that Gregory was at Rome at the time, and witnessed both the sufferings during the siege and Pelagius's intervention on behalf of the city. In any case, the Rome that Gregory knew was a far cry from the ancient glory of the empire. Shortly after Totila's victory, Belisarius and the Byzantines retook the city, only to lose it again. After years of neglect and repeated sieges, the city was in a grave state of chaos and mismanagement. Many of its ancient monuments and buildings had been destroyed in order to provide stones for repairing the walls. The aqueducts and the system of drainage had fallen into disrepair, and disease was rife.

Little is known of Gregory's early years in this beleaguered city. He may have been an important Roman official—a career for which he was undoubtedly trained by his family, which was of aristocratic origin. After he became a Benedictine monk, Pope Benedict made him a deacon—that is, a member of his administrative council. The next pope, Pelagius II, appointed Gregory his ambassador before the court at Constantinople. There Gregory spent six years, and was often involved in the theological controversies and political intrigues that were constantly boiling in the great city. Finally, in 586, Pelagius sent another ambassador, and Gregory was able to return to his monastery in Rome, where he was made abbot.

At that time the situation in Rome was serious. The Lombards had finally united, and intended to conquer the whole of Italy. Although some resources were sent from Constantinople for the defense of Rome, and although the Lombards were occasionally being attacked from the rear by the Franks, there was great danger that the city would fall.

This Gospel illumination with the symbol of Luke (the winged ox) may well have come from a copy of the Gospels sent to England by Gregory.

To make matters worse, an epidemic broke out in Rome. Shortly before, floods had destroyed much of the store of food. Since those who were ill frequently had hallucinations, rumors began circulating. Someone had seen a great dragon emerging from the Tiber. Death was seen stalking the streets. Fire had rained from heaven. Then Pope Pelagius, who with the help of Gregory and other monks had organized the sanitation of the city, the burial of the dead, and the feeding of the hungry, himself became ill and died.

Under such circumstances, there were not many who coveted the empty post. Gregory himself had no wish to become pope, but the clergy and the people elected him. He sought to have his election annulled by writing to the emperor and asking that his appointment not be confirmed—by that time it had become customary to request the approval of Constantinople before consecrating the bishop of an important see. But his letter was intercepted. Eventually, although reluctantly, he was made bishop of Rome.

Gregory then set about his new tasks with unbounded zeal. Since there was nobody else to do it, he organized the distribution of food among the needy in Rome, and he also took measures to guarantee the continuing shipments of wheat from Sicily. Likewise, he supervised the rebuilding of the aqueducts and of the defenses of the city, and the garrison was drilled until morale was restored. Since there was little help to be expected from Constantinople, he opened direct negotiations with the Lombards, with whom he secured peace. Thus, by default, the pope was acting as ruler of Rome and the surrounding area, which soon came to be known as "Saint Peter's Patrimony." Much later, in the eighth century, someone forged a document, the so-called *Donation of Constantine,* which claimed that the great emperor had granted these lands to Saint Peter's successors.

But Gregory considered himself above all a religious leader. He preached constantly in the various churches in Rome, calling the faithful to renewed commitment. He also took measures to promote clerical celibacy, which was slowly becoming the norm throughout Italy, and which many claimed to follow but did not. Also, as bishop of Rome, Gregory saw himself as patriarch of the West. He did not claim for himself universal authority, as Leo had done earlier. But he took more practical steps, which did in fact increase his authority in the West. In Spain, he was instrumental in the conversion of the Visigothic population to Nicene Catholicism. To England, he sent Augustine's mission, which would eventually extend the authority of Rome to the British Isles. His letters to Africa, dealing with the Donatist schism, were not as well received by the local bishops, who wished to guard their independence. He also tried to intervene in the various Frankish territories, seeking more autonomy for the church. But in this he did not succeed, for the Frankish rulers wished to have control of the church, and saw no reason to yield to the pope's entreaties.

However, it is not only for these reasons that Gregory is called "the Great." He was also a prolific writer whose works were very influential throughout the Middle Ages. In these writings, he did not seek to be original or creative. On the contrary, his greatest pride was not to say anything that had not been held by the great teachers of earlier centuries, particularly Saint Augustine. To him, it sufficed to be a disciple of the great bishop of Hippo, a teacher of his teachings. But in spite of such wishes, there was a chasm between Gregory and his admired Augustine. Gregory lived in a time of obscurantism, superstition, and credulity, and to a degree he reflected his age. By making Augustine an infallible teacher, he contradicted the spirit of that teacher, whose genius was, at least in part, in his inquiring spirit and venturesome mind. What for Augustine was conjecture, in Gregory became certainty. Thus, for instance, the theologian of Hippo had suggested the possibility that there was a place of purification for those who died in sin, where they would spend some time before going to heaven. On the basis of these speculations of Augustine, Gregory affirmed the existence of such a place, and thus gave impetus to the development of the doctrine of purgatory.

It was particularly in that which refers to the doctrine of salvation that Gregory mitigated and even transformed the teachings of Augustine. The Augustinian doctrines of predestination and irresistible grace were set aside by Gregory, who was more concerned with the question of how we are to offer satisfaction to God for sins committed. This is done through penance, which consists of contrition, confession, and the actual punishment or satisfaction. To these must be added priestly absolution, which confirms the forgiveness granted by God. Those who die in the faith and communion of the church, but without having offered satisfaction for all their sins, will go to purgatory before they attain their final salvation. The living can help the dead out of purgatory by offering masses in their favor. Gregory believed that in the mass or communion Christ was sacrificed anew (and there is a legend that the crucified appeared to him while celebrating mass). This notion of the mass as sacrifice eventually became standard doctrine of the Western church—until it was rejected by Protestants in the sixteenth century.

Gregory tells the story of a certain monk who had died in sin. The abbot—Gregory himself—ordered that daily masses be said on behalf of the deceased, whose soul appeared to a brother after thirty days, declaring that he was now free of purgatory, and had moved on to heaven. This and similar stories were not Gregory's invention. They were rather part of the atmosphere and beliefs of the time. But, while earlier Christian teachers had sought to preserve Christian faith free of popular superstition, Gregory readily accepted the stories circulating at his time as if they were simple and direct confirmation of the Christian faith.

Under Gregory's successors, the papacy fell on evil days. Constantinople insisted on asserting its authority over Rome. Since at that time, as we shall see in the next chapter, the Eastern church was divided by christological controversies, the emperors demanded that the popes support their theological positions. Those who refused were treated harshly. Thus, it came about that Pope Honorius (625–638) declared himself a *Monothelite*—that is, a follower of a christological heresy claiming that Jesus Christ had two natures but only one will. When, years later, Pope Martin I disobeyed the emperor's command that there was to be no more discussion of these christological issues, he was kidnapped and taken to Constantinople. His main supporter, the monk Maximus, had his tongue and his right hand cut off by imperial order, and was also sent into exile. From then on, all the theological controversies with which we shall deal in the next chapter had serious repercussions in Rome, which could not free itself from the overwhelming power of the emperors of Constantinople. During all this time, and until Gregory III (731–741), the election of a pope had to be confirmed by the authorities in Constantinople before the candidate could be consecrated as bishop of Rome.

Then, as Byzantine power in Italy began to wane, the ever present threat of the Lombards forced the popes to find new support elsewhere, and they turned to the Franks. It was for this reason that Pope Zacharias agreed to have Childeric III, "the Stupid," deposed, and Pepin crowned in his stead. Although Zacharias died the same year that Pepin was crowned (752), his successor, Stephen II, collected the debt that Pepin had acquired with the papacy. When the Lombards again threatened, Stephen appealed to Pepin, who twice invaded Italy, and granted to the pope several cities that the Lombards had taken. The protests of the government at Constantinople need not be heeded, and the popes became rulers of a vast portion of Italy. From that point, the alliance between the Franks and the popes grew closer. Finally, Pope Leo III crowned Charlemagne emperor of the West on Christmas Day, 800 CE.

THE ARAB CONQUESTS

Early in the seventh century, it seemed that order was about to be restored in most of the ancient Roman Empire. Most of the Arian invaders had embraced Nicene orthodoxy. The Franks, who from the beginning had been converted to that faith, were beginning to unite in Gaul. In the British Isles, the first fruits of Augustine's mission could be seen. The Byzantine Empire still enjoyed many of the results of Justinian's conquests—particularly in North Africa, where the Vandal kingdom had disappeared.

Then something unexpected happened. Out of Arabia, a forgotten corner of the world that had been generally ignored by both the Roman and the Persian Empires, a tidal wave of conquest arose that threatened to engulf the world. In a few years, the Persian Empire had vanished, and many of the ancient Roman territories were in Arab hands.

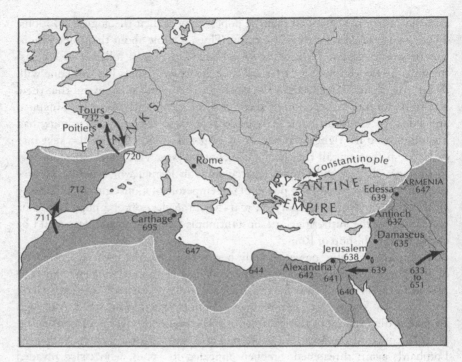

The Arab conquests.

The driving force behind this human avalanche was the teachings of Muhammad, an Arab merchant who had always had deep religious interests, and who had come in contact with both Judaism and the various Christian sects that existed in Arabia—some of them rather unorthodox. A deeply religious man, he had a series of dreams and visions calling him to his task as prophet and giving him the message he was to proclaim. This message, which he claimed had been revealed to him by Gabriel, was that of a single God, both just and merciful, who rules all things and requires obedience from all. It was often presented in rhythmic fashion that could be memorize and recited, like those of the ancient Hebrew prophets—indeed, from his very first vision Muhammad was commended to "recite in the name of your Lord the Creator . . . recite!" and the title of the *Qur'an* means "recitation." Muhammad claimed that he was not preaching a new religion, but simply the culmination of what God had revealed in the Hebrew prophets and in Jesus, who was a great prophet, although not divine as Christians claimed.

This religion had five basic points, which to this day are called the Five Pillars of Islam. The first is radical monotheism, and Muhammad's role in preaching it under divine guidance: "There is no god but God, and Muhammad is his Prophet." The second is ritual prayer, prescribed at specific times. The third is *zakat*, which is often translated as "almsgiving," but whose full meaning includes taxation, and specifically that the poor have a right to some of the wealth of the rich. Of the Five Pillars, it is this that has been most debated and modified in various Muslim communities. The fourth pillar is fasting during the month of Ramadan, in celebration of the month when the Qur'an was originally given to Muhammad. Finally, the fifth pillar is pilgrimage to Mecca or *hajj*, which every adult male who is able must make at least once in his lifetime.

Partly because they feared it would affect their business, the merchants in Mecca opposed the preaching of Muhammad, who took refuge at the nearby oasis where Medina would eventually become a great city. The date of that flight, 622 CE, is the beginning of the Muslim era, from which years are counted. There Muhammad founded the first Muslim community, in which worship, as well as civil and political life, followed the guidelines set out by him. Then he and his followers set out on a military and political campaign that eventually gave them control over Mecca. At that point, Muhammad decreed that his former enemies were forgiven, although all idols must be overthrown. By his death in 632, a goodly part of Arabia was in Muslim hands.

Then leadership passed on to the *caliphs*—from an Arabic word which means "successor." Under Abu Bakr (632–634), power over Arabia was consolidated, and the Muslims achieved their first victory over the Byzantine armies. Under Omar (also known as 'Umar ibn al-Khattab, 634–644) the Arabs invaded Syria. In 635 they took Damascus, and Jerusalem in 638. Two years later, they were masters of the entire region. At the same time, another Muslim army invaded Egypt, founded what would one day become Cairo, and took Alexandria in 642. By 647, under the leadership of the third caliph, Otman (also known as 'Uthman ibn Affan, 644-656), they were again marching westward along the northern coast of Africa. Meanwhile, a Muslim army invaded the Persian Empire, whose last king died in 651. After that, experiencing only minor setbacks, the Muslims swept through what had once been one of the most powerful kingdoms on earth.

During the second half of the century, the Muslim advance was somewhat slowed by the inner strife that had marked it from the beginning. Of the first four caliphs, three were assassinated. The struggle between the fourth caliph, Ali (Ali ibn Abi Talib, 656-661), and his rivals resulted in a great division that would continue to persist through the centuries: the Shiites supporting Ali, and the Sunni his rivals. While their theological differences were minor, they disagreed on some matters of ritual, and in particular on whether only a direct descendant of Muhammad could be his successor—a position held by the Shiites, and denied by the Sunni.

Even while torn asunder by inner conflict, however, Islam continued to advance. Carthage fell in 695, and soon many of the inhabitants of North Africa, who had lived through so much strife between Catholics, Donatists, Arians, and Byzantines, accepted Islam. By 711, a small band crossed the Straits of Gibraltar—whose name is derived from that of their leader, Tariq—and found the Visigothic kingdom so weakened that they overran it. Soon all of Spain, except for the extreme northern areas, was under Muslim rule. From there they crossed the Pyrenees and threatened the very heart of Western Europe. In 732, they were finally defeated by Charles Martel at the battle of Tours, which marked the end of the first wave of Muslim expansion.

This enormous expansion was made possible by disaffection among those who had been subjected to the Byzantine and Persian empires. In the specific case of the Byzantine Empire, such disaffection had already played a role in the growth of Monophysitism in areas such as Syria and Egypt. Now Muslim rule presented itself as an alternative to Byzantine oppression, and promised those who had been disaffected for religious reasons that their views and goods would be respected. The proclamation issued at the time of the conquest of Jerusalem is typical, although of particular interest due to the later history of religious relations in that city. In that proclamation the general promised that Jews and Christians would be respected in their property and their customs, but would only be required to pay tribute "like the inhabitants of other cities." As to Christians, "their churches and their crosses" would be respected. And there would be "no pressure or coercion on religious matters." Only the "Greeks"—meaning the Byzantines—would be forced to leave the city, and they would be given a safe conduct to do so.

These invasions had enormous significance for Christianity. For one thing, many of the ancient centers of Christianity—Jerusalem, Antioch, Damascus, Alexandria, and Carthage—were now under Muslim rule. Although seldom persecuted, Christians in those areas were placed under severe handicaps. Most often conversion to Christianity was harshly punished. Although the church in these areas produced a number of notable apologists, at times any defense of Christianity was considered an offense against Muhammad, punishable by death. In Carthage and the surrounding area, Christianity completely disappeared. In the rest of the vast Arab holdings it was tolerated, but ceased growing, and eventually was content with holding its own.

The Byzantine Empire, which until then had vast territories in the Near East and the northern coast of Africa, was pushed back to what is now Turkey, and to its holdings in Europe. In the next chapter we shall see that, since many of those within that empire who had dissented from its policies were now under Muslim rule, and therefore the Byzantine emperors no longer felt the need to take their views into account, Byzantine Orthodoxy could now ignore the objections of Monophysites and Nestorians.

Furthermore, the entire geographic configuration of Christianity changed. Until then, Christianity had developed along the Mediterranean basin. Now, it would find its center along an axis that ran from north to south, including the British Isles, the Frankish kingdom, and Italy. Constantinople would be increasingly alienated from that axis. Therefore it is no coincidence that a few years after the Arab conquests, in 800 CE, the pope felt inclined to crown Charlemagne emperor of the West, and both he and Charlemagne were ready to ignore the protests that came from Constantinople.

In the field of theology, Islam affected Christianity, not only in that the latter produced a number of apologies—written both within and beyond the borders of Muslim power—but also in the manner in which Christian leaders sought to respond to Islamic criticism. This was particularly true in the debate regarding the use of images, which would rage in the eighth century, and in the need to clarify the doctrine of the Trinity, which Muslims claimed was a denial of monotheism.

But above all, the Muslim invasions, and Christian reaction to them, continued and accelerated a process of militarizing Christianity that had long been developing. The earliest Christians, following the teachings of Jesus, had been strict pacifists. Slowly, however, as Christianity made way among the ranks of the military, concessions began to be made. Even before Constantine's conversion, some Christian writers held that strict pacifism was required only of monastics. After Constantine Christians, now finding themselves responsible for the safety and order of the state, developed the Just War Theory, which made it acceptable for Christians to use violence under some circumstances. Then came Germanic invasions from the north, and Muslim invasions from the south. The Germanic peoples were assimilated, and in the process the church came to adopt many of their traditional warlike customs. To the East and South, Islam presented itself as a constant threat to be held back only by armed force, with the result that Christianity became radically militarized, and a few centuries later would undertake an offensive against Islam—the Crusades—whose violence and cruelty equaled any perpetrated earlier by the Muslim invaders. Thus was created an atmosphere of violence and suspicion that would continue to bear its bitter fruit half a millennium later.

28

Eastern Christianity

When I have no books, or when my thoughts, torturing me like thorns,
do not let me enjoy reading, I go to church, which is the cure available
for every disease of the soul. The freshness of the images draws my
attention, captivates my eyes . . . and slowly leads my soul to divine
praise.

JOHN OF DAMASCUS

Although in the last chapter our attention has centered on Western Christianity, one must not forget that at the same time there was an Eastern
branch of the church. For Christians at that time, both East and West, the
church was one. Historians, however, can now see that by the early Middle Ages
the two branches of the church were drifting apart, and that the final schism,
which took place in 1054, was long in the making. Apart from the obvious
cultural differences between the Latin-speaking West and the Greek-speaking
East, the political course of events produced entirely different situations in the
two branches of the church. In the West, the demise of the empire created a
vacuum that the church filled, and thus ecclesiastical leaders—particularly the
popes—also came to wield political power. In the East, the empire continued
for another thousand years. It was often beleaguered by foreign invasion or by
inner turmoil, but it survived. Its autocratic emperors kept a tight rein on ecclesiastical leaders. This usually led to civil intervention in ecclesiastical matters,
particularly in theological debates. Theological discussion came to be tainted
with the ever-present possibility of appealing to the emperor to take one's side,
and thus crushing an enemy one could not overcome by mere argument. Given
that power, many emperors made theological decisions on the basis of political
considerations, which led to even greater acrimony. For these reasons, theological controversy became one of the hallmarks of Eastern Christianity during the
early Middle Ages.

This is not to say that such controversies were not important. The issues at
stake were often central to the gospel. Furthermore, since Christians at that

time considered themselves members of the same church, the decisions made in the East, sometimes with little or no Western participation, came to be regarded as normative by both East and West. Finally, out of these debates the first permanent schisms developed within Christianity, giving rise to separate churches that still exist.

THE CHRISTOLOGICAL DEBATES TO
THE COUNCIL OF CHALCEDON

The question of the divinity of the second person of the Trinity (and of the Holy Spirit) had been settled by the Councils of Nicea (325) and Constantinople (381). Although the conversion to Arianism of some of the Germanic people beyond the borders of the empire, and their subsequent invasion of Western Europe, brought about a brief resurgence of Arianism, this eventually disappeared, and Christians were in basic agreement on trinitarian doctrine. But there were still other issues that would cause sharp theological disagreement. Foremost among these was the question of how divinity and humanity are joined in Jesus Christ. This is the fundamental christological question.

On this question, there were in the East two different currents of thought, which historians have conveniently labeled the *Antiochene* and the *Alexandrine*—although not all those who followed the Alexandrine way of thinking were from Alexandria, nor were all the Antiochenes from Antioch. Both sides were agreed that the divine was immutable and eternal. The question then was, how could the immutable, eternal God be joined to a mutable, historical man? At this point, the two schools followed divergent paths. The Alexandrines, like Clement and Origen centuries earlier, stressed the significance of Jesus as the teacher of divine truth. In order to be this, the Savior had to be a full and clear revelation of the divine. His divinity must be asserted, even if this had to be done at the expense of his humanity. The Antiochenes, on the other hand, felt that for Jesus to be the Savior of human beings he had to be fully human. The Godhead dwelt in him, without any doubt; but this must not be understood in such a way that his humanity was diminished or eclipsed. Both sides agreed that Jesus was both divine and human. The question was how to understand that union.

As one now looks back at that question, it appears that the way it had been posed made it impossible to answer. In the preceding generations, guided mostly by earlier Greek philosophy, Christian theologians had come to define God in terms of contrast with all human limitations. God is immutable; humans are constantly changing. God is infinite; humans are finite. God is omnipotent; human power is limited. God is eternal and omnipresent; humans can only be present at one place in a particular time. When divinity and humanity are thus defined, the incarnation of God in Jesus Christ—the presence and full union of the divine and the human—becomes a contradiction. (I have said elsewhere that it is like asking someone to produce hot ice cream. One can melt the ice cream; one can mix the ingredients; one can put both ice cream and something hot on the same plate; but one can never produce ice cream that, without ceasing to be ice cream, is hot.) The only solutions to such a quandary, when matters are posed in such terms, are to declare that the divinity and the humanity are not really joined in one—which was the Antiochene way of thinking—or to be willing to have the divinity overwhelm the humanity, overcoming its natural limitations—which was the Alexandrine position.

In the West, such questions did not create the same stir. For one thing, after the Germanic invasions, there were other urgent matters that required attention. For another, the West simply revived Tertullian's old formula—that in Christ there were two natures united in one person—and was content to affirm this. Thus, the West played a balancing role between the two factions in the East, and for that reason would come out of the controversies with enhanced prestige.

The first stages of the controversy began even before the trinitarian issue was settled. One of the defenders of the Nicene position regarding the Trinity, Apollinaris of Laodicea, thought that he could help that cause by explaining how the eternal Word of God could be incarnate in Jesus. This he attempted to do by claiming that in Jesus the Word of God, the second person of the Trinity, took the place of the rational soul. Like all human beings, Jesus had a physical body, and this was activated by the same principle that gives life to all human beings. But he did not have a human intellect. The Word of God played in him the role that the intellect or "rational soul" plays in the rest of us.

Although this explanation seemed satisfactory to Apollinaris, soon many began to see flaws in it. A human body with a purely divine mind is not really a human being. From the Alexandrine point of view, this was quite acceptable, for all that was needed was that Jesus really speak as God, and that he have the body necessary to communicate with us. But the Antiochenes insisted that this was not enough. Jesus must be truly human. This was of paramount importance, because Jesus took up humanity so that humankind could be saved. Only if he really became human did he really save us. If any part of what constitutes a human being was not taken up by him, that was not saved by him. Gregory of Nazianzus (one of the Cappadocian Fathers) put it this way:

> If any believe in Jesus Christ as a human being without human reason, they are the ones devoid of all reason, and unworthy of salvation. For that which he has not taken up he has not saved. He saved that which he joined to his divinity. If only half of Adam had fallen, then it would be

Ephesus, where the Third Ecumenical Council met (431), was also the site of the Robber Synod of 449.

possible for Christ to take up and save only half. But if the entire human nature fell, all of it must be united to the Word in order to be saved as a whole.[40]

After some debate, the theories of Apollinaris were rejected, first by a number of leading bishops and local synods called by them, and eventually by the Council of Constantinople in 381—the same council that reaffirmed the decisions of Nicea against Arianism.

The next episode of the christological controversies was precipitated by Nestorius, a representative of the Antiochene school who became patriarch of Constantinople in 428. There were always political intrigues surrounding that office, for the patriarchate of Constantinople had become a point of discord between the patriarchs of Antioch and Alexandria. The Council of Constantinople had declared that the bishop of Constantinople should have in the East precedence similar to that which the bishop of Rome had in the West. This was a simple acknowledgment of political reality, for Constantinople had become the capital of the Eastern empire. But the bishops of the older churches in Antioch and Alexandria were not content with being relegated to a secondary position. They responded, among other things, by turning the bishopric of Constantinople into a prize to be captured for their own supporters. Since Antioch was more successful at this game than Alexandria, most of the patriarchs of Constantinople were Antiochenes, and therefore the patriarchs of Alexandria regarded them as their enemies—a process we have already seen when dealing with the life of John Chrysostom. For these reasons, Nestorius's position was not secure, and the Alexandrines were looking to catch him at his first mistake.

This happened when Nestorius declared that Mary should not be called *Theotokos*—that is, bearer of God—and suggested that she be called *Christotokos*—bearer of Christ. It is difficult for Protestants to understand what was at stake here, for we have been taught to reject the notion that Mary is the "Mother of God," and at first glance this seems to be what was at issue here. But in truth, the debate was not so much about Mary as about Jesus. The question was not what honors were due to Mary, but how one was to speak of the birth of Jesus. When Nestorius declared that Mary was the bearer of Christ, but not of God, he was affirming that in speaking of the incarnate Lord one may and must distinguish between his humanity and his divinity, and that some of the things said of him are to be applied to the humanity, and others to the divinity. This was a typically Antiochene position, which sought to preserve the full humanity of Jesus by making a very clear distinction between it and his divinity. Nestorius and the rest of the Antiochenes feared that if the two were too closely joined together, the divinity would overwhelm the humanity, and one would no longer be able to speak of a true man Jesus.

In order to explain this position, Nestorius declared that in Jesus there were "two natures and two persons," one divine and one human. The human nature and person were born of Mary; the divine were not. What he meant by this is not altogether clear, for the terms "person" and "nature" could be used with different meanings. But his enemies immediately saw the danger of "dividing" the Savior into two beings whose unity consisted of agreement rather than in any real joining together. Soon many others were convinced that Nestorius's doctrines were indeed dangerous.

As was to be expected, the center of opposition to Nestorius was Alexandria, whose leader, Bishop Cyril, was a much more able politician and theologian than Nestorius. Cyril made certain that he had the support of the West, for which the doctrine of two persons in Christ was anathema, as well as of emperors Valentinian III and Theodosius II, who then called an ecumenical council to be gathered at Ephesus in June 431.

Nestorius's main supporters, John of Antioch and his party, were delayed. After waiting for them for two weeks, the council convened, in spite of the protests of the Roman legate and several dozen bishops. They then dealt with the case of Nestorius and, without allowing him to defend himself, declared him a heretic and deposed him from his see.

John of Antioch and his party arrived a few days later, and they then convened a rival council, which was much smaller than Cyril's, and which declared that Cyril was a heretic and reinstated Nestorius. In retaliation, Cyril's council reaffirmed its condemnation of Nestorius and added to it the names of John of Antioch and all who had taken part in his council. Finally, Theodosius II intervened, arrested both Cyril and John, and declared that the actions of both councils were void. Then followed a series of negotiations that led to a "formula of union" to which both Cyril and John agreed in 433. It was also decided that the actions of Cyril's council against Nestorius would stand. As to Nestorius, he spent the rest of his life in exile, first in a monastery in Antioch, and then, when he became too embarrassing to his Antiochene friends who had abandoned him, in the remote city of Petra.

Thus, the second episode in the christological controversies ended with a victory for Alexandria, and with a truce that would not hold for long. In 444, when Dioscorus succeeded Cyril as patriarch of Alexandria, the stage was set for a third and even more acrimonious confrontation, for Dioscorus was a convinced defender of the most extreme Alexandrine positions, and a rather unscrupulous maneuverer.

The storm centered on the teachings of Eutyches, a monk in Constantinople who lacked theological subtlety, and who held that, while the Savior was "of one substance [*homoousios*] with the Father," he was not "of one substance with us." He also seems to have been willing to say that Christ was "from two natures before the union, but in one nature after the union." Exactly what this meant is not altogether clear. In any case, Patriarch Flavian of Constantinople, whose theology was of the Antiochene tradition, felt that Eutyches's teachings were close to Docetism and condemned him. Through a series of maneuvers, Dioscorus had the affair grow into a conflict that involved the entire church, so that a council was called by Emperor Theodosius II, to meet at Ephesus in 449.

When this council gathered, it was clear that Dioscorus and his supporters had taken all the necessary steps to predetermine the outcome. Dioscorus himself had been appointed president of the assembly by the emperor, and given the authority to determine who would be allowed to speak. This council took an extreme Alexandrine stand. When Pope Leo's legates tried to present before the assembly a letter that Leo had written on the subject at hand—commonly known as Leo's *Tome*—they were not allowed to do so. Flavian was manhandled so violently that he died in a few days. The doctrine that there are in Christ "two natures" was declared heretical, as were also all who defended the

Antiochene position, even in moderate form. Furthermore, it was decreed that any who disagreed with these decisions could not be ordained.

In Rome, Leo fumed, and called the council a "Robber Synod." But his protests were to no avail. Theodosius II and his court, who apparently had received large amounts of gold from Alexandria, considered the matter ended.

Then the unexpected happened. Theodosius's horse stumbled, and the emperor fell and broke his neck. He was succeeded by his sister Pulcheria and her husband Marcian. Pulcheria had agreed earlier with the Western position, that Nestorius should be condemned, for it imperiled the union of the divine with the human. But she was not an extreme Alexandrine, and felt that the proceedings at Ephesus in 449 had left much to be desired. For this reason, at the behest of Leo, she called a new council, which met at Chalcedon in 451 and which eventually became known as the Fourth Ecumenical Council.

This council condemned Dioscorus and Eutyches, but forgave all others who had participated in the Robber Synod of Ephesus two years earlier. Leo's letter was finally read, and many declared that this expressed their own faith. It was a restatement of what Tertullian had declared centuries earlier, that in Christ there are "two natures in one person." Finally, the council produced a statement that was not a creed, but rather a *Definition of faith*, or a clarification of what the church held to be true. A careful reading of that "Definition" will show that, while rejecting the extremes of both Alexandrines and Antiochenes, and particularly the doctrine of Eutyches, it reaffirmed what had been done in the three previous great councils (Nicea in 325, Constantinople in 381, and Ephesus in 431):

> Following, then, the holy Fathers, we all with one voice teach that it is to be confessed that our Lord Jesus Christ is one and the same God, perfect in divinity, and perfect in humanity, true God and true human, with a rational soul and a body, of one substance with the Father in his divinity, and of one substance with us in his humanity, in every way like us, with the only exception of sin, begotten of the Father before all time in his divinity, and also begotten in the latter days, in his humanity, of Mary the Virgin bearer of God.
>
> This is one and the same Christ, Son, Lord, Only-begotten, manifested in two natures without any confusion, change, division or separation. The union does not destroy the difference of the two natures, but on the contrary the properties of each are kept, and both are joined in one person and *hypostasis*. They are not divided into two persons, but belong to the one Only-begotten Son, the Word of God, the Lord Jesus Christ.

All this, as the prophets of old said of him, and as he himself has taught us, and as the Creed of the Fathers has passed on to us.

It will be readily seen that this *Definition* does not seek to "define" the union in the sense of explaining how it took place, but rather in the sense of setting the limits beyond which error lies. Thus, it rejected the notion that the union destroyed "the difference of the two natures" and also the view that the Savior is "divided into two persons"—thus rejecting the most extreme Alexandrine and Antiochene positions. It is clear that this manner of speaking of the Savior is far distant from that of the Gospels, and has been deeply influenced by extrabiblical patterns of thought. But, given the manner in which the issue was posed, it is difficult to see what else the bishops gathered at Chalcedon could have done in order to safeguard the reality of the incarnation.

The *Definition of faith* soon became the standard of christological orthodoxy in the entire Western church, and in most of the East—although there were some in the East who rejected it, and thus gave rise to the first long-lasting schisms in the history of Christianity. Some, mostly in Syria and Persia, insisted on a clear distinction between the divine and the human in Christ, and were eventually called "Nestorians." Many others took the opposite tack, rejecting the doctrine of "two natures," and for that reason were dubbed "Monophysites"—from the Greek *monos* (one) and *physis* (nature). Very few of these, however, adhered to the teachings of Eutyches. Rather, their concern was that the divine and the human in the Savior not be so divided that the incarnation be rendered meaningless. To this were joined political and nationalist considerations which added fire to the theological debates that raged for centuries.

FURTHER THEOLOGICAL DEBATES

The Chalcedonian *Definition* did not put an end to christological debates, particularly in the East. There were many in Egypt who considered Dioscorus a martyr, and believed that Flavian and Leo were heretics. A large number of believers in Syria held similar views. In both cases, their theological objections were also spurred by resentment against the central government in Constantinople, which collected taxes in the provinces and did not return to them proportional benefits. To this were added cultural and ethnic tensions that existed since the time of the first Roman conquests, and had never been resolved. In order to regain the loyalty of these people, the emperors sought theological compromises that would satisfy both them and those who held to the decisions of Chalcedon. It was an impossible task, for the reasons for disaffection were not purely theological. On balance, all that the emperors achieved was to alienate both the Chalcedonians and the others, and to force the church into endless controversy.

The first to follow this unwise policy was Basiliscus, who had deposed Emperor Zeno, and who in 476 annulled the decisions of Chalcedon and called a new council. But this never met, for Zeno regained the throne and Basiliscus's projects were abandoned. Then Zeno himself published a *Henotikon* ("Edict of Union") in 482, in which he simply directed that all should return to what was commonly held before the controversy. But this created a new stir, for many, particularly Pope Felix III, declared that the emperor had no authority to prescribe what was to be believed. Since Zeno had the support of Patriarch Acacius of Constantinople, the dispute resulted in an open breach between the bishops of Rome and Constantinople. Called the Schism of Acacius, this separated the East from the West until 519, well after the death of both principals. At that time, Emperor Justin and Pope Hormisdas reached an agreement that was in fact a return to the decisions of Chalcedon.

Justin was succeeded by his nephew Justinian, the ablest emperor of the Byzantine Empire, who restored its military glory by reconquering North Africa and Italy, rebuilt Hagia Sophia, and codified the entire system of law. He was convinced that the differences between Chalcedonians and Monophysites were mostly verbal, and that the two parties could be reconciled through a series of meetings and dialogues. Much later, historians of Christian thought would come to the conclusion that on this score he was probably correct. But he seems not to have realized that to a great extent what appeared to be purely theological disagreements were in fact the results of much more difficult and intractable cultural, social, economic, and political conflicts. Thus, Justinian restored to their sees several of the Monophysite bishops who had been deposed during the reign of Justin, and some were even invited to visit the emperor and his wife Theodora at their palace, where they were received cordially and respectfully.

In 532, at the emperor's urging, a theological conference took place in Constantinople. The most distinguished Chalcedonian theologian of the time, Leontius of Byzantium, interpreted the Chalcedonian *Definition* in such a way that some of the leading Monophysites declared that the way was open for a rapprochement. One of them even declared that he was ready to accept the Chalcedonian *Definition*. At the end of the conference, many hoped that the schism would soon be healed.

But the emperor erred in thinking that he could regain the allegiance of his subjects who still rejected the council of Chalcedon by condemning, not the council itself, but the writings of three Antiochene theologians who were particularly distasteful to those who rejected the council—Theodore of Mopsuestia, Theodoret of Cyrus, and Ibas of Edessa. What ensued is usually called the

Justinian, shown with his court in a mosaic in Ravenna, led the empire in a brief revival of its power.

Controversy of the Three Chapters. Justinian was correct in that these three were among the Antiochene theologians whose christological views most offended the Monophysites. But this created such a stir that eventually Justinian was forced to call a council, which gathered at Constantinople in 553. At Justinian's prodding, the council, which eventually came to be known as the Fifth Ecumenical Council, condemned the Three Chapters. (Many objected to the condemnation of people who had been dead for quite some time, and whose contemporaries did not consider heretics. Therefore, rather than condemning them, the council condemned those among their writings that the Monophysites found most offensive.) But this did not satisfy those who wished to see the decisions of Chalcedon withdrawn, and therefore Justinian achieved little for all his efforts.

The last emperor who sought to regain the allegiance of those opposed to Chalcedon was Heraclius, early in the seventh century. Patriarch Sergius of Constantinople proposed that, while there are indeed two natures in Christ, there is only one will. Although Sergius's position is not altogether clear, it seems that he meant that in Christ the divine will took the place of the human will. In any case, this was how he was interpreted, and thus the objections raised against his view were similar to those raised earlier against Apollinaris: a man without a human will is not fully human. Sergius's position, which came to be

known as *Monothelism*—from the Greek *monos* ("one"), and *thelema* ("will")—
gained the support of Pope Honorius, and long debates ensued. But then came
the Arab conquests, which overran Syria and Egypt. Since those were the areas
where opposition to Chalcedon was strongest, imperial policy no longer sought
to reconcile the anti-Chalcedonians. In 648, Constans II prohibited any further
discussion on the will or wills of Christ. Finally, the Sixth Ecumenical Council, gathered at Constantinople in 680–681, condemned Monothelism, and
declared Pope Honorius to have been a heretic. (Much later, in the nineteenth
century, this condemnation of a pope as a heretic came to the foreground in the
discussions surrounding the proclamation of Papal Infallibility.)

Then came the controversy regarding the use of images. In a way, this was
a final episode in the christological debates. In the early church, there seems
to have been no objection to the use of images, for the catacombs and other
early places of worship were decorated with paintings depicting communion,
baptism, and various biblical episodes. Later, when the empire embraced Christianity, several leading bishops expressed concern that the masses now flocking
to the church would be led to idolatry, and therefore they preached, not against
the images themselves, but against their misuse as objects of worship. In the
eighth century, several Byzantine emperors took steps against images. Emperor
Leo III (who ruled in 717–741, and is not to be confused with the pope of the
same name, who ruled in 795–816) opened the controversy when he ordered the
destruction of a statue of Jesus that was highly regarded by many of the faithful. In 754 Constantine V, Leo's son and successor, called a council that forbade
the use of images and condemned those who defended them. The reasons for
these decisions are not altogether clear. Certainly, the presence of Islam, with
its strong teaching against any physical representation, was a factor. Also, the
emperors may have wished to curb the power of the monks, who were almost
unanimously in favor of images—and part of whose income came from the
production of images or icons. In any case, the entire empire was soon divided
between "iconoclasts"—destroyers of images—and "iconodules"—worshipers
of images.

The most influential theologian among the iconodules was John of Damascus, who lived under Muslim rule and was a high official in the caliph's government before he resigned from that position to become first a monk and then a
priest. His *Exposition of the Orthodox Faith* is significant both as a systemati-
zation of Eastern Orthodox doctrine and as the first major Christian writing
written in the context of Islam and in response to it. John is also famous for his
theological distinction between what can be known (the *kataphatic*) and what is
by its very nature a mystery and cannot be known (the *apophatic*).

John of Damascus and the rest of the iconodules saw their position as a cor-

*A deacon in the cathedral of Hagia
Sophia reads the Decree of 843 that put
an end to the iconoclastic controversy.*

ollary of christological orthodoxy. If Jesus was truly human, and in him God
had become visible, how could one object to representing him? Furthermore,
the first maker of images was God, who created humans after the divine image.
John, whose theology was such that he was among those condemned by the
council of Constantine V, argued:

> Why do we venerate one another, if not because we are made after
> the image of God? . . . To depict God in a shape would be the peak of
> madness and impiety. . . . But since God . . . became true man . . . the
> Fathers, seeing that not all can read nor have the time for it, approved
> the descriptions of these facts in images, that they might serve as brief
> commentaries.[41]

The controversy raged for years. The West simply ignored the imperial
edicts, while the East was rent asunder. Finally, the Seventh Ecumenical Council gathered at Nicea in 787. This assembly distinguished between worship
in the strict sense, *latria,* which is due only to God, and a lesser worshipful
veneration, *dulia,* which is to be given to images. Although the iconoclasts
regained power for a time, in 842 images were definitively restored—an event
that many Eastern churches still celebrate as the "Feast of Orthodoxy." In the
West, the decisions of the council of 787 were not well received, for the distinction between *latria* and *dulia* was difficult to make in Latin. But eventually the
difficulties were overcome, and most Christians agreed on the use of images in
church, and on the restricted veneration due to them.

THE DISSIDENT CHURCHES OF THE EAST

Although the various councils came to positions that eventually gained general
acceptance in the West and within the borders of the Byzantine Empire, such
decisions were not always well received by churches beyond the confines of the

empire. One of these was the Persian church. Since Persia was a traditional enemy of the Roman Empire, Christians in that nation took pains to show that their faith did not make them foreign agents. When they did not succeed in this, they were cruelly persecuted. In 410, the Persian church organized itself as an autonomous church, under the leadership of the patriarch of Ctesiphon—the Persian capital. When Nestorius was condemned shortly thereafter, a number of theologians of Antiochene inclinations, fearing further reprisals, crossed over to Persia, where they settled in the city of Nisibis and founded a school that eventually became the main center of theological education in Persia. As a result, the Persian church came to hold views that other Christians called "Nestorian." At its high point, this church had flourishing missions in Arabia, India, and even China. But political adversities eventually diminished its numbers, and the few thousand Nestorians who now remain are scattered all over the world.

Within the borders of the Byzantine Empire, the main strongholds of "Monophysism" were Egypt and Syria. In Egypt, opposition to the decisions of the council was coupled with unrest on the part of the people of ancient Egyptian stock, the Copts, who felt exploited and oppressed by the empire. In the cities, there were many Greek-speaking Christians who felt quite satisfied with the existing order, and who generally accepted the Chalcedonian *Definition of Faith*. After the Arab conquests, the Coptic Church became the main Christian body in Egypt. Those who held to Chalcedonian orthodoxy were dubbed *Melchites*—that is, "imperial" Christians. Both churches—the Coptic and the Melchite—have continued existing side by side until the present day, although the Coptic Church is the larger of the two. Since the church in Ethiopia had always had close ties with Egypt, and few directly with the rest of the church, it followed the lead of the Coptic Church in rejecting the Council of Chalcedon, and thus becoming "Monophysite."

Something similar happened in Syria, although the country was more evenly divided between Chalcedonians and "Monophysites." The great leader of the latter was Jacob Baradaeus, an indefatigable traveler and organizer, and for that reason their church came to be called "Jacobite."

The other major "Monophysite" body is the Armenian church. By 450, when the Persians tried to impose their religion on Armenia, Christianity—which had arrived there through the work of Gregory the Illuminator—had become the rallying point of Armenian nationality. This was just before the Council of Chalcedon, and the Armenians hoped that the Roman Empire would come to their aid as fellow Christians. But then Theodosius II, who had promised such aid, died, and his successors Pulcheria and Marcian simply let Armenia be invaded by the Persians. With 1,036 soldiers who fought to the last man, the Armenians defended the mountain passes, hoping that this delay would

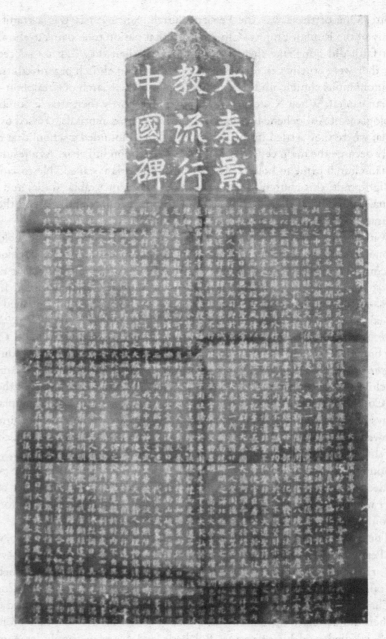

This inscription, commonly known as the Nestorian tablet, dates from 781, and marks the presence of Nestorian Christianity in China at least a century and a half earlier. The heading reads: Memorial of the Propagation in China of the Luminous Religion.

give the Romans time to intervene. But it was all in vain, and the country was overrun by the Persians. Since it was precisely at that time that Pulcheria and Marcian called the Council of Chalcedon, it is not surprising that the Armenians rejected the decisions of that council. For that reason, they were dubbed "Monophysites." They in turn declared that those who had gathered at the council—who had declared that in Christ there are "two natures," the divine and the human—were not only traitors, but also heretics.

Under the Persians, the Armenians proved unwilling to give up their religion and traditions, and were granted a measure of autonomy. Then came the Arabs, under whose regime, in spite of sporadic persecution, Armenian Christianity flourished. In the eleventh century, the Turks took the country, and their harshness led many Armenians to emigrate to Asia Minor, where they founded Little Armenia. But eventually this region was also taken by the Turks, who ruled it with an iron hand. Early in the twentieth century, they massacred thousands of Armenians. Entire villages were wiped out. The survivors scattered throughout the world. Meanwhile, the older Armenia continued its traditions, first most of it under Soviet rule, and then as the independent Republic of Armenia.

While these various bodies continued existing into the present, by the second half of the twentieth century they had been touched by the ecumenical movement, and there were in all of these churches—as well as in those that had always held to the *Definition* of Chalcedon—growing numbers that felt that many of their disagreements were verbal rather than real, and thus a rapprochement had begun.

EASTERN ORTHODOXY AFTER THE ARAB CONQUESTS

Although it is obvious that every church thinks of itself as orthodox, that title has become such a hallmark of Eastern Chalcedonian Christianity that it is often called the Orthodox Church.

After the Arab conquests, the Orthodox Church was blocked to the south and east by Islam, and thus its expansion was in a northerly and northwesterly direction. Those areas of Eastern Europe were populated mostly by Slavs, who had invaded them after the Germanic peoples. They occupied most of what is today Poland, the Baltic countries, Russia, Slovakia, Serbia, and Greece. Those who had crossed the Danube were, at least nominally, part of the Byzantine Empire. The rest were divided among many tribes and nations. Then a new group of invaders, the Bulgars, conquered a vast portion of the Danube basin, where they ruled over a mixed population of Slavs and other former subjects of the Byzantine Empire.

Such was the situation in 862, when a letter arrived in Constantinople from King Rostislav of Moravia, one of the Slavic kingdoms:

> Many Christians have arrived in our midst, some Italian, some Greek, and some German, and they have spoken to us in their different ways. But we Slavs are simple people, and have no one to teach us the truth. . . . Therefore we pray you to send us someone capable of teaching us the whole truth.[42]

Rostislav was not as naive as he made his letter sound. He feared that the Western missionaries in his kingdom would serve as a spearhead for conquest, as had already happened in other areas where missionaries from the Frankish Empire had worked. He was also aware of the rivalry between Eastern and Western Christians, and his letter was an attempt to use that rivalry to safeguard his kingdom.

In any case, the request was well received in Constantinople as an opportunity to extend Byzantine influence. In response to Rostislav's request, two brothers, Cyril and Methodius, were sent as missionaries. They had grown up in the Balkans, among Slavs, and therefore already knew something of the language. They had also shown their mettle in a previous mission to Crimea. In Moravia, they were well received. Cyril devised a way to write Slavonic—the Cyrillic alphabet, still used by most Slavic languages—and translated the Bible, several other books, and the liturgy. But they soon ran into opposition from German missionaries, who claimed that the only proper liturgical languages were Latin, Greek, and Hebrew. Finally, Cyril and Methodius went to Rome, where the pope decided in their favor, but put them under his jurisdiction. Thus, for years the Moravian church was torn by a three-way contest between Constantinople, Rome, and the Germans. Finally, in 906, the Hungarians invaded the area, and the kingdom of Moravia disappeared. However, the pioneer work of Cyril and Methodius bore fruit among all the Slavic peoples, some of whom eventually joined Western Christianity, while others became Orthodox.

Meanwhile, the Bulgarians had grown strong in the Balkans. They too had been visited by both Western and Orthodox missionaries when their leader, King Boris, decided to become a Christian. After being baptized, Boris requested of Photius, the patriarch of Constantinople, that an archbishop be named for his kingdom. Since Photius asked questions and demanded that certain conditions be met, Boris turned to Pope Nicholas, who sent him two bishops but refused him an archbishop. Finally, Photius's successor to the see of Constantinople did consecrate an archbishop and several bishops to lead the newly formed Bulgarian Orthodox Church. After a brief pagan reaction, Christianity was consolidated under Boris's son Simeon. In 917, Simeon asserted his independence from Byzantium by taking the title of "czar"—meaning caesar or emperor—and ten years later a similar action was taken in ecclesiastical matters when the archbishop was given the title of patriarch. Although at first Byzantine authorities took these actions to be a usurpation of power, they eventually were reconciled to them.

The greatest missionary success of the Orthodox Church, however, was the conversion of Kievan Rus, and eventually Russia. Around 950, Queen Olga, who ruled the principality of Kiev, was converted and baptized by Germanic missionaries. But it was under her grandson Vladimir (980–1015) that Christianity began making significant progress. For reasons that are not altogether clear, Vladimir sent for missionaries, not from the West, but rather from the Byzantine Empire. He and many of his subjects were baptized in 988, and this date is usually given as the beginning of both the Ukrainian and the Russian church—for the princes of Kiev would eventually rule in Moscow, which at the time of Vladimir's conversion was just a small village. There is also some question as to how much force Vladimir used to induce his subjects to become Christians. His son Yaroslav the Wise (1019–1054) strengthened the ties with Constantinople, and moved further away from Rome. By 1240, when the Mongols invaded Russia and ruled the country for over two centuries, Christianity

Queen Olga's grandson, now known as St. Vladimir, was the Grand Prince of Kiev, and led his subjects into the Christian faith. In this painting, commissioned for the celebration of the millennium of that event, Vladimir stands at the center, with his wife Anna of Constantinople and his son Yaroslav, who would continue his work. At the left, the ancient religion is overthrown. The artist, Peter Andrusiw, has painted himself in the baptismal waters, almost directly below St. Vladimir.

was the national bond of unity that allowed Russia to survive as a nation, and eventually to be rid of the invaders. In the sixteenth century, after Constantinople had been taken by the Turks, Russia declared that Moscow was "the Third Rome," its rulers took the imperial title of czars, and the bishop of Moscow that of patriarch.

After the Arab conquests, relations between Rome and Constantinople grew steadily worse. The restoration of the Western empire under Charlemagne meant that the popes no longer needed the support of the Byzantine Empire. And the prolonged controversy over the use of images convinced the West that the Eastern church was a puppet in the hands of the emperor. All this led to what the West called the Photian Schism (867). Photius had been made patriarch of Constantinople following a revolution that deposed Patriarch Ignatius. Both Photius and Ignatius turned to Pope Nicholas for support, and he took the side of Ignatius. Photius then declared that the entire West was heretical, because it had tampered with the Nicene Creed by including in it the word *Filioque* ("and from the Son"). The old creed said that the Holy Spirit proceeds "from the Father." Photius argued that in adding "and from the Son," the Westerners were tampering both with the creed itself and with the ancient understanding of the Trinity, which affirms that the Spirit proceeds "from the Father, *through* the Son."

It seems that this alteration of the Nicene Creed arose first in Spain, and from there was taken to France. By Charlemagne's time, the Creed recited in the royal chapel at Aachen included the *Filioque*. When some Frankish monks visiting the East recited the Creed with that clause in it, they created a scandal among the Orthodox, who demanded to know who had given the Franks authority to alter the ancient Creed of the great council. To this were added political rivalries between the ancient Byzantine Empire and the Frankish upstarts, as well as the traditional distrust between East and West.

One by-product of this controversy was the resurgence of the Old Roman Creed, now called the Apostles' Creed. The pope, wishing to alienate neither the Byzantines nor the Franks, began using that old, almost forgotten creed instead of the Nicene. Eventually, through the influence of Rome, the Apostles' Creed supplanted the Nicene Creed as the most commonly used among Western Christians.

When political circumstances changed in Constantinople, Ignatius was restored as patriarch, and there was an agreement that Photius would be the next patriarch. But the bitterness engendered by the schism continued, and would eventually bear fruit.

The final schism came in the eleventh century. The Bulgarian archbishop, Leo of Ochrid, accused the West of error because it made clerical celibacy a universal rule, and because it celebrated communion with unleavened bread. When the dispute grew, Pope Leo IX sent an ambassador to Constantinople to deal with it. But his choice was most unfortunate. Cardinal Humbert, his legate, knew no Greek and did not care to learn it. He was a zealous reformer whose program included clerical celibacy and the autonomy of the church from civil rulers. To his mind, the Eastern married clergy, and the authority that the Byzantine emperor had over the church, were the very enemies which he had vowed to destroy. He and patriarch Michael Cerularius exchanged insults. Finally, on June 16, 1054, when the patriarch was preparing to celebrate communion, Cardinal Humbert appeared at the cathedral of Hagia Sophia, walked to the high altar and, in the name of the pope—who actually had died shortly before—placed on it a sentence of excommunication against "heretic" Michael Cerularius, as well as any who dared follow him. Cardinal Humbert then left, shook the dust from his feet, and set out for Rome. The break between East and West was finally accomplished.

29

Imperial Restoration and Continuing Decay

> Let the powerful beware . . . of taking to their own condemnation that
> which belongs to the church, . . . knowing that ecclesiastical properties
> are the promises of the faithful, the patrimony of the poor, the price for
> the remission of sin.
>
> HINCMAR OF REIMS

On Christmas Day 800 in Saint Peter's Basilica in Rome, three hundred
and four years after the baptism of Clovis, Pope Leo III took a crown in
his hands, approached Charles, king of the Franks, and placing the crown on
his head exclaimed: "May God grant life to the great and pacific emperor!"
Three hundred and twenty-four years earlier, the last emperor of the West
had been deposed. In crowning Charles—or Charlemagne, as he came to be
called—Leo revived the ancient Roman Empire, now reborn under the aegis of
the church.

CHARLEMAGNE'S REIGN

When Leo crowned Charlemagne, almost all of Western Christendom was
under the emperor's rule. The main exception was the British Isles. But even
before being crowned emperor, while he was only king of the Franks, Charlemagne had extended his domains beyond the borders of the ancient Roman
Empire. This he did through a series of campaigns against the Saxons and their
Frisian allies, on the Eastern borders of his empire.

The campaigns against the Frisians and Saxons were long and bloody.
Repeatedly, Charlemagne invaded their territory and forced them to submit,
only to have them rebel again as soon as he was away. Charlemagne resolved to
drown the rebellion in blood and in the waters of baptism. Those who proved
intractable were slaughtered. The rest were forced to accept baptism. By 784,
the Frisians gave up the struggle; a year later, the final resistance of the Saxons

Under Charlemagne's leadership, the Western empire was resurrected.

was broken, and thousands were forcibly baptized. This was an important step, for many Saxons seem to have believed that in accepting baptism they were forsaking their gods, who in turn would forsake them. Thus, once baptized, one had no god to turn to but the Christian God. In any case, these forced baptisms had such results that soon there were Christian leaders among the Saxons, who then employed similar methods for the conversion of their neighbors.

Charlemagne also extended his power to the west. His first campaign into Spain was a disaster. He invaded the peninsula because he had been assured of support from some Muslim leaders, and that support never materialized. On the way back, his rearguard was ambushed, probably by Basques, at Ronces-valles—an event that inspired the earliest existing major work in French, the *Chanson de Roland,* and left its mark on later literature on medieval chivalry.

Later, Charlemagne's armies did establish a foothold in Spain, conquering the land as far as the river Ebro, and establishing there the province known as the Spanish March. Also, Charlemagne supported the efforts of Alfonso II of Asturias, who was beginning the long process of reconquering the peninsula from the Moors.

As emperor, Charlemagne felt called to rule his people both in civil and in ecclesiastical matters. He appointed bishops just as he named generals, although always seeking men of worth. He also enacted laws ordering that there be preaching in the language of the people, that Sunday be kept as a day of worship and rest, and that tithes be collected as if they were a tax. Monasticism had lost a great deal of its original zeal, with many abbots who viewed their office as a means to riches and power, and Charlemagne decided that the entire institution was in need of reform. For this he counted on Benedict (not to be confused with Benedict of Nursia, who wrote the *Rule*) a man respected for his wisdom and piety who had abandoned the court in order to become a monk, and whom now Charlemagne appointed to head the royal abbey of Aniane, which was to serve as a model to bring other monasteries in Charlemagne's domains into compliance with the Benedictine *Rule*.

Charlemagne, although not himself an educated man, was a patron of learning. He revived and reformed the schools that already existed, and called to his court deacon Alcuin of York, whom he had met in Italy, and who reintroduced among the Franks the knowledge that had been preserved first in Irish and then in British monasteries. From Spain, Charlemagne brought Theodulf, whom he made bishop of Orleans, and who ordered that throughout his diocese there should be a school in every church, and that these were to be open to the poor as well as to the rich. Soon other bishops followed Theodulf's example, and there was a significant revival of learning that was aided by the many scholars who flocked to Charlemagne's domains.

The glory of Charlemagne's empire did not last long after the great emperor's death. His son Louis "the Pious" was a conscientious ruler, but not a good judge of character. Louis was committed to monastic reform, and even before he became emperor in 814 he had requested Benedict of Aniane to undertake the reform of monasteries in Aquitaine, over which Louis ruled as king. After Louis became emperor, the imperial diet of 817, following his wishes, ordered that all monasteries be reformed under the leadership of Benedict of Aniane, and that bishops and other clerics should not wear jewels or ostentatious attire. The same diet also declared tithes to be obligatory for all, and ordered that two-thirds of the money received as tithes be given to the poor. Finally, the diet sought to give the church more autonomy by reverting to the old custom of allowing bishops to be elected by the people and the clergy. But there were many, including some bishops, who took advantage of Louis's good nature, and the last years of his reign were marred by civil wars in which Louis's sons and their partisans fought each other as well as the emperor. Repeatedly, after defeating various rebellious groups, Louis would forgive his adversaries; but rather than gaining wider support, such magnanimity encouraged additional rebellions, and even those who had been forgiven rose again against the emperor. When he died, his possessions were divided among his three sons. Under his grandson Charles "the Fat" of France, emperor from 881 to 887, most of the ancient empire was reunited, only to be divided again after Charles's death. To these inner divisions and internecine warfare were added raids and invasions by Norsemen and others.

The Arab conquests also had enormous consequences for the economic and political life of Western Europe. Before those conquests, there was widespread commerce along the Mediterranean, and even with the Orient. Now the Arabs blocked the route to the Orient and ruled the southern and eastern shores of the Mediterranean. Although there was still some shipping in the Adriatic and on the northern shores of Europe, trade on a large scale was interrupted, and each area had to become more self-sufficient. There came a time when money almost ceased circulating, Western Europe moved into a barter economy, and gold coins became rare.

Under such circumstances, the main source of wealth was land, rather than money. Kings and other lords often paid for services by granting land to those they wished to reward. Thus was feudalism born. It was a hierarchical system, based on land holdings; each feudal lord, while receiving homage from those who owed their lands to him, paid homage to the greater lord from whom he had received his. At first, grants of land were made for a lifetime. But eventually they became hereditary. Because a vassal often held land under various lords, the obligations of vassalage could always be evaded by claiming a conflicting allegiance to another lord. The result of all this was the political and economic fragmentation of Western Europe, and the decline of all centralized power, including that of kings.

The church was also affected. Since bishoprics and abbeys often had vast holdings of land, bishops, abbots, and abbesses became magnates whose support everyone sought. Therefore, the question of who possessed the authority to name those who would fill such positions became one of enormous political significance.

THEOLOGICAL ACTIVITY

The revival of learning that Charlemagne had sought bore fruit throughout the ninth century. Wherever there was a strong ruler and a measure of peace, schools flourished, manuscripts were copied, and there was a measure of theological activity. However, during all that time Western Europe produced only one systematic thinker of stature, while most theological activity centered on controversies over a single point of doctrine or worship.

The great systematic thinker during the reign of the Carolingians—the dynasty of Charlemagne—was John Scotus Erigena, a native of Ireland who had fallen heir to the knowledge of antiquity that had been preserved in Irish monasteries. Toward the middle of the ninth century, he settled at the court of Charles "the Bald"—one of the three heirs of Louis the Pious—and there came to enjoy great prestige for his erudition. Well versed in Greek, he translated into Latin the works of the false Dionysius the Areopagite. In the fifth century, someone had written these works, which were purported to be by the same Dionysius who had heard Paul at the Areopagus. When they were introduced into Western Europe during the reign of Charles "the Bald," no one doubted their authenticity. Erigena's translation was read as the word of one whose authority was almost apostolic. Since these works expounded a form of Neoplatonic mysticism, soon this was confused with Paul's theology, and the apostle was read as if he too had been a Neoplatonist.

Erigena's great writing, *On the Division of Nature,* followed along the same lines, and many of his tenets can now be recognized as more Neoplatonic than Christian. However, his tone was so erudite, and his speculation so abstract, that not many read his work, fewer understood it, and no one seems to have become his follower. Later, those few who had taken from Erigena one point or another often found themselves condemned as heretics.

One of the main theological controversies of the Carolingian period centered on the teachings of Spanish Bishops Elipandus of Toledo and Felix of Urgel. There remained in Spain many Christians whose ancestors had not fled at the time of the Muslim conquests, and who now lived under Moorish rule. These Christians, the *Mozarab*s, kept their ancient traditions dating back to pre-Islamic times, including their form of worship, known as the *Mozarabic liturgy*—which is still celebrated in the Cathedral of Toledo. When Charlemagne began reconquering some of the lands that had previously been under Islamic rule, the Mozarabs clung to their traditions, which the Franks sought to replace with those of France and Rome. Thus, there was tension between Franks and Mozarabs even before the controversy broke out.

The conflict began when Elipandus, on the basis of some phrases in the Mozarabic liturgy, declared that, according to his divinity, Jesus was the eternal Son of the Father, but that, according to his humanity, he was son only *by adoption.* This led many to call Elipandus and his followers adoptionists. But there was a vast difference between what Elipandus taught and true adoptionism. The latter claims that Jesus was a "mere man" whom God had adopted. Elipandus, on the other hand, affirmed that Jesus had always been divine. But he felt the need to insist on the distinction between divinity and humanity in the Savior, and he did this by speaking of two forms of sonship, one eternal and one by adoption. Thus, rather than adoptionism in the strict sense, this was the sort of christology that earlier theologians of the Antiochene school had held, and whose extreme form was condemned by the Council of Ephesus.

Against these views, others insisted on the close union of the divine and human in Jesus. Beatus of Liebana, for instance, wrote:

> Unbelievers could see nothing but a man in the one whom they crucified. And as a man they crucified him. They crucified the Son of God. They crucified God. My God suffered for me. For me was my God crucified.[43]

Soon the teachings of Elipandus and his follower Felix of Urgel were condemned both by Frankish theologians and by the popes. Felix was forced to recant, and was kept away from Urgel, where Mozarabic influence was strong. Elipandus, however, was living in Moorish lands, and refused to recant. After the death of both Elipandus and Felix, the controversy subsided.

Meanwhile, however, other controversies had developed in the West. We have already discussed the clash with Constantinople on the interpolation of *Filioque* in the Nicene Creed. Of the many other issues debated among Western theologians, the most significant were predestination and the presence of Christ in communion.

The main figure in the controversy regarding predestination was Gottschalk of Orbais, a monk who had carefully studied the writings of Augustine and had come to the conclusion that the church had departed from the teachings of the great bishop of Hippo, particularly in the matter of predestination. While he understood the content of Augustine's views on predestination better than his contemporaries—and in this he was right—he expounded and defended them with a bitterness that was far from the spirit of Augustine. Indeed, some commentators have declared that he seemed to rejoice over the conviction that his enemies were reprobates condemned to eternal damnation. For a number of reasons, Gottschalk made enemies among his superiors, and when he made his views known there were those who were prompt to attack him. Among these were the abbot of Fulda, Rabanus Maurus, and the powerful Bishop Hincmar of Reims. After a debate that involved many distinguished theologians—including John Scotus Erigena, but also Rabanus and most particularly Hincmar—Gottschalk was declared a heretic and imprisoned in a monastery, where he is said to have gone mad shortly before his death.

The other great controversy of the Carolingian period had to do with the presence of Christ in communion. The occasion for the debate was a treatise

On the Body and the Blood of the Lord, by Paschasius Radbertus, a monk of Corbie who would later be declared a saint. In his treatise, Radbertus declared that when the bread and wine are consecrated they are transformed into the body and blood of the Lord. They are no longer bread and wine, but the very body that was born of the Virgin Mary, and the same blood that ran at Calvary. According to Radbertus, although this transformation takes place mysteriously, and human senses cannot usually perceive it, there are extraordinary cases in which a believer is allowed to see the body and blood of the Lord instead of bread and wine.

When King Charles the Bald read Radbertus's treatise, he had doubts about it, and asked Ratramnus of Corbie to clarify the matter. Ratramnus answered that, although the body of Christ is truly present in communion, this is not the same sort of presence of any other physical body, and that in any case the eucharistic body of Christ is not the same as the historical body of Jesus, which is sitting at the right hand of God.

This controversy shows that, by the Carolingian period, there were some who held that in communion the bread and wine cease to be such, and become the body and blood of Christ. But it also shows that still at that time many theologians took this to be the result of popular exaggeration and inexact use of language. Shortly thereafter, some began to speak of a "change in substance," and finally in the thirteenth century the Fourth Lateran Council (1215) would proclaim the doctrine of transubstantiation.

These are just a sampling of the many controversies that took place during the Carolingian revival of learning. That revival, however, was brief, and its promise was cut short by divisions among the successors of Charlemagne, as well as by new waves of invaders who once again brought fear and chaos to Western Christianity.

NEW INVASIONS

For a time, Charlemagne and his successors seemed to have brought Western Europe out of the confusion created by the Germanic invasions of the fourth and fifth centuries. But in truth those invasions, which had subsided for a while, had not ended, and would start afresh at a time that coincided with the decline of the Carolingian empire.

For centuries, extreme northern Europe had been inhabited by Scandinavians. During the eighth century, these heretofore sedentary people developed the art of shipbuilding to such a point that they mastered the neighboring seas. Their ships, sixty or seventy feet in length and propelled by sail and oars, could carry up to eighty men. In them, the Scandinavians began their expeditions to the rest of Europe, where they were called Norsemen. As the Carolingian

King Canute was master of England as well as Scandinavia. Here he places a cross on the altar of a church in England.

empire began to disintegrate, the northern coasts of France became vulnerable to attack, and the Norsemen soon discovered that they could land on them, sack churches, monasteries, and palaces, and return to their lands with booty and slaves. Since they often attacked churches and monasteries in pursuit of the treasures they held, they were taken to be enemies of God.

At first, the Norsemen limited their attacks to the nearby coasts of the British Isles and northern France. But they soon grew more daring, both in reaching farther afield and in settling down as conquerors in new lands. In England, the only one who offered significant resistance was King Alfred the Great of Wessex, but by the eleventh century King Canute of the Danes was master of all of England—as well as of Denmark, Sweden, and Norway. In France, they took and sacked such cities as Bordeaux, Nantes, and even Paris, which they reached in 845. In Spain, they looted the Christian shrine of Santiago de Compostela, as well as the Muslim city of Seville, far south. They crossed the Straits of Gibraltar, and made their presence felt in the Mediterranean. Eventually they settled in Sicily, which they took from the Muslims, and in southern Italy, and founded a kingdom in those lands. Others settled in northern France, in the region that came to be Normandy. From there, they would later cross to England, and conquer that land.

Eventually, the Norsemen became Christians. Many simply took over the faith of those whom they had conquered and among whom they settled.

Others, mostly in Scandinavia itself and in distant Iceland, were led to baptism by the example—and sometimes the coercion—of their leaders. By Canute's time, in the first half of the eleventh century, almost all Scandinavians had been baptized.

At about the same time as the Scandinavians invaded from the north, others were coming from the east. These were the Magyars, whom the Latin West called "Hungarians" because they brought memories of the ancient Huns. After settling in what is now Hungary, they repeatedly invaded Germany, and crossed the Rhine more than once. Even distant Burgundy trembled under the hooves of their horses, and into southern Italy they marched, victorious and destructive. Finally, in 933 and 955, Henry the Fowler and his son Otto I of Germany dealt them crushing defeats, and most of their attacks ceased.

The Hungarians assimilated much of the culture of their German neighbors, as well as of the Slavs they had conquered. Missionaries went to Hungary both from Germany and from the Byzantine Empire, and late in the tenth century their king was baptized. The next king, who took the name of Stephen and is generally known as Saint Stephen of Hungary, forced the conversion of all his subjects.

The incursions of Scandinavians and Hungarians made of the tenth century what an historian has called "a dark century of lead and iron." Although toward the end of the century the empire enjoyed a certain revival under Otto the Great and his immediate successors, it too was an empire of lead and iron. And the papacy, reflecting the times, fell to the lowest depths of its entire history.

DECAY IN THE PAPACY

The crowning of Charlemagne put the papacy in an ambiguous position. On the one hand, since the popes seemed to have the right to crown emperors, they enjoyed great prestige beyond the Alps. But, on the other hand, in Rome itself chaos often reigned. Thus, those who had the power to dispose of the empire seemed unable to govern their own city. And this in turn made the papacy an easy prey for the ambitious, one to be had by bribery, deceit, or even violence.

The decline of the papacy was not as rapid as that of the Carolingians. As imperial authority waned, there was a brief period during which the popes were seen as the only source of universal authority in Western Europe. Consequently, the reign of Pope Nicholas I, which lasted from 858 to 867, was the most outstanding since that of Gregory the Great, three centuries earlier. His authority was reinforced by a collection of documents, supposedly ancient, which granted popes great power. These documents, the *False Decretals,* were probably forged by members of the lower echelons in the German ecclesiastical hierarchy, who sought to bolster the authority of the pope over their direct superiors. In any case, both Nicholas and the rest of Europe believed that the *Decretals* were genuine, and on that basis he acted with unprecedented energy. He was particularly active in curbing the warring inclinations of the powerful, who often seemed to make war as a sport, while the common folk suffered most of the consequences.

His successor, Hadrian II, followed a similar policy. He clashed with Lothair II, king of Lorraine, whom Nicholas had already reprimanded for marital irregularities. In Monte Cassino, when the king appeared for communion, the pope cursed him and his court. When a terrible epidemic broke out in the king's court, and Lothair was among the dead, the pope's prestige knew no bounds.

But the reign of the next pope, John VIII, saw the first signs of decline. In order to respond to the threat of Muslim invasion, he sought the support of Charles the Fat, as well as of the Byzantines, and found that neither of them would come to his aid. He was murdered in his own palace, and it is said that when the aide who had poisoned him saw that he was slow in dying, he broke the pope's skull with a mallet.

From then on, pope succeeded pope in rapid sequence. Their history is one of intrigues too complicated to follow here, as the papacy became the prize for which the various rival parties in Rome and beyond the Alps fought. Popes were strangled, or died of starvation in the dungeons where they had been thrown by their successors. At times there were two popes, or even three, each claiming to be the one true successor of Saint Peter.

Some instances will suffice to illustrate the mood of the times. In 897 Pope Stephen VI presided over what came to be known as the "Cadaveric Council." One of his predecessors, Formosus, was disinterred, dressed in his papal robes, and exhibited on the streets. Then he was tried, found guilty of a multitude of crimes, and mutilated. Finally, what remained of the body was thrown into the Tiber.

In 904, Sergius III had his two rivals, Leo V and Christopher I, incarcerated and killed. He had come to power with the support of one of the most powerful families of Italy. This family was headed by Theophylact and his wife Theodora, whose daughter, Marozia, was Sergius's lover. Shortly after the death of Sergius, Marozia and her husband Guido of Tuscia captured the Lateran palace and made John X their prisoner, subsequently suffocating him with a pillow. After the brief pontificates of Leo VI and Stephen VII, Marozia placed on the papal throne, with the name of John XI, the son whom she had had from her union with Sergius III. Thirty years after the death of John XI, that papacy was in the hands of John XII, a grandson of Marozia. Later, her nephew became John XIII. His successor, Benedict VI, was overthrown and strangled by Crescentius, a brother of John XIII. John XIV died of either poison or starvation in the dungeon where he had been thrown by Boniface VII, who in turn was poisoned.

For a while, Emperor Otto III was able to determine who would be pope. His first choice was his own nephew, who became pope at twenty-three years of age, and took the name of Gregory V. Then he named the famous scholar Gerbert of Aurillac, who became Sylvester II and made a valiant but unsuccessful effort to reform the papacy as well as the entire church.

When Otto died, the family of Crescentius—which was also the family of Theophylact, Theodora, and Marozia—once again gained control of the papacy, until the counts of Tusculum gained the upper hand and named Benedict VIII, John XIX, and Benedict IX. The latter was fifteen years old when he became pope. Twelve years later, in 1045, he abdicated on the basis of having been promised a financial settlement. His godfather, Gregory VI, tried to reform the church, but then Benedict IX withdrew his abdication, and Crescentius's family put forth its own pope, whom they called Sylvester III.

Finally, King Henry III of Germany intervened. After an interview with Gregory VI he gathered a council that deposed all three popes and named Clement II. The same council also enacted a series of decrees against ecclesiastical corruption, particularly simony—the practice of buying and selling positions in the church.

Clement II crowned Henry emperor, and died shortly thereafter. Henry then decided to offer the papacy to Bruno, bishop of Toul, already known for his reforming zeal. But Bruno refused to accept the papacy unless he was elected to it by the people of Rome. To that end he left for the ancient capital, in the company of two other monks of similar ideas, Hildebrand and Humbert. As it approached Rome, that small party carried with it the beginnings of a new age for the church.

30

Movements of Renewal

What would the bishops of yesteryear have done, had they had to live through all of this? . . . Every day a banquet. Every day a parade. On the table, all sorts of delicacies, not for the poor, but for sensual guests. Meanwhile, the poor, to whom these things rightfully belong, are not allowed in, and they perish in hunger.

PETER DAMIAN

The violence and corruption that followed the decline of the Carolingian empire awakened in many a deep yearning for a new order. The sight of the papacy turned into a bone of contention for petty rivals, bishoprics bought and sold, and the entire life of the church put at the service of the powerful was a scandal for many who took their faith seriously. Given the options open at that time, it was to be expected that most of those who yearned for reform had taken up the monastic life. Thus, it was out of monasteries that a wave of reform arose that conquered the papacy, clashed with the powerful, and was felt even in the distant shores of the Holy Land.

MONASTIC REFORM

Monasticism itself was in need of reformation. Many monasteries had been sacked and destroyed by Norsemen and Hungarians. Those in more sheltered areas became toys for the ambitions of abbots and prelates. The nobles and bishops who were supposed to be their guardians used them for their own ends. Just as the papacy and the episcopacy had become means of personal aggrandizement, so had the great abbeys. Some became abbots by buying their posts, or even through homicide, and then gave themselves to an easy life on the basis of the abbey's income. The *Rule* of Benedict was generally ignored, and monks and nuns who sincerely felt called to the monastic life found that violence was done to their vocation. One such was Hildegard of Bingen (1098–1179), a German Benedictine abbess whose mystical writings became popular among those who sought a more profound spiritual life. But although there were numerous nuns

Thanks to a long series of extraordinarily able abbots, Cluny Abbey in France became the center of a vast renewal of monasticism that eventually made an impact on all of Western Europe.

and monks whose commitment to reformation led them to found new monastic houses, eventually the prevailing corruption would affect them too.

Two centuries before Hildegard's time, in 909, Duke William III of Aquitaine had founded a small monastery, hoping that it would be better than the existing ones. In itself, this was not new, for such actions had become common on the part of powerful nobles. But several wise decisions and providential circumstances turned that small monastic house into the center of a vast reformation.

In order to lead his new monastery, William called on Berno, a monk who was well known for his steadfast obedience to the *Rule* and for his efforts for the reformation of monasticism. At Berno's request, William set aside Cluny, his own favorite hunting place, for the use of the monastery. This, with the necessary lands for the sustenance of the monastery, was deeded over to "Saints Peter and Paul," thus placing the new community under the direct jurisdiction and protection of the pope. Since at that time the papacy was at its nadir, such protection would only amount to forbidding the intervention of nearby bishops and feudal lords, including William himself or his heirs. Also, in order to guarantee that the new monastic foundation did not fall prey to a corrupt papacy, the deed explicitly forbade the pope from invading or otherwise taking what belonged only to the two holy apostles. This and other similar donations to abbeys and monasteries may well have been part of a general attempt on the part of many to be reconciled with God as the end of the first millennium approached, for Augustine and others had suggested that, since a thousand years are as a day in the eyes of God, the end of the first millennium would bring about the consummation of creation.

Berno ruled at Cluny until 926. Not much is known of those early years, for Cluny was only one of several monasteries that Berno set out to found or to reform. But after his death the house was led by a series of able and high-minded abbots who turned Cluny into the center of a vast monastic reform: Odo (926–944), Aymard (944–965), Mayeul (965–994), Odilo (994–1049), and Hugh (1049–1109). Six abbots of extraordinary dedication, ability, and length of life ruled Cluny for a total of two hundred years. Under their leadership, the ideals of monastic reform expanded ever farther. The seventh abbot, Pontius (1109–1122) was not of the caliber of the rest. But his successor, Peter the Venerable (1122–1157) regained much of what had been lost in Pontius's time. One of the characteristics of the Cluniac reformation of monastic life was that all their houses had to have clear title to their property, thus freeing them from subjection to the whims of a feudal lord.

At first, the purpose of the monks of Cluny was simply to have a place where they could follow the *Rule* of Benedict in its entirety. But then their horizons widened, and the abbots of Cluny, following Berno's example, set out to reform other houses. Thus there appeared an entire network of "second Clunys," which were directly under the abbot of the main monastery. It was not an "order" in the strict sense, but rather a series of independent monasteries, all under the rule of a single abbot, who normally appointed the prior of each community. This reformation also gained way in women's monastic communities, the first of which, Marcigny, was founded in the eleventh century, when Hugh was abbot of Cluny.

The main occupation of these monks and nuns, as the *Rule* commanded, was the Divine Office, or the celebration of the hours of prayer and scripture reading that had been set by Benedict. To this the Cluniacs devoted their undivided attention, to such a point that at the height of the movement 138 psalms were sung in a single day. This was done in the midst of ceremonies that became more and more complicated with the passing years, and therefore the Cluniacs came to spend practically all their time at the Divine Office, neglecting the physical labor that was so important for Benedict. This departure from the *Rule* was justified by arguing that the monks' function was to pray and to praise God, and that they could do this with more purity if they were not soiled in the fields.

A monastery served as a center of learning and worship, as shown in this Spanish manuscript.

At its high point, the reforming zeal of the Cluniacs knew no bounds. After ordering the life of hundreds of monastic houses, they set their sights on the reformation of the entire church. This was the darkest hour of the papacy, when pontiffs succeeded one another with breathtaking frequency, and when popes and bishops had become feudal lords, involved in every intrigue that was brewing. In such circumstances the monastic ideal, as it was practiced at Cluny, offered a ray of hope. Many who were not Cluniacs joined in the goal of a general reformation following the monastic model. In contrast with the corruption that reigned in the highest offices of the church, the Cluniac movement seemed to many a miracle, a divine intervention to bring about a new dawn.

Thus, the goal of ecclesiastical reformation was seen in the eleventh century as an extension of what was taking place in many monastic communities. This was the vision that Bruno of Toul, and his companions Hildebrand and Humbert, took with them on their way to Rome, where Bruno would become pope under the name of Leo IX. Just as Cluny had been able to carry on its great work because it was independent of all civil power, so was the dream of those reformers a church whose leaders would be free from every obligation to civil authorities, be they kings or nobles. Simony (the buying and selling of ecclesiastical posts) was therefore one of the worst evils to be eradicated. The appointment and the investiture of bishops and abbots by nobles, kings, and emperors, although not strictly simony, was dangerously close to it, and must also be forbidden, particularly in those areas whose rulers were not zealous reformers.

The other great enemy of reformation thus conceived in monastic terms was clerical marriage. For centuries, many had practiced celibacy, and there had been earlier attempts to promote it, but never as a universal rule. Now, fired by the monastic example, these reformers made clerical celibacy one of the pillars of their program. Eventually, what earlier had been required only of monks and nuns would also be required of the clergy.

This was not achieved without much pain, heartbreak, and even violence. At some point in the process, apparently in Milan, the "Patarines" arose. These were overzealous promoters of clerical celibacy who held that the marriage of priests was really a form of concubinage, called priest's wives harlots, and insisted that they must simply be expelled from their husband's households. In Florence, many refused to accept sacraments celebrated by married priests. When the bishop tried to appeal to reason and tradition, the Patarines accused him of simony. John Gualbert of Vallombrosa—later canonized as a saint—paraded through the streets of the city proclaiming that the bishop was indeed a simoniac—which the bishop denied. Hildebrand entered into the fray in support of John Gualbert. Peter Damian, a respected reforming monk, called for calm, moderation, patience, and love. Finally someone suggested that the matter be settled by trial of fire. On the outskirts of the city, a bonfire was built, a monk who supported the Patarines walked across it, and this was taken as proof that the accusations against the bishop were true. The bishop had to flee the city, where clergy families were forcibly pulled out of their homes and thrown out in the streets.

The powerful had great influence in the life of the church. Here King Henry I of France makes a grant to an abbey.

Obedience, another cornerstone of Benedictine monasticism, would also be fundamental to this reformation of the eleventh century. Just as monks owed obedience to their superiors, so must the entire church (in fact, all Christendom) be subject to the pope, who would head a great renewal in which his role would be similar to that of the abbots of Cluny in the monastic reform.

Finally, when it came to poverty, both Cluniac monasticism and the general reformation that it inspired were ambivalent. A good monk should own nothing, and must lead a simple life. The monastery, however, could have property and vast expanses of land. These grew constantly through gifts and inheritance from the faithful who admired the monastic way of life, or who simply wished to earn merit toward their salvation. Eventually, this made it difficult for monks to lead the simple life which the *Rule* required. In the case of Cluny itself, the time came when it and its sister houses were so rich that their monks could spend all their time at the Divine Office and neglect physical labor. Likewise, the reformers criticized the luxurious life of many bishops, but at the same time insisted on the right of the church to its holdings of land and to all the wealth it had accumulated over the centuries. In theory, this was not for the use of the prelates, but for the glory of God and to help the poor. But in truth it hindered the proposed reformation, for it invited simony, and the power that bishops and abbots had as feudal lords led them to be constantly involved in political intrigue.

The wealth that it accumulated was one of the main causes of the decline of the Cluniac movement. Inspired by the holiness of the monks, rich and poor alike made gifts to their monasteries. Cluny and its sister houses adorned their chapels with gold and jewels. Eventually, the simplicity of life that had been Benedict's ideal was lost, and other movements of more recent foundation, and more insistent on poverty, took the place of Cluny. Likewise, one of the main causes of the final failure of the reformation of the eleventh century was the wealth of the church, which made it very difficult for it to set aside the intrigues of the powerful, and take the side of the poor and the oppressed.

Discontent with the ease of Cluny soon gave rise to other movements. Peter Damian, for instance, sought to outdo the Benedictine principle according to which a monk should be content with what is sufficient, and advocated living in extreme need. The next great movement of monastic reform, however, began late in the eleventh century, when Robert of Molesme founded a new monastery at Citeaux. Since the Latin name of this place was *Cistertium,* the movement came to be called "Cistercian." Robert returned to his original monastery, but a community continued existing in Citeaux, and eventually gave rise to a wave of monastic reform similar to that which had been lead earlier by the abbots of Cluny.

The great figure of the Cistercian movement was Bernard of Clairvaux, who was twenty-three years old when he presented himself at Citeaux (in 1112 or 1113) in the company of several relatives and friends, and requested admission to the community. He had decided to join that monastery, and before even presenting himself for admission he had convinced several others to follow him. This was an early indication of his great powers of persuasion, which would eventually be felt throughout Europe and would even send many to the Holy Land. When the number of monks at Citeaux grew too large, he was ordered to found a new community at Clairvaux. This grew rapidly, and soon became a center of reformation.

Bernard was first and foremost a monk. He was convinced that, as Jesus had told the two sisters at Bethany, Mary's was a better lot than Martha's, and all he wished to do was to spend his time meditating on the love of God, particularly as revealed in the humanity of Christ. But he soon found himself forced to take on the role of Martha. He was a famous preacher—so much so, that he came to be known as "Doctor Mellifluous," for the words from his mouth were like honey. Examples of this are two hymns attributed to him and still popular: "O Sacred Head, Now Wounded" and "Jesus, the Very Thought of Thee." His fame forced him to intervene as an arbitrator in many political and ecclesiastical disputes. His personality dominated his time, for he was at once the mystic devoted to the contemplation of the humanity of Christ, the power behind and above the papacy (especially when one of his monks became pope), the champion of ecclesiastical reform, the preacher of the Second Crusade, and the enemy of all theological innovation. Bernard's fame gave the Cistercian movement great impetus, and soon it came to play a role similar to that which Cluny had played more than a century before.

This brief overview of the two main movements of monastic reform from the tenth to the twelfth centuries has forced us to move ahead in our story. Therefore, let us return to where we had left our narrative at the end of the previous chapter, to the year 1048, when Odilo was still abbot of Cluny, and rejoin Bruno of Toul and his companions as they made their way to Rome.

CANONICAL AND PAPAL REFORM

There were other efforts at reforming the entire church through legislation and through the centralization of power in the hands of reforming popes. In the field of legislation, the *Decretum* usually called "of Gratian"—although its author is unknown—was compiled around 1140, and was an effort to compile and coordinate the many laws that supposedly governed the life of the church. Joined to five other main documents, it came to form the *Corpus Juris Canonici*, which was the basis for the law of the Roman Catholic Church until 1917.

But it was a series of reforming popes that led the way to reformation as they understood it. The small band of pilgrims on their way to Rome in 1048 was headed by Bruno, to whom the emperor had offered the papacy, and who had preferred to enter the city as a pilgrim. If, once there, the people and the clergy elected him, he would accept. But to take the office of pope from the hands of the emperor was dangerously close to simony—or, as Hildebrand had told Bruno, it would mean going to Rome "not as an apostle, but as an apostate."

Another member of the small party was Humbert, who in his monastery in Lotharingia had devoted himself to study and to a constant campaign against simony. This had never been attacked as forcefully as in his treatise *Against the Simoniacs,* which was a blistering attack on the powerful of his time. Humbert was a man of fiery temperament, and in his attack against simony he went so far as to declare that sacraments offered by simoniacs were not valid—a position that Augustine had rejected centuries earlier in his debates with the Donatists. It was also he who later, in 1054, would lay the sentence of excommunication against Patriarch Michael Cerularius on the high altar of Hagia Sophia, and thus seal the schism between East and West.

The third and most remarkable member of that party was the monk Hildebrand, a man of humble origins—his father was a carpenter in Tuscany—who had entered a monastery in Rome at a very early age. While a monk at Rome he had met the future pope Gregory VI. As was said at the end of the last chapter, Gregory VI hoped to reform the church. To that end he called Hildebrand to his side. But then a situation developed in which there were three who claimed to be the rightful pope, and Gregory abdicated for the sake of peace and unity. Hildebrand went with him into exile, and it is said that he closed the saintly man's eyes on his deathbed. Two years later, Bruno, on his way to Rome, asked Hildebrand to join him in the task of reformation that lay ahead.

Hildebrand has often been depicted as the ambitious man behind several popes. Until he felt ready to take power for himself, however, the sources of the time seem to indicate that in truth he wished nothing more than the reformation of the church. It was apparently on that basis that he supported the work of several popes, until the time came when it seemed that reformation could best be served by accepting the papacy himself, which he took under the name of Gregory VII.

For the time being, however, the man called to be pope was Bruno of Toul, who went to Rome as a barefooted pilgrim in an act of personal devotion. As he crossed northern Italy on his way to Rome, multitudes lined the roads and cheered him, and soon people began to talk of miracles that supposedly had taken place during that pilgrimage. After entering Rome barefooted and being acclaimed by the people and the clergy, Bruno accepted the papal tiara, and took the name of Leo IX.

As soon as he saw himself on Saint Peter's throne, Leo began his work of reformation by calling to his side several people who were known for holding similar ideas. One of these was Peter Damian, who had long rued the state of the church, and had convinced many of the need for reformation—although without the fiery zeal of Humbert and Hildebrand, for he insisted that reformation must be a work of love and charity. The program of reformation of the entire group was based on the promotion of clerical celibacy and the abolition of simony. There was a connection between these two, for in that feudal society the church was one of the few institutions in which there still existed a measure of social mobility. Hildebrand, for instance, was of humble origin, and would eventually become pope. But this social mobility was threatened by the practice of simony, which would guarantee that only the rich would occupy high offices in the church. If to this was added clerical marriage, those who held high office would seek to pass it on to their children, and thus the church would come to reflect exclusively the interests of the rich and the powerful. Thus, the movement for reformation by abolishing simony and promoting clerical celibacy had the support of the masses, who seem to have understood that here was an opportunity for wresting from the powerful the control of the church.

After taking a number of reforming measures in Italy, Leo decided that the time had come to carry the movement across the Alps. He went to Germany, where Emperor Henry III had already taken some steps against simony, and reaffirmed the emperor's decisions while making it clear that this did not mean that the emperor could rule the life of the church in his domains. While in Germany, he excommunicated Godfrey of Lorraine, who had rebelled against the emperor, and forced him to submit. Then he saved the rebel's life by interceding for him before the emperor.

In France simony was widespread, and Leo sought to put an end to it. With this in mind, he decided to visit that country. Although the king and several prelates let him know that he would not be welcome, Leo went to France and called a council that deposed several prelates who had been guilty of simony. The same council also ordered that married bishops should set their wives aside, but this order was not generally obeyed.

Leo made two grave errors during his pontificate. The first was to take up arms against the Norsemen who had settled in Sicily and southern Italy. Peter Damian urged him to desist, but he marched at the head of the troops, which were defeated by the Norsemen. Captured by those whom he had hoped to conquer, Leo remained a prisoner until shortly before his death. His other error was to send Humbert as his legate to Constantinople. Humbert's rigidity and lack of interest in the concerns of the Byzantines led to the schism of 1054, shortly after Leo's death.

The election of the new pope was a difficult matter. To ask the emperor to select him would be tantamount to the control of the church by the state, which the reformers deplored. To let the Roman clergy and people proceed to the election risked having the papacy fall again in the hands of one of the Italian families who wished to have it as a means to their own political ends. Eventually it was decided that the Romans would elect the new pope, but that this had to be a German—thus making it impossible for any of the various parties in Rome to capture the papacy. The new pope, Victor II, continued Leo's policies. When emperor Henry III found himself in difficulties—Godfrey of Lorraine had rebelled again—the pope went to his aid, and on the emperor's death was entrusted with the care of his young son, Henry IV. Thus for a time Victor held the reins of both church and empire, and the reformation that he advocated progressed rapidly.

After that time, with one exception, there was a succession of reforming popes. That exception led the reformers, under the leadership of Nicholas II, to call the Second Lateran Council, which determined the manner in which popes were to be elected thereafter. The power of election was to rest with the cardinals who also held the title of bishops, who would then seek the consent of the rest of the cardinals, and, finally, of the Roman people. (The origins of the title "cardinal" are obscure, and need not detain us here. By the time of the Second Lateran Council, in 1059, the cardinalate was an ancient institution.) Since the cardinals were committed to reform, and since the popes elected by them would name any new cardinals, the power of the reforming party seemed assured. The next pope, Alexander II, was duly elected by the cardinals and continued the work of reformation, although some of the powerful Roman families, with support from the Germans, set up a rival pope.

When Alexander died, Hildebrand was elected pope, although the order prescribed by the Second Lateran Council was reversed, for it was the people who demanded his election, and the cardinals who agreed. He took the name of Gregory VII, and continued the work of reformation in which he had been engaged for years. His dream was of a world united under the papacy, as one flock under one shepherd. Among the many steps he took in this direction, he declared that the Bible should not be translated into vernacular languages, for the ministry of teaching and interpretation must be in the hands of Rome. His vision of unity included not only Western Europe, but also the Byzantine church as well as the lands then under Muslim control. For a while he sought to organize a great military offensive against Islam, with a western front in Spain and another in the East, where Latin Christians would go to the succor of beleaguered Constantinople—a project that two decades later would result in the Crusades. But these plans, as well as his efforts to extend his authority to the East, never came to fruition.

In Western Europe, Gregory VII continued the campaign against simony and the marriage of clergy. A synod gathered in 1070 condemned simony and ordered that clergy be celibate. Gregory reinforced the synod's decisions by forbidding the laity from receiving the sacraments from the hands of simoniacs. He also named legates who would travel, ensuring that these orders were obeyed. In response, some accused Gregory of heresy, for long before his time Augustine had declared—and the rest of the church had agreed—that sacraments administered by schismatics were nonetheless valid. In truth, Gregory did not declare that such sacraments were invalid; he simply ordered people to abstain from them. In France, King Philip I would not heed Gregory's admonitions. With his support, the French clergy refused to obey Gregory's reforming decrees. Indeed, the two-pronged offensive against simony and clerical marriage was unwise, for it created an alliance between the powerful prelates who profited from ecclesiastical posts, and the many worthy members of the lower clergy who bemoaned simony, but who were married and refused to set their wives aside. By joining the monastic ideal of celibacy to his reformation, Gregory and his friends made it much more difficult for their plans to succeed.

Gregory was most successful in England, where William the Conqueror now ruled. When he was still a papal advisor, Hildebrand had supported William's plans to invade England from Normandy, and now the Conqueror, who in any case was in favor of ecclesiastical reform, supported the pope's campaign against simony.

THE PAPACY AND THE EMPIRE IN DIRECT CONFRONTATION

Gregory's reforming zeal soon clashed with the interests of Emperor Henry IV. As a young boy, Henry had been under the care of one of the reforming popes, and therefore Gregory believed that he, of all rulers, should support the program of reformation. But Henry felt that the power of bishops and other prelates was such that, for the political survival of the empire, the emperor must be free to appoint those who would support him. The conflict finally broke out when, in response to riots in Milan provoked by Patarine extremists who sought to enforce clerical celibacy, Henry deposed the bishop and appointed another in his place. Gregory responded by ordering Henry to appear at Rome by a certain date, and declaring that if he failed to do so he would be deposed and his soul condemned to hell. On Christmas Eve, 1075, two months before the deadline set by Gregory, a military contingent attacked the pope while he was celebrating mass, beat him, and took him prisoner. In response, the Roman populace rose up, besieged and then took the tower where Gregory was being held. The man who had led the attack against the pope had to flee, and was able to save his life only because Gregory ordered those who were pursuing him to spare him on condition that he go on pilgrimage to Rome. The emperor, who had recently had significant success and was therefore at the height of his power, responded to Gregory's ultimatum by calling a council that gathered a few days before the deadline set by the pope and declared that Gregory was deposed on grounds of tyranny, adultery, and the practice of magic. Then, in the council's name, Henry sent notification of these decisions "to Hildebrand, not a pope, but a false monk."

Gregory gathered a synod of his supporters, who advised stern measures against the emperor. On the next day, precisely the date for which he had summoned Henry to Rome, Gregory issued his sentence:

In the name of the Father, the Son, and the Holy Ghost, by the power and authority of Saint Peter, and for the defense and honor of the church, I place king Henry . . . under interdict, forbidding him to rule in any of the kingdoms of Germany or Italy. I also free from their oaths any who have sworn or would swear loyalty to him. And I forbid that he be obeyed as king.[44]

At first, Henry was resolved to continue in the course he had set. But his support began eroding. Many who had other reasons to disobey him now had the pope's sentence as an excuse. The more superstitious began spreading the word that to be near him was to call a curse on oneself. This was given credence when one of his staunchest supporters died unexpectedly. Finally, Henry felt that his only recourse was to appeal to Gregory's mercy. This he would do as privately as possible, and thus set out to meet Gregory in Italy. Gregory was not sure whether the emperor was coming in peace, or rather intended to use violence. His suspicions increased when many in northern Italy received Henry as a hero and rallied to him. But Henry did not wish to gamble his throne on the uncertain outcome of battle, and therefore refused to organize his supporters into an army.

The two finally met at Canossa, where the pope had taken residence because the city was well fortified. Henry had hoped for a private interview where he would make his obeisance before Gregory. But the latter insisted on public

Henry was forced to appear at Canossa to beg Gregory's forgiveness. To their left is Matilda, owner of the castle.

penance, and Henry had to beg entrance into Canossa, as a penitent, for three days before he was admitted to Gregory's presence. Finally, since it was impossible for one who claimed to be the leader of Christ's disciples to do otherwise, Gregory granted the pardon that Henry begged, and withdrew his sentence against the emperor.

Henry then returned hastily to Germany, where his enemies, encouraged by his difficulties with Gregory, had rebelled. Although Gregory had withdrawn his sentence against Henry, he did nothing to discourage the rebels, who elected their own emperor. The pope's ambiguous posture encouraged civil war, and it soon became clear that Henry would overcome his foes. But Gregory did not trust him, and therefore decided to cast his lot with the usurper. Once again he excommunicated Henry, whose imminent death he also foretold. But this time the emperor's followers did not heed the pope's sentence, and a rival pope, who took the name of Clement III, was elected. Finally, the usurping emperor was killed in battle, and Henry was left as sole master of the empire.

As soon as the ice thawed in the passes through the Alps in the spring of 1081, Henry marched on Rome. Gregory's only possible support were the Normans who ruled in southern Italy, and who had been his allies before. But he had also excommunicated them. He then appealed to Byzantium, but to no avail. The Romans defended their city valiantly. But when it became clear that the pope would not negotiate with the invader, they opened the gates of the city, and Gregory had to flee to the castle of Sant'Angelo. Henry entered in triumph, and Clement III took possession of the city. Then the Normans intervened, and Henry abandoned the city. The Normans acted as masters of the city, and many citizens were killed, buildings burned, and thousands taken away to be sold as slaves.

After several days of violence and depredation, the people of Rome rebelled, and a long period of violence and chaos ensued in which Clement III and his supporters were able to reclaim a part of the city. Gregory, who had fled to Monte Cassino and then to Salerno, continued thundering against Henry and Clement III. But his words were to no avail. It is said that when he died in 1085 his last words were: "I have loved justice and hated iniquity. Therefore I die in exile."

Before his death, Hildebrand had declared that his successor should be the aged abbot of Monte Cassino. These wishes were followed, and the old man, who had no desire to be pope, was forced to accept. He took the name of Victor III, and was restored to Rome by his allies. But he became ill, and withdrew to Monte Cassino to die in peace.

The reforming party then elected Urban II, who was able to regain the city of Rome and expel Clement III. He is mostly known for having proclaimed the First Crusade—with which we shall deal in the next chapter. But he also continued the policies of Gregory VII. This led him into further conflicts with Philip I of France, whom he excommunicated for having set aside his wife in favor of another. In Germany, he encouraged the rebellion of Henry's son Conrad, who promised that if he were made emperor he would give up any claim to the right to the appointment and investiture of bishops. But Henry reacted vigorously, defeated his son, and had him disinherited by a diet of the empire.

Urban's successor, Paschal II (1099–1118), hoped that the schism would end when Clement III died. But the emperor made certain that another was appointed to take Clement's place, and therefore the schism continued.

Henry IV died in 1106, when he was preparing to wage war against his son Henry, who had also rebelled against him. Pope Paschal was ready to make peace, and declared that all consecrations that had taken place during the previous reign, even under lay appointment and investiture, were valid. But he also made it clear that any future lay investiture was unacceptable, and that any who disobeyed him on this point would be excommunicated. Thus, while clearing the slate, he also threw down the gauntlet before the new emperor.

Henry V waited three years to respond to the pope's challenge. Then he invaded Italy, and Paschal was forced to reach a compromise. What Henry proposed, and Paschal accepted, was that the emperor would give up any claim to the right of investiture of bishops, as long as the church gave up all the feudal privileges that prelates had, and which made them powerful potentates. Paschal agreed, with the sole stipulation that "Saint Peter's patrimony" would remain in the hands of the Roman church. Henry's proposal cut to the heart of the matter, for civil rulers could not afford to give up the right to name and invest bishops as long as these were also powerful political figures. And, if the reformers were consistent on their application of monastic principles to the reform of the church, they should be willing to have the church follow the way of poverty.

But this decision, reasonable though it seemed, was not politically viable. There soon was a violent reaction among prelates who saw themselves deprived of temporal power. Some were quick to point out that the pope had been very liberal with their possessions, but had retained his. The high nobility in Germany began to suspect that the emperor, having strengthened his position by stripping the bishops of their power, would turn on them and abolish many of their ancient privileges. Then the people of Rome rebelled against the emperor, who left the city taking as prisoners the pope as well as several cardinals and bishops. Finally, the emperor returned the pope to Rome, and the latter in turn crowned him at St. Peter's—with the doors closed for fear of the populace. The emperor then returned to Germany, where urgent matters required his presence.

In Germany, Henry encountered new difficulties. Many of the high clergy and the nobility, fearing the loss of their power, rebelled. While Paschal remained silent, many of the German prelates excommunicated the emperor.

The castle of Sant'Angelo, where Pope Gregory VII was forced to take refuge.

Then several regional synods followed suit. When Henry protested that by his attitude Paschal was breaking their agreement, the pope suggested that the emperor call a council in order to solve the dispute. This Henry could not do, for he knew that the majority of the bishops, who saw their possessions and power threatened by the emperor's policies, would decide against him. Therefore, he opted for renewed use of force. As soon as the situation in Germany allowed him to do so, he again invaded Italy, and Paschal was forced to flee to the castle of Sant'Angelo, where he died.

The cardinals then hastened to elect a new pope, lest the emperor intervene in the election. The new pope, Gelasius II, had a stormy and brief pontificate (1118–1119). A Roman potentate who supported the emperor made him a prisoner and tortured him. Then the people rebelled and freed him. But the emperor returned to Rome with his armies, and Gelasius fled to Gaeta. Upon returning to Rome, he was again captured by the same Roman magnate, but he fled and finally fell exhausted in the middle of a field, where some women found him, almost naked and lifeless. He then sought refuge in France, where he died shortly thereafter in the abbey of Cluny.

The decision of Gelasius to flee to France was a sign of the new direction in which papal policy was being forced. Since the empire had become its enemy, and since the Normans in the south had proven unreliable allies, popes began looking to France as the ally who would support them against the German emperors.

The next pope, Calixtus II (1119–1124), was a relative of the emperor, and both he and his kinsman were convinced that the time had come to end the dispute. After long negotiations, interspersed with threats and even military campaigns, both parties came to an agreement by the Concordat of Worms (1122). It was decided that prelates would be elected freely, according to ancient usage, although in the presence of the emperor or his representatives. Only proper ecclesiastical authorities would henceforth have the right to invest prelates with their ring and crosier, symbols of pastoral authority; but the granting of all feudal rights, privileges, and possessions, as well as of the symbols thereof, would be in the hand of civil authorities. The emperor also agreed to return to the church all its possessions, and to take measures to force any feudal lords holding ecclesiastical property to do likewise. This put an end to this series of confrontations between papacy and empire, although similar conflicts would develop repeatedly through the centuries.

In the end, the program of the reforming popes succeeded. The rule of clerical celibacy became universal in the Western church, and was generally obeyed. For a while, simony almost disappeared. And the power of the papacy continued to grow, until it reached its apex in the thirteenth century.

However, the controversy over the appointment and investiture of prelates shows that the reformist popes, while they insisted on the monastic ideal of celibacy, did not do the same with the ideal of poverty. The question of

The conflict between the empire and the papacy continued. In this piece of propaganda against the pope, the latter is seen dallying with a woman (in the window at upper right) while Henry begs admittance to the Castle of Canossa.

investitures was important for civil authorities—especially the emperor—because the church had become so rich and powerful that an unfriendly bishop was a political power to be feared. Bishops could afford rich courts and even armies. Therefore, in the interest of self-preservation, rulers had to make sure that those who occupied such important positions were loyal to them. Henry V had pointed to the heart of the matter when he suggested that he was willing to relinquish all claim to the investiture of bishops in his realm, as long as those bishops did not have the power and resources of great feudal lords. As the reformist popes saw matters, the possessions of the church belonged to Christ and the poor, and therefore could not be relinquished to the civil authorities. But in fact those possessions were used for personal profit, and for achieving the ambitious personal goals of bishops and others who in theory were not owners, but guardians.

31

The Offensive Against Islam

I say it to those who are present. I command that it be said to those who
are absent. Christ commands it. All who go thither and lose their lives,
be it on the road or on the sea, or in the fight against the pagans, will be
granted immediate forgiveness for their sins. This I grant to all who will
march, by virtue of the great gift which God has given me.

URBAN II

Among the many ideals that captivated the imagination of Western Christendom during the Middle Ages, no other was as dramatic, as overwhelming, or as contradictory, as was the crusading spirit. Tragically romanticized by
many, the Crusades have the distinction of being one of the most blatant of the
many instances in which Christianity, fueled in part by its own zeal, has contradicted its very essence—on this score, only the Inquisition can be compared
with it. For several centuries, Western Europe poured its fervor and its blood
into a series of expeditions whose results were at best ephemeral, and at worst
tragic. The hope was to defeat the Muslims who threatened Constantinople,
to save the Byzantine Empire, to reunite the Eastern and Western branches of
the church, to reconquer the Holy Land as well as other territories that Islam
had previously taken by means of a similar use of military force (see chapter
27), and—in so doing—to win heaven. Whether or not this last goal was
achieved is not for us to decide. All the others were achieved, but none of them
permanently. The Muslims, at first defeated because they were divided among
themselves, eventually were united in a common front that expelled the crusaders. Constantinople, and the shadow of its empire, survived until the fifteenth
century, but then were swept by the Ottoman Turks. The two branches of the
church were briefly reunited by force as a consequence of the Fourth Crusade,
but the final result of that forced reunion was greater suspicion and hatred
between the Christian East and the Christian West. The Holy Land was in
the hands of the crusaders for approximately a century, and then returned to
Muslim control.

THE FIRST CRUSADE

For centuries, Christians had held the Holy Land in high esteem, and pilgrimages to its holy places had become one of the highest acts of devotion. Already in the fourth century, Constantine's mother had considered a visit to the holy places of Palestine an act of devotion. Shortly thereafter, a Spanish nun named Etheria, but commonly known as Egeria, traveled to the Holy Land and left detailed notes of its places, customs, and Christian rituals. Her account, the *Peregrinatio Aetheriae*, was still circulating in the eleventh century, and is an example of the manner in which the Christian West looked to the holy places as objects of devotion.

Those holy places had been in Muslim hands for centuries. But now the rise of the Seljuk Turks, who had become Muslim and were threatening the Byzantine Empire, reminded many of the earlier losses at the time of the Arab conquests. If the West were to save the Byzantines from that threat, it was to be expected that relations between the two branches of the church, broken since 1054, would be restored. Thus, Gregory VII had already envisioned a great Western army that would save Constantinople and retake the Holy Land. But the time was not yet ripe, and it was Urban II who, at the Council of Clermont in 1095, responding to a request for support against the Turks from Byzantine Emperor Alexis I, proclaimed the great enterprise, to which those present responded with cries of *Deus vult*—"God wills it."

It was a difficult time in many parts of Europe, where crops had failed and disease ran rampant. Therefore, the call to go to a foreign land as soldiers of Christ was received with enthusiasm by many, both of the lower classes and of the nobility. The apocalyptic dreams that for centuries had been repressed, and that had been revitalized earlier, in expectation of the new millennium, now emerged again. Some had visions of comets, angels, or the Holy City suspended over the eastern horizon. Soon a disorganized mob, under the very loose leadership of Peter the Hermit, set out from Cologne for Jerusalem. Along the way, they fed on the land, on which they fell like locusts, and had to fight other Christians who defended their goods and crops. They also practiced their war against the infidel by killing thousands of Jews. Eventually, most of this initial wave lost their lives, and a few joined the ranks of the more organized crusaders.

The formal Crusade was led by Adhemar, bishop of Puy, whom Urban had named his personal representative. Other leaders were Godfrey of Bouillon, Raymond of Saint-Gilles, Bohemond, and Tancred. By various routes, the crusaders converged at Constantinople, where they were well received by Emperor Alexius, and where Peter the Hermit joined them with the remnant of his ragged army. With the help of the Byzantines, they took Nicea, which had been the capital of the Turks—and which the Byzantines entered first, for the

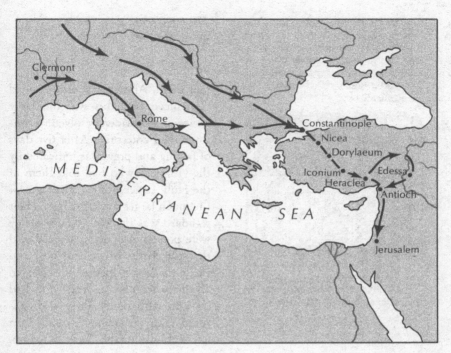

The First Crusade.

emperor feared that the crusaders would sack the city. They then marched on Antioch, and endured many sufferings while crossing Asia Minor. Before the walls of Tarsus, Tancred and Baldwin, Godfrey's younger brother, quarreled, and Baldwin decided to abandon the enterprise and accept the offer of the Armenians to establish himself as their leader, under the title of Count of Edessa. The rest continued their long march to Antioch, to which they finally laid siege, as they had done earlier before Nicea.

The siege of Antioch was a difficult enterprise. The besieged had more supplies than the crusaders, who were about to run out of food and had been plagued by desertions, when an Armenian Christian who resided in the city opened a gate to them. At the cry of "God wills it," the crusaders entered the city, while its Turkish defenders sought refuge in the citadel. But four days later a large Turkish army arrived, and the crusaders found themselves besieged while the citadel itself had not yet surrendered to them. Hungry and discouraged, the crusaders began to doubt the wisdom of the entire enterprise.

Then someone said he had a vision, that the Holy Lance with which Christ's side had been pierced lay buried in Antioch. Led by the seer, they dug where he

milhomer apie dechcualierr trefergenz
Acheueur zdhaubcrz ozenr c mile sllour
furent engranr nolenre trefturr defeltrer
nef teleur guertef bien emploier zmoir
tefurment sihaurement enprendre lenr
puunier fer quetoutef lef aultref genz
lef entourassenr

Elarre denique sacher quele fu
foin lenethie tenicomede Alef ien
rereref costanins lafifi oster telpour acel

told them. And they found a spear! Convinced that this was the Holy Lance, the crusaders resolved to continue their enterprise. After five days of fasting and prayer, as indicated by the visionary who had told them of the Holy Lance, they sallied against the much larger Turkish army. Their standard was the Holy Lance. They were possessed of such frenzied zeal that the Turks broke and ran, and the crusaders helped themselves to all the provisions that the Turks had brought with them. They also captured many women who had been left behind in the Turkish camp, and an eyewitness boasting of the holiness of the Christian army says: "We did nothing evil to them, but simply speared them through."

Bishop Adhemar, the appointed leader of the Crusade, had died of fever during the siege, and the army was headless. After much bickering and delay, Godfrey of Bouillon emerged as the new leader, and the army finally caught its first glimpse of the Holy City on June 7, 1099.

Those defending Jerusalem were not Turks, but Fatimite Arabs from Egypt—so named because they claimed descent from Fatima, Muhammad's daughter. Indeed, the reason why the crusaders had achieved their measure of success was that the Muslims were not united—much as earlier the Arabs had been able to conquer vast territories because their enemies were similarly divided. Those whom the crusaders had fought in Nicea and Antioch were Turks, who had become Sunni, while the Fatimites who held Jerusalem were Shiites. Furthermore, according to Arab chronicler Ibn Al-Athir the crusaders had come to Syria at the behest of the Fatimites, who feared the growing power of the Turks.

The garrison in Jerusalem was ready for a long siege. The surrounding land had been razed, and the wells poisoned, to deny supplies to the besiegers. The crusaders also expected a long siege. But in early July they received news of a large Fatimite army approaching, and came to the conclusion that they had to take the city or withdraw. Since theirs was a religious enterprise, they begged God for support, marching around the city barefooted and singing penitential hymns. A few days later, they attacked the walls. Resistance was strong. But finally a single knight was able to climb to the top of the wall, and there to hold a space where others could follow him. As the breach grew, resistance melted. The defenders fled from the walls, and the crusaders swept into the city that was the goal of their long campaign. It was July 15, 1099.

Although some scholars today tend to think that there is a measure of exaggeration in them, contemporary reports declare that all the defenders were killed, as well as many civilians. Women were raped, and infants thrown against walls. Many of the city's Jews had taken refuge in the synagogue, and the crusaders set fire to the building with them inside. At the Porch of Solomon horses waded in blood.

Then the Crusaders set out to organize the conquered lands in the fashion of Western Europe. Godfrey of Bouillon was made "Protector of the Holy Sepulcher," but his brother Baldwin, who succeeded him in 1100, took the title of King of Jerusalem. The main vassals of this kingdom were Bohemond, Prince of Antioch, Baldwin, Count of Edessa, and Raymond of Toulouse, Count of Tripoli.

LATER HISTORY OF THE CRUSADES

Many of the crusaders now felt that their task was done, and prepared to return home. Godfrey of Bouillon was scarcely able to retain the knights necessary to meet the Muslim army that was already marching on Jerusalem. At Ashkelon, the crusaders defeated the Muslims, and thus the survival of the Latin Kingdom of Jerusalem was assured for a brief span. But reinforcements were sorely needed, and thus it became customary for small bands of armed men to leave Europe for a time of service in the Holy Land. While many of these remained, others simply returned after what amounted to an armed pilgrimage.

The fervor of the Crusade also continued among the masses. Repeatedly, there were those who had apocalyptic visions and collected a motley following as they marched toward Jerusalem. There were also those who claimed that, since God valued innocence, children were to play a special role in the entire enterprise. Thus developed several "Children's Crusades," which were no more than masses of children and adolescents marching eastward, only to die along the way or to be enslaved by those whose territories they crossed.

Since the crusading spirit, and crusading columns, were a constant feature for centuries, it is not altogether correct to speak of the "Crusades" as a series of isolated campaigns. But there were high points in the entire enterprise, which are usually referred to as the "Second Crusade," the "Third Crusade," and so on. An outline of these will show some of the subsequent course of the crusading spirit.

The occasion for the Second Crusade was the Fall of Edessa, taken by the Sultan of Aleppo in 1144. Once again, popular preachers arose who called for the masses to invade the Holy Land. Along the way, some also said, Jews should be exterminated. The preaching of Bernard of Clairvaux was very different, for it sought both to organize an army of relief for the Kingdom of Jerusalem, and to refute the fiery preaching of those who advocated a mad rush to Jerusalem. Finally, under the leadership of Louis VII of France and Conrad III of Germany, an army of almost two hundred thousand left for the Holy Land. They were repeatedly defeated by the Turks, and accomplished little.

For a while the kingdom of Jerusalem grew strong, and under Amalric I it even extended as far as Cairo. But then the Muslims began to regroup and, under the leadership of the Sultan of Egypt, Saladin, took Jerusalem in 1187.

The news shook Christendom, and Pope Clement III called for a renewal of the crusading enterprise. This Third Crusade was led by three sovereigns: Emperor Frederick Barbarossa, Richard the Lionhearted of England, and Philip II Augustus of France. This too failed. Frederick drowned, and his army dissolved. Richard and Philip achieved nothing but taking Acre after a siege that lasted two years. Philip then returned to Europe, hoping to take advantage of Richard's absence to take some of the latter's lands. Richard himself, on his way home, was captured by the emperor of Germany and kept a prisoner until an enormous ransom was promised.

The Fourth Crusade, called by Innocent III, was an even greater disaster. Its goal was to attack Saladin at his headquarters in Egypt. A famous preacher, Foulques de Neuilly, was entrusted with the task of raising armies and funds for the Crusade. Foulques was a radical opponent of usury and all forms of social injustice who was incensed at the manner in which the developing monetary economy allowed the rich to use their money to become even richer, while the poor remained in poverty. In preaching the Crusade, Foulques declared that the poor were elected by God to fulfill this great task. All could participate in this project. Those who could not go on Crusade, no matter how poor, should support others who could. The rich must also join, for in so doing their exploitations were forgiven. Thus an army was raised eager to attack Saladin in his own capital.

But, unbeknownst to Foulques and even to Pope Innocent, there were other plans afoot. The throne in Constantinople was disputed by two rivals, one of whom asked Innocent to send the Crusade first to Constantinople to place him on the throne. In exchange, he would then support the Crusade against Saladin. Innocent refused, but the Venetians, whose fleet was charged with the task of transporting the crusaders to Egypt, agreed to take them instead to Constantinople in exchange for large sums of money. Thus, the Crusade was rerouted to Constantinople, which the crusaders took. They then named Baldwin of Flanders emperor of Constantinople, and thus was founded the Latin Empire of Constantinople (1204–1261). A Latin patriarch of Constantinople was also named, and thus, in theory at least, East and West were reunited. Innocent III, at first incensed by this misuse of the Crusade, eventually decided that it was God's way of reuniting the church. But the Byzantines did not accept matters so easily, and continued a long resistance, founding various states that refused to accept the authority of the Latin emperors. Finally, in 1261, one of these splinter states, the Empire of Nicea, retook Constantinople, and ended the Latin Empire. The net result of the entire episode was that the enmity of the Greek East toward the Latin West grew more intense.

The Fifth Crusade, led by the "King of Jerusalem"—who claimed this title even though the city had been in Muslim hands for a long time, and he had never seen it—attacked Egypt, and accomplished very little. The Sixth, led by excommunicated emperor Frederick II, had better success than the rest, for the emperor and the sultan came to an agreement granting Jerusalem, Nazareth, and Bethlehem to Frederick, as well as the roads linking those holy places to Acre. Frederick entered Jerusalem and, since no one else would do it, crowned himself King of Jerusalem. The pope who had excommunicated him, Gregory IX, fumed, but Europe rejoiced and called Frederick the "Liberator of Jerusalem." The Seventh and Eighth Crusades, led by Louis IX of France (Saint Louis) were major disasters. The king was captured by the Muslims in the Seventh Crusade, and forced to pay a large ransom. In the Eighth, he died of fever in Tunis. It was the year 1270, and the Crusades had run their course.

THE SPANISH RECONQUISTA

The ancient Visigothic kingdom of Spain had been destroyed by the Muslims in the eighth century, and only small remnants of it continued a precarious existence in the region of Asturias, in northern Spain. Later, the Franks established their influence farther east. Out of these two foci would come the long struggle against Islam known in Spain as the *Reconquista* ("the reconquest"). Although later legend characterized this as this an almost continuous Christian effort against the infidel, the truth is much more complicated, for Christians seem to have fought as much among themselves as against Muslims, and alliances across religious lines—as well as marriages between Muslims and Christians—were not uncommon.

In the unification of Christian Spain, the "discovery" of the tomb of Saint James played an important role. By the ninth century, this had become one of

As the myth of the Reconquista developed, Rodrigo Díaz de Vivar, commonly known by his Arabic title of El Cid, became a symbol of national identity and unity. This statue in his native village of Vivar honors him.

the main places of pilgrimage for Christians from all over Western Europe, and thus the road to Santiago—Saint James—brought northern Spain into constant contact with the rest of Western Christendom. Eventually, Saint James became the patron saint of the struggle against the Muslims, and thus came to be known as *Santiago Matamoros*—"Saint James the Moors slayer."

The Muslims of Spain had not always been united. Their greatest time came after Amir Abd-al-Rahman of Cordoba took the title of caliph in 929. But this Caliphate was eventually weakened by internecine wars, and when the last of the caliphs of Cordoba was deposed by rival parties in 1031, Muslim lands were soon divided into a multitude of small kingdoms. It was then that the Spanish Reconquista gained strength. By 1085, the Spanish kingdom of Castile had taken Toledo, the old Visigothic capital. This called forth a reaction from the Moors, who sent reinforcements from North Africa. In 1212, however, the Christian kings joined together in defeating the Moors at the Battle of Las Navas de Tolosa, and thereafter the Reconquista marched apace. By 1248, the only Moorish state in the peninsula was the kingdom of Granada, which survived by paying tribute to the king of Castile. Such would be the situation until 1492, when Granada finally fell to the armies of Ferdinand and Isabella.

Spain and Sicily—the latter taken by the Normans in the eleventh century—were the only areas where the military campaign against Islam was permanently successful.

CONSEQUENCES OF THE OFFENSIVE AGAINST ISLAM

The most obvious consequence of these various episodes was the increased mistrust and enmity between Christians and Muslims, as well as between Latin and Byzantine Christians. The events of the Crusades, and the blood spilled, would not be forgotten easily, and the consequences would still be felt as late as the twenty-first century. At the time of the Crusades, Iraqi poet al-Abiwardi wrote words that remind us of much that we hear in our own time:

> Must the foreigners feed on our ignominy, while you trail behind you the
>   train of a pleasant life, like men whose world is at peace?
> When the white swords' points are red with blood, and the iron of the
>   brown lances is mixed with gore?
> This is war, and he who lies in the tomb at Medina seems to raise his voice
>   and cry: "O sons of Hassim!
> I see my people slow to raise the lance against the enemy: I see the Faith
>   resting on feeble pillars."[45]

In Western Europe, the Crusades and the Spanish Reconquista enhanced the power of the papacy. Since it was the popes who called for the Crusades and appointed their leaders, and since they also took a special interest in Spain, the papacy gained further international authority. When Urban II called for the First Crusade, his authority was in doubt, particularly in Germany. By the time of Innocent III, when the Fourth Crusade took Constantinople, the papacy had reached the apex of its power.

The Crusades also had an impact on Christian piety. Increased contacts with the Holy Land turned people's attention to the historical narratives of the Bible, and devotion came to center on the humanity of Jesus. Bernard of Clairvaux, the preacher of the Second Crusade, was also a mystic devoted to the contemplation of the humanity of Jesus. Poems and entire books were written about every

The shape of reliquaries sometimes indicated the nature of the relics kept in them.

detail of the passion. For similar reasons, the veneration of relics, which had ancient roots, gained momentum as Europe was flooded with pieces of the True Cross, bones of patriarchs, teeth of biblical figures, and so forth.

The monastic ideal took a new direction with the founding of the military orders. Members of these orders made the traditional vows of obedience, poverty, and chastity. But instead of spending their time in meditation or in study, they were warriors. The Order of Saint John of Jerusalem (which later moved its headquarters to Malta), the Templars, and others were founded in the Holy Land. In Spain there were the similar Orders of Calatrava, Alcantara, and Santiago. Long after the Crusades, these orders continued existing, and some of them held enormous power. The Templars gained such wealth and power that in 1307 King Philip IV of France accused them of heresy, witchcraft, and moral aberration, with the connivance of Pope Clement V (1305–1314), had their leaders in France executed, and confiscated their enormous wealth. In 1312 Clement suppressed the order throughout all Christendom. Soon, partly on the basis of the false accusations against them, legends arose claiming that the Templars were indeed a heretical society that held to ancient Gnostic teachings. The Order of Calatrava was sufficiently powerful in Spain that in their attempt to unify the land under their rule, Isabella and Ferdinand made the latter Grand Master of the order. The Knights of Saint John of Jerusalem ruled in Malta until Napoleon overthrew them in 1798.

The crusading spirit was also used to combat heresy. In southern France and some sections of Italy, doctrines had spread that were similar to those of the ancient Manichaeans, who believed in a cosmic struggle between equally powerful forces of good and evil. It appears that they were imported from Bulgaria, in the Byzantine Empire, where a sect of "Bogomils" had long held a Manichaean dualism. They were also called *Cathars* (a word derived from the Greek for "pure") or *Albigensians*, since many came from the town of Albi, in southern France. Against them, Innocent III called a Crusade, and in 1209 ambitious noblemen from northern France invaded the south. Atrocities similar to those that had taken place in Muslim lands were committed, both against Albigensians and against their Catholic neighbors who came to their defense. This was an indication that for years to come the crusading ideal would be used in different circumstances, quite apart from the original intent of retaking the Holy Land.

In the field of theology, renewed contact with the Muslim world had far-reaching consequences. Muslim Spain, and to a lesser degree Muslim Sicily, had been centers of learning. The greatest Jewish and Muslim philosophers of the Middle Ages, Maimonides and Ibn Rushd (known in Western literature as *Averroes*) had been born in Cordoba. They and others had revived a

Cordoba, long a center of Muslim power and learning, made a significant contribution to the development of Christian theology in the period immediately following the Crusades. The two most influential Cordoban figures in this process were the Muslim Averroes and the Jew Maimonides, now honored by these two monuments in Cordoba.

great deal of the philosophy of antiquity, and related it to Jewish and Islamic theological questions. Averroes in particular had written commentaries on Aristotle, and these were so widely used that he came to be known simply as "the Commentator." From Spain and Sicily, the works of these philosophers, as well as of Aristotle himself, were introduced into Western Europe, where in the thirteenth century they would give rise to a great deal of philosophical and theological activity.

Finally, there is a complex relationship between the Crusades and a series of economic and demographic changes which took place in Europe at approximately the same time. Although it is clear that the Crusades contributed to these changes, there were several other factors involved, and historians are not in agreement as to their relative importance. In any case, the age of the Crusades witnessed the development of cities and of an economy where trade once again became active. Until then, most trade was by barter, and the only important source of wealth was land. Therefore economic power was in the hands of the nobles and prelates who had control of the land. But the development of an economy where trade was increasingly important and was done on the basis of money and letters of credit gave rise to new sources of wealth. This in turn contributed to the growth of cities, where a new class, the bourgeoisie, began to emerge. This class, whose name means precisely "those who live in the city," was formed mostly by merchants whose economic and political power was on the rise. Soon they would be allies of the monarchy against the excessive power of the high nobility; eventually, in the French Revolution, they would overcome both the crown and the nobility.

32

The Golden Age of Medieval Christianity

Just as God established two great luminaries in the heavens, the greater to preside over days, and the lesser to preside over nights, so did he establish two luminaries in the heavens of the universal church.... The greater to preside over souls as over days, and the lesser to preside over bodies as over nights. These are pontifical authority and royal power.

INNOCENT III

As the Crusades were drawing to a close, medieval Christianity reached its high point. Once again, this was seen primarily in developments that took place in the two foci of medieval religious life: monasticism and the papacy. And it also found expression in theology, in missionary work, and in architecture. Therefore, very briefly, we shall turn our attention to each of these in order: the development of mendicant monastic orders, the rising power of the papacy, theological activity, missionary endeavors, and architecture.

THE MENDICANT ORDERS

The growth of cities, trade, and the monetary economy brought about changes that were not always welcome. The use of money had replaced bartering for goods, and while promoting more specialized production and thus increasing the collective wealth, the use of money had the great disadvantage of making economic transactions less direct and human, and of promoting a growing chasm between rich and poor. The growth of cities, and the movement of population that it involved, also made it difficult for the traditional parish ministry to fill the needs of those who flocked to the towns. Thus, it is not surprising that monasticism, which through the ages has shown its enormous adaptability, would take new shapes that both questioned the mores of the monetary economy and responded to the needs of a population on the move. The monastics that did so were called the *mendicants*—those who lived by begging.

Francis is best known for the stigmata—the marks of the cross—which he bore on his body.

A precursor of the mendicant orders was Peter Waldo, a twelfth-century merchant from Lyons who heard the story of a monk who practiced extreme poverty and was moved by it to devote himself to a life of poverty and preaching. He soon gathered a number of followers, but the archbishop forbade their activities, which seemed a critique of the rich and would undermine his own authority and control of religious life. They appealed to Rome, and the theologians appointed to hear their case treated them with derision for their ignorance. In spite of this and despite repeated condemnations, they continued preaching. Persecution then forced them to withdraw to remote valleys in the Alps, where they continued existing until the Protestant Reformation. At that time, they were approached by Reformed theologians whose teachings they accepted, and thus became Protestant.

In its early stages, the Franciscan movement was very similar to the Waldensians. Francis (c. 1181–1226), like Peter Waldo, belonged to the merchant class. An Italian, his true name was Giovanni. But his mother was French, his father had trade relations with France, and he himself was fond of the songs of French troubadours. Therefore, soon friends in his native Assisi called him "Francesco"—the little Frenchman—and by that name he is known to this day.

Like Peter Waldo, Francis had a profound religious experience that led him to embrace a life of poverty. It is said that one day his friends noticed that he was exceptionally happy.

"Why are you so happy?" they asked him.
"Because I have married."
"Whom have you married?"
"Lady Poverty!"

The Portiuncula.

He then gave to the poor all he had. If his parents gave him more, he immediately gave it away. Dressed in rags, he spent his time praising the beauty of poverty to any who would listen, or rebuilding an abandoned chapel, or enjoying the beauty and harmony of nature. His father put him in a cellar and appealed to the authorities. The bishop finally decided that, if Francis was not willing to use his family's goods wisely, he must give them up. Upon receiving the verdict, he gave up his inheritance, returned to his father the clothes he was wearing, and left naked into the woods, where he lived as a hermit and spent much of his time in the reconstruction of a small and dilapidated chapel called the Portiuncula.

Then, late in 1209, he heard the reading of the Gospel (Matt. 10:7-10), where Jesus sent his disciples to preach, taking with them no gold or silver. Until then, he had been concerned almost exclusively with voluntary poverty and the joy he found in it. Now he saw the possibility of joining poverty with preaching. His place would not be in quiet solitude, but in the bustle of the cities, wherever people were, preaching to them, helping the poor and the sick. Now voluntary poverty was not only a means of self-discipline, but even more, a means to identify with those who were poor out of necessity.

Led by this new vision, Francis left his retreat and returned to Assisi, there to preach and to face the insults of his former friends. Slowly, however, a small following gathered around him, and he and a few others went to Rome to ask authorization from the pope to found a new monastic order. The pope was Innocent III—the most powerful man, and one of the wisest, ever to occupy that position. Innocent was not inclined to grant what Francis requested. It is said that Innocent told Francis that he looked like a pig, and should go and wallow among pigs. Frances went to a pig sty, and then returned to Innocent covered in mud and saying, "Father, I have done as you ordered; now, will you do as I request?" No matter whether the story is true or not, the fact is that Innocent was wiser than his predecessors, and, after testing Francis's mettle, yielded.

Francis returned to Assisi to continue his work with papal approval. Soon people began flocking to his new "order of lesser brothers"—or *Friars Minor*. Saint Clare, a spiritual sister of Francis, founded an order for women that became commonly known as the *Clarisses* or *Poor Clares*. Franciscans preaching, singing, and begging became a common sight throughout Western Europe.

Francis was concerned that the success of the movement would be its downfall. When his followers began to be respected, he began to fear for their humility. It is said that, when a novice asked him if it was lawful to have a Psalter, he replied: "When you have a Psalter, you will want a Breviary. And when you have a Breviary you will climb to the pulpit like a prelate."

The story is also told of a friar who returned joyful, because someone had given him a gold coin. Francis ordered him to take the coin between his teeth, and bury it in a dung heap, pointing out that such was the best place for gold.

Well aware of the temptations that success placed before his order, Francis made a will forbidding his followers to possess anything, or to appeal to the pope or to anyone else to have the *Rule* that he had given them made less stringent.

At the general chapter of the order that met in 1220, he gave up the leadership of the order, and knelt in obedience before his successor. Finally, on October 3, 1226, he died at the Portiuncula, the chapel that he had rebuilt in his youth. It is said that his last words were: "I have done my duty. Now, may Christ let you know yours. Welcome, sister Death!"

The founder of the other major mendicant order was Saint Dominic. He was some twelve years older than Francis, but his work as the founder of an order was somewhat later. He was born in the town of Caleruega, in Castile, to an aristocratic family whose tower still dominates the landscape of Northern Spain.

After some ten years of study in Palencia, Dominic became a canon of the cathedral of Osma. Four years later, when he was twenty-nine, the chapter of the cathedral resolved to follow the monastic rule of the Canons of Saint Augustine. This meant that the members of the cathedral chapter lived in a monastic community, but without withdrawing from the world nor setting aside their ministry to the faithful.

In 1203, Dominic and his bishop, Diego of Osma, visited southern France. He was moved by the success of the Albigensians, and by the efforts to convert

Statue honoring St. Dominic in his native Caleruega.

them to Catholicism by force. Their dualistic division of the world into material (bad) and spiritual (good) was easily grasped, but theological heresy. Dominic also noted that the Albigensians' main attraction was the asceticism of their leaders, which contrasted with the easy life of many orthodox priests and prelates. Convinced that there were better means of combating heresy, Dominic set out to preach and teach orthodoxy. This he joined to a disciplined monastic life and rigorous study in order to make use of the best possible arguments against heresy. On the foothills of the Pyrenees he founded a school for noblewomen who were converted from among the ranks of the Albigensians. The archbishop of Toulouse, encouraged by his success, gave him a church in which to preach, as well as a house in which to organize a monastic community.

Shortly thereafter, with the support of the archbishop, he went to Rome in order to request permission from Innocent III to found a new order, with its own rule. The pope refused, for he was concerned over the proliferation of different monastic rules. But he encouraged Dominic to continue his work, and to adopt one of the existing monastic rules. Upon returning to Toulouse, Dominic and his followers adopted the rule of the Canons of Saint Augustine. Then, through further legislation, they adapted that rule to their own needs. They also adopted the rule of poverty and mendicancy, perhaps following the example of early Franciscanism, but certainly as a means to refute the arguments of the Albigensians, who claimed that orthodox Christians were too worldly.

From its very beginnings, the Order of Preachers—for such was the official name of the Dominicans—emphasized study. In this Dominic differed from Saint Francis, who did not wish his friars to have even a Psalter, and who was suspicious of study. The Dominicans, in their task of refuting heresy, must be well armed intellectually, and for that reason their recruits received solid intellectual training. They soon gave to the church some of its most distinguished theologians—although the Franciscans, who entered the theological field somewhat later, were not far behind.

Both mendicant orders spread throughout most of Europe. They had sister organizations for women, and even a "third order" of people who followed the piety and practices of the Franciscans or the Dominicans, but without becoming monastics nor abandoning their secular roles in society. These third orders were instrumental both in spreading Franciscan and Dominican piety and in providing support for the mendicants themselves. Soon there were other similar movements, or ancient orders that now followed the example of the Franciscans and Dominicans. In general, the subsequent course of the Order of Preachers was much less turbulent than that of the Franciscans.

From the beginning, Dominicans had seen poverty as an argument that strengthened and facilitated their task of refuting heresy. Their main objective was preaching, teaching, and study, and poverty was seen as a means to that end. Therefore, when new circumstances seemed to make it advisable for the order to have property, this was done without major difficulties, and the ideal of living by begging was set aside. Also, since such a step agreed with their original impulse, they soon established a foothold in the universities, which were beginning to blossom at the same time.

The two main centers of theological studies at the time were the nascent universities of Paris and Oxford. The Dominicans founded houses in both cities, and soon had professors teaching in the universities. Before long, such Dominicans as Albert the Great and Thomas Aquinas would bring great prestige to the order in intellectual circles.

The Franciscans also established a foothold in the universities. In 1236, a professor at the University of Paris, Alexander of Hales, joined the Franciscans, and thus the Friars Minor had their first university professor. Before long, there were Franciscan teachers in all the major universities of Western Europe.

In spite of its early success—and perhaps because of it—the order founded by Saint Francis had a stormy history. Francis himself had always feared that his friars would become rich and comfortable. For that reason he ordered absolute poverty, not only for individual friars, but also for the order as a whole. And he nailed down this command by reaffirming it in his will, and forbidding his followers to seek any change in the *Rule* he had given them.

Shortly after Francis's death, two parties had developed within the order. The rigorists insisted on strict obedience to the founder's instructions. The moderates argued that changed circumstances required a less literal interpretation of the *Rule*, and that the order ought to be able to accept property given to it to further its mission. In 1230, Gregory IX declared that the will of Francis was not binding, and that the order could therefore ask Rome to alter the rule of poverty. In 1245, the order began owning property, although the Holy See held title to it and the Franciscans had only the right to use it. Eventually, even this fiction was abandoned, and the order came to own vast holdings.

While all this was taking place, the rigorists became increasingly alienated from the hierarchy of the church. They viewed what was taking place as a great betrayal of Saint Francis. Soon some began saying that the prophecies of Joachim of Fiore, who had lived a generation before Francis, were being fulfilled. Joachim had proposed that history consisted of three successive stages: the era of the Father, the era of the Son, and the era of the Spirit. The first, from Adam to Jesus, lasted forty-two generations. Since God loves order and symmetry, Joachim had argued, the era of the Son will last the same number of generations. At thirty years per generation, Joachim arrived at the year 1260 as the end of the age of the Son, and the beginning of that of the Spirit. During the age of the Son, monks, who are more spiritual than the rest of believers, are heralds of the age of the Spirit.

Since the year 1260 was approaching, it was natural that a number of rigorist Franciscans, alienated as they were from the hierarchy, would adopt Joachim's scheme. The present difficulties, they believed, were but the last struggles before the next age would dawn, when they would be vindicated. Meanwhile, the pope and other leaders of the church were at best believers of a lower sort, and there would soon be no need for them.

Calling themselves "spirituals," those Franciscans set out to preach the theories of Joachim of Fiore. The minister general of the order, John of Parma, leaned in their direction to such a degree that he had to defend himself against accusations of heresy. Thus, for a time it appeared that the Franciscans would follow a path similar to that of the earlier Waldensians, and break with the hierarchical church. But the next minister general, Bonaventure, who had also served as a professor at the University of Paris, was able to combine profound piety with strict obedience to the hierarchy, and the spirituals lost momentum. The same ideas reemerged in the fourteenth century among the *Fraticelli*—Italian for "little brothers"—who were ruthlessly persecuted until they disappeared.

ONE FLOCK UNDER ONE SHEPHERD

The Concordat of Worms (1122), which granted the emperor the power to invest bishops with secular authority but *not* with sacred authority, did not end the difficulties of the papacy. In Rome there were still powerful families that sought to capture it for their own purposes, and soon there were once again two claimants to the See of Saint Peter. Europe would have been divided in its allegiance to them had it not been for the decisive support of Bernard of Clairvaux for Innocent II. Having lost Rome to his rival claimant, Innocent sought refuge in France, which sided with him. England and Germany, France's traditional enemies, hesitated in their allegiance. But Bernard convinced both sovereigns to side with Innocent. Eventually, with the support of imperial troops, Innocent was able to return to Rome.

But then the emperor died, and Innocent's relations with the new emperor deteriorated. Republican ideas were circulating in Italy, and the pope subversively encouraged them in the imperial cities of the north, while the emperor did the same in Rome. A number of imperial cities rebelled and proclaimed themselves republics. The people of Rome also rebelled, proclaimed a republic, elected a senate, and declared that they would obey the pope's spiritual authority, but not his temporal rule. The next few popes were seldom able to reside in the city. Tension between papacy and empire grew under the next emperor, Frederick Barbarossa (1152–1190), who finally had a series of rival popes elected. But he was unable to impose his policy in Italy, where the rebellious imperial cities, united in a Lombard League, defeated him. After years of struggle, Barbarossa made peace with the pope, at that time Alexander III. The rival pope, Calixtus III, resigned in 1178. Alexander accepted his resignation gracefully, and even appointed him to high ecclesiastical office.

Frederick strengthened his hand by marrying his son Henry to the heir of the throne of Sicily, a traditional ally of the popes. Then Frederick drowned in the Third Crusade, and was succeeded by his son Henry VI, who was both emperor of Germany and king of Sicily. Soon it was clear that Henry sought to control the papacy, and Pope Celestine III excommunicated him. Open warfare seemed inevitable when both the emperor and the pope died.

Since the empire had not yet recovered from the unexpected death of Henry VI, the cardinals were able to elect a new pope without undue pressure. Their choice fell on Lotario de' Conti di Segni, thirty-seven years old, who under the name of Innocent III became the most powerful pope in the history of Christianity.

Henry's widow feared that her infant son, Frederick, would be destroyed by some of those vying for power in Germany, and therefore placed the child under the protection of the pope by declaring the kingdom of Sicily a fiefdom of the papacy. Thus was averted the threat to the papacy which that kingdom had been under Henry VI.

The imperial crown, which Henry had also held, was not hereditary. Rather, the emperor was elected from among the nobles. Young Frederick was obviously too young to be emperor, especially since it was certain that this would not be an easy crown to hold. Those who had supported Henry VI and his house of Hohenstaufen elected Henry's brother Philip. But a rival faction elected Otto IV, who soon had the support of Innocent III. It is clear that Philip had been duly elected. But Innocent declared that he was tainted by his brother's crimes in opposing the pope, and that in any case the pope has the authority to determine the rightful emperor. The temporal power and the spiritual power, he claimed, have both been instituted by God. They are like the moon and the sun. But, just as the moon receives its light from the sun, so does the emperor receive his power from the pope. On this basis, Innocent declared that Otto was the rightful ruler, and a civil war ensued that lasted ten years, and which ended only when Philip was murdered.

After he had undisputed control of the empire, Otto IV broke with the pope who had supported his claim. Once again the main reason for discord was the emperor's effort to increase his power in Italy, and the pope's refusal to allow him to do so. As in previous generations, Otto's agents encouraged the republican party in Rome, while he prepared to invade the kingdom of Sicily, which, in theory at least, belonged to the papacy, for young Frederick was Innocent's vassal.

In retaliation, Innocent excommunicated Otto, declared him deposed, and affirmed that the legitimate emperor was young Frederick. With the pope's support, Frederick, now grown, crossed the Alps, appeared in Germany, and wrested the imperial crown from his uncle. This was a strange victory for both Frederick and Innocent. By supporting Frederick, Innocent had contributed to the restoration of the house of Hohenstaufen, traditional enemies of the papacy. But it was also true that Frederick II, the new emperor, had reached that position on the basis of the papal claim to authority over emperors and kings. Thus, while Innocent acknowledged Frederick, the new emperor had tacitly affirmed that the pope had been within his rights in assuming authority to determine who was the rightful ruler.

Germany was not the only country in which Innocent III intervened. Indeed, there was hardly a European monarch who did not feel the weight of his authority.

In France, he intervened in the marital life of King Philip Augustus. The king had been widowed and remarried to a Danish princess, but then he had repudiated his second wife and taken a third. Innocent admonished the king to return to his rightful wife, and when Philip refused he placed the entire country under an interdict, forbidding the celebration of sacraments. Philip called a gathering of nobles and bishops, with the hope that they would support him against the pope. But they took the opposite stance, and Philip was forced to leave his third wife and return to the second. The deposed queen died shortly thereafter, suffering from intense depression. The restored queen spent the rest of her life complaining that her supposed restoration was in truth constant torture. In any case, the pope's authority had prevailed over one of the most powerful sovereigns of the time.

In England, the ruler was John Lackland, brother and heir to the great military leader, crusader and king, Richard the Lionhearted. Although John's marital life had been much more disorderly than Philip's, Innocent did not intervene, for at the time he desperately needed England's support in his efforts to establish Otto on the throne of Germany. But later Innocent and John clashed over the question of who was the legitimate archbishop of Canterbury. There were two rival claimants to that see, the most important in England, and both appealed to the pope. Innocent's response was that neither was the legitimate archbishop. Instead, he named Stephen Langton to that post. John Lackland refused to accept the papal decision, and Innocent excommunicated him. When this proved insufficient, Innocent declared John deposed from his throne, released all his subjects from their vows of obedience to him, and called a crusade against him. This was to be under the leadership of Philip Augustus of France, who gladly prepared to obey the pope in this matter. Fearing that many of his subjects were not loyal to him, and that he would not be able to defend his throne, John capitulated and made his entire kingdom a fief of the papacy, as had been done earlier with the kingdom of Sicily.

Innocent accepted John's submission, canceled the crusade that Philip of France was preparing, and thereafter became a staunch supporter of his new ally. Thus, when the English nobility, with the support of Stephen Langton, forced John to sign the Magna Carta, limiting the power of the king vis-à-vis the nobility, Innocent declared that this was a usurpation of power. But all his protests were to no avail.

Innocent also intervened repeatedly in Spain. Pedro II of Aragon was forced to turn his kingdom into a fief of the papacy, thus giving credence to Innocent's claim that all lands conquered from unbelievers—by which he meant Muslims—belonged to the papacy. One of the ironies of history is that this king, known as "the Catholic," died while supporting the Albigensians against the crusade that Innocent had proclaimed against them. The kingdoms of Leon and Castile also felt Innocent's hand, for the pope refused to allow the marriage of the King of Leon with the daughter of his first cousin, the King of Castile. And a further irony of history is that one of the sons of that forbidden union, Ferdinand III of Castile and Leon, became a saint of the church.

These are just a few of the many examples of Innocent's far-reaching international policies. His authority was felt in his personal intervention in the affairs of Portugal, Bohemia, Hungary, Denmark, Iceland, and even Bulgaria and Armenia. Although this was done against his wishes, the Fourth Crusade, in taking Constantinople and establishing there a Latin Empire, further extended the reach of his power.

But this was not all. It was during Innocent's reign that the two great mendicant orders of the Franciscans and Dominicans were founded, that the Christian kingdoms of Spain joined to defeat the Moors in the battle of Navas de Tolosa, and that the great Crusade against the Albigensians took place. In all of these events, Innocent played a leading role.

Innocent's program for the reformation of the church found expression in the decrees of the Fourth Lateran Council, which gathered in 1215. It was this council that promulgated the doctrine of transubstantiation, which holds that in communion the substance of the body and blood of Christ takes the place of the substance of the bread and wine. During its brief three sessions, this council approved an entire program of reformation dictated by the pope. It condemned the Waldensians, the Albigensians, and the doctrines of Joachim of Fiore. It instituted episcopal inquisition, which meant that every bishop should inquire as to the presence of heresy in his diocese, and destroy it. It determined that no new monastic orders, with new rules, could be founded. It ordered that every cathedral have a school, and that education in such schools be open to the poor. It ordered the clergy to abstain from the theater, games, hunting, and other such pastimes. It decreed that all the faithful must confess their sins and receive communion at least once a year. It forbade the introduction of new relics without papal approval. It required all Jews and Muslims in Christian lands to wear distinctive garments that would set them apart from Christians. And it made it unlawful for priests to charge for the administration of sacraments. Since the council accomplished all this, and more, in only three sessions, each of which lasted a single day, it is clear that most of these measures were not the result of the assembly's deliberation, but that they were rather part of a program that Innocent had determined, and which he had the council approve.

For all of these reasons, it was under Innocent III that Christendom most nearly approached the ideal of being "one flock, under one shepherd"—the pope. Thus, it is not surprising that his contemporaries came to believe that the pope was more than human, and that by right he had an authority that extended to every human endeavor.

Innocent died in 1216, and for several decades his successors basked in the light of his prestige. Between 1254 and 1273, Germany went through a period of disorder, and eventually it was the papacy, under Gregory X, that restored order by supporting the election of Rudolf of Hapsburg. In return, the new emperor declared that Rome and the papal states were independent of the empire.

Meanwhile, France's power was increasing, and the popes repeatedly found support in it. Also, the prestige of the mendicant orders was such that many hoped for popes elected from within their ranks. The first Dominican pope was Innocent V, who reigned very briefly in 1276. The first Franciscan was Nicholas IV, who was pope from 1288 to 1292.

When Nicholas died, there was disagreement among the cardinals. Some insisted that the pope should be experienced in worldly matters, a man who understood the intrigues and ambitions of the world; others held to the Franciscan ideal, and sought the election of a candidate embodying it. Finally, the latter group prevailed, and Celestine V was elected. He was a Franciscan of the "spiritual" wing of the order. When he appeared barefoot and riding a donkey, many thought that the prophecies of Joachim of Fiore were coming true. Now was the age of the Spirit beginning, and the church would be led by the humble and the poor. Two hundred thousand hopeful believers went on pilgrimage to greet him. Shortly after his election, he gave the spiritual Franciscans authority to leave the order, whose rule of poverty previous popes had relaxed, and live as poor hermits. The famous poet Jacopone da Todi, a spiritual Franciscan who agreed with the views earlier expressed by Joachim of Fiore, declared that the hopes of the world were laid on Celestine's shoulders, and that were he to fail great woes would ensue. And fail he did. Since he knew nothing—and wished to know nothing—of the political realities of his time, he soon became a tool of Charles II of Naples, who used the pope to advance his own political agenda. Finally, less that a year after his election, Celestine decided to abdicate after a brief pontificate. He appeared before the cardinals, shed the papal robes, and literally sat on the ground, vowing that he would not change his mind. He then withdrew once again to a strict monastic life, which he led until his death less than five years later.

His successor was a man of entirely different inclinations, who took the title of Boniface VIII (1294–1303). His bull *Unam Sanctam* marked the high point of papal claims to temporal power:

> One sword must be under the other, and temporal authority must be subject to the spiritual . . . . Therefore, if earthly power strays from the right path it is to be judged by the spiritual . . . But if the supreme spiritual authority strays, it can only be judged by God, and not by humans. . . .
> We further declare, affirm, and define that it is absolutely necessary for salvation that all human creatures be under the Roman pontiff.[46]

However, as we shall see in the next chapter, such high claims were belied by events, for it was during the reign of Boniface VIII that it became apparent that the power of the papacy was declining.

THEOLOGICAL ACTIVITY: SCHOLASTICISM

The thirteenth century, which marked the apex of papal power and the birth of the mendicant orders, was also the high point of medieval scholasticism. This theology, which developed in the schools, had its own characteristic methodology. It took root first in monasteries, but in the twelfth-century cathedral schools became the center of theological activity, only to be supplanted, early in the thirteenth century, by universities. In a way, this is another consequence of the growth of cities. From monasteries, which usually existed apart from centers of population, theology moved to cathedral schools, that is, to schools connected with churches that had bishops—and therefore were usually in cities. Then it centered in universities, which were vast associations of scholars gathered in the principal cities.

The most important forerunner of scholasticism was Anselm of Canterbury. A native of Italy, he had joined the monastery of Bec, in Normandy, in 1060. He was attracted to that particular monastery by the fame of its abbot, Lanfranc, who left in 1078 to become archbishop of Canterbury. In 1066, William of Normandy had conquered England, and was now drawing on Normandy for leaders both in ecclesiastical and in civil matters. In 1093, Anselm himself was called to England to succeed Lanfranc as archbishop of Canterbury. He went reluctantly, for he knew that he would soon clash with the king over the question of the relative authority of church and state. (Seventy years later, Thomas Becket, then archbishop of Canterbury, would be murdered at the cathedral for similar reasons.) Indeed, first under William, and then under his son Henry, Anselm spent most of his career exiled from Canterbury. He made use of those periods of exile, as he had done with his years at Bec, by meditating and writing on theological issues.

Anselm's significance for the development of scholasticism lies in his desire to apply reason to questions of faith. What he sought in doing this was not to prove something that he did not believe without such proof, but rather to understand more deeply what he already believed. This may be seen in his prayer in the first chapter of his *Proslogion*:

> I do not seek, Lord, to reach your heights, for my intellect is as nothing compared to them. But I seek in some way to understand your truth, which my heart believes and loves. For I do not seek to understand in order to believe, but rather believe in order to understand.[47]

Anselm believed in the existence of God. But he sought to understand more deeply what that existence meant. It was for this reason that he developed in the *Proslogion* what is known as the ontological argument for the existence of

Scholarship and the copying of manuscripts had long been main occupations of monks.

God. Briefly stated, Anselm's argument is that when one thinks of God, one is thinking of *that than which no greater can be thought*. The question is then, is it possible to think of *that than which no greater can be thought* as not existing? Clearly not, for then an existing being would be greater than it. Therefore, by definition, the idea of *that than which no greater can be thought* includes its own existence. To speak of God as not existing makes as much sense as to speak of a triangle with four sides. The exact interpretation, significance, and validity of this argument have been discussed by scholars and philosophers through the ages, and are still discussed. What is important for our purposes, however, is the method of Anselm's theology, which applies reason to a truth known by faith, in order to understand it better.

The same is true of Anselm's treatise *Why Did God Became Man?* There he explores the question of the reason for the incarnation, and offers an answer that would eventually become standard in Western theology. In this scheme, clearly shaped by feudal views on crime and its penalties, the importance of a crime is measured in terms of the one against whom it is committed. Therefore, a crime against God (sin) is infinite in its import. But, on the other hand, only a human being can offer satisfaction for human sin. This is obviously impossible, for human beings are finite, and cannot offer the infinite satisfaction required by the majesty of God. For this reason, there is need for a divine-human, God incarnate, who through his suffering and death offers satisfaction for the sins of all humankind. This view of the work of Christ, which was by no means the generally accepted one in earlier centuries, soon gained such credence that most Western Christians came to accept it as the only biblical one. Again, what is significant here is Anselm's use of reason to seek to understand more fully the incarnation in which he already believes.

Another important forerunner of scholasticism was Peter Abelard. Born in Brittany in 1079, Abelard spent his youth studying under the most famous scholars of his time. He found them wanting, and let them know his opinion of them. He thus collected some of the many enemies that would make his life a *History of Calamities*—the title of his autobiography. He then went to Paris, where a canon of the cathedral entrusted him with the education of his very gifted niece, Heloise. The teacher and the student became lovers and had a child. Heloise's uncle, outraged, had some ruffians break into Abelard's room and emasculate him. Abelard then withdrew to a life of monastic retreat, but was followed by his many enemies, and by those who were convinced that his bold use of reason was heresy. Foremost among these was the saintly Bernard of Clairvaux, who had Abelard condemned as a heretic in 1141. When Abelard appealed to Rome, he found that Bernard had already closed that door. Thus, toward the end of his career, Abelard came to view his life as a series of calamities. He died in 1142, having reconciled with the church (and with Heloise, who had continued correspondence with him), and had his remains moved from Cluny to the monastery he had founded and been forced to leave, the Oratory of the Paraclete.

Abelard's main contribution to the development of scholastic theology was the book *Yes and No*, in which he took up 158 theological questions and then showed that various authorities, including the Bible and the ancient Christian writers, did not agree on their answers.

Naturally, such a book aroused great opposition, especially coming from one who was at best suspected of heresy. Abelard's purpose, however, does not seem to have been to discredit the authorities he set against each other, but simply to show that theology must not be content with citing authorities. It was necessary, as he saw matters, to find ways to reconcile such apparently contradictory authorities. Eventually, scholasticism used this method. The typical scholastic work began by posing a question and then quoting authorities who seemed to support one answer, and then other authorities who seemed to support another. What the scholastics did (and Abelard did not do) was to then offer an answer and "solutions," which demonstrated how it was possible for all the authorities quoted to be correct.

The third main forerunner of scholasticism was Peter Lombard, who wrote *Four Books of Sentences*, a systematic treatment of the main themes of Christian theology, from the doctrine of God to eschatology ("the last things"). At first some disagreed with a number of the opinions expressed in it, and sought to have it condemned. Eventually, however, it became the basic textbook for teaching theology in the universities, where scholars were usually expected to comment on the *Sentences* of Peter Lombard. Therefore the works of major scholastic theologians often include a *Commentary on the Sentences* written during the early years of their teaching careers.

A very important point on which Peter Lombard left his mark in theology was his determination that there are seven sacraments: baptism, confirmation, eucharist, penance, anointing of the sick, holy orders, and matrimony. This point had not been at all clear before his time but due to his influence it has been the official teaching of the Roman Catholic Church to this day.

Besides these forerunners, two developments were significant for the early history of scholasticism: the growth of universities and the reintroduction of the teachings of Aristotle into Western Europe.

The universities were in part the result of the growth of cities. Students congregated in urban centers, first at the cathedral schools, and then at others, and all of these were eventually united in what came to be known as "general studies." Out of these evolved the main universities of Europe. But these were not so much institutions like our modern universities as they were guilds of scholars, both teachers and students, organized in order to defend the rights of their members, and to certify the level of proficiency achieved by each.

The oldest universities in Western Europe date from the late years of the twelfth century; but it was the thirteenth that witnessed the growth of universities as the main centers of study. Although in all of them one could acquire a basic education, soon some became famous for a particular field of study. Those who wished to study medicine, for example, endeavored to go to the universities

This medieval classroom at the University of Salamanca shows the benches and tables on which students sat and worked, as well as the pulpit from which the professor spoke. When the professor was commenting on a text, this text was presented by a reader seated in the special section just below the professor.

in Montpelier or Salerno, while the universities in Ravenna, Pavia, and Bologna were famous for study in law. For theology, the main centers were Paris and Oxford.

Those who aspired to become theologians first had to spend several years studying philosophy and humanities in the Arts Faculty. Then they entered the Faculty of Theology, where they began as "hearers," and could progressively become "biblical bachelors," "bachelors on the sentences," "formed bachelors," "licensed masters," and "doctors." By the fourteenth century, this process required fourteen years after having completed one's studies in the Faculty of Arts.

Theological academic exercises consisted of commentaries on the Bible or the *Sentences,* sermons, and "disputations." The latter were the academic exercise par excellence. Here a debatable question was posed, and those present and qualified to do so were given opportunity to offer reasons for answering the question one way or the other, usually on the basis of the authority of scripture or of an ancient writer. Thus was compiled a list of opinions that seemed to contradict each other, similar to Abelard's *Yes and No.* Then the teacher was given time to prepare an answer, for in the next session he had to express his own opinion, and to show that this did not contradict any of the authorities that had been adduced for the opposite view. Eventually, this method was so generalized that the various *Commentaries on the Sentences* followed it, as did Thomas Aquinas in his *Summa Contra Gentiles* and in his *Summa Theologica*.

The other development that made a great impact on scholasticism was the reintroduction of Aristotle into Western Europe. From the time of Justin in the second century, most Christian theologians, particularly in the West, had grown accustomed to what was essentially a Platonic or Neoplatonic philosophy, which tended to distrust the senses as a source of knowledge. Although some of Aristotle's works were read and used, these had to do mostly with logic, and did not contradict the essentially Platonic world view of early medieval theology. But then the Crusades, and especially renewed contacts with Muslims in Spain and Sicily, brought about greater knowledge of Aristotle's philosophy, and it was clear that this differed in many ways from what was generally accepted—particularly in valuing the senses as part of the process leading to true knowledge. Furthermore, since Aristotle's most famous commentator was Averroes, many of the latter's views entered Western Europe. This was especially true in the Faculty of Arts at the University of Paris, where there was keen interest in the "new" philosophy.

Several professors in the arts faculty at Paris embraced the new philosophical ideas with enthusiasm. Since they generally read Aristotle through the eyes of the Muslim commentator Averroes, they have been called "Latin Averroists." There were several elements in their philosophy that profoundly disturbed the theologians. Foremost of these was the insistence on the independence of reason and philosophy from any constraint imposed by faith and theology. The Averroists insisted that the path of reason should be followed to the end, and that if its conclusions somehow differed from those of theology, this was a problem for theologians, and not philosophers, to solve. This position then allowed them to accept a number of doctrines of Aristotle and Averroes that contradicted traditional Christian teaching. For instance, they said that, according to reason, matter is eternal—which contradicted the doctrine of creation out of nothing; and that all souls are ultimately one—which contradicted the Christian doctrine of individual life after death.

Some theologians responded to this challenge by affirming the traditional Platonic and Augustinian outlook. Saint Bonaventure, for instance, who was the most distinguished Franciscan theologian of the thirteenth century, insisted that faith is necessary in order to achieve correct understanding. For example, the doctrine of creation tells us how the world is to be understood, and those who do not set out from that doctrine can easily come to the erroneous conclusion that matter is eternal. Furthermore, all knowledge comes from the Word of God who was incarnate in Christ, and to claim any knowledge apart from him is to deny the very core and source of the knowledge that one claims.

There was, however, an alternative that existed between that of the Averroists and that of traditional Augustinian theology. This was to explore the possibilities for a better understanding of Christian faith that the new philosophy offered. This was the path followed by the two great teachers of the Dominican Order: Albert the Great and Thomas Aquinas.

Albert, whose academic career in Paris and Cologne was frequently interrupted by the many tasks assigned to him, made a clear distinction between philosophy and theology. Philosophy operates on the basis of autonomous principles, which can be known apart from revelation, and seeks to discover truth by a method that is a strictly rational. A true philosopher does not seek to prove what the mind cannot understand, even if the question at hand is a doctrine of faith. The theologian, on the other hand, does set out from revealed truths, which cannot be known by reason alone. This does not mean that theological doctrines are less sure. On the contrary, revealed data are always more certain than those of reason, which may err. But it does mean that philosophers, as long as they remain within the scope of what reason can attain, should be free to pursue their inquiry, without having to turn at every step to the guiding hand of theology.

On the question of the eternity of the world, for instance, Albert frankly confesses that as a philosopher he cannot prove creation out of nothing. At best he can offer arguments of probability. But as a theologian he knows that the world was made out of nothing, and is not eternal. What we have here is a case in which reason cannot attain truth, for the object of inquiry is beyond the scope of human reason. A philosopher who claims to prove the eternity of the world, and a philosopher who claims to prove its creation out of nothing, are both poor philosophers, for they ignore the limits of reason.

Albert's most famous disciple was Thomas Aquinas. Born about 1224 in the family castle of Roccasecca, on the outskirts of Naples, Thomas was reared in an aristocratic family. All his brothers and sisters eventually came to occupy places of distinction in Italian society. His parents had intended an ecclesiastical career for him, with the hope that he would one day hold a post of power and prestige. He was five years old when they placed him in the Benedictine abbey of Monte Cassino, there to begin his education. At fourteen, he began studies at the University of Naples, where he first encountered Aristotelian philosophy. All this was preparation for the career his parents had planned for him. In 1244, however, he decided to become a Dominican. The new order, still in its early years, was regarded with disapproval by many of the wealthy. Therefore, his mother and brothers—his father had died by then—tried to persuade him to change his mind. When this failed, they locked him up in the family castle, where they kept him for more than a year while trying to dissuade him using

The ruins of Roccasecca, where Thomas Aquinas was born.

threats and temptations. He finally escaped, completed his novitiate among the Dominicans, and went to study at Cologne under Albert.

Many who knew Thomas in his early years failed to see his genius. He was so big and quiet that his fellow students called him "the dumb ox." But slowly his intelligence broke through his silence, and the Dominican Order acknowledged his intellectual gifts. He thus came to spend most of his life in academic circles, particularly in Paris, where he became a famous professor.

Thomas's literary production was astonishing. His most famous works are the *Summa Contra Gentiles*—perhaps written as a manual on theology for missionaries among Muslims—and the huge *Summa Theologica*. But he also wrote commentaries on the *Sentences,* on scripture, and on several works of Aristotle, as well as a number of philosophical and theological treatises. He died in 1274, when he was scarcely fifty years old. Some time before that, he had a series of mystical experiences and started to write less and less, until about a year before he died. Apparently after an experience while saying mass, Thomas told a friend, "I can write no more. I have seen things that make all my writings like straw." Albert, his teacher, outlived him, and became one of the staunchest defenders of his views.

It is impossible to review here even the salient points of Thomism. Therefore, we shall limit our discussion to the relationship between faith and reason, which is at the heart of Thomism (the name given to his system), and to his

Thomas became one of the most influential theologians of all time.

arguments for the existence of God, which illustrate the difference between Thomas's theology and that of his predecessors. Finally, a word will be added regarding the significance of Thomas's work.

On the relationship between faith and reason, Thomas follows the path outlined by Albert, but defines his position more clearly. According to Thomas, some truths are within the reach of reason, and others are beyond it. Philosophy deals only with the first; but theology is not limited to the latter. The reason for this is that there are truths that reason can prove, but which are necessary for salvation. Since God does not limit salvation to those who are intellectually gifted, all truth necessary for salvation, including that which can be reached by reason, has been revealed. Thus, such truths are a proper field of inquiry for both philosophy and theology.

One example of how this is applied is the manner in which Thomas deals with the question of the existence of God. It is impossible to be saved without believing that God exists. For that reason, the existence of God is a revealed truth, and the authority of the church suffices to believe in it. No one can plead lack of intelligence, for the existence of God is an article of faith, and even the most ignorant person can accept it on that basis. But this does not mean that the existence of God is a truth beyond the reach of reason. In this case, reason can prove what faith accepts. Therefore, the existence of God is a proper subject for both philosophy and theology, although each arrives at it following its own method. Furthermore, rational inquiry helps us to understand better that which we accept by faith.

That is the purpose of Thomas's "five ways" or arguments for the existence of God. The five ways are parallel, and do not have to be expounded here. Let it suffice to say that each of them starts from the world as it is known through the senses, and then shows that such a world requires the existence of God. The first way, for instance, begins by considering movement, and argues that, since what is moved must have a mover, there must be a prime mover, and this is God.

It is interesting to compare these arguments with Anselm's. Anselm distrusted the senses, and thus starts, not by looking at the world, but by examining the idea of God itself. Thomas's arguments follow the opposite route, for they start with the data known through the senses, and from them move on to the existence of God. This is a clear example of the manner in which Thomas's Aristotelian orientation contrasts with Anselm's Platonist views. Whereas Anselm believed that true knowledge is to be found in the realm of pure ideas, Thomas held that sense perception is the beginning of knowledge.

Thomas's work was of great significance for the ongoing development of theology. This was partly due to the systematic structure of his thought, but above all to the manner in which he joined traditional doctrine with what was then a new philosophical outlook.

As to the systematic character of his work, Thomas's *Summa Theologica* has been compared to a vast Gothic cathedral—a work which like many Gothic cathedrals, was never finished. As we shall see in the next section of this chapter, the great Gothic cathedrals were imposing monuments in which each element of creation and of the history of salvation had a place, and in which all elements stood in perfect balance. Likewise, the *Summa* is an imposing intellectual construction. Even those who disagree with what Thomas says in it cannot deny its architectural structure and its symmetry, in which each element seems to be in its proper place and balanced with all the others.

But Thomas's significance is even greater in his ability to turn a philosophy that many considered a threat into an instrument in the hands of faith. For centuries, Western theology—and much of Eastern theology as well—had been dominated by a Platonic bias. This had come about through a long process that involved such figures as Justin Martyr, Augustine, Pseudo-Dionysius, and many others. That philosophy had helped Christianity in various ways, particularly in its early struggles with paganism, for it spoke of an invisible Supreme Being, of a higher world that the senses cannot perceive, and of an immortal soul. Yet, Platonism also had its own dangers. By interpreting the Christian faith in Platonic terms, it was possible that Christians would come to undervalue the present world, which according to the Bible is God's creation. It was also possible that the incarnation, the presence of God in a physical human being, would be pushed to the background, for Platonism was not interested in temporal realities—which could be dated and located at a particular place—but rather in immutable truth. There was therefore the danger that theologians would pay less attention to Jesus Christ as a historical figure, and more to the eternal Word of God—again conceived in Neoplatonic terms.

The advent of the new philosophy threatened much of traditional theology. For that reason many reacted against it, and the reading and teaching of Aristotelianism were often forbidden. Condemnations of Aristotle often included some theses held by Thomas, and therefore there was a struggle before Thomism was considered an acceptable theological system. But eventually its value was acknowledged, and Saint Thomas—as he came to be known—was recognized as one of the greatest theologians of all time.

The importance of Thomas and his work cannot be overstated. Not only did he help the church cope with new ideas coming out of the Aristotelian revival, but in doing so he opened the way for modern science and observation. Traditional Platonism, with its distrust of the senses, was not particularly well suited to observation and experimentation. It had produced among Christians an attitude toward the physical and natural world that was typified in Augustine's lament that he had spent some time looking at a lizard and its movements, when he should have been contemplation God's truths; or in Anselm's like-minded assertion, that the soul is made for contemplating the divine, and if for only one instant it pulls its sight away from God to contemplate even the highest of creatures, this is sin. In contrast, Thomas's teacher, Albert, wrote about animals and plants, about heavenly and earthly bodies. Thomas himself, by making

Aristotelianism more palatable to Christian theologians, made it possible for others to continue Albert's lead, and this eventually led to scientific methods of observation, experimentation, and corroboration. On the basis of all this, one could even say that it was Thomas who opened the way for Western modernity.

MISSIONARY ENDEAVORS

Francis had been passionately interested in the conversion of Muslims, and in 1219 traveled to Damietta, in Egypt, where he had an interview with al-Kamil, an Ayyubid sultan, and was apparently treated with respect. Perhaps out of that experience, the last section of his *Rule* takes for granted that some of his followers will be missionaries, and commands that "those who under divine inspiration seek to go among Saracens (Muslims) and other infidels" must seek approval from their superiors in the order.

Following Francis's impulse, his followers preached not only to Christians, but also to others. Very soon there were Franciscan missionaries in Muslim lands in Spain and in North Africa, and even as far east as Beijing. The Franciscan John of Monte Corvino visited Persia, Ethiopia, and India, and in 1294, after a journey of three years, arrived at Cambaluc—now Beijing. In a few years, he had made several thousand converts. The pope then made him archbishop of Cambaluc, and sent seven other Franciscans to serve under him as bishops. Of these, only three reached their destination.

Also, after the failure of the Crusades, Franciscans were the main missionary body remaining in the Holy Land—an endeavor that over the centuries has produced more than two thousand martyrs.

Others were not Franciscans, but were inspired by Francis and the Friars Minor, and undertook similar work. Most notable among these was Raymond Lull, who spent much time trying to convince European church leaders to establish schools for the study of Arabic and Eastern languages, and died of his wounds after having been stoned in a mission to the Muslims in Majorca.

Dominicans also tried to convert Muslims and Jews. The most famous preacher among Muslims in the early years was William of Tripoli. Among Jews in Spain, Vincent Ferrer played a similar role. In both cases, however, some of their success was due to the use of force—by the Crusaders against Muslims in Tripoli, and by Spanish Christians against Jews in Spain.

Sadly, while Franciscans, Dominicans, and others were trying to bring people to Christian faith through the power of persuasion, others felt that the best way to achieve the conversion of non-believers was through a continuation of the crusading ideal. This was particularly true of the Teutonic knights, a military monastic order that forced the conversion of many along the Baltic coast. Similarly, the king of Sweden led a Crusade against the Finnish.

Among the Eastern churches, the most remarkable expansion took place out of Russia. When this land was conquered by the Mongols in the thirteenth century, Christianity became a rallying point for Russian nationalism. Thus, even though the period of Mongolian rule presented challenges for the church, when the Mongols were finally overthrown, Russian Christianity not only had developed deeper roots in the nation, but also had expanded toward Finland, Lapland, and the White Sea.

STONES THAT BEAR WITNESS: ARCHITECTURE

Medieval churches had two purposes, one didactic and one cultic. Their didactic purpose responded to the needs of an age when books were scarce, and there were not many who could read them. Church buildings thus became the books of the illiterate, and an attempt was made to set forth in them the whole of biblical history, the lives of great saints and martyrs, the virtues and vices, the promise of heaven and the punishment of hell. Today it is difficult for us to read these architectural books. But those who worshiped in them knew their most minute details; in them their parents and grandparents had read stories and teachings that they in turn had learned from earlier generations.

The cultic purpose of church buildings centered on the medieval understanding of communion. This was seen as the miraculous transformation of the bread and wine into the body and blood of the Lord, and as the renewal of the sacrifice of Christ. Inasmuch as possible, a church building had to be worthy of such miraculous events, and of the body of Christ that was reserved in it even after the service. The church was not seen primarily as a building for meeting or even for worship, but as the setting in which the great miracle took place. Thus, what a town or village had in mind in building a church was to build a setting for its most precious jewel.

The earlier basilicas evolved into a style of architecture called Romanesque—that is, Roman-like. There were three main differences. First, the sanctuary was elongated, so that while the earlier basilicas had the shape of a Tau cross (a T), Romanesque churches tended toward our more common Latin cross. This was done mostly because there was a growing distinction between the people who attended services, and the priests and monks who officiated and sang in it. As the number of the latter grew, particularly in monastic chapels, it became necessary to enlarge the sanctuary. Second, whereas the earlier churches had wooden roofs, Romanesque buildings had stone roofs. This was done by building a series of semicircular arches. Because arches (or vaults resulting from the juxtaposition of a series of arches) cause the weight of the structure to produce a lateral thrust, it was necessary to build thicker walls, with very few windows, and supported on the outside by heavy buttresses—pillars of stone that added

There was a marked contrast between Romanesque and Gothic architectural styles. Above: The Romanesque cathedral, Southwell Minster, England. Below: The Gothic Cathedral of Notre-Dame, Chartres, France.

The apse of Saint Vincent's Basilica, in Avila, Spain, is a good example of Romanesque architecture. Note the heavy walls and semicircular arches.

weight to the wall and balanced the outward thrust of the vault. For this reason, Romanesque churches had very little light, and windows were generally limited to the facade and the apse. Third, during the Middle Ages it became customary to add a belfry to churches, which could be either part of the main structure or a separate building.

Toward the middle of the twelfth century, however, Romanesque architecture began to be supplanted by Gothic. The name Gothic was given to this style much later, by critics who thought that it was barbaric, something worthy only of the Goths, but has been kept as a designation for an architectural style worthy of appreciation. In spite of the great differences between the two styles, Gothic architecture grew out of Romanesque. Therefore, the basic plan of churches remained the same, and roofs were made by vaults based on the principle of the arch. But Gothic architects perfected that principle by using pointed arches rather than semicircular ones, and by building the ceilings, not on the principle of the "barrel vault" used by Romanesque, but rather with "groined" and "ribbed" vaults whose great advantage was that the weight rested on columns in the corners, rather than on entire walls. By repeating the process, long and high roofs could be built without having to place them

Flying buttresses in the cathedral of Seville.

on thick walls. But the lateral thrusts of such vaults was enormous, and thus it became necessary to increase the inward thrust of the buttresses. This was done, not by simply building heavier ones, but by use of "flying buttresses," in which, again using the principle of the arch, a pillar built some distance from the wall exerted a lateral thrust that balanced the weight of the vault. Thus, it was possible to erect a building whose main lines were so vertical that it seemed to soar to heaven. This effect was then enhanced by adding towers and spires, and by making the "nerves" of the vaults stand out and run along the columns all the way to the ground.

The entire structure no longer needed the heavy walls of Romanesque buildings, and this in turn made wide spaces available for stained-glass windows that illuminated the building with mysterious light effects, and also served to depict biblical stories, lives of saints, and the like.

The final outcome of these developments was—and still is—impressive. Stone seemed to take flight and rise to heaven. The entire building, inside and out, was a book in which the mysteries of faith and all creation were reflected. Inside, the long naves and slender columns, the multicolored windows, and the play of lights provided a worthy setting for the eucharistic miracle.

The Gothic cathedrals that still dominate the skyline of many cities are the legacy of the Middle Ages to future generations. There were cases, such as

One of the most famous Gothic cathedrals is Notre Dame in Paris, whose steeples were never finished.

that of the cathedral of Beauvais, where the vault collapsed because architects sought to impose on stone an ideal verticality of which it was not capable. Perhaps this too was a symbol of an age when the lofty ideals of Hildebrand, Francis, and others sought to overcome the resistance of human nature, and often failed.

33

The Collapse

It is better to avoid sin, than to flee from death. If you are not ready
today, how will you be ready tomorrow? The morrow is uncertain. How
do you know that you will live until then?

KEMPIS

The thirteenth century was the high point of medieval civilization. With
Innocent III, the papacy reached the apex of its power. At the same time,
the mendicant orders set out to bring the world to Christ, the universities developed impressive theological systems, and in Gothic art even the weight of stone
seemed to have been overcome. In theory, Europe was united under a spiritual
head, the pope, and a temporal one, the emperor. And, since the crusaders had
taken Constantinople, it seemed that the schism between the Eastern and Western branches of the church had been healed.

But in all of these elements of unity there were tensions and weak points that
would eventually bring down the imposing edifice of medieval Christianity.
Already in 1261, the Latin Empire of Constantinople had come to an end, and
so had the fictitious union between East and West that the Fourth Crusade had
accomplished. During the fourteenth and fifteenth centuries, new economic
and political conditions would challenge the papacy and cause it to lose much
of its authority. Nationalism, war, plague, corruption, and invasion would shat-
ter the dreams of the thirteenth century, and open the way for the new order of
the Modern Age.

NEW CONDITIONS

The monetary economy, which had been developing during the last two centuries, became a dominant factor toward the end of the Middle Ages. Credit
systems, trade, and manufacturing—obviously, in a minor scale by today's
standards—gave increasing power to the bourgeoisie. The interests of this
rising class clashed with those of the feudal lords. The frequent petty wars between nobles, the taxes that each imposed on goods crossing their lands, and

the desire of the great barons to be self-sufficient, deterred trade and made it less profitable. For the bourgeoisie, a strong centralized government was highly desirable, for this would protect trade, suppress banditry, regulate coinage, and put an end to petty wars. Therefore, the bourgeoisie tended to support the efforts of kings to curtail the power of the high nobility.

Kings also profited from that alliance. Powerful nobles could afford to disobey their monarchs only as long as the latter did not have the resources to raise armies against them. These resources the kings obtained from the bourgeoisie. Thus, during the late Middle Ages, the growth of centralized monarchies went hand in hand with the rising power of bankers and merchants.

Out of this process developed several modern states. France, England, and the Scandinavian countries were the first to be united under relatively strong monarchies. Spain was divided among several Christian kingdoms and the Muslim one in Granada, and was not united until the end of the Middle Ages. Germany and Italy were not united until much later.

Nationalism became a significant factor during this period. Earlier, most Europeans had considered themselves natives of a county or a city. But now there was more frequent talk of a French nation, for instance, and the inhabitants of that nation began having a sense of commonality over against the rest of Europe. This took place even in those areas that were not united under a powerful monarch. Late in the thirteenth century, several Alpine communities rebelled and founded the Helvetic Confederation, which during the following century continued growing, and repeatedly defeated imperial troops sent against them. Finally, in 1499, Emperor Maximilian I had to acknowledge the independence of Switzerland. In Germany, although the country was not united, there were many indications that the inhabitants of the various electorates, duchies, free cities, and the like began to feel German, and to bewail and resent the foreign interventions that German disunity allowed.

Nationalism in turn undermined the papal claims to universal authority. If the popes seemed to lean toward France, as was indeed the case during their residence in Avignon, the English were ready to disobey and even oppose them. If, on the other hand, a pope refused to be a docile instrument of French interests, France simply had a rival pope elected, and all of Europe was divided in its allegiance to two different popes. The net result was that the papacy as an institution lost a great deal of its prestige and authority, and many began hoping for a reformation of the church that would come from sources other than the popes.

The dominant political and military event of the fourteenth and fifteenth centuries was the Hundred Years' War (1337–1475). Although basically a conflict between France and England, this war so involved the rest of Europe that some historians suggest that it be called the "First European War." Edward III of England claimed the throne of France, held by his first cousin, Philip VI, and this, together with the English invasion of Scotland, and France's support for King David of Scotland, led to war. Through a series of alliances, the war soon involved Emperor Louis of Bavaria, the kings of Navarre, Bohemia, and Castile, and innumerable other participants. Repeatedly the English invaded France, won impressive victories on the battlefield—Crecy and Agincourt—and then were forced to withdraw for lack of funds. When a peace treaty was signed by both major parties, war broke out in Spain, and soon France and England were at war once again, now drawn into it by their alliances with the warring parties in the Iberian Peninsula. The English gained the upper hand when Charles VI came to the throne of France. The new French king gave signs of madness; and, when it became necessary to appoint a regent, two opposing parties developed that eventually led to civil war. The English took sides in the affair, and again invaded the country. They and their French allies were winning when Charles VI died. His son the Dauphin, whose party had been losing the war, declared that he was now king, and took the name of Charles VII. He was besieged in Orleans, and had little hope of truly becoming the ruler of France, when many of his former enemies decided that, now that his father was dead, they should support him. It was also at that time that he first heard of Joan of Arc, a young woman from the village of Domrémy.

Joan of Arc claimed that she had had visions of Saints Catherine and Margaret, and of Archangel Michael, ordering her to lead the Dauphin's troops to break the siege of Orleans, and then to have him crowned at Rheims, the place where kings of France were traditionally crowned. On hearing this, Charles sent for her in what appeared to be disbelief, and perhaps to amuse himself. But Joan convinced him to trust her, and she was sent to try to bring into the city supplies that were sorely needed and which were stored in Blois. This she did, somehow crossing the enemy lines. Then she was allowed to lead a sortie against the besiegers, again with incredible success. Rumors circulated in the enemy camp of this young maiden clad in armor who every day came out of the city, and every day took one of their bastions. Finally, the siege was broken, and the enemy withdrew. The "Maid of Orleans"—as she was then called—did not allow the Dauphin's troops to follow the retreating armies, pointing out that it was Sunday, a day for prayer and not for battle. From that point on, the course of the war changed. The French, tired of civil war, flocked to the Dauphin's standards, and Joan was able to accompany him in triumphal march to Rheims. This and other cities that had long held out against him opened their gates, and he was finally crowned in the Cathedral of Rheims, while the Maid of Orleans stood by the altar.

She wished to return to Domrémy, but the king would not allow it, and she had to continue fighting until she was captured and sold to the English. Her former allies abandoned her, and it seems that the king did not even try to negotiate for her ransom. The English sold her for ten thousand francs to the bishop of Beauvais, who wished to try her as a heretic and a witch.

The trial took place in Rouen. She was accused of heresy for claiming to receive orders from heaven, for insisting that these orders were given to her in French, and for dressing as a man. She agreed to sign a recantation, and was condemned to life imprisonment. But then she said that Saints Catherine and Margaret had spoken to her again, and rebuked her for her recantation, which she now withdrew. In consequence, she was taken to the Old Market Square in Rouen, and burned alive. Her last request to the priest who accompanied her was to hold the crucifix high, and speak the words of salvation loudly, so she could hear them above the roar of the flames. Twenty years later, Charles VII entered Rouen and ordered an inquiry which, as was to be expected, exonerated her. In 1920, Benedict XV granted her sainthood within the Roman Catholic Church. But long before that she had become the national hero of France.

By the time Joan died, in 1431, Charles VII had the upper hand. Soon the civil war in France ended, and by 1453 hostilities between England and France had been reduced to a series of skirmishes. When peace was finally signed, in 1475, all English possessions on the Continent, except Calais, were in French hands. (Calais would become French in 1558.)

This long war had enormous consequences for the life of the church, as we shall see in the rest of this chapter. Since during part of the war the popes resided in Avignon under the shadow of the French, the English came to see the papacy as their enemy. Later, during the Great Schism in which the entire Western church was divided in its allegiance to two rival popes, nations chose their allegiance partly on the basis of alliances and enmities created by the Hundred Years' War—and the war itself made it more difficult to put an end to the schism. Finally, in France, England, and Scotland, the enduring international conflict strengthened nationalist sentiments, and thus weakened the claims of the papacy to universal authority.

Another event that set the stage for the life of the church in the later Middle Ages was the Great Plague of 1347. There were at that time weather changes that historians now call "the little ice age." This reduced agricultural production, increased famines, and in general left the population more vulnerable to disease. Bubonic plague, we now know, is transmitted by fleas, and black rats act as intermediary hosts. Trade had improved greatly, particularly since the Genovese had defeated the Moors and opened the Straits of Gibraltar to Christian shipping. Thus, there was constant contact between northern Europe and the

Mediterranean, and when plague broke out in the Black Sea, and moved on to Italy, it soon appeared also in northern Europe. Suddenly, and with no apparent reason, people began developing strange symptoms that usually began with a fever, then led to loss of balance, and produced enormously swollen lymph nodes, often accompanied by symptoms of dementia. By the fifth day, most who had developed these symptoms were dead. In a few months, between 1348 and 1350, the plague swept the entire continent. According to some estimates, a third of the population died of the plague or of related causes. After those three years, the storm abated, although there were new outbreaks every ten or twelve years. In these subsequent outbreaks, the dead were mostly among the young, apparently because their elders had developed a degree of immunity to the disease.

The plague had far-reaching consequences. Economically, all Europe was disrupted. Entire markets disappeared. Unemployment increased drastically in areas where mortality had not been as high as in the rest of Europe. This in turn created political turmoil, riots, and further economic disruption. It would take Europe several centuries to find a measure of demographic and economic stability.

The plague also had enormous religious consequences. In the subsequent outbreaks those who died were mostly the young, who had not developed any immunity, so it seemed to some people that Death had come to prefer younger victims. The nature of the disease itself, which attacked people who seemed perfectly healthy, led many to doubt the rationally ordered universe of earlier generations. Among intellectuals, this led to doubts regarding the ability of

The Black Plague swept through Western Europe, killing most of the population in some areas.

reason to grapple with the mysteries of existence. Among the general populace, it encouraged superstition. Since death was always at the threshold, life became a preparation for it. Many went on pilgrimage to the Holy Land, to Rome, or to Santiago. Those who were too poor to contemplate such long journeys went on pilgrimage to local shrines. The veneration of relics, and trade in supposed relics, gained momentum—in spite of the prohibitions of the Fourth Lateran Council. Fear was everywhere: fear of the plague, fear of hell, fear of the supreme judge, whom many were having to face sooner than expected.

For many Jews, the plague brought death by violence beyond the disease itself. Christians could not understand why the plague seemed to make less headway in Jewish neighborhoods. Today some suggest that there were more cats and fewer rats in those areas, because among Christians cats had been associated with witchcraft. Whatever the case may be, at the time of the plague some came up with the simple explanation that Jews had poisoned the wells from which Christians drank. The result was violence and massacre. It was a time of fear, and fear demanded its victims.

While all of this was taking place, Constantinople led a precarious existence. Its standing had been weakened by the Fourth Crusade and the ensuing period of Latin rule. When the Byzantine Empire was restored, some areas that had become independent from Constantinople during the struggle against the Latin invaders retained their independence. The Byzantine Empire, in spite of its high-sounding name, was little more than the city of Constantinople and its surroundings. The Turkish menace grew, and was stemmed only because the Turks themselves were more concerned with other enemies—the Albanians, Hungarians, and, in the East, the Mongols. In 1422, the Turks besieged Constantinople, but had to abandon the enterprise when they were attacked by other enemies. By mid-century, it was clear that the great dream of Sultan Muhammad II was to take Constantinople and make it the capital of his empire.

The Byzantine emperors had no other option than to appeal to the West. The price that the popes demanded was ecclesiastical reconciliation, and this was achieved at the Council of Ferrara-Florence in 1439. But this did not help the Byzantine Empire, for the Pope was unable to convince Western Christians to come to the help of the beleaguered city, and the actions of the council did convince many of the empire's subjects that their leaders had capitulated before heresy, and should not be defended. In 1443, the patriarchs of Jerusalem, Alexandria, and Antioch rejected the decisions of the council, and thus broke communion with Constantinople. The Russians took a similar position. Thus, Constantinople was friendless, and Constantine XI, who was then emperor, had no option but to continue his plans of union with Rome, and hope that somehow Western Europe would come to his help. Late in 1452, after more than four centuries of mutual excommunication, the Roman mass was celebrated in Hagia Sophia.

The days of Constantinople were numbered. On April 7, 1453, Muhammad II laid siege to the city. The ancient walls were no match for his artillery, which Christian engineers in search of profit had built. The besieged fought bravely, but the wall crumbled around them. On May 28, there was a solemn service in the cathedral of Hagia Sophia. On May 29, the city fell. Emperor Constantine XI Paleologus died in battle. The Turks broke through the walls and the city was sacked for three days and three nights, as the sultan had promised his troops. Then Muhammad II took formal possession of it. In Hagia Sophia, the great cathedral of the East, now resounded the name of the Prophet. Constantine's dream of a new Christian Rome had come to an end, and eventually the city he had named after himself would be renamed as Istanbul.

THE PAPACY UNDER THE SHADOW OF FRANCE

The foregoing section has dealt with a series of events that took place during the thirteenth and fourteenth centuries. They were the context in which the church moved in those difficult times. We now return to the end of the thirteenth century, where we left our story in the previous chapter—with the election of Boniface VIII (1294).

There was a marked contrast between the previous pope, Celestine V, and Benedetto Gaetani, who now became Boniface VIII. Celestine had failed because, in his austere simplicity, he was unable to understand the duplicity and intrigues of those with whom he had to deal. Gaetani, on the other hand, was well at home with kings and potentates, and in his diplomatic career had gained a deep understanding of the intrigues that were always brewing in European courts. Both were sincere men who sought to reform the church. But whereas Celestine had tried to achieve that reformation through Franciscan simplicity, Boniface would seek the same end through power politics. Celestine was one of the humblest men ever to occupy the throne of Saint Peter; Boniface, one of the haughtiest.

Not all were happy with Boniface's election. Besides the powerful Colonna family in Italy, who had hoped to capture the papacy, there were the extreme Franciscans or *Fraticelli*, around whom many had rallied in support of Celestine. Among the Fraticelli, as well as among some of the lower classes whose only hope was for a new age to dawn, many had come to believe that the election of Celestine had been the beginning of the "age of the Spirit" that Joachim of Fiore had announced. His resignation was a severe blow, and many refused to accept it, claiming that Gaetani had forced it. Others contended that, even if Celestine's resignation was voluntary, the powers of the pope did not include the right to abdicate, and that therefore, even against his own will, Celestine was still pope. When Celestine died, those who held such positions spread the word—probably false, or at least grossly exaggerated—that Boniface had mistreated him, and that this had caused his death.

In spite of such opposition, the early years of Boniface's reign were eminently successful. He felt called to pacify Italy, and in this he succeeded to a great extent. Against the Colonna, his most powerful opponents in Italy, he called a Crusade that deprived them of their lands and castles, and forced them into exile. In Germany, Albert of Hapsburg rebelled against Adolf of Nassau and killed him. Boniface called him a rebel and a regicide, and Albert was forced to seek reconciliation under terms that enhanced the prestige of the pope. England and France were threatening to go to war in what proved to be a prelude to the Hundred Years' War, and Boniface resolved to make peace between them. When Philip IV of France and Edward I of England refused to heed his entreaties, he used greater force, and in 1296 issued the bull *Clericis laicos,* forbidding the clergy to make any kind of contribution to the secular power. With this he hoped to bring economic pressure to bear on the two kings, who in turn responded with measures against the clergy and the papacy, and continued their war. This, however, brought no results, for neither side was able to gain a decisive advantage, and finally both kings had to accept Boniface's mediation—although Philip made it clear that he accepted the mediation of the private person Benedetto Gaetani, and not of the pope. Meanwhile Scotland, faced with English invasion, declared itself a fief of the papacy. Although England generally ignored the protection that this was supposed to grant Scotland, Boniface saw in it further confirmation of the universal power of the pope.

Then came the year 1300, which marked the high point of his papacy. Boniface proclaimed a great year of jubilee, promising plenary indulgence to all who visited the tomb of Saint Peter—meaning that when they died they would be spared the time they would otherwise have to remain in purgatory being cleansed of their sins. Rome was flooded with pilgrims who came to render homage, not only to Saint Peter, but also to his successor, who seemed to be the foremost figure in Europe.

But relations with France grew tense. King Philip granted asylum and support to Sciarra Colonna, one of Pope Boniface's bitterest enemies. He further challenged the pope by confiscating ecclesiastical lands, and by offering his sister's hand to Albert, the German emperor whom Boniface had denounced as a usurper and regicide. The correspondence between France and Rome verged on insults. The French ambassador before the papal court was offensive to the pope, and the king complained that Boniface's legate was just as offensive.

Early in 1302, a papal bull was burned in the king's presence, and later that year Philip called the Estates General—the French parliament—in order to muster support for his policies toward Rome. It is significant that this session of the Estates General was the first to include, besides the traditional two "estates" of the nobility and clergy, the "third estate" of the bourgeoisie. This assembly sent several communiqués to Rome supporting Philip's policies.

Boniface's response was the bull *Unam Sanctam*, which was quoted in the last chapter as the high point of papal claims to universal power, both ecclesiastical and political. He then convoked the French prelates to a meeting in Rome, there to discuss what was to be done with King Philip. The latter issued a decree forbidding all bishops to leave the kingdom without his permission, under penalty of confiscation of all their property. He also hastened to make peace with King Edward of England. The pope, on his part, conveniently forgot that Emperor Albert of Germany was a usurper and a regicide, and made an alliance with him, while he ordered all German nobles to accept him as emperor. At a session of the French Estates General, William Nogaret, one of Philip's closest advisors, accused Boniface of being a heretic, a sodomite, and a false pope. In compliance with the king's wishes, the assembly asked Philip, as "guardian of the faith," to call a council to judge the "false pope." In order to assure himself of the support of the clergy before the council gathered, Philip issued the "Ordinances of Reform," by which he reaffirmed all the ancient privileges of the French clergy.

Boniface's last weapon was the one his predecessors had used against other recalcitrant rulers, excommunication. He gathered his closest advisors in Anagni, his native town, and there prepared a bull of excommunication that was to be issued on September 8. But the French were aware that the confrontation was reaching its climax. Sciarra Colonna and William Nogaret were in Italy making ready for such an occasion and, drawing on Philip's credit with Italian banks, they organized a small armed band. On September 7, the day before the planned sentence of excommunication, they entered Anagni and kidnapped the pope, while his home and those of his relatives were sacked by mobs.

Nogaret's purpose was to force Boniface to abdicate. But the elderly pope was firm and declared that, if they wished to kill him, "here is my neck, here my head." Nogaret struck him, and then they humiliated him by forcing him to sit backwards on a horse, and thus parading him through town.

Only two of the cardinals who were present at Anagni (Peter of Spain and Nicholas Boccasini) remained firm supporters of the humiliated pope. Finally, Boccasini was able to move some of the people, who reacted against the outrage, freed the pope, and expelled the French and their partisans from the city.

But the evil had been done. Back in Rome, Boniface was no longer able to inspire the respect he had commanded earlier. He died shortly after the episode of Anagni. His enemies circulated rumors that he had committed suicide, but it seems that he died quietly, surrounded by his closest advisors.

In such difficult circumstances, the cardinals hastened to elect Boccasini as the next pope, who took the name of Benedict XI. He was a Dominican of humble origin and sincere piety who sought to follow a policy of reconciliation. He restored to the house of Colonna the lands that Boniface had confiscated, forgave all the enemies of Boniface, except Nogaret and Sciarra Colonna, and extended an offer of peace to Philip. But this was not enough. Philip insisted on the project of calling a council to judge the dead pope. This Benedict could not accept, for it would be a serious blow to papal authority. On the other side, there were those who accused the new pope of excessive concessions to those who had attacked the papacy. He was thus besieged and criticized by both sides when he died, after a very brief pontificate (1303–1304). Soon the rumor spread that he had been poisoned, and each party accused the other. But there is no proof that Benedict was in fact poisoned.

The election of the next pope was a difficult matter, for each party insisted on one of its members being elected. Finally, through a subterfuge, the pro-French party obtained the agreement of the cardinals on the election of Clement V. This agreement was possible because the new pope, while appearing to take the side of the defenders of Boniface's memory, had been in contact with the French. A pope elected under such circumstances would not be a model of fortitude or firmness. During his entire reign (1305–1314), Clement V did not visit Rome once. Although the citizenry of Rome insisted on his establishing residence in the city, Philip kept him occupied in France, and therefore under his thumb. During his pontificate, Clement V named twenty-four cardinals, and all but one were French. Furthermore, several of them were his relatives, thus creating and encouraging the nepotistic practices that would be one of the great ills of the church until the sixteenth century.

Clement's defense of Boniface's memory was no more forceful. He also refused to agree to the council that the French wished. But the council was not necessary, for little by little Clement undid all that Boniface had done, forgave Nogaret and his companions, and even declared that in the whole affair Philip had acted with "admirable zeal."

The most shameful event of this weak papacy, however, was the arrest and trial of the Templars. This was one of the military orders founded during the Crusades, and therefore it had become obsolete. But it was also rich and powerful. At a time when the king of France was affirming his rule over the ancient nobility, the power and wealth of the Templars were an obstacle to his policy of centralization. Since they were a monastic order, they could not be subjected directly to temporal power, and therefore Philip resolved to accuse them of heresy and force weak Clement to suppress the order in such a manner that most of its wealth would benefit the French treasury.

Unexpectedly, all the Templars who happened to be in France were arrested. Under torture, some were forced to confess that they were in truth a secret order opposed to the Christian faith, that in their worship they practiced idolatry, cursed Christ, and spit on the cross, and that they were sodomites. Although many stood firm under torture, those who broke down and agreed to confess what was required of them provided the excuse to continue legal proceedings against the entire order. Among those who yielded was the grand master of the order, Jacques de Molay, who may have been convinced that the accusations were so preposterous that no one would give them credence.

The Templars hoped that the pope would defend them and protest against the injustice that was being done. But Clement did exactly the opposite. When he received the report from the king's officers as to what the Templars had confessed, he ordered the arrest of all the members of the order who were not in France, and thus precluded any action they might take against their incarcerated brothers. When he learned that the supposed confessions had been obtained through torture, he ordered that this be stopped, declaring that he would judge the Templars, and that the civil authorities had no jurisdiction over them. But the accused remained in prison, and the pope did nothing to free them. The king then accused Clement of being the instigator of the evils that the Templars supposedly practiced, and Clement, yielding once more, agreed to have a council judge the matter.

The council, which Philip and Nogaret had hoped would be malleable to their desires, proved sterner than the pope. Perhaps the bishops were shamed by the weakness of their leader. However, they insisted on hearing the case anew, and on giving the accused an opportunity to defend themselves. Finally, while the council dealt with other matters, Philip and Clement came to an agreement. Instead of trying the Templars for their supposed crimes, the order would be abolished by administrative decision of the pope, and the property it held would be transferred to another military order. The council, no longer having jurisdiction over the case, was dissolved. As to the wealth of the Templars, Philip took most of it by sending the pope an enormous bill for their trial, and insisting that payment for this bill take precedence over any other disposition of the property of the Templars.

Many of the Templars spent the rest of their life in prison. When Jacques de Molay and a companion were taken to the cathedral of Notre Dame in Paris in order to confess publicly their sins and thus silence those who said that a grave

For several decades the popes resided in Avignon, on the border of France.

crime had been committed, they recanted and declared that all the accusations were lies. That very day they were burned alive.

Clement V died in 1314. His pontificate was a sign of things to come. In 1309 he had begun residing in Avignon, a papal city at the very borders of France. For nearly seventy years, while still claiming to be bishops of Rome, the popes would generally remain in Avignon. This period, often called the "Avignon Papacy" or the "Babylonian Captivity of the Church," was marked, not only by the absence of the popes from Rome, but also by their willingness to serve as tools of French policy.

After Clement's death, the cardinals were unable to reach an agreement as to who would be the next pope. They finally elected a seventy-two year old man, expecting that his pontificate would be brief and that during that time they would be able to reach a consensus. But this pope, who took the name of John XXII, surprised the world with his vitality and the length of his pontificate (1316–1334). With the help of the French, he sought to assert the power of the papacy in Italy, which was therefore involved in constant wars. In order to finance these, as well as his court at Avignon, John developed an elaborate system of ecclesiastical taxes that produced widespread resentment, particularly among those who opposed his pro-French policies.

Benedict XII (1334–1342), while promising the Romans that he would return to their city, ordered a great palace to be built in Avignon. He also contradicted his promises to the Romans by having the papal archives moved to Avignon. Since he put all the resources of the papacy at the service of the French crown, and it was the time of the Hundred Years' War, his policies alienated England and its main ally, the Holy Roman Empire—which at that time was centered in Germany. Clement VI (1342–1352) tried to mediate between the French and the English, but it was clear that the latter saw him as a partisan of the former, and therefore his efforts were fruitless. During his pontificate, which was marked by nepotism, the court at Avignon rivaled those of great secular lords in its pomp and luxury. Since this was the time of the plague, many believed that this was divine punishment for the popes' absence from Rome. The next pope, Innocent VI (1352–1362) began making arrangements to return to Rome, but died before this could be accomplished. Urban V (1362–1370) was a man of reforming ideas who led a rigorously disciplined life. He reformed the court at Avignon, sending away those who would not follow his example of austerity. In 1365 he returned to Rome, and was received with great demonstrations of joy. But then he proved unable to hold the loyalty of his Roman subjects, and all over Italy there was such disorder that he decided to return to Avignon. The next pope was Gregory XI (1370–1378), who had been made a cardinal by his uncle Clement VI when he was seventeen years old. It was at the time of his election that Catherine of Siena came forth, calling the pope to return to Rome.

As a young girl, Caterina de Icopo di Benicasa, now known as St. Catherine of Siena, had shown an inclination to the monastic life. Her middle-class family, unhappy with such prospects, sought to dissuade her. But in spite of entreaties, threats, and punishment, she remained firm in her inclination, refusing to consider the prospect of marriage. The death of her sister Bonaventura—one of twenty-five children born to the family—was the final turning point for Catherine. Following the guidance of a relative who was a Dominican priest, Catherine joined the "Sisters of the Penance of St. Dominic," or Third Order of the Dominicans. This was a very flexible organization whose members continued living at home, but devoted themselves to a life of penance and contemplation. Two years later, she had a vision in which Jesus joined her in mystical marriage, and ordered her to serve others. Then began a second stage in her life, during which she spent a great deal of time helping the poor and the sick. She became famous as a teacher of mysticism, and gathered around her a circle of men and women, many of them more educated than she, whom she taught the principles and practice of contemplation. Several of these disciples were Dominicans who were well versed in theological questions, and from them Catherine learned enough theology to avoid the errors of other mystics who had been condemned by the church.

In 1370, the same year of Gregory's election, she had another mystical experience. For four hours she lay so quietly that her friends thought she had died. But then she woke up, declared that she had had a vision, and set out on a campaign to have the papacy return to Rome. In order to do this, it was necessary to pave the way in Italy, where constant wars made it unsafe for the pope to reside. To that end she began a pilgrimage from city to city, and was received by multitudes who flocked to see her, and among whom stories circulated about

Catherine's mystical nuptials. Painting by Francisco de Zurbarán (1598-1664).

her many miracles. All the while she wrote humbly but firmly to the pope, whom she called "our sweet father," but to whom she also complained of "seeing God thus offended" by the long stay at Avignon. To what degree this influenced Gregory's decisions, it is impossible to know. But in any case on January 17, 1377, amid general rejoicing, Gregory entered Rome. The long period of exile in Avignon had ended—but worse was to follow.

Catherine died three years after that event. A century later she was made a saint of the Roman church, and in 1970 Paul VI gave her the title of "doctor of the church"—one of two women who have been so honored.

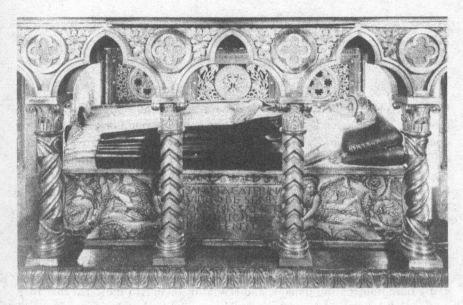

St. Catherine's tomb in Siena.

In summary, the long period of the popes' residence in Avignon had disastrous consequences for the life of the church. Since this was the time of the Hundred Years' War, and the popes were tools of French policies, those countries which were at war with France grew accustomed to seeing the papacy as a foreign power, and in them nationalism was soon linked with resentment toward the papacy. Since the court at Avignon, and the constant wars and intrigues in which it was involved, required abundant funds, John XXII and his successors devised means to acquire them. When a position was vacant, its income for one year was to be sent to Avignon. If the vacancy lasted longer, the income continued going to Avignon. Therefore, the popes had a vested interest in frequent and unfilled vacancies. This did not benefit the pastoral ministry of the church, which was repeatedly interrupted by frequent and prolonged vacancies. To this was added the sale of ecclesiastical posts—the very simony that Gregory VII and other advocates of reform had deplored. Since ecclesiastical positions proved a good means of income, there were some who held several of them, and who therefore were usually absent from their charges. The evils of simony, pluralism, and absenteeism, were compounded by another practice for which many popes set the example: nepotism—the naming of relatives to positions of power. By the end of the "Babylonian Captivity of the Church," there were many who were clamoring for a reformation of the church. Since the papacy itself was in need of reform, this clamor was often joined by attempts to limit the power of popes, or to restrict the hand of the papacy to purely spiritual matters.

THE GREAT WESTERN SCHISM

Catherine of Siena's dream seemed to have been fulfilled when Gregory XI brought the papacy back to Rome. But the political conditions that had produced the "Babylonian Captivity of the Church" had not disappeared. Soon the difficulties were such that Gregory began considering the possibility of returning to Avignon, and probably would have done so had death not interrupted his plans. It was then that a situation developed that was even worse than the Babylonian Captivity.

With the papacy vacant, the people of Rome feared that a pope would be elected who would be inclined to return to Avignon, or who at least would again be willing to serve the interests of France, as had been done by a long series of popes. There were grounds for such fears, since the French cardinals vastly outnumbered the Italians, and several of them had indicated that they preferred Avignon to Rome. There was the possibility that the cardinals would leave Rome and meet someplace else, perhaps under French protection, to elect a French pope who would be willing to reside in Avignon. The rumor of a possible flight on the part of the cardinals created a riot. The place where the conclave was to meet in order to elect a new pope was invaded by a mob that would not leave until they had searched the entire building and made certain that there was no way for the cardinals to escape. All the while, the mob, both in the building and outside, clamored for the election of a Roman, or at least of an Italian.

Under such circumstances, the conclave did not dare elect a French pope. After long deliberation, they chose the archbishop of Bari, an Italian, who took the name of Urban VI. With great pomp, and the participation of all the cardinals, both French and Italian, Urban was crowned on Easter Sunday, 1378.

The crowning of Urban VI seemed to be the beginning of a new age. He was a man of humble origins and austere life, who would clearly undertake the reformation for which so many were calling. But it was also clear that in this he would clash with the many cardinals who were used to luxury, and for whom their office was a means to riches and to the aggrandizement of their families. Even the most cautious and levelheaded pope would find great difficulty in implementing the much-needed reform.

But Urban was neither cautious nor levelheaded. In his zeal to put an end to absenteeism, he declared that those bishops who formed part of his court, and therefore were not in their dioceses, were traitors to Christ and guilty of perjury.

From the pulpit he thundered against the cardinals' ostentatiousness, and then affirmed that a prelate receiving any gift whatsoever was guilty of simony and should therefore be excommunicated. Trying to wrest power from the hands of the French, he decided to appoint a vast number of Italian cardinals, so that they would be the majority. And then he committed the indiscretion of announcing his plan to the French before actually implementing it.

All this was no more than the reformation that so many wished. But Urban's actions against the cardinals gave credence to reports that he had gone mad. His reactions to such reports were such as to make them even more credible. Also, while claiming that he wished to reform the church, he continued appointing relatives to positions of importance, thus making himself vulnerable to the charge of nepotism.

An ever-increasing number of cardinals joined the opposition. First the French, and then many of the Italians, fled from Rome and gathered in Anagni. There they declared that they had elected Urban under coercion, and that such an election was not valid. They conveniently forgot that after the election all of them had participated in the coronation, and that they had not raised a single voice of protest. And they also forgot that for several months they had been part of Urban's papal court, without ever expressing any doubts as to the validity of his election.

Urban responded by appointing twenty-six new cardinals from among his staunchest supporters. This would give his partisans the majority in the college of cardinals, and therefore those who had defected declared that cardinals elected by a false pope were not true cardinals, and that it was time to proceed to the proper election of a pope.

Gathered in conclave, the same cardinals—except one—who had elected Urban, and who for some time had served him, elected a new pope whom they declared to be the legitimate successor of Saint Peter. The Italian cardinals who were present abstained from the election, but did not protest.

Thus an unprecedented situation developed. On several earlier occasions there had been more than one claimant to the papacy. But now for the first time there were two popes elected by the same cardinals. One of them, Urban VI, repudiated by those who had elected him, had created his own college of cardinals. The other, who took the name of Clement VII, had the support of those cardinals who represented continuity with the past. Therefore, all Western Christendom was forced to take sides.

The decision was not easy. Urban VI had been duly elected, in spite of the tardy protests of those who had elected him. His rival, by the very act of taking the name of Clement, announced his inclination to continue the policies of the popes who had resided in Avignon. But it was also true that Urban gave no signs of the wisdom necessary to lead the church in such difficult times, while Clement was an able diplomat—though certainly not a pious man, as even his supporters conceded.

As soon as he was elected, Clement took arms against Urban, and attacked the city of Rome. Being repulsed, he took up residence in Avignon. The result was that there were now two popes, one in Rome and one in Avignon, each with his court and his college of cardinals, and each seeking the recognition of the various courts in Europe.

As was to be expected, France opted for the pope in Avignon, and in this was followed by Scotland, its old ally in the war against England. This in turn meant that England took the opposite tack, for the papacy in Avignon was a threat to its interests. Scandinavia, Flanders, Hungary, and Poland also took the side of Urban. In Germany, the emperor, who was an ally of England against France, followed the same policy, but many of the nobles and bishops who had reason to oppose the emperor declared for Clement. Portugal changed sides repeatedly. Castile and Aragon, at first supporters of Urban, eventually decided in favor of Clement. In Italy, each city and each ruler followed its own course, and the important kingdom of Naples changed its allegiance repeatedly.

Catherine of Siena devoted the few years she had left to Urban's cause. But it was a difficult cause to defend, particularly since Urban decided to create a principality for his nephew, and to that end became involved in a series of senseless wars. When some of his cardinals suggested that he change this policy, he had them arrested, and to this day the manner of their death is not known.

Since the schism was due to conflicting interests that went beyond the existence of two popes, when these died others were elected to continue their line. When Urban died, in 1389, his cardinals named Boniface IX. By taking that name, the new pope indicated that he would follow the policies of Boniface VIII, whose great enemy had been the French crown. But this new Boniface left aside Urban's program of reform, and his papacy gave new impetus to the practice of simony. Indeed, the schism itself encouraged simony, for each of the rival popes was in need of funds in order to compete with his adversary, and the sale of ecclesiastical posts was a convenient way to obtain such funds. In 1394, the theologians of the University of Paris presented a proposal to the king that outlined three ways in which the schism could be healed: the first was that both popes resign, and a new one be elected; the second, that the question be settled by negotiation and arbitration; the third, that a general council be called to decide on the matter. Of these three solutions, the theologians preferred the first, since the other two would pose the difficult questions of who would be the arbitrator, or who had the authority to call a council. The king, Charles VI, fol-

The Castle of Peñíscola, on the Mediterranean coast of Spain, was the last stronghold of Benedict XIII, with whose death the line of Avignon popes came to an end.

lowed the advice of the theologians, and when Clement VII died he asked the Avignon cardinals not to elect a new pope, for he hoped that the pope in Rome could be persuaded to abdicate.

But the schism, created in part by French interests, now had a life of its own. The cardinals in Avignon feared that if they did not have a pope their case would be weakened, and they hastened to elect Spanish cardinal Pedro de Luna, who took the name of Benedict XIII (whom the Roman Catholic church considers an antipope, and is not to be confused with another Benedict XIII, who occupied the papacy in the eighteenth century). If the king wished to insist on his solution, and force both popes to resign, he would have to face two parties, each of which had a pope, and not a Roman pope opposed only by a headless college of cardinals in Avignon. Charles VI pursued the new course he had set. His ambassadors tried to persuade the various courts in Europe to pressure both popes into resigning. In France itself, a national council withdrew its obedience from Benedict. French troops then laid siege to Avignon. But Benedict was able to hold out until changing political circumstances forced Charles to abandon his project, and declare himself once again in favor of the papacy in Avignon.

These events showed that Christendom was growing weary, and that if the two rival popes did not end the schism, others would. For these reasons Benedict XIII and the Roman popes—first Boniface IX, then Innocent VII, and finally Gregory XII—began a series of maneuvers to make it appear that they were seeking to end the schism, and that it was the other party that refused to negotiate. These maneuvers came to the point where Benedict XIII and Gregory XII agreed to meet in September 1407. By May of the following year, the meeting had not taken place. The two rivals were only a few miles apart, and Benedict finally went to the appointed meeting place, but Gregory refused to budge.

Before such refusal, and conscious that Europe was growing weary, the Roman cardinals broke with their pope and began their own negotiations with the Avignon party. France then withdrew her support for Benedict and his party, and once again took up the efforts to end the schism. The conciliar movement, which had been developing over the years, was about to see its day.

34

In Quest of Reformation

> Therefore, the pope is not the head, nor are the cardinals the whole body
> of the holy, Catholic and universal church. Only Christ is the head, and
> his predestined are the body, and each is a member of that body.
>
> JOHN HUSS

The sorry state of the church during the fourteenth and fifteenth centuries
gave impetus to various movements of reform, each with its own program.
One of these, the conciliar movement, hoped both to heal the schism and to put
an end to such corrupt practices as simony and nepotism without substantially
challenging accepted Christian dogma. Others, such as John Wycliffe and John
Huss, came to the conclusion that it was not only the life, but also the doctrine
of the church that ought to be reformed. Still others vented the apocalyptic
expectations that so frequently take hold of the hopes of the poor and the oppressed. To these various movements of reformation we now turn. The reader
should note, however, that for the sake of clarity we are not following a strictly
chronological order. Thus, while we continue our narrative at the point where
we left it in the previous chapter, when Europe was seeking a solution to the
Great Schism, we shall then have to return to John Wycliffe, who lived before
the heyday of the conciliar movement.

THE CONCILIAR MOVEMENT

Back in the fourth century, when Constantine saw the church threatened with
schism over the Arian controversy, he had called a council. At other times in the
centuries immediately thereafter, other crises had been solved by similar means.
Later, as the popes gained power, the councils became instruments for their policies and programs, as we saw in the case of the Fourth Lateran Council, which
endorsed a long series of measures that Innocent III put forth. Now, as the
moral authority of the papacy waned through the long decades of the Babylonian Captivity and the ensuing Great Schism, there were many who hoped that
a universal council could destroy the great evils of the time, both by restoring

unity and by reforming the church. As the conciliar theory developed, its proponents came to hold that a universal council, representing the entire church, had more authority than the pope. If this were the case, then it would seem that the question of who was the legitimate pope could best be settled, not by the popes themselves, who obviously could not agree on the matter, but rather by a council. The great difficulty standing in the way of such a simple solution was the question of who had authority to call an ecumenical council. If one party or the other convoked the assembly, there was always the danger that the outcome would be prejudiced, that its decisions would not be universally accepted, and that as a result the schism would not be healed.

This difficulty was solved when the cardinals of both parties, weary of the popes' refusal to negotiate, issued a joint call to a great council that was to gather in Pisa in 1409. Each of the two rival popes then called his own council to pre-empt the one at Pisa, but both failed. While still claiming to be the legitimate pope, each of the two withdrew to a fortified stronghold.

When the council finally gathered in Pisa, it had the support of both colleges of cardinals, as well as of most of the courts of Europe. Rather than trying to determine who was the rightful pope, the council declared that both were unworthy and that therefore both the legitimate pope—whoever that might be—and his rival were deposed. The council then went on to take measures against simony and other evils, while the cardinals elected Alexander V to take the place of the deposed pope and his rival. Shortly thereafter, convinced that it had put an end to the schism, the council adjourned.

But the situation was now even worse, for the two earlier claimants to the papacy refused to accept the decisions of the council, and therefore now there were three popes. Although Alexander V was acknowledged by most of Europe, each of his two rivals had enough support to insist on his claims. Less than a year after being elected, Alexander died, and the cardinals elected John XXIII to take his place. Neither Alexander nor John was able to end the schism, and political turmoil forced John to flee Italy and seek shelter with Emperor Sigismund of Germany—one of three claimants to the throne, each of the three supported by a different pope—who then decided that the time had come to call another council to put an end to the schism. (At this point, the reader may be asking, how is it that there was a Pope John XXIII in the fifteenth century, and another Pope John XXIII in the twentieth? The answer is that the Roman Catholic Church accepts as legitimate the line of popes who resided in Rome, that is, Urban VI and his successors. The rival popes in Avignon, as well as the two "Pisan popes" Alexander V and John XXIII, are considered antipopes.)

Since the Hundred Years' War was going against France at that time, Sigismund, the emperor whose refuge Pope John sought, was the most powerful

The council gathered at Pisa in 1409, seeking to end the schism and decide who was the rightful pope.

sovereign of Europe. He offered protection to the fugitive pope, on condition that he agree to the convocation of another general council. This was done, and when the council gathered at Constance in 1414 John XXIII expected that the assembly would support him. But it soon became clear that his ambitions and lifestyle were not in agreement with the reformist goals of the council, and that he could not count on the outcome of its sessions. When the council demanded his resignation, John fled. For several months, he was a fugitive. But all his supporters failed him, and he was captured, taken back to Constance, and forced to resign. He was then condemned to prison for the rest of his life, lest he attempt to claim the papacy once more. Shortly thereafter, Gregory XII, the Roman pope, resigned, as he had promised to do if his rivals did likewise. After passing some decrees for the reformation of the church, the council took steps for the election of a new pope. The cardinals present, jointly with a commission named by the council, elected Martin V. As to Benedict XIII, the last of the Avignon line, he took refuge in the fortress of Peñíscola, on the Mediterranean coast of Spain, where he continued claiming that he was the legitimate pope. But no one paid much attention to him, and when he died in 1423 no successor was elected.

Those who gathered at Constance had hoped, not only to end the schism, but also to begin the long process of ridding the church of heresy and corruption. It was with the first of these in mind that they condemned John Huss—to whom we shall return later in this chapter. However, when it came to evils such as simony, pluralism, and absenteeism, the council found that it could do little more than issue some fairly general decrees. It therefore resolved to take measures for the continuation of what it had begun, and ordered that similar councils should meet periodically in order to make certain that the reformation that began at Constance would continue.

The next council, called by Martin V as had been ordered at Constance, gathered at Pavia in 1423, and then moved to Siena fleeing from the plague. Attendance was scarce, and once the council had passed a number of minor decrees Martin had no difficulty in having it adjourn.

As the date for the next council (1430) approached, Martin seemed disinclined to convoke it. But he became aware that conciliarism was still strong, and that his failure to call the council would provoke a crisis. He died shortly after the council gathered, this time in Basel, and his successor, Eugene IV, declared it dissolved. But the council refused to adjourn, and there was talk of sitting in judgment of the pope. At that point Emperor Sigismund intervened, and Eugene withdrew the decree of dissolution. By then the council, which at first had attracted little notice, had become the center of attention, and seemed to have gained supremacy over the pope. There were even those who suggested that it should meet indefinitely and rule the church directly.

Then a request for help came from Constantinople, which was threatened by the Turks. In order to secure such help, the Byzantine emperor and the patriarch of Constantinople declared that they were willing to rejoin the Western church and take part in its council, if it would move to a city closer to Constantinople. Eugene seized the opportunity to transfer the council to Ferrara. Most of the council refused to obey, but others, in the hope of ending the centuries-old schism between East and West, joined the pope's council at Ferrara. Thus, it

The seal of the council of Basel.

happened that the conciliar movement, which had come to power as a response to schism in the papacy, was itself divided, and there were now two councils and one pope.

The Council of Ferrara, which subsequently moved to Florence, gained widespread recognition when, forced by circumstances, the emperor and the patriarch of Constantinople accepted its formula for reunion, which included papal supremacy.

Meanwhile, the council of Basel became more and more radical. One by one, its most distinguished leaders left it and joined the pope's council. What was left of the old council declared Eugene deposed and named Felix V in his stead. Thus, now there were two councils and two popes, and the conciliar movement, which had ended the papal schism, had resurrected it. But the remnant of the council of Basel, and the pope whom it named, made little impact on the life of the church. Eventually, the last members of the council moved to Lausanne, where they finally disbanded. In 1449, Felix V gave up his claim to the papacy. By then, it was clear that the papacy had won, and that from that time councils would be subject to it, and not vice versa.

JOHN WYCLIFFE

In order not to interrupt our narrative, we have followed the course of the papacy and of the conciliar movement until the middle of the fifteenth century. In the conciliar movement, we have seen a program of reformation addressed mainly at moral and pastoral issues, such as simony and absenteeism. But at the same time there were other movements that sought to reform, not only the life,

Wycliffe became the center of a vast movement seeking the reformation of the church.

but also the doctrines, of the church. The two most outstanding leaders of this type of reformation were John Wycliffe and John Huss. Wycliffe lived during the Avignon papacy, and died in 1384 just after the beginning of the Great Schism. Huss, to whom we shall devote the next section of this chapter, died just over thirty years later at the Council of Constance.

Little is known of Wycliffe's early years. The name by which he is known comes from the Yorkshire village of Wycliffe-on-Tees, where he was born and where his family owned land. He was about twelve years old when the village itself came under the jurisdiction of John of Gaunt, King Edward III's second son, with whom Wycliffe's life would be entwined. He spent most of his career at Oxford, where he began studying in 1345, when he was some fifteen years old, and eventually became famous for his erudition and his unflinching logic—although not for his sense of humor, which he totally lacked. He had strong support among his colleagues, although eventually he left the university to serve the crown, first as a diplomat, and then as a polemicist.

Those were crucial and unsettled times in the life of England, which was affirming its nationhood. When Wycliffe was born, Norman French was still the language of the elites and of government; but in 1362, while Wycliffe was a student at Oxford, English became the language of the courts, and shortly after his death it was the primary language in elementary schools—at Oxford and other centers of higher learning, Latin was still the language of instruction. It was the time of the papacy in Avignon, which was at the service of French interests and therefore created resentment and resistance in England. A series of English statutes (1351, 1353, 1363) sought to limit papal influence, first by making election to ecclesiastical positions independent of the pope, and then by forbidding appeals to courts outside of England. Therefore, the English authorities welcomed Wycliffe's arguments on the nature and limits of lordship or dominion, which he expressed in two major works, *On Divine Dominion* and *On Civil Dominion*. According to him, all legitimate dominion comes from God. But such dominion is characterized by the example of Christ, who came to serve, not to be served. Any lordship used for the profit of the ruler rather than for that of the governed is not true dominion, but usurpation. The same is true of any dominion, no matter how legitimate, which seeks to expand its power beyond the limits of its authority. Therefore, any supposed ecclesiastical authority that collects taxes for its own benefit, or seeks to extend its power beyond the sphere of spiritual matters, is illegitimate.

Naturally, these views were well received by civil authorities in England, involved as they were in a constant quarrel with the papacy precisely over the questions of taxation and of the temporal authority of popes. These conflicts led to a conference at Bruges in 1374, where Wycliffe was sent as one of the English representatives. Perhaps as a reward for such services, he was granted the parish of Lutterworth, which he held and where he preached until he suffered two strokes, one in 1382, and another in 1384, which caused his death.

But Wycliffe meant every word he said, and soon his logic led him to point out that what he had affirmed regarding the limits of ecclesiastical dominion was also true of civil power. This too must be measured according to the service that it renders its subjects. In consequence, Wycliffe soon lost the support of those who had earlier rejoiced in his forthrightness.

At this time, his position also grew more radical. The scandal of the Great Schism encouraged this, and he began teaching that the true church of Christ is not the pope and his visible hierarchy, but rather the invisible body of those who are predestined to salvation—a point he drew from Saint Augustine of Hippo. Although it is impossible to know exactly who has been predestined, there are indications in the fruits that each produces, and this would seem to indicate that many ecclesiastical leaders are in truth reprobate. Toward the end of his life, Wycliffe declared that the pope was among those who were probably reprobate.

According to Wycliffe, it is true that scripture is the possession of the church, and that only the church can interpret the Bible correctly. But this church that owns scripture is the body of all who are predestined, and therefore the Bible ought to be put back in their hands, and in their own language. It was because of this claim that Wycliffe began translating the Bible from the Vulgate into English, a task that his followers continued after his death. (A century earlier, King Alfonso the Wise of Castile had ordered that the Bible be translated into Spanish, and this directive had resulted in the *Biblia alfonsina*, one of the earliest translations of the Bible into the vernaculars of Western Europe.) This translation of scripture into English was not an isolated phenomenon, for as we have seen it was during Wycliffe's lifetime that English became the language of the courts; and it was also during his lifetime that Archbishop John Toresby of York had the catechetical instructions for both clergy and laity translated into English.

However, the point at which Wycliffe's doctrines aroused most controversy was his understanding of the presence of Christ in communion. The Fourth Lateran Council, in 1215, had affirmed the doctrine of transubstantiation. In his treatise *On the Eucharist*, Wycliffe rejected this because he saw in it a denial of the principle manifested in the incarnation. When God was joined to human nature, the presence of the divinity did not destroy the humanity. Likewise, what takes place in communion is that the body of Christ is indeed present in the bread, but without destroying it. In a "sacramental" and "mysterious" way, the body of Christ is present in communion. But so is the bread.

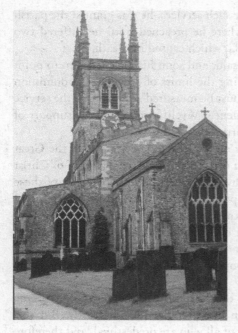

Wycliffe retired to his parish at Lutterworth.

By 1377, partly due to his theology, and partly because John of Gaunt was not supporting him as firmly as before, Wycliffe was coming under repeated attacks. That year, Pope Gregory XI issued five bulls against him—one sent to King Edward III, one to the University of Oxford, and three jointly to the archbishop of Canterbury and the bishop of London. Since his views contradicted what was then official dogma of the church, Wycliffe was declared a heretic by many at Oxford, where he had returned when his popularity with the civil authorities began to wane. Although he was incarcerated for some time, his prestige was such that he was allowed to continue his studies and his writing.

Finally, in 1381, he retired to his parish at Lutterworth. The fact that he had a parish, and that he had received this from the crown in gratitude for services rendered to it, shows the degree to which the evils that the reformers so deplored had spread throughout the church. Even Wycliffe, an ardent advocate of reform, had financed his life at Oxford with the proceeds of an ecclesiastical appointment. And later, when he was in need of ready cash, he exchanged that appointment for a less productive one, plus a sum of money.

The year 1381 was also marked by the first great peasant revolt in England, led by Wat Tyler. Since he expressed support for some of the peasants' claims, Wycliffe was accused of having instigated the revolt—which he apparently did not. In 1382, Archbishop William Courtenay, who had long opposed Wycliffe, summoned a court to examine Wycliffe's writings and teachings. The gathering was marked by an earth tremor which each side claimed was a sign of God's displeasure with the other. In the end, ten of Wycliffe's tenets were declared heretical, his writings were placed under the ban, and the archbishop began putting pressure on his followers, many of whom recanted—although by then Wycliffe had gained wide support among what came to be known as the "Lollards" (a pejorative title of obscure origin, probably meaning that they mumbled their prayers). But still, Wycliffe's prestige was such that he was able to retain his parish, and was not excommunicated.

Wycliffe died of a stroke in 1384. Since he died in the communion of the church, he was buried in consecrated ground. But the Council of Constance subsequently condemned him, and his remains were disinterred and burned. His ashes were then thrown into the river Swift.

Even while Wycliffe was alive, some of his disciples set out to preach his doctrines. It is not clear that this was done at his instigation, nor even that all who eventually received the name of *Lollards* were in fact Wycliffites. But in any case there was soon a substantial number of people who held beliefs similar to those of Wycliffe, and who set out to translate the Bible into English and to preach their understanding of the Christian faith. They were convinced that the Bible belonged to the people and should be returned to them, that pastors should not hold civil offices, and that the worship of images, and enforcing clerical celibacy and pilgrimages, as well as other such abuses were an abomination. They also rejected the doctrine of transubstantiation, and prayers for the dead. In many of these tenets, they were forerunners of the Protestant Reformation.

At first, Lollardism had a significant number of adherents among the nobility, although it soon became a popular movement. At one point, they sought to have Parliament change the laws regarding heresy. But in this they failed, and their situation became precarious. Most of the Lollards among the nobility recanted and returned to the official church. A few persisted, and in 1413 Sir John Oldcastle led an abortive rebellion that led to his capture and execution. The movement then lost most of its support among the gentry. But it continued spreading among the lower classes, where it became more radical. A Lollard conspiracy, discovered in 1431, hoped both to reform the church and to overthrow the government. In spite of constant persecution, Lollardism never disappeared. Early in the sixteenth century, it enjoyed a revival, and many of its followers were condemned to death. Eventually, the Lollard remnant swelled the ranks of Protestants in England. But long before that time, Wycliffe's teachings made an impact on distant Bohemia.

JOHN HUSS

Bohemia, in what is now the Czech Republic, became the home of another reformist movement that ecclesiastical authorities were not able to suppress. Its leader was John Huss (1362–1415), a deeply devout man who in 1393, shortly before the beginning of the controversy, spent most of his funds in purchasing an indulgence for his sins. At that time he was a student—and not on outstanding one—at the University of Prague. But Huss was a diligent worker and an eloquent preacher, with the result that in 1401 he became dean of the faculty of philosophy at the university, and in 1402 was appointed preacher at the Chapel of Bethlehem, which had been founded in 1391 as a center for preaching in the vernacular.

It was a time of increasing nationalism among Czechs, who generally resented what they considered the excessive influence of Germans in their country. They were ruled by King Wenceslas (Václav), who was a half-brother of Sigismund, and who should not be confused with the Good King Wenceslas of song (who was in fact only a duke, and lived three centuries earlier). Wenceslas had been deposed as Holy Roman emperor by Sigismund, but still claimed the title. It was the time of the Great Western Schism, when two rivals, one in Rome and one in Avignon, claimed the see of Peter. Since the Roman pope, Boniface IX, had supported the deposition of Wenceslas, the king supported the Avignon papacy, and fomented Czech nationalism as a way to strengthen his own hand in the political game he was playing.

It was also a time when there were close ties between Czech professors and students at the University of Prague and their counterparts at Oxford, whose King Richard II was married to a Bohemian princess. As a result of these ties, the writings of Wycliffe were taken to Bohemia by a number of Czechs who had studied in England. These writings caused a great stir at the university, although at first the debate centered on technical points in Wycliffe's philosophical views. The university was divided between Germans and Czechs, and soon that division was reflected in the positions taken by various teachers vis-à-vis Wycliffe's philosophy, for the Czechs accepted it and the Germans rejected it, mostly claiming that it was outdated. Then some of the German scholars injected into the controversy the question of Wycliffe's orthodoxy, and thus put the Czechs in the difficult position of defending the writings of a man whose theology was questionable, and with whom in any case they did not completely agree. Huss in particular, while defending scholars' rights to read and discuss the works of Wycliffe, disagreed with him on the question of the presence of Christ in communion, and held the traditional doctrine of transubstantiation. Eventually, with the support of the king of Bohemia, the Czechs gained the upper hand, and the German teachers left Prague in order to found their own university at Leipzig. On leaving, they declared that they were doing so because Prague had become a hotbed of heresies, particularly those of Wycliffe. Thus, the debate over Wycliffe's writings contributed to give the rest of the world the impression that the Czechs were heretics.

Meanwhile, from the pulpit of the nearby Chapel of Bethlehem, Huss was advocating a reformation similar to what the conciliarists of his time were proposing. At first, he had no intention of altering the traditional doctrines of the church, but only of restoring Christian life, and particularly the life of the clergy, to its highest ideals. His fiery preaching was aimed particularly at the corruption of the clergy, whom he called "the Lord's fat ones," and accused of fornication, absenteeism, and enriching themselves at the expense of the people. His attacks on simony targeted the highest ranks of the church, for it was widely known that in 1402, when he was twenty-five years old, Archbishop Zbynek had bought his post. In all of this, Huss was continuing a movement that had deep roots among the Czech people, for some thirty years earlier a movement combining nationalism and a call for reformation had been headed by Jan Milic, a wealthy prelate who had renounced his wealth as part of his call to reformation. Actually, the Chapel of Bethlehem, where Huss preached, had been founded by some of Milic's followers, and its practice of preaching in the vernacular reflected the nationalism that had marked that movement.

While controversy was raging in Bohemia, the Great Western Schism grew worse. The Council of Pisa had tried to end the Great Western Schism, with the unintended result that there were now three popes instead of two. Wenceslas now supported the Pisan popes—first Alexander V and then John XXIII. Zbynek at first resisted the directives of the crown, but eventually relented, and he too came to support the Pisan popes. He then appealed to the first of these, Alexander V, for help against Huss. In response, Alexander ordered an investigation into the spread of Wycliffe's doctrines in Bohemia, and also ordering that preaching should take place only in cathedrals, parish churches, and monasteries. Since the Chapel of Bethlehem did not fall in any of these three categories, the papal decree practically amounted to silencing Huss. After deep soul-searching, Huss decided that he could not obey, and continued preaching. Zbynek responded by burning Wycliffe's books; but the public reaction was such that he had to flee Prague and take refuge in a castle. In 1410, Huss was summoned to Rome to answer for that act of disobedience and for others that followed. He refused to go, and was excommunicated in 1411. But he had the support of the king and the people of Bohemia, and therefore the papal sentence had little effect. Zbynek, on his part, issued an interdict against Prague, hoping that the lack of sacraments would force his opponents to relent. But Queen Sophia, who had always supported Huss, urged her husband to stand firm, and also wrote to Pisan Pope John XXIII urging him to allow Huss to continue preaching—which in any case Huss was already doing.

As these events unfolded, the conflict with the Pisan papacy led Huss to more radical views. First, he declared that an unworthy pope is not to be obeyed. He did not question the Pisan popes' legitimacy. What he questioned was their authority when it was clear that they were acting in their own interests, and not for the welfare of the church. He thus came to the conclusion that the Bible is the final authority by which the pope as well as any Christian is to be judged. A pope who does not obey the Bible is not to be obeyed.

Thus far, Huss had said little that the more radical conciliarists could not accept. But then John XXIII proclaimed a Crusade against Naples, mostly for reasons relating to Italian politics, and determined that the Crusade would be financed through the sale of indulgences—the remission of the time to be spent in purgatory in purification and punishment for sins. Huss, who had bought an indulgence twenty years earlier, by then had come to the conclusion that only God could grant forgiveness, and that to sell what comes only from God is usurping God's power. In this particular case, he was also incensed by the notion of a war among Christians being sanctified simply because it suited the pope's ambitions.

The king, who needed Pope John's support, ordered Huss to silence his protest. But by then his views were known, and there were public demonstrations against the exploitation of the Czech people by the papacy. John XXIII excommunicated Huss once again, and this time the reformer, who did not wish to involve the entire nation in the controversy, left Prague and his pulpit, withdrew to the countryside, and continued writing on the need for reformation. He was there when he received news that a great council was to gather in Constance, and that Sigismund invited him to defend himself before the assembly, and granted him safe-conduct to attend the council.

The great council promised to be the dawn of a new age for the church, and therefore Huss could not refuse the invitation. Perhaps he would be able to contribute to the great reformation that the council would undertake. Upon arriving at Constance, however, it was clear that John XXIII wished to try him directly, apart from the council. Huss was taken to the papal consistory and ordered to recant his heresy. To this he responded that he would gladly recant if someone could show him that he was a heretic. After that stormy interview, he was treated as a prisoner, first in his own residence, then in the bishop's palace, and finally in cells in various monasteries. The emperor protested against this violation of his safe-conduct. But, when he realized that Huss's cause was not popular, and that he would appear as a supporter of heretics, he prudently washed his hands of the entire affair. It is said that when John XXIII fled from Constance he gave Sigismund the keys to Huss's cell, so that he could be freed; but Sigismund decided that this would interfere with his political ambitions, and actually had Huss transferred to a more secure cell. Shortly before his death, Huss wrote to a friend blaming Sigismund's weakness and deceit for his impending death, and praying that God would forgive him.

On June 5, 1415, Huss was taken before the council. A few days earlier John XXIII, who had fled the city, had been brought back as a prisoner. There was reason to hope that the council would see Huss as an enemy of John, and dismiss the charges against him. But the council, like the emperor, wished to appear as a stern defender of orthodoxy. Therefore, Huss was in chains when he appeared before the assembly. Its leaders wished to have him submit to the council, and declared that all he had to do was recant his heresies. He insisted that he had never held the doctrines of which they accused him. They retorted that all he had to do was recant. This Huss could not do, for then he would be admitting that he had been a heretic, and that his Czech friends and followers were heretics. Finally, convinced that he could not obtain a fair hearing from those present, he declared: "I appeal to Jesus Christ, the only judge who is almighty and completely just. In his hands I place my cause, since he will judge each, not on the basis of false witnesses and erring councils, but on truth and justice." He was then sent back to prison, where many went to plead with him; for what the leaders of the council sought was a recantation that would affirm the assembly's authority, not a condemnation that would cause many to question its wisdom.

Finally, on July 6, Huss was taken to the cathedral. There he was dressed in his priestly garments, which were then torn from him. His tonsure was erased by shaving his head, which was then covered with a paper crown decorated with demons. On his way to the stake, they led him past a pyre where his books were being burned. When he was tied to the stake, they gave him a last chance to recant, and once again he refused. He then prayed aloud, "Lord Jesus, it is for thee that I patiently endure this cruel death. I pray thee to have mercy on my enemies." He was heard reciting the Psalms as he died. A few days later his colleague Jerome of Prague, who had been the main proponent of Wycliffe's views in Bohemia and had decided to join Huss at Constance, was also burned. Their executioners gathered the ashes and threw them into the lake, so that nothing would remain of the heresiarchs. But some Czechs took back with them bits of the soil where Huss had died, to serve as a memorial of the crime committed at Constance.

The Bohemians were indignant, and almost unanimously repudiated the council. Four hundred and fifty-two noblemen gathered in solemn assembly and announced their agreement with Huss, that an unworthy pope ought not be obeyed. The council countered by ordering that the University of Prague be dissolved, summoning the rebellious nobles to Constance, and declaring that the king of Bohemia was abetting heresy.

In Bohemia itself, several different groups came together in their opposition to the council. The original Hussites were mostly members of the nobility and the bourgeoisie, but they soon had accepted the support of more radical movements arising from the lower classes. Most notable of these was the Taborites, an apocalyptic movement that had spread among the peasants

In spite of assurances that he had been granted safe-conduct, John Huss was condemned and burned at the stake.

even before the time of Huss. The Taborites rejected everything that was not to be found in scripture, whereas the true Hussites were willing to retain everything except what was explicitly rejected by the Bible. Another movement similar to that of the Taborites, but less radical in its apocalypticism, was that of the Horebites.

The threat of armed intervention led these various groups to agree to *Four Articles* that would become the basis of Bohemian resistance. The first was that the Word of God was to be preached freely throughout the kingdom. The second, that communion would be given "in both kinds"—that is, that the cup, and not only the bread, was to be given to the laity. This was a conclusion that Huss had reached toward the end of his life, and which soon became one of the main demands of all Hussites. Third, all agreed that the clergy should be deprived of its wealth, and live in "apostolic poverty." Finally, the fourth article stated that gross and public sin, especially simony, would be properly punished.

Then King Wenceslas died (1419), and his legitimate successor in ruling Bohemia was Sigismund, the German emperor who had failed Huss at Constance.

The Bohemians demanded that he agree to the *Four Articles,* that he grant freedom of worship, and that he promise not to name Germans to public posts. Sigismund would not accept these conditions, and at his request the pope called a Crusade against the Hussites. Sigismund and his troops marched to the vicinity of Prague, but there they were crushed by a Bohemian army whose main contingent was Taborite. The Taborites had been joined by John Zizka, a member of the lesser nobility, who organized them into a fighting force. His main weapon was the peasants' carts, which Zizka armed with blades and turned into fearsome war chariots. In a second battle, the remnants of Sigismund's Crusade were utterly destroyed. A year later, in 1421, an army of a hundred thousand crusaders fled before Zizka's carts. A third Crusade, 1422, dissolved before it even met the enemy. Shortly thereafter Zizka, who had lost his one good eye in a battle in 1421, left the Taborites, who had become too visionary for his tastes, and joined the Horebites. He died of the plague in 1424. But the Bohemians continued the struggle, and defeated two other Crusades in 1427 and 1431.

By then, the Council of Basel had come to the conclusion that the Council of Constance had dealt unwisely with the Bohemian question, and invited the Hussites to attend this new council, in order to settle their differences with the Catholics. But the Hussites feared a repetition of the events surrounding the trial and death of Huss, and demanded guarantees that the council considered offensive. Once more, the Catholics organized a Crusade against Bohemia. And once more they were defeated.

This last defeat finally convinced the Catholics that negotiation was necessary. As a result of that negotiation, the church in Bohemia rejoined the rest of Western Christendom, but was allowed to retain communion in both kinds as well as certain other elements of the *Four Articles.* Many Hussites, particularly those among the nobility, agreed to this, and finally Sigismund was able to become king of Bohemia—although he died sixteen months later.

But not all Bohemians accepted this agreement. Many left the established church, and eventually formed the *Unitas Fratrum*—or "Union of Brethren." Their numbers grew rapidly, not only in Bohemia, but also in nearby Moravia. During the Protestant Reformation of the sixteenth century, they established close ties with protestantism, and for some time it seemed likely that they would become Lutherans. Shortly thereafter, the Hapsburg emperors, staunch supporters of Roman Catholicism, persecuted them. They were dispersed, and the *Unitas Fratrum* almost disappeared. From exile, their leader, Bishop John Amos Comenius (1592–1670), encouraged them and interceded on their behalf, hoping that some day the plant that had been so brutally cut would bloom again. These hopes were fulfilled long after his death, for later in our story we shall see the impact of a remnant of the *Unitas Fratrum,* who were by then called simply Moravians. Another remnant became one of many churches following Calvinist theology.

GIROLAMO SAVONAROLA

Late in the spring of 1490, a Dominican friar stood at the gates of Florence. A native of Ferrara, Girolamo Savonarola had spent most of his thirty-three years in study and devotion. This was not his first visit to Florence, where he had lived before. But the Florentines, who admired his biblical scholarship, had not liked his vehement preaching and his "foreign" accent—from Ferrara. Now he was returning at the invitation of Lorenzo de Medici the Magnificent, who practically owned Florence, and to whom he had been recommended by the famous philosopher Pico della Mirandola.

In the monastery of St. Mark, which he joined, Savonarola began a series of sessions expounding scripture to his fellow friars. Soon many others were attending the sessions, which were moved from the garden to the church, and the lectures became sermons. By Lent, 1491, his fame was such that he was invited to preach at the main church in Florence. What he said there about the evils of the time, and about the contrast between true Christian life and the love of luxury, offended many among the powerful. Lorenzo de Medici was particularly displeased, and hired another preacher to attack Savonarola. This failed,

Savonarola was an eloquent and fiery preacher.

since the people of Florence took the side of Savonarola, and the other preacher decided to leave for Rome, there to plot against his rival.

When Savonarola was elected prior of St. Mark, some of the friars told him that it was customary on such an occasion to visit Lorenzo and thank him for his support of the monastery. The new prior responded that he owed his post to God, not to Lorenzo, and that therefore he would withdraw and thank God in prayer. Shortly thereafter, he sold a great deal of the property of the convent and gave the proceeds to the poor. He also reformed the inner life of the community, to the point that people commented on the holiness and spirit of service of the friars. Other monastic houses then asked to join in the reformation that had thus begun. Even Lorenzo, when he was about to die, called on the saintly friar to join him at his bedside.

Pietro de Medici, Lorenzo's successor, lost the respect of the Florentines. Charles VIII of France was marching south to claim the crown of Naples. Unwilling or unable to organize the defense of Florence, which lay on Charles's path, Pietro tried to buy him off. The Florentines were incensed, and sent their own embassy, led by Savonarola. Meanwhile, they expelled Pietro from the city. When Charles entered Florence, and made unreasonable demands from it, once again it was Savonarola who intervened, garnering more reasonable agreement, and as a result the Florentines became allies of France.

When Charles and his troops left, Savonarola's prestige was such that the Florentines turned to him for guidance as to their form of government. As he recommended, they established a republic, and took steps to restore the economic life of the city, which had been interrupted. Meanwhile, he also recommended that the gold and silver of the churches be sold in order to feed the poor.

It was at this point that Savonarola's program of reformation reached its high point. Although he has often been depicted as a fanatical and ignorant monk, he believed that study should be at the center of the needed reformation. For that reason, under his leadership the friars in Saint Mark's studied Latin, Greek, Hebrew, Arabic, and Chaldean. But he was also convinced that the luxuries of the time, and all the things that the rich valued so much, were vanity, and that lust for them was at the root of the evils that he deplored. Therefore, under his leadership, there were periodic "burnings of vanities." A great wooden pyramid was built in the main square, and under it were piles of straw and firewood laced with gunpowder. On the steps of the pyramid people then placed their "vanities"—dresses, jewelry, wigs, ostentatious furniture, and the like. Then, in the midst of much singing, processions, and other ceremonies, the entire structure was set on fire. Those great bonfires came to take the place of the carnival, the traditional celebration just before the beginning of fasting for Lent that Savonarola and his followers had banned.

Savonarola's call for reformation found echo in neighboring cities. The republic of Siena, a rival of Florence, requested his help. He arrived at Siena with twenty fellow friars, and for a time the proposed reformation flourished. But soon resistance grew, led by some monks whom Savonarola had expelled from their convent, and Savonarola eventually left the city, shaking off the dust from his feet. He was more successful at Pisa, then under Florentine rule, where he expelled from the convent of Santa Caterina a group of monks who objected to his rigorous demands, and from there his reformation expanded to other neighboring monastic houses.

Savonarola's downfall was brought about by political circumstances. The pope—Alexander VI, one of the worst popes ever—made an alliance against France that included much of Italy, Germany, and Spain. It would have been advantageous for Florence to join the pope's party. But Savonarola insisted on keeping the promises made to Charles VIII. The pope responded with a series of harsh measures, first against Savonarola, and then against the entire city. It soon became clear to many Florentines that they were losing a great deal of their trade because their preacher insisted on keeping his word. Opposition to Savonarola and his policies grew among the wealthy. Those who supported him became increasingly convinced that he was a prophet, and demanded miracles of him. When something he had foretold became true, they grew even more enthusiastic. But when he failed to perform the miracles they demanded, they too turned against him.

Finally, a mob invaded St. Mark's. Savonarola refused to defend himself, or to have his friends take up arms against other Florentines in order to save him. He was taken by the mob, tied, beaten, and turned over to the authorities, some of whom had been plotting precisely such an event.

It was now necessary to find something of which to accuse him. He was tortured for several days, and the most his tormentors could make him confess was that it was not true that he could foretell the future—which in any case he had never claimed. The pope sent his legates to participate in the judicial process, and these too tortured Savonarola. All they could obtain was his "confession" that he had planned to appeal to a council. Savonarola himself came to recognize that perhaps he had been too proud in his calls for reformation, declaring, "Lord, if even Peter, on whom you had bestowed so many gifts and graces, failed so thoroughly, what else could I do?" Giving up hope to be able to bring more specific charges against him, the judges finally decided to condemn Savonarola and two of his closest collaborators as "heretics and schismatics," without specifying the nature of their heresy. They were then turned over to the "secular arm" to be executed, for the church must not kill. The only mercy they received was that they were hanged before their bodies

After Savonarola and two of his associates were hanged, their bodies were burned, and their ashes thrown into the river.

were burned. All three died valiantly. Their ashes were then thrown into the river Arno, to erase all memory of them. But in spite of this there were many who kept relics of the holy friar. When, years later, Rome was sacked by the Germans, some saw in this the fulfillment of Savonarola's prophecies. At various times since then, and even to this day, there have been in the Roman Catholic Church those who have argued that the Dominican friar was in fact a saint, and that as such his name should be added to the official list of saints of the church.

THE MYSTICAL ALTERNATIVE

In spite of their many evils, and perhaps in part because of them, the fourteenth and fifteenth centuries were a time when mystics abounded. In Spain, England, and Italy there were remarkable mystics whose works were an inspiration for generations to come. But it was in Germany and the Low Countries, along the borders of the Rhine, that mysticism flourished.

The great teacher of German mysticism was Eckhart von Hochheim, generally known as Meister Eckhart, who lived in the late thirteenth and early fourteenth centuries. His mystical doctrine was essentially Neoplatonic, for its goal was the contemplation of the divine, the ineffable One. According to Eckhart, all words about God are inexact, and therefore, strictly speaking, false. "If I say, 'God is good,' that is not true. I am good. God is not." Declarations such as this were open to misinterpretations, giving the impression that Eckhart lacked respect for the godhead. Actually, his intention was exactly the opposite. What he meant was certainly not that God is evil, but rather that all language about God is analogical, and therefore inexact. In any case, his words show the character of his mystical thought, where he sought to exalt God by showing that no human concept can grasp the divine, and that therefore true knowledge of God is not rational, but intuitive. God is known, not by study or rational argument, but by mystical contemplation in which one is finally lost in the divine.

From all eternity, all creatures are in God. Before the foundation of the world, the ideas of all things that would exist were in the mind of God, the Great Artificer. This too is a characteristic theme of the entire Platonic tradition, and of the Neoplatonic mysticism that Eckhart embraced. On the basis of these views, he declared:

> Within that true essence of the godhead, which is beyond all being and every distinction, there I already existed. There I willed myself. There I knew myself. There I wished to create the man I am. For that reason, I am my own cause according to my being, which is eternal, although not according to my becoming, which is temporal.[48]

This statement, and others like it, led many to consider him a heretic. It was said that he taught that the world and all the creatures were eternal, and that he confused God and the world, thus falling into pantheism—the belief that all creatures are part of the divine. He was especially accused of holding that the soul, or part of it, is not created, but rather eternal. Eckhart protested repeatedly that such charges were based on mistaken interpretations of his teachings, and it is true that he tried to avoid pantheism, as well as the doctrine of the divinity of the soul. But his expressions often left him open to such interpretations. Toward the end of his career, he was formally charged with heresy, and convicted of it. He then appealed to Rome, but died before the case was settled.

Although much of what was said about Eckhart's teachings was an oversimplification or an exaggeration, there is no doubt that there is a vast difference between his Neoplatonic mysticism and the christocentric mysticism of Bernard of Clairvaux and Francis of Assisi. These two had found their inspiration in the contemplation of Jesus as a historical human being, as God incarnate in a particular time and place. Eckhart, on the other hand, was not particularly interested in the historical time or the geographical place of biblical events. "Jerusalem," he said, "is as close to my soul as is the place where I stand right now." What he meant by this is that one finds God through inner contemplation, by "allowing oneself to be carried," and thus coming to God "without intermediaries."

Although during his life he was accused of heresy, after his death Meister Eckhart had many followers, particularly in his own Dominican order. Most famous among these were John Tauler and Henry Suso. These two, although less erudite than their teacher, were able to expound his views in terms that were much more accessible to those who had not been trained in theology. Through their works, Eckhart's mysticism gained widespread acceptance.

Further down along the Rhine lived the Flemish mystic John of Ruysbroeck. Although he probably read Eckhart's works, and on some points followed the German master, Ruysbroeck's mysticism was more practical, and more directly related to everyday life. This was carried further by Gerhard Groote, another Flemish mystic who was greatly influenced by Ruysbroeck.

Ruysbroeck and Groote gave shape and popularity to what came to be known as the "modern devotion"—*devotio moderna*. This consisted mainly of a life of disciplined devotion centered on the contemplation of the life of Christ, and on its imitation. The most famous writing of this school is *The Imitation of Christ* of Thomas à Kempis, which through the centuries has been one of the most widely read devotional works.

Ruysbroeck, Groote, and their followers also found it necessary to reject the teachings of the "Brethren of the Free Spirit." These were mystics who claimed that, since they had a direct experience with God, they had no need of intermediaries such as the church or the Bible. Some may even have claimed that, since they were spiritual, they were free to let their bodies follow their own inclinations.

Perhaps Groote's greatest contribution was the founding of the Brethren of the Common Life. He gave up the sinecure from which he, like so many in his time, derived his income, and set out to attack corruption in the church and to call his followers to renewed holiness and devotion. But, in marked contrast with many others who had preached similar reformations, Groote did not call his followers to the monastic life. Rather, he insisted that, unless they had a genuine monastic vocation, they were to continue in their callings—the "common life"—and in them to follow the principles of the modern devotion. In spite of this, eventually many of his disciples did take up the monastic life, taking the rule of the Augustinian canons. But they never lost their interest in the "common life" of those who were not called to monasticism. For that reason the Brethren of the Common Life founded excellent schools where they trained, not only those who were to follow the monastic life, but also many who had other plans for their lives. Those schools stressed both scholarship and devotion, and became centers for the renewal of the church, for most of their alumni were possessed of a critical and reforming spirit. The most famous of these alumni was Erasmus of Rotterdam, who was a leading figure in the sixteenth century.

With few exceptions, German and Flemish mystics avoided enthusiastic excesses. Mystical contemplation as they saw it did not lead to turbulent emotions, but rather to an inner peace. This was to be attained, not through emotional stimulation of passions that waver, but rather through inner and firm intellectual contemplation.

Among the many who devoted their lives to religion and contemplation, Dame Julian of Norwich (1342–c.1417) deserves special mention. When she was almost thirty years old, in 1373, and in the context of a serious illness, she had a series of fifteen visions of Christ and the Virgin. The following night, when she began doubting the validity of her earlier experience, a new vision came to confirm the previous ones. In contrast to other mystics, she had only those visions, and no more; but she devoted the rest of her life to meditate on them, delving into their most profound meaning. She made arrangements to be enclosed in a cell adjacent to the church. There she would spend the rest of her life. This cell had only one door leading to an enclosed garden, and windows through which she could communicate with a servant and with her many visitors, and also look on the altar of the church during communion. Although many came to ask her advice and consolation, she is particularly famous for her *Showings*, of which there are two versions (one earlier and shorter than the other), and in which she explores the meaning of her one set of visions. Her daring metaphors, jointly with her theological wisdom, have made her book one of the most admired and discussed documents of medieval devotional writing. Other notable English mystics are Richard Rolle (1290–1349) and Margery Kempe (1373–1438).

The mystic movement itself was not opposed to the church nor to its hierarchy. Although some of its leaders criticized the abuses of prelates, and above all their ostentatiousness, most of them were content with the inner peace of their devotion, and felt no need to oppose ecclesiastical authorities. But, on the other hand, the mystical impulse itself tended to weaken the authority, not only of corrupt prelates, but of the hierarchical church itself. Indeed, if through direct contemplation one can achieve communion with the divine, such traditional means of grace as the sacraments, preaching, and even Scripture lose their importance. The mystics of the fourteenth and fifteenth centuries rarely reached such radical conclusions—and those who did, such as the Brethren of the Free Spirit, were refuted by most of the leading mystics as well as by the rest of the church. But their teachings introduced a germ of doubt that in subsequent years would increasingly weaken the authority of the hierarchy.

POPULAR MOVEMENTS

Most of the foregoing has dealt with movements of reform among the wealthy and the educated. For obvious reasons, most of the extant sources deal with such movements. The poor and the ignorant do not write books about their dreams, which only find their way into books of history when they explode in violent confrontation with the powerful. But such dreams were numerous among the common folk in the later Middle Ages.

Wycliffe's teachings survived, not so much among the learned at Oxford or the nobles who espoused them, as among the Lollards who went from village to village, preaching a gospel that contradicted a great deal of what the villagers heard from the authorities of the church. The Hussites, at first mostly gentry and scholars, found their greatest support among the Taborites, who probably preceded them, and who derived many of their doctrines, not from Huss, but rather from common religiosity and from the apocalyptic expectations of the poor.

Something similar took place among women. For them, monasticism was practically the only way in which to lead a life free from direct dependence on their fathers, husbands, or sons. Thus, women flocked to orders such as the Franciscans and Dominicans. Soon the male leaders of these orders began to limit the number of women who could be admitted to the feminine branches of the orders. This, however, could not restrain the monastic impulse among women, and some of them began joining in small groups in order to live together in prayer, devotion, and relative poverty. Such women were dubbed *beguines*, and their houses, *beguinages*. Although the origin of these words is obscure, there is no doubt that it was pejorative, and it was probably somehow connected with heresy, of which such women were often suspected. Although a few bishops supported the movement, others banned it. Late in the thirteenth century, and for years to come, the church enacted laws against this sort of life which, while not part of an order under properly constituted authority, often shamed those who belonged to the official monastic orders. When men took up a similar life, they were called "beghards," and they too became suspect.

Another popular movement was that of the flagellants. They first appeared in 1260, but it was the fourteenth century that saw their numbers swell. Whipping oneself in penance for sin was not new, since it was a common practice in many monastic houses. But now it became a popular craze, with little connection to the hierarchy of the church. Thousands of Christians from all walks of

The flagellants followed a prescribed rite of flagellation and other self-mortification.

life, convinced that the end was near, or that God would destroy the world if humankind did not show repentance, lashed themselves till the blood flowed.

This was not a momentary or disorderly hysteria. On the contrary, the movement had a rigid and sometimes even ritualistic discipline. Those who wished to join did so for thirty-three-and-a-half days, and during that time owed absolute obedience to their superiors. After that initial period, although they returned home, flagellants were committed to whipping themselves every year on Good Friday.

During the thirty-three days of their obedience, flagellants were part of a group that followed a prescribed ritual. Twice a day they would march in procession to the local church, two by two, while singing hymns. After praying to the Virgin in the church, they would return to the public square, still singing. There they would bare their backs, form a circle, and kneel in prayer. While still kneeling, they resumed their singing, and beat themselves vigorously, until their backs were bloody. Sometimes one of their leaders would preach to them, usually on the sufferings of Christ. After the flagellation they would arise, cover their backs, and withdraw in procession. Besides these two public flagellations every day, there was a third one, to be done in private.

At first, the hierarchy saw no danger in the movement. But when the flagellants began speaking of their ritual as a form of penance and as a "second baptism"—as the early church had spoken of martyrdom—they were accused of seeking to usurp the "power of the keys," given only to St. Peter and his successors. In several countries they were persecuted. Eventually, the practice of public flagellation was abandoned. But the movement continued a clandestine existence for several generations. (One could still find echoes of the medieval flagellants in the Americas even into the twenty-first century, for instance, among the *penitentes* of New Mexico.)

Another movement that illustrates the mood of the time was led by Hans Böhm. In the village of Nicklashausen, in the diocese of Wurzburg, there was an image of the Virgin that had become a center of pilgrimage. In Lent of 1476, a young shepherd by the name of Hans Böhm began preaching among the pilgrims. Times were bad, for the crops had failed, and the bishop of Wurzburg oppressed the poor with ever higher taxes. At first Böhm preached mostly on the need for repentance. But soon he was moved by the poverty of his hearers, and his message took more radical overtones. He pointed to the contrast between the commands of the gospel and the greed and corruption of the clergy. Then he announced that the day would come when all would be equal, and all would work for a living. Finally, he urged his followers, by then more than fifty thousand, to act in advance of that great day, refusing to pay taxes and tithes. And he set a date when all would march together to claim their rights.

How Böhm intended to do this is not known, for on the eve of the appointed day the bishop's soldiers arrested him and dispersed the crowd with artillery shots. Böhm was burned as a heretic. His followers, however, continued gathering at Nicklashausen. The bishop pronounced an interdict on the entire village. But still they came. Finally, the archbishop of Mainz intervened and ordered that the church in the village be destroyed. Having no leader and no center around which to rally, Böhm's followers disbanded. But it is quite likely that they contributed to the radical Anabaptist movement of the sixteenth century.

This was just one among many similar episodes. The last years of the Middle Ages were a time of unrest in which social causes joined with religious dissatisfaction and expectation. Ecclesiastical authorities benefitted from the existing order, and usually gave their support to the powerful as they suppressed every movement of protest. In that atmosphere anticlericalism flourished, finding its basic inspiration, not in modern secularizing currents, but rather in ancient hopes of justice.

35

Renaissance and Humanism

> Oh, supreme liberality of the Father God! Oh, most high and marvelous
> joy of the human creature, to whom has been granted to have what it
> chooses, to be what it decides!
>
> PICO DELLA MIRANDOLA

The last centuries of the Middle Ages saw a bifurcation of thought and
philosophy. On the one hand, there were those who continued the traditions of scholastic theology; and on the other, there were those who looked back
to classical antiquity for guidance and inspiration, and who gave birth to the
Renaissance.

THE LATER COURSE OF SCHOLASTICISM

After reaching its high point in Thomas Aquinas, scholastic theology was
marked by three characteristics. The first was its constant search for ever subtler
questions to pose, and for fine distinctions with which to answer them—for instance, can God make a stone so big that even God cannot move it? And, does
God always do what is good, or is whatever God does good simply because God
does it? This was joined with the development of a dense style and technical
vocabulary that were far beyond the reach of the uninitiated. Its second characteristic was the increasing rift between philosophy and theology, between what
reason can discover and what is known only through divine revelation. Finally,
the tendency of Western theology to make salvation a goal to be attained by
human action reached its high point in late medieval theology, for which even
attendance at communion became a pious work meriting salvation. As we shall
see, the Reformation of the sixteenth century was to a large degree a reaction to
these tendencies of late medieval theology.

Saint Thomas and his contemporaries had held that there was a basic continuity between faith and reason. This meant that certain revealed truths—such
as the existence of God—could also be reached by the proper use of reason. But

shortly after the death of the great Dominican theologian, others began questioning the basic assumption of continuity between faith and reason.

John Duns Scotus, the most famous Franciscan theologian after the time of Bonaventure, was appropriately known as "the Subtle Doctor." This was intended as a sign of respect. But it also points to a characteristic of late medieval theology that would soon turn many intellectuals against it. His subtlety and fine distinctions are such and so many, that his writings can only be understood by those who have spent many years studying the philosophy and theology of the time. Even so, it is clear that Scotus disagreed with those theologians of an earlier generation who believed that doctrines such as the immortality of the soul or divine omnipresence could be proven to be true by the sole and proper use of reason. As to the existence of God, Scotus rejected both the ontological argument of Anselm, that it is self-evident, and the cosmological arguments of Thomas Aquinas, that it can be proven on the basis of the existence of other beings. He did not deny these doctrines. Nor did he deny that they were compatible with reason. What he did deny was that reason could prove them. At most, reason could show that they are possible.

This tendency became clearer in the fourteenth and fifteenth centuries. Typical of the time were William of Occam (c. 1280–1349; frequently spelled "Ockham") and his disciples. Occam is famous mostly for what is known as "Occam's razor," or the "law of parsimony." Briefly stated, this is Occam's principle that one should not pose the existence of anything not necessary to respond to a question or explain an event—or, in other words, the simplest explanation is usually the best one. Although after Occam's time this principle has been employed as an argument against the existence of God, this was not Occam's purpose, for he was convinced that God does exist, even though such existence cannot be proven by rational argument, but simply accepted by faith. And faith affirms not only that God exists, but also that God is omnipotent. Starting from divine omnipotence, Occam and his followers reached the conclusion that human natural reason can prove absolutely nothing regarding God or the divine purposes. Most of them distinguished between God's "absolute" and "ordered" power. Given divine omnipotence, the "absolute" power knows no bounds. Whatever God pleases to do is possible. Nothing is above the absolute power of God—not even reason, nor the distinction between good and evil. Were it not so, one would be forced to declare that God's absolute power is limited by reason, or by the distinction between good and evil. It is only according to the "ordered" power that God acts reasonably, and does what is good. Strictly speaking, one should not say that God always does good, but rather that whatever God does, no matter what it might be, is good. It is God who determines what is good, and not vice versa. Likewise, it is incorrect to say that God has to act reasonably. Reason does not determine God's action. On the contrary, it is the sovereign will of God that determines what is to be reasonable and then, by the "ordered" power of God, acts according to those directives.

This meant that all the traditional arguments whereby theologians had tried to prove that a doctrine was reasonable, or even "fitting," lost their power. Take, for instance, the doctrine of incarnation. Anselm, and practically all theologians after him, had claimed that the incarnation of God in a human being was reasonable, since humankind's debt before God, being infinite, could only be paid by God made human. But theologians in the fourteenth and fifteenth century pointed out that, no matter how reasonable this may seem from our point of view, it is not so if we take into account God's absolute power. By that power, God could have canceled our debt, or simply declared that humans are not sinners, or have counted as meritorious something else, quite apart from the merits of Christ. We are saved by Christ's merits, and this is so, not because it had to be so, nor because the incarnation and passion of Christ were the most fitting means to that end, but simply because God decided that it would be so.

This also means that we are not to delude ourselves into thinking that there is something in the human creature which makes it particularly suited for the incarnation of God. The presence of God in a creature is always a miracle, having nothing to do with our capacity to receive God. For this reason, some of Occam's disciples went so far as to declare that God could have become incarnate in an ass.

All this is not to imply that these theologians were unbelievers who enjoyed asking difficult questions for the mere joy of it. On the contrary, all that is known of their lives would seem to indicate that they were devout and sincere believers. Their purpose was to praise the glory of God. The Creator is infinitely above the creature. The human mind cannot fathom the mysteries of God. The divine omnipotence is such that before it all our efforts to understand it must cease.

This was not a disbelieving theology, willing to believe only that which reason could prove. It was rather a theology which, after showing that reason could not reach the depths of God, placed everything in God's hands, and was ready to believe anything that God had revealed. And to believe it, not because it made sense, but because it had been revealed.

This in turn meant that the question of authority was of paramount importance for theologians in the fourteenth and fifteenth centuries. Since reason cannot prove that a doctrine is true or false, one must make such determinations on the basis of infallible authorities. Occam himself believed that both the pope and a universal council could err, and that only the Bible was infallible. But later, as the Great Western Schism gave further impetus to the conciliar movement, many became convinced that a universal council was the final authority to which all opposition must yield. For this reason, at the Council of Constance the famous theologians Gerson and d'Ailly demanded that John Huss submit to the authority of the council. If he was given the opportunity to argue against the council, the assembly's authority would be jeopardized. And, since the power of reason was as little as they had claimed, there would be no authority left to put an end to the schism, to reform the church, or to determine what doctrines were true.

These late medieval theologians stressed the importance of faith, not only as belief, but also as trust. God has ordered the divine power for our good. Therefore, all of God's promises must be trusted, even though reason might lead us to doubt them. The divine omnipotence is above all our enemies. Those who trust in it will not be put to shame. This theme, typical of the late Middle Ages, would reappear later in Martin Luther.

Yet, no matter how devout these theologians were, their subtleties and their insistence on precise definitions and fine distinctions provoked the reaction of many who deplored the contrast between the complexity of academic theology and the simplicity of the gospel. Part of that reaction was the "modern devotion." The best-known book inspired by it, *The Imitation of Christ*, expressed an opinion that was a commonly held:

> What good is it for you to be able to discuss the Trinity with great profundity, if you lack humility, and thereby offend the Trinity?
>   Verily, high sounding words do not make one holy and just. But a life of virtue does make one acceptable to God.
>   Were you to memorize the entire Bible and all the sayings of the philosophers, what good would this be for you without the love of God and without grace?
>   Vanity of vanities. All is vanity, except loving God and serving only God.[49]

In summary, during the last centuries of the Middle Ages, scholasticism followed a path that could not but provoke a negative reaction among many devout people who declared that this sort of theology, far from being an aid to piety, was an obstacle to it. With ever-growing urgency, the cry was heard for a return to the simplicity of the gospel.

THE REVIVAL OF CLASSICAL LEARNING

While scholastic theology continued along its road of ever-increasing complexity, others sought to revive the glories of classical antiquity. This gave rise to the Renaissance and to its counterpart in the field of literature, humanism. Both of these terms—Renaissance and humanism—have been used in so many different ways that they require some clarification.

The very name Renaissance, or rebirth, as applied to a historical period, implies a negative judgment on the preceding age. Those who first used it meant it precisely that way. They called the thousand years since the Fall of Rome the "Middle Ages," because they saw in them little more than a negative intermission between classical antiquity and their own time. In calling the best medieval art "Gothic," they showed the same prejudice, for the word itself meant that this art was the work of barbaric Goths. Likewise, in giving the name of "Renaissance" to the intellectual and artistic movement that sprang up in Italy and spread to the rest of Western Europe in the fourteenth and fifteenth centuries, they vented their prejudice against the centuries immediately preceding them, and claimed that what was taking place was a glorious rebirth of theretofore forgotten antiquity. The truth is that the Renaissance, while drinking from the sources of antiquity, also drew from the centuries immediately preceding it. Its art had deep roots in Gothic; its attitude toward the world was inspired as much by St. Francis as by Cicero; and its literature was deeply influenced by the medieval songs of the troubadours. Once this has been said, however, there is still ample reason to call this movement "the Renaissance." Many of its main figures believed that the immediate past, and perhaps even the present, was a period of decadence when compared with classical antiquity, and therefore made every effort to promote a rebirth of ancient civilization.

The ambiguity is even greater in the use of the term humanism. This is the name often given to the tendency to place humans at the center of the universe, and to make them the measure for all things. But humanism is also the study of the humanities—what we call liberal arts today. In this last sense, it was employed by many scholars at the end of the Middle Ages and in the sixteenth century, who called themselves humanists because they were devoted to the study of liberal arts. It is true that many of them were humanists also in the other sense, because their study of classical antiquity produced in them a sense of awe before human creativity. But this was not always the case, for many of the humanists had a profound sense of sin and of the limits of human achievement. Therefore, when in the present chapter we speak of humanism, this simply means a literary movement that sought to return to the sources of classical literature, and to imitate its style.

The revival of antiquity had many advocates, first in Italy, and then throughout Western Europe. One of these advocates was the Italian poet Petrarch, who in his youth had written sonnets in Italian, but later preferred to write in Latin, imitating Cicero's style. He soon had many followers, who also emulated classical letters. Many began copying and circulating manuscripts of ancient Latin authors. Others visited Constantinople, and returned with copies of the works of Greek writers. When Constantinople fell to the Turks in 1453, Byzantine exiles flooded Italy with their knowledge of classical Greek literature. The result was a literary awakening that began in Italy and then spread beyond the Alps.

This interest in antiquity also manifested itself in the arts. Painters, sculptors, and architects sought their inspiration, not in the Christian art of the centuries immediately preceding them, but rather in the pagan art of the classical age. Naturally, they did not entirely abandon their own traditions, and for that reason Gothic art did influence their works. But the ideal of many Italian artists of the Renaissance was to rediscover the classical canons of beauty, and to apply them to their work.

This awakening of interest in classical learning coincided with Johan Gutenberg's invention of the movable-type printing press in 1439. Printing had long been employed in the form of woodcuts that were inked and pressed on paper. Gutenberg's invention had a profound impact on humanism. At first, the printing press was not seen as a means of popularizing literature. On the contrary, most of the early books printed were difficult to read, and were in either Latin or Greek. Furthermore, typography sought to imitate handwritten books, including the frequent abbreviations that copyists used at the time. (Gutenberg himself did not publicize his invention, for his purpose was to produce large numbers of books that he could then sell as expensive manuscripts. To that end, rather than simplifying the printed page, he made it as elaborate as any traditional manuscript.) For the early humanists, the printing press was an excellent medium for communication among scholars, or for duplicating the writings of antiquity, but not for popularizing their ideas. Those ideas remained the exclusive property of an intellectual aristocracy. With minor exceptions, the printing press was not used for communication to the masses until the time of the Reformation eighty years later.

In spite of this, the press did have an impact on the literature of the Renaissance. Books were now more accessible, and scholars became increasingly aware of the degree to which various manuscripts of the same work differed. Although earlier generations had been aware of these divergences, all they could do was to be very careful in the copying of manuscripts. But now it was possible to produce several hundreds of copies of a book, without any new errors creeping into them. If a scholar, by comparing several manuscripts, produced a reliable text of an ancient writing, and supervised its printing, that work would be of permanent value, for it would not have to be entrusted again to a multitude of copyists who might introduce new errors. Thus the discipline of textual criticism arose, whose purpose was to compare existing manuscripts, and to apply all the resources of historical research to the task of restoring the works of antiq-

A page of the Gutenberg Bible, which sought to imitate manuscript writing.

uity. Soon there were scholars working on "critical editions" of Cicero, Jerome, and the New Testament.

The discovery of the extent to which mistakes had crept into ancient texts led to doubts as to the authenticity of some of the texts themselves. Since the manuscripts were not entirely trustworthy, was it not possible that some of the writings that supposedly were very old were in truth the product of a later age?

Some of the most respected documents of the Middle Ages, when measured by the tools of historical research, were found to be spurious. Such was the case with the *Donation of Constantine*, in which the great emperor supposedly gave the popes jurisdiction over the West. The scholar Lorenzo Valla studied this document and came to the conclusion that its style and vocabulary proved that it was written long after the time of Constantine. Likewise, Valla offered strong arguments against the legend according to which the Apostles' Creed was composed by the apostles, each contributing a clause.

The consequences of these studies to the life of the church were not as immediate or as drastic as one might expect. Valla was a secretary to the pope, who does not seem to have minded Valla's studies and conclusions. The reason for this was that the results of such studies were circulated only among an intellectual aristocracy whose members were not interested in influencing the masses with their newly found knowledge. It would take some time for the notion to spread, that Christianity as it then existed was not what it had always been, and that a return to its roots was necessary. This notion would be a contributing factor to the Protestant Reformation.

A NEW VISION OF REALITY

Italy was going through a period of prosperity. In its principal cities there were financial resources for erecting great buildings and for adorning them with works of art. Sculptors, painters, and architects flocked to such places. Since the nobles and the rich bourgeoisie were the patrons of the arts, most of the works of this period were not created to extol the glories of heaven but rather of those who paid for them. Therefore art, which had up until that time been devoted almost exclusively to religious instruction and to the glory of God, turned its attention to human splendor. In the classical works of Greece and Rome, there had been an admiration for the human creature that medieval art seemed to forget, and which the painters and sculptors of the Renaissance now expressed in paint and stone. The Adam that Michelangelo painted in the Sistine Chapel, receiving from God's finger the power to rule over creation, is very different from the frail Adam of medieval manuscripts. He embodies the Renaissance view of what it means to be fully human, born to create, to leave one's imprint on the world.

This vision took flesh in Leonardo da Vinci. There were few areas of human endeavor into which this great genius of the Renaissance did not delve. Although today Leonardo is known primarily as a painter and sculptor, he also did significant research and work in engineering, jewelry making, ballistics, and anatomy. His goal—which coincided with the ideal of his time—was to be the universal man. His grand ideas for inventions that would channel rivers,

Leonardo da Vinci embodied the Renaissance ideal of the "universal man."

serve as new weapons, and allow people to fly and move underwater, never fully materialized. Many of his paintings remained unfinished, or did not go beyond the stage of preliminary sketches which are now valued as great artistic treasures. But in spite of the often fragmentary and unfinished nature of his work, Leonardo became the embodiment and symbol of the universal man that characterized the Renaissance.

That vision of humanity as having unlimited capabilities, both for good and for evil, was the main theme of Pico della Mirandola, one of the authors of the period. According to Pico, we have been given by God all kinds of seeds, so that we can decide which we are to sow within ourselves, and therefore what we become. Those who choose the "vegetative" seed, or the "sensitive," will be little more than a plant or a brute. But any who choose the "intellectual" seed, and cultivate it in themselves, "will be angels and children of God." And if, dissatisfied with being creatures, such persons turn toward the center of their own soul, "their spirit, joined with God in its dark solitude, will arise above all these things." All this lead Pico to exclaim, in a strange word of praise that epitomizes the Renaissance view of human potentiality, "Who can help but admire this strange chameleon that we are?"

THE POPES OF THE RENAISSANCE

Although the Renaissance was for Italy a time of great prosperity, it was also a time of upheaval. The Babylonian Captivity of the papacy in Avignon, and the Great Schism that followed, had affected Italy more directly than the rest of Europe. Italy had been the almost-constant battlefield for rival popes, or for the nobles and republics that supported one side or the other. At the time of the Renaissance, conflict between the old aristocracy and republican sentiments was constant, and therefore in cities such as Florence and Venice there were repeated upheavals that often led to armed encounters, not only in the cities themselves, but also in the surrounding areas. To this were added the constant intrigues of foreign powers—particularly France and Germany—which vied for influence in the region.

It was within this context of prosperity, intrigues, turmoil, and Renaissance ideals that the papacy existed during the final generations before the Reformation. When we last spoke of the popes, Eugene IV had finally asserted his authority over the Council of Basel. His reign was marked by his efforts to embellish the city of Rome, to which he drew artists such as Fra Angelico and Donatello. This was an early indication that the spirit of the Renaissance was taking hold of the papacy. Since then and until the outbreak of the Protestant Reformation, the goals and ideals of most popes would be those of the Renaissance: most of them were enthusiasts of the arts, who used their reign to attract to Rome the best artists, and to adorn the city with palaces, churches, and monuments worthy of its place as the capital of Christendom. Some were profoundly captivated by literature, and did much to enlarge the papal library. In all of these artistic endeavors—and particularly in the enormous undertaking that was the construction of Saint Peter's Basilica—the popes of the Renaissance invested much of the financial resources of the church. And, not content with that, many devised new sources of income that would allow them to continue their aggrandizement of Rome and its art.

But not all the popes of the Renaissance focused their interest on the arts. Others were more like warlords who spent most of their time in military campaigns. Still others sought to increase their power through intrigue and diplomacy. Most of them were carried away by the spirit of the age, as could be seen in their love of pomp, despotic power, and sensual pleasure.

Pope Eugene IV was succeeded by Nicholas V, who spent most of his pontificate (1447–1455) trying to gain political dominance for Rome over other Italian states. His goal was to turn the city into the intellectual capital of Europe, and to that end he sought to attract the best authors and artists. His personal library was reputed to be the best in Europe. He was ruthless with those who opposed his power, and had several of them executed. The fall of Constantinople took place during his reign, and he hoped to use the occasion to promote a great crusade that would enhance his prestige throughout Europe. But in this he failed, for his call went unheeded.

His successor was Calixtus III (1455–1458), the first pope of the Spanish family of Borja—known in Italy as *Borgia*. All that he took from the ideals of the Renaissance was the dream of becoming a great secular prince. With the pretext that it was necessary to unify Italy in order to resist a possible Turkish attack, he paid more attention to military campaigns than to his priestly duties. During his reign, nepotism reached new heights. One of the many relatives on whom he heaped honors was his grandson Rodrigo, whom he made a cardinal, and who would later become the infamous Alexander VI.

The next pope, Pius II (1458–1464), was the last of the Renaissance popes to take his office seriously. He commissioned Nicholas of Cusa to develop a plan for the reformation of the church, but this came to naught, mostly due to the opposition of the cardinals and other prelates. His achievements were not great, but at least he did not turn the papacy into a means to increase his power or that of his family. As a scholar, Pius began, but never completed, a vast *Cosmography*, whose view of the world would later lead Christopher Columbus in his attempt to reach the Indies by sailing West.

Paul II (1464–1471) was an opportunist who, upon learning that his uncle had been made pope (Eugene IV), had decided that an ecclesiastical career was more promising than his current occupation in trade. His main interest was collecting works of art—particularly jewelry and silver. His penchant for luxury became proverbial, and his concubines were publicly acknowledged in the papal court. His main project was the recovery of the architectural and monumental glory of pagan Rome, to which he devoted a great deal of wealth and attention. According to some chroniclers, he died of apoplexy, as a consequence of his excesses.

Sixtus IV (1471–1484) bought the papacy by promising gifts and privileges to the cardinals. During his reign, corruption and nepotism reached new heights. The main thrust of his policy was to enrich his family, particularly his five nephews. One of these, Giuliano della Rovere, would later be pope under the name of Julius II. Under Sixtus, the church became a family business, and all Italy was involved in a series of wars and conspiracies whose sole purpose was to enrich the pope's nephews. His favorite nephew, Pietro Riario, was twenty-six years old when he was made a cardinal, patriarch of Constantinople, and archbishop of Florence. Another, Girolamo Riario, plotted the murder of a member of the Medici family who was killed before the altar while saying mass. When the dead man's relatives took revenge by hanging the priest who had murdered their kinsman, the pope excommunicated the entire city of Florence and declared war on it. In order to support his intrigues and the enormous expenses of his nephews and their supporters, he imposed a heavy tax on wheat. The best grain was sold to fill the papal coffers, while the Roman populace ate bread of the lowest quality. In spite of all this, posterity has forgotten most of Sixtus's misdeeds, and remembers him mostly for the Sistine Chapel, which is named after him.

Before his election, Innocent VIII (1484–1492) made a solemn vow not to name more than one member of his family to high office, and to put the Roman see in order. But as soon as he was made pope he declared that, since papal power was supreme, he was not bound by his oath, especially since it had been given under pressure. He was the first pope to acknowledge several of his illegitimate children, on whom he heaped honors and riches. The sale of indulgences became a shameless business proposition, under the management of one of his sons. In 1484 he ordered that Christendom be cleansed of witches, and the result was the death of hundreds of innocent women.

After Innocent's death, Rodrigo Borgia bought the cardinals' votes and became pope under the name of Alexander VI (1492–1503). Under him, papal corruption reached its peak. He was a strong and implacable man, who was said to commit publicly all the capital sins—except gluttony, for his digestion was not good. A chronicler affirms that the people used to say: "Alexander is ready to sell the keys, the altars, and even Christ himself. He is within his rights, since he bought them." While Europe trembled before the threat of the Turks, the pope had secret dealings with the sultan. His concubines, who were legally the wives of others in his court, gave him several children whom he acknowledged publicly. The most famous of these were Cesare and Lucrezia Borgia. Even though the worst stories told about this family are probably untrue, those that are undeniable are still enough to convict the pope of corruption and boundless lust for power. Italy, bathed in blood due to his plots and his wars, was ready to believe the worst of him, and the prestige of the papacy suffered accordingly.

Alexander VI died unexpectedly—some said that he took by mistake a potion that he had prepared for someone else. His son Cesare, who had hoped to take hold of the papacy at his father's death, was in bed suffering from the same disease—or the same poison—and was therefore unable to set his plans in motion. The election thus fell on Pius III, a man of reforming zeal who undertook the difficult task of bringing peace to Italy. But he died after being pope for twenty-six days, and the new pope was a worthy successor of Alexander VI.

Julius II (1503–1513), who had been made a cardinal by his uncle Sixtus IV, took that name to indicate that his model was not a Christian saint, but rather Julius Caesar. Like most of the popes of that period, he was a patron of the arts. It was during his pontificate that Michelangelo finished painting the Sistine Chapel, and Raphael decorated the Vatican with his famous frescoes. But Julius's favorite pastime was war. He reorganized the papal guard, dressed it in colorful uniforms that Michelangelo is said to have designed, and led it to battle. His military and diplomatic abilities were such that some even thought that he might finally achieve the unification of Italy, with Julius as its leader.

The infamous Borgia pope, Alexander VI.

France and Germany opposed these plans, but Julius defeated them both in diplomacy and on the battlefield. In 1513, death put an end to the projects of this pope, whom his contemporaries called "the Terrible."

He was succeeded by a son of Lorenzo the Magnificent, Giovanni de Medici, who took the name of Leo X (1513–1521). Following his father's example, Leo was a patron of the arts. He also tried to consolidate the political and military gains of Julius II. In this he failed, and in 1516 he was forced to sign an agreement with Francis I of France that gave the king enormous authority in French ecclesiastical affairs. His passion for the arts overshadowed any religious or pastoral concerns, and his great dream was to complete the great basilica of St. Peter, in Rome. The financing of that project was one of the purposes of the sale of indulgences that provoked Luther's protest. Thus, the man occupying the papacy when the Protestant Reformation began was unequal to the challenge before him.

SUGGESTED READINGS

Aziz S. Atiya. *History of Eastern Christianity.* Notre Dame: University of Notre Dame Press, 1967. Oxford: Oxford University Press, 2003.

Renate Blumenfeld-Kisinski. *Poets, Saints and Visionaries of the Great Schism, 1378–1417.* University Park: Pennsylvania University Press, 2006.

Henry Chadwick. *East and West: The Making of a Rift in the Church from Apostolic Times until the Council of Florence.* Oxford University Press, 2003.

G. R. Evans. *John Wyclif: Myth and Reality.* Downers Grove: InterVarsity, 2005.

Justo L. González. *A History of Christian Thought,* Vol. 2. Nashville: Abingdon, 1971.

Carole Hildebrand. *The Crusades: Islamic Perspectives.* New York: Routledge, 2000.

David Knowles. *From Pachomius to Ignatius: A Study of the Constitutional History of Religious Orders.* Oxford: Clarendon Press, 1966.

Gordon Leff. *Heresy in the Later Middle Ages.* 2 vols. Manchester: Manchester University Press, 1967.

Gordon Leff. *Medieval Thought: St. Augustine to Ockham.* Baltimore: Penguin Books, 1958.

Christine Meek and Catherine Lawless. *Pawns or Players? Studies on Medieval and Early Modern Women.* Dublin: Four Corners, 2003.

H. St. L. B. Moss. *The Birth of the Middle Ages: 395–814.* Oxford: University Press, 1935.

Thomas F. X. Noble and Julia M. H. Smith, eds. *The Cambridge History of Christianity: Volume 3: Early Medieval Christianities, c.600–c.1100.* Cambridge, UK: Cambridge University Press, 2008.

George Ostrogorsky. *History of the Byzantine State.* New Brunswick: Rutgers University Press, 1957.

Roberto Ridolfi. *The Life of Girolamo Savonarola.* London: Routledge and Kegan Paul, 1959.

Miri Rubin and Walter Simons, eds. *The Cambridge History of Christianity: Vol. 4: Christianity in Western Europe, c. 1100–c.1500.* Cambridge, UK: Cambridge University Press, 2009.

R. V. Sellers. *The Council of Chalcedon: A Historical and Doctrinal Survey.* London: S.P.C.K., 1953.

Desmond Seward. *The Hundred Years War.* New York: Atheneum, 1978.

Barbara W. Tuchman. *A Distant Mirror: The Calamitous 14th Century.* New York: Alfred A. Knopf, 1978.

Herbert B. Workman. *The Evolution of the Monastic Ideal.* London: Charles H. Kelly, 1913.

PART IV

THE BEGINNINGS OF COLONIAL CHRISTIANITY

Chronology

Events	Date
†Henry the Navigator	1460
Surrender of Granada; Columbus' first voyage	1492
Vasco da Gama travels to India	1497–1498
Alvares Cabral discovers Brazil	1500
Portuguese settle in Goa	1510
Balboa reaches the Pacific	1513
Ponce de León to Florida; Siege and fall of Tenochtitlan	1521
Capture of Atahualpa	1532
De Soto reaches the Mississippi	1541
†Francis Xavier	1552
Villegagnon settles in Brazil	1555
Portuguese settle in Macao	1557
Jean Ribaut in Florida	1562
†Las Casas	1566
†Luis Beltrán	1581
Ricci in Beijing	1601
†Toribio Alfonso de Mogrovejo	1606
†Pedro Claver	1654
Jesuits expelled from Spanish colonies	1767
Tupac Amaru rebellion	1780

NOTE: Since this period coincides chronologically with others discussed in the second volume, the reader may refer to the chronologies in that volume for dates of popes, rulers, and events in Europe.

36

Spain and the New World

> Because of your cruelty and oppression of these innocent people, you
> are in mortal sin. You live and die in mortal sin. Who gave you the right
> to subject these Indians to cruel and terrible slavery? Who gave you the
> right to make war on people who lived in peace and quiet in their own
> lands? . . . Are they not human?
>
> ANTONIO DE MONTESINOS

Toward the end of the Middle Ages, and during the time of the Protestant
Reformation, Spain and Portugal began a process of expansion that would
have enormous impact on the subsequent history of the church. Protestant
church historians, preoccupied with the momentous events that were taking
place in Europe at the time, often forget that it was precisely during this period
that Catholicism enjoyed its most rapid expansion. The same is true of many
Catholic historians, for whom the Catholic Reformation—often called the
Counter-Reformation—takes center stage. Such an omission, which was perhaps defensible at an earlier time, became inexcusable in the twentieth century
after the Second Vatican Council, and even more so in the twenty-first. At that
council, and in the life of the church thereafter, the impact of Roman Catholics
from Latin America, Asia, and Africa has been prominent. Therefore, in order
to understand the present course of Roman Catholicism it is necessary to understand the forces that shaped it in those lands.

THE NATURE OF THE SPANISH ENTERPRISE

When, on October 12, 1492, Christopher Columbus and his companions set
foot in the New World, neither he nor anyone in Europe had the remotest idea
of the significance of that event. But as soon as Ferdinand and Isabella had an
inkling of the vast lands and huge sums that could be involved, they took steps
to limit Columbus's power. Their reason for doing this was not simple greed,
but the experience of long years of struggle to assert their authority in Spain.
There, with the help of the bourgeoisie, they were finally managing to curb

the power of the potentates, both lay and clerical, who had wrecked the earlier reign of Isabella's brother, Henry IV of Castile. Therefore, they feared the rise of similar magnates in the New World, and their policies were aimed at curbing them. Columbus, as Admiral of the Ocean Sea, Viceroy and Governor General, and as beneficiary of one-tenth of all trade with the New World, would have been able to refuse obedience to the crown, and therefore the sovereigns could not grant him such wealth and power.

In the New World, this usually resulted in the crown enacting laws for the protection of those whom Columbus mistakenly dubbed "Indians." Ferdinand and Isabella feared that, if the Spanish conquistadores were not curbed in their exploitation of the Indians, they would become powerful feudal lords with the same independent spirit as the grandees of Spain. This gave rise to constant conflicts between the crown and the Spanish settlers. Repeatedly, laws were enacted in Spain that were not obeyed in the New World. The net result was that the Indians were exploited and decimated, while Spaniards on both sides of the ocean deliberated as to what was the best course to follow.

Religious policies in the new lands followed the patterns that had been established during the Middle Ages. In their wars against the Moors in Spain, Christian Spaniards had drawn on the ideals and principles of the Crusades, and now they applied the same principles to the conquest of the Indian "infidels." Also, shortly before the discovery of the New World, Castile had conquered the Canary Islands and Granada, and the popes had granted the crown extraordinary powers over the church in the newly conquered lands. These precedents were now applied in the New World. In a series of bulls from 1493 to 1510, Popes Alexander VI and Julius II gave enormous authority to the Spanish crown. The kings of Spain were given the right of *patronato real*—"royal patronage"—over the church in the new lands. As this evolved, it meant that the kings had the right to nominate—and therefore practically to appoint—bishops and other high ecclesiastical officers for the New World. With few exceptions, the crown was also to administer tithes and other offerings, and to be responsible for all the expenses of the church. The result was that the church in Spanish America had very few direct dealings with Rome, and became practically a national church under the leadership of the Spanish kings and their appointees. Although some of the bishops selected by the crown were faithful pastors of their flocks, most of them, especially in later years, were political appointees who had no understanding of, nor concern for, the plight of the masses in Spanish America.

There was, however, another side to the church in the New World. Those who carried out missionary work—usually Franciscans, Dominicans, or Jesuits—lived among the people, and knew their plight. The vows of poverty of these missionaries, and the simplicity of their lifestyle, made it possible for them

Isabella and Ferdinand met with Columbus in Granada, and granted him vast powers and privileges which they would later rescind.

to live among the Indians, and to see the disastrous results of colonial policies. Thus, many friars became the defenders of the Indians against the depredations of European settlers. In the early stages of the enterprise, the Dominicans took the lead in the defense of the Indians. In the eighteenth century, that defense was one of the factors contributing to the suppression of the Jesuits, first by the Spanish and other rulers in Europe, and eventually even by the pope (see Vol. 2, chapter 19). And all the while, far above this church that showed concern for the poor, there was the hierarchical church, led by those who owed their posts to their contacts in the Spanish court. Thus, from the very beginning, there were two faces to the Roman Catholic Church in Spanish America: on the one hand, most of the hierarchy and of the diocesan or secular clergy, and some friars, supported the exploitation of the native population for the benefit of the Spanish settlers, while on the other hand many friars criticized such exploitation and became defenders of the oppressed native population.

In the nineteenth century, when the old colonies began their struggle for independence, the church would be divided along similar lines, and for that reason, while most of the bishops were loyalists, many parish priests and friars cast their lot with the rebels. In the latter half of the twentieth century and well into the twenty-first, the revival of Roman Catholicism in Latin America, and the leading role it took in many social struggles, would be due in part to the inroads that the church of the poor was making among the hierarchy. Thus the "two faces of the church" that began taking shape in the early stages of colonization would continue to exist side-by-side for centuries.

THE PROTEST

The first open protest against the exploitation of the Indians was a sermon preached in Santo Domingo in 1511 by the Dominican Antonio Montesinos, quoted at the beginning of this chapter, and in which he concluded that the settlers were no closer to salvation than were "the Moors or Turks." This sermon did not express only Montesinos's views, for his fellow Dominicans had commissioned him to raise the voice of protest and warning against the exploitation of the native population. Local authorities tried to silence Montesinos, but his fellow Dominicans rallied to his support, and eventually the dispute reached the court in Spain.

Among those who heard Montesinos was Bartolomé de Las Casas. He had settled in Santo Domingo almost ten years earlier, and at some point had been ordained a priest—probably the first ever to be ordained in the New World. But he was not overly troubled by the exploitation of the Indians. In fact, he himself held several of them in *encomienda*.

The system of *encomiendas*—trusts—was the main abuse against which the Dominicans protested. It was forbidden to enslave the Indians. But, supposedly in order to civilize them and to teach them Christian doctrine, groups of them were "entrusted" to a settler. In exchange for the settler's guidance, the Indians were to work for him. The result was even worse than outright slavery, for those who held trusts—the *encomenderos*—had no investment in the Indians, and therefore no reason to be concerned for their well-being.

Las Casas had an *encomienda* when Montesinos began preaching against this practice. When the debate broke out, he chose to remain silent. Then, on Pentecost 1514, he had a radical change of heart. He gave up his *encomienda*, and from that point on openly declared that Christian faith was incompatible with the exploitation of the Indians by the Spanish. With Montesinos, he traveled to Spain, and convinced authorities to appoint a commission to investigate the matter. When he found that the members of the commission would listen only to the *encomenderos*—those who held Indians "in trust"—he broke with them and returned to Spain. Thus began a long career of repeated crossings of the Atlantic, obtaining in Spain legislation protecting the Indians, and finding in the New World that the authorities were unwilling or unable to apply such legislation. At one point, he tried to set an example of pacific evangelization in Venezuela. But neighboring settlers provoked violence, and finally the Indians rebelled. He then returned to Santo Domingo, where he finally joined the Dominican order. Further travels took him to Central America, Mexico, and again to Spain. He had many sympathizers in the Spanish court, and was made bishop of Chiapas, in southern Mexico. After many clashes with the *encomenderos* in his flock, he resigned and returned to Spain. There he spent thirty-nine years of advocacy for the Indians, partly through direct appeals and partly through his books. He died in 1566, when he was ninety-two years old.

Las Casas's books caused quite a stir, and many came to doubt the morality of the entire Spanish enterprise in the New World. But eventually the vested interests of those who profited from the colonial empire prevailed. In 1552, while Las Casas still lived, his books were banned in Peru. By the middle of the following century, they were included in the Inquisition's list of forbidden books.

Another Dominican who questioned the Spanish enterprise in the New World was Francisco de Vitoria, a professor of theology at the University of Salamanca. Disturbed by the news of the conquest of Peru, and of the ruthless exploitation on the natives, their lands and mines, Vitoria gave a series of lectures questioning the right of the Spanish to take the territories of the Indians.

The main result of the protests of Las Casas, Vitoria, and others were the *New Laws of Indies,* enacted by Charles V in 1542. These laws limited the power of the Spanish settlers over the Indians, and outlawed war against any Indians who were willing to live in peace with the Spanish. They were largely ignored in the New World. In Peru, the settlers openly revolted. Eventually, the *New Laws* were forgotten. Throughout the colonial period, however, there were in Spanish America Christians who protested against the exploitation of the Indians, and who devoted their lives to the betterment of their lot.

THE CARIBBEAN

In his second voyage, in 1493, Columbus took with him seven missionaries whose appointed task was to convert the Indians. But when they arrived in Hispaniola at the small fort that Columbus had built during his first voyage, they found distressing news. Their mistreatment, exploitation, and rape by the Spaniards had provoked the Indians to revolt, and they had destroyed the fort and killed the entire garrison. Columbus ordered the "pacification" of the island, giving his lieutenants instructions to cut the ears and nose of any who would not submit. Soon, however, there were also rebels among the Spaniards. Reports of mismanagement and tyranny in the colony provoked Isabella to action, and Columbus was deposed and taken back to Spain in chains.

Under Columbus's successors, things were no better for the Indians. They were ordered to pay a quarterly tax to the Spaniards in gold or cotton. Those who were unwilling or unable to pay the tax were enslaved. The Indians then took to the mountains, where they were hunted with dogs. As to the missionaries, they seem to have done little more than take some of the sons of Indian chiefs into their homes, there to educate them as Christians. In 1503, orders arrived from Spain that the Indians were to live in their own villages, each with a representative of the Spanish government and a chaplain. This was done in some cases. But then those able to work were marched off to mine for gold, and kept away from their families for months. In the end, forced labor, diseases imported by the Spanish, and mass suicides destroyed most of the native population. Similar events took place in Puerto Rico, Cuba, Jamaica, and several of the lesser islands.

The loss of Indian labor led the Spanish to import black slaves. The first arrived from Spain in 1502, but for another few years Indian labor was still too cheap to encourage black slavery. In 1516, Las Casas, in his zeal for the well-being of the Indians, suggested that slaves be imported from Africa. He soon recanted, and became a defender of blacks as well as of Indians. But by 1553 tens of thousands of Africans were being imported as slaves. It is significant that the few theologians who objected did so, not on the basis of opposition to slavery, but rather because they had doubts as to how the profits should be distributed. In any case, what happened in the Caribbean was repeated throughout the Spanish colonies. Wherever the Indian population was scarce, black African slaves took their place. To this day, blacks are more numerous in areas where the Indian population was low in the sixteenth century.

MEXICO

In his march to Tenochtitlan—the capital city of the Aztec empire—Cortez destroyed the idols of the various tribes he visited. He did not do this, however, in the case of the Tlascalans, who were a powerful tribe whose support he needed for the conquest of the Aztec empire. Thus, an odd combination of political expediency and fanatical zeal set the tone for Spanish religious policies in Mexico.

Although two priests accompanied the original expedition, these were clearly not enough. Cortez, who in spite of his greed and violence was a sincere Catholic, requested from Charles V that mendicant friars, and not secular priests or prelates, be sent to Mexico. His argument was that the friars would live in poverty, and would be able to set a good example for the natives, whereas the secular priests and prelates would live in scandalous luxury and would not be actively interested in the conversion of the Indians. In response to this request, twelve Franciscans went to Mexico. On their arrival, Cortez knelt and kissed their hands. But their task was not easy, for there was great resentment against the Spanish and their religion among the Indians. On the other hand, it seemed clear to the Indians that the Christian God had defeated their own gods, and therefore many Indians, while not forgetting the violence being done against them, rushed to request baptism, thus hoping to gain the support of the powerful Christian God.

Little by little, the twelve original friars, and many others who followed them, gained the respect and even the love of their Indian flock. There were times when the Indians rioted upon learning that their priest was being sent elsewhere, and forced the authorities to change their plans.

There were many conflicts and disputes in the nascent Mexican church. The Franciscan missionaries baptized any who wished to receive the holy rite, requesting only that they knew that there is only one God and that Jesus is our redeemer, and that they could recite the Lord's Prayer and the Hail Mary. In some cases, even these minimal requirements were waived. There were reports of missionaries baptizing hundreds in a single day, sometimes merely sprinkling several of them at the same time. The secular priests—that is, those who did not belong to monastic orders—had reason to be jealous of the friars' success, although most of them did little for the instruction of the Indians. In any case, they accused the friars of oversimplifying baptism—not of lowering the requirements, as one might expect, but of omitting certain elements in the administration of the rite itself. Eventually, the dispute was settled by Pope Paul III, who declared that there had been no sin in the previous simplified baptismal rites, but that from that time on certain directives must be followed. But even after this papal intervention the strife between the friars and the seculars continued for generations.

The first bishop—and then archbishop—of Mexico was a Franciscan, Juan de Zumárraga. He was convinced that the church was in need of reformation, and that this would be achieved by proper instruction of the faithful and by the development of an educated priesthood. With this in mind, he had a printing press taken to Mexico—the first in the Western hemisphere—and with it printed many books for the instruction of the Indians. Among these was included a book whose author Zumárraga did not name, but who was later condemned by the Spanish Inquisition as a Protestant. Zumárraga also took steps for the founding of the University of Mexico; and he was an ardent defender of the Indians against any who would exploit them, no matter how exalted.

However, like most Christians of his time, this otherwise open-minded bishop had little tolerance for what he considered heresy. In 1536, he was made "apostolic inquisitor" for New Spain—the name then given to Mexico. Between that time and 1543, 131 people were tried for heresy. While most of the accused were Spaniards, thirteen were Indians. The most famous of these was chief Carlos Chichimectecotl, who had studied with the Franciscans, and was accused of worshiping idols, living in concubinage, and lacking respect for priests. He confessed that he lived with his niece. A search of his home produced some idols that he said he kept for historical curiosity. No one had seen him worship them. The case would probably have ended in some minor penalties had not a witness declared that he had heard Chichimectecotl declare that the religion of Christians was doubtful, since many of them were promiscuous drunkards whose priests could not control them. On that basis, he was condemned to be burned at the stake.

Since Chichimectecotl was an educated man, his trial renewed the arguments of those who opposed the education of the Indians. Generally, their argument was not that Indians were incapable of learning. On the contrary, what was said was that if they learned how to read and write they would be able to communicate among themselves from one ocean to the other, and that this would make them dangerous. This fear lay behind the low level of education given to the Indians for several generations. It was also the main reason why even the most progressive Spaniards had doubts about ordaining them. In 1539, a gathering of church leaders under the presidency of Bishop Zumárraga opened to Indians the possibility of receiving the four lowest levels of holy orders, but none that had sacramental functions. Even less progressive than the Franciscans, the Dominicans declared that Indians should not be ordained or educated at all. The same spirit prevailed in monasteries. The Franciscans, again the most open-minded in such matters, allowed Indians to live in their monastic communities, and to wear a special brown cassock. But they were not permitted to make vows, nor to become even lay brothers. If one of them was not considered fit by the Spanish Franciscans, they simply expelled him, no matter how long he had been part of the community. In 1588, Philip II's royal order opened both priestly orders and monastic vows to Indians. But in 1636 King Philip IV lamented that too many "mongrels, bastards and other defective people" were being ordained.

It is within such a setting that the legend and devotion of the Virgin of Guadalupe must be understood. The legend states that the Virgin appeared to an Indian, Juan Diego, with a message for Zumárraga. The bishop did not believe what the Indian told him, until a series of miracles forced him to believe. As a result, and under direct instructions from the Virgin, a chapel was built at the place of the apparitions. Historians have searched in vain for any indication in the records of Zumárraga and his contemporaries that any part of this story is true. Furthermore, an early Christian chronicler declares that the place where the Virgin supposedly appeared was the very hill where the Indians worshiped a goddess called *Tonantzin*, the "mother of the gods," and that the Indians simply continued worshiping the old goddess under a new name. But no matter what may be the events behind it, the legend itself is a vindication of the oppressed Indian over against the Spanish bishop. In the end, the bishop had to do what the Indian told him. Ever since, the Virgin of Guadalupe has been more than an object of devotion. She became the symbol and rallying point of Mexican national sentiment against any form of foreign intervention.

The Aztec empire did not include all of present-day Mexico. But its downfall led many of the neighboring states to submit to the Spanish. Toward the south, there were the remnants of the ancient Mayan civilization. Their conquest took years, mostly due to the rugged terrain and the dense vegetation. It was not until 1560 that Spanish lordship over Yucatan was sufficiently established to name a bishop for that area.

After the initial conquest, the Spanish continued moving north in quest of two illusory goals. The first, a sea pass connecting the Atlantic to the Pacific, led them to explore the Gulf of California, for during a long time it was believed that Baja California was an island, and that the Gulf of California somehow joined the Atlantic Ocean. The other chimera was the "Seven Golden Cities" of which some Indians spoke to the Spanish, and which drew the Spanish almost directly north, toward New Mexico. At a later time, the threat of the French advancing from Louisiana, and of the Russians moving down the Pacific Coast, led the Spanish to settle in Texas and in California.

In Baja California, missionaries were more successful than colonizers and explorers. The first who settled in the area, first on the eastern shore of the Gulf of California, and then on the peninsula itself, were the Jesuits. Outstanding among them was Eusebio Francisco Kino, an Italian by birth, who founded a chain of missions extending far beyond the limits of Spanish rule, into present-day Arizona. When he died in 1711, he was planning a mission among the Apaches. But in 1767 the Jesuits were expelled from all Spanish territories. Some of their missions were entrusted to Franciscans, Dominicans, and others. Many were simply abandoned.

In California, Franciscan missionaries centered their efforts on Alta California—what is now the state of California. In the eighteenth century, when the authorities organized an expedition to explore and settle the area, the Franciscan Junípero Serra joined it. He then founded a long chain of missions, many far beyond the reach of Spanish protection. In those areas where the Indians had to live under Spanish rule, Serra was a zealous defender of their rights vis-à-vis the Spanish. But this did not free him from the prejudice, paternalism, and sometimes even the cruelty, that characterized most of his countrymen, with the result that, while today many extol Serra's work, others view him as simply one more example of the religious justification of genocide.

But the Franciscans' main thrust was directly north, where conquistadores searched for the fabled Seven Cities. Sometimes with the conquistadores, at other times after them, but most often before them, Franciscans crossed the center of Mexico and entered New Mexico. There the Spanish founded in 1610 the *Villa Real de la Santa Fe de San Francisco de Asís* ("The Royal City of the Holy Faith of Saint Francis of Assisi")—now known simply as Santa Fe. Twenty years later, fifty missionaries were pastors to sixty thousand baptized Indians in New Mexico. The great Indian uprising of 1680 killed some four

The Virgin of Guadalupe became the rallying point of Mexican national sentiment against all foreign intervention.

hundred Spaniards, among whom were thirty-two Franciscans. When the Spanish undertook the reconquest of the area, the Franciscans returned with them.

Spanish expansion from Mexico was also directed westward, across the Pacific. Magellan had visited the Philippines in 1521, and was killed by the natives of that archipelago. Later, a series of expeditions were sent from Mexico. Finally, under the leadership of Miguel López de Legazpi, the conquest of the islands was undertaken in 1565. There the Spanish found many Muslims, whom they called *Moros* after the Moors who had ruled Spain for centuries. These, and the Chinese in some of the islands, offered strong resistance. But eventually the entire archipelago was conquered. Once again, policies were followed that were similar to those applied in the Western hemisphere, and which provoked great resentment among the original inhabitants of the islands. The Spanish had hoped that these islands would become a stepping stone for missions into the Far East; but they were unwilling to educate the Filipinos, and for that reason this project failed.

GOLDEN CASTILE

The area that is now Central America and Panama had drawn the attention of Spanish authorities from an early date. Columbus had sailed along its coast, hoping to find a passage to the West. By 1509, the first attempts at conquest and colonization were undertaken. These failed until an adventurer called Vasco Núñez de Balboa overthrew the appointed leader and took charge of the enterprise. In contrast with most other conquistadores, Balboa knew how to establish cordial relationships with the Indians, although he too was capable of atrocities. It seems that the main reason why he befriended the Indians was that he was convinced that this was the best way to obtain gold and women from them. Thanks to Indian help, he was able to send gold to Spain, hoping to legitimize his rule. And with the same help he reached the Pacific Ocean, which he called "South Sea" because in that particular area of Panama the Pacific is south of the Caribbean.

Balboa's move in sending gold to Spain backfired. Authorities there decided that this land was too valuable to be entrusted to Balboa, and another leader was appointed to the colony, which was now named *Castilla del Oro*—or Golden Castile. The two men clashed, and eventually the new governor had Balboa executed. His policy was to force the Indians to produce gold. Many were distributed among the colonizers in *encomiendas*. Others were killed because they would not or could not produce as much gold as was demanded. Finally, most of the Indians fled, and fought as guerillas against the conquistadores. Since there were no crops, food became scarce. More than five hundred Spaniards died, many of them of hunger. The bishop who had been appointed to oversee the church in the colony, as well as the Franciscan missionaries, returned to Spain in protest against the poor management of the colony. It was decades before there was any semblance of order.

Probably the most interesting character in the early history of the church in Central America was father Juan de Estrada Rávago, who was a renegade Franciscan, ambitious conquistador, failed courtier, and benevolent missionary. He was ready to return to Spain, in obedience to a royal decree ordering all renegade friars to leave the colonies, when he learned that a proposed expedition to Costa Rica was in need of funds. He provided them and joined the expedition, of which he eventually became the head. He learned the language of the Indians and, with a single exception, refrained from violence against them. He traveled throughout the area teaching the Christian faith, baptizing people, and building churches. With his own resources he bought clothes, food and seeds for both Indians and settlers. Twelve Franciscans from Mexico joined him, and the church developed rapidly.

By the end of the sixteenth century, most of the original inhabitants of Central America called themselves Christian. But there were still vast areas that the Spanish had not explored, where the Indians kept their ancient religions and government. In supposedly Christianized areas, priests were scarce, and their work was greatly hampered by the resentment provoked by the conquistadores. Golden Castile never produced great amounts of the precious metal, and therefore Spain paid little attention to it.

FLORIDA

From an early date, the Spanish were aware of lands north of Cuba. In 1513, Juan Ponce de León, governor of Puerto Rico, received a royal charter authorizing him to explore and colonize the land of *Bimini*, where there was rumored to exist a fountain whose waters restored youth, or at least produced wonderful cures. Ponce's expedition landed in Florida, so named because they took possession in the name of the king on Easter—*Pascua Florida*. After exploring the coasts both along the Atlantic and in the Gulf, and some violent encounters with the Indians, the expedition returned to Puerto Rico. Several years later, Ponce de León organized a second expedition. But he was wounded by the Indians and withdrew to Cuba, where he died.

Other expeditions fared no better. One in 1528 was wiped out by the Indians. Eight years later, four survivors appeared in Mexico, after having walked halfway across the continent. Hernando de Soto explored the area in 1539 and 1540, but did not attempt to colonize it. Another colonial enterprise undertaken twenty years later was abandoned after two years of hardship and little success.

It was the presence of the French in the area that finally forced the Spanish to invest the resources necessary to take possession of it. In 1562, French settlements were started in Florida and South Carolina under the leadership of Jean Ribaut. To make matters worse from the Spanish point of view, most of the French settlers were Protestants. In reaction to this invasion of lands supposedly granted to Spain by the popes, the Spanish government commissioned Pedro Menéndez de Avilés to destroy the settlements. He attacked the French with a powerful squadron. Many fled inland, where they were eventually killed by the Indians. The Spanish captured the rest, and put 132 men to the sword. Only women and children under fifteen years of age were spared. Ribaut, who was absent at the time, was shipwrecked and surrendered to the Spanish, who executed him and more than seventy others who had survived the shipwreck. Menéndez de Avilés then founded the city of Saint Augustine, which became his center of operations.

Ribaut and his companions were avenged. A Frenchman who was a close friend of Ribaut secretly prepared an expedition that landed at the exact place of the earlier massacre, captured a number of Spaniards, and hanged them. Menéndez de Avilés had declared that he had killed Ribaut and his company, "not as Frenchmen, but as Lutherans. " Now the French left a sign that said their victims had been killed "not as Spaniards, but as traitors, thieves, and murderers." Then, before reinforcements could arrive from Saint Augustine, they sailed for France.

From Florida, and now due to the threat of the English, who were showing interest in the New World, the Spanish moved on to Guale (Georgia), Santa Elena (the Carolinas), and Ajacán (Virginia).

In all these lands most of the Spanish were either military or missionaries. These missionaries, mostly Jesuits, with some Franciscans and Dominicans, had to work against enormous difficulties. The Spanish had provoked the hostility of the Indians, and therefore many missionaries were killed as soon as they lacked the protection of Spanish arms. The settlements and missions north of Florida were ephemeral. In 1763, the Spanish ceded Florida to England in exchange for Havana, which the British had taken. Twenty years later, Florida was restored to Spanish rule. Finally, in 1819, it was formally ceded to the United States, which had invaded the area.

Of the ancient Spanish missions in that vast land, nothing remained but the memory, some scattered ruins, and the bones of the missionaries who gave up their lives in a cause that their fellow citizens had made well-nigh impossible.

COLOMBIA AND VENEZUELA

Columbus had visited the coast of South America on his second voyage. The conquest of the coast of present-day Colombia was begun in 1508, but failed. It was begun anew in 1525, with the founding of Santa Marta by Rodrigo de Bastidas. Bastidas was convinced that Indians should be treated humanely, and for that reason the other settlers forced him to return to Hispaniola. Then began a wave of terror against the Indians, trying to force them to tell the secret location of El Dorado—another of those incredible fables that the conquistadores believed. With Santa Marta as their base of operations, the Spanish moved west, where they founded Cartagena, and south, where they defeated chief Bogotá and founded the city of Santa Fe de Bogotá.

Very soon after the founding of the first cities, the transplanting of the Spanish church was completed with the establishment of a series of bishoprics and the introduction of the Inquisition. At first the latter was used almost exclusively against Spaniards, but soon the oppressed Indians and enslaved blacks—they were imported from a very early date—learned that if their masters were about to punish them, all they had to do was to cry, "I deny God," which put them under the somewhat more benevolent jurisdiction of the Inquisition. Eventually, a tacit agreement was reached, that only in extreme cases would the Inquisition intervene against Indians or black slaves. Since by that time the British were making their appearance in the Caribbean, the Inquisition was also used against them, and a number were killed for their Protestant convictions.

The two great Christian figures of this area were Saints Luis Beltrán and Pedro Claver. Luis Beltrán was one of the hundreds of missionaries who sought to bring Christianity to the Indians, and to undo the evil done by the conquistadores and the settlers. A Dominican, he spent the earlier part of his career as master of studies in the Dominican house of his native Valencia. The news from the New World, about the millions who needed someone to minister to them, moved him, and he decided that he had to find out if he was called to be a missionary. In 1562, when he was thirty-six years old, he landed in Cartagena. He repeatedly clashed with the *encomenderos,* and his preaching about justice often resounded with echoes of the Old Testament prophets. But he was still uncertain about his vocation and finally returned to Spain, where his piety and holiness gained him many admirers. Luis Beltrán died in 1581. In 1671, pope Clement X added his name to the official list of saints of the church—the first with any connection with the New World.

Spanish-born Pedro Claver, the other great Colombian saint, led a very different life. He was born in 1580, shortly before Beltrán's death, and from early youth decided to join the Jesuits and become a missionary to the New World. His superiors thought that he lacked intelligence, and he was still a novice when he arrived at Cartagena in 1610. He had ample opportunity to see the sufferings of black slaves, and therefore when he was finally allowed to make his final vows in 1622 he added a further vow to his signature: *Petrus Claver, aethiopum semper servus* ("Pedro Claver, forever a servant to blacks").

Since the languages the slaves spoke were too many for him to learn, he tried to borrow other slaves to serve as his interpreters. But the slaveholders were not willing to lose the labor of these interpreters, and Claver persuaded his monastery to buy a number of slaves to serve as interpreters. This created friction with his fellow Jesuits, some of whom persisted in treating the slaves as such. Claver insisted that these were brothers in Christ, to be treated as equals. Eventually, by sheer stubbornness, he forced the other Jesuits to agree, at least in theory.

As soon as a slave ship arrived, Claver and his interpreters ran to meet it. Sometimes they were allowed to enter the hold of the ship, but most often they had to wait until the slaves had been transferred to the barracks that would be their temporary homes until they were sold. These quarters were not as cramped as the ships, and slaves were now fed more abundantly, in order to prepare them for auction. Still, many died from the effects of the crossing, or because they refused to eat, fearing that they were being fattened in order to be eaten. Stark naked, the sick and the healthy lay together with the dead on the floor of broken bricks, until Claver and his companions came in and carried out the bodies of the dead. Then they would return with fresh fruit and clothes, and seek out the weakest among the slaves. If these seemed to be seriously ill, Claver would carry them to a small hospital he had built nearby. Then he would return and begin trying to communicate the gospel to those who were well enough to listen to him.

His methods were dramatic. He gave them water, of which they had not had a sufficient supply since they had boarded their ships, and then explained to them that the waters of baptism quench the thirst of the soul. Getting together a group who spoke the same language, Claver would sit them in a circle, sit among them, and give the only chair to the interpreter, who sat in the center and explained to the bewildered slaves the rudiments of the Christian faith. Sometimes he would tell them that, just as a snake changes its skin as it grows, so must one change one's life at baptism. He would then pinch himself all over, as if he were removing his skin, and explain to them the characteristics of the old life that must be left behind. Sometimes, in order to show their assent, they too would pinch themselves. At other times he explained the doctrine of the Trinity by folding a handkerchief so that three corners could be seen, and then showing that it was a single piece of cloth. This was all done in a warm spirit of friendliness and sometimes even humor.

Claver's concern, which was first shown at the arrival of the slave ships, was evident in many other ways. Since leprosy was a common disease among slaves, and those who had it were simply expelled by their masters, Claver founded a leprosarium where he spent most of his time when there were no slave ships in the bay, or slaves in the barracks waiting to be sold. There he was often seen embracing and trying to console a poor leper whose rotting body made others

Cartagena, in Columbia, witnessed the work of Sts. Luis Beltran and Pedro Claver.

shy away. Also, during the years of his ministry there were three outbreaks of smallpox in Cartagena, and in all three occasions Claver took upon himself the task of cleaning the sores of infected blacks who had been cast out to die.

Although his superiors always considered him imprudent and unintelligent, Claver knew full well how far he could go before the white population of Cartagena would crush his ministry. He never attacked or criticized the whites, but the entire city knew that as he walked along the streets he only greeted blacks and those few whites who supported his work. He soon let it be known that when he heard confessions he would follow an inverse order to that of society, listening first to the slaves, then to the poor, and finally to the children. Those who did not fall in any of these categories would do better to find another confessor.

He found much support among the slaves of Cartagena. On the great festivities of the church, some of these slaves helped him prepare banquets for the lepers, slaves, and beggars of the city. Others took up the ministry of giving decent burial to deceased slaves. Still others visited the sick, gathered fruit for the hungry and for the recent arrivals, collected and mended clothing, and in many other ways ministered to their fellow slaves.

During most of this time, white society in Cartagena paid little attention to this strange Jesuit who spent most of his time among slaves. Those who had anything to do with him mostly tried to dissuade him from his labors, for they feared that giving the slaves a sense of dignity was a dangerous thing to do. His superiors were constantly sending reports to Spain, to the effect that Father Claver had neither prudence nor intelligence.

Toward the end of his days, he was struck by a paralyzing disease and was hardly able to leave his cell. His last outing took him to the pier, where his eyes filled with tears before so much pain that he could no longer assuage. His fellow Jesuits trusted his care to a slave, and Claver had to suffer in his own flesh the consequences of the evil that his race had inflicted upon the black race, for the slave treated him cruelly, letting him lie in his own filth, and in many other ways reproducing on his sickbed many of the tortures of the slaves' Atlantic passage.

At the very last moment, Cartagena realized that a saint was about to pass away. The cream of society came to visit him in his cell, and all wanted to carry away a relic. Not even his crucifix was left to the poor Jesuit, for when a marquis declared that he wanted it Claver's superiors ordered him to relinquish it. His death, in 1654, was bemoaned by many who had scorned him while he lived. More than two hundred years later, his name was added to the official list of Catholic saints.

THE FOUR CORNERS OF THE EARTH:
THE INCAN EMPIRE

The western part of South America was under the control of the Incas. Although the Spanish eventually called the heartland of this area "Perú," the Incas called their empire *Tahuantinsuyu* ("the four corners of the world"), meaning that their power extended in every direction, and that what was not under their control was not really part of the world. With borders that are now difficult to determine, this empire included all or part of Peru, Ecuador, Bolivia, Chile, and Argentina—a total of somewhere between 350,000 and 440,000 square miles.

The conquest of this vast empire was accomplished by Francisco Pizarro through a combination of luck, daring, and treachery. When Pizarro, with a force of 168 men, set out to conquer the territory, the Incan Empire was divided by civil war. The previous *Sapa Inca* ("Supreme Ruler") had died of smallpox, and his two sons were contesting his succession. (It is interesting to note that, in spite of the speed of the Spanish conquest in the Americas, smallpox, brought to these lands by the Europeans, advanced at a much faster pace.)

In 1532, Pizarro captured Inca Atahualpa, the pretender who at that time had the upper hand. The episode of that capture, known as the Incident of Cajamarca, is illustrative of much that took place during the time of the conquest. Pizarro was in Cajamarca awaiting Atahualpa and his court, who were coming to see them mostly out of curiosity. When he learned that the Sapa Inca was coming, Pizarro hid his men at the edges of the city's main plaza. Atahualpa arrived with an entourage of several thousand, expecting no violence and confident that all was under his control, for, as he boasted, in all of Tahuantinsuyu not a bird could fly without his permission. Pizarro attempted to intimidate the Inca by galloping on his horse right up to him; but Atahualpa would not flinch. Then Pizarro ordered a priest who accompanied him—and who was also one of the main investors in the enterprise—to read the *Requerimiento*. This was a curious document that shows to what extent the conquistadores felt the need to justify their enterprise, and to what strange lengths they were willing to take their efforts to do so. Since war, conquest, and enslavement needed a justification, beginning in 1514 it was ordered that, before making war on the native inhabitants, they would be invited to accept Christianity and Spanish rule, on the basis that the pope, God's representative on earth, had granted these lands to the Spanish, and that this invitation would take place through the reading of the *Requerimiento*—usually in Spanish, and without benefit of translation. This document was now read to Atahualpa, and when the Inca responded with contempt, Pizarro gave the signal for his men to open fire, taking care not to hit the Inca himself. In the panic that ensued several thousand were killed, and Atahualpa was made a prisoner. Pizarro then offered the Inca his freedom in exchange for a

The Spanish conquest of the Incan Empire was made possible by a civil war in which that empire was engaged at the time of the conquest. Here Atahualpa's troops hold his rival and half-brother Huascar captive.

ransom consisting in a room full of gold. While the ransom was being collected, Atahualpa, apparently still not aware of the enormity of the events surrounding him, ordered the death of his half-brother and rival claimant to the throne, who was being held captive by Atahualpa's supporters. After the ransom arrived, Pizarro had Atahualpa tried for fratricide, and garroted to death.

This did not put an end to upheavals and civil wars. While the Indians continued a valiant and spirited resistance, the Spanish fought among themselves. When King Charles of Spain sent a viceroy, the settlers refused to obey him, and it was necessary to bring in reinforcements to quell the rebellion. All the while, Indian resistance continued until as late as 1780. At that time Tupac Amaru, who claimed to be a descendent of the last Inca, led a revolt that gained the support of much of the population—including some poor whites who felt exploited by the Spanish aristocracy.

The role of the church in these events, as in the entire Spanish enterprise in the New World, was twofold. On the one hand, it supported conquest and exploitation. On the other, some of its members raised vigorous voices of protest. The priest who read the *Requerimiento* in the betrayal through which Atahualpa was captured was rewarded by being made bishop of Cuzco—the capital of the empire. The enormous wealth of Peru seems to have corrupted even many of the friars, who in other areas were noted for their sacrificial ministry among the Indians. Rumors of licentiousness and greed prompted Spain to send an envoy to investigate the matter. He died mysteriously before he even reached Peru. When it was decided to have separate churches for whites and Indians, there was hardly a voice of protest. Among the Indians, some chiefs killed those who accepted baptism, which had now become a symbol of subjection to the invader. It took many years even for those who were baptized to gain a basic understanding of the Christian faith. Even then, priests paid by the *encomenderos* made certain that this faith was understood in such a way that it made them docile.

In 1581, Toribio Alfonso de Mogrovejo was made archbishop of Lima. This was an enormous archdiocese, for it included what is now Nicaragua, Panama, part of Colombia, all of Ecuador, Peru, Bolivia, Paraguay, and parts of Chile and Argentina. In response to the Protestant Reformation, the Council of Trent—which will be discussed in the next volume—had ordered a number of measures of reform, and Mogrovejo was convinced that these were necessary. In the New World, however, it was not easy to impose the discipline required by Trent. The new archbishop called a provincial synod in order to reform the church. One of the items of business was the corruption of the bishop of Cuzco, which was amply documented. But when the synod gathered, the bishop of Tucumán, a friend of the accused, wrenched the documents from the archbishop's hands and burned them in the oven of a bakery. In spite of such conditions, the archbishop was able to institute some reforms. He also prepared a catechism that was translated into several Indian languages, and which for three hundred years was the main means of Christian instruction in vast areas of Spanish America. He repeatedly clashed with civil authorities, particularly on the issue of better treatment for the Indians. But he never spoke a word against the fundamental injustice of the regime itself. In 1726, 120 years after Mogrovejo's death, his name was added to the official list of Catholic saints.

The Peruvian church produced three others who are now counted among such saints. Saint Rosa of Lima (1586–1617) followed the path of ascetic mysticism, and had experiences of ecstasy. Saint Martín de Porres (1579–1639) entered a Dominican monastery, but was never allowed to become a full member of the order because he was a mulatto. He spent many years taking care of the sick, both humans and animals, and planting fruit trees in the countryside, hoping that someday they would help someone who was hungry. Finally, Saint Francisco Solano (1549–1610) was a quiet and humble man who in 1604 was suddenly possessed of an apocalyptic vision, and ran through the streets declaring that Lima had become a new Ninevah, and that God would destroy it in an earthquake if the population did not repent. The message of this new Jonah was heeded, and people flocked to the churches to confess their sins and do penance.

But probably the most remarkable figure of that early period was the Dominican Gil González de San Nicolás, who spent many years as a missionary among the Indians in Chile, and came to the conclusion that the war that was being waged against them was unjust. To attack others with the sole purpose of taking their lands and property, he declared, was a mortal sin, and therefore those who were involved in such activities should be denied the consolation of penance. His preaching found echo among other Dominicans and Franciscans, who refused to grant absolution—and therefore communion—to any who participated in, or profited from, such wars. Civil and ecclesiastical authorities sought an excuse to silence the preacher. Finally, they accused him of heresy, for he had declared that future generations of Spaniards would be punished for the crimes that were taking place, and this was tantamount to affirming that actual sin—and not only original sin—is transmitted from generation to generation. On that basis, González was silenced, and others who had supported him were forced to recant.

LA PLATA

The territories that are now Argentina, Uruguay, and Paraguay were the last to be occupied by the Spanish. After several unsuccessful settlements, in 1537 they built a fort in what is now the city of Asuncion, in Paraguay. Since they were isolated, and knew that they depended on the Indians for their subsistence, the Spanish in Asunción were fairly moderate in their treatment of the Indians. Many of these were gathered in a number of small towns founded by Franciscan missionaries who taught them European methods of agriculture, as well as the rudiments of the Christian faith. One of these missionaries also translated St. Toribio's catechism into Guarani, the language of the local Indian population.

It was, however, the Jesuits who applied this method most successfully. In many other parts of the Spanish empire, notably in northern Mexico, missionaries had founded towns where Indians lived under their direction. But the common experience was that the proximity of Spanish settlers usually hindered the work of the missionaries, and sometimes even destroyed it. Therefore, rather than follow the Franciscans by organizing Indian villages near Asuncion, the Jesuits decided to venture into areas where European influence was barely felt. Roque González, a Jesuit who had grown up in Asunción, and who therefore spoke Guarani with ease, was the driving force behind these missions. Since he knew the language and customs of the Indians, he was able to defuse a great deal of their hostility, and was thus able to found villages whose inhabitants were there voluntarily, without any coercion by the Spanish.

These towns were actually small theocracies. Although the Indians elected their leaders, they were under the final authority of the missionary, whose word was final, not only in matters of religions and morals, but also in all the practical affairs of the community. Thus, while these Jesuit missions did much to protect the Indians and to introduce new crops and animal husbandry, they were also marked by a high degree of paternalism, making the entire enterprise dependent on the presence and guidance of the missionaries.

The basic layout of these towns was fairly uniform. In the center there was a big open plaza, where meetings, festivals, and processions took place. Facing it was the church, which included living quarters for the missionary. There were rows of apartments for families, and a separate building for widows and orphans. A large warehouse stored food, seeds, and other common property. Several other buildings housed workshops of all kinds.

Although individuals were allowed to have small private gardens, most property was held in common. This included the vast majority of the land as well as the herds, tools, seeds, and so forth. All had to work a certain number of hours in the common fields, but they also had time that they could devote to their family gardens or to developing and using other skills. In some of these towns, craftsmen became so skilled that they were able to build organs of exceptionally good quality.

But there were difficulties. Near each town there were other Indians who refused to join, and who constantly invited others to leave or to rebel. It was in one such rebellion that Roque González, the founder of the entire enterprise, was killed. He was declared a saint in 1934. The worst enemies of these missions, however, were whites, both Spanish and Portuguese. The latter, settled in Brazil, feared that Jesuit missions would serve as the vanguard of Spanish penetration. But the main source of their hostility was that the Jesuits prevented them from enslaving the Indians. The Spanish settlers opposed the Jesuit missions for similar reasons. They felt that, were it not for the Jesuits, all these Indians would be available to work for the Spanish under the system of *encomiendas*.

In 1628, some Portuguese out of São Paulo began attacking the Jesuit missions. They razed villages and carried away native inhabitants to be sold as slaves. In some cases, the Jesuits followed their flocks until the slavers forced them back. The Jesuits then moved their villages farther away from Brazil. But they were soon followed by the slavers, who simply penetrated deeper into the territory.

Given this situation, the Jesuits decided to arm the Indians. Their shops were converted into arms factories, and a standing army was organized under the leadership of one of the Jesuits. Pope Urban VIII excommunicated any who

The Jesuit missions were veritable towns, as these ruins in Paraguay attest.

would venture into Jesuit territory to hunt Indians, and King Philip IV declared that the Indians were free and not subject to slavery. But still the Portuguese came, often with the help of Spanish settlers who wished to destroy the entire enterprise. In 1641, in a pitched battle, the Indians and Jesuits defeated the invaders. Repeated accusations that the Jesuits were illegally arming the Indians found no support in either Rome or Madrid, both of which declared that the Jesuits had the right to arm themselves and their flock, because they were doing it in self-defense. Under such conditions, the missions flourished, and by 1731 there were more than 140,000 Indians living in them.

Opposition did not cease. It was rumored that the Jesuits hid vast quantities of gold that rightfully belonged to the crown. Repeated investigations found that there was no basis for this charge. Then it was said that the Jesuits aspired to create an independent republic, and even that they already had a leader: "King Nicholas I of Paraguay." At that time there were similar accusations circulating in Europe against the Jesuits, and since the house of Bourbon, which now ruled in Spain and in several other European lands, was following an anti-Jesuit policy (partly because the Jesuits had been supporters of the house of Hapsburg), in 1767 the crown ordered that all Jesuits must leave all Spanish colonies. Upon receiving these orders, the Spanish governor feared rebellions. But the Jesuits encouraged the Indians to accept the new situation, and left in peace.

The plan was that Franciscans and Dominicans would take the place of the Jesuits. But there were similar vacancies throughout the Spanish empire, and there were not enough Dominicans and Franciscans to fill them. Lacking leadership, many missions disappeared. Civil authorities began exploiting the Indians, and since the new missionaries did little to prevent such abuses, the Indians began distrusting them. Soon the Portuguese were again invading the area, hunting slaves. Some Spaniards did likewise. By 1813, the missions were reduced to a third of the size they had once been, and their decline continued. The missions of Paraguay, a discordant witness at a time when Christianity used to oppress and exploit the Indians, could not withstand the pressures of boundless greed.

37

The Portuguese Enterprise

If the Indians had a spiritual life and would acknowledge their Creator
and their vassalage to Your Majesty and their obligation to obey Christians . . . men would have legitimate slaves captured in just wars, and
would have also the service and vassalage of the Indians in the missions.

MANOEL DA NÓBREGA

AFRICA

Portugal completed the conquest of its lands from the Moors in the thirteenth
century, long before Castile. Since the latter hemmed them in, the only route
left for the Portuguese to expand was the sea. In the first half of the fifteenth
century, Prince Henry the Navigator encouraged the exploration of the west
coast of Africa. Under his auspices, and after fourteen unsuccessful attempts,
Portuguese sailors weathered Cape Bojador and reached Sierra Leone. This
exploration had several aims. One was to reach the Orient by sailing around
Africa, or by crossing that continent, and thus to circumvent the Muslims who
at that time controlled the most direct land routes between Europe and the Far
East, rich in silk and spices. Also, vague rumors of the existence of Ethiopia
had reached European courts, and there was the hope of finding this Christian kingdom, establishing an alliance with it, and launching a great Crusade
that would attack the Muslims from two different directions at the same time.
Finally, the slave traffic soon became an important factor in the exploration and
colonization of Africa.

In 1487, Portuguese explorers finally rounded the Cape of Good Hope. Ten
years later, Vasco da Gama sailed along the east coast of Africa, crossed the
Indian Ocean, and returned to Europe with proof that it was possible to circumvent the Muslims and establish direct commercial links with India.

While these early explorations were taking place, the Portuguese were busily
establishing alliances and colonies on the African coast. In 1483, an expedition
landed at the mouth of the Congo River and learned that this land, and vast

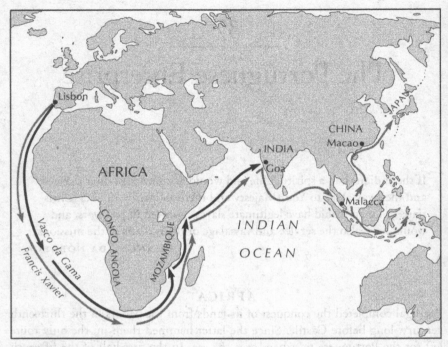

The Portuguese in Africa and the Orient

territories in the interior of the continent, were ruled by a man named Nzinga a Nkuwu who was the *mani kongo* ("king"). Because they hoped to reach Ethiopia by sailing up the Congo, the Portuguese treated the mani kongo's subjects respectfully. Four Portuguese remained behind, and four Africans were taken as guests to the court of Lisbon. When they returned with stories of the wonders of European civilization, and of their fair treatment in Lisbon, King Nzinga a Nkuwu decided to become an ally of the Portuguese, who in turn sent missionaries and craftsmen to the Congo. After a month of listening to Christian preaching, Nzinga a Nkuwu was baptized and took the Christian name of João, after the king of Portugal. (The king's son was also baptized and became Afonso I Mvemba a Nzinga.) Later, Portuguese military support in wars against his neighbors convinced King João I Nzinga a Nkuwu that he had made the right choice.

The next mani kongo, Afonso, was even more favorable to the Portuguese and their missionaries. In 1520, after long negotiations, Pope Leo X consecrated Henrique, a brother of Afonso, as bishop of the Congo. On his return to his land, however, the new bishop found that many European clerics paid little attention to his directives. He died in 1530, and two years later the church in the Congo was placed under the jurisdiction of the Portuguese bishop of the nearby island of São Tomé. The mission begun with such cordial relationships produced ever-increasing friction. After Afonso's death, civil war broke out, in part because many Congolese resented the presence and influence of the Portuguese. The latter intervened militarily, and in 1572 Mani kongo Alvaro declared himself a vassal of Portugal. By then resentment and suspicion had replaced the earlier friendly relations.

South of the Congo lay the lands of a ruler known as the "Ngola." These lands—now Angola—were seen from the beginning as a source of slaves. In the Congo, the mani kongo controlled the slave trade. In Angola, through the use of force, Portuguese slavers obtained greater advantages. Eventually, the coast became a Portuguese colony. Although Portugal claimed vast lands in the interior of the continent, those territories, seldom visited by them, were seen mostly as a vast source of slaves, usually taken to the coast by African slavers. Although churches were established, these were mostly for the Portuguese and for a few Africans along the coast. Since there were other lands that appeared more important to Portuguese eyes, the church in Angola was generally entrusted to what amounted to the dregs of Portuguese clergy.

The Portuguese enterprise on the eastern coast of Africa was even more violent. When Vasco da Gama arrived at a town in Mozambique and discovered that many of its inhabitants were Muslim, he bombarded the city with cannon fire. Proceeding to Mombasa, he did the same. He finally established an alliance with Malindi, a rival of both areas he had bombarded earlier. In 1505, Portugal sent a fleet of twenty-three vessels to India, with instructions to stop along the way and establish Portuguese rule in eastern Africa. In five years, the entire coast was subject to the Portuguese. In 1528, Mombasa gave signs of rebelliousness, and was bombarded for a second time.

The first Portuguese priests arrived at Mozambique in 1506. Their main task was not converting Africans, but rather to serve as chaplains to the Portuguese garrisons. In 1534, when the bishopric of Goa, in India, was founded, the entire eastern coast of Africa was placed under its jurisdiction.

Although most Portuguese priests remained in posts along the coast, under the protection of Portuguese cannon, a number of Jesuits and Dominicans did undertake missions to the interior. The most famous of them was the Jesuit Gonzalo de Silveira, who reached Zimbabwe and converted and baptized its king. Some African traders, fearing that the missionary's success would open the way for Portuguese traders, convinced the king that the Jesuit was a spy and a practitioner of evil magic. When he learned that the king had resolved to kill him, Silveira decided not to flee, but rather to remain in his post, where he was

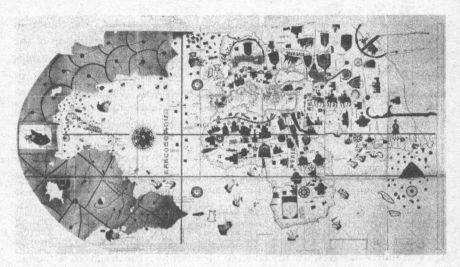

This old Portuguese trade map shows their understanding of the route around Africa and to the Orient.

strangled in his sleep. Like him, there were many missionaries who gave their lives in the next fifty years, and who in doing so gained the admiration of many Africans. But in spite of these martyrs, the vast majority of the clergy showed little concern for the Africans, and in this they were simply reflecting the attitude of Portugal itself, which by now was much more interested in the Far East, and paid little attention to its African colonies.

TOWARD THE RISING SUN

When, after the first discoveries of Columbus, the pope apportioned the entire non-Christian world between Spain and Portugal, the latter received, not only Africa, where Portuguese explorers had been active for some time, but also the entire Orient, which had always been the goal of the exploration of Africa. Upon Vasco da Gama's return, it became clear that the vast territories and teeming populations of India, Japan, and China could not be conquered by Portugal. Since products from the Orient—silk and spices—brought a high price in European markets, Portugal settled on a policy of trade rather than conquest.

In order to make trade with the East truly profitable, the Portuguese must have control of it. This was the purpose of a vast network of military bases that could both serve as refitting stations for Portuguese ships and as guardians of the sea lanes. Having established themselves on both sides of Africa, the Portuguese closed the Red Sea by taking the island of Socotra and other neighboring areas. In India, they took Goa and fortified it. By establishing a base in Ceylon, they controlled shipping around the southern tip of India. Farther East, their presence in Malacca closed the way to China to any daring Europeans who would venture that far. Finally, in China itself, Macao served as the channel for all trade with that enormous nation. Many of these places were taken by force. In others, such as Macao, the Portuguese were allowed to settle because the local or national authorities wished to trade with them. But even in those places where their original settlement took place through the force of arms, the Portuguese were interested in trade, not in conquest, and therefore avoided any missionary efforts that might lead to conflict, and thus interrupt trade.

King João III of Portugal, having heard of the zeal of the recently founded Jesuit order, requested that six Jesuits be sent to his colonies in the Orient. Loyola, the founder of the order, could only spare two. One of these was Francis Xavier, who upon learning what he was commanded to do took time only to mend his cassock and left for Lisbon. There the king and his court were so impressed with the Jesuits that they insisted that one of them remain in Portugal, and Francis Xavier was sent as the sole missionary to the Orient.

In May of 1542, after a voyage of more than a year, Xavier arrived at Goa, the center of Portuguese operations in the East. He was scandalized by the life of the Portuguese, but soon discovered that all his recriminations were to no avail. He then hit upon a method that became characteristic of him. He would walk along the streets with a bell, inviting children to come with him to church, where he taught them the catechism and the moral teachings of the church. Then he would send them home to share with their parents what they had learned. Little by little, Xavier gained the respect of the adults, who eventually flocked to hear him preach. Then followed scenes of mass penance reminiscent of Florence in Savonarola's time.

But it was not to preach to the Portuguese that Xavier had gone to India. His sojourn in Goa was only an interlude while he prepared for his vaster mission to those who had not heard the name of Christ. Therefore, after spending five months in Goa, Xavier left for the nearby Fishery coast—so named because of its pearl fisheries. This was an area frequently visited by Portuguese traders, and many of the Indians there had accepted Christianity simply because it was the religion of the powerful Portuguese. Xavier took with him two young clergymen who knew the language of the area, and with them as interpreters preached and taught for some time. From neighboring villages came requests that he go and preach to them. Since it was impossible to respond to all such requests, Xavier trained some of his converts, who then traveled about preaching and baptizing.

Most of Xavier's converts, as well as most of those won in other parts of India, belonged to the lower castes. The caste system was deeply ingrained

Portuguese traders being greeted on their arrival in Japan by Japanese officials and Franciscan Portuguese missionaries.

in Indian society, and there was no way to break out of it. People of different castes were not allowed to eat together. Since Christians partook of communion together, many members of the lower castes believed that if they became Christians this meant that they had joined the caste of the Portuguese. Therefore, for many converts conversion and baptism came to have a dimension of social liberation. But, for the same reason, many members of the higher castes opposed the preaching of Christianity, which they saw as subversive. In many areas there were martyrdoms similar to those of the early years of the church. Xavier himself was attacked in various occasions, and once was wounded by arrows. For a time, he sought to use Portuguese military power to protect his converts. Such military action was ruled out by the Portuguese authorities, not out of pacifist ideals, but rather because it would interrupt trade.

In 1546, leaving others in charge of the work begun in India, Xavier sailed for more distant lands. Three Japanese whom he met in his travels invited him to visit their land. After spending some time back in Goa, Xavier undertook this new mission. In 1549, with the three Japanese converts and two fellow Jesuits, Xavier sailed for Japan. There he was well received, and the number of his converts was such that he was convinced that he had built the foundation of what would soon be a flourishing church. He had no way of knowing that shortly after his death a great persecution would break out, and his newly founded church would almost disappear. (It actually seemed to have been completely destroyed until, three centuries later, Protestant missionaries found that there were about a hundred thousand Christians in Nagasaki and the neighboring area.)

On his return to Malacca, Xavier learned that the Jesuit order had decided to organize a new province that included all territories east of the Cape of Good Hope, and that he had been named its head. These new administrative responsibilities forced him to return to Goa, and to postpone his dream of preaching the Gospel in China.

Finally, in 1552, he sailed for China. Before leaving Goa, he wrote to the King of Portugal: "What encourages us is that God has inspired this thought in us . . . and we do not doubt that the power of God is infinitely superior to that of the king of China." But in spite of such confidence, Xavier was never able to enter China, whose government was averse to any foreign influence. He died on an island at the fringes of the Chinese empire where he had settled in order to prepare for the day when that vast land would be open to him.

Xavier and his fellow missionaries did not make a clear distinction between European culture and the Christian faith. When their converts were baptized, they were given "Christian"—that is, Portuguese—names, and encouraged to dress in Western clothes. Many of these converts actually believed that when they accepted baptism they became subjects of the King of Portugal. For similar reasons, the cultured and the powerful in the various countries that the missionaries visited viewed Christianity as a foreign influence, undermining both traditional culture and the existing social order.

A younger generation of Jesuits, all under Portuguese auspices, but many of them Italians by birth, questioned this identification of Christianity with Portuguese power and culture, and sought ways in which the preaching of the Gospel could be adapted or "accommodated" to the ancient Eastern cultures. Most notable among this younger generation were Roberto di Nobili and Matteo Ricci—the first a missionary to India, and the latter to China.

Di Nobili began his missionary career in the Fishery coast, and there became aware that, while many members of the lower castes embraced Christianity as a way to break away from their inferior status, this also meant that those of the higher castes were not willing to listen to a message associated with what they saw as the dregs of society. Therefore, when he was transferred to a different region di Nobili decided to follow another method. Arguing that he was of noble birth in his own country, he dressed as a Brahman and took the title of "teacher." He also took up the vegetarian diet of all good Hindus, and learned Sanskrit. By such methods, he gained the respect of many among the higher castes. When some of these were converted, he set them apart in a church of their own, and ordered that no members of the lower castes be allowed to worship with his privileged converts.

Di Nobili justified these actions claiming that the caste system, although evil, was a cultural matter, and not a religious one. It was necessary to respect the culture of the Hindus, and to preach the gospel following the lines of caste. If this were done, he argued, the lower castes would follow the example of their betters, and all would be converted. Such arguments were refuted by others who pointed out that justice and love are part of the gospel, and that to deny these is not to preach true Christianity. Eventually, di Nobili's most extreme propositions were rejected. For a long time, however, there continued existing in India separate churches—or separate areas within a church—for different castes.

Matteo Ricci followed in China a policy similar to di Nobili's in India, but less extreme. China was hermetically closed to any foreign influence, except the small window for trade provided by Macao. Shortly after Xavier's death, a Spanish missionary from the Philippines who had tried to visit China had declared that "with or without soldiers, to try to enter China is like trying to reach the moon." But, in spite of these difficulties, the Jesuits did not abandon Xavier's dream. Seeing that China was a highly civilized country that looked upon the rest of the world as barbarians, the Jesuits decided that the only way to make an impact on that vast land was to learn, not only its language, but also its culture. To this end, a group of Jesuits settled at the borders of the Chinese empire, and devoted itself to such studies. Slowly, some Chinese intellectuals in the nearby areas came to the conclusion that these Europeans, unlike the many adventurers who came to China after riches, were worthy of respect. Finally, after protracted negotiations, they were granted permission to settle in the provincial capital of Chaochin, but not to travel to other areas.

Ricci was among those who settled in Chaochin. He had become proficient in Chinese language and culture, and was also a geographer, astronomer, mathematician, and clockmaker. Aware that friendship was an important virtue among the Chinese, he wrote a treatise on that subject, following the canons of Chinese literature, and joining the wisdom of that land with material drawn from Western philosophy. Soon people began speaking of "the wise man from the West," and scholars would visit him to discuss astronomy, philosophy, and religion. A map of the world drawn by Ricci, which included vast areas unknown to the Chinese, drew the attention of the court in Beijing. His explanations of the movement of heavenly bodies according to complicated mathematical principles gained him even greater respect. Finally, in 1601, he was invited to the imperial court in Beijing, where he was given the necessary resources to build a great observatory, and where he remained until his death in 1615.

Ricci's strategy consisted of penetrating China without necessarily seeking large numbers of converts. He feared that, were he to cause a great religious stir, he and the other missionaries would be expelled from the country, and their

Matteo Ricci adopted the customs of China.

work would come to naught. Therefore, he never built a church or chapel, and he didn't he preach to multitudes. It was in his home, in a small circle of friends and admirers who gathered to discuss clockmaking and astronomy as well as religion, that he gained his only converts. When he died, he left a nucleus of believers, all members of the intellectual elite. But through the years these in turn converted others, and eventually there was a substantial number of Christians in the country—still led by the Jesuits, who continued serving the court at Beijing as its official astronomers.

As in the case of di Nobili, Ricci's methods met with objections from other Catholics. In this case, the point at issue was not the caste system, but rather ancestor worship and Confucianism. The Jesuits argued that Confucianism was not a religion, and that there was much in the teachings of Confucius that could be used as a point of entry for the gospel. As to ancestor worship, they claimed that this was not true worship, but rather a social custom whereby one showed respect for one's ancestors. Their opponents, mostly Dominicans and Franciscans, argued that such worship was in fact idolatry. Another point at issue was which of two possible Chinese words should be used to refer to the Christian God. When the emperor of China learned that this particular dispute had reached Rome, and that the pope was going to settle it, he was incensed at the notion that a barbarian who did not know a word of Chinese presumed to teach the Chinese how to speak their own language.

Whereas in China the question of "accommodation" had to do mostly with cultural issues, in India the question posed was whether one can actually claim to preach the gospel when such preaching is lacking in any word of judgment on human injustice and oppression. Is a Christian faith that accepts the caste system truly Christian? This question, or others like it, would become crucial in later centuries.

BRAZIL

By the time Columbus returned to Europe with news of his voyage, the Portuguese had long been exploring the coasts of Africa in search of a new route to the East. Hoping to avoid conflicts, the pope established a line of demarcation west of which the Spanish could explore and colonize, while the Portuguese retained their rights east of the line. Since the prevailing winds often forced Portuguese sailors trying to sail south along the coast of Africa to make a wide westward detour, the line of demarcation was moved more to the west. At that time, no one knew that the eastern tip of South America spanned the line of demarcation. In 1500, a Portuguese squadron sailing for the Orient gave the coast of Africa a wide berth in order to avoid contrary winds, and accidentally sighted what is now Brazil. After exploring the area, most of the squadron continued on its way to the Orient, while one ship was sent back to Lisbon with news of the land that had been discovered, in what seemed the middle of the Atlantic Ocean. Several preliminary explorations led to the conclusion that the only source of wealth to be found in the area was brazilwood, which could be used for making dyes. King Manoel of Portugal granted the monopoly on brazilwood to a group of Portuguese merchants, whose representatives established trading centers along the coast. There they traded knives, scissors, needles, and the like for brazilwood that the Indians cut and carted to warehouses along the coast. When brazilwood became scarce, the Portuguese turned their attention to sugar cane, which could easily be grown in the area. Since at that time sugar demanded very high prices in Europe, there were fortunes to be made in it. The king granted captaincies to fifteen of his favorites, giving each fifty leagues of seashore, and as far back inland as the beginning of Spanish territory. Only ten of the captaincies were ever settled, and eight of these failed. The two that succeeded were the beginning of the permanent colonization of Brazil.

Growing and processing sugar cane required abundant cheap labor, and the Portuguese sought to obtain this by enslaving the Indians. In theory, only those Indians who were already slaves of other Indians, and those captured in a just war, could be enslaved. But soon all sorts of excuses were found for supposedly just wars, and eventually even appearances were cast aside as slavers sailed along the coast, capturing and enslaving any Indians who were unwary enough to be caught. The Portuguese also incited wars between different Indian tribes, who would then sell their captives in exchange for tools, knives, and the like.

These methods, however, did not produce sufficient slaves, and many of those captured escaped into the jungle at the first opportunity. It was then that the Portuguese began importing slaves from Africa, which lay fairly close across the Atlantic. Blacks and Portuguese came to make up the majority of the population of eastern Brazil as the natives moved to the interior, died, or were absorbed by the rest of the population.

Reports reaching Lisbon from Brazil were uninspiring. The cruelty and licentiousness of the colonizers provoked a strong reaction. In 1548, with a view both to establishing order and to enlarging his coffers, the king of Portugal abolished the captaincies, bought back the land of those that had not failed and declared Brazil a royal colony. Jesuit missionaries arrived with its first governor. Their leader was Manoel da Nóbrega, whose words, quoted at the beginning of this chapter, give a clear indication of his understanding of his mission. The first bishop, appointed in 1551, was not much better. He quarreled with the colonizers, and paid no attention to the plight of Indians and Africans. He was returning to Portugal, in order to complain about the settlers, when he was shipwrecked. He and his entire company were killed and eaten by Indians.

The Jesuits whose presence the Portuguese crown had requested founded missions very similar to those of Paraguay, except for one important difference: instead of placing them as far as possible from the settlers, they built them where the Indians could serve on the plantations. The missionaries were grateful for the support of the Portuguese, and in exchange offered the labor of the Indians in what practically amounted to slavery. As one missionary said, "They quake in fear before the governor, and that fear . . . is enough for us to teach them. It helps them to hear the Word of God."

However, as the Jesuits became better established, some turned a more critical eye on the abuses of the colonizers. Best known among the Jesuits was António Vieira (1608–1697) who had been raised in Bahia and had studied at one of the many schools the Jesuits had founded—most of them for Portuguese settlers and their children. He was known as a defender of the Jews in Portugal, where he had gone to pursue his studies and his career as a priest. After returning to Brazil as a missionary, he also became an ardent defender of the Indians. When he preached, he asked, "Do you think that because you were born farther away from the sun this gives you a right over those who were born closer to it?" And then, in words reminiscent of Montesinos a century and a half earlier, Vieira told the Portuguese settlers that they were living off the blood of the Indians, and that "you are all going straight to hell, there to join many others who are there already." The settlers were so enraged that Vieira had to return to Portugal, where he spent three decades in advocacy similar to Las Casas's in Spain during the previous century. Vieira finally returned to Brazil a few years before his death.

In spite of Vieira and people like him, the preaching and teaching of Christianity in Brazil followed the path suggested by da Nóbrega in the mid-sixteenth century: it sought to justify the colonial enterprise and to make the Indians more docile. The Indian reaction took the form of a messianic cult that combined Christian elements with others derived from ancient beliefs. When a smallpox outbreak killed thousands of Indians, talk began of a savior whom the Indians called "Santo," who would come and free them from the Portuguese yoke. This new religion, *Santidade,* gained ground both among the Indians under Portuguese tutelage and among those who remained free beyond the reach of the Portuguese, and served as a bridge between the two groups. Likewise, black slaves developed various combinations of Christianity and their ancestral religions. Both of these movements allowed oppressed blacks and Indians a sense of dignity that official Christianity denied them.

From an early date, the French had competed with the Portuguese in the brazilwood trade, and some of them had hoped to establish a permanent settlement in Brazil. This was attempted in 1555 by Nicholas Durand de Villegagnon, who started a colony on an island in the bay of Guanabara, near present-day Rio de Janeiro. Villegagnon established friendly relations with the Tamoyo Indians, who helped him fortify the island. He also wrote to Calvin, and in response to his request was sent several Protestant pastors to serve those among the settlers who were Protestant. This, and many other issues, created grave difficulties in the settlement, which was eventually wiped out by the Portuguese. The Tamoyo Indians, and a number of French refugees who lived among them, continued resisting for some time. Later the tribe moved inland to escape from the Portuguese. When, late in the sixteenth century, a British adventurer persuaded them to return to the coast and fight for their rights, they were wiped out. Ten thousand of them were killed, and twice that many were captured and sold into slavery.

All told, the early story of Christianity in the various Portuguese colonies, as in so many other lands in that period of colonial expansion, is not an inspiring one. Brazil became a land to be colonized for farming and mining, where most of the hard labor was placed on the shoulders of slaves brought from Africa. Africa itself was seen mostly as a source for slaves and as an obstacle on the way to the riches of the East. And in the East all the Portuguese were able to accomplish was to establish trade posts such as Goa in India and Macao in China, and a series of fortified positions to protect their own shipping and defend their monopoly. In all of this, missionary work was at best a secondary concern, and often made to serve the interests of colonizers, traders, and slavers. It would be many years before the negative consequences of such inauspicious beginnings could be overcome.

38

The New World and the Old

They don't claim anything as their private property, but have all things
in common. They live in harmony without a ruler or an authority, for all
are like lords.

AMERIGO VESPUCCI

The impact of the Iberian enterprise in the Western Hemisphere was so
momentous—and so tragic—that it tends to eclipse the parallel impact
of the Western Hemisphere on Europe and the events taking place there. This
is true in the field of religion, but also in other aspects of European life, which
was drastically changed by the New World. Indeed, it was the "discovery"
and colonization of the Americas that allowed Europe to continue feeding its
population for the next several centuries. Until that time, the cereals grown
in Europe produced very limited yields in terms of the ratio between seeds
planted and grain harvested. This meant that normally at least a fifth of a
given year's harvest had to be reserved for planting the following year, and
that the consequences of a failed crop were felt for several years, until enough
seed could be produced and saved for new planting. In contrast to such cereals, American corn—maize—would produce yields of several hundred to one.
One grain of corn could produce a stalk with one or more ears, and each of
these ears could in turn produce hundreds of seeds. Thus larger populations
could be supported, and if a crop failed only a small portion of it had to be
preserved for next year's planting.

Even more than corn, potatoes shaped the life and diet of much of Europe. It
was in the Andean highlands that potatoes were first cultivated. By the time the
Spanish arrived, hundreds of varieties of potatoes were grown, capable of feeding the large population of the Incan Empire in spite of its rugged terrain and
limited agricultural land. Taken to Europe, potatoes—now ironically known as
"Irish potatoes"—became a staple that allowed significant population growth,
which would later produce new waves of emigration as these new crops failed.
Although the most important, corn and potatoes were not the only American

crops that affected European diet and life; there was also the impact of tomatoes on Italy, chocolate on Switzerland, and tobacco throughout the world.

The impact of the New World on the Old went far beyond food. The gold and other riches that flowed from the Americas made Spain—recently united into a single kingdom—one of the dominant powers in sixteenth-century Europe. Charles V used American gold to pay off the enormous debt he had acquired as he sought election as emperor. Spanish—actually, American—gold financed the industrial development of poorer lands such as Flanders and England, as the now-rich Spanish preferred purchasing textiles and other products from those lands rather than producing them themselves. The result was that, while in the sixteenth century Spain was the hegemonic power in Western Europe, by the end of that century such hegemony was waning, and ceding its place to England and other northern lands. Soon, those northern lands would begin challenging the Spanish in the Caribbean, and wrestling from them islands such as Jamaica and most of the Lesser Antilles, where sugar cane further enriched the new colonial powers. Then they began settling in some of the poorer or less developed areas in North America—particularly the British along the Atlantic coast, and the French at the mouth of the Mississippi. All of this would greatly change life in Europe, and would also result in new centers of missionary activity—now mostly Protestant.

In the field of religion, it was the New World that was most drastically impacted by the Old, as ancient gods failed and religions disappeared or were radically changed, and as Christianity came to take their place—although often with an admixture of those ancient religions. But even on religious matters the New World had an impact on the Old. The very "discovery" of lands until then unknown challenged much of the traditional worldview, and therefore also much of the theological tradition that had shared and bolstered that worldview. For centuries, theologians had declared that there are signs or vestiges of the Trinity in all of creation, and that one of these signs is in the tripartite nature of the world itself, which consists of Europe, Africa, and Asia. But now a fourth part of the world suddenly appeared—and a part much larger than Europe itself. If the theologians had been wrong in declaring that there were three parts to the world, could they be equally wrong in other matters? For centuries, it had been thought that the apostles had preached the gospel in every land. There were even legends ascribing particular territories to specific apostles, and arguing that the ancestors of the unbelievers now living in those areas had been given their opportunity to believe at the time of the apostles, and that those now living were condemned as a result of the obstinacy of their ancestors. Now there were lands where apparently no apostle had even been. Were these people condemned to eternal damnation for no apparent reason? Did they not have souls worthy of salvation? Could it be that the stories about the apostles travel-ing throughout the world were not true?

Others looked at the New World with a more positive attitude. Immedi-ately after his early encounters with the natives of the Americas, Columbus had declared that he thought he had discovered the lost Eden, where people lived unashamedly in almost total nakedness. Although Columbus himself had changed his mind when he discovered that the Indians would not do as he wished, there were still reports of peaceful natives who needed to toil little in a land of quiet and abundance. Out of such glowing reports arose the notion of the noble savage, untainted by civilization and its greed, not know-ing words such as *mine* or *thine*, ruled by love and simplicity. In this view, even American corn itself, with what seemed its miraculous yield, was the fulfillment of ancient millenarian dreams of fields so fertile that crops would produce at rates of a hundred to one. Thus, the New World nurtured the utopian dreams of the Old—including Sir Thomas More's famous *Utopia*. By the seventeenth century the New World was also providing a place where such utopian dreams could be tried out in various attempts to give humankind a new start, and to establish a new society untainted by the greed, inequalities, and incredulity of the Old.

While Spain and Portugal were building vast overseas empires, and planting Roman Catholicism in distant lands, the Protestant Reformation was taking place in Europe. The year 1521, when Luther valiantly stood before Charles V at the Diet of Worms, was also the year when Cortés captured Tenochtitlan. Even though neither Luther nor Charles—much less Montezuma—knew it, the consequences of the two events would be linked in many ways. For example, it was the gold of Tenochtitlan that allowed Charles to pursue his policies for the aggrandizement of the house of Hapsburg and the suppression of Protestant-ism. A few years earlier many of those yearning for a reformation of the church expected it would come out of Spain, but now Spain and the house of Hapsburg became the staunchest defenders of traditional religion in the face of the Prot-estant Reformation.

Living as we do, only five centuries after both the Reformation and the co-lonial expansion of Iberia, it may be too early to decide which of the two will eventually have greater significance to the course of Christianity. The one re-sulted in major divisions that exist to this day, as well as in a renewal of biblical scholarship and theology. The other resulted in the largest expansion of Chris-tianity in both number of followers and geographic reach since its very incep-tion. Events in the late twentieth and early twenty-first centuries may well tilt the balance in the direction of the discovery and colonization of America, for at a time when Christianity is generally waning in the areas that had been rent by the Reformation of the sixteenth century, it is showing significant signs of vitality and creativity in the lands colonized in the sixteenth century.

In the next volume of this history, we shall return to Europe, and resume the narrative of the quest for renewal and reformation, and of those who gave their lives to that quest. But we will soon find ourselves crossing the Atlantic once again, now to look at momentous developments, first in the former British colonies in the Americas, and then also in the Iberian colonies, both of which are crucial for understanding the subsequent course and present state of Christianity.

SUGGESTED READINGS

Germán Arciniegas. *America in Europe: A History of the New World in Reverse.* San Diego: Harcourt Brace Jovanovich, 1975.

Stephen Clissold. *The Saints of South America.* London: Charles Knight, 1972.

Vincent Cronin. *The Wise Man from the West.* New York: Dutton, 1955.

George H. Dunne. *Generation of Giants: The Story of the Jesuits in China in the Last Generations of the Ming Dynasty.* London: Burns & Oates, 1962.

John Hemming. *Red Gold: The Conquest of the Brazilian Indians.* Cambridge, Massachusetts: Harvard University Press, 1978.

Ondina W. González and Justo L. González. *Christianity in Latin America: A History.* Cambridge UK: Cambridge University Press, 2008.

Samuel Eliot Morison. *The European Discovery of America: The Southern Voyages, A.D. 1492–1616.* New York: Oxford University Press, 1974.

Stephen Neill. *Colonialism and Christian Missions.* London: Lutterworth, 1966.

J. H. Parry. *The Discovery of South America.* New York: Taplinger, 1979.

John Frederick Schwaller. *The Church in Colonial Latin America.* Wilmington, DE: Scholarly Resource Books, 2000.

APPENDIX

The Ecumenical Councils

*In 1054, the church was divided between East and West. After that date, councils listed are only western.

Number	Date	Name	Primary Decisions
1	325	I Nicea	Condemnation of Arius Son of one substance with Father Creed of Nicea
2	381	I Constantinople	Reiteration of Nicea Divinity of Holy Spirit Condemnation of Apollinaris
3	431	Ephesus	Condemnation of Nestorius Mary *theotokos*–"bearer of God"
4	451	Chalcedon	Condemnation of Eutyches Two natures–divine and human–in Christ
5	553	II Constantinople	Condemnation of "Three Chapters": Theodore of Mopsuestia Theodoret Ibas of Edessa
6	680–681	III Constantinople	Condemnation of Monothelism Condemnation of Pope Honorius
7	787	II Nicea	Condemnation of iconoclasts Images worthy of veneration *(dulia)* but not worship *(latria)*
8	869–870	IV Constantinople	Ended schism of Photius
9	1123	I Lateran	Confirmed Concordat of Worms between Papacy and Empire
10	1139	II Lateran	Compulsory clerical celibacy
11	1179	III Lateran	Determined method of papal election
12	1215	IV Lateran	Transubstantiation Confession and communion at least yearly Condemned Joachim of Fiore, Waldensians, and Albigensians Regulated Inquisition
13	1245	I Lyons	Declared Emperor Frederick II desposed
14	1274	II Lyons	New regulations for papal elections (basically those employed to the present) Nominal reunion with Constantinople
15	1311–1312	Vienne	Suppression of the Templars

Number	Date	Name	Primary Decisions
16	1414–1418	Constance	End of Great Schism Condemnation of John Huss Council has authority over pope Plans for reformation and other councils
17	1431–1445	Basel/Ferrara Florence	Nominal reunion with Constantinople, with Armenia, and with Jacobites
18	1512–1517	V Lateran	Condemned schismatic Council of Pisa
19	1545–1563	Trent	Condemned Protestants Authority of Scripture *and* tradition Consolidated Catholic Reformation
20	1869–1870	I Vatican	Papal infallibility
21	1962–1965	II Vatican	Liturgical renewal (use of vernacular) Church responsive to modern world: international economic inequities, nuclear war, religious freedom, openness to other Christians

Notes

CHAPTER 3: **The Church in Jerusalem**
1. *Against Heresies*, 1.26.2.

CHAPTER 5: **First Conflicts with the State**
2. *Annals* 15.44.
3. *Annals* 15.44.

CHAPTER 6: **Persecution in the Second Century**
4. *Apology* 1.2.
5. Ignatius, *Romans* 1.2–2.1.
6. *Martyrdom of Polycarp* 14.
7. *Meditations* 2.5.

CHAPTER 7: **The Defense of the Faith**
8. Origen, *Against Celsus* 3.55.
9. *Octavius* 12.
10. Origen, *Against Celsus* 4.3.
11. *Prescription against Heretics* 1.7.
12. *To Diognetus* 5.1–11.

CHAPTER 8: **The Deposit of the Faith**
13. Giovanni Filoramo, *A History of Gnosticism* (Oxford, U.K.: Basil Blackwell, 1990), p. 170.

CHAPTER 9: **The Teachers of the Church**
14. *Prescription against Heretics* 8.
15. *Prescription against Heretics* 8, 7.
16. *Against Praxeas* 1.

CHAPTER 10: **Persecution in the Third Century**
17. *Martyrdom of Perpetua and Felicitas* 5.3.

CHAPTER 11: **Christian Life**
18. *Armenian Gospel of the Infancy*, 23.2-3.
19. *I Apol.*, 67.3-6.
20. *I Apol.* 14.2.
21. *I Apol.* 65.1-3.
22. Rodney Stark, *Cities of God* (San Francisco: HarperSanFrancisco, 2006), 225.

CHAPTER 12: **The Great Persecution and the Final Victory**
23. *Church History* 8.17.6–10.

CHAPTER 13: **Constantine**
24. See the Appendix for a list of all the Ecumenical Councils, with dates and primary decisions.

CHAPTER 17: **The Arian Controversy and the Council of Nicea**
25. Eusebius of Caesarea, *Life of Constantine* 3.7.
26. Eusebius of Caesarea, *Epistle to the Caesareans*.

CHAPTER 20: **The Great Cappadocians**
27. *Homily on Luke's Words, "I'll tear down my barns. . ."* 1.

CHAPTER 21: **Ambrose of Milan**
28. *Commentary on Luke*, 2.41.
29. *Duties of the Clergy* 2.137.
30. *Sermon against Auxentius* 5.
31. Sozomen, *Church History* 7.25.

CHAPTER 22: **John Chrysostom**
32. *On the Priesthood* 6.
33. *Homily* 2.4.

CHAPTER 23: **Jerome**
34. *Epistle* 28.2.
35. *Epistle* 71.3.
36. *Epistle* 112.19.
37. *Commentary on Ezequiel,* prefaces to
     books 2 and 7.

CHAPTER 24: **Augustine of Hippo**
38. *Confessions,* 2.3.8.
39. *On Christian Doctrine,* 28.

CHAPTER 28: **Eastern Christianity**
40. Gregory of Nazianzus, *Epistle* 101.
41. *On the Orthodox Faith* 4.16.
42. Quoted in G. Zananiri, *Histoire de
     l'église byzantine* (Paris: Nouvelles édi-
     tions latines, 1954), p. 185.

CHAPTER 29: **Imperial Restoration and
Continuing Decay**
43. *Epistle to Elipandus* 1.4.

CHAPTER 30: **Movements of Renewal**
44. Gregory VII, *Register* 3.10a.

CHAPTER 31: **The Offensive Against
Islam**
45. Quoted in Francesco Gabrieli, *Arab
     Historians of the Crusades* (New York:
     Dorset, 1957), 12.

CHAPTER 32: **The Golden Age of
Medieval Christianity**
46. *Corpus of Canon Law* 2.1245.
47. *Proslogion,* 1.

CHAPTER 34: **In Quest of Reformation**
48. *Sermon on Blessed Are the Poor in Spirit.*

CHAPTER 35: **Renaissance and
Humanism**
49. *The Imitation of Christ* 1.1.3.

Index

Page numbers of illustrations appear in italics.

Abbots, 167, 168, 279; of Cluny, 328–29
Abgarus of Edessa, 253, 254
Abiwardi, al-, 353
Absenteeism, 401, 403, 409, 411, 417
Absolution, 288, 468
Acts, 1–2, 13, 25–27, *28*, 31, 33, 36, 42, 76, 79, 108
Acts of the Martyrs, 49
Acts of Thomas, 38
Address to Diognetus, 62, 68
Address to the Greeks (Tatian), 62, 64
Adiabene, 254
Adolf of Nassau, 394
Adoptionism, 319–20
Adrianople, battles of, 135, 259, 271
Africa: Angola, 475; colonial Portuguese, 473–76, *474*; Congo, 473–75; Donatist schism, 173–79, *177*, 248, 287; early church, 103, 282; Eastern Christianity in, 270; Mauritania and Numidia, 176–78; Mozambique, 475; Muslim, 270–71, *289*; Proconsular, 176, 242, 259; Vandal kingdom, 289; Zimbabwe, 475
Against Celsus, 62, 94, 105

Against Heresies, 84
Against Praxeas, 92
Against the Galileans, 197
Against the Gentiles (Athanasius), 200
Albert of Hapsburg, 394
Albert the Great, 362, 375, 376–77
Albigensians, 354, 360–61
Albina, 234
Alcantara, order of, 354
Alcuin of York, 317
Alexander II, 337
Alexander III, 364
Alexander V, 408–18
Alexander VI, 424, 443, 444, *445*, 451
Alexander of Alexandria, 184–85, 191, 199, 201
Alexander of Hales, 362
Alexander the Great, 13–14, 19, 21
Alexandria, 19, 37, 86–87, 88, 93, 94, 96, 163, 184–86, 202–4, 207, 291; bishops of, 93, 143, 184, 203, 207; Museum of, 139; synod of, 206
Alexius, 346
Alfonso II of Asturias, 317
Alfred the Great, 321, 413
Ambrose, St., 144, 206, 219–24, *220*, *221*, 231, 233, 245

Anchorite, 161, 167, 172
Angels, 11, 85, 86, 247
Angles, 274, 275
Anselm, 369–71, 435
Anthony, St., 157, *160*, 161, 162–63, 168, 199, 246
Antioch, 31, 33, 37, *52*, 185, 207, 210, 225, 227, 234; as apostolic church, 89; bishops, 80; Ignatius, martyrdom of, 51–53; siege, 347–48
Anti-Semitism, 30, 43, 60, 61, 73, 142, 223, 392
Apaches, 458
Apocryphal Gospels, 106–7
Apocalypticism, 346, 349, 407, 420, 429, 468
Apollinaris, 297, 304
Apologists, 57, 59–68, 83, 107
Apology (Justin Martyr), 55
Apology (Tertullian), 63
Apostles, 2, 25–29, *32*, 79–80, 89, 94; apostolic churches, 89; facts and legends, 36–39, *37*; mission to the Gentiles, 31–39
Apostles' Creed, 77–79, 189, 312, 440; "R," 77, 78, 79
Apostolic fathers, 83
Apostolic succession, 79–81, 89
Aphrahat, 256

Aquinas, St. Thomas, 362, 375–80, *376, 377*, 433, 434
Arabia, 256, 289, 307;
Arabs: conquests, 289–93, 305, 307, 319, 318; Fatimites, 348
Arcadius, *216*, 227–31
Archimandrites, 167
Architecture. *See* Art and architecture
Argentina, 465, 469
Arianism, 141, 151, 152, 163, 181–82, 200, 201, 213, 214–17, 219, 221; Blasphemy of Sirmium, 205; Constantius II and, 202–5; Germanic people and, 257–58, 260–61, 271–72, 276–77, 283, 289; Valens and, 207, 211, 213
Aristides, 62, 66
Aristotle, 63, 90, 355, 374–79
Arius, 184–85, 187–88, 190–91, 201
Arizona, 458
Arles, Synod of, 140, 142
Armenia, 255, 307, 309, 347, 366
Arsenius, 201–2
Art and architecture, 117, 140; basilicas, 137, 145–47, *145*; Dura-Europas, *110*, 111, 143, 145, 256; flying buttresses, 384, *384*; Gothic, 281–85, 378–79, *382, 384*, 437–38; medieval, 76, *183*, 378–86; mosaics, 146; *Pantokrator*, 146; Renaissance, *122*, 437–38, 440–44, *441*; Romanesque, 381–82, *382, 383*; Rome and papal patronage, 442–44; Vatican and, 444
Asceticism, 148, 158–59, 161–65, 168–69

Asia Minor, 33, 36, 48, 52, 56, 86, 96, 254, 346
Atahualpa, 465–67, *466*
Athanasius, 161–62, 163, 164, 169, 185, 188, 191, 199–207, *200*, 246, 255
Athenagoras, 62
Athens, 194, *195*, 210; Academy, 139
Attila the Hun, 282–83
Augustine of Canterbury, 275, 277
Augustine of Hippo, 169, 172, 173, 179, 222, 233, 237–38, 241–52, *243, 251*, 282, 288, 320, 334, 374–75, 413
Averroes (Ibn Rushd), 354–55, *355*, 374
Avignon, *397*; papacy in, 390, 398–406, *405*, 407–8, 410, 412
Aztecs, 455, 457

Baja California, 457–58
Balboa, Vasco Núñez de, 459
Baldwin, 346, 349
Balkans, 271, 309–10
Baptism, 86, 88, 96, *110*, 111–13, *112*, 147. 154, 248, administration of, 176; baptistry, 147; conquest and conversion, 315–16, 323, 455, 464, 467; creeds, 77, 79, 112; infant, 113; teaching and, 35, 112, 144–45
Barbarians, 64, 97, 100, 131, 132, 137, 257; fall of Rome, 259–61; spread of Christianity, 253, 269–77
Barnabas, 31, 33, 35, 116
Basel, Council of, 410, *410*; 421, 442
Basil the Great, 169, 172, 194, 209, 211–13, *212*, 233
Basiliscus, 303
Bastidas, Rodrigo, 462

Beatus of Liebana, 320
Becket, Thomas, 369
Beghards, 429
Beguines, 429
Beltrán, Luis, 462
Benedict, St., 277–81, 333
Benedict I, 285
Benedict VI, VIII, and IX, 324–25
Benedict XI, 395, 396
Benedict XII, 398
Benedict XIII (Avignon pope), 405–6, *405*, 409
Benedict XV, 390
Benedictine Order, 277–81; *Rule* and, 281, 327–29
Benedict of Aniane, 317
Bernard of Clairvaux, 333–34, 350, 353, 363–64, 371, 426
Berno, 328–29
Bethlehem, 145, 237, 239, 351
"Be Thou My Vision," 274
Biblia alfonsina, 413
Bishops, 67, 80, 89, 113–14, 157, 165, 171, 172, 275; appointment, 273, 317, 331, 337, 341, 451; authority, 80–81, 103; election, 187; investiture, 331, 341; joint office, 247; origins, 28; wealth and power, 333, 344
Boethius, 276–77
Bogomils, 354
Bohemia, 366, 415–22
Böhm, Hans, 431
Bolivia, 465
Bonaventure, St., 363, 374
Boniface VII, 325
Boniface VIII, 368, 393, 396
Boniface IX, 406, 416
Borgias, 442–43, 444, *445*
Boris of Bulgaria, 310–11
Bourbon, house of, 471
Brazil, 470, 482–84; *Santidade*, 484
Brethren of the Common Life, 427, 428

Brethren of the Free Spirit, 427, 429
Breviary, 280
Britain: Christian conversion, 273–76, 315–16; colonies, 488; Norse invasion, 321–22, *322*; Scotch-Irish Church, 274–75. *See also* England; Scotland
Bulgaria, 309–12, 354, 366
Burning of vanities, 423
Byzantine Empire, 137, 231, 259, 260, 284, 288–89, 312; Belisarius and conquests, 270, 277, 283; fall of, 392–93; images and, 305–6; Justinian and, 277, 284; Muslim invasion, 292–93; schism with Rome, 303; theology of, 292–93. *See also* Constantinople
Byzantium, 133, 135, 136

Cadaveric Council, 324
Caecilian, 174–75, 176
Caesarea, 16–17, 93, 149, 152, 210, 212, 255; Baptismal creed of, 79; bishops of, 116, 151, 213
Calatrava, order of, 354
California, 457–58
Calixtus, 92, 104
Calixtus II, 342–43
Calixtus III, 442–43
Calixtus III (antipope), 364
Calvin, John, 422, 484
Canary Islands, 451
Canons of St. Augustine, 169, 361
Canute, 322, *322*
Cardinals, 337
Caribbean, 454
Carolingians, 319
Carthage, 88, 103, 142, *175*, 242, 244, 269; Proconsular Africa and, 176–77, *177*; Muslim conquest, 292; rival bishops in, 174; society and economics, 177–78
Castile, 352, 366, 389, 404
Catechumens, 35, 93, 112
"Cathedral," 146
Catherine of Siena, 399–400, *400*, *401*, 402, 404
"Catholic," 66
Celestine III, 364
Celestine V, 368, 394
Celibacy, 159–61, 172, 210, 227, 271, 287, 312–13, 331, 336, 338, 343–44, 415, 417; Patarines, 331, 338
Celsus, 60, 61–62, 67, 105, 115
Central America, 453, 459–60
Chalcedon, Council of, 255, 256, 300–302
Chanson de Roland, 316
"Chapel"/"Chaplain," 171
Charlemagne, 273, 277, 289, 293, 312, 315–18, *316*
Charles Martel, 273, 292
Charles the Bald, 319
Charles the Fat, 324
Charles V, 453, 455, 467, 488, 489
Charles VI, 389, 404–5
Charles VII, 389–90
Charles VIII, 423–24
Chichimectecotl, Carlos, 456
Childeric III, 273, 289
Chile, 465, 467
China: Christianity in, 307, *308*, 380; Beijing, 380, 480; missionaries to, 477–82; trade with, 476
Chi-Rho, *116*, 126, 138, 140
Choir, 144, 146
Christ. *See* Jesus Christ
Christmas, 112
Christology, 92, 319; Alexandrine, 296–97, 300–301, 302; Antiochene, 296–300,
302, 320; controversies, 256, 289, 296–306, *306*, 319–20; heresy and, 78
Christopher I, 324
Church: authority, 75–81, 83, 89–90, 278, 428; body and bride of Christ, 104, 176; Christ as head of, 86; government, 28, 67, 113–15, 274–75, 334–38; hierarchy, 113–14, 154, 428–29; invisible, 413; necessary for salvation, 104; schisms in, 104, 173–79; state and, 179, 181–82, 196–97, 273, 284–87, 289, 295, 336–44, 363–68, 369, 394–95, 445 (*see also* Bishops; Papacy)
Church History (Eusebius), 150, 152
Circumcellions, 178–79, 248
Cistercians, 333, 334
Cities, growth of, 355–57, 369, 372–75
City of God, 250, *251*
Clare, St., 360
Clarisses/Poor Clares, 360
Claudius, 42, 254
Claver, Pedro, 462–65, *463*
Clement II, 325
Clement III (antipope), 349, 389
Clement V, 396–98
Clement VI, 398–99
Clement VII (Avignon pope), 403–5
Clement X, 462
Clement of Alexandria, 83, 86–88, 98, 105, 107, 182, 183, 200, 296
Clement of Rome, 83, 282
Clergy: Ambrose and, 221; John Chrysostom and, 227–28; council of Toledo and, 271, Fourth Lateran Council and, 367; reformation, 416–17
Clericis laicos, 394

Clermont, Council of, 346
Clovis of Gaul, 273
Cluny Abbey/Cluniacs, *328*, 329–34, 342, 371
Colombia, 462–65; Cartagena, *463*, 464–65
Colonial Christianity: Caribbean, 454; Central America, 459–60; Columbia and Venezuela, 462–65; Florida, 460–61; Incan empire, 465–68; Mexico, 455–59; New World, *450*, 450–71; protest of, 452–54; South America, 469–71
Colonna, Sciarra, 394–96
Columba, 274, 277
Columbus, Christopher, 443, 449, 450, 454, 459, 462, 489
Comenius, John Amos, 421
Commodus, 57
Communion, 86, 96, 107–13, 147, 154, 164, 168, 175, 288, 313, 320–21, 381, 413, 417, 478; early, 27, 35; fragmentum, 111; "in both kinds," 420; rumors and, 60; as sacrifice, 288, 381
Conciliar movement, 406–11, 416, 435–36
Concordat of Worms, 343, 363
Confession, 288, 367
Confessions (Augustine), 250
Confessors, 102, 103, 174, 274
Conrad III of Germany, 350
Constance, 133, 135; Council of, 409–10, 412, 415, 418–21, 436
Constans, 191, 202, 203
Constans II, 305
Constantine, 43, 76, 123–26, *125*, 131–45, *132*, *133*, 150, 152–53, 163, 174, 178, 181–82, 184–86, 193, 196, 201, *284*;

Arch of, *151*; baptism, 191; Constantinople, 136–37; conversion, 126, 137–41, 153–54; Council of Nicea, 186–92, *187*; death and succession, 202–5; family, *191*, vision of, 125–26, 139
Constantine II, 191, 202, 203
Constantine V, 305
Constantine XI, 392–93
Constantinople, 37, 136–37, 140, 179, 196, 202, 210, 215, 216, *216*, 297–98, 345, 410; bishops, 216–17, 227; Crusades and, 351; Councils of, *206*, 207, 213, 217, 234, 298, 301, 304, 305; fall of, 392–93, 438, 442; Latin Empire, 351, 366, 387, 392; Roman rivalry, 312; waning power of, 284
Constantius, 141, 193, 194, 195–96
Constantius Chlorus, 119, 122, 204
Constantius II, 191–96, 202–5, *204*
Controversy of the Three Chapters, 303–4
Copts, 163, 199, 307
Cornelius, 31, 33
Cornelius Fronto, 61, 105
Corpus Juris Canonici, 334
Cortez, Hernán, 455
Cosmography (Pius), 443
Creation, 1, 66, 69, 70, 73, 74, 78, 84, 91, 94, 374–75
Creeds, 77–80, 112; Apostles', 77–78, 79, 189; Nicene, 79, 181, 189–90
Crusades, 345–56, 366, 367, 374, 380, 419–21, 442, 473; antecedents, 337; children's, 349; consequences of, 352–56;

Eighth, 351; Fifth, 351; First, 340, 346–49, *347*; Fourth, 345, 350–51, 353, 366, 392; leaders, 346, 350–51; Second, 349, 353; Seventh, 351; Sixth, 351; Third, 350
Cuba, 454, 460
Cyprian, 97, 103, 181, 282
Cyprus, 31, 33
Cyril and Methodius, 310
Cyril of Alexandria, 197, 299–300
Cyrilic alphabet, 310
Czechoslovakia, 415–17

Da Gama, Vasco, 473
Da Vinci, Leonardo, 440–41, *441*
Damascus, 31, 292
David of Scotland, 389
De Molay, Jacques, 397–98
De principiis (Origen), 94
De Soto, Hernando, 460
Dead Sea Scrolls, 17
Dead, prayers for the, 415
Decius, 93, 97, 100–102, *100*, *101*, 119
Decretum (of Gratian), 334
Defense of Origen (Eusebius), 150
Definition of Faith, 301–302, 307, 309
Demons, 95, 162–63, 247
Demonstration of Apostolic Preaching (Irenaeus), 84
Demonstration on Persecution (Aphrahat), 256
Denmark, 366
Dialogue with Trypho (Justin), 62
Diatessaron (Tatian), 254
Didache, 83, 113, 144
Diego of Osma, 360
Diet of Worms, 489
Diocletian, 119, 120–23, *120*, *122*, 150
Dionysius the Aeropagite, 319
Dioscorus, 255, 300–302

Divine Office, 280, 329, 333

Divinization, 85

Docetism, 72, 78, 300

Dominic, St., 360–61, *361*

Dominicans, 361–62, 367, 375, 399, 422–25, 429, 451; Catherine of Siena and, 399–400; Meister Eckhart and, 426–27; missionaries, 380, 451–53, 456–58, 462, 468, 471, 475, 480

Domitian, 46–48

Donation of Constantine, 287, 440

Donatism, 173–79, *177*, 248, 287, 334

Donatus, 174

Dualism, 244, 354

Duns Scotus, John, 434

Dura-Europas, *110*, 111, 143, 145, 256

Duties of the Clergy (Ambrose), 221

Easter, 111–13, 275–76

Eastern Orthodoxy, 309–13; after Arab conquests, 309–13; dissident churches, 306–9; Feast of Orthodoxy, 306;

Ebionites, 29–30

Eckhart (Meister), 426–27

Ecuador, 465

Edessa, 254; Count of, 347, 349

Edessius, 255

Education: catechumens, 35, 93, 112; cathedral schools, 369, 372; of early Christians, 35; imperial church, 144–45; universities, 362, 369, 372–74, *373*

Edward I, 394, 395

Edward III, 389, 412, 414

Egypt, 14, 211, 236–37; Cairo, 291; Council of Chalcedon and, 255, 301, 307; early

Christians, *28*, 255; gods of, 21; Jews in, 17–18, 19; monastics in, 148, 161, 167, 168, 277; Muslim/Arab invasion, 291, 305. *See also* Copts

Elipandus of Toledo, 319–20

Elvira, Council of, 142

Encomiendas, 452–53, 459, 462, 470

England: Canterbury as ecclesiastical capital, 275, 369; Crusades, 350–51; Germanic invasions, 274; Hundred Years' War, 388–89, 394, 398, 408; Magna Carta, 366; papacy and, *286*, 287, 338, 364, 366, 394, 412; peasant revolt, 414; Scotch-Irish Christianity, 274–75

Ephesus, 33, 36, 52, 80, *112*, 229; Council of, 256, *298*, 299–301; 320; Robbers' Synod, 301

Epiphany, 112

Erasmus, 428

Eschatology, 17, 69, 91, 95, 154, 430

Essenes, 17

Estrada Rávago, Juan de, 460

Ethelbert of Kent, 275

Ethiopia, 255, 258, 307, 380, 473

Etymologies (Isidore), 271

Eudoxia, 227, 228–29, 230

Eugene IV, 410, 442, 443

Eusebius of Caesarea, 121, 124, 125, 147, 149–55, 157, 186–88, 254

Eusebius of Nicomedia, 135, 187, 190, 191, 201, 202

Eustochium, 234, *235*, 236–39

Eutyches, 300–302

Evil: Gnostics and, 70, 72; Marcion and, 74; origin of, 244–45, 247; sexuality and, 159

Exhortation to the Pagans (Clement), 87

Exposition of the Orthodox Faith (John of Damascus), 305

Faith: and pagan culture, 63–66, 67; reason and, 87–88, 369–80, 433–36; as trust, 436

False Decretals, 323–24

Fasting, 27, 111, 112, 113

Felicitas, 56

Felix III, 303

Felix V (antipope), 411

Felix of Urgel, 319–20

Ferdinand II of Aragon, 352, 449–50, *451*

Ferdinand III of Castile, 367

Ferrara-Florence, Council of, 392, 410–11

Feudalism, 319, 335, 387–88

Filioque, 312, 320

Filorama, Giovanni, 73

Final judgment, 63, 74, *79*, 233

First Clement, 48, 82

Fish, as symbol, 117

Flagellants, 429–31, *430*

Flavia Domitilla, 47–48, 105

Flavian of Constantinople, 300, 301

Flavius Clemens, 47–48

Florida, 460–61

Florence, 331, 422–25, 443

Formosus, 324

Formula of reunion, 300

Foulques de Neuilly, 350–51

Four Articles, 420, 421

France, 259, 269; Christianity in, 249–50, 273, 342; colonial, 484, 488; Crusades and, 350–51; Dominicans in, 361; Hundred Years' War, 388–89, 394, 398, 408; invasions of, 322, 323; papacy and, 365, 367–68, 388, 393–402, *398*

Francis, St., 358–60, *358*,
    362, 385, 426
Francis I, 445
Franciscans, 359–60,
    362–63, 367, 374, 429,
    434, 451; missionaries,
    380, 451, 455–59, 461,
    468, 469, 471, 482; as
    pope, 368
Franks, 273, 277, 285–89,
    293
Fraticelli, 363, 393
Frederick Barbarossa, 350,
    364
Frederick II, 365
Frederick II of Germany, 351
Free will, 84, 247, 248–49
Fritigil, Queen, 224
Frumentius, 255

Galerius, 119, 120–21,
    123–24
Gallus (Julian's brother),
    193, 194, 195
Gaul, 56, 272–73, 289
Gelasius II, 342
Gentiles, 28; admission into
    church, 25, 31–39, 181;
    dominance in church, 30,
    42, 112; teaching of, 35
Germanic people, 259;
    assimilation of, 293;
    kingdoms and invasions,
    269–77, *270*, *272*, 321;
    spread of Christianity to,
    257–58
Germany: confrontation
    with papacy, 338–44;
    house of Hohenstaufen,
    365; Magyar invasions,
    323; mysticism in, 425–
    29; papacy and, 336–
    29; 353; 364–65, 367, 388,
    404; reformation and,
    416–22
Gervasius and Protasius,
    144, 223
Gnosticism, 70–73, *71*,
    75–81, 95, 158, 181,
    242, 244; Elkesaites, 256;

eons, 71, 73; Gospels, 76;
    Nag Hammadi, 70, 73;
    refutation of, 84
God, 84, 107; divine cre-
    ation and, 1, 66, 69, 70,
    78, 84, 94; Eckhart's
    view, 426; existence,
    369–70, 278, 433–36;
    existence of evil and, 244,
    247; as Father, 183, 188,
    190; immutable,182,
    183; ineffable, 88, 107;
    Marcion and, 74; nature
    of, 183–92, *183*, 296–97;
    omnipotent, 61, 67, 69,
    77, 90, 434–36; personal,
    183–84; as supreme
    being, 64–65, 71, 138,
    182–83; Word of, 3; as
    Yahweh, 74
Godfrey of Bouillon, 345,
    349
Godfrey of Lorraine, 336
González de San Nicolas,
    Gil, 468
González, Roque, 469
Gospel of Judas, 70
Gospel of Thomas, 70, 75
Gospel of Truth, 70, 75
Gospels, 75–76, 91;
    Apocryphal, 106–7;
    Diatessaron, 254;
    Gregory's copy, *286*;
    Ulfila's Gothic version,
    257, *258*
Goths, 221, 239, 239, 257–
    58, *258*, 259, *260*, 383
Gottschalk of Orbais, 320
Grace, 249, 250, 288, 428
Gratian, 141, 222
Great Cappadocians, 207,
    209–17, 220
Greece: classical culture
    and Christianity, 63–66;
    early Christianity in, 33,
    42, 48, 105; gods of,
    21, 66; Greco-Roman
    world, 19–23, *20*;
    Julian the Apostate and,
    194–97; language of

apologists, 62; language
    of Eastern church, 96,
    184, 220; language of
    Scripture, 18
Gregorian chant, 237
Gregory I (the Great), 275,
    282, 285–88, *286*
Gregory III, 289
Gregory V, 325
Gregory VI, 325, 335
Gregory VII, 325, 331, 334–
    38, 340, *342*, 346, 385
Gregory IX, 351, 362–63
Gregory X, 367
Gregory XI, 399, 401, 414
Gregory XII, 406, 408
Gregory of Nazianzus, 214–
    17, *215*, 297–98
Gregory of Nyssa, 209, 211,
    213–14
Gregory Thaumaturgus, 116
Gregory the Illuminator,
    255, 307
Groote, Gerhard, 427
Guido of Tuscia, 324

Hadrian, 273
Hadrian II, 324
Hagia Sophia, 216, 228, 229,
    284, *306*, 313, 335, 393
Hebrew, 234, 237, 239, 253
Helena, 144, 145
Hellenism, 14–15, 19, 22,
    23, 25–26, 31, 32, 203
Helvetic Confederation, 388
Henry I of England, 369
Henry III of Germany, 325,
    336
Henry IV of Castile, 450
Henry IV of Germany,
    336–40, *330*; at Canossa,
    339–40, *343*
Henry V of Germany, 341–44
Henry VI of Germany, 364
Henry the Fowler, 323
Henry the Navigator, 473
Heraclius, 304
Heresy, 70–81; Abelard
    and, 371; creeds and,
    77, 78; Crusades and,

354; Dominicans and, 361–62; inquisition and, 367; John Huss and, 418–19; pagan philosophy as source, 63, 90; refutations and doctrine, 84–96, 179. *See also specific heresies*
Hersiologists, 70
Herod Agrippa, 28, 37, 41
Herod the Great, 15
Hexapla, 93–94
Hilarius, 283
Hilary of Poitiers, 171
Hildebrand. *See* Gregory VII
Hildegard of Bingen, 327–28
Hincmar, 315, 320
History: as revelatory, 78, 83, 84, 85–86, 185; Augustine's view, 250; Eusebius's view, 153–54; God enters, through Christ, 185; Irenaeus' view, 86; of Israel, 85; Joachim's stages, 363; Origen's view, 95; rule of God over, 78, 83, 84, 85–86
History of Calamities, 371
Holy Land, 144, 236–37, 346, 380
Holy Spirit, 2, 85, 91, 94, 217, 312
Homoiousios and *Homoousios*, 189–90, 205–6, 217, 300
Honorius, *216*, 227, 230, 289, 305
Horebites, 420, 421
Hormisdas, 283, 303
Hosius of Cordova, 138, 185–86, 192, 204
Hours of prayer, 280, 329
Humanism, 436–40, 441
Humbert, 313, 325, 331, 334, 335
Hundred Years' War, 388–390, 394, 398, 408
Hungary, 309–10, 323, 366, 404; Magyars, 323

Huss, John, 407, 409, 412, 415–22, *420*, 436
Hussites, 419–20, 429
Hymns, 88, 206, 274, 334

Ibas of Edessa, 303
Iceland, 366
Iconoclasts vs. iconodules, 305–6
Idolatry, 63, 117, 305–6, 397, 482
Ignatius of Antioch, 49, 51–53, 115
Ignatius of Constantinople, 312
Imitation of Christ (Kempis), 427, 436
Inca Empire, 465–68, *466*
Incarnation, 65–66, 73, 74, 85–86, 88, 94, 153, 200, 221, 371, 374, 413, 435
India, 38, 256–57, 307, 380, 382; caste system, 477–78, 482; Goa, 476–78
Indians (of New World), 450–71, 482–84
Indulgences, 418, 444, 445
Innocent I, 230
Innocent II, 364
Innocent III, 350, 353–55, 357, 361, 364–67
Innocent V, 368
Innocent VI, 399
Innocent VII, 406
Innocent VIII, 444
Inquisition, 367, 453, 456, 462
Ireland, 257, 274, *274*; monasteries, 257, 319
Irenaeus, 29, 84–86, 87, 95, 96, 98, 153
Isabella, 352, 449–50, *451*, 454
Isidore of Seville, 271
Islam. *See* Muslims
Italy; early Christianity, 33; Eastern Roman Empire, 283; Germanic invasions, 276–77, 282–83; Great Schism, 404; Norse inva-

sions, 322, 336; unification, 388, 443

Jacob Baradaeus, 307
Jacobites, 307
Jamaica, 454, 488
James (brother of Jesus), 28, 29
Japan, 476, 478–79, *478*
Jerome, 136, 161–62, 169, 172, 191, 199, 204, 233–39, *235*, *236*, *239*, 259
Jerome of Prague, 419
Jerusalem, 132, 236; Constantine and, 152; Church of the Holy Sepulchre, 152; Crusades and, 346, 348–49, 350; early Christians in, 25–30, *26*, 31–33; Latin Kingdom, 349–50; Muslim rule, 291, 350; "new," 48, 107; rebuilding of Temple, 197; Roman destruction, 14, 16, 17, 29, 46, 70
Jesuits, 47; as missionaries, 451, 457–58, 461–65, 469–71, *470*, 475, 477–84
"Jesus, the Very Thought of Thee" (Bernard), 334
Jesus Christ, 1, 2, 16, 29, 73; birth, 1, 78; death, 3, 78; divinity and incarnation, 65–66, 184, 188, 217, 371, 427; followers, class of, 105–6; humanity of, 72, 333, 353; legends of, 107, 254; meaning of "Christ," 18–19; Muslims and, 290; nature of, 256, 289, 296–306; Pharisees and, 16; resurrection, 27, 36, 91, 154; salvation and, 184–85; as Second Adam, 86; as the Son, 319–20; work of, 86, 95, 296. *See also* Incarnation; Logos

Jewish Christianity, 25–30, 31, 254
Jews. *See* Judaism/Jews
Joachim of Fiore, 363, 367–68, 393
Joan of Arc, 389–90
João III of Portugal, 477
John, 26, 28, 31, 36, 38
John, Gospel of, 36, 65–66
John I, 276
John VIII, X, XI, XIII, and XIX, 324–35
John XXII, 398, 401
John XXIII, 408
John XXIII (Pisan Pope), 408, 417–18
John Chrysostom, 142, 217, 225–31, *226*, 233
John Gualbert, 331
John Lackland, 366
John of Antioch, 299–300
John of Damascus, 295, 305–6
John of Gaunt, 412, 414
John of Monte Corvino, 380
John of Parma, 363
John of Ruysbroeck, 427
John Scotus Erigena, 319, 320
Jovian, 141, 207
Judaism/Jews; antiquity of, 64; anti-Semitism, 30, 43, 60, 61, 73, 142, 223, 392, 367; basis of Christian beliefs, 78; conflict with Christians, 42–43; conversion, 380; Crusaders' murder of, 349; Diaspora, 17–19, *18*, 253; early Christians as Jews, 25–30, 31, 36, 41–43, 254; expulsion from Rome, 42; Gnostic, 70; Godfearers, 33, 35; Hellenism and, 14–15, 19, 23, 32, 64; Jewish War, 29, *29*; Julian the Apostate and, 197; Law and, 16, 17, 32–33, 35, 42, 87, 91; Maccabees, 15, *15*; Marcion and, 54;

Massada, 16; Messiah and, 17, 41; monotheism of, 17, 21, 66; Muslims and, 290; in Palestine, 13–17; Passover, 111; persecution, 42, 47, 98, 142, 223, 346, 380; Pharisees, 16, 17, 69; redemption and, 85; Roman rule and, 15–16, 17, 20, 29, *29*, 42–43, 46–47, 61; Sadducees, 16, 17; Sanhedrin, 26; in Spain, 271; synagogue, 17; Zealots, 16, 17
Julian of Norwich, 428
Julian the Apostate, 141, 148, 170, 178, 193–97, *194*, 205, 210, 215; religious policy, 196–97, 207
Julius II, 443, 444–45, 451
Justin Martyr, 55, 56, 62, 64–66, 88, 105, 106, 109–11, 115, 182, 183, 254
Justin, 303
Justina, 222–23
Justinian, 270, 277, 284, *284*, 303–4, *304*
Just War Theory, 179, 293

Kempe, Margery, 428
Kempis, Thomas, 387, 427
Kingdom of God, 86, 107, 154, 158–59
Kino, Eusebio Francisco, 457–58
Kiss of peace, 109, 112
Knights of Malta, 354

Lactantius, 124, 138
Langton, Stephen, 366
Lapsed Christians, issue of, 102–4, 173–74, 181, 187
Las Casas, Bartolomé de, 452–53
Lateran Councils, 321, 337, 367, 392, 407, 413
Latin America, 449, *450*, 459–60, 462–71, 482–84

Latin language, 63, 93, 96, 220, 237, 254, 260, 412
Law: Judaic, 16, 17, 22–23, 42, 87, 91; natural, 23; Roman, 19
Leipzig, university of, 416
Leo I, 282, 283, 300–302
Leo III, 289, 315
Leo V and VI, 324
Leo IX, 313, 331, 331, 334, 335–36
Leo X, 445, 474
Leo of Orchid, 312
Letter to Diogneus, 62, 68
Libanius, 225
Liberius of Rome, 192, 204
Licinius, 123–26, 132–35, *134*, 138, 150, 184, 185
Life of Constantine, 186
Life of St. Anthony, 169, 199
Life of St. Martin, 169–70
Logos or Word, 1, 65–66, 85, 153, 182–84, 374; Arianism, 184, 188, 189
Lollards, 414–15, 429
Lombard League, 364
Lombards, 276–77, 281, 284–86, 289
López de Legazpi, Miguel, 459
Lothair II, 324
Louis VII of France, 350
Louis IX of France, 351
Louis of Bavaria, 389
Louis the Pious, 317, 318
Luke, Gospel of, 74, 75–76, 79
Lull, Raymond, 380
Luther, Martin, 436, 489
Lyons, 56, 59, 358

Macrina, 209–11
Maimonides, 354–55, *355*
Malta, 354
Manichaeism, 242, 244, 247–48, 354
Manoel of Portugal, 482
Marcella, 234
Marcellina, 220, 234

Marcion/Marcionism, 73–
80, *79*, 91, 95
Marcus Aurelius, 55–57,
60, 105
Marius Victorinus, 245–46
Marozia, 324–25
Marriage, 89, 114–15, *115*
Martin I, 289
Martin V, 409–10
Martin of Tours, 142, 169–
71, *170*
Martyrdom, 47–48, 49,
51–56, 93, 98, 99,
101–2, 115–16, 121,
150, 158, 179, 277, 380;
commemorating, 144;
spontaneous, 55
Martyrdom of Polycarp, 55,
111
*Martyrdom of Saints Perpetua
and Felicitas*, 98–99
Mary, 76, 77, 78, 301;
Theotokos, 299
Mary, Pachomius' sister, 166
Mason, Lowell, 88
Matter/material world, 78,
94, 242; eternal, 374;
Gnostics on, 70
Maxentius, 124–25, 132
Maximian, 119, 123–24
Maximilla, 91
Maximinus Daia, 123–26,
133, 150
Maximus, 222–23, 289
Mayas, 457
Medici, Lorenzo de, 422–23,
445
Medici, Pietro de, 423
Meditations (Marcus
Aurelius), 55
Melchites, 307
Mendicants, 357–63, *358*,
359, *361*, 367
Menéndez de Avilés, Pedro,
461
Merovingian dynasty, 273
Messiah, 17, 18–19, 27,
35, 41
Mexico, 454–60, *458*, 469;
university of, 356

Michael Cerularius, 313, 335
Michelangelo, 440, 444
Milac, Jan, 417
Milan, 217–18, *221*,
223–24, 241, 244–45;
Edict of, 126, 135, 150;
Patarines, 331, 338
Military orders, 354, 380
Minucius Felix, 61, 63
Miracles, 107, 116, 223, 255
Missionaries, 4, 5; accom-
modation, 480, 481–82;
Africa, 475–76; Brazil,
483–84; China, 480–82,
481; early, 30–39,
115–17; Eastern Europe,
381; India, 476–77,
482; Iona and, 274, *274*;
Japan, 478–79; Scotch-
Irish, 273–76; methods,
115–17, 480–82; monas-
tics as, 172, 380–81 (*see
also specific orders*); New
World, 451–52, 453,
457–65, 469–71
Modalism, 92
"Modern devotion," 427
Modernity, 380
Mogrovejo, Toribio Alfonso
de, 467–69
Monasticism, 147–48,
157–72, 211, 214, 226,
246, 277–81, *328*,
329–34, 359–63, 367;
429; Athanasius and,
199–200, 204; Basil and,
210–13; Benedictine
Rule, 281, 327–29; celibacy and, 159–61, 343;
cenobitic, 165–68; eco-
nomic impact, 280–81;
Egyptian, 161, 167, 277;
female, 114, *158*, 167,
168, 209–11, 220, 278,
328–29, 360, 399; Fourth
Lateran Council and,
367; Franciscan *Rule*,
360, 362, 380; Irish, 319;
as learning center, *330*;
mendicants, 357–63, *358*,

359, *361*, 367; military
orders, 354, 380; missionary work, 172, 380–81;
"monk," 161; origins,
157–64; poverty, ideal of,
166, 280, 332–33, 341,
343–44, 358–59, 363;
reform, 317–18, 327–34;
sacking by invaders, 327;
Scotch-Irish, 274–75,
274; social services, 281,
281; spread of ideal, 168–
72; wealth and power,
332–33, *322*, 402; west-
ern vs. eastern, 277–78.
See also specific orders
Monophysites, 255, 256,
301, 304, 307, 309
Monotheism, 17, 21, 22,
66, 184
Monothelism, 304
Montanus/Montanism,
91–92, 98
Monte Cassino, 278, 281,
324, 340, 375
Montesinos, Antonio, 452
Moors, 272, 352
Moravians, 310, 421–22
More, Sir Thomas, 489
Moses, 64
Mozarabic litury, 319
Muhammad, 256, 290–91
Muhammad II, 393
Muslims: beliefs, 290–91,
305; Caliphs, 291;
Christians and, 292, 293;
conquests, 179, 270–72,
289–93; consequences of
offensive against, 352–
56, 367; conversion, 380;
Crusades, 293, 345–56;
Fatimites, 348; Mecca
and Medina, 291; Moors,
272, 352; Reconquista
and, 351–52, 353. *See
also* Averroes
Mystery religions, 21, 194
Mysticism, 70, 209, 214,
244, 319, 376, 399–400,
400, 425–29, 468

Naples, 368, 404, 418, 423;
University of, 375
Nationalism, 387, 388, 390,
401, 416, 417
Neoplatonism, 244–46, 319,
374, 426
Nepotism, 401, 403, 407,
443
Nero, 36, 43–46, *44*
Nestorius/Nestorians, 256,
299–302, 307, *308*, 309
New Laws of Indies, 453
New Mexico, 457, 458
New Testament, 1–2, 3, 18,
36, 42, 48, 91; canon,
75; Syriac (Peshitta), 254
New World: impact on Old,
487–90. *See also* Central
America; Latin America;
Mexico; North America
Nicea, *185*, 346, *348*;
Council of, 140, 143,
151–52, 159–60,
186–92, *187*, *190*, 199,
202–4, 205, 212, 217,
257, 301; II Council of,
306
Nicene Creed, 79, 181, 189–
90, 312, 320; *Filioque*,
312, 320
Nicholas I, 310, 323
Nicholas II, 337
Nicholas IV, 368
Nicholas V, 442
Nicholas of Cusa, 443
Nobili, Roberto di, 479–80,
481
Nóbrega, Manoel de, 473,
483
Nogaret, William, 395–96,
397
Normans, 340, 342
North America, 487–90
Notre Dame, Chartres, *382*
Notre Dame, Paris, *385*, 397
Novatian, 103, 104

Obedience, 166, 172, 185,
278, 332, 431
Occam, William of, 434

Octavius, 63
"Of the Father's Love
Begotten," 206
Old Testament, 1, 13, 75,
85; antiquity of, 64;
Hexapla, 93–94; Marcion
and, 74; translations, 18,
75, 253–54
Oldcastle, Sir John, 415
Olga, Queen, 311, *311*
Onesimus, 52
On Baptism (Tertullian), 88
On Divine Dominion
(Wycliffe), 412
*On the Body and Blood of the
Lord* (Paschasius), 321
*On the Consolation of
Philosophy*, 276
On the Division of Nature
(Erigena), 319
On the Eucharist (Wycliffe),
413
On the Holy Ghost (Basil), 220
*On the Incarnation of the
Word* (Athanasius), 200
*On the Resurrection of the
Dead* (Athenagoras), 62
On the Witness of the Soul, 89
Orange, Synod of, 250
Order of St. James, 38
Order of St. John, 354
Origen, 62, 88, 93–96, 99,
102, 105, 115, 149–50,
158, 182, 183–84, 188,
200, 296
"O Sacred Head, Now
Wounded," 334
"O Splendor of God's Glory
Bright," 206
Ostrogoths, 276–77, 278;
283, 285
Otto I (the Great), 323
Otto III, 325
Otto IV, 364–65
Oxford, university, 362, 373,
412, 414

Pachomius, 165–68
Pacifism, 63, 138–39, 179,
293

Pagan/paganism, 116–17,
140, 143, 182; cen-
ters of learning, 139;
and Christian faith,
63–66, 67; Christian
festivals substituted for,
116; Constantine and,
139–40; criticism of
Christians, 60, 61–63,
105; Decius's plan to
restore, 100–102, *101*;
early Christians and, 45,
46, 47, 50, 52, 56, 57,
88, 93; Germanic inva-
sions and, 277; Julian the
Apostate and, 193–97;
loss of status, 141–42;
persecution of, 141–42;
philosophy, 19, 63–66
Palestine, 13–17, *14*;
Caesarea, 15, 150
Pamphilus of Caesarea,
149–50
Panama, 459–60
Pantaenus, 86
Pantokrator, 78, 146, 217
Papacy, 281–89; alliance
with Lombards, 277; in
Avignon, 393–402, 412;
Constantinople and, 289;
decay in, 323–25; and
Empire, 336, 338–44,
339, *343*; *False Decretals*
and, 323–24; Innocent
III and power of,
364–67; nepotism and,
399, 403, 443; Papal
Infallibility, 305; "pope,"
281; reform, 334–38,
343–44, 407–31;
Renaissance and, 441–
45, *445*; rival popes, 283,
337, 340, 363–64; rules
of election, 289, 336–37;
wealth and power, 287,
323, 343, 353, 364–68,
387–88, 412
Papal states, 368
Papias of Hierapolis, 36
Paraguay, 469–71, *470*

Paris, university of, 362, 373, 374, 376, 404

Paschal II, 341–42

Paschasius Radbertus, 321

Patrick, 257

Patripassianism, 92, 188, 190

Paronato real, 451

Paul, 2, 19, 26, 27, 28, 33–35, *34*, 36, 38, 42, 43, 48, 52, 66, 89, 105, 116, 159, 181, 241; Epistles of, 74, 76, 79, 83

Paul II, 443

Paul III, 355

Paul VI, 400

Paul the Hermit, 161–62, 163, 168, 199

Paula, 234, *235*, 236–38

Paulus Orosius, 269

Pavia-Siena, Council of, 410

Pedro II of Aragon, 366

Pelagianism/Pelagius, 238, 248–50

Pelagius II, 285, 386–87

Pella, city of, 28–29

Penance, 104, 288, 429–31, 468

Pentecost, 2, 25, *32*, 91, 112

Pepin the Short, 273, 289

Perpetua and Felicitas, 98–99, 105

Persecution, 21–22, 26, 28, 29, 36, 43–58, *58*, 67, 86, 93, 97–104, 151, 153, 157, 197; end of Roman, 126, 131, 150; Great, Diocletian, 119–26, 163, 256; Japanese Christians, 478–79; Jews, 42, 47, 142, 346, 380; in North Africa, 173; by Ostrogoths, 276–77; pagans, 141–42; Waldensians, 358, 363, 367; women, 444

Persia, 17, 121, 136, 195, 197, 255, 301; Christianity in, 255–56, 257, 307, 380; Muslims in, 291

Peru, 453, 465–68

Peter, 25–28, 31, 36, 37, *37*, 38, 46, 81, 89, 282

Peter Abelard, 371–72; and Heloise, 371

Peter Damian, 327, 331, 333, 335, 336

Peter Lombard, 372

Peter of Spain, 395

Petrarch, 437–38

Philip, 26, 31, 37, 114

Philip the Arabian, 99

Philip I of France, 337, 341

Philip II Augustus, 350, 365

Philip IV of France, 394, 396–97

Philip IV of Spain, 470–71

Philip VI of France, 389

Philippines, 459

Philo of Alexandria, 19

Philosophy (classical), 22–23, 63–66, 87, 94, 95, 354–55; body vs. soul traditions, 159; nature of God and, 182–83; rift with theology, 433; scholasticism and, 373–80, 433; source of heresies, 63, 90; truth, pursuit of, 242

Photinus, 68

Photian Schism, 312

Pico della Mirandola, 422, 433, 441

Pierius of Alexandria, 149

Pilgrimage, 144, 236–37, 346, 392, 394, 415

Pisa, Council of, 408, *409*, 417

Pius II, 443

Pius III, 444

Pizarro, Francisco, 465–66

Plague, 390–92, *391*, 399, 421

Plato, 22, 64, 65, 66, 87, 158, 182

Platonism, 22, 87, 88, 94, 95, 374–75, 378–79

Plea for the Christians, A (Athenagoras), 62

Pliny, 49–50, 54, 56, 109, 114

Pluralism, 401, 409

Poland, 404

Polycarp of Smyrna, 52, 53–55, 84, 115

Ponce de León, Juan, 460

Pontius Pilate, 45, 77, 78

Pope. *See* Papacy; *specific popes*

Porres, Martin de, 468

Portugal, 366, 404; colonial, 449, *450*, 471, 473–85, 489

Poverty, ideal of, 343, 358–59, 362, 363, 420. *See also* Mendicants

Prague, university of, 415, 419

Praxeas, 92

Predestination, 249, 288, 320, 413

Prescription against the Heretics, 89, 91

Priests, 143, 164

Printing press, 438, *439*, 456

Priscilla, 91

Proslogion, 369–70

Protestant Reformation, 90, 104, 252, 358, 421, 433, 442, 445, 489

Protoevangelium of James, 76

Puerto Rico, 454, 460

Pulcheria and Marcian, 301, 307, 309

Purgatory, 288

Quadratus, 62

Rabanus Maurus, 320

Raphael, 444

Ratramnus of Corbie, 320

Reason, 87–88, 392, 433–36; Anslem's arguments and, 371. *See also* Faith

Recared, 271, 272

Recesvinth, 272

Redemption, 85

Reformation: Conciliar movement, 407–11, 416, 435–36; John Huss and, 415–22, 436; John Wycliffe and, 411–15;

Reformation *(continued)*
mystical alternative, 425–
29; popular movements,
429–31; Savonarola and,
422–25

Relics, 111, 144, *353*, 354,
367, 392

Renaissance, 433–45; art
and reality, 440–41; pa-
pacy and, 441–45, *445*;
scholasticism in, 433–36;
revival of classical learning, 436–40

Resurrection: apologists' arguments, 66–67; bodily,
62, 65, 69, 74, 77, 78; of
Jesus, 86, 91, 154

Revelation, book of, 36, 41,
48, 76, 113

Ribaut, Jean, 461

Ricci, Matteo, 479, 480–82.
481

Richard II of England, 416

Richard the Lionhearted,
350

Robert of Molesme, 333

Rolle, Richard, 428

Roman Empire:
Constantine's conquest
and rule, 124–26,
131–45, 153, 178–79;
conversion, 137–41, 256;
criticism of Christians,
59–62; Eastern, 137,
179, 196, 284 (*see also*
Byzantine Empire); em-
peror worship, 20, 22,
43, 51, 67; fall of, 137,
239, 250, 259–61, 270;
gods of, 21–22, *22*, 43,
51, 100–102, *100*, *101*,
139–42, 143; Imperial
Church and, 131–260;
invasion and collapse of,
179; in Palestine, 15–16;
persecution of Christians,
21–22, 26, 28, 29, 36,
43–58, 67, 97–104,
119–26, 153; persecution
of Jews, 42, 46–47, 98;

spread of Christianity in,
19–20, 116–17. *See also
specific emperors*

Rome (city/state), 136, 137,
234, 340; Athanasius
exile in, 202–3;
Augustine in, 244;
bishops of, 80, 83, 89,
92, 99, 113–14, 174,
186, 202, 230, 281–82;
burning of, and Nero,
44; Carthage and,
177–78; early Christians
in, 33, 36, 48, 52–53,
56; Colosseum, *47*;
Constantinople rivalry
with, 312; expulsion of
the Jews, 42; Gregory
the Great and, 285–87;
Lateran palace, 140,
324; Montanists in, 92;
papacy and, 281–89,
363–64, 398–99, 402;
pilgrimage to, 394; "R"
and, 77; sacking of, 239,
259, 260, 270, 283

Romulus Augustulus, 276

Rosa of Lima, 468

Rostislav of Moravia, 310

Rudolf of Hapsburg, 367

Rufinus, 255

Rule of St. Benedict,
278–80, *279*, 317, 327,
328, 329

Rule of St. Francis, 360, 362,
380

Russia, 147, 189, 309, 311–
12, *311*, 381; Mongols
and, 311, 381

Ruysbroeck, John of, 427

Sabbath, 27

Sacraments, 428; practice of
charging for, 367; validity
(and Donatism), 175–76,
179, 248

St. Irene, church of, 137,
145, *206*

St. Peter's Basilica, 341, 442,
445

St. Peter's Patrimony, 287,
341

Saints' days, 111, 144

Saladin, 350

Salamanca, university of,
373, 453

Salvation, 1, 70, 71, 74,
91, 96, 104, 131, 154,
184–85, 242, 278, 288,
368, 433, 435

Samaria, 26–27, 31

Santiago, order of, 354

Satan, 86, 95, 157, 158

Savonarola, 422–25, *422*,
425

Saxons, 274, 315–16

Scandinavia, 321–22, 380,
404

Schisms: of Acacius, 303;
Donatist, 103, 173–79;
East and West, 283–84,
295, 313, 334–36; Great
Western, 390, 393–11,
412, 417, 435; John
Chrysostom and, 231;
Photian, 312

Scholastica, 278

Scholasticism, 369–80, *370*,
373, *376*, *377*, 433–36

Scotland, 389, 394, 404;
Scotch-Irish Christianity,
274–75, *274*

Scripture, 75, 244, 428; as
allegory, 19, 87, 182–83,
245; authority of, 248,
418, 422, 435; belonging
to the church, 89, 90,
413; canon, 69, 75–81;
Greek philosophy and,
19, 87; *Hexapla*, 93–94;
interpretations, 62, 88;
monasteries and, 280;
reading, during worship,
109; translations, 18, 234,
237, 253–54, 310, 413

Semi-Pelagianism, 250

Sentences (Peter Lombard),
372, 376

Septimius Severus, 57, 86,
93, 97–99

Septuagint, 18, 75, 237, 254
Sergius III, 324
Sergius of Constantinople, 304–5
Serra, Junípero, 458
Severus, 104
Sex, 143, 159–61, 234, 235. *See also* Celibacy
Shepherd of Hermas, 83
"Shepherd of tender youth" (hymn), 88
Sicily, 270, 322, 336, 352, 354, 364–65, 374
Sigismund, 272, 408, 410, 416, 418, 420–21
Silveira, Gonzalo de, 475
Simeon, St., 29
Simeon of Bulgaria, 311
Simon Magnus, 31
Simony, 143, 331, 333–35, 337–38, 343, 401, 404, 407, 409, 411, 417, 420
Simplicius, 283
Sin, 2, 92, 249, 288, 371, 379, 387, 420, 429, 437, 449, 468; Adam, Eve, and the Fall, 85, 95, 249; consequences of, 85, 248–49; forgiveness, 83; free will and, 249; lapsed Christians and, 104
Sistine Chapel, 440, 443
Sixtus IV, 443, 444
Slavery, 453, 454, 462, *463*, 464–65, 471, 473, 475, 483, 484
Slavic Church, 309–10
Smyrna, 52, 53–55
Society and economics: bourgeoisie, 356, 388, 395, 440, 449; Crusades and, 355–56, 346; early Christians, 61, 64, 67, 105–7, *106*, 115, 117, 138; Egyptian, 73, 199; 14th and 15th centuries, 387–88; monetary economy, 357, 387–88; plague and, 390–92, *391*; riches as divine favor,

153–54; social mobility, 335–36
Socrates, 22, 65, 66
Solano, Francisco, 468
Son, divinity of, 78, 217, 319. *See also* Logos; Monophysites
Soul, 89; classical philosophy and, 159; immortality, 22, 65, 434; Neoplationism and, 245, 426; not created, 426; preexistence, 95; scholastics and, 379; unity of, 374
Spain: Arianism , 271; colonialism and expansion, 449–71, *450*, *451*, 488–89, 490; early Christians, 33, 36, 37–38, *37*; Germanic conquests, 269, 271, 287; Innocent III and, 366; Mozarabic liturgy and, 319; Muslims/Moors in, 271, 292, 351, 352, 354, 367, 374; philosophers, 354–55, *355*; Reconquista, 351–52, *352*, 353; unification, 388
Spirit, 70–71, 94–95
Spirituals, 363
Stephen, 26, 41
Stephen II, 289
Stephen VI, 324
Stephen VII, 324
Stephen of Hungary, 323
Stoicism, 22, 23, 159
Suetonius, 42
Sulpitius Severus, 169, 171
Summa Contra Gentiles, 374, 376
Summa Theologica, 374, 376, 278–79
Suso, Henry, 427
Switzerland, 388
Sylvester II, 325
Syncretism, 20–21, 69, 87, 97–98
Syria, 14, 86, 96; Chalcedon "definition" and, 301,

307, 309; Crusades and, 348; Jacobite Church, 307; monastics in, 148; Muslim invasion, 292, 305; Seleucids, 15
Syriac language, 253–54; *Diatessaron* and, 254; spread of Christianity, 254, 255–56

Taborites, 419–20, 421, 429
Tacitus, 44–46, 105
Tamoyos, 411
Tatian, 62, 64, 254
Tauler, John, 427
Taxes, 137, 142, 174
Templars, 354, 396–98
Tertullian, 50–51, 63, 88–93, 96, 98, 101, 188, 282, 297, 301
Tertullianists, 92
Teutonic Knights, 380
Textual criticism, 438–39
Thaddeus, St., 254
Thelica, Martyr, 119
Theodora, Empress, 284
Theodore of Mopsuestia, 303
Theodoret, 143
Theodoret of Cyprus, 303
Theodosius, 216, 217, 223–24, 227, 231
Theodosius II, 137, 299–301, 307
Theodulf, 317
Theophilus of Alexandria, 142, 227, 229–30
Theophilus of Antioch, 62
Theophylact and Theodora, 324
Thomas, 38, 256
Thomism, 376–80
Tithes, 317, 451
To Autolycus, 62
To His Wife (Tertullian), 89
Toledo: battle for, 352; Cathedral of, 319; council of, 271, 319
Tome (Leo), 300
Toresby, John, 413

Tours, 413; battle of (or Poitiers), 273, 292
Traditores, 174, 175
Tradt of Armenia, 255
Trajan, 49–50, 51, 55–54, 57, 114
Transubstantiation, 320, 367, 413–14
Trent, Council of, 467
Trinity, 85, 92, *183*, 205–6, 213, 217, 220, 253, 272, 293, 297–306, 435, 464; creeds and, 78; hymns affirming, 206
True Word, The (Celsus), 60
Tupac Amaru, 467
Turkey, 292
Turks: Armenia and, 309; fall of Constantinople, 393, 410; Nicea and, 346
Tyre, synod of, 201–2

Ulfila (Wulfila), 257, *258*
Unam Sanctam, 368, 395
Unitas Fratrum, 421
Universities, 362, 369, 372–74, *373*
Urban II, 340–41, 345, 353
Urban V, 399
Urban VI, 402–4
Urban VIII, 470
Uruguay, 469
Utopia (More), 489

Valens, 207, 210, 213
Valentinian II, 141, 222–23
Valentinian III, 299
Valentinus, 70
Valla, Lorenzo, 440
Vandals, 179, 252, 269–70, 283, 289

Vatican Council II, 449
Venezuela, 453, 462
Vespucci, Amerigo, 487
Victor II, 336
Victor III, 340
Vieira, António, 483–84
Villegagnon, Nicholas Durand de, 484
Vincent Ferrer, 380
Vincent of Lerins, 250
Virgen del Pilar, 37
Virgin birth, 78
Virgin of Guadalupe, 457, *458*
Visigoths, 271–72, 292
Vitoria, Francisco de, 453
Vladimir, 311, *311*
Vulgate Bible, 237, 254

Waldo, Peter and Waldensians, 358, 363, 367
Wenceslas, 416, 420
Whitby, synod of, 237
Why Did God Become Man? (Anselm), 371
William III of Aquitaine, 328
William of Tripoli, 380
William the Conqueror, 338
Women: consecrated widows, 56, 114; contributions to church history, 4; as "doctor of the church," 400; in early church, 50, 56, 73, 91, 114; Gnosticism and, 73; Jerome's supporters, 234, *235*, 236–38; monasticism and orders, 114, *158*, 167, 168, 209–11, 220, 278, 328–29, 360,

399, 429; mystics, 399–400, 428; social status of, 115; virginity, 158, 159; witchcraft, 444
Word. *See* Logos; Son
World, 65, 69, 70, 71–72, 73, 376, 426. *See also* Creation
Worship, 83, 85, 86; buildings for, 381; calendar, 111; in catacombs, 110, 111; Constantinian changes and imperial protocol, 143–44, 154; early Christian, 35, 50, 59–60, 67, 107–13, *108*, *110*, *112*; feast days and holidays, 111–12; incense, 143; *latria* vs. *dulia*, 306; locations for, 110, 111, 143; prayer, 280; Processionals, 144; Scriptural canon and, 77; Sunday services, 27, 108, 109, 111, 140, 143, 147, 165, 168, 317, 389. *See also* Art and architecture
Wycliffe, John, 407, 411–15, *411*, *414*, 417, 419, 429

Xavier, Francis, 477–79

Yaroslav the Wise, 311
Yes and No (Abelard), 371–72, *373*
Yucatan, 457

Zacharias, 273, 289
Zeno, 276, 303
Zizka, John, 421
Zumárraga, Juan de, 456–57

CREDITS

Page 15: Wall painting of Judas Maccabeus by Taddeo di Bartolo; Italian, fifteenth century. / Page 18: Menorah mosaic from Hamman-Lif, Tunisia; third to fifth century A.D.; The Brooklyn Museum, Museum Collection Fund. / Page 21: Courtesy Justo L. González / Page 22: Roman bronze sculpture; The Metropolitan Museum of Art, Gift of Henry G. Marquand, 1897. / Page 26: Marilyn Silverstone, Magnum Photos, Inc. / Page 28: The Pierpont Morgan Library. / Page 29: A silver shekel from the first year of the Jewish War. Permission: British Museum, Department of Coins and Medals. / Page 32: Manuscript illumination of the Apostles (Codex Monacensis Lat. 23338); Bayer. Staatssbibliothek, Munich. / Page 34: Early Christian ivory plaque; The Metropolitan Museum of Art, Gift of George Blumenthal, 1941. / Page 37: Courtesy Justo L. González / Page 44: Coin with portrait of Emperor Nero, A.D. 54-68; The American Numismatic Society. / Page 47: Italian Government Tourist Office. / Page 52: Princeton University, Department of Art and Archaeology. / Page 58: Probably Constantinople, ca. A.D. 1300; Dumbarton Oaks, Washington, D.C., courtesy of the Byzantine Collection. / Page 65: From Vase of Duris; Kunsthistorisches Museum, Berlin; The Bettman Archive. / Page 71: Gnostic gem engraved with serpent and the name *Chnoubis*; Agyptisches Museum, Staatliche Museen, Berlin. / Page 79: The Last Judgment by Andrea Orcogna; Pisa, Italy; The Bettman Archive. / Page 100: Decius Addressing the Legions by Peter Paul Rubens, ca. 1617; National Gallery of Art, Washington, D.C., Samuel H. Kress Collection, 1957. / Page 101: P. Mich. Inv. 263 (libellus from the Decian persecution, 250 A.D.), Regents of the University of Michigan. / Page 106: Early Christian shrine ca. first century A.D.; courtesy, Elek Books Limited. / Page 108: The Bettman Archive. / Page 110: Reconstruction of the Baptistery at Yale University Art Gallery, Christian Building at Dura-Europas. Courtesy Yale University Art Gallery, Dura-Europos Collection. / Page 112: Courtesy Justo L. González / Page 115: Gold leaf etching on glass bowl, ca. third or fourth century, A.D.; The Metropolitan Museum of Art, Rogers Fund, 1915. / Page 116: British Museum, Prehistoric and Romano British Department. / Page 122: Francisco Gallego, *Acacius and the 10,000 Martyrs on Mount Ararat*, c. 1490. Meadows Museum, SMU, Dallas, Algur H. Meadows Collection, MM.68.02; Photography by Michael Bodycomb. / Page 125: Courtesy Justo L. González / Page 133: Marble head of Constantine I, ca. A.D. 325; The Metropolitan Museum of Art, Bequest of Mrs. F. F. Thompson, 1926. / Page 134: Coin with portrait of Licinius, ca. A.D. 310; The American Numismatic Society. / Page 145: Courtesy Justo L. González / Page 151: Courtesy Justo L. González / Page 158-159: Limestone relief of seated nuns from altar of the abbey church in Werden, Germany, ca. 1066-1081. Bildarchiv Foto Marburg. / Page 160: Engraving by Martin Schongauer; German, ca. 1445-1491; Metropolitan Museum of Art, Rogers Fund, 1920. / Page 164: Courtesy Justo L. González / Page 170: Courtesy Justo L. González / Page 175: Ruins of the Roman theatre, Carthage; The Bettman Archive. / Page 183: Tiroler Volkskunstmuseum, Innsbruck, Austria. / Page 185: Courtesy Justo L. González / Page 187: Historical Pictures Service, Chicago. / Page 190: Chronicle of Nüremberg, 1493. Special Collections, Bridwell Library, Perkins School of Theology, Southern Methodist University. / Page 194: Capitonline Museum, Rome; The Bettman Archive. / Page 195: The Bettman Archive / Page 200: Statue of St. Athanasius; detail of the Throne of St. Peter by Gianlorenzo Bernini, 1657-1666; St. Peter's Cathedral, The Vatican, Rome; Saskia/Art Resource. / Page 204: Constantius II / Page 206: Courtesy Justo L. González / Page 212: Fresco, Cathedral of St. Sophia Ochrid. / Page 215: Ca. 880; Bibliotheque Nationale, Paris. / Page 216: Courtesy Justo L. González / Page 220: Altarpiece panel detail in the basilica dedicated to St. Ambrose; Milan, ninth century, Bildarchiv Foto Marburg. / Page 221: Courtesy Justo L. González / Page 226: Mosaic, tenth century; Cathedral of St. Sophia, Instanbul. / Page 235: St. Jerome with St. Paula and St. Eustochium by Francisco de Zurbaran; Spanish, seventeenth century; National Gallery of Art, Washington, D.C., Samuel H. Kress Collection, 1952. / Page 236: Juan Martín Cabezalero, Saint Jerome, *1666*. Meadows Museum, SMU, Dallas. Museum Purchase, Meadows Museum Acquisition Fund, MM.86.01. Photography by Michael Bodycomb. / Page 239: The Last Communion of St. Jerome by Sandro Botticelli; Italian fifteenth century; The Metropolitan Museum of Art, Bequest of Benjamin Altman,1913. / Page 243: St. Augustine by Sandro Botticelli; Italian, fifteenth century; Ognissanti, Florence; Scala/Art Resource / Page 251: 1489 Basel (Amerbach) edition of Augustine's *De civitate Dei*. Special Collections, Bridwell Library, Perkins School of Theology, Southern Methodist University. / Page 258: Silver ink on purple-stained parchment; fourth century; Uppsala Universitet, Sweden. / Page 260: Fifth-century seal; Kunsthistoriches Museum, Vienna / Page 272: Whalebone moneybox; third century; British Museum, Medieval Department. / Page 274: Courtesy Justo L. González / Page 279: MS Hatton 48, Fol. I A.D. 529; Bodleian Library, Oxford, England. / Page 281: Courtesy Justo L. González / Page 284: Courtesy Justo L. González / Page 286: Courtesy Masters and Fellows of Corpus Christi College, Cambridge, England. / Page 298: George Rodger, Magnum Photos, Inc. / Page 304: Mosaic in San Vitale, Ravenna, Italy, A.D. 547; Scala/Art Resource. / Page 306: Miniature manuscript illustration, mid eleventh century; Princeton University Library, Princeton, N.J. / Page 308: Photo of the reproduction of the Nestorian Tablet. Courtesy Nanjing Union Theological Seminary, China. / Page 311: Courtesy of the Metropolitan Archeparchy of Philadelphia of the Ukrainian Catholic Church / Page 316: Gold reliquary in the form of the head of Charlemagne, ca. 1350. Cathedral Treasury, Aachen, Germany; Bildarchiv Foto Marburg. / Page 322: Tenth century; The British Library / Page 328: Bildarchiv Foto Marburg. / Page 330: The Pierpont Morgan Library, New York City. / Page 332: Manuscript illumination; The British Library / Page 339: Miniature manuscript illustration; Canossa, early twelfth century; The Bettman Archive. / Page 342: Courtesy Justo L. González / Page 343: John Foxe's *Actes and Monuments...*, London, 1563: Henry IV at Canossa. Special Collections, Bridwell Library, Perkins School of Theology, Southern Methodist University. / Page 348: Illumination from *Les Estoires d'Outremer* by William of Tyre, thirteenth century, Bibliotheque Nationale, Paris / Page 352: Courtesy Justo L. González / Page 353: The Bettman Archive / Page 355: Courtesy Justo L. González / Page 358: Alonso López de Herrera, *St. Francis of Assisi Receiving the Stigmata*, 1639. Meadows Museum, SMU, Dallas. Museum Purchase, Meadows Acquisition Fund, MM.88.08.a-b. Photography by Michael Bodycomb. / Page 359: Courtesy Justo L. González / Page 361: Courtesy Justo L. González / Page 370: Illumination of St. Gregory writing, Add. MS. 39943, The British Library. / Page 373: Courtesy Justo L. González / Page 376: Courtesy Justo L. González / Page 377: Alonso López de Herrera, St. Thomas Acquinas, 1639. Meadows Museum, SMU, Dallas. Museum Purchase, Meadows Acquisition Fund MM.88.08.a-b. Photography by Michael Bodycomb. / Page 382: The Bettman Archive / Page 383: Courtesy Justo L. González / Page 384: Courtesy Justo L. González / Page 385: The Bettman Archive / Page 391: Miniature illustration from the Toggenburg Bible; Imperial Collection of Vienna; The Bettman Archive / Page 398: The Bettman Archive / Page 400: Francisco de Zurbarán, *The Mystic Marriage of Saint Catherine of Siena*, 1640-60. Meadows Museum, SMU, Dallas. Algur H. Meadows Collection, MM.67.14. Photography by Michael Bodycomb. / Page 401: Tomb of St. Catherine of Siena, attributed to Isaia da Pisa; Santa Maria sopra Minerva, Rome; Scala/Art Resource / Page 405: Courtesy Justo L. González / Page 409: Italian Government Travel Office / Page 410: Seal of the Council of Basel, 1431-1449; Kunsthistorisches Museum, Vienna / Page 411: Courtesy Justo L. González / Page 414: Courtesy Justo L. González / Page 420: From Ulrich von Reichental's *Chronicle of the Council of Constance*; Bohemian, early fifteenth century; The British Library. / Page 422: G. Gruyer, *Les illustrations des écrits de Jérome Savonarola* (Paris, 1879). Special Collections, Bridwell Library, Perkins School of Theology, Southern Methodist University. / Page 425: Museo di San Marco, Florence; Alinari/Art Resource / Page 430: Chronicle of Nüremberg, 1493. Special Collections, Bridwell Library, Perkins School of Theology, Southern Methodist University. / Page 439: An illuminated page from a facsimile copy of the Gutenberg Bible, issued ca. 1455. New York Public Library, Rare Book Room. / Page 441: Self-portrait in red chalk, ca. 1514; Biblioteca Reale, Turin;The Bettman Archive. / Page 445: Detail of a painting by Pinturicchio, 1492-1503; Vatican Palace, Rome; Alinari/Art Resource / Page 451: Courtesy Justo L. González / Page 458: Courtesy Museum of New Mexico. / Page 463: Courtesy Parroquia San Pedro Claver, Cartegena. / Page 466: Royal Library, Copenhagen, Denmark / Page 470: Courtesy Justo L. González / Page 476: The New York Public Library, Map Division / Page 478: Painting on a screen, early seventeenth century. Kobe Municipal Museum, Japan. / Page 481: The Bettman Archive

CPSIA information can be obtained
at www.ICGtesting.com
Printed in the USA
LVHW041009100920
665531LV00022B/2613